SOCIETY AND THE LEGAL ORDER

SOCIETY AND THE LEGAL ORDER / CASES AND MATERIALS IN THE SOCIOLOGY OF LAW /

EDITED BY *Richard D. Schwartz*
AND *Jerome H. Skolnick*

Basic Books, Inc., *Publishers*

NEW YORK / LONDON

TO

Richard C. Donnelly

AND

Fowler V. Harper

Preface

For several years, both editors have taught courses exploring the relationship between law and the social sciences. Our collaboration began when we were colleagues on the faculty of the Yale Law School and participants in its program in Law and Behavioral Science. Our work there was aided by an institutional grant from the National Institute of Mental Health. Upon moving to Northwestern and Berkeley, respectively, we had the good fortune to participate in programs in law and social science that, at both institutions, are supported by grants from the Russell Sage Foundation. We are particularly grateful to Leonard S. Cottrell, Jr., of the Russell Sage Foundation for his steady support of these programs.

To expedite our teaching, we early began to search out materials that would help in teaching the sociology of law. The present compilation includes many of the selections that we have found most useful for the purpose. Where possible, we have juxtaposed cases and research materials to raise questions as to how sociology and the law relate to each other. Except for introductory comments, however, we have left to the reader the job of formulating the nature of this relationship. Our students have regularly demonstrated the diversity of ways in which this can be done. We hope that readers of this book will do the same, and that the book will thus contribute to the search for a systematic and comprehensive view of the field.

In assembling these materials, we have benefited from advice and criticism of several colleagues and students, especially John E. Coons, Gerald M. Caplan, Robert Rabin, and Sheldon Messinger.

The work of getting the manuscript into shape for publication has been efficiently and willingly carried out by Sali Balick and Miriam Ritman in Evanston, and Emily Knapp in Berkeley. Above all, we salute our students, whose interest in the subject encourages us to feel that the enterprise is worthwhile.

Evanston, Ill.　　　　　　　　　　　　　　　　　　RICHARD D. SCHWARTZ
Berkeley, Calif.　　　　　　　　　　　　　　　　　JEROME H. SKOLNICK
May 1970

Contents

Part II

THE SOCIAL BASES OF LAW

Part III

ORGANIZATION FOR THE ADMINISTRATION OF LAW

Part IV

THE CAPACITY OF LAW TO AFFECT SOCIAL BEHAVIOR

SOCIETY AND THE LEGAL ORDER

Introduction

In principle, legal phenomena should be extremely interesting to sociologists. Sociology is committed to the understanding of the social order; law provides the framework of formal norms within which complex societies function. Sociology concerns itself with the processes of social control and social change; legal institutions comprise a major agency through which society seeks authoritatively to exercise its control function and to limit or direct social change. Sociology studies the forms of organization through which men seek to accomplish their collective purposes; legal organization provides a fascinating mixture of purposive action and unanticipated consequence.

Why, then, have legal phenomena been so carefully ignored by American sociologists prior to the current decade? Avoidance of the unfamiliar constitutes part of the explanation. Most American sociologists know very little about the law. Their ignorance is in large part a consequence of the distinctive manner in which legal training has been carried out in this country.

It is rare for students in American colleges and universities to be introduced to law in their liberal arts training. Because of egalitarian tendencies in American society the practice of law tended to be a service occupation toward which people of little formal education could aspire. Thus, law in America was not seen as an intellectual pursuit, by and large, but as a vocation. Indeed, the aspiring lawyer had a training relation to his master similar to that of an apprentice to a skilled craftsman. This sort of apprenticeship system evolved into the law school structure of today, and it is still true that law training is unconnected with, though usually preceded by, a liberal arts education.

As a result of the technical nature of legal training, most professional sociologists tend to be frightened off by law or studies of law; they are likely to assume that sociological studies of law presuppose formal legal training. In fact, this is not true. Most of the time, when sociologists do study law, they work in a relatively limited context. This is not to suggest that no additional training is necessary; only that the magnitude of the training consists of taking a couple of additional courses. A social scientist need not go through the socialization process of becoming a lawyer to engage in research on legal subjects. Indeed,

3

such training—which involves learning to see the world in a certain way—may serve to obscure sociological issues presented by legal phenomena.

In Europe, by contrast, it is more typical for law to be an integral part of liberal arts training. Consequently, the scholar who goes on to another social science field will have had some exposure to legal training, if not a legal education. To put it another way, law in Europe can be studied as another major— like sociology, economics, or history in the United States—rather than as a vocation such as medicine. Thus, European sociologists were better equipped than Americans for the study of law as a social phenomenon.

In light of this background, it is not surprising that European scholars provided the best early studies in the sociology of law. Both Durkheim and Weber, to take the outstanding examples, tried to relate the legal system to a fundamental feature of the society, namely, its underlying socio-economic structure. This approach is clear in their best known treatises in the sociology of law.

In *The Division of Labor in Society*,[1] Durkheim examined the fundamental sociological issue of what holds the society together by exploring the relationship of criminal and civil law to distinctive types of social solidarity. He characterized criminal law as a set of norms embodying the basic moral principles of the society. Although he recognized the importance of criminal law in advanced society, he further reasoned that criminal law predominates as a social tie in societies where the division of labor is minimal. By contrast, civil law implies greater diversity in standards of conduct, and will be found in societies characterized by a higher degree of division of labor. In such societies, the ties of solidarity will be anchored, according to Durkheim, on a recognition of the mutual interdependence of diverse actors. Sanctions in such a society tend to be restitutive rather than retributive, emphasizing and implementing reciprocity rather than restraint as the dominant principle of social order.

In *Law in Economy and Society*,[2] Weber dealt with the development of formal rationality in law, which for him constituted the basis of the modern state. The social conditions that aided this development were a nascent capitalistic economy and an increasingly differentiated legal profession. In turn, the introduction of predictability or rationality into the legal system provided a basis for further expansion of capitalistic economic enterprise. This had not been possible, according to Weber, in political organizations based upon the personality of a leader (charisma) or the traditional domination of the kinship group, since decisions in these types of political organization were apt to be "irrational" in the sense of being motivated by subjective considerations.

It should be noted that these men viewed law as a sociological phenomenon in more ways than one. Their interest in relating law to the fundamental institutions of society is patent. Less obvious, perhaps, is their insistence that legal phenomena are to be treated as social facts subject to the same conceptual analysis as other social facts. Thus, laws were seen as types of norms, the legal profession as a vocation, and legal penalties as sanctions. Attention was given, of course, to the distinctive characteristics of legal norms, personnel and sanctions, but even these distinguishing properties were phrased in sociologically meaningful terms.

In Durkheim's *Division of Labor,* for instance, law was adopted as the key indicator of type of solidarity. Like all norms, it served to express the "collective representations" of the society, the deep-set socially anchored orientations that Durkheim felt were at the heart of the social order. He assumed that legal and non-legal norms were conceptually equivalent. Legal norms assumed a central position in his analysis not because they were different in form from other norms but because they constituted an especially valid index of the normative order.

Weber was similarly interested in using legally based phenomena to understand society. Thus, he studied, as part of his sociology of law, the manner in which an organized staff affects the development of a normative system for which it bears specialized responsibility. This was an issue which he had also examined in his detailed studies of ancient religions. In analyzing the development of European law, he was able to pose the same general questions with illuminating results. In a concise analysis, Weber showed the relationship between the relatively unstructured training of the English lawyer and the pragmatic evolution of common law. By contrast, he pointed out that the standardized legal training and structured authority system of the continental advocates harmonized with the promulgation of their organized codes.

The classical works dealt particularly with the effects of social organization on the legal process. This is apparent not only in the previously mentioned writings of Durkheim and Weber, but also in other works of the period. Maine, for example, asserted that, as kin ties decline, there is a growing tendency for relationships to be governed by legal norms. Most significant is his analysis of the effects of the antecedent system of social organization on the growth and form of legal obligations. Testamentary succession by a non-relative, one of his most famous illustrations, is first accomplished under the cloak of adoption, a form that uses the normative support already established for the kin relationship. Only after the arrangement has acquired recognition and social acceptance in this form does it emerge as an independent relationship, sanctioned by legal norms that are no longer obscured and protected by the legal fiction of adoption. Thus, Maine concerned himself with social conditions both as they promote new legal relationships and as they affect the manner in which these new arrangements are introduced.[3]

Simmel too was interested in law as a product of the structure of society. Like Maine, he noted that formal law emerges in more complex societies. He analyzed this finding in terms of the growth of numbers in society. As the social group increases in size it tends to become differentiated. For Simmel, this relationship is inevitable, given the number of relationships and the necessity for organizing the resultant interactions. But the growth of size and differentiation affects the kinds of norms that can be effectively applied to the entire group. Accordingly, only those customary norms are applied which represent the minimal standards of conduct necessary for the persistence of the group.

These minimal standards tend to be proscriptions which are likely to be most readily enforceable upon all the members. To ensure their enforcement, negative sanctions are provided, since positive rewards are decreasingly effective as group size and complexity increase. The resultant norms have, then, the characteristic properties of laws: proscriptions enforced by the threat of punishment.[4]

These examples illustrate the tendency of nineteenth-century sociologists to view law primarily as a dependent variable. They were interested in the ways in which law was affected by social and cultural conditions. Those sociologists who did inquire into the *consequences* of law were likely to reach the conclusion that the capacity of law to achieve independent effects on social behavior was relatively limited.[5]

It takes a closer reading to discern the alternative interest in classical sociological writing. Nevertheless, the treatment of law as an independent variable is implicit at least in the writing of the men we have discussed. All of them were concerned with the contribution of law to social order. While this theme is often phrased in terms of the social conditions leading to changes in law, the explanations are frequently functional in form: certain social conditions give rise to the development of a legal system or a particular kind of law *because* law produces some needed results for the social system. In Weber's analysis, predictability is required for capitalism; for Simmel, minimal standards of conduct are needed to make a social order viable; and for Maine, the modifiable social relationships must substitute for a kin-based social order in a dynamic society.

Durkheim, however, carried the functional approach furthest. In *Professional Ethics and Civic Morals* [6] he developed his analysis of law more fully than had been done in the *Division of Labor*.[7] In *Professional Ethics* he stressed the complex relationship between law and the associations of which the individual is a member. These associations he found essential in providing appropriate restraints and guidance for the individual. If they did not exist, the state would have the entire responsibility for control.

In the United States, the sociology of law has developed in the perspective of European sociology, as has all American sociology to a degree. In addition, however, it is evident that the sociology of law has addressed itself in America to the more or less apparent social contradictions existing in the United States. For example, presented with the fact of social stratification within a society characterized by egalitarian norms, the sociology of law in America has looked into the consequences of the social stratification system for the administration of justice. This concern is most evident in studies of the legal profession and the functioning of courts. To the general tendency toward depersonalization and urbanization, the sociology of law has responded with studies that seek to understand the difficulties of realizing ideals of individual justice in a mass industrial society. Finally, to the increasing of centralization of power over the lives of individuals, the sociology of law has responded with a concern for the fate of legal ideals in private government and public regulatory agencies. Such social trends and tendencies are by no means an exclusively American phenomenon and we may anticipate that sociologists of law in other nations will address similar issues.

This volume was organized not so much as a basis for preparation for research in the sociology of law, as a set of materials for teaching a high-level introductory course. Thus, we have omitted much reference to methodological concerns, and have concentrated instead upon readings and cases that would provide an interesting basis for discussion of certain fundamental issues. The book has four parts which we hope have raised or touched upon most of the major issues and controversies within the sociology of law.

In Part I, we have attempted to look at the effect of social values on the development of the legal order. We believe that law does not develop in a vacuum, and that it is strongly influenced by the values and beliefs prevailing in the society that promulgates the law. Consequently, to the extent that there are conflicts in such values, they will be reflected in certain difficulties in developing law and in administering it.

Part II is a more explicit examination of some of the issues raised in Part I. Both parts I and II deal with the question of how substantive law is developed in a society, that is, what factors affect the development of substantive law. Thus, in Part II, we look at certain specific phenomena such as custom and public opinion in the development of law.

Part III takes the substantive law as given, and begins to consider as problematic the organizations that are developed for the administration of law. It is in this part that we look to such legal organizational phenomena as the jury, the legal profession, and the courts, and attempt to raise major questions that sociologists, political scientists, and legal scholars have considered concerning the operation of the administration of law.

In Part IV we go from the legal administrative structures themselves to the question of how law affects social behavior. Law is usually a means to an end, and while the ends may be problematic, as discussed in Part I, it is also important to understand what roadblocks there are to the achievement of specified ends through the instrumentality of legal rules.

In reviewing these materials one important fact should become apparent to the reader: there is no "party line" regarding important research in the sociology of law. Useful research in the field ranges from intensive factual studies of narrowly defined questions to research on a very broad historical and comparative level. It is possible to do analyses deriving from the theory of organizations, and analyses deriving from theories of deviance. In this respect, the sociology of law is quite typical of any field of sociology that defines a social phenomenon as its chief interest. That phenomenon may be observed from a variety of perspectives, and it is our hope that we have suggested this variety with enough of a conception of unity to make this book of readings worthwhile for the teachers and students who we hope will be using it.

NOTES

1. Emile Durkheim, *The Division of Labor in Society,* George Simpson, trans. (Glencoe: Free Press, 1960).
2. Max Rheinstein, ed., *Max Weber on Law in Economy and Society* (Cambridge, Mass.: Harvard, 1954).
3. Henry Sumner Maine, *Ancient Law* (London: Oxford University Press, 1931).
4. George Simmel, "The Persistence of Social Groups," Albion W. Small, trans., *American Journal of Sociology,* V (1897), 662–698, 829–836, and IV (1898), 35–50. See also his "The Number of Members as Determining the Sociological Form of the Group," Albion W. Small, trans., VIII (1902), 1–46, 158–196.
5. William Graham Sumner is almost universally cited as the extreme example of this view. A more moderate interpretation of his position is given in Harry V. Ball, George Eaton Simpson, and Kiyoshi Ikeda, "Law and Social Change: Sumner Reconsidered," *American Journal of Sociology,* LXVII (1962), 532–540.
6. Emile Durkheim, *Professional Ethics and Civic Morals,* Cornelia Brookfield trans. (Glencoe: Free Press, 1958).
7. Published in 1893, *Division of Labor* preceeded *Professional Ethics* by at least five years.

Part I SOCIAL VALUES AND THE LAW

Editors' Introduction

Part I addresses itself to some of the most fundamental and perplexing issues in the sociology of law, especially the nature and functions of law in reflecting and implementing societal values. Law cannot be understood without relating it to the values of the society and the norms which express them. Some of these values may be embodied in constitutional provisions, such as the protection of freedom of speech. Others may be unstated, may be part of the most deeply held sentiments of a society. In particular, this section examines the meaning of legality, the problems of conflicting values, and the implementation of legal standards in the light of value conflict.

Section One begins with a discussion by an anthropologist, a sociologist, and two legal scholars, all of whom write extensively on the philosophy of law. There is first a short statement by E. A. Hoebel, who takes a functionalist view of the role of law in society. Hoebel's view, the simplest of the four, sees law as a means of settling disputes, of defining relationships within the society. Hoebel's point of view derives from his and other anthropologists' first hand observations of primitive societies. His writings raise the issue of whether it is possible to generalize about the functions of law from simple to more complex societies.

Philip Selznick, a sociologist, draws attention to the distinction between positive law, which is the product of legal problem-solving, and the ideal of legality as a commitment to the search for truth, as revealed by consistency of thought, evidence, classifications, and analogies. By going beyond the simple concept of positive law as the development of rules for the solution of social problems, Selznick relates law to the fundamental value assumptions underlying science. Thus he asserts that "judicial conclusions gain in legal authority as they are based on good reasoning including sound knowledge of human personality, human groups, human institutions."

Selections from Fuller and Noonan are complementary to the position taken by Selznick. Fuller asserts that the legal order rests on an implicit or internal morality, a morality defined by distinctive ideals and purposes. The brief selection from Fuller's *The Morality of Law* suggests that legal procedures must conform to certain requirements for a system of rules which they implement to be properly considered a legal system at all. In effect, he provides a specification of the elements of legality whose fundamental significance is asserted by Selznick.

Similarly, John T. Noonan, Jr., in examining natural law reasoning against contraception indicates that if one looks at the history of the development of these rules, one finds that the intent of the rules was to protect certain values. Noonan suggests that the values protected by the rules were four: procreation, life, dignity, and love. By viewing these rules in the context of values, asserts Noonan, the issue is drawn to a discussion of the rationality of the rules. The rationality of rules may vary with changes in values; rules that are rational for the achievement of one set of values may become irrational as the values they were designed to serve undergo change.

Section Two indicates the problems that are created for a legal order when there is a striking discrepancy in fundamental values between the governor and those who are governed. The murder trial of the Eskimo Sinnisiak for killing a Catholic missionary priest is probably the most striking illustration in case law of the problem of deep cultural conflict. The case raises the fundamental issue of whether it is at all possible to achieve the sort of legality contemplated by writers such as Selznick and Fuller when the population against whom the laws are being enforced has a totally different conception of the world from that held by the dominant legal order. This is the classic case of colonial justice, or, as the reader may feel after reading it, colonial injustice.

Petition of McCord, like *Rex v. Sinnisiak,* raises the issue of the extent to which colonial law, used as a means of education, approaches the totalitarian concept of justice. Law, under such a conception, is seen as a teacher rather than as a reflection of the norms of all elements of society. Harold Berman states this conception in describing the paternalistic character of Soviet legality and its consequences: "Soviet law cannot be understood unless it is recognized that the whole of Soviet society is conceived to be a single great family, a gigantic school, a church, a labor union, a business enterprise. The state stands at its head, as a parent, the teacher, the priest, the chairman, the director. As the state, it acts officially through the legal system, but its purpose in so acting is to make its citizens into obedient children, good students, ardent believers, hard workers, successful managers. This, indeed, is the essential characteristic of the law of a total state."

Thus, one question that might be raised regarding both the *Sinnisiak* and *McCord* cases is the extent to which colonial justice is inherently a form of totalitarian justice. To what extent must the governed participate in the making of laws for the legal order to be considered as fair and just? Must law be based upon an elementary level of coincidence between the values of those who are being governed and those who are enforcing the rules? The final selection in Section Two, by C. K. Meek, would suggest that the contrasts between various non-Western legal systems and Western legal systems are so considerable as to preclude the possibility of governing non-Western peoples on the basis of Western standards.

Section Three brings the issue of a conflict of moral standards closer to home. The subjects are not exotic Eskimos, but white Protestant Americans, members of a Mormon sect know as Fundamentalists. These Americans exhibit all of the puritanical virtues save one. They are God-fearing, thrifty, industrious, honest, and polygamous. They not only believe in plural marriage, they practice it; in so doing they appear to violate not only certain state laws but may, as the case of *Cleveland v. United States* demonstrates, also violate federal law as well. There is an interesting debate in the decision as to whether the Fundamentalist's practice of polygamy is "motivated solely by lust," as contended by Justice Douglas, or whether, as dissenting Justice Murphy argues, "plural marriage is a form of marriage built upon a set of social and moral principles . . . [and] must be recognized and treated as such." Other questions are also lurking which may be of interest to the student. One is the question of what we mean by plural marriage. For instance, the writer of the decision, Justice Douglas, has since taken two additional wives, although, to be sure, they were wedded only after the divorce of previous spouses, a pattern that has been described as "serial polygyny." In most states, even if adultery or the taking of a mistress is technically a crime, it is rarely enforced. In New York State, for example, literally thousands of divorces were granted on the grounds of adultery with nary a prosecution. The question then is raised as to the purpose of laws prohibiting plural marriage. Is the "creation" of such a "deviation" required to justify the existence of a fundamental institution? Durkheimians might argue that society requires that such deviance be denied to explicate the boundaries of social propriety. Is the law against a plural marriage not an especially pertinent example of this social process? Or are there better reasons that may be given for the laws against plural marriage? If the chief reason is to sustain the moral standards, is such instrumentalism a necessary and proper part of the legal system? Does it in any sense violate the notions of legality that were set forth in the first chapter?

These readings also raise another set of issues regarding the relation between social knowledge and law. Would Justice Douglas have written his decision in just the same way had he been privy to an anthropological report on the fundamentalist Mormons? Or suppose he had seen Jessop's article on "Why I Have Five Wives," would it and should it have made any difference to Justice Douglas? Would the facts of the problems of enforcement and of social disorganization resulting from a prosecution of such communities as that of Short Creek have made any difference to a Supreme Court justice? Should they have? Should there be some facility for bringing such facts to the attention of the court other than the briefs provided by the defense counsel? Finally, this section raises the issue of the extent to which the law should attempt to enforce the moral standards of the majority against the moral standards of a minority. Or, is this a feature of law that cannot be avoided? Is all law of this character, and therefore the question, of little concern?

The case of Michael Boutilier raises similar issues as the case of *Cleveland v. United States.* Is Justice Douglas's dissent in this case consistent with the stance he adapts in *Cleveland?*

The selection by Skolnick, part of a more general paper on the enforcement of morals published by The President's Commission on Law Enforcement and Administration of Justice, attempts to summarize some of the thinking of sociologists on the reasons for the attempt to enforce morality in a society. The emphasis here is on the symbolic functions of law in exhibiting the dominance of values held by certain groups in the society, and what may happen when the political dominance of such groups changes.

Section Four indicates that questions of morality are a problem where organized groups do not exist, as well as where organized groups having a separate set of moral standards do exist. The chapter concentrates upon cases where the law finds itself in a position of having to assess and shape contemporary moral standards without there being an organized group manifesting such standards, as the Mormon Fundamentalists. The case of *Repouille v. United States* is a euthanasia or "mercy killing" case. The student is invited first of all to ask himself whether he would have decided the case as Judge Hand did; and second, as to whether the standards of public opinion discussed by Judges Hand and Frank are appropriate; or whether any other standard ought to be introduced.

The reading by St. John-Stevas raises the whole issue of whether public opinion ought to play the predominant role in deciding matters of life and death. It raises very fundamental issues for law; to what extent are acts to be considered absolutely right or absolutely wrong, regardless of their seemingly salutary consequences in any particular case? If murder is wrong, are there to be excuses for murder based upon the need of the person who is doing the murdering, or the "benefit" that is intended for the individual who is being put to death, or for mankind in general? The case of *The Queen v. Dudley and Stevens* raises this issue in another context and also poses the question of whether it is possible for people to develop their own sets of rules outside of conventional society based upon the existential needs that they are presently experiencing.

The case of *Painter v. Bannister* raises the issue of moral standards in the area of child custody. The student should here ask himself first whether he agrees with the outcome of the case; second, if he does not, under what principle he thinks the case was decided; whether he would substitute a different principle, and if so, which one? If he raises these questions, he may find that he would invoke a principle suggesting that there is a natural right of parenthood, and that, in this case, the court gave greater weight to the principle of the good of the child. Those students who feel that the court assessed the well-being of the child wrongly would be well advised to ask whether the court could have done otherwise than to decide, on the basis of its own best judgment, what was good for the child? Does the student believe that the court did not decide on those grounds? If not, what evidence is there to support such a contention?

Finally, the selection from Emile Durkheim raises some fundamental issues regarding the necessity for a pluralistic political order. Durkheim argues that if the state is to be the liberator of the individual, it must be counterbalanced and restrained by other collective forces. He concludes that it is out of this conflict of social forces that individual liberties are born. The question for the student is whether he believes that it is possible to have a legal order that does not represent the conflict of diverse social forces. But do the cases in this section suggest that the conflict of social forces will necessarily result in the enhancement of individual liberty?

SECTION ONE *On the Nature and Functions of Law*

1

The Functions of Law

E. A. HOEBEL

Law performs certain functions essential to the maintenance of all but the very most simple societies.

The first is to define relationships among the members of a society, to assert what activities are permitted and what are ruled out, so as to maintain at least minimal integration between the activities of individuals and groups within the society.

The second is derived from the necessity of taming naked force and directing force to the maintenance of order. It is the allocation of authority and the determination of who may exercise physical coercion as a socially recognized privilege-right, along with the selection of the most effective forms of physical sanction to achieve the social ends that the law serves.

The third is the disposition of trouble cases as they arise.

The fourth is to redefine relations between individuals and groups as the conditions of life change. It is to maintain adaptability.

Purposive definition of personal relations is the primary law-job. Other aspects of culture likewise work to this end, and, indeed, the law derives its working principles (jural postulates) from postulates previously developed in the nonlegal spheres of action. However, the law's important contribution to the basic organization of society as a whole is that the law specifically and explicitly defines relations. It sets the expectancies of man to man and group to group so that each knows the focus and the limitations of its demand-rights on others, its duties to others, its privilege-rights and powers as against others, and its immunities and liabilities to the contemplated or attempted acts of others. This is the "bare-bones job," as Karl Llewellyn likes to call it. It is the ordering of the fundamentals of living together.

From *The Law of Primitive Man* (Cambridge: Harvard University Press, 1954), pp. 275–276. Reprinted by permission of the author and publisher.

2

The Ideal of Legality

PHILIP SELZNICK

The impulse to create a legal order is, in the first instance, a practical one. From the standpoint of the rulers, power is made more secure when it is legitimate; from the standpoint of the ruled, fears of oppression are allayed. Thus legalization is rooted in the problems of collective life. It is not, in its primitive forms, an expression of social idealism. It is obvious, moreover, that communities survive and even flourish without going very far toward legalization. We do not suppose that the values associated with law must necessarily be realized. Other values, for example, religious or aesthetic values, may define a world more appealing.

To understand what legalization entails for the life of a political community or a specialized institution, however, we should consider its ideal or developed state. In what follows we shall briefly explicate what is meant by "legality," which we take to be a synonym for "the rule of law."

The essential element in the rule of law is the restraint of official power by rational principles of civic order. Where this ideal exists, no power, including the democratic majority, is immune from criticism or entirely free to follow its own bent, however well-intentioned it may be. Legality imposes an environment of constraint, of tests to be met, standards to be observed, ideals to be fulfilled.

Legality has to do mainly with *how* policies and rules are made and applied rather than with their content. The vast majority of rules, including judge-made rules, spell out policy choices, choices not uniquely determined by the requirements of legality. Whether contracts must be supported by consideration; whether a defendant in an accident case should be spared liability because of plaintiff's contributory negligence; whether minors should be relieved of legal consequences that might otherwise apply to their actions—these and a host of other issues treated in the common law are basically matters of general public policy. For practical and historical reasons, a great many of these policy matters are decided by the courts in the absence of, or as a supplement to, legislative determination. In making these decisions, and in devising substantive rules, the courts are concerned with dimensions of justice that go beyond the ideal of legality. Legality is a part of justice, but only a part.

Nevertheless, there are times when the ideal of legality does determine the

---

From *Law, Society, and Industrial Justice* (New York: Russell Sage Foundation, 1969), pp. 11–18. Reprinted by permission of the author and publisher.

content of a legal rule or doctrine. This occurs when the purpose of the rule is precisely to implement that ideal, the most obvious illustration being the elaboration of procedural rules of pleading and evidence. In addition, principles of statutory interpretation, including much of constitutional law, directly serve the aim of creating and sustaining the "legal state." Some of these rules are "merely" procedural, chosen because some device was necessary, for which some other procedure might readily be substituted. Others are vital to the protection of just those substantial rights which the ideal of legality is meant to protect. These include primarily all that we term civil rights, the rights of members of a polity to act as full citizens and to be free of oppressive and arbitrary official power. Again, it is not the aim of this ideal to protect the individual against *all* power, but only against the misuse of power by those whose actions have the color of authority. Later we shall argue that in modern society we must extend our notions of who it is that acts "officially."

The effort to see in law a set of standards, an internal basis for criticism and reconstruction, leads us to a true *Grundnorm*—the idea that a legal order faithful to itself seeks progressively to reduce the degree of arbitrariness in positive law and its administration. By "positive law" we mean those public obligations that have been defined by duly constituted mechanisms, such as a legislature, court, administrative agency, or referendum. This is not the whole of law, for by the latter we must mean the entire body of authoritative materials—"precepts, techniques, and ideals" [1]—that guide official decision-making. Law is "positive" when a particular conclusion has been reached by some authorized body—a conclusion expressed in a determinate rule or judgment.

Plainly, positive law includes an arbitrary element. For him who must obey it, it is to some extent brute fact and brute command. But this arbitrary element, while necessary and inevitable, is repugnant to the ideal of legality. Therefore the proper aim of the legal order, and the special contribution of legal scholarship, is to minimize the arbitrary element in legal norms and decisions. This objective may be compared to the scientific ideal of "reducing the degree of empiricism," that is, the number of theoretically ungrounded factual generalizations within the corpus of scientific knowledge.

If the reduction of arbitrariness is central to legality, three corollaries may be suggested:

1. Legality is a variable achievement. A developed legal order is the product of continuing effort and posits values that are always incompletely fulfilled. We can unblushingly speak of more or less legality, meaning nothing more obscure than that some systems of rules, and some modes of decision, are less arbitrary than others. A major topic in legal sociology is the study of empirical conditions that reduce or exacerbate the arbitrary element in making or applying rules. For example, studies of police discretion locate systematic sources of arbitrary decision in the handling of juveniles; "treatment" is seen as a cover for unsupervised control; the low visibility of decisions in administrative agencies tends to encourage self-serving discretion.

This is not to suggest that the notion of "arbitrary" is completely clear, or that it has a simple meaning. Rules are made arbitrarily when appropriate interests are not consulted and when there is no clear relation between the rule enunciated and the official end to be achieved. Rules are arbitrary when they reflect confused policies, are based on ignorance or error, and when they suggest no inherent principles of criticism. Discretion is arbitrary when it is whimsical, or governed by criteria extraneous to legitimate means or ends. All of this is a matter of degree. Few decisions are completely arbitrary, yet we may compare, at least crudely, the more and the less.

The reduction of arbitrariness cannot be equated with the elaboration of formal rules and procedures. "Formal justice" equalizes parties and makes decisions predictable; it is therefore a major contribution to the mitigation of arbitrary rule. But legal "correctness" has its own costs. Like any other technology, it is vulnerable to the divorce of means and ends. When this occurs, legality degenerates into legalism. Substantive justice is undone when there is too great a commitment to upholding the autonomy and integrity of the legal process. Rigid adherence to precedent and mechanical application of rules hamper the capacity of the legal system to take account of new interests and circumstances, or to adapt to social inequality. Formal justice tends to serve the status quo. It therefore may be experienced as arbitrary by those whose interests are dimly perceived or who are really outside "the system."

Formal attributes of equality or certainty may run counter to the continuities of culture and social organization. One student of the role of British law in India has noted:

> The common law proceeds on the basis of equality before the law while indigenous dispute-settling finds it unthinkable to separate the parties from their statuses and relations. The common law gives a clear-cut "all or none" decision, while indigenous processes seek a face-saving solution agreeable to all parties; the common law deals only with a single isolated offense or transaction, while the indigenous system sees this as arbitrarily leaving out the underlying dispute of which this may be one aspect; the common law has seemingly arbitrary rules of evidence, which do not permit that which is well-known to be proved and that which is not can be proved; the common law then seems abrupt and overly decisive, distant, expensive, and arbitrary.[2]

The limits of formalism suggest that the reduction of arbitrariness requires a union of formal and substantive justice.

Properly understood, the concept of legality is more critical than celebrationist. To say that legality is a variable achievement is to leave room for the conclusion that, at any given time, the system of positive law is "congealed injustice."[3] An affirmative approach to legal values need not accept the defensive rhetoric of men in power. On the contrary, it offers principles of criticism to evaluate the shortcomings of the existing system of rules and practices.

2. Legality extends to administration as well as adjudication. Wherever there is official conduct, the possibility of arbitrary decision arises. That conduct may be far removed from rule-making or adjudication, at least in spirit or purpose. It may be a practical effort to get a job done. Yet the question of

legitimacy—of power exercised in the light of governing norms—is always appropriate. Furthermore, the problem of arbitrariness is at issue whenever rights are determined, something that may occur quite incidentally, in the course of administrative decision and policy-making. Thus any official decision, whether it be a purchase, a hiring, a deployment of police power, or any other active effort to accomplish a defined social purpose, may be criticized in the name of legality.

It has been said that "reliance on the action of abstract rules governing the relations between individuals . . . is the essential basis of the Rule of Law." [4] That formulation is too sweeping, for it limits the legal ideal to the adjudicative mode. It precludes a law-governed, arbitrariness-minimizing sphere of administrative action.

In adjudication, whether conducted by an administrative agency or a court, there is a quest for and application of rules that are logically, if not historically, prior to the case at hand. It is not a rule tailored to the needs and circumstances of a particular plaintiff or defendant, with the idea of achieving a particular outcome. The same rule is applied to every member of a legally defined class of cases. A particular case cannot be handled, without risk to legality, unless it belongs to a category, unless it can be so classified that a general rule, applicable to the entire class of cases, can be invoked.

The application of general rules does not preclude "tempering justice with mercy," taking account of special strengths or weaknesses, or any other effort to adapt the administration of justice to the actual circumstances before the court or administrative tribunal. In principle, this is only a matter of specifying more closely the category to which the case belongs, often by combining a set of applicable concepts or doctrines, for example, that a contract made by a minor is voidable but that unjust enrichment will not be allowed. The only important criterion is: Would another litigant in the same circumstances be judged according to the same criteria?

Thus, in the determination of rights, "discretion" is compatible with the rule of law when it remains essentially judicial rather than administrative. Like any other discretion, judicial discretion involves a certain freedom of choice. The choice, however, is of a special kind. From among many possible ways of classifying the events at hand, the court selects that particular classification which will fix the rights and obligations of the parties. To this end, judicial discretion may carpenter doctrines and otherwise rework the legal materials. But the objective remains: Find a rule or a rule-set that will do justice in a special class of situations.

Administrative discretion is of another order.[5] The administrator (where he is not really a judge) is also interested in diagnosing and classifying the world. But he properly looks to an end-in-view, the refashioning of human or other resources so that a particular outcome will be achieved. A judge becomes an administrator when his objective is to reform a criminal, avert a strike, or abate a nuisance. For then his aim is not justice but accomplishment, not fairness but therapy.

Administration may be controlled by law, but its special place in the division of labor is to get the work of society done, not to realize the ideals of legality. Adjudication also gets work done, in settling disputes, but this is secondary and not primary. The primary function of adjudication is to discover the legal coordinates of a particular situation. That is a far cry from manipulating the situation to achieve a desired outcome.

This line of reasoning suggests that administration, even in a developed legal order, is distinguished from adjudication by a weaker commitment to the ideal of legality. It does not follow, however, that legality is foreign to the ethos of administration. Its relevance appears in two ways. First, there is a common commitment to objective and impersonal decision-making. Second, administration can contain within it machinery that approximates adjudication when rights are affected.

Objective decisions call for *universalistic* rather than *particularistic* criteria of assessment—a distinction that is as subtle in logic as it is precarious in experience. The model of particularism is found in ties of common association —religious, political, kinship, friendship, even conspiratorial. The claim of a particular individual to be treated in a distinctive way is recognized. The prototypical case is nepotism. However, the nepotistic response may be made in the light of a general norm governing how one should treat a relative or friend. The tension is created by competing norms, not by a difference between decision in the light of what is general as distinguished from what is specific. The norm of particularism is subversive of objective and impartial judgment because it introduces extraneous, person-centered criteria of decision into settings where there should be a sovereignty of institutional purpose.

Universalism is as pertinent to administration as it is to adjudication. Universalism asks only that criteria of decision transcend the special interests of persons or groups. Situations may be dealt with according to the special requirements, and specific outcomes may be sought, but the integrity of official decision is retained so long as there is an objective relation between the course of decision-making and the requirements of institutional purpose. The official can then give reasons for his actions and expose them to criticism in the light of publicly acknowledged ends.

3. Legality applies to public participation as well as to the conduct of officials. If legality aspires to minimize the arbitrary element in law, then public participation must itself be subject to scrutiny and criticism. Positive law is a product of both will and reason; the mixture is variable and unstable. Although positive law cannot be *merely* an expression of social power, neither is it free of that element. The actions of an electorate and the decisions of a legislature may conform to procedural standards and yet contain strong arbitrary elements. Some statutes are passed under the heavy pressures of special interests or in a mood of panic, confusion, or unreason. And the quality of decision by a popular majority may be marred and distorted under conditions of collective excitement, irrelevant symbolism, or misinformation. When the public acts officially, or influences official conduct, it may do so arbitrarily. Legality recognizes the arbitrary element in law, and even protects some of

those elements, such as the right of a legitimate decider to prevail for the time being despite some acting out of power or whim. But the larger aspiration of a community dedicated to law is to enlarge the role of reason and fairness in all public decision.

The general public contributes to legality, not only through the quality of democratic decision-making, but also insofar as it has the competence, and recognizes the duty, of criticizing authority. To be sure, there must be public respect for law, and appropriate self-restraint, but in a vital legal order something more is wanted than submission to constituted authority. A military establishment places very great emphasis on obedience to lawful commands, yet such a setting is hardly a model of institutionalized legality. So too, a conception of law as the manifestation of awesome authority encourages feelings of deference and is compatible with much arbitrary rule. In a community that aspires to a high order of legality obedience to law is not submissive compliance. The obligation to obey the law is closely tied to the defensibility of the rules themselves and of the official decisions that enforce them.

Thus understood, legality has a strong affinity with the ideal of political democracy. This is most readily manifest in democracy's dependence on limited governmental authority, and on the possibility of appeal, beyond majority will, for the protection of minority rights and the free creation of new majorities. But there is also an affinity of fundamental values—above all, to the role of reason in official judgment. Legality does not require the machinery of democratic decision-making. But it does require that the civic participant be treated as a "legal man," a right-and-duty bearing entity invested with the presumption of competence and guaranteed access to tribunals that are committed to the impartial assessment of evidence and argument.

4. Legality is an affirmative ideal. The rule of law is a practical ideal, which is to say it rests in part on pessimistic premises regarding the nature of man and society. "Free government," wrote Thomas Jefferson, "is founded in jealousy, and not in confidence, it is jealousy, and not confidence, which prescribes limited constitutions, to bind down those whom we are obliged to trust with power; . . . in questions of power, then, let no more be heard of confidence in man, but bind him down from mischief by the chains of the Constitution." [6] The assumption is that no man, no group of men, is to be trusted with unlimited power. No amount of wisdom or good will can justify a transfer of untrammeled power to mortal men.

This view does not require the belief that any man, given the chance, would misuse power; rather, the premise is that there is a sufficient *risk* of such misuse to forbid *reliance upon* the idealism and good will of men in authority. Nor does Jefferson's pessimism necessarily deny that power and authority can be ennobling, summoning ordinary men to political and moral heights.

Legality begins as a practice of constraint, but it promises more than a way of moderating the uses of power. The "progressive reduction of arbitrariness" knows no near stopping-place. The closer we look at that process, the more we realize that it calls for an affirmative view of what it means to participate in a legal order, whether a citizen, judge, or executive. In its richest connotation, legality evokes the Greek view of a social order founded in reason, whose constitutive principle is justice.[7]

NOTES

1. See Roscoe Pound, *Jurisprudence* (St. Paul: West Publishing Co., 1959), II, 107: "Law in the sense we are considering is made up of precepts, techniques and ideals: A body of authoritative precepts, developed and applied by an authoritative technique in the light of or on the background of authoritative traditional ideals."
2. Marc Galanter, "Hindu Law and the Development of the Modern Indian Legal System" (mimeo.; prepared for delivery at the 1964 Annual Meeting of the American Political Science Association), p. 25. On the relation between formal and substantive justice, see Max Weber's discussion in Max Rheinstein, ed., *Max Weber on Law in Economy and Society* (Cambridge: Harvard University Press, 1954), pp. 224 ff.
3. Howard Zinn, *Disobedience and Democracy: Nine Fallacies on Law and Order* (New York: Vintage Books, 1968), p. 4.
4. F. A. Hayek, *The Political Ideal of the Rule of Law* (Cairo: National Bank of Egypt, 1955), p. 32.
5. In his *Administrative Law Treatise* (St. Paul: West Publishing Co., 1958), K. C. Davis assimilates the administrative process to adjudication by defining an "administrative agency" as "a governmental authority other than a court and other than a legislative body, which affects the rights of private parties through either adjudication or rule-making" (I, 1). He suggests a distinction between the "executive process" and the "administrative process" (ibid., p. 57). It seems better to maintain the more conventional usage and see administration as fundamentally task-oriented.
6. See E. D. Warfield, *The Kentucky Resolutions of 1798* (New York: G. P. Putnam's Sons, 1887), pp. 157–158.
7. See Werner Jaeger, "Praise of Law," in Paul Sayre (ed.), *Interpretations of Modern Legal Philosophers* (New York: Oxford University Press, 1947), pp. 352–375.

3

The Morality That Makes Law Possible

LON L. FULLER

This chapter will begin with a fairly lengthy allegory. It concerns the unhappy reign of a monarch who bore the convenient but not very imaginative and not even very regal-sounding name of Rex.

From *The Morality of Law* (New Haven: Yale University Press, 1964), pp. 33–39. Reprinted by permission of the author and Yale University Press. Copyright © 1964 by Yale University.

Eight Ways to Fail to Make Law

Rex came to the throne filled with the zeal of a reformer. He considered that the greatest failure of his predecessors had been in the field of law. For generations the legal system had known nothing like a basic reform. Procedures of trial were cumbersome, the rules of law spoke in the archaic tongue of another age, justice was expensive, the judges were slovenly and sometimes corrupt. Rex was resolved to remedy all this and to make his name in history as a great lawgiver. It was his unhappy fate to fail in this ambition. Indeed, he failed spectacularly, since not only did he not succeed in introducing the needed reforms, but he never even succeeded in creating any law at all, good or bad.

His first official act was, however, dramatic and propitious. Since he needed a clean slate on which to write, he announced to his subjects the immediate repeal of all existing law, of whatever kind. He then set about drafting a new code. Unfortunately, trained as a lonely prince, his education had been very defective. In particular he found himself incapable of making even the simplest generalizations. Though not lacking in confidence when it came to deciding specific controversies, the effort to give articulate reasons for any conclusion strained his capacities to the breaking point.

Becoming aware of his limitations, Rex gave up the project of a code and announced to his subjects that henceforth he would act as a judge in any disputes that might arise among them. In this way under the stimulus of a variety of cases he hoped that his latent powers of generalization might develop and, proceeding case by case, he would gradually work out a system of rules that could be incorporated in a code. Unfortunately the defects in his education were more deep-seated than he had supposed. The venture failed completely. After he had handed down literally hundreds of decisions neither he nor his subjects could detect in those decisions any pattern whatsoever. Such tentatives toward generalization as were to be found in his opinions only compounded the confusion, for they gave false leads to his subjects and threw his own meager powers of judgment off balance in the decision of later cases.

After this fiasco Rex realized it was necessary to take a fresh start. His first move was to subscribe to a course of lessons in generalization. With his intellectual powers thus fortified, he resumed the project of a code and, after many hours of solitary labor, succeeded in preparing a fairly lengthy document. He was still not confident, however, that he had fully overcome his previous defects. Accordingly, he announced to his subjects that he had written out a code and would henceforth be governed by it in deciding cases, but that for an indefinite future the contents of the code would remain an official state secret, known only to him and his scrivener. To Rex's surprise this sensible plan was deeply resented by his subjects. They declared it was very unpleasant to have one's case decided by rules when there was no way of knowing what those rules were.

Stunned by this rejection Rex undertook an earnest inventory of his personal strengths and weaknesses. He decided that life had taught him one clear lesson, namely, that it is easier to decide things with the aid of hindsight than it is to attempt to foresee and control the future. Not only did hindsight make it easier to decide cases, but—and this was of supreme importance to Rex—it made it easier to give reasons. Deciding to capitalize on this insight, Rex hit on the following plan. At the beginning of each calendar year he would decide all the controversies that had arisen among his subjects during the preceding year. He would accompany his decisions with a full statement of reasons. Naturally, the reasons thus given would be understood as not controlling decisions in future years, for that would be to defeat the whole purpose of the new arrangement, which was to gain the advantages of hindsight. Rex confidently announced the new plan to his subjects observing that he was going to publish the full text of his judgments with the rules applied by him, thus meeting the chief objection to the old plan. Rex's subjects received this announcement in silence, then quietly explained through their leaders that when they said they needed to know the rules, they meant they needed to know them *in advance* so they could act on them. Rex muttered something to the effect that they might have made that point a little clearer, but said he would see what could be done.

Rex now realized that there was no escape from a published code declaring the rules to be applied in future disputes. Continuing his lessons in generalization, Rex worked diligently on a revised code, and finally announced that it would shortly be published. This announcement was received with universal gratification. The dismay of Rex's subjects was all the more intense, therefore, when his code became available and it was discovered that it was truly a masterpiece of obscurity. Legal experts who studied it declared that there was not a single sentence in it that could be understood either by an ordinary citizen or by a trained lawyer. Indignation became general and soon a picket appeared before the royal palace carrying a sign that read, "How can anybody follow a rule that nobody can understand?"

The code was quickly withdrawn. Recognizing for the first time that he needed assistance, Rex put a staff of experts to work on a revision. He instructed them to leave the substance untouched, but to clarify the expression throughout. The resulting code was a model of clarity, but as it was studied it became apparent that its new clarity had merely brought to light that it was honeycombed with contradictions. It was reliably reported that there was not a single provision in the code that was not nullified by another provision inconsistent with it. A picket again appeared before the royal residence carrying a sign that read, "This time the king made himself clear—in both directions."

Once again the code was withdrawn for revision. By now, however, Rex had lost his patience with his subjects and the negative attitude they seemed to adopt toward everything he tried to do for them. He decided to teach them a lesson and put an end to their carping. He instructed his experts to purge the code of contradictions, but at the same time to stiffen drastically every requirement contained in it and to add a long list of new crimes. Thus, where before the citizen summoned to the throne was given ten days in which to report, in the revision the time was cut to ten seconds. It was made a crime, punishable by ten years' imprisonment, to cough, sneeze, hiccough, faint or fall down in the presence of the king. It was made treason not to understand, believe in, and correctly profess the doctrine of evolutionary, democratic redemption.

When the new code was published a near revolution resulted. Leading citizens declared their intention to flout its provisions. Someone discovered in an ancient author a passage that seemed apt: "To command what cannot be done is not to make law; it is to unmake law, for a command that cannot be obeyed serves no end but confusion, fear and chaos." Soon this passage was being quoted in a hundred petitions to the king.

The code was again withdrawn and a staff of experts charged with the task of revision. Rex's instructions to the experts were that whenever they encountered a rule requiring an impossibility, it should be revised to make compliance possible. It turned out that to accomplish this result every provision in the code had to be substantially rewritten. The final result was, however, a triumph of draftsmanship. It was clear, consistent with itself, and demanded nothing of the subject that did not lie easily within his powers. It was printed and distributed free of charge on every street corner.

However, before the effective date for the new code had arrived, it was discovered that so much time had been spent in successive revisions of Rex's original draft, that the substance of the code had been seriously overtaken by events. Ever since Rex assumed the throne there had been a suspension of ordinary legal processes and this had brought about important economic and institutional changes within the country. Accommodation to these altered conditions required many changes of substance in the law. Accordingly as soon as the new code became legally effective, it was subjected to a daily stream of amendments. Again popular discontent mounted; an anonymous pamphlet appeared on the streets carrying scurrilous cartoons of the king and a leading article with the title: "A law that changes every day is worse than no law at all."

Within a short time this source of discontent began to cure itself as the pace of amendment gradually slackened. Before this had occurred to any noticeable degree, however, Rex announced an important decision. Reflecting on the misadventures of his reign, he concluded that much of the trouble lay in bad advice he had received from experts. He accordingly declared he was reassuming the judicial power in his own person. In this way he could directly control the application of the new code and insure his country against another crisis. He began to spend practically all of his time hearing and deciding cases arising under the new code.

As the king proceeded with this task, it seemed to bring to a belated blossoming his long dormant powers of generalization. His opinions began, indeed, to reveal a confident and almost exuberant virtuosity as he deftly distinguished his own previous decisions, exposed the principles on which he acted, and laid down guidelines for the disposition of future controversies. For Rex's subjects a new day seemed about to dawn when they could finally conform their conduct to a coherent body of rules.

This hope was, however, soon shattered. As the bound volumes of Rex's judgments became available and were subjected to closer study, his subjects were appalled to discover that there existed no discernible relation between those judgments and the code they purported to apply. Insofar as it found expression in the actual disposition of controversies, the new code might just as well not have existed at all. Yet in virtually every one of his decisions Rex declared and redeclared the code to be the basic law of his kingdom.

Leading citizens began to hold private meetings to discuss what measures, short of open revolt, could be taken to get the king away from the bench and back on the throne. While these discussions were going on Rex suddenly died, old before his time and deeply disillusioned with his subjects.

The first act of his successor, Rex II, was to announce that he was taking the powers of government away from the lawyers and placing them in the hands of psychiatrists and experts in public relations. This way, he explained, people could be made happy without rules.

The Consequences of Failure

Rex's bungling career as legislator and judge illustrates that the attempt to create and maintain a system of legal rules may miscarry in at least eight ways; there are in this enterprise, if you will, eight distinct routes to disaster. The first and most obvious lies in a failure to achieve rules at all, so that every issue must be decided on an ad hoc basis. The other routes are: (2) a failure to publicize, or at least to make available to the affected party, the rules he is expected to observe; (3) the abuse of retroactive legislation, which not only cannot itself guide action, but undercuts the integrity of rules prospective in effect, since it puts them under the threat of retrospective change; (4) a failure to make rules understandable; (5) the enactment of contradictory rules or (6) rules that require conduct beyond the powers of the affected party; (7) introducing such frequent changes in the rules that the subject cannot orient his action by them; and, finally, (8) a failure of congruence between the rules as announced and their actual administration.

A total failure in any one of these eight directions does not simply result in a bad system of law; it results in something that is not properly called a legal system at all, except perhaps in the Pickwickian sense in which a void contract can still be said to be one kind of contract.

4

The Natural Case Against Contraception

JOHN T. NOONAN, JR.

The attitude toward rhythm, like the older attitude toward the marriage of the sterile, must be a source of surprise and discomfort for anyone who takes literally the statement, "Coitus is naturally generative, contraception is against nature." The same surprise and discomfort would have been experienced by anyone who had taken literally the statements, "Money is naturally sterile, usury is against nature," and had then considered the attitude of the Church on the *societas,* the *census,* the sale of foreign exchange, and the rent *ad pompam.* In both cases, the statements projected values; confusion resulted only from mistaking the function the statements performed.

Like the statements on money, the statements on the generative act and organ functioned in relation to a rule, an absolute prohibition of the Church. Like the statements on money, the first function of these statements on nature was to place the prohibition within the realm of the rational. If the rule was founded on nature, neither biblical texts nor ecclesiastical pronouncements would, in the long run, be as influential as the judgment of reasoning human beings. The appeal to nature was, in effect, an invitation to exercise reason.

The absolute rule of the Church here, like the absolute rule on usury, protected certain values. Can one identify the "nature" asserted with the values protected? An answer to this question depends on an inspection of the values. I would suggest that the values protected by the rule were four: procreation, life, dignity, and love. In the first place, the prohibition of contraception asserted that procreation was good. For thirteen hundred years there were major movements within the Church, or in competition with it, which taught that procreation was evil: Gnosticism, Manicheanism, Priscillianism, Bogomilism, Catharism. Against these movements, the assertion that contraception was against nature was, in large part, an affirmation that procreation was a good act of cooperation with a good God.

Second, prohibition of contraception embodied an assertion of the sanctity of life. In the Greco-Roman society in which Christians first condemned contraception there was widespread insensitivity to infant and embryonic life. Infanticide, abandonment of babies, and abortion were practiced without legal restraint and with little moral criticism. The Christians appeared as defenders of the rights of the infant and the embryo. Destruction of any human life, they maintained, was murder. The defense of the sacredness of existing life ex-

From *Natural Law Forum,* X (1965), 232–235. Abridged without notes. Reprinted by permission of the author and publisher.

tended to a defense of the sacredness of the process by which life was engendered. There were two main reasons for this extension of concern. No clear line existed between seed and embryo; if, with Tertullian, one said, "He kills a man who kills a man to be," the statement seemed to apply equally to both. In practice, it was difficult to distinguish between the abortifacient and contraceptive effects of the potions that were the most popular contraceptives. The protection of existing life seemed to require the proscription of means affecting conception. The valuation given life thus played a part in the judgment formed on contraception.

Third, some sexual acts in marriage appeared to be destructive of the personal dignity of a spouse. These acts expressed or fostered the belief that a spouse, usually the wife, was a thing given the other to be enjoyed and exploited. The treatment of oral intercourse and anal intercourse as unnatural may be read as assertions, in the language of an age unacquainted with personalist philosophy, that the spouses, united in marriage, must relate to each other as persons.

Finally, the sanctity attached to coitus was an implicit assertion of the value of sexual love. Not promiscuously outside of marriage, not even without reverence within marriage, could love be expressed in sexual acts. In the treatment of coitus as a sacral union, the mystery and the importance of sexual love were obscurely acknowledged.

That protection of procreation and of life were in the minds of those framing the absolute rule seems to me to be established by evidence. That protection of personal dignity and of love was also in their minds rests on evidence also; but here we attribute to earlier theologians concepts which they did not use explicitly; we reinterpret and explicate. We are using our concepts to describe the way the rule functioned; we are hypothesizing that these values gave vitality to the rule.

The argument that contraception was against nature supported the absolute rule just as the argument that usury was against nature supported the usury prohibition. Again, it is possible to see the argument as making absolute a rule which could have been expressed in more discriminating and flexible terms. Again, the question arises why the argument based on nature seemed so superior; and again, psychological and rhetorical satisfactions would seem to account for the choice. The sacral character of coitus to which the argument based on nature finally appeals seems to be no stronger than the usury argument's appeal to the sacred character of time. This characterization asserts the reality of the rule, the seriousness of the violation, but adds no new evidence or insight. The claim that coitus was naturally fertile continued long after acceptance of the marriage of the sterile, intercourse in pregnancy, intercourse to express love, and the use of rhythm. Although coitus might often be lawfully sterile, theologians still asserted that to make it sterile was self-stultifying. To demonstrate the rule on contraception by claiming that a contraceptive act was self-contradictory apparently yielded psychological and rhetorical gratifications.

To look only at the negative aspects of the argument based on nature would be to overlook its most important function. Like its counterpart on usury, it asserted that there was an evil in contraception which man could grasp. The prohibition of contraception was not simply a Jewish law, a Christian idiosyncrasy, a papal aberration, a divine whim. There were values which the practice of contraception endangered which should be dear to all men. Contraception was in a given society an evil. The argument based on nature stood for this proposition. It announced the rational character of the rule on coitus. It taught that there was a measure in marital acts which could be found by examination; it invited scrutiny which could lead to revision of the rule.

A comparison of arguments based on the nature of money with arguments based on the nature of sex may seem to bring together two hopelessly dissimilar subjects. "For love or money": the dichotomy seems eternal. Nature itself would seem to cry out against an attempt to extract from such diverse natures any common themes. The considerations appropriate to an ethics of moneylending, the specialized function of a few, would seem so remote from the considerations relevant to the sexual conduct of all married persons that only accident or force could bring them both together.

In the present essay I have tried to show that in fact both topics have been approached in much the same way by Catholic theologians employing the concept of natural law. Conclusions similar to mine have been reached by a more abstract examination of natural law in general; but they lack concreteness and could be viewed as the results of a preference for "subjectivism." Here I have drawn conclusions from the way natural law concepts actually functioned in two specific moral problems. The conclusions suggested are true at least in these two cases.

"Nature" has a rhetorical function. The acts and purpose designated as natural occur in experience, but their controlling normative role is assigned them by an authoritatively proclaimed rule. It is evident to everyone today that the "sterile nature" of money was a concept employed for didactic and psychological reasons; it added no fresh evidence for the usury rule which invoked it. An analogous function is equally clear in the employment of the concept of the "fertile nature" of coitus. In each case the vitality of the moral rule itself depended not on the concept of nature employed but on the values protected. These values were not discoverable from an inspection of the nature of an act. They depended on human purposes, and so on human persons. The truly vital function of the argument based on nature, however, was to draw an issue into discussion by men. The argument based on natural law demanded the exercise of rationality; it rejected the view that behavior in a given area of life was purposeless, measureless, uncontrollable, or arbitrary. It assumed that there was an order for human purposes, and so a human nature whose mark was reason. It called for a process of rationality which began in argument and ended in reasoned decision.

SECTION TWO *Culture Conflict and the Law*

5

A Remarkable Murder Trial:
Rex v. Sinnisiak

EDWIN R. KEEDY

Sinnisiak was charged with the murder of Rev. Father Rouviere, a priest of the order Oblates of Mary Immaculate, at Bloody Falls on the Coppermine River near Coronation Gulf on the Arctic Ocean in November, 1913. . . .

I

During the summer of 1913 the Rev. Fathers Rouviere and LeRoux, both members of the Oblate Order, left Fort Norman on the Mackenzie River for the northeast shores of Great Bear Lake for missionary work among the Eskimos. They expected to be absent for about two years. Nothing was ever heard from them, but in the spring of 1915 rumors reached the authorities at Fort Norman that the priests had been killed by Eskimos. Inspector LaNauze and two constables of the Royal Northwest Mounted Police [later The Royal Canadian Mounted Police] were sent with supplies to investigate the rumors and clear up the mystery of the missing priests. The officers, accompanied by an interpreter, reached Great Bear Lake in the fall of 1915 and encamped there for the winter. In the spring of 1916 Inspector LaNauze with his party proceeded to the shore of Coronation Gulf near the mouth of the Coppermine River, where he learned that the priests had been killed by Sinnisiak and Uluksak. Inspector LaNauze was shortly afterward joined by Corporal Bruce of the Mounted Police who with several guides had set out from Herschel Island in the Arctic Ocean to make an independent search for the missing priests and had obtained from the Eskimos the vestments and breviaries of the priests and articles for the Mass used by them.

Inspector LaNauze, who held a commission as a justice of the peace, on the complaint of Corporal Bruce, issued a warrant for the arrest of Sinnisiak who was located in a deerskin tent, engaged in making a wooden bow, and was arrested on the warrant. In his report the Inspector stated that "he appeared to be stunned with fear and I learned afterward that he expected to be stabbed right then." The interpreter, who accompanied the Inspector, stated that Sinnisiak said, "If the white men kill me I will make medicine and the ship will go

From *University of Pennsylvania Law Review*, XLVIII (1951), 49–67. Copyright © 1951 by the University of Pennsylvania Law Review. The original notes, which were deleted for this volume, contained extensive comments on Canadian territorial procedures.

down in the ice and all will be drowned." Following the arrest of Sinnisiak, the Inspector, in his capacity as a justice of the peace, conducted a preliminary examination, at which Sinnisiak, after being warned that he need not make any statement, freely admitted that the priests were killed by him and Uluksak. He was accordingly committed for trial. Several days later Uluksak was arrested and, after a preliminary examination at which he admitted taking part in the killing, was committed for trial.

Inspector LaNauze in his report stated the following:

> I have not deceived the murderers in any way, I have had it carefully explained to them that it is not for me to judge them but that the Big White Chief must decide what he will do with them. But it is hard for them to grasp the meaning of this, in their life they have no chief, everyone is equal, and their word "Ishumatak" for "chief" literally translated means "the thinker," the man who does the deciding or thinking for the party. As regards their religion they have none. . . .
>
> In conclusion, I might mention we were dealing with a still practically primitive people, a people who six years ago were discovered living in what might be termed a stone age, and hidden away in the vast sub-Arctic spaces of the Northland of Canada.

It required more than a year for the officers to bring Sinnisiak and Uluksak from the Coppermine River to Edmonton. They also brought two interpreters and an elderly Eskimo, Koeha, who was to be a witness at the trial.

II

Although the crime charged against the defendants was committed in the region of the Arctic Ocean more than two thousand miles from Edmonton, the trial in that city was authorized by a statute providing that an offense committed in any part of Canada not in a province duly constituted may be tried in any province as may be most convenient.

The Chief Justice of the Supreme Court of Alberta presided at the trial, and the Canadian Minister of Justice appointed able and experienced counsel to represent the Crown and to conduct the defense. Although both the Eskimos had been charged with the murder of the two priests, Crown counsel elected to proceed against Sinnisiak alone for the murder of Father Rouviere.

At the start of the trial the courtroom presented a dramatic spectacle. On the bench was the Chief Justice wearing a black silk gown, a similar gown being worn by each of the counsel. Appearing as witnesses for the Crown were the members of the Northwest Mounted Police, who had investigated the crime and brought the defendants from the Arctic Ocean, the Inspector in a uniform consisting of a dark blue tunic and light blue breeches, while the Corporal and the Constable wore breeches of the same color with scarlet tunics. Also appearing as witnesses for the Crown were several priests of the Oblate Order, each wearing a long black cassock with a large silver crucifix hanging by a chain from the neck. Displayed as exhibits were the vestments of Fathers

Rouviere and LeRoux with the articles for the Mass used by them. In order that the jury, which was composed of prominent citizens, might observe the defendants as they appeared in their native habitat, they were dressed, at the opening of the trial, in the garments which they wore when taken into custody, consisting of a loose smock and hood of sealskin with loose trousers and soft boots of the same material. As the summer temperature at Edmonton was much too warm for such apparel each of the defendants was provided with a washtub, filled with water and blocks of ice, into which he placed his feet. After the first session of the trial the defendants wore suits of blue denim.

In his opening address to the jury Crown counsel stated that "The long arm of British Justice has reached out to the shore of the Arctic Ocean, and has made prisoners of two of the aboriginal inhabitants of the Arctic Shore, suspected of committing the crime in question." He also stated that "the great importance of the trial consists in this: that for the first time in history these people, these Arctic people, prehistoric people, people who are as nearly as possible living today in the Stone Age, will be brought in contact with and will be taught what is the white man's justice."

The first witness was Father Duchasoir, of the Oblate Order, who identified the vestments of Father Rouviere and the articles for the Mass used by him, also letters received from him by his superiors at Fort Norman.

The second witness was Corporal Bruce who described his search for the priests and his discovery of their vestments and articles for the Mass.

On cross-examination he was questioned as follows regarding the Eskimos of the Coppermine River, generally known as the Copper Eskimos:

Q. What manner of people did you find them?
A. Very simple, kindly as a rule.
Q. What about their intelligence?
A. Well, they are very clever in their work, but their minds don't work like ours.
Q. They compare more with children, don't they, than with grown-up people as far as we are concerned?
A. As regards our ways, it is a hard question to answer.
Q. That is what I say, as regards our ways, our methods of doing things, they are simple like children?
A. Yes; they want to examine everything; they are very curious to find out about things, how it is made and how it is done.
Q. What you would call primitive?
A. Yes, they are primitive.

The witness was also questioned regarding the religion of the Copper Eskimos. The following questions and answers are significant:

Q. Do you know anything about these people's religion?
A. Yes, that is, according to ethnologists, their religion consists of a series of taboos.

Q. Good spirits and evil spirits?

A. Yes.

Q. Things they should do and things they should not do?

A. Yes.

Q. I understand they think these spirits come to them in human form?

A. Yes. Those are imaginary spirits they call down. They sometimes say they see spirits, performing that way.

When asked to name some of the "taboos," the witness stated "they are not supposed to eat caribou meat on the ice" and "women are not supposed to sew in the full of the moon."

When asked about the custom after a caribou was killed the witness said "they generally cut a little piece off of it and throw it to one side." Then followed these questions and answers:

Q. Do you know the reason for that? Did you ever hear of that because the caribou has spirits?

A. I understood it to be that.

Q. Spirits go along with the caribou, and they have to appease those spirits?

A. Yes.

When asked whether the Eskimos practiced any form of punishment the witness replied, "Not that I know of except they have blood feuds there."

On cross-examination regarding his approach to the village where Sinnisiak was arrested, the witness testified that he did not carry a gun because he didn't want to cause any fear among the Eskimos.

After testimony by the Constable who accompanied Inspector LaNauze, confirming the testimony of Corporal Bruce regarding the arrest of Sinnisiak, Koeha, the elderly Eskimo, who was brought to Edmonton with the defendants, was called as a witness. After being sworn by the formula "Whatever you speak now you speak straight, don't speak with two tongues," the witness testified through an interpreter. He first stated that the priests were given Eskimo names, Kuleavik for Father Rouviere and Ilogoak for Father LeRoux. He also identified photographs of the priests. He was then questioned by Crown counsel regarding his knowledge of the killing of the priests. This involved the asking of many leading questions, some of which were objected to by counsel for the defense. The judge, however, allowed Crown counsel considerable latitude in this respect. Much difficulty was experienced with the interpreter, who did not always understand the questions put to the witness. In some instances these were translated to the interpreter in "pigeon English" by one of the Mounted Police. The extent of the difficulty with the interpreter is indicated by the following dialogue:

MR. WALLBRIDGE: My lord, the interpreter Patsy informs me that this interpreter is putting him [the witness] through the third degree, is accusing him of lying, and trying to get him to give an answer which the Eskimo doesn't want to give.

THE COURT: Ilavinik, just ask him the question that counsel gives you. Do not say any more to him. Just get him to answer that. You can explain that to him, but do not ask him anything else, and do not say anything else to him.

At this point in the trial Crown counsel offered in evidence the statement made by Sinnisiak at the preliminary hearing. The Court of its own motion directed that the interpreter, Ilavinik, who was the interpreter at the preliminary hearing, be questioned as to whether he interpreted correctly. Ilavinik was accordingly sworn as a witness and testified that Sinnisiak's statement was the result of questions put to him, the answers being correctly interpreted. He stated that he put questions to Sinnisiak "pretty nearly all day." The statement of Sinnisiak, which was then admitted in evidence, was as follows:

The accused being duly warned in the usual manner makes the following statement:

I was stopping at the mouth of the Coppermine River and was going fishing one morning. A lot of people were going fishing. When the sun had not gone down I returned to camp and saw that the two priests had started back up the river. They had four dogs. I saw no other men.

I slept one night. Next morning I started with one dog. I help people coming from the south. All day I walked along and then I left the river and traveled on the land, I was following the priests' trail. I met the priests near a lake, when I was close to them one man came to meet me. The man Ilogoak, the big man, came to me and told me to come over to the camp. Ilogoak said to me, "if you help me pull the sled I will pay you in traps." We moved off the same day I arrived to be near wood, Uluksak was with me and we pulled the sled. We could not make the trees, it was hard work and we made camp.

The next day we started back and the priests were going ahead, it started to storm and we lost the road. After that the dogs smelt something and Uluksak went to see what it was and I stayed behind. Uluksak found it was a cache of the priests and told me to come over. As soon as we got there the priests came back.

Ilogoak was carrying a rifle, he was mad with us when we started back from their camp and I could not understand his talk. I asked Ilogoak if he was going to kill me and he nodded his head. Ilogoak said "Come over to the sled" and pushed me with his hand.

The priests wanted to start again and he pushed me again and wanted me to put on the harness and then he took his rifle out on top of the sled. I was scared and I started to pull.

We went a little way and Uluksak and I started to talk and Ilogoak put his hand on my mouth.

Ilogoak was very mad, and was pushing me. I was thinking hard and crying and very scared and the frost was in my boots and I was cold.

I wanted to go back, I was afraid. Ilogoak would not let us. Every time the sled stuck Ilogoak would pull out the rifle.

I got hot inside my body and every time Ilogoak pulled out the rifle I was very much afraid.

I said to Uluksak, I think they will kill us, I can't get back now. I was thinking I will not see my people any more, I will try and kill him. I was pulling ahead of the dogs. We came to a small hill. I took off the harness quick and ran to one side and Ilogoak ran after me and he pushed me back to the sled. I took off my belt and told Ilogoak I was going to "relieve myself" as I did not want to go to the sled. After that I ran behind the sled, I did not want to relieve myself. Then Ilogoak turned around and saw me, he looked away from me and I stabbed him in the back with a knife. I then told Uluksak, "You take the rifle." Ilogoak ran ahead of the sled and Uluksak went after him. The other white man wanted to come back to the sled. I had the knife in my hand and he went away again. Uluksak and Ilogoak were wrestling for the rifle and after that Uluksak finished up Ilogoak. I did not see Uluksak finish him. The other man ran away when he saw Ilogoak die. I asked Uluksak is he dead, and he said yes already. I then said to Uluksak, "Give me the rifle." He gave it to me. The first time I shot I did not hit him, the second time I got him. The priest sat down when the bullet struck him. I went after him with the knife, when I was close to him he got up again, both of us were together. I had the knife in my hand and I went after him when he got up again.

Uluksak told me, "Go ahead and put the knife in him." The priest fell down on his back. I said to Uluksak, "Go ahead you I fixed the other man already." Uluksak struck first with the knife and did not strike him the second time he got him. The priest lay down and was breathing a little. I struck him with an axe I was carrying across the face. I cut his legs with the axe. I killed him dead.

One man is in a creek, the first one alongside the sled.

After they were dead I said to Uluksak before when white men were killed they used to cut off some and eat some. Uluksak cut up Ilogoak's belly. I turned around.

Uluksak gave me a little piece of the liver. I eat it. Uluksak eat too.

We covered up both bodies with snow when we started to go back. We each took a rifle and cartridges. We took 3 bags of cartridges each. We started back in the night time. We camped that night.

Next morning we got back to camp as soon as it was light.

I went into Kormik's tent. Kormik was sleeping and I woke him up. I told him I kill those two fellows already. I can't remember what Kormik said. Kormik, Koeha, Angibrunna, Kallun, Kingordlik went to get the priests' stuff. They started in the morning and came back the same night. Kormik had two church shirts and some clothing. I can't remember the other things. Kormik sold the two church shirts to A. Nautallik. I do not know what he got for them. I can't tell any more. If I knew more I would tell you, I can't remember any more.

WITNESS and INTERPRETER:
    WITNESS (Sgd). W. V. Bruce, Cpl.
    INTERPRETER (Sgd). X Ilavinik
        C. D. LaNauze, J.P.

The next witness was Inspector LaNauze, who described his search for the priests and told of his meeting with Corporal Bruce at the mouth of the Coppermine River in the spring of 1916. He stated that he obtained an interpreter, Ilavinik, who had been with [Vilhjalmur] Stefansson when he made his trip to this region. He then described the arrest of Sinnisiak. He stated that he entered a tent where he was informed he would find Sinnisiak. He then said: "The first thing I saw was a man sitting at the far end of the tent. He was engaged in the manufacture of a bow, and he sat there trembling, in fact he was shaking all over."

Regarding the attitude of the Eskimos, who were present when Sinnisiak was arrested, the witness testified as follows: "I simply explained our mission, and rather curious to relate, the people were all on our side. They turned around and said, 'You must do what the white man tell you; you have got to go with them' and after that we got quietly away from the camp."

On cross-examination of the witness the following dialogue occurred:

Q. And the story you got from all of them, as well as the story you got from this prisoner, the information you got was that these men had killed the priests out of fear?
A. Out of fear?
Q. Yes.
A. No, I don't know.
Q. Your report says that they had killed them in self-defense?
A. I said they might have, I think.

Questioned regarding the arrest of Sinnisiak, he stated that Sinnisiak undoubtedly thought that he was going to be killed "on the spot."

Counsel for the defense then read to the witness the following statement from Stefannson's book, *My Life among the Eskimos:* "Like our distant ancestors, no doubt, these people fear most of all things the evil spirits that are likely to appear to them at any time in any guise, and next to that they fear strangers." The witness was then asked whether this was "a fair statement," to which he replied, "Well, Stefannson is an authority."

The attention of the witness was called to the following statement of his report: "Their own defense of being ill-treated is their strongest point, and the prosecution has no witness that will deny this." He was then asked: "You were unable to find any?" To which he replied "No." The witness also confirmed that his report contained the following statement: "The unfortunate priests may have been the victims of a premeditated murder for the possession of their rifles and ammunition, or may have brought on the crime by their own untactfulness." He was then asked: "I want to know whether you had any information that would suggest this untactfulness?" To this he replied: "Yes, I thought so possibly by the prisoner's statements." [1]

The witness was asked: "And if a white man, a stranger, holds a gun on an Eskimo, the Eskimo hasn't any other notion but what it is going to be used? There is no doubt?" The answer was "No doubt."

Koeha, being recalled as a witness, testified regarding the priests' relations with the Eskimos. He was asked: "Had the priests been pretty good to the Eskimos, to the Huskies?" To this he replied: "Yes, they had been good." He also stated that the priests had taught the Eskimos to catch fish with nets. Following is a portion of the cross-examination:

Q. Did you know the first time you saw Ilogoak that he was a priest, a missionary? Do you know what a priest is?

A. No.

Q. Did you know that Kuleavik was a priest?

A. I didn't know.

Q. Did you think they were trappers or traders?

A. I think they come down for caribou, think they were hunters and traders.

During the cross-examination the witness was questioned about spirits as follows:

Q. Do you like to talk about spirits?

THE INTERPRETER: He doesn't want to speak.

Q. Are you afraid to speak about spirits?

A. I am not afraid.

Q. (To interpreter) But he doesn't like to speak about spirits?

THE INTERPRETER: No.

Q. Is it unlucky to speak about spirits?

A. Yes.

At the completion of the testimony of Koeha, the Crown rested.

Sinnisiak, the defendant, was then called as a witness and sworn by the interpreter. Counsel for the defense then directed the interpreter to make the following statement to the defendant:

Tell him, first, I want him to speak to the big chief, and I want him not to be afraid, and to say everything. You tell him that. Tell him not to be afraid because all these people are here, to just talk to me as if he was talking to me alone.

On direct examination the testimony of the defendant was substantially the same as his statement made at the preliminary hearing, which had previously been put in evidence by Crown counsel. He testified specifically that "When we started off—every time we tried to get out of the harness the priest had his gun and was going to shoot me." He testified further that he thought he was going to be killed.

Regarding spirits the defendant testified as follows:

Q. Why did you eat a piece of the dead man's liver?

A. Because I heard from my grandfather. I heard about it from my grandfather.

Q. Did you know what it was going to do for you to eat the liver?

A. The man might get up again if I didn't eat his liver.[2]

Q. Do you like to talk about spirits?

A. I don't know.

Q. You don't know what? Do you like to talk about spirits?

A. I don't know how to speak about spirits.

Q. Do you know about spirits? Do you know anything about spirits?
A. I know about spirits.
Q. Has the eating of the liver anything to do with spirits?
A. I think maybe the spirits make the man alive.

The defendant testified that before the arrival of the priests he had seen three white men, Stefansson and two prospectors.

At the conclusion of the defendant's testimony Crown counsel stated that he would not cross-examine him, but would "go to the jury on the evidence in the shape in which it is."

Counsel for the defendant now addressed the Court and jury. He contended that the defendant should be judged by the standard of his own people and not by the standard of civilized persons. He argued for an acquittal on two grounds: (1) that the defendant should be treated as a young child and should be judged by the standard of his own people and (2) that he acted in self-defense, reasonably believing that he was in danger of being killed by the priests.

In his closing address to the Court and jury, Crown counsel stated by way of introduction the following:

> The object of giving these people the advantage of British justice and British fair play is to make it known that if the white men, traveling in that country, are killed, that the tribe will not be exterminated, that no punitive expedition will exterminate them, but that they will be given the same fair trial as any white man, Englishman or Canadian, would get under similar circumstances.

Crown counsel contended that the evidence showed the defendant and Uluksak planned to murder the priests for their rifles. With regard to the argument of counsel for the defense that the defendant should not be judged by the ordinary standard of civilized persons Crown counsel replied that this argument did not apply to the question of guilt but to mitigation of punishment, and should be addressed not to the judge and jury but to the Governor in Council after conviction.

The Court commenced his charge to the jury by stating the following:

> The fact that he is a poor, ignorant benighted pagan, who comes from beyond the borders of our civilization, does not stand in the way of his receiving all the protection that our law can give any person charged with any offence. As you have seen he has been furnished with counsel, not some junior counsel who might be desirous of getting the experience of defending an important case, but he has been provided as counsel with one of the leaders of the bar, who has left no stone unturned during the course of this trial to see that no unfair advantage was taken of the accused, and to see that everything that might be brought out in his favor should be brought out. Owing to the circumstances of this case, the particular circumstances, I instructed the sheriff, when empanelling the jury, to see that no person was put on the panel of jurors except men of the highest standing in the community. I thought it only fair that the prisoner should have the best that our country can afford in answering a charge such as this.

Regarding the contention that the defendant should be judged by the standard of his own people the Court charged as follows:

> Much has been suggested in the present case about the prisoner's lack of knowledge of our law and our customs, and his own custom. Of course, that applies to a greater or less extent to many of the foreigners who have come into our country; to the Indians, although they have to become gradually more and more accustomed to our laws, but that cannot be dealt with by the court such as this is in considering the liability for the crime. In law a person must be considered liable. In fact, there is a very great difference. That is a matter to be dealt with in the matter of punishment.

The Court disposed of the claim of self-defense as follows:

> The question then would seem largely to be one between culpable homicide and excusable or justifiable homicide. Now, homicide is justified if it is done in self-defense, but self-defense does not mean prevention. We have, of course, in the last two or three years had pressed upon us very frequently the question of self-defense in a way that is more or less applicable to this. Germany has declared that she is making this war as a war of self-defense. Assuming that she is honest, all of us consider it is not self-defense as we look upon self-defense. It may be for the purpose of preventing what she fears, but it is not defending herself against an attack because she attacked first. That perhaps is her view of self-defense, and that is a view of self-defense that has been advanced as an excuse for killing within our own memory. We have accounts of it in the early unsettled portions of the country where the law is not strictly enforced of people taking the law in their own hands. Where they feared, and had good reasons to fear, men might kill them, they kill the person to prevent it. That is not self-defense. That is an attempt to prevent, but it is not under our law permissible. Now, the self-defense, as it is known to our law, that is, the excuse for the killing, is the defense against attack, a defense against an assault of some sort.

In conclusion the Court charged as follows:

> It is your duty to deal with this case calmly and deliberately and not to be affected by your sympathies, but allow your judgment full sway. I say that is your duty. You are human, however, and you have your sympathies as you cannot help having them, and they, no doubt, will have some effect upon you; and I want to say to you, therefore, that while it is your duty to find a verdict of murder, if you view the case largely as I have suggested it to you and on that verdict, if you find it, it will be my duty to pass the sentence of death; that would be the only sentence that I could pass. Yet I have no hesitation in saying to you that I would consider it a crime that this man should be executed for the act with which he has been, and for which he is being, charged here. It is there that his condition, his absence of knowledge, his customs, and his absence of knowledge of our customs should have effect, and I would be bound, in the exercise of my duty, to recommend that the sentence of death should not be carried out, and I have no doubt whatever that the authorities would recommend to His Excel-

lency, the Governor-General, that he should not be executed, but that some other form of punishment would be imposed which would meet the requirements of the case, and which would take home to him and to the members of his tribe the knowledge of our laws and our measure of justice. I have no doubt that some such punishment as that would be given to him, and not that the extreme penalty of the law would be exercised. I tell you that so that you may feel freer perhaps to do what the law demands of you, but which might perhaps be abhorrent to your sentiments of humanity if you felt that the strict letter of the law would have to be carried out.

The jury retired to consider their verdict at 12:03 o'clock and at 1:10 P.M. returned the following verdict: "Not guilty."

III

After the acquittal of Sinnisiak for the murder of Father Rouviere the authorities decided to try both Sinnisiak and Uluksak jointly for the murder of Father LeRoux. Acting under a statute which gives the court authority to change the venue, Chief Justice Harvey directed that the trial should occur in Calgary, about 200 miles south of Edmonton. The trial started six days after the close of the trial in Edmonton and lasted three days. The evidence for the prosecution was in substance the same as in the trial at Edmonton. Both Sinnisiak and Uluksak testified as witnesses for the defense. Sinnisiak's testimony was practically identical with that given by him in the Edmonton trial. When Uluksak took the stand he was asked how old he was. He replied: "Maybe I am eight years old (holding up fingers of both hands)." Ulusak's testimony was the same as his statement made at the preliminary hearing. The addresses of counsel and the charge of the Court were similar to those at Edmonton. There was an added statement by defense counsel regarding the independent nature of the Eskimos. He said, "There are natives who can be treated with the whip, natives of Africa I understand, thrashed into the way of the white man, made to do his bidding. But that is not the way with the Eskimo; he is a free, independent man. You cannot coerce him. You can coax him; you can make him do your bidding by kindness, but you cannot coerce him. His motto is the one made famous by Patrick Henry, 'Give me liberty or give me death.' " With regard to the eating of portions of the priest's liver Crown counsel stated the following: "That comes under the head of cannibalism as described in the *Encyclopaedia Britannica* which says it may be divided according to the motives of the act, and he mentions a species of cannibalism called protective cannibalism 'which consists in the consumption of a small portion of the body of a murdered man, in order that his ghost may not trouble the murderer.' That was the idea, that the ghost of these men would haunt them."

Following the Court's charge the jury, after deliberating for 45 minutes, returned the following verdict: "We find the prisoners guilty of murder, with the strongest possible recommendation to mercy that the Jury can give." The Court then addressed the jury: "Gentlemen of the jury: You have performed a very unpleasant duty and, I think, have come to exactly the correct conclusion in all respects. I think the verdict is the only honest verdict that could be rendered on the evidence and the recommendation is most proper. It will be submitted by me with my own recommendations to the same effect at once."

The Court then announced sentence would be deferred. He then directed the interpreter to tell the defendants to stand, whereupon he spoke the following: "Patsy, tell them that the jury have found that they were guilty of killing the priests without right to do it; that under our law when people kill others that way they have to give their lives, but the great white chief further away than the distance they have come may interfere and show them mercy, may be kind to them."

The Court then remanded the defendants to the custody of the police to be taken back to Edmonton and stated that he would telegraph at once to the Minister of Justice.

Several days later in Edmonton the Chief Justice imposed sentence as follows:

> Patsy, tell the prisoners to stand up. Tell them what I have to say. You told them in Calgary the other day that I would ask the Big Chief far away not to be too hard on them, and I have asked him by the way we have here, a long way, by telegraph, and he says because they did not know our ways, that they did not know what our laws are, he will not have them put to death for the killing of these men this time. They must understand though that for the future they know now what our law is and if they kill any person again then they have to suffer the penalty.
>
> I am going to pass sentence. I do not think it is necessary to explain the particulars of it now, but in the usual course action will be taken so that it will not be carried out. I impose the sentence of death in the usual form, and I will fix the 15th of October as the date of execution. That is, of course, under the circumstances, something more or less a matter of form, but it is a form the Minister desires to have the proceedings take so that the commutation of the sentence may be in the usual way. He authorizes me to state the sentence will be commuted. You may tell them just what will be done I cannot say, but they will know in a few days. They will probably be punished in some way, but I do not know just in what form it will be.
>
> Patsy, you might tell them when they get back home, if they do, they must let their people know that if any of them kill any person, they will have to suffer death. They know now what our law is.

The sentence of death was commuted, on August 19, by the Governor in Council to life imprisonment at the Mounted Police guard room at Herschel Island in the Arctic Ocean. The following day the place of detention was changed to Fort Resolution on Great Slave Lake in the Northwest Territories.

On May 15, 1919, by order of the Governor in Council, Sinnisiak and Uluksak were released from custody and permitted to return to the region from which they were taken. The following conditions formed part of the order of release:

It has been determined that they may be set at liberty conditionally upon their undertaking solemnly for the future to respect human life and property, and to make known to members of their band and native associates, in addition to the facts aforesaid, that the Eskimos live and are governed under a system of law which, with equality as against white man, Indian, and Eskimo, exacts speedy and rigorous punishment for crime according to the degree, and that by mandate of the law, capital punishment must follow a capital offence; and moreover that while for the reason aforesaid these prisoners have been visited by a dispensation of mercy whereby their lives have been spared, notwithstanding the offence which they committed, these reasons are not likely to be permitted to avail on another occasion, either for them or for any other Eskimo, seeing that the proceedings in the present case have served to inform them of their responsibilities, and that they are solemnly charged with their duty to serve God and honor the King and carefully to observe his laws.

NOTES

1. Stefansson, writing in 1921, stated that "the only practicable method of treating Eskimos who meet a white man for the first time is to deal with them as equals." He then expressed the opinion that failure to do this was the reason why Fathers Rouviere and LeRoux were killed. *The Friendly Arctic* (1921), p. 432.
2. It has also been pointed out that among some of the primitive peoples in Africa the liver is believed to be the seat of the spirit. Crawley, *The Idea of the Soul* (1909), p. 93.

6

Petition of McCord

McCarrey, District Judge.

This matter comes before the court upon a petition for a writ of habeas corpus.

Emil McCord is being held to answer for statutory rape. It is charged that he, being a male person 23 years of age, did carnally know and abuse a female person under the age of 16 years, to wit, 14 years of age. Andrew Nickanorka is held to answer on the same charge. It is alleged that he, being a male person 29 years of age, did carnally know and abuse another female person under the age of 16 years, to wit, 14 years of age.

From United States District Court, Alaska, 151 F. Supp. 132 (1957).

While being held in custody by the United States Marshal to answer to the Grand Jury, the petitioners filed habeas corpus proceedings before this court to obtain their release from the United States Marshal, upon the grounds that it is contrary to the law to hold them upon the territorial crime of statutory rape, in that title 18 U.S.C. § 1153, makes such a crime inapplicable to the act charged. The petitioners allege that they and the female victims are full-blooded Indians and that they all reside at Tyonek, Alaska, which is within the limits of an area set aside for their use by Executive Order No. 2141, issued in 1915.

There is no dispute as to the fact that the petitioners and the victims are full-blooded Indians and that they and their ancestors, for a long period of time, have resided in this area set aside by the order *supra,* which is administered by the Alaska Native Service, an administrative unit of the Bureau of Indian Affairs. Further, that the tribe is governed by a council elected at general meetings of the tribe.

One of the petitioners testified at the hearing that the chief of the tribe, one Simeon Chickalusion, died on Easter Sunday and as of this date the tribe has not called a meeting to elect a new chief. He further testified that there are six members of the council and that these members are chosen by a vote of the members at a general meeting called for that purpose. Some testimony was adduced from this witness to the effect that the chief and the council take action to correct any infractions of the law set up by the council. The witness referred specifically to the violation of fish location jumping, fishing being the principal source of livelihood and income of this Indian tribe, since fur trapping has virtually become extinct, due to the depletion of fur-bearing animals.

All of the inhabitants in that area, excepting one white schoolteacher who resides there a portion of the year, and a Hawaiian who is married to a member of the tribe, are all native Indians and members of the tribe.

The petitioners contend that the crimes alleged to have taken place were committed, if at all, within "Indian country" which is within the definition of 18 U.S.C. § 1151 et seq., and as a result thereof, they are outside the jurisdiction of the Territory of Alaska and its penal laws. Their additional argument is that the crime of statutory rape is not within any of the crimes set forth in 18 U.S.C. § 1153, which is more commonly referred to as the "Ten Major Crimes" statute, applicable to Indian offenses within Indian country.

The Government, on the other hand, takes the position that Tyonek is not within "Indian country," as defined in 18 U.S.C. § 1151, and that Alaska natives are in a different position as concerns the jurisdiction of criminal offenses than the Indians in the United States proper. The Government further contends that, in any event, the crime of statutory rape is within the provisions of 18 U.S.C. § 1153.

The administration of criminal law in areas occupied by members of Indian tribal bodies has been the subject of prolonged legislative activity, extensively recited in the case of *United States v. Jacobs,* D.C.E.C. Wis. 1953, 113 F.

Supp. 203. Congress, for a considerable length of time, has removed the trial and punishment of criminal offenses from the courts of the states and territories of the United States within which the Indians are located and substituted federal jurisdiction over the major crimes and left the minor crimes to the tribal organization. *United States v. Chavez,* 1933, 290 U.S. 357, 54 S. Ct. 217, 78 L. Ed. 360. A number of reasons have been forwarded for this, two of which are covered in *Ex parte Crow Dog,* 1883, 109 U.S. 556, 3 S. Ct. 396, 27 L. Ed. 1030, perhaps the leading case on this subject. The Supreme Court there rules that the courts of the Territory of Dakota had no jurisdiction over members of the Sioux tribe within Indian country, reasoning that their independent status, established by treaty, evidences of Congressional intent to relieve them of the rule of the Territory, and, second, that the tribes must be protected from the restraints of a society they do not understand and into which they have not yet become assimilated. A third reason is suggested in *United States v. Chavez,* 290 U.S. 357, at page 361, 54 S. Ct. 217, 78 L. Ed. 360, that the federal court system may afford the Indian protection from a frequently unfriendly and occasionally hostile community until the time arrives when he is more adequate to defend himself. Perhaps a fourth reason has been the reluctance of the state authorities to assume the government of a large and tax-free population within its borders. Whatever may be the determinative reason behind this policy, Congress has evidenced an intent to continue the existing system by revising the legislation pertaining to this subject in 1948 (62 Stat. 757; 63 Stat. 94). At the same time, however, recent enactments of Congress removing certain areas in certain states from the exclusive jurisdiction of the United States Courts (67 Stat. 588, 18 U.S.C. § 1162) indicate an intent to place Indian peoples within the same society as their white neighbors just as rapidly as they are able to adapt themselves to that society. It is certainly to be desired that a time will come when there is no need for this type of legislation, but that time must be determined by Congress, not by this Court.

The principal issue presented at the hearing on the writ was whether the Tyonek area fits within the meaning of "Indian country" in 18 U.S.C. § 1153. The Act defines the term as:

(a) all land within the limits of any Indian Reservation under the jurisdiction of the United States government . . . (b) all dependent Indian communities within the borders of the United States whether within the original or subsequently acquired territory thereof, and whether within or without the limits of a state, and (c) all Indian allotments, the Indian titles to which have not been extinguished . . . (18 U.S.C. § 1151).

The Government's suggestion that the meaning of the terms is confined to lands reserved to the Indians by treaty is not compatible with the definition and their contention that the definition is as to areas within the several states seems also to be incorrect. The Supreme Court in the *Chavez* case, 54 S. Ct. 217, 220, defined the term "Indian country" as:

. . . Any unceded lands owned or occupied by an Indian nation or tribe of Indians. . . .

I feel that this interpretation is broad enough to include an area, such as the Tyonek area, which is set aside and treated as Indian land, even though the executive order separating the land from the public domain fails to indicate its exact purpose. The Court of Appeals for this circuit has indicated that the recent amendments of the provisions applicable to these situations have served to enlarge the meaning of the term, rather than to diminish it. *Williams v. United States,* 9 Cir., 1954, 215 F. 2d 1; *Guith v. United States,* 9 Cir., 1956, 230 F. 2d 481. In this light, I think I am warranted in concluding that the Tyonek area is "Indian country."

The prosecution's argument that Alaska natives have a different status than Indians of the States is a rather novel concept which I regard as inaccurate. The district court in *United States v. Kie,* D.C. Alaska 1885, Fed. Cas. 15, 528a, indicated that the Territory of Alaska as a whole was not Indian country and that the natives of this area had not achieved independent status by treaty. With these observations I can concur, but I do not feel that this acts to remove them from the definitions of Congress otherwise applicable to them and not limited by the legislative pronouncement. See *In re Sah Quah,* D.C. Alaska 1886, 31 F. 327 in this regard. In view of the opinions expressed by these courts and the definition of Congress, however, any extension of the definition beyond those areas set apart from the public domain and dedicated to the use of the Indian people, and within which is found an operational tribal organization, would be unwarranted.

The next question is whether the crime of statutory rape is one of those crimes within the terms of 18 U.S.C. § 1153 of which the federal courts will take jurisdiction. The provision states:

Any Indian who commits against the person . . . of another Indian . . . any of the following offenses, namely . . . rape . . . shall be subject to the same laws and penalties as all persons committing any of the above offenses, within the exclusive jurisdiction of the United States. As used in this section, the offense of rape shall be defined in accordance with the laws of the State in which the offense was committed.

In *United States v. Jacobs,* D.C., 113 F. Supp. 203, the court concluded, after an extensive discussion of the Congressional activities concerning the provision cited, that it was not the intent of Congress to include the offense of statutory rape or carnal knowledge of a female under a certain age in those crimes enumerated in the Act. The same conclusion has been reached by the Supreme Court of Wisconsin in *State v. Rufus,* 1931, 205 Wis. 317, 237 N.W. 67. The reasoning adopted in these cases is quite convincing and the deletion of a proposed amendment to the Act which would have provided for this offense would certainly indicate that Congress preferred to leave this matter to the tribal courts. At any rate, as the *Jacobs* case states, any doubt in this direction must be resolved in favor of the accused:

It is axiomatic that statutes creating and defining crimes cannot be extended by intendment, and that no act, however wrongful, can be punished under such a statute, unless clearly within its terms. There can be no constructive offenses, and before a man can be punished, his case must be plainly and unmistakably within the statute (113 F. Supp. 207).

We have no indication that the particular acts in question will subject the petitioners to punishment by the tribe. It is with interest that one observes the Indian race in the United States is fast advancing in the adoption of the white man's society. This is commendable and the realization of a goal sought. A large part of our Indian population is at last shedding the distrusts and fear of our society which they have evidenced in the past. Many are entering commercial activities with their Caucasian neighbors. A small but encouraging number have entered the professions and our institutions of education are beginning to feel the influx of Indian students, which has been so long desired but, until recently, little realized. The records of the past series of armed conflicts in which the United States has engaged illustrates a most commendable achievement by members of the Indian elements of our population. In the interest of further acquainting the members of the tribe with the society with which they must soon become members, it would certainly be injudicious to allow the petitioners to escape without any sanctions applied to them. However, the sanctions to be applied by the chief and the council must be left to the tribe, in the absence of Congressional action. *United States v. Quiver,* 1916, 241 U.S. 602, 36 S. Ct. 699, 60 L. Ed. 1196.

Since it follows as a corollary that if the Indian people want to take advantage of the opportunities afforded them under our democracy, there must, of necessity, and corollary to these opportunities, follow the paralleling responsibility of abiding by the laws and precepts of government that have been adopted by the white race and which have made our democracy great. However, I cannot avoid agreeing with Judge Tehan in the *Jacobs* case, 113 F. Supp. 203, when he says:

It may well be that the description of the Indian people set out in *Ex parte Crow Dog* (109 U.S. 556, 3 S. Ct. 396, 27 L. Ed. 1030) is no longer warranted, and that the time has come to make Indians subject to more of the laws governing other citizens or residents of the United States. But this is a matter for the legislature and not the courts. It is for Congress to change a policy that has been long established and has been repeatedly recognized by the courts.

This decision should not be interpreted by members of the native groups, be they Indian or Eskimo, as a general removal of the territorial penal authority over them, for the reason that this court will take judicial notice that there are few tribal organizations in Alaska that are functioning strictly within Indian country as defined in 18 U.S.C. § 1151 et seq. As I have said, only when the offense fits distinctly within the provisions of the applicable federal law will territorial jurisdiction be ousted. Testimony indicates that the Tyonek area, unlike most areas inhabited by Alaska natives, has been set aside for the use of and is governed by an operational tribal unit. Under these conditions, I can see no alternative but to order the release of the petitioners.

7

Contrasts Between Ibo and Western Legal Systems

C. K. MEEK

As the law of any society is an expression of its own culture, and as Ibo culture is totally different from ours, it follows that in spite of many points of contact with our legal system, that of the Ibo presents marked divergences. Their sense of values does not coincide with ours. Thus, to accuse an unsophisticated Ibo of practicing witchcraft would be a much more serious matter than charging him with having embezzled a large sum of money, whereas to an Englishman the former charge would mean nothing at all. Again, in English law adultery is never anything more than a private injury, whereas in Ibo law it may be treated as a private injury if committed in a house but if committed on a farm it is a public abomination. Similarly, to steal from a farm a yam valued at one shilling would be a very different matter from stealing one shilling in cash.[1] Then again there is the native attitude toward homicide, which differs from ours in a variety of ways. Thus to the Ibo vendetta was a duty, and so was the killing of witches and twins. And death or enslavement was imposed for numerous offenses which to us would appear to be comparatively trivial.

And yet it is not so long ago that in England persons convicted of witchcraft were judicially executed, and during the early part of the nineteenth century English law awarded death to anyone who stole five shillings' worth of goods from a dwelling-house, or broke a window and tried to lift a latch, or forged a

From *Law and Authority in a Nigerian Tribe* (London: Oxford University Press, 1937), pp. 337–339. Abridged with renumbered notes. Reprinted by permission of the publisher.

will, or made the counterfeit of the smallest coin. And in the eyes of the Ibo we appear brutal and unjust even at the present day in awarding death to those courageous and public-spirited persons who rid the community of witches and of twins.

Moreover, in judging of the severity of Ibo laws we must not forget that, in the absence of prisons, the community had no other means than death or selling into slavery by which it could rid itself of a habitual criminal. Indeed, today it is a frequent cause of complaint that prisons only give temporary relief, and that habitual criminals keep returning to the community after terms of imprisonment, fortified by good food to continue their depredations! Prison conditions, it is said, are too pleasant to act as a sufficient deterrent, and imprisonment has not yet come to be regarded as a social disgrace.

Another important factor differentiating Ibo from English legal conceptions is that in Ibo society a man's conduct is largely conditioned by his status. Everybody has a fixed place in society with definite duties assigned to his grade. Persons of the same status form a class of their own, as it were, and are responsible for each other, and observe certain patterns of behavior toward classes above or below them. The Ozo society is a close corporation of privileged bureaucrats. Age-grades impose certain standards of conduct on their members and punish any dereliction. A senior wife can lord it over a junior, an elder brother over a younger, and so on. Now one effect of this system, and it is an important effect which may be misunderstood by European administrative or judicial officers, is that a person of junior status should not sue a person of senior status directly; he should do so through the mediumship of a person of similar status.[2] And thus it is that in judicial proceedings a prosecution or defense may be conducted by someone who, to a European observer, has no connection with the case at all. Serious offense can be given by ignoring native etiquette in such matters, in deference to the English principle of complete personal responsibility.

This brings us to another important aspect of native law, namely, collective responsibility. This is the direct outcome of the form of the social organization, and is based primarily on the kinship unit which we have called the extended-family or kindred, the members of which are so closely bound together that the conduct of one may affect them all. But the sense of collective responsibility, being founded ultimately on the principle that union is strength, extends also to the local group composed of many kindreds. It is a powerful factor, therefore, in promoting social cohesion, and when it is allowed full play in matter of law and authority is of immense value as a means of imposing a high standard of conduct on the members of the group. Numerous instances have been given to show how the heads of kindreds and local groups constantly warned the younger men to exercise self-restraint, lest the ill-advised conduct of one of their number should implicate them all. Not that the principle of collective responsibility was applied indiscriminately, for the group did not hesitate to repudiate blatant ill behavior on the part of any of its members.

The principle of collective responsibility still operates in various ways at the present time. Thus, it may induce the group of a person charged with an offense to protect him from arrest, or, if he is arrested and fined, to pay his fine. And the Nigerian Government recognizes the principle to some extent, for one of its laws [3] provides that punishment may be imposed on an entire group in certain (unusual) circumstances for an offense committed by a member or members of that group. . . .

Then again there is a vast difference between the sanctions of English laws and those of the Ibo. For the most part regulations are obeyed in all communities because they are recognized as necessary for the proper functioning of society. But to give these regulations the force of law, sanctions are required, that is rewards or penalties for their observance or non-observance. The nature of the sanctions in any community depends on its cultural complex, and as the cultural complex of the Ibo is totally different from that of the English, their sanctions must also be different. Thus, to take an example, Ibo society includes the dead no less than the living; and hence, as has been repeatedly shown, the ancestors were in the past (and still are) a governing factor in the maintenance of law and order. The law was in fact what the ancestors had considered good or bad in the past, and in every case of importance they were believed to be present to see that there was no deviation from traditional practice, and that the proceedings were conducted in a spirit of equity and truth. The *ofo* of the elders were a symbol and indeed the medium of their presence, and a means of securing truthful evidence, as any witness might be called on to swear on his *ofo*.

Then, too, there was Ala the Earth-deity, a disciplinary force of great authority acting in conjunction with, but wholly distinct from, the ancestors. Just as Jupiter, the ancient deity of the sky, by whom men were wont to swear, became among the Romans the embodiment of justice, so did Ala, the Earth-deity, come to be regarded by the Ibo as the guardian and indeed the source of morality. Most of the offenses classed as "abominable" were considered to be offenses against Ala, and, even when the offense had been expiated by punishment, the community had still to be cleansed by sacrifice. The whole system of magic and taboo served as a solid buttress of the law, a means of conferring a feeling of security, of protecting property, and constraining people to perform their innumerable obligations. . . .

NOTES

1. It is not possible to say why adultery and thefts committed on farms are regarded as especially heinous. It may be due to magico-religious beliefs connected with fertility; or the magico-religious attitude may have been evolved as the best method of preventing offenses which are particularly easy to commit without detection.
2. Mr. Driberg has drawn attention to this aspect of African law in a suggestive article published in the *Journal of Comparative Legislation and International Law* (November, 1934).
3. The Collective Punishments Ordinance. But this Ordinance is now virtually a dead letter.

SECTION THREE   *Conflict in American Society: The Mormons*

8

Cleveland v. United States

Mr. Justice Douglas delivered the opinion of the Court.

Petitioners are members of a Mormon sect, known as Fundamentalists. They not only believe in polygamy; unlike other Mormons,[1] they practice it. Each of petitioners, except Stubbs, has, in addition to his lawful wife, one or more plural wives. Each transported at least one plural wife across state lines,[2] either for the purpose of cohabiting with her, or for the purpose of aiding another member of the cult in such a project. They were convicted of violating the Mann Act on a trial to the court, a jury having been waived (56 F. Supp. 890). The judgments of conviction were affirmed on appeal. 146 F. 2d 730. The cases are here on petitions for certiorari which we granted in view of the asserted conflict between the decision below and *Mortensen v. United States,* 322 U.S. 369.

The Act makes an offense the transportation in interstate commerce of "any woman or girl for the purpose of prostitution or debauchery, or for any other immoral purpose." The decision turns on the meaning of the latter phrase, "for any other immoral purpose."

United States v. Bitty involved a prosecution under a federal statute making it a crime to import an alien woman "for the purpose of prostitution or for any other immoral purpose." The Act was construed to cover a case where a man imported an alien woman so that she should live with him as his concubine. Two years later the Mann Act was passed. Because of the similarity of the language used in the two acts, the *Bitty* case became a forceful precedent for the construction of the Mann Act. Thus one who transported a woman in interstate commerce so that she should become his mistress or concubine was held to have transported her for an "immoral purpose" within the meaning of the Mann Act. *Caminetti v. United States,* 242 U.S. 470.

It is argued that the *Caminetti* decision gave too wide a sweep to the Act; that the Act was designed to cover only the white slave business and related vices; that it was not designed to cover voluntary actions bereft of sex commercialism; and that in any event it should not be construed to embrace polygamy which is a form of marriage and, unlike prostitution or debauchery or the concubinage involved in the *Caminetti* case, has as its object parenthood and the creation and maintenance of family life. In support of that interpreta-

From Supreme Court of the United States, 329 U.S. 14 (1946). Abridged with re-numbered notes.

tion an exhaustive legislative history is submitted which, it is said, gives no indication that the Act was aimed at polygamous practices.

While *Mortensen v. United States* (322 U.S.), rightly indicated that the Act was aimed "primarily" at the use of interstate commerce for the conduct of the white slave business, we find no indication that a profit motive is a *sine qua non* to its application. Prostitution, to be sure, normally suggests sexual relations for hire.[3] But debauchery has no such implied limitation. In common understanding the indulgence which that term suggests may be motivated solely by lust.[4] And so we start with words which by their natural import embrace more than commercialized sex. What follows is "any other immoral purpose." Under the *ejusdem generis* rule of construction the general words are confined to the class and may not be used to enlarge it. But we could not give the words a faithful interpretation if we confined them more narrowly than the class of which they are a part.

That was the view taken by the Court in the *Bitty* and *Caminetti* cases. We do not stop to reexamine the *Caminetti* case to determine whether the Act was properly applied to the facts there presented.

But we adhere to its holding, which has been in force for almost thirty years, that the Act, while primarily aimed at the use of interstate commerce for the purposes of commercialized sex, is not restricted to that end.

We conclude, moreover, that polygamous practices are not excluded from the Act. They have long been outlawed in our society. As stated in *Reynolds v. United States,* 98 U.S. 145, 164:

> Polygamy has always been odious among the northern and western nations of Europe, and, until the establishment of the Mormon Church, was almost exclusively a feature of the life of Asiatic and of African people. At common law, the second marriage was always void (2 Kent, Com. 79), and from the earliest history of England polygamy has been treated as an offense against society.

As subsequently stated in *Church of Jesus Christ of L.D.S. v. United States,* 136 U.S. 1, 49, "The organization of a community for the spread and practice of polygamy is, in a measure, a return to barbarism. It is contrary to the spirit of Christianity and of the civilization that Christianity has produced in the Western world." And see *Davis v. Beason,* 133 U.S. 333. Polygamy is a practice with far more pervasive influences in society than the casual, isolated transgressions involved in the *Caminetti* case. The establishment or maintenance of polygamous households is a notorious example of promiscuity. The permanent advertisement of their existence is an example of the sharp repercussions that they have in the community. We could conclude that Congress excluded these practices from the Act only if it were clear that the Act is confined to commercialized sexual vice. Since we cannot say it is, we see no way by which the present transgressions can be excluded. These polygamous practices have long been branded as immoral in the law. Though they have different ramifications, they are in the same genus as the other immoral practices covered by the Act.

The fact that the regulation of marriage is a state matter does not, of course, make the Mann Act an unconstitutional interference by Congress with the police powers of the States. The power of Congress over the instrumentalities of interstate commerce is plenary; it may be used to defeat what are deemed to be immoral practices; and the fact that the means may have "the quality of police regulations" is not consequential. *Hoke v. United States*, 227 U.S. 308, 323; see *Athanasaw v. United States*, 227 U.S. 326; *Wilson v. United States*, 232 U.S. 563.

Petitioners' second line of defense is that the requisite purpose was lacking. It is said that those petitioners who already had plural wives did not transport them in interstate commerce for an immoral purpose. The test laid down in the *Mortensen* case was whether the transportation was in fact "the use of interstate commerce as a calculated means for effectuating sexual immorality," 322 U.S. 375. There was evidence that this group of petitioners in order to cohabit with their plural wives found it necessary or convenient to transport them in interstate commerce and that the unlawful purpose was the dominant motive. In one case the woman was transported for the purpose of entering into a plural marriage. After a night with this petitioner she refused to continue the plural marriage relationship. But guilt under the Mann Act turns on the purpose which motivates the transportation, not on its accomplishment. *Wilson v. United States*, supra (232 U.S. 570, 571).

It is also urged that the requisite criminal intent was lacking since petitioners were motivated by a religious belief. That defense claims too much. If upheld, it would place beyond the law any act done under claim of religious sanction. But it has long been held that the fact that polygamy is supported by a religious creed affords no defense in a prosecution for bigamy. *Reynolds v. United States*, supra. Whether the act is immoral within the meaning of the statute is not to be determined by the accused's concepts of morality. Congress has provided the standard. The offense is complete if the accused intended to perform, and did in fact perform, the act that the statute condemns: the transportation of a woman for the purpose of making her his plural wife or cohabiting with her as such.

We have considered the remaining objections raised and find them without merit.

Affirmed.

Mr. Justice Black and Mr. Justice Jackson think that the cases should be reversed. They are of opinion that affirmance requires extension of the rule announced in the *Caminetti* case and that the correctness of that rule is so dubious that it should at least be restricted to its particular facts.

Mr. Justice Rutledge concurs.

Mr. Justice Murphy dissenting.

Today another unfortunate chapter is added to the troubled history of the

White Slave Traffic Act. It is a chapter written in terms that misapply the statutory language and that disregard the intention of the legislative framers. It results in the imprisonment of individuals whose actions have none of the earmarks of white slavery, whatever else may be said of their conduct. I am accordingly forced to dissent.

The statute in so many words refers to transportation of women and girls across state lines "for the purpose of prostitution or debauchery, or for any other immoral purpose." The issue here is whether the act of taking polygamous or plural wives across state lines, or taking girls across state borders for the purpose of entering into plural marriage, constitutes transportation "for any other immoral purpose" so as to come within the interdict of the statute.

The Court holds, and I agree, that under the *ejusdem generis* rule of statutory construction the phrase "any other immoral purpose" must be confined to the same class of unlawful sexual immoralities as that to which prostitution and debauchery belong. But I disagree with the conclusion that polygamy is "in the same genus" as prostitution and debauchery and hence within the phrase "any other immoral purpose" simply because it has sexual connotations and has "long been branded as immoral in the law" of this nation. Such reasoning ignores reality and results in an unfair application of the statutory words.

It is not my purpose to defend the practice of polygamy or to claim that it is morally the equivalent of monogamy. But it is essential to understand what it is, as well as what it is not. Only in that way can we intelligently decide whether it falls within the same genus as prostitution or debauchery.

There are four fundamental forms of marriage: (1) monogamy; (2) polygyny, or one man with several wives; (3) polyandry, or one woman with several husbands; and (4) group marriage. The term "polygamy" covers both polygyny and polyandry. Thus we are dealing here with polygyny, one of the basic forms of marriage. Historically, its use has far exceeded that of any other form. It was quite common among ancient civilizations and was referred to many times by the writers of the Old Testament; even today it is to be found frequently among certain pagan and non-Christian peoples of the world. We must recognize then, that polygyny, like other forms of marriage, is basically a cultural institution rooted deeply in the religious beliefs and social mores of those societies in which it appears. It is equally true that the beliefs and mores of the dominant culture of the contemporary world condemn the practice as immoral and substitute monogamy in its place. To those beliefs and mores I subscribe, but that does not alter the fact that polygyny is a form of marriage built upon a set of social and moral principles. It must be recognized and treated as such.

The Court states that polygamy is "a notorious example of promiscuity." The important fact, however, is that, despite the difference that may exist between polygamy and monogamy, such difference does not place polygamy in the same category as prostitution or debauchery. When we use those terms we are speaking of acts of an entirely different nature, having no relation whatever to the various forms of marriage. It takes no elaboration here to point out that marriage, even when it occurs in a form of which we disapprove, is not to be compared with prostitution or debauchery or other immoralities of that character.

The Court's failure to recognize this vital distinction and its insistence that polygyny is "in the same genus" as prostitution and debauchery do violence to the anthropological factors involved. Even etymologically, the words "polygyny" and "polygamy" are quite distinct from "prostitution," "debauchery," and words of that ilk. There is thus no basis in fact for including polygyny within the phrase "any other immoral purpose" as used in this statute.

One word should be said about the Court's citation of *United States v. Bitty*, 208 U.S. 393, and the statement that the interpretation of the statute there involved is a forceful precedent for the construction of the White Slave Traffic Act. The thought apparently is that the phrase "any other immoral purpose," appearing in the White Slave Traffic Act, was derived from the identical phrase used in the statute regulating the immigration of aliens into the United States, the statute which was under consideration in the *Bitty* case. [February 20, 1907] 34 Stat. 898, c 1134. That case concerned itself with the portion of the immigration statute forbidding "the importation into the United States of any alien woman or girl for the purpose of prostitution, or for any other immoral purpose." Significantly, however, the statute made separate provision for the exclusion of "polygamists, or persons who admit their belief in the practice of polygamy." Thus the phrase "any other immoral purpose," following the reference to prostitution, certainly did not comprehend polygamy. And if that statute, or the interpretation given it in the *Bitty* case, is to be any authority here, the conclusion to be drawn is inconsistent with the result reached by the Court today. As a matter of fact, Congress has always referred to polygamy by name when it desired to deal with that subject, as distinguished from immoralities in the nature of prostitution. See, for example, 8 U.S.C.A. § 364, 18 U.S.C.A. § 513.

The result here reached is but another consequence of this Court's long-continued failure to recognize that the White Slave Traffic Act, as its title indicates, is aimed solely at the diabolical interstate and international trade in white slaves, "the business of securing white women and girls and of selling them outright or of exploiting them for immoral purposes." House Report No. 47, 61st Cong., 2d Sess., p. 11; Senate Report No. 886, 61st Cong., 2d Sess., p. 11. The Act was suggested and proposed to meet conditions that had arisen in the years preceding 1910 and which had revealed themselves in their ugly details through extensive investigations. The framers of the Act specifically stated that it is not directed at immorality in general; it does not even attempt to regulate the practice of voluntary prostitution, leaving that problem to the various states. Its exclusive concern is with those girls and women who are "unwillingly forced to practice prostitution" and to engage in other similar immoralities and "whose lives are lives of involuntary servitude." A reading of the legislative reports and debates makes this narrow purpose so clear as to remove all doubts on the matter. And it is a purpose that has absolutely no relation to the practice of polygamy, however much that practice may have been considered immoral in 1910.

Yet this Court in *Caminetti v. United States,* 242 U.S. 470, over the vigorous dissent of Justice McKenna in which Chief Justice White and Justice Clarke joined, closed its eyes to the obvious and interpreted the broad words of the statute without regard to the express wishes of Congress. I think the *Caminetti* case can be factually distinguished from the situation at hand since it did not deal with polygamy. But the principle of the *Caminetti* case is still with us today, the principle of interpreting and applying the White Slave Traffic Act in disregard of the specific problem with which Congress was concerned. I believe the issue should be met squarely and the *Caminetti* case overruled. It has been on the books for nearly 30 years and its age does not justify its continued existence. *Stare decisis* certainly does not require a court to perpetuate a wrong for which it was responsible, especially when no rights have accrued in reliance on the error. *Helvering v. Hallock,* 309 U.S. 106, 121, 122. Otherwise the error is accentuated; and individuals, whatever may be said of their morality, are fined and imprisoned contrary to the wishes of Congress. I shall not be a party to that process.

The consequence of prolonging the *Caminetti* principle is to make the federal courts the arbiters of the morality of those who cross state lines in the company of women and girls. They must decide what is meant by "any other immoral purpose" without regard to the standards plainly set forth by Congress. I do not believe that this falls within the legitimate scope of the judicial function. Nor does it accord the respect to which Congressional pronouncements are entitled.

Hence, I would reverse the judgments of conviction in these cases.

NOTES

1. The Church of Jesus Christ of Latter-Day Saints has forbidden plural marriages since 1890. See *Toncray v. Budge,* 14 Idaho 621, 654, 655, p. 26.
2. Petitioners' activities extended into Arizona, California, Colorado, Idaho, Utah, and Wyoming.
3. "Of women: The offering of the body to indiscriminate lewdness for hire (esp. as a practice or institution): whoredom, harlotry." *Oxford English Dictionary,* VIII.
4. "Vicious indulgence in sensual pleasures." *Oxford English Dictionary,* III, 79.

9

Arizona Raided Short Creek—Why?

WILEY S. MALONEY

For years the whispers had been heard in Arizona, Utah, Idaho, and other Western states: somewhere in each of those states was a cult of practicing polygamists, men with as many as six or seven wives and literally dozens of children: fundamentalist Mormons, still adhering to the concept of plural marriage that was outlawed by the U.S. Supreme Court and the heads of the Mormon Church in 1890.

In Fredonia, Arizona, and Hurricane, Utah, there were more than whispers; there were hard facts. Midway between those towns was the parched, ramshackle, almost inaccessible border community of Short Creek, situated in a remote area first explored in 1860 by the frontier scouts of Brigham Young, great leader of the Latter-Day Saints. The practice of polygamy had never ceased in Short Creek. In 1935, the state of Arizona had raided the community and had obtained three convictions for "open and notorious misconduct." In 1944, the Federal Bureau of Investigation had raided the town again (along with several other places in Utah, Idaho, and Arizona); there had been a few more convictions. Nevertheless, visitors reported, there were still men in Short Creek with more than one wife and many children, and the community was growing larger every year.

In Kingman, Arizona, seat of Mohave County, Superior Court Judge J. W. Faulkner collected some of the facts. County officials reported that in hard times welfare requests would pour in from the isolated little village, and often a number of women applying for relief would list the same man as their husband.

There was another, more disquieting, report: some of the wives were youngsters 13 to 15 years old. In Arizona, the age of consent is 18. Parents may permit their daughters to marry at 16, but no younger, even if the child is pregnant. Pregnancy at that age is presumptive evidence of statutory rape.

Deeply disturbed, Judge Faulkner brought his facts to the attention of Governor Howard Pyle in March 1951. He pointed out that the residents of Short Creek, living a cooperative communal life, considered themselves a "charitable and philanthropic organization" under the law, and were paying no property taxes, yet were demanding expanded school facilities to take care of the community's rapid growth. The population was increasing not only from normal

From *Collier's* (November 13, 1953), pp. 30–31. Abridged. Reprinted by permission of Crowell Collier and Macmillan, Inc.

causes but through a vigorous recruitment program. Even more troubling were reports that Short Creek was not a unique community; there were other groups of fundamentalist Mormons in Utah, Colorado, Idaho, Mexico, and Canada.

To Judge Faulkner, plural marriage was lawless, immoral and, if allowed to continue, dangerous, no matter how sincerely religious in intent. He was concerned about the children: Might they not become the victims of this archaic doctrine?

Aroused, the governor asked the state legislature for funds to conduct an investigation. The state lawmakers appropriated $10,000, and the Burns Detective Agency in Los Angeles was hired for the job. For several months after that, the people of Short Creek, always hard pressed for cash, were cheered by the prospect of finding work as movie extras: Film scouts had appeared in town, asking questions, taking photographs, and talking of using the region as the scene of a Western thriller.

• • •

Early this year, Governor Pyle and Attorney General Ross F. Jones felt that the time had come for action. In the two years that had elapsed since Judge Faulkner had spoken to them, Short Creek's population had risen to 368. The community was fast becoming the second largest in Mohave County; residents were predicting a population of 2,000 in another couple of years, which would put Short Creek almost in a class with Kingman, the county seat. And the larger the village grew, the harder it would be to break up the cult.

The Short Creek raid was planned for months in strictest secrecy, lest the families of the community learn about it and thwart arrest by drifting across the state line to Utah (they learned anyhow, but did nothing). The $50,000 appropriation required to finance the operation was embodied in an omnibus appropriation bill and listed as part of the governor's emergency fund; only a few leaders of the legislature knew what the money was for. At one point, a bill actually was drafted appropriating the money for "grasshopper control."

The governor and attorney general of Utah were informed of Arizona's plan, and so were the leaders of the Mormon Church in Salt Lake City, which had long been embarrassed by the activities of the Fundamentalists.

Last July 1, Arizona's governor quietly transferred the $50,000 fund to the attorney general's office and declared that a state of insurrection existed in Short Creek, the necessary legal step to justify taking action.

There was one big problem: There is no legal penalty for polygamy in Arizona. Both Arizona and Utah had been specifically required to outlaw multiple marriage as a condition of statehood, back around the turn of the century, but when Arizona's code of laws was written, a statute covering penalties for polygamy was somehow omitted. Attorney General Jones had to find other grounds for prosecuting the Short Creek group. After some study, he concluded that the community constituted a conspiracy against the state.

In 1942, Short Creek had been legally organized as the United Effort Plan, a commune which claimed ownership of all the property and earnings of its residents, with the exception of six persons who lived in Short Creek but were not members of the fundamentalist sect: novelist Jonreed Lauritzen and his wife; Lauritzen's brother-in-law, Clifford Black; Mohave County sheriff's deputy Alphonso Nyborg (who was notified of the raid in advance, and who helped bring it about) and his wife; and Don Covington, the town's only bachelor.

The trustees of the United Effort Plan controlled all its assets, expenditures, membership applications, and marriages. No man could take a wife without their approval; the reason, authorities believe, was to enable the elders to keep close watch of blood lines and avoid inbreeding in the small community. Even so, families at Short Creek were thoroughly scrambled. Some men were married to their wives' daughters by previous marriage. Eighty-four-year-old patriarch Joseph Smith Jessop (who died soon after the raid) was the father of 28 children, including a four-year-old child who is the great-aunt by marriage of another four-year-old in the community.

According to the attorney general's office, every adult member of the Short Creek United Effort Plan is a participant in the conspiracy. Under the blanket conspiracy charge, many counts were listed, ranging from adultery, bigamy, and rape to misappropriation of school funds, falsification of public records, and failure to comply with state corporation laws. In all, 122 warrants were prepared, one for each of the 36 men and 86 women in the community.

• • •

The ending of the Short Creek story now rests with the courts.

10

Why I Have Five Wives

EDSON JESSOP

I am thirty-four years old. I have five wives and twenty children. I am what the world calls a polygamist; a Mormon: one of those "heathenish Short Creek cultists" you may have read about. In my grandfather's day Mormons were thought to have horns, and maybe I seem equally strange to you now.

From *Collier's* (November 13, 1953), pp. 27–30. Abridged. Reprinted by permission of Crowell Collier and Macmillan, Inc.

Actually, I'm not strange at all; I'm merely living celestial marriage, which is the law of God.

But despite my obedience to the covenant, despite the size of my family, today I am the loneliest man in the world. Shortly after thirty-nine of us had been arrested for our beliefs, we were released from the jail in Kingman, Arizona, to await trial. I arrived home at night to find my house abandoned, my family gone, the rooms dark and silent. Unless you've lived through it, you can't imagine what that means. No sound, no hushed childish giggles, nothing. Only the wind and, in the flare of my match, the red sand seeping beneath the doorsills, the red sand that conquers everything but the grave in my country.

• • •

Short Creek isn't much to look at, and it's hard to reach. That's why we live here. Many years ago the Mormon leader, Brigham Young, was urged to move to the Salt Lake valley-desert because "nobody else wants it." Brother Brigham agreed, saying: "If there is a place on this earth that nobody else wants, that's the place I am hunting for." So with us. We don't like to live on parched soil, we don't like to go without modern plumbing and refrigerators any more than you would. We have windmills and wells, but there isn't enough water for farming, and certainly not enough for the flowers and lawns we'd grow if we could. Yet it is just because Short Creek is barren and rejected that it was to us the promised land. If nobody else wanted it, we figured that maybe the world would let us have it, and here live in peace.

I am a carpenter, and men who work with their hands are not supposed to notice stuff like scenery. But I notice. As one comes to appreciate a plain but good woman, I have come to appreciate this hard land. Carving out our life here has been like planing rough lumber: It takes sweat and time for the pattern to show up. But now I love the pattern: the smell of sage after the rain, and the changing lights on the cliffs. I love this house, which I planned and am building myself. It has nineteen rooms and an encircling veranda, and will have French doors that open.

• • •

My grandparents on both sides were Latter-Day Saints, and they stood side by side with Brigham Young a century ago during those earlier persecutions. After Brigham died, they watched the church leaders give in to their persecutors and exchange the old dream of the State of Deseret, that paradise all their own, for Utah and union and peace. But like hundreds of other Mormons, my grandparents—on both sides—never gave in. Plural marriage runs strong in my family. My great-grandfather was one of those early polygamists who served time in the Utah State Penitentiary. I am next to the oldest of thirty-three children. My mother had twenty-six brothers and sisters, although she was the only one to accept the fullness of the gospel.

Originally my people settled in Millville, a little town in northern Utah. I was born there, but lived for twenty-one years in Salt Lake City, where I grew up like any Mormon boy. In high school I hated to diagram sentences and loved to play basketball. And always I was active in the church. After high school I was apprenticed to my father, a carpenter, and later worked at the trade myself, doing fine cabinetwork and helping to build houses, all the while continuing with my religious duties.

In 1942, when I was twenty-two years old, I married Margaret Hunter. Margaret, five years my junior, was an Idaho girl with the same kind of Mormon background as my own. (She now has two brothers in the Short Creek group.) Like any other young Mormon couple in love, we were married and sealed to each other for "Time and Eternity." We were very happy.

But it was wartime. Shortly after our marriage I was drafted, and then, within a few months, discharged because of rheumatism. The experience lasted just long enough to upset the routine of our lives. While we were still uprooted Margaret and I came to realize that something was lacking in our existence. We both longed for a way to shut out the hate and evil in the world, to draw closer somehow to our heavenly Father, to live the gospel more fully. After much prayer and study of the Scriptures we came to see that the only way to live the gospel spiritually was to live it physically, which the church had not done since 1890, when Mormon President Wilford Woodruff issued the manifesto outlawing polygamy.

The Argument for Plural Marriages

No mortal can set aside a decree of God; the manifesto was not a revelation but merely a political agreement between the heads of the church and Congress. If plural marriage was once commanded of God, it is still commanded of God. The church had apostatized and gone against the commandment, but that was no excuse for us to do so.

Therefore, in the spring of 1943 Margaret and I moved to Short Creek, to join the community of fundamentalist Mormons. The trip was brief in hours, but it spanned an eternity in the changes it brought in our lives.

The revelation that motivates the people of Short Creek is clearly set forth in Section 132 of our Doctrine and Covenants: "If any man espouse a virgin and desire to espouse another, and the first give her consent, and if he espouse the second, and they are virgins, and have vowed to no other man, then is he justified. . . . For behold! I reveal unto you a new and an everlasting covenant; and if ye abide not that covenant, then are ye damned; for no one can reject this covenant, and be permitted to enter unto my glory. . . . All covenants . . . that are not made . . . and sealed by the Holy Spirit . . . are of no efficacy."

To us, the foundation of Mormonism is its priesthood organization, representing God's authority on earth, the authority He restored in the spring of 1829 when Peter, James, and John appeared to Joseph Smith, the Prophet. It is this priesthood authority (which the church as a whole lost with the Manifesto) that directs us, and which the state of Arizona is now fighting.

Most churches dream of going back to the bosom of Abraham, and Abraham and other prophets of the Bible such as Moses, Jacob, David, and Solomon were polygamists. How can you enter the glory of Abraham except by living the laws of Abraham? All Latter-Day Saints believe that as we are now God once was, and as God is now we may become. That is, perhaps thousands of years from now, each of us may become a god and, under the direction of our Saviour, each may create and populate his own world. To enter into godhood, we must live all the laws of the gospel and to us the laws of the gospel include plural marriage and the United Order (we in Short Creek call it the United Effort, but it means the same: donating all property to the community, which, in turn, measures and supplies the needs of each member).

Some of the newspapers claimed that we in the United Effort had gullibly enriched our leaders in Salt Lake and elsewhere by contributing tithes. Actually, Short Creek could not have made the grade without the help of our Salt Lake brethren. This much I will say: Living the United Order, as well as celestial marriage, calls for all a man's self-discipline. Loving your neighbor as yourself is not always easy. But the faithful are rewarded with a joy that others cannot fathom. I know that Margaret and myself, once we entered the movement, felt dedicated.

Those now arrayed against us are trying to put new minds in our bodies, and it cannot be done. If some of us have to suffer to give the world our testimony, so be it. We can only hope that our children, raised in this belief, continue faithful.

Shortly after we settled in Short Creek (and while Margaret and I were awaiting the arrival of our first child), we discussed whom I should take as second wife. Call her Marie. She was pretty and bright; she had been a part of our high-school crowd and she was near Margaret's age. What interested us in Marie was that she came from a background like ours and was idealistic and of an inquiring mind. I should like to state that she came to Short Creek of her own volition, once I had written her, and that Margaret stood up with us at our sacred rite. Of course there was no civil ceremony. However, my second sealing was fully as harmonious as my first. Today Margaret and I have five daughters, Marie and I three.

Soon after Marie joined the family my brother Jay was killed while felling trees not far from Short Creek. Seventeen months older than I, Jay seemed the younger; a good man and true to the gospel, but more fun-loving. Jay had taken both his wives in Salt Lake City. His first wife, whom I'll call Rayola, is a gay girl with snapping brown eyes. I courted her before she met Jay, but she probably found me too much of a sobersides. Girls like Rayola sometimes find celestial marriage difficult; after her first baby was born, Jay took his second wife, Patty, and Rayola said later: "When Jay first mentioned Patty I thought I'd have to black his eyes, but you learn to swallow some mighty big swallows!"

After my brother died, I was obligated, according to the laws of Israel under Moses, to assume his responsibilities and take to wife his widows and "raise unto him a posterity." So Rayola and Patty were sealed to me, still just one month before my own first child was born. Rayola already had two children and Patty one; they now have five children each.

Four years later I took my fifth wife, whom I'll call Alice. A year older than Margaret and Marie, she was a northern Utah girl with the same interests as the others. She, too, came to Short Creek and the covenant of her own free will. I now have two children by Alice. Altogether I have twenty sons and daughters, of whom the eldest (Rayola's first-born, Jay) is twelve, and the youngest is four months.

At this stage of my story I can anticipate your question: Can a man love five women at once? I've heard the question before; always I answer: Can a man love five children at once, or five friends, or five brothers and sisters? Show me the monogamous outsider who has not had a mistress, at least in his heart. Here in Short Creek we do not love in secret disgrace, we love in honor; we do not have abortions, we have children.

Not that we in Short Creek are without faults. In any family, children quarrel; but I've observed less quarreling in a large family where each child necessarily accepts responsibilities almost from the moment he is born. As for my wives, show me five women anywhere who will not harbor some jealousies. But the revelation charges: "Prepare your heart." Until our women have conquered self, they know better than to attempt the covenant.

Naturally, a great deal depends on the husband. And although intimate matters are my own business, as with any decent-minded man, I will say that I try to be impartial. You must realize that a plural family is, above all, a unit. My wives trust me. A man of our faith never walks the chalk line as does the man with only one wife. I spend my time where I'm most needed, perhaps where there is sickness or trouble. My wives trust me to do whatever is best for the family as a whole.

Of course, a man has to be something of a diplomat. Even when my families lived separately, I rotated my evenings; once a week we met together at our Home Evening. When you pray and sing together, air your problems and your grudges, play games and visit, and afterward sample Marie's special angel-food cake or Alice's cream puffs, you not only have fun, you forge bonds that will endure through eternity.

Naturally a man values his wives for different qualities, just as he values his friends. Perhaps one wife has pretty hair, and another is wonderful with the children; perhaps one is witty and keeps him cheerful, and another brings him closer to God. Nevertheless, he should be chary in praise as in blame. We believe in covering our bodies and we frown upon make-up; silence itself is reproof enough if one's wives come out with short sleeves or painted faces. If a wife burns her bread, a man learns to keep still until she turns out a batch he can praise.

Fortunately my wives are nearly all of an age, and good friends. They cooperate efficiently, one handling the sewing for the family, another the cooking and so forth. What counts is not the number of wives, but the number of united wives. In fact, there are times when I wish mine would at least get mad at me separately, instead of all together.

I suppose our way of life might seem pious and boring to you. Actually we have a lot of fun, although to prevent bedlam, we have certain routines. It is wonderful to see all my youngsters in the morning at family prayer, each kneeling beside his chair at the table, hand over eyes, while a little one lisps out a plea to God to bless "Jay in his arithmetic today . . ." After the prayer there's always a scramble as the children climb into their chairs. Usually I sit at the head of the table with Margaret at my right, Marie at my left, and my other wives dispersed among the kids. Before we eat, one of the youngsters asks the blessing on the food, and then confusion! Believe me, it's a job to teach table manners to twenty hungry youngsters.

I think it is the evening hours that are most holy to me: the family prayer preceding supper, the twilight story-and-counsel time when the children are weary from school and play . . . then bedtime. There is nothing like a houseful of healthy, happy, sleeping children to make a man feel that he has inherited the earth and the fullness thereof.

As a people we have been called many names. But the epithet that hurts most is "lascivious." In Short Creek we observe a law of strict chastity. We believe in continence except for procreation, and a wife is honored by her husband while expectant and for months after the baby is born. We have been called immoral, yet you will never hear the Lord's name taken in vain in our homes; and you will hear very little backbiting or evilspeaking.

Our children are branded as "underprivileged." Why? None of my twenty children has ever had a serious illness, just the usual measles, whooping cough, and the like. In fact, with two hundred sixty-three children in our town, we've never had polio or diphtheria, there are no mentally retarded, and only one deformed, and he was born elsewhere. They say our children are undernourished. Yet on any winter morning a Short Creek child loads up on hot oatmeal, fresh milk and eggs, home-baked whole-wheat toast and jam. Last summer one of my wives put up 2,500 quarts of fruit and vegetables.

It's true that we don't have much fresh meat, because we can't afford a deep freeze; recently we acquired cold-storage lockers, but because of the arrests they're not even unpacked. But once a year we kill and can a beef, and every fall we get venison.

We residents of Short Creek have been called backward. Yet of the four teachers in our grade school, three are working on their master's degrees. Among our housewives are several college graduates and three registered nurses. Almost every family in town owns a piano. We have movies, and my children are experts on classical music. Short Creek has its own orchestra, which includes instruments like the viola, cello, and French horns that the boys taught themselves to play from self-instruction books. Nearly every family in town subscribes to magazines. Last winter, I attended adult-education classes three evenings a week; studying physiology, practical science, organic culture, dramatic art, and square dancing. We make our own entertainment;

writing, directing, and acting in our own plays and often composing the musical scores.

Also, through the United Effort, the community has been slowly accumulating material possessions such as a potato-and-grain farm, a sawmill, a shingle mill, cannery, automobile repair shop, dairy herd, fruit drier, and carpentry shop. When we can, we men contract for outside jobs. Of course these group projects have had to precede home building. Being the Effort carpenter, I helped with other homes before I could start my own.

I've mentioned my house, but I'd like to tell you more about it. It's of the finest cinder blocks, and when it is finished it will have three stories, ten bedrooms, a big playroom for the kids, two kitchens, a sewing room, three bathrooms, a dining room, a living room, and a den for me. I've assembled the beds, but our new kitchen range still sits outside, and, because my children begged so hard, I stopped shingling to fix up their playground in the garden: a community swing that holds several little ones at once, single swings, whirligigs, teeter-totters, bars, and the dollhouse.

But today I can't be sure I'll ever finish my house—this long dream of my wives—or that my children will ever again use these swings and teeter-totters. Our people have known other polygamy raids. But they say this time our families are to be broken up, our property confiscated, a shameful procedure in a country whose constitution guarantees every citizen the right to worship God according to the dictates of his own conscience.

Although we'd been alerted for weeks to expect a raid, it was a shock when it happened, that unforgettable night of July 26. When the lights of those 100 cars came in sight, grinding over the roads from Fredonia to the east and Hurricane to the west, we barely had time to set off the dynamite, not for retaliation, as they claim, but as a warning to our women and kids back in town to get up and dress. At the showdown I was proud of our people, assaulted by strange, angry voices, yet standing there in the schoolyard under the Stars and Stripes, singing "America."

The next day the state of Arizona set up its portable soup kitchens in a vacant field and forced us to line up, plate in hand, like so many refugees. Then we had to hunker down on the ground, in the sun and the flies, eating tasteless food brought from Phoenix within sight of our own homes, stocked with fresh garden vegetables, milk, eggs, home-baked bread, and the civilized comfort of chairs and white tablecloths. They even broke into our community store to feed us canned stuff from our own shelves. Any deputy could have had the key just by asking. But no. Having declared us criminals, Arizona had to bust a few locks to prove it.

The jailing problem stumped them: Short Creek has no jail. So they had to incarcerate us "criminals" in our church.

We could laugh at that. But being shamed before our children was another matter. I admit it hurt when the embarrassed deputy entered my home and read the warrant for my arrest before my family. It hit hard to have my children hear their father accused of "unlawful and notorious cohabitation," "bastardy," "rebellion," and "insurrection"—I, Edson Jessop, who in all my life have never lifted a finger in violence. It hurt until I had to blink tears when my little girls, scared and bewildered, clung to my legs and cried and kissed me good-by as I climbed into the deputy's car to go to jail.

But nothing hurt like the home-coming to an empty hearth—our discovery that the state of Arizona had spirited one hundred fifty-four innocent women and children away to Phoenix just to keep us husbands and fathers from our families.

What will be the outcome?

We shall never give up. We have taken our wives in good faith. Before we abandon them as concubines and our children as illegitimates we shall fight the state of Arizona with all our strength. We shall commit no violence; we'll passively resist, as Gandhi did.

If God made the heavens and earth, if He could save the Hebrew children in the fiery furnace and Daniel in the lions' den, cannot He prompt the courts of America? Our wives and our children are in His hands.

11

The Law v. Plural Marriages

RALPH NADER

The Short Creek raid proved itself a costly failure. By 1955 when the children were released from state custody, after expenses of $110,000 were incurred for their care, the colony slowly resumed its normal life and now is prospering once again. No further enforcement is planned by either county or state officials. Nor did anything materialize out of the hearings held at Short Creek in 1955 by the Senate Subcommittee to Investigate Juvenile Delinquency. Senator Langer had promised a full report and action

In Utah the limitations of enforcement have lately resulted in the formation of an Anti-Polygamy Citizen League. Its initial public report, issued last November, emphasized the detrimental effect that children of plural marriages have on other children in the community. The survey also stressed the low economic status of polygamists, allegedly due to the inability of one man to support several families, and the lowering of neighboring property values "as a result of poor property maintenance and care." These allegations, which have

From *Harvard Law Record,* XXXI, No. 1 (1960), 10–12. Reprinted by permission of the author and publisher.

been repeated many times previously to whip up community fervor, are questioned by more impartial observers who point to facts showing the contrary. As an action program, the League advocates broader legislation, boycotting of known polygamists' shops and businesses, and the discharge of cultists currently on Civil Service rolls at Hill Air Force Base.

Why have law enforcement efforts generally failed? First, in eradicating fundamentalist polygamy, it is necessary to break the hold of strong religious commitment, not masculine concupiscence. Judge Tuller of the Superior Court of Pima County, Arizona, told a group of violators: "You have an unshakeable belief that it is the rest of the world that is out of step. . . . Nothing short of life imprisonment would prevent you from committing the same crime in the future." He added that confronted by such immutable beliefs, punishment would neither deter nor rehabilitate the offenders. The separation principle was probably based, to a degree, on a common-sense recognition of the law's limitations in the area of religious persuasions.

Problems of investigation and prosecution also hamper enforcement. How can a suspected polygamist, an expert at evasion and cloaking his activities, be brought to trial? His arrangements do not exactly correspond to an oriental seraglio. Wives are often situated in two or more of the mountain states; colonies are situated in remote areas; the children of one wife may be placed with another; birth certificates are falsified and sympathetic neighbors are reluctant to divulge incriminating information.

The proper charge presents difficulties. The charge of polygamy, frequently used at the turn of the century, has to surmount the barrier of proving the second marriage. Plural marriages take place secretly; no certificate is made out, the service is performed by a sect member, often a relative, and only one wife will assume her husband's name. Technical pitfalls in a prosecution for bigamy in other states are well known, perhaps none better than the "trigamy as a defense to bigamy" Maryland case. *Wright v. State,* 81 *A. 2d* 602 (1951).

In recent times, other more flexible charges are brought including unlawful cohabitation, fornication, marrying the spouse of another, and contributing to the delinquency of a minor.

The cost of caring for children of these marriages, after their parents have been convicted, can be very costly and even prohibitive to many counties. Caring for the Short Creek children amounted to a year's budget for Mohave County, had it paid the entire bill.

Prohibition by law of plural marriages is based on a rationale which proceeds from felt assumptions to foregone conclusions. Courts have characterized them as "crimes against the family" and a "contemptible evil." And with sweeping righteousness, the Supreme Court of Utah has objurgated the offenders: "The good name of this state and its people, committed to sustaining a high moral standard, must not be obliged to suffer because of the unsavory social life of appellants and others claiming the constitutional right under the guise of religious freedom to bring shame and embarrassment to the people of this state."

It seems that what most concerns articulate anti-polygamists is the contaminating or epidemic potential of a religiously based practice toward igniting pure licentiousness and a moral breakdown among non-cultists. This fear could explain the extremes in which their execrations are couched.

In our monogamous system that admits of no exceptions, the solution of the problem of polygamy may require more than legal control or enforcement attempts. These but inspire greater furtiveness and vigilance by the sects. A more sophisticated use of informal social approaches may succeed where attempts at enforcement have failed.

12

Boutilier v. Immigration and Naturalization Service

Mr. Justice Clark delivered the opinion of the Court.

The petitioner, an alien, has been ordered deported to Canada as one who upon entry into this country was a homosexual and therefore "afflicted with psychopathic personality" and excludable under § 212 (a) (4) of the Immigration and Nationality Act of 1952. 66 Stat. 182, 8 U.S.C. § 1182 (a) (4).[1] Petitioner's appeal from the finding of the Special Inquiry Officer was dismissed by the Board of Immigration Appeals, without opinion, and his petition for review in the Court of Appeals was dismissed, with one judge dissenting, 363 F. 2d 488. It held that the term "psychopathic personality," as used by the Congress in § 212 (a) (4), was a term of art intended to exclude homosexuals from entry into the United States. It further found that the term was not void for vagueness and was, therefore, not repugnant to the Fifth Amendment's Due Process Clause. We granted certiorari, 385 U.S. 927, and now affirm.

I

Petitioner, a Canadian national, was first admitted to this country on June 22, 1955, at the age of 21. His last entry was in 1959, at which time he was re-

Supreme Court of the United States, 387 U.S. 118 (1967). Abridged with renumbered notes.

turning from a short trip to Canada. His mother and stepfather and three of his brothers and sisters live in the United States. In 1963 he applied for citizenship and submitted to the Naturalization Examiner an affidavit in which he admitted that he was arrested in New York in October 1959, on a charge of sodomy, which was later reduced to simple assault and thereafter dismissed on default of the complainant. In 1964, petitioner, at the request of the Government, submitted another affidavit which revealed the full history of his sexual deviate behavior. It stated that his first homosexual experience occurred when he was fourteen years of age, some seven years before his entry into the United States. Petitioner was evidently a passive participant in this encounter. His next episode was at age 16 and occurred in a public park in Halifax, Nova Scotia. Petitioner was the active participant in this affair. During the next five years immediately preceding his first entry into the United States petitioner had homosexual relations on an average of three or four times a year. He also stated that prior to his entry he had engaged in heterosexual relations on three or four occasions. During the eight and one-half years immediately subsequent to his entry, and up to the time of his first statement, petitioner continued to have homosexual relations on the average of three or four times a year. Since 1959 petitioner has shared an apartment with a man with whom he has had homosexual relations.

The 1964 affidavit was submitted to the Public Health Service for its opinion as to whether petitioner was excludable for any reason at the time of his entry. The Public Health Service issued a certificate in 1964 stating that in the opinion of the subscribing physicians petitioner "was afflicted with a class A condition, namely, psychopathic personality, sexual deviate" at the time of his admission. Deportation proceedings were then instituted. "No serious question," the Special Inquiry Officer found, "has been raised either by the respondent [petitioner here], his counsel or the psychiatrists [employed by petitioner] who have submitted reports on the respondent as to his sexual deviation." Indeed, the officer found that both of petitioner's psychiatrists "conclude that the respondent has been a homosexual for a number of years but conclude that by reason of such sexual deviation the respondent is not a psychopathic personality." Finding against petitioner on the facts, the issue before the officer was reduced to the purely legal question of whether the term "psychopathic personality" included homosexuals and if it suffered illegality because of vagueness.

II

The legislative history of the Act indicates beyond a shadow of a doubt that the Congress intended the phrase "psychopathic personality" to include homosexuals such as petitioner.

Prior to the 1952 Act the Immigration Law excluded "persons of constitutional psychopathic inferiority." 39 Stat. 875, as amended, 8 U. S. C. § 136 (a) (1946 ed.). Beginning in 1950, a subcommittee of the Senate Committee on the Judiciary conducted a comprehensive study of the immigration laws and in its report found "that the purpose of the provisions against 'persons with constitutional psychopathic inferiority' will be more adequately served by changing that term to 'persons afflicted with psychopathic personality' and that the classes of mentally defective should be enlarged to include homosexuals and other sex perverts." Senate Report No. 1515, 81st Cong., 2d Sess., p. 345. The resulting legislation was first introduced as S. 3455 and used the new phrase "psychopathic personality." The bill, however, contained an additional clause providing for the exclusion of aliens "who are homosexuals or sex perverts." As the legislation progressed (now S. 2550 in the 82d Congress), however, it omitted the latter clause "who are homosexuals or sex perverts" and used only the phrase "psychopathic personality." The omission is explained by the Judiciary Committee Report on the bill:

> The provisions of S. 716 [one of the earlier bills not enacted] which specifically excluded homosexuals and sex perverts as a separate excludable class does not appear in the instant bill. The Public Health Service has advised that the provision for the exclusion of aliens afflicted with psychopathic personality or mental defect which appears in the instant bill is sufficiently broad to provide for the exclusion of homosexuals and sex perverts. *This change of nomenclature is not to be construed in any way as modifying the intent to exclude all aliens who are sexual deviates.* [Emphasis supplied.] Senate Report No. 1137, 82d Cong., 2d Sess., p. 9.

Likewise, a House bill, H. R. 5678, adopted the position of the Public Health Service that the phrase "psychopathic personality" excluded from entry homosexuals and sex perverts. The report that accompanied the bill shows clearly that the Committee adopted the recommendation of the Public Health Service that "psychopathic personality" should be used in the Act as a phrase that would exclude from admission homosexuals and sex perverts. House Report No. 1365, 82d Cong., 2d Sess. It quoted at length, and specifically adopted the Public Health Service report which recommended that the term "psychopathic personality" be used to "specify such types of pathologic behavior as homosexuality or sexual perversion." We, therefore, conclude that the Congress used the phrase "psychopathic personality" not in the clinical sense, but to effectuate its purpose to exclude all homosexuals and other sex perverts.

Petitioner stresses that only persons *afflicted* with psychopathic personality are excludable. This, he says, is "a condition, physical or psychiatric, which may be manifested in different ways, including sexual behavior." Petitioner's contention must fall to his own admissions. For over six years prior to his entry petitioner admittedly followed a continued course of homosexual conduct. The Public Health Service doctors found and certified that at the time of his entry petitioner "was afflicted with a class A condition, namely, psychopathic personality, sexual deviate, at the time of his admission." It was stipulated that if these doctors were to appear in the case they would testify to this effect and that "no useful purpose would be served by submitting this additional psychiatric material [furnished by petitioner's doctors] to the United States Public Health Service." The Government clearly established that petitioner was a homosexual at entry. Having substantial support in the record, we do not now disturb that finding, especially since petitioner admitted being a homosexual at the time of his entry. The existence of this condition over a continuous and uninterrupted period prior to and at the time of petitioner's entry clearly supports the ultimate finding upon which the order of deportation was based.

III

Petitioner says, even so, the section as construed is constitutionally defective because it does not adequately warn him that his sexual affliction at the time of entry could lead to his deportation. It is true that this Court has held the "void for vagueness" doctrine applicable to civil as well as criminal actions. See *Small Co. v. Am. Sugar Ref. Co.*, 267 U. S. 233, 239 (1925). However, this is where "the exaction of obedience to a rule or standard . . . was so vague and indefinite as really to be no rule at all." In short, the exaction must strip a participant of his rights to come within the principle of the cases. But the "exaction" of § 212 (a) (4) never applied to petitioner's conduct after entry. The section imposes neither regulation nor sanction on conduct. In this situation, therefore, no necessity exists for guidance so that one may avoid the applicability of the law. The petitioner is not being deported for conduct engaged in after his entry into the United States, but rather for characteristics he possessed *at the time of* his entry. Here, when petitioner first presented himself at our border for entrance, he was already afflicted with homosexuality. The pattern was cut, and under it he was not admissible.

The constitutional requirement of fair warning has no applicability to standards such as are laid down in § 212 (a) (4) for admission of aliens to the United States. It has long been held that the Congress has plenary power to make rules for the admission of aliens and to exclude those who possess those characteristics that Congress has forbidden. See *The Chinese Exclusion Case*, 130 U. S. 581 (1889). Here Congress commanded that homosexuals not be allowed to enter. The petitioner was found to have that characteristic and was ordered deported. The basis of the deportation order was his affliction for a long period of time *prior to entry*, six and one-half years before his entry. It may be, as some claim, that "psychopathic personality" is a medically ambiguous term, including several separate and distinct afflictions. Noyes, *Modern Clinical Psychiatry* (3d ed.) (1941), p. 410. But the test is what the Congress intended, not what differing psychiatrists may think. It was not laying down a clinical test, but an exclusionary standard which it declared to be inclusive of those having homosexual and perverted characteristics. It can hardly be disputed that the legislative history of § 212 (a) (4) clearly shows that Congress so intended.

But petitioner says that he had no warning and that no interpretation of the section had come down at the time of his 1955 entry. Therefore, he argues, he was unaware of the fact that homosexual conduct engaged in after entry could lead to his deportation. We do not believe that petitioner's post-entry conduct is the basis for his deportation order. At the time of his first entry he had continuously been afflicted with homosexuality for over six years. To us the statute is clear. It fixes "the time of entry" as the crucial date and the record shows that the findings of the Public Health Service doctors and the Special Inquiry Officer all were based on that date. We find no indication that the post-entry evidence was of any consequence in the ultimate decision of the doctors, the hearing officer, or the court. Indeed, the proof was uncontradicted as to petitioner's characteristic at the time of entry and this brought him within the excludable class. A standard applicable solely to time of entry could hardly be vague as to post-entry conduct.

The petitioner raises other points, including the claim that an "arriving alien" under the Act is entitled to medical examination. Since he is not an "arriving alien" subject to exclusion, but a deportable alien within an excludable class—who through error was permitted entry—it is doubtful if the requirement would apply. But we need not go into the question since petitioner was twice offered examination and refused to submit himself. He can hardly be heard to complain now. The remaining contentions are likewise without merit. Affirmed.

Mr. Justice Brennan dissents for the reasons stated by Judge Moore of the Court of Appeals, 363 F. 2d, 488, 496–499.

Mr. Justice Douglas, with whom Mr. Justice Fortas concurs, dissenting.

The term "psychopathic personality" is a treacherous one like "communist" or in an earlier day "Bolshevik." A label of this kind when freely used may mean only an unpopular person. It is much too vague by constitutional standards for the imposition of penalties or punishment.

Cleckley defines "psychopathic personality" as one who has the following characteristics:

1. Superficial charm and good "intelligence."
2. Absence of delusions and other signs of irrational "thinking."
3. Absence of "nervousness" or psychoneurotic manifestations.
4. Unreliability.
5. Untruthfulness and insincerity.
6. Lack of remorse or shame.
7. Inadequately motivated antisocial behavior.
8. Poor judgment and failure to learn by experience.
9. Pathologic egocentricity and incapacity for love.
10. General poverty in major affective reactions.
11. Specific loss of insight.
12. Unresponsiveness in general interpersonal relations.
13. Fantastic and uninviting behavior with drink and sometimes without.
14. Suicide rarely carried out.

15. Sex life impersonal, trivial and poorly integrated.
16. Failure to follow any life plan. Cleckley, *The Mask of Sanity* (1941), pp. 238–255.

The word "psychopath" according to some means "a sick mind." Guttmacher and Weihofen (1952), p. 86:

> In the light of present knowledge, most of the individuals called psychopathic personalities should probably be considered as suffering from neurotic character disorders. They are, for the most part, unhappy persons, harassed by tension and anxiety, who are struggling against unconscious conflicts that were created during the very early years of childhood. The nature and even the existence of these conflicts that drive them restlessly on are unknown to them. When the anxiety rises to a certain pitch, they seek relief through some antisocial act. The frequency with which this pattern recurs in the individual is dependent in part upon the intensity of the unconscious conflict, upon the tolerance for anxiety, and upon chance environmental situations that may heighten or decrease it. One of the chief diagnostic criteria of this type of neurotically determined deliquency is the repetitiveness of the pattern. The usual explanation, as for example, that the recidivistic check-writer has just 'got in the habit of writing bad checks' is meaningless. *Id.,* pp. 88–89.

Many experts think that it is "a meaningless designation . . . not yet is there any common agreement . . . as to classification or . . . etiology." Noyes, *Modern Clinical Psychiatry* (3d ed.) (1941), p. 410. "The only conclusion that seems warrantable is that, at some time or other and by some reputable authority, the term psychopathic personality has been used to designate every conceivable type of abnormal character." Curran & Mallinson, "Psychopathic Personality," *Journal of Mental Science,* XL, 278. It is much too treacherously vague a term to allow the high penalty of deportation to turn on it.

When it comes to sex, the problem is complex. Those "who fail to reach sexual maturity (heterosexuality), and who remain at a narcissistic or homosexual stage" are the products "of heredity, of glandular dysfunction, [or] of environmental circumstances." Henderson, *Mental Abnormality and Crime* (1949), p. 114.

The homosexual is one who, by some freak, is the product of an arrested development:

> All people have originally bisexual tendencies that are more or less developed and which in the course of time normally deviate either in the direction of male or female. This may indicate that a trace of homosexuality, no matter how weak it may be, exists in every human being. It is present in the adolescent stage, where there is a considerable amount of undifferentiated sexuality. Abrahamsen, *Crime and the Human Mind* (1944), p. 117.

Many homosexuals become involved in violations of laws; many do not. Kinsey reported:

It is not possible to insist that any departure from the sexual mores, or any participation in socially taboo activities, always, or even usually, involves a neurosis or psychosis, for the case histories abundantly demonstrate that most individuals who engage in taboo activities make satisfactory social adjustments. There are, in actuality, few adult males who are particularly disturbed over their sexual histories. Psychiatrists, clinical psychologists, and others who deal with cases of maladjustment, sometimes come to feel that most people find difficulty in adjusting their sexual lives; but a clinic is no place to secure incidence figures. The incidence of tuberculosis in a tuberculosis sanitarium is no measure of the incidence of tuberculosis in the population as a whole; and the incidence of disturbance over sexual activities, among the persons who came to a clinic, is no measure of the frequency of similar disturbances outside of clinics. The impression that such "sexual irregularities" as "excessive" masturbation, pre-marital intercourse, responsibility for a pre-marital pregnancy, extra-marital intercourse, mouth-genital contacts, homosexual activity, or animal intercourse, always produce psychoses and abnormal personalities is based upon the fact that the persons who do go to professional sources for advice are upset by these things.

It is unwarranted to believe that particular types of sexual behavior are always expressions of psychoses or neuroses. In actuality, they are more often expressions of what is biologically basic in mammalian and anthropoid behavior, and of a deliberate disregard for social convention. Many of the socially and intellectually most significant persons in our histories, successful scientists, educators, physicians, clergymen, businessmen, and persons of high position in governmental affairs, have socially taboo items in their sexual histories, and among them they have accepted nearly the whole range of so-called sexual abnormalities. Among the socially most successful and personally best adjusted persons who have contributed to the present study, there are some whose rates of outlet are as high as those in any case labeled nymphomania or satyriasis in the literature, or recognized as such in the clinic. Kinsey, *Sexual Behavior in the Human Male* (1948), pp. 201–202.

It is common knowledge that in this century homosexuals have risen high in our own public service—both in Congress and in the Executive Branch—and have served with distinction. It is therefore not credible that Congress wanted to deport everyone and anyone who was a sexual deviate, no matter how blameless his social conduct had been nor how creative his work nor how valuable his contribution to society. I agree with Judge Moore, dissenting below, that the legislative history should not be read as imputing to Congress a purpose to classify under the heading "psychopathic personality" every person who had ever had a homosexual experience:

Professor Kinsey estimated that "at least 37 per cent" of the American male population has at least one homosexual experience, defined in terms of physical contact to the point of orgasm, between the beginning of adolescence and old age.[2] Kinsey, p. 623. Earlier estimates had ranged from one per cent to 100 per cent. *Id.*, at 616–622. The sponsors of Britain's current reform bill on homosexuality have indicated that one male in 25 is a homosexual in Britain.[3] To label a group so large "excludable aliens" would be tantamount to saying that Sappho,

Leonardo da Vinci, Michelangelo, André Gide, and perhaps even Shakespeare, were they to come to life again, would be deemed unfit to visit our shores.[4] Indeed, so broad a definition might well comprise more than a few members of legislative bodies. 363 F. 2d 488, 497–498.

The Public Health Service, from whom Congress borrowed the term "psychopathic personality" (House Rep. No. 1365, 82d Cong., 2d Sess., 46–47), admits that the term is "vague and indefinite." *Id., at* 46.

If we are to hold, as the Court apparently does, that any acts of homosexuality suffice to deport the alien, whether or not they are part of a fabric of antisocial behavior, then we face a serious question of due process. By that construction a person is judged by a standard that is almost incapable of definition. I have already quoted from clinical experts to show what a wide range the term "psychopathic personality" has. Another expert[5] classifies such a person under three headings:

Acting: (1) inability to withstand tedium, (2) lack of a sense of responsibility, (3) a tendency to "blow up" under pressure, (4) maladjustment to law and order, and (5) recidivism.

Feeling: they tend to (1) be emotionally deficient, narcissistic, callous, inconsiderate, and unremorseful, generally projecting blame on others, (2) have hair-trigger emotions, exaggerated display of emotion, and be irritable and impulsive, (3) be amoral (socially and sexually), and (4) worry, but do nothing about it.

Thinking: they display (1) defective judgment, living for the present rather than for the future, and (2) inability to profit from experience, that is, they are able to realize the consequences intelligently, but not to evaluate them.

We held in *Jordan* v. *DeGeorge,* 341 U. S. 223, that the crime of a conspiracy to defraud the United States of taxes involved "moral turpitude" and made the person subject to deportation. That, however, was a term that has "deep roots in the law." *Id.,* at 227. But the grab-bag "psychopathic personality" has no "deep roots" whatsoever. Caprice of judgment is almost certain under this broad definition. Anyone can be caught who is unpopular, who is off-beat, who is nonconformist.

Deportation is the equivalent to banishment or exile. *Fong Haw Tan* v. *Phelan,* 333 U. S. 6, 10. Though technically not criminal, it practically may be. The penalty is so severe that we have extended to the resident alien the protection of due process. *Wong Yang Sung* v. *McGrath,* 339 U. S. 33. Even apart from deportation cases, we look with suspicion at those delegations of power so broad as to allow the administrative staff the power to formulate the fundamental policy. See *Watkins* v. *United States,* 354 U. S. 178, 203–205; *Kent* v. *Dulles,* 357 U. S. 116. In the *Watkins* case we were protecting important First Amendment rights. In the *Kent* case we were protecting the right to travel, an important ingredient of a person's "liberty" within the meaning of the Fifth Amendment. We deal here also with an aspect of "liberty" and the requirements of due process. They demand that the standard be sufficiently clear as to forewarn those who may otherwise be entrapped and to provide full opportunity to conform. "Psychopathic personality" is so broad and vague as to be hardly more than an epithet. The Court seeks to avoid this question by saying that the standard being applied relates only to what petitioner had done prior to his entry, not to his post-entry conduct. *But at least half of the questioning of this petitioner related to his post-entry conduct.*

Moreover, the issue of deportability under § 212 (a) of the Act turns on whether petitioner is "afflicted with psychopathic personality." On this I think he is entitled to a hearing to satisfy both the statute and the requirement of due process.

One psychiatrist reported:

On psychiatric examination of Mr. Boutilier, there was no indication of delusional trend or hallucinatory phenomena. He is not psychotic. From his own account, he has a psychosexual problem but is beginning treatment for this disorder. Diagnostically, I would consider him as having a Character Neurosis, believe that the prognosis in therapy is reasonably good and do not think he represents any risk of decompensation into a dependent psychotic reaction nor any potential for frank criminal activity.

Another submitted a long report ending as follows:

The patient's present difficulties obviously weigh very heavily upon him. He feels as if he has made his life in this country and is deeply disturbed at the prospect of being cut off from the life he has created for himself. He talks frankly about himself. What emerged out of the interview was not a picture of a psychopath but that of a dependent, immature young man with a conscience, an awareness of the feelings of others and a sense of personal honesty. His sexual structure still appears fluid and immature so that he moves from homosexual to heterosexual interests as well as abstinence with almost equal facility. His homosexual orientation seems secondary to a very constricted, dependent personality pattern rather than occurring in the context of a psychopathic personality. My own feeling is that his own need to fit in and be accepted is so great that it far surpasses his need for sex in any form.

I do not believe that Mr. Boutilier is a psychopath.

In light of these statements, I cannot say that it has been determined that petitioner was "afflicted" in the statutory sense either at the time of entry or at present. "Afflicted" means possessed or dominated by. Occasional acts would not seem sufficient. "Afflicted" means a way of life, an accustomed pattern of conduct. Whatever disagreement there is as to the meaning of "psychopathic personality," it has generally been understood to refer to a consistent, lifelong pattern of behavior conflicting with social norms without accompanying guilt. Cleckley, *supra,* at 29. Nothing of that character was shown to exist at the time of entry. The fact that he presently has a problem, as one psychiatrist said, does not mean that he is or was necessarily "afflicted" with homosexuality. His conduct is, of course, evidence material to the issue. But the informed judgment of experts is needed to make the required finding. We cruelly mutilate the Act when we hold otherwise. For we make the word of the bureaucrat supreme, when it was the expertise of the doctors and psychiatrists on which Congress wanted the administrative action to be dependent.

NOTES

1. "Sec. 212. (a) Except as otherwise provided in this Act, the following classes of aliens shall be ineligible to receive visas and shall be excludable from admission into the United States: (b) Aliens afflicted with psychopathic personality, epilepsy, or a mental defect.

   "Section 241 (a)(1) of the Immigration and Nationality Act, 66 Stat. 204, 8 U. S. C. § 1251 (a)(1), provides that: 'Any alien in the United States . . . shall, upon the order of the Attorney General, be deported who—(1) at the time of entry was within one or more of the classes of aliens excludable by the law existing at the time of such entry.' "

2. "Homosexual activity in the human male is much more frequent than is ordinarily realized. In the youngest unmarried group, more than a quarter (27.3 per cent) of the males have some homosexual activity to the point of orgasm. The incidence among these single males rises in successive age groups until it reaches a maximum of 38.7 per cent between 36 and 40 years of age.

   "High frequencies do not occur as often in the homosexual as they do in some other kinds of sexual activity. Populations are more homogeneous in regard to this outlet. This may reflect the difficulties involved in having frequent and regular relations in a socially taboo activity. Nevertheless, there are a few of the younger adolescent males who have homosexual frequencies of 7 or more per week, and between 26 and 30 the maximum frequencies run to 15 per week. By 50 years of age the most active individual is averaging only 5.0 per week.

   "For single, active populations, the mean frequencies of homosexual contacts rise more or less steadily from near once per week for the younger adolescent boys to nearly twice as often for males between the ages of 31 and 35. They stand above once a week through age 50." Kinsey, pp. 259–260.

3. Report, Committee on Homosexual Offenses and Prostitution (1957).

4. Sigmund Freud wrote in 1935:

   "Homosexuality is assuredly no advantage, but it is nothing to be ashamed of, no vice, no degradation, it cannot be classified as an illness; we consider it to be a variation of the sexual function produced by a certain arrest of sexual development. Many highly respectable individuals of ancient and modern times have been homosexuals, several of the greatest men among them (Plato, Michelangelo, Leonardo da Vinci, etc.). It is a great injustice to persecute homosexuality as a crime, and cruelty too. If you do not believe me, read the books of Havelock Ellis." Ruitenbeck, *The Problem of Homosexuality in Modern Society* (1963), p. 1.

5. Caldwell, "Constitutional Psychopathic State (Psychopathic Personality) Studies of Soldiers in the United States Army," *J. Crim. Psychopath*, III (1941), 171–172.

13

Morality and Social Dominance

JEROME H. SKOLNICK

When an automobile manufacturer attempts to effect a reduction in the excise tax on automobiles, or when an oil and gas producer seeks to maintain or increase depletion allowances, such conduct may be challenged, but it is understood as rational by all interested parties. The self-interested profit motive is easily comprehended, with no questions asked as to why the entrepreneur is behaving as he does even by those who oppose him. Thus, there may be conflict between consumer lobbies and producer lobbies, or between different industries interested in increasing their own profits, but the motives of each are conventional and understandable to all. By contrast, the motives of those engaged in moral advocacy are not so clear, precisely because they do not fall clearly into the domain of apparent self-interests that are usually thought to motivate human effort. In the past decade, there has been an increasing interest on the part of sociologists, especially those concerned with deviance and social control, to interpret the basis of such motivation.

This concern reflects an emphasis on the study of deviant behavior that places less stress on the "deviant" and his personal characteristics as the "cause" of deviant behavior, than upon the reaction of a society or of other individuals that defines the behavior in question as deviant. Thus, Howard S. Becker has argued in his influential book *Outsiders* that:

> Social groups create deviance by making the rules whose infraction constitutes deviance, and by applying those rules to particular people and labeling them as outsiders. From this point of view, deviance is not a quality of the act the person commits, but rather a consequence of the application by others of rules and sanctions to an "offender." The deviant is one to whom the label has been successfully applied; deviant behavior is behavior that people so label.

Similarly, John Kitsuse has suggested as a central problem for theory and research in the sociology of deviance the following:

> What are the behaviors that are defined by members of the group, community, or society as deviant, and how do those definitions organize and activate the societal reactions by which persons come to be differentiated and treated as

From Jerome H. Skolnick, "Coercion to Virtue," *Southern California Law Review*, XLI, No. 3 (1968), 607–611. Abridged without notes. Reprinted by permission of the publisher.

deviants? In formulating the problem this way, the point of view of those who interpret and define behavior as deviant must explicitly be incorporated into a sociological definition of deviance. Accordingly, deviance may be conceived as a process by which the members of a group, community, or society (1) interpret behavior as deviant, (2) define persons who so behave as a certain kind of deviant, and (3) accord them the treatment considered appropriate to such deviants.

Becker, in particular, has been interested in analysis of the motivations of individuals or social groups that "create" deviance, especially those that "create" crime. He regards people who take the initiative in reordering the content of rules as "moral entrepreneurs," the prototype of whom is the crusading reformer. Becker is not ungenerous in assessing the motives of those who engage in moral crusades. He recognizes that in the moral crusader there is not only the motive of the meddling busybody but also the spirit of the humanitarian. "It is appropriate," he writes, "to think of reformers as crusaders because they typically believe that their mission is a holy one. The prohibitionist serves as an excellent example, as does the person who wants to suppress vice and sexual delinquency or the person who wants to do away with gambling."

The motivation of moral entrepreneurship is explored in greater detail in Joseph Gusfield's analysis of the temperance movement. The movement to suppress the use of alcoholic beverages was part of a general effort to improve the human condition. "Temperance" supporters were to be found prominently in such related movements as sabbatarianism, abolition, women's rights, agrarianism, and in humanitarian attempts to improve the lot of the poor. There was a great concern, especially on the part of the Women's Christian Temperance Union (WCTU), to improve the welfare of the lower classes, to secure penal reform, to shorten working hours, to raise wages for workers, to improve working conditions, to abolish child labor, and to protect working girls from the exploitation of men. The breadth of the reform movement mirrors a concern with fundamental values, and any intrusion on these values constitutes a threat to the social position of the group. Thus, Gusfield analyzes moral reform as one way that a "cultural group acts to preserve, defend, or enhance the dominance and prestige of its own style of living within the total society."

For those whose immediate interests are being gratified within the framework of the established and operative social system, the intense dedication of a moral crusade may appear erratic and beyond understanding. But if we perceive the crusader's concern with a moral issue as symbolic of the preservation or assertion of a style of living that represents a configuration of values, then the crusader may be rational in his own terms. Or, to put it another way, the weight of "liberal and informed thinking" on the subject of drinking would doubtless today argue that while social drinking may sometimes result in medical and social problems, the use of alcoholic beverages should not be prohibited by criminal law. But seen from the viewpoint of the prohibitionist advocate of, say, the early twentieth century, the issue of national prohibition was not merely a question of drinking; it involved a test of strength between conceptions of social order: on the one side, the social order associated with the villages, and farms, and sectarian and fundamentalist Christianity; on the other side, the threat posed by the ever increasing social influence and style of life of the cities, of industrialization, of a Romanized and Anglicized Christianity, and of immigration. Thus, for the prohibitionist, legalization of social drinking represented the subversion of a way of life. As Walter Lippmann wrote in 1927, when it was becoming increasingly evident that the dominion of rural America was waning in American life:

> The evil that the old fashioned preachers ascribe to the Pope, to Babylon, to atheists, and to the devil, is simply the new urban civilization, with its irresistible scientific and economic and mass power. The Pope, the devil, jazz, the bootleggers, are a mythology that expresses symbolically the impact of a vast and dreaded social change. The change is real enough. . . . The defense of the Eighteenth Amendment has, therefore, become much more than a mere question of regulating the liquor traffic. It involves a test of strength between social orders, and when that test is concluded, and if, as seems probable, the Amendment breaks down, the fall will bring down with it the dominion of the older civilization. The Eighteenth Amendment is the rock on which the evangelical church militant is founded, and with it are involved a whole way of life and an ancient tradition. The overcoming of the Eighteenth Amendment would mean the emergence of the cities as the dominant force in America, dominant politically and socially as they are already dominant economically.

The absence of societal consensus did not deter the ardent advocate of public opinion. On the contrary, that public opinion seemed increasingly to be marshalled against his cause spurred him to advocacy. Public opinion was for him not irrelevant, but subject to a different interpretation than the "moderate liberal" would make of it. The growth of the "forces of evil" demanded an even greater commitment to the good cause, which was the dominance of sectarian Christianity in the echelons of government, in the respect accorded to his way of thinking, in the social position of the sectarian Christian in the community. Thus, the Wickersham Commission observed in 1931 that:

> It is safe to say that a significant change has taken place in the social attitude toward drinking. This may be seen in the views and conduct of social leaders, business and professional men in the average community. It would not have been possible a generation ago. It is reflected in a different way of regarding drunken youth, in a change in the class of excessive drinkers, and in the increased use of distilled liquor in places and connections where formerly it was banned. It is evident that, taking the country as a whole, people of wealth, businessmen and professional men, and their families, and, perhaps, the higher paid workingmen and their families, are drinking in large numbers in quite frank disregard of the declared policy of the National Prohibition Act.

The subjective side of the sense of status decline is given by one of Joseph Gusfield's WCTU interviewees who lamented: "We were once an accepted group. The leading people would be members. Not exactly the leading people, but upper-middle class people and sometimes the leaders. Today they'd be ashamed to belong to the WCTU. . . . Today it's kind of lower-bourgeois. It's not fashionable any longer to belong."

Such a statement discloses something fundamental about the relation between societal consensus and the regulation of public morality. For those who affirm a strong moral position, the capacity to regulate public morality may document their status in society. . . .

The greater the commitment to a declining way of life, the more important is validation of public recognition through public power. Genuine custom requires less State support than mere convention, which is spurious custom. Thus, in this instance the once dominant WCTU'er reveals the personal psychology of the deviant. She is now the "outsider," by social definition. Drinking has become part of the American way of life, and those who continue to seek its prohibition are ejected from its mainstream.

SECTION FOUR   *Defining Moral Standards*

14

Repouille v. United States

L. Hand, Circuit Judge.

The District Attorney, on behalf of the Immigration and Naturalization Service, has appealed from an order, naturalizing the appellee, Repouille. The ground of the objection in the district court and here is that he did not show himself to have been a person of "good moral character" for the five years that preceded the filing of his petition. The facts were as follows. The petition was filed on September 22, 1944, and on October 12, 1939, he had deliberately put to death his son, a boy of 13, by means of chloroform. His reason for this tragic deed was that the child had "suffered from birth from a brain injury which destined him to be an idiot and a physical monstrosity malformed in all four limbs. The child was blind, mute, and deformed. He had to be fed; the movements of his bladder and bowels were involuntary, and his entire life was spent in a small crib." Repouille had four other children at the time toward whom he has always been a dutiful and responsible parent; it may be assumed that his act was to help him in their nurture, which was being compromised by the burden imposed upon him in the care of the fifth. The family was altogether dependent upon his industry for its support. He was indicted for manslaughter in the first degree; but the jury brought in a verdict of manslaughter in the second degree with a recommendation of the "utmost clemency"; and the judge sentenced him to not less than five years nor more than ten, execution to be stayed, and the defendant to be placed on probation, from which he was discharged in December, 1945. Concededly, except for this act he conducted himself as a person of "good moral character" during the five years before he filed his petition. Indeed, if he had waited before filing his petition from September 22, to October 14, 1944, he would have had a clear record for the necessary period, and would have been admitted without question.

Very recently we had to pass upon the phrase "good moral character" in the Nationality Act;[1] and we said that it set as a test, not those standards which we might ourselves approve, but whether "the moral feelings, now prevalent generally in this country" would "be outraged" by the conduct in question: that is, whether it conformed to "the generally accepted moral conventions current at the time."[2] In the absence of some national inquisition, like a

United States Court of Appeals, Second Circuit, 165 F. 2d 152 (1947). Abridged with renumbered notes.

Gallup poll, that is indeed a difficult test to apply; often questions will arise to which the answer is not ascertainable, and where the petitioner must fail only because he has the affirmative. Indeed, in the case at bar itself the answer is not wholly certain; for we all know that there are great numbers of people of the most unimpeachable virtue, who think it morally justifiable to put an end to a life so inexorably destined to be a burden to others, and—so far as any possible interest of its own is concerned—condemned to a brutish existence, lower indeed than all but the lowest forms of sentient life. Nor is it inevitably an answer to say that it must be immoral to do this, until the law provides security against the abuses which would inevitably follow, unless the practice were regulated. Many people—probably most people—do not make it a final ethical test of conduct that it shall not violate law; few of us exact of ourselves or of others the unflinching obedience of a Socrates. There being no lawful means of accomplishing an end, which they believe to be righteous in itself, there have always been conscientious persons who feel no scruple in acting in defiance of a law that is repugnant to their personal convictions, and who even regard as martyrs those who suffer by doing so. In our own history it is only necessary to recall the Abolitionists. It is reasonably clear that the jury that tried Repouille did not feel any moral repulsion at this crime. Although it was inescapably murder in the first degree, not only did they bring in a verdict that was flatly in the face of the facts and utterly absurd—for manslaughter in the second degree presupposes that the killing has not been deliberate—but they coupled even that with a recommendation which showed that in substance they wished to exculpate the offender. Moreover, it is also plain, from the sentence which he imposed, that the judge could not have seriously disagreed with their recommendation.

One might be tempted to seize upon all this as a reliable measure of current morals; and no doubt it should have its place in the scale; but we should hesitate to accept it as decisive, when, for example, we compare it with the fate of a similar offender in Massachusetts, who, although he was not executed, was imprisoned for life. Left at large as we are, without means of verifying our conclusion, and without authority to substitute our individual beliefs, the outcome must needs be tentative; and not much is gained by discussion. We can say no more than that, quite independently of what may be the current moral feeling as to legally administered euthanasia, we feel reasonably secure in holding that only a minority of virtuous persons would deem the practice morally justifiable, while it remains in private hands, even when the provocation is as overwhelming as it was in this instance.

However, we wish to make it plain that a new petition would not be open to this objection; and that the pitiable event, now long passed, will not prevent Repouille from taking his place among us as a citizen. The assertion in his brief that he did not "intend" the petition to be filed until 1945 unhappily is irrelevant; the statute makes crucial the actual date of filing.

Order reversed; petition dismissed without prejudice to the filing of a second petition.

Frank, Circuit Judge (dissenting).

This decision may be of small practical import to this petitioner for citizenship, since perhaps, on filing a new petition, he will promptly become a citizen. But the method used by my colleagues in disposing of this case may, as a precedent, have a very serious significance for many another future petitioner whose "good moral character" may be questioned (for any one of a variety of reasons that may be unrelated to a "mercy killing") in circumstances where the necessity of filing a new petition may cause a long and injurious delay.[3] Accordingly, I think it desirable to dissent.

The district judge found that Repouille was a person of "good moral character." Presumably, in so finding, the judge attempted to employ that statutory standard in accordance with our decisions, that is, as measured by conduct in conformity with "the generally accepted moral conventions at the time." My colleagues, although their sources of information concerning the pertinent mores are now shown to be superior to those of the district judge, reject his finding. And they do so, too, while conceding that their own conclusion is uncertain, and (as they put it) "tentative." I incline to think that the correct statutory test (the test Congress intended) is the attitude of our ethical leaders. That attitude would not be too difficult to learn; indeed, my colleagues indicate that they think such leaders would agree with the district judge. But the precedents in this circuit constrain us to be guided by contemporary public opinion about which, cloistered as judges are, we have but vague notions. (One recalls Gibbon's remark that usually a person who talks of "the opinion of the world at large" is really referring to "the few people with whom I happened to converse.")

Seeking to apply a standard of this type, courts usually do not rely on evidence but utilize what is often called the doctrine of "judicial notice," which, in matters of this sort, properly permits informal inquiries by the judges.[4] However, for such a purpose (as in the discharge of many other judicial duties), the courts are inadequately staffed,[5] so that sometimes "judicial notice" actually means judicial ignorance.

But the courts are not utterly helpless; such judicial impotence has its limits. Especially when an issue importantly affecting a man's life is involved, it seems to me that we need not, and ought not, resort to our mere unchecked surmises, remaining wholly (to quote my colleagues' words) "without means of verifying our conclusions." Because court judgments are the most solemn kind of governmental acts—backed up as they are, if necessary, by the armed force of the government—they should, I think, have a more solid foundation. I see no good reason why a man's rights should be jeopardized by judges' needless lack of knowledge.

I think, therefore, that, in any case such as this, where we lack the means of determining present-day public reactions, we should remand to the district judge with these directions: The judge should give the petitioner and the government the opportunity to bring to the judge's attention reliable information

on the subject, which he may supplement in any appropriate way. All the data
so obtained should be put on record. On the basis thereof, the judge reconsider his decision and arrive at a conclusion. Then, if there is another appeal,
we can avoid sheer guessing, which alone is now available to us, and can reach
something like an informed judgment.[6]

NOTES

1. §707(a) (3), Title 8 U.S.C.A.
2. *United States v. Francioso*, 2 Cir., 164 F. 2d 163.
3. Consider, for example, the case of a professional man, unable during a long delay,
   incident to his becoming a citizen, to practice his profession in certain states of this
   country.
4. In this very case, my colleagues have relied on informally procured information with
   reference to "the fate of a similar offender in Massachusetts."
5. Think how any competent administrative agency would act if faced with a problem
   like that before us here.
6. Of course, we cannot thus expect to attain certainty, for certainty on such a subject
   as public opinion is unattainable.

15

The Thalidomide Tragedy

NORMAN ST. JOHN-STEVAS

The trial opened at Liège (Belgium) on Monday, November 5, 1962. Accused
of murdering Corinne van de Put was her mother, Suzanne van de Put. Also
arraigned as aiders and abettors, and, in fact, as equal partners, were her husband, her mother, her sister, and Dr. Jacques Casters, the family doctor, but
Madame van de Put was the center of the trial. It was she who was alleged to
have administered the poison that killed the child. She had taken 11 thalidomide tranquilizer pills prescribed to her before pregnancy by Dr. Casters. On
May 22, 1962, her child was born with no arms or shoulder structure, and
with deformed feet. Appalled, the family held a council and, according to the
indictment, this ended with the unanimous decision "to condemn the child to
death." Dr. Weerts, the gynecologist, was then approached to kill the infant;
he refused. So did Sister Philomene, the nun who had been the midwife attendant at the birth. In the end, the mother administered the poison herself. Bar-

From *The Right to Life* (New York: Holt, Rinehart and Winston, 1963), pp. 5–8, 14–
16. Abridged with renumbered notes. Copyright © by Norman St. John-Stevas. Reprinted by permission of Holt, Rinehart and Winston, Inc.

biturate was mixed in honey and water and placed in the baby's feeding bottle. "Go away," Madame van de Put is alleged to have said to her relatives, "I want to do it alone." The accused did not deny the child had been killed, but pleaded that it had been done to save the baby from a life of suffering. Twelve male jurors had to decide the issue of guilt or innocence.

The President of the court asked Madame van de Put why she had not put the baby in a home, as had been suggested by the gynecologist. "I did not want it," was the reply. "Absolutely not. For me, as an egoist, I could have been rid of her. But it wouldn't have given her back her arms." The President pointed out that the child was mentally normal. "That was only worse," said Madame van de Put. "If she had grown up to realize the state she was in, she would never have forgiven me for letting her live." In her evidence, Madame van de Put said that she had approached Dr. Weerts to help her and he had repeated three times, "I can do nothing," with emphasis on the "I." This was denied by Dr. Weerts, who stated his own position in court. "I am a doctor. I cannot kill. I must let live. The day doctors start killing I shall change my profession." Madame van de Put's husband stated that originally he had been against the killing of the child, but now believed that his wife had been right. Dr. Casters said that there could be no question of fitting artificial limbs, since there was no shoulder structure, only cartilage. Dr. Hoet, Professor of Pathological Embryology at the Catholic University of Louvain, testified that there was not one chance "in 100,000" that the child was not a thalidomide baby. In his opinion she did not have more than one or two years to live.

Forty witnesses came forward in the course of the trial to give evidence in favor of the accused. Testimony in favor of Dr. Casters was extremely strong. Patients and friends came forward to refer to him as "the doctor of the poor" and "the idol of the quarter." The local parish priest stressed that "he acted according to his conscience, with all his patients, always."

At the conclusion of the evidence the prosecutor demanded a verdict of guilty, although he indicated he would support a recommendation from the jury for a royal pardon. An acquittal, he maintained, would set a "terrible" precedent and open the door to all abuses. No one had said of Corinne, "This is my child; should I do anything to make it like other children?" Experts, he said, had given the baby a chance of life of one in ten. "Why did Corinne not have her chance?' The child had never experienced a single gesture of maternal love, "and if there is a paradise for unloved children, then Corinne is there with only the smile of Sister Philomene having passed over her cradle." The Defense asked for an acquittal. "Personally," said counsel, "I do not think their solution was the only one, but it is not possible to condemn them for having chosen it." Society was more to blame than Madame van de Put. Society had done nothing to prevent the tragedy; the rules about dangerous drugs were there but nothing had been done to enforce them until the child's death.

At the end of the six-day trial the jury acquitted all five defendants, and they were released from custody. The verdict was greeted with frenzied joy by the thousand people who had crowded into the court for the last day of the trial. Their rejoicing was taken up by the crowds outside the court when the news became known; traffic in the center of the city was blocked for more than an hour. "Passing trams," records an eyewitness, "rang their bells, drivers honked their horns, and the indescribable din could be heard even above the noise around the courtroom." Such an explosion of pent-up joy and relief was to be expected but as it subsided, other voices were to be heard expressing uneasiness about the verdict and its possible consequences. . . .

. . . The grounds for condemning the Liège verdict are thus clear. The felicific calculus is quite inadequate to measure the worth of human life. Handicaps can be overcome, and useful lives led. A case in point is Beethoven, for whom, on Benthamite grounds, there might have been a strong case for suppression at birth.[1] . . .

. . . The last point to be made against the Liège verdict is that it is fundamentally uncivilized and dangerous. It invites imitation. Within a few days of the verdict a Belgian housewife was remanded in custody for having killed her three-year-old mentally retarded daughter. Over the centuries, society has contrived to limit the taking of human life to the state, under rigidly defined circumstances. The van de Put case, in effect, confers on the individual citizen a license to kill, a license with no clear limiting terms. . . .

NOTE

1. Maurice Baring used to tell the following story. One doctor to another: "About the terminating of a pregnancy, I want your opinion. The father was syphilitic; the mother tuberculous. Of the four children born, the first was blind, the second died, the third was deaf and dumb, the fourth also tuberculous. What would you have done?" "I would have ended the pregnancy." "Then, you would have murdered Beethoven."

16

The Queen v. Dudley and Stephens

Indictment for the murder of Richard Parker on the high seas within the jurisdiction of the Admiralty.

At the trial before Huddleston, B., at the Devon and Cornwall Winter Assizes, November 7, 1884, the jury, at the suggestion of the learned judge,

14 Queens Bench 273 (1884). Abridged.

found the facts of the case in a special verdict which stated "that on July 5, 1884, the prisoners, Thomas Dudley and Edward Stephens, with one Brooks, all able-bodied English seamen, and the deceased also an English boy, between 17 and 18 years of age, the crew of an English yacht, a registered English vessel, were cast away in a storm on the high seas 1,600 miles from the Cape of Good Hope, and were compelled to put into an open boat belonging to the said yacht. That in this boat they had no supply of water and no supply of food, except two one-pound tins of turnips, and for three days they had nothing else to subsist upon. That on the fourth day they caught a small turtle, upon which they subsisted for a few days, and this was the only food they had up to the twentieth day when the act now in question was committed. That on the twelfth day the remains of the turtle were entirely consumed, and for the next eight days they had nothing to eat. That they had no fresh water, except such rain as they from time to time caught in their oilskin capes. That the boat was drifting on the ocean, and was probably more than 1,000 miles away from land. That on the eighteenth day, when they had been seven days without food and five without water, the prisoners spoke to Brooks as to what should be done if no succor came, and suggested that someone should be sacrificed to save the rest, but Brooks dissented, and the boy, to whom they were understood to refer, was not consulted. That on the 24th of July, the day before the act now in question, the prisoner Dudley proposed to Stephens and Brooks that lots should be cast who should be put to death to save the rest, but Brooks refused to consent, and it was not put to the boy, and in point of fact there was no drawing of lots. That on that day the prisoners spoke of their having families, and suggested it would be better to kill the boy that their lives should be saved, and Dudley proposed that if there was no vessel in sight by the morrow morning the boy should be killed. That next day, the 25th of July, no vessel appearing, Dudley told Brooks that he had better go and have a sleep, and made signs to Stephens and Brooks that the boy had better be killed. The prisoner Stephens agreed to the act, but Brooks dissented from it. That the boy was then lying at the bottom of the boat quite helpless, and extremely weakened by famine and by drinking sea water, and unable to make any resistance, nor did he ever assent to his being killed. The prisoner Dudley offered a prayer asking forgiveness for them all if either of them should be tempted to commit a rash act, and that their souls might be saved. That Dudley, with the assent of Stephens, went to the boy, and telling him that his time was come, put a knife into his throat and killed him then and there; that the three men fed upon the body and blood of the boy for four days; that on the fourth day after the act had been committed the boat was picked up by a passing vessel, and the prisoners were rescued, still alive, but in the lowest state of prostration. That they were carried to the port of Falmouth, and committed for trial at Exeter. That if the men had not fed upon the body of the boy they would probably not have survived to be so picked up and rescued, but would within the four days have died of famine. That the boy, being in a much weaker condition, was likely to have died before them. That at the time of the act in question there was no sail in sight, nor any reasonable prospect of relief. That under these circumstances there appeared to the prisoners every probability that unless they then fed or very soon fed upon the boy or one of themselves they would die of starvation. That there was no appreciable chance of saving life except by killing someone for the others to eat. That assuming any necessity to kill anybody, there was no greater necessity for killing the boy than any of the other three men." But whether upon the whole matter by the jurors found the killing of Richard Parker by Dudley and Stephens be felony and murder the jurors are ignorant, and pray the advice of the court thereupon, and if upon the whole matter the Court shall be of opinion that the killing of Richard Parker be felony and murder, then the jurors say that Dudley and Stephens were each guilty of felony and murder as alleged in the indictment.

• • •

Lord Coleridge, C. J.:

• • •

There remains to be considered the real question in the case: whether killing under the circumstances set forth in the verdict be or be not murder.

• • •

Is there any authority for the proposition which has been presented to us? Decided cases there are none. The American case cited by my brother Stephen in his Digest, from Wharton on *Homicide,* in which it was decided, correctly indeed, that sailors had no right to throw passengers overboard to save themselves, but on the somewhat strange ground that the proper mode of determining who was to be sacrificed was to vote upon the subject by ballot, can hardly, as my brother Stephen says, be an authority satisfactory to a court in this country.

• • •

We are dealing with a case of private homicide, not one imposed upon men in the service of their Sovereign and in the defense of their country. Now it is admitted that the deliberate killing of this unoffending and unresisting boy was clearly murder, unless the killing can be justified by some well-recognized excuse admitted by the law. It is further admitted that there was in this case no such excuse, unless the killing was justified by what has been called "necessity." But the temptation to the act which existed here was not what the law has ever called necessity. Nor is this to be regretted. Though law and morality are not the same, and many things may be immoral which are not necessarily illegal, yet the absolute divorce of law from morality would be of fatal consequence; and such divorce would follow if the temptation to murder in this case were to be held by law an absolute defense of it. It is not so. To preserve one's life is generally speaking a duty, but it may be the plainest and the highest duty to sacrifice it. War is full of instances in which it is a man's duty not to live, but to die. The duty, in case of shipwreck, of a captain to his crew, of the crew to the passengers, of soldiers to women and children, as in the noble case of the *Birkenhead;* these duties impose on men the moral necessity, not of the preservation, but of the sacrifice of their lives for others, from which in no country, least of all, it is to be hoped, in England, will men ever shrink, as indeed, they have not shrunk. It is not correct, therefore, to say that there is any absolute or unqualified necessity to preserve one's life. It is not needful to point out the awful danger of admitting the principle that has been contended for. Who is to be the judge of this sort of necessity? By what measure is the comparative value of lives to be measured? Is it to be strength, or intellect, or what? It is plain that the principle leaves to him who is to profit by it to determine the necessity that will justify him in deliberately taking another's life to save his own. In this case the weakest, the youngest, the most unresisting, was chosen. Was it more necessary to kill him than one of the grown men? The answer must be "No."

> So spake the Fiend, and with necessity,
> The tyrant's plea, excused his devilish deeds.

It is not suggested that in this particular case the deeds were "devilish," but it is quite plain that such a principle once admitted might be made the legal cloak for unbridled passion and atrocious crime. There is no safe path for judges to tread but to ascertain the law to the best of their ability and to declare it according to their judgment; and if in any case the law appears to be too severe on individuals, to leave it to the Sovereign to exercise that prerogative of mercy which the Constitution has intrusted to the hands fittest to dispense it.

It must not be supposed that in refusing to admit temptation to be an excuse for crime it is forgotten how terrible the temptation was; how awful the suffering; how hard in such trials to keep the judgment straight and the conduct pure. We are often compelled to set up standards we cannot reach ourselves, and to lay down rules which we could not ourselves satisfy. But a man has no right to declare temptation to be an excuse, though he might himself have yielded to it, nor allow compassion for the criminal to change or weaken in any manner the legal definition of the crime. It is therefore our duty to declare that the prisoners' act in this case was willful murder, that the facts as stated in the verdict are no legal justification of the homicide; and to say that in our unanimous opinion the prisoners are upon this special verdict guilty of murder.[1]

The court then proceeded to pass sentence of death upon the prisoners.[2]

NOTES

1. My brother Grove has furnished me with the following suggestion, too late to be embodied in the judgment but well worth preserving: "If the two accused men were justified in killing Parker, then if not rescued in time, two of the three survivors would be justified in killing the third, and of the two who remained the stronger would be justified in killing the weaker, so that three men might be justifiably killed to give the fourth a chance of surviving."
2. This sentence was afterward commuted by the Crown to six months' imprisonment.

17
Painter v. Bannister

Stuart, Justice.

We are here setting the course for Mark Wendell Painter's future. Our decision on the custody of this seven-year-old boy will have a marked influence on his whole life. The fact that we are called upon many times a year to determine custody matters does not make the exercising of this awesome responsibility any less difficult. Legal training and experience are of little practical help in solving the complex problems of human relations. However, these problems do arise and under our system of government, the burden of rendering a final decision rests upon us. It is frustrating to know we can only resolve, not solve, these unfortunate situations.

The custody dispute before us in this habeas corpus action is between the father, Harold Painter, and the maternal grandparents, Dwight and Margaret Bannister. Mark's mother and younger sister were killed in an automobile accident on December 6, 1962, near Pullman, Washington. The father, after other arrangements for Mark's care had proved unsatisfactory, asked the Bannisters to take care of Mark. They went to California and brought Mark to their farm home near Ames in July, 1963. Mr. Painter remarried in November, 1964, and about that time indicated he wanted to take Mark back. The Bannisters refused to let him leave and this action was filed in June, 1965. Since July, 1965, he has continued to remain in the Bannister home under an order of this court staying execution of the judgment of the trial court awarding custody to the father until the matter could be determined on appeal. For reasons hereinafter stated, we conclude Mark's better interests will be served if he remains with the Bannisters.

Mark's parents came from highly contrasting backgrounds. His mother was born, raised, and educated in rural Iowa. Her parents are college graduates. Her father is agricultural information editor for the Iowa State University Extension Service. The Bannister home is in the Gilbert Community and is well kept, roomy, and comfortable. The Bannisters are highly respected members of the community. Mr. Bannister has served on the school board and regularly teaches a Sunday-school class at the Gilbert Congregational Church. Mark's mother graduated from Grinnell College. She then went to work for a newspaper in Anchorage, Alaska, where she met Harold Painter.

Supreme Court of Iowa, 140 N.W. 2d 152 (1966).

Mark's father was born in California. When he was two and a half years old, his parents were divorced and he was placed in a foster home. Although he has kept in contact with his natural parents, he considers his foster parents, the McNellys as his family. He flunked out of a high school and a trade school because of a lack of interest in academic subjects, rather than any lack of ability. He joined the Navy at seventeen. He did not like it. After receiving an honorable discharge, he took examinations and obtained his high school diploma. He lived with the McNellys and went to college for two and a half years under the G.I. bill. He quit college to take a job on a small newspaper in Ephrata, Washington, in November, 1955. In May, 1956, he went to work for the newspaper in Anchorage that employed Jeanne Bannister.

Harold and Jeanne were married in April, 1957. Although there is a conflict in the evidence on the point, we are convinced the marriage, overall, was a happy one with many ups and downs as could be expected in the uniting of two such opposites.

We are not confronted with a situation where one of the contesting parties is not a fit or proper person. There is no criticism of either the Bannisters or their home. There is no suggestion in the record that Mr. Painter is morally unfit. It is obvious the Bannisters did not approve of their daughter's marriage to Harold Painter and do not want their grandchild raised under his guidance. The philosophies of life are entirely different. As stated by the psychiatrist who examined Mr. Painter at the request of the Bannisters' attorneys: "It is evident that there exists a large difference in ways of life and value systems between the Bannisters and Mr. Painter, but in this case there is no evidence that psychiatric instability is involved. Rather, these divergent life patterns seem to represent alternative normal adaptations."

It is not our prerogative to determine custody upon our choice of one of two ways of life within normal and proper limits and we will not do so. However, the philosophies are important as they relate to Mark and his particular needs.

The Bannister home provides Mark with a stable, dependable, conventional, middle-class, Middle West background and an opportunity for a college education and profession, if he desires it. It provides a solid foundation and secure atmosphere. In the Painter home, Mark would have more freedom of conduct and thought with an opportunity to develop his individual talents. It would be more exciting and challenging in many respects, but romantic, impractical, and unstable.

Little additional recitation of evidence is necessary to support our evaluation of the Bannister home. It might be pointed out, however, that Jeanne's three sisters also received college educations and seem to be happily married to college graduates.

Our conclusion as to the type of home Mr. Painter would offer is based upon his Bohemian approach to finances and life in general. We feel there is much evidence that supports this conclusion. His main ambition is to be a free-lance writer and photographer. He has had some articles and picture stories published, but the income from these efforts has been negligible. At the time of the accident, Jeanne was willingly working to support the family so Harold could devote more time to his writing and photography. In the ten years since he left college, he has changed jobs seven times. He was asked to leave two of them; two he quit because he didn't like the work; two because he wanted to devote more time to writing and the rest for better pay. He was contemplating a move to Berkeley at the time of trial. His attitude toward his career is typified by his own comments concerning a job offer:

About the Portland news job, I hope you understand when I say it took guts not to take it; I had to get behind myself and push. It was very, very tempting to accept a good salary and settle down to a steady, easy routine. As I approached Portland, with the intention of taking the job, I began to ask what, in the long run, would be the good of this job; (1) it was not really what I wanted; (2) Portland is just another big farm town, with none of the stimulation it takes to get my mind sparking. Anyway, I decided Mark and myself would be better off if I went ahead with what I've started and the hell with the rest, sink, swim, or starve.

There is general agreement that Mr. Painter needs help with his finances. Both Jeanne and Marilyn, his present wife, handled most of them. Purchases and sales of books, boats, photographic equipment, and houses indicate poor financial judgment and an easy come, easy go attitude. He dissipated his wife's estate of about $4,300, most of which was a gift from her parents and which she had hoped would be used for the children's education.

The psychiatrist classifies him as "a romantic and somewhat of a dreamer." An apt example are the plans he related for himself and Mark in February, 1963: "My thought now is to settle Mark and myself in Sausalito, near San Francisco; this is a retreat for wealthy artists, writers, and such aspiring artists and writers as can fork up the rent money. My plan is to do expensive portraits ($150 and up), sell prints ($15 and up) to the tourists who flock in from all over the world. . . ."

The house in which Mr. Painter and his present wife live, compared with the well-kept Bannister home, exemplifies the contrasting ways of life. In his words "it is a very old and beat-up and lovely home." They live in the rear part. The interior is inexpensively but tastefully decorated. The large yard on a hill in the business district of Walnut Creek, California, is of uncut weeds and wild oats. The house "is not painted on the outside because I do not want it painted. I am very fond of the wood on the outside of the house."

The present Mrs. Painter has her master's degree in cinema design and apparently likes and has had considerable contact with children. She is anxious to have Mark in her home. Everything indicates she would provide a leveling influence on Mr. Painter and could ably care for Mark.

Mr. Painter is either an agnostic or atheist and has no concern for formal religious training. He has read a lot of Zen Buddhism and "has been very much influenced by it." Mrs. Painter is Roman Catholic. They plan to send

Mark to a Congregational Church near the Catholic Church, on an irregular schedule.

He is a political liberal and got into difficulty in a job at the University of Washington for his support of the activities of the American Civil Liberties Union in the university news bulletin.

There were "two funerals" for his wife. One in the basement of his home in which he alone was present. He conducted the service and wrote her a long letter. The second at a church in Pullman was for the gratification of her friends. He attended in a sport shirt and sweater.

These matters are not related as a criticism of Mr. Painter's conduct, way of life, or sense of values. An individual is free to choose his own values, within bounds, which are not exceeded here. They do serve however to support our conclusion as to the kind of life Mark would be exposed to in the Painter household. We believe it would be unstable, unconventional, arty, Bohemian, and probably intellectually stimulating.

Were the question simply which household would be the most suitable in which to raise a child, we would have unhesitatingly chosen the Bannister home. We believe security and stability in the home are more important than intellectual stimulation in the proper development of a child. There are, however, several factors that have made us pause.

First, there is the presumption of parental preference, which though weakened in the past several years, exists by statute. Code of Iowa, Section 668.1; *Finken v. Porter,* 246 Iowa 1345, 72 N.W. 2d 445; *Kouris v. Lunn,* Iowa, 136 N.W. 2d 502; *Vanden Heuvel v. Vanden Heuvel,* 254 Iowa 1391, 1399, 121 N.W. 2d 216. We have a great deal of sympathy for a father who, in the difficult period of adjustment following his wife's death, turns to the maternal grandparents for their help and then finds them unwilling to return the child. There is no merit in the Bannister claim that Mr. Painter permanently relinquished custody. It was intended to be a temporary arrangement. A father should be encouraged to look for help with the children from those who love them without the risk of thereby losing the custody of the children permanently. This fact must receive consideration in cases of this kind. However, as always, the primary consideration is the best interest of the child and if the return of custody to the father is likely to have a seriously disrupting and disturbing effect upon the child's development, this fact must prevail. *Vanden Heuvel v. Vanden Heuvel, supra; In re Guardianship of Plucar,* 247 Iowa 394, 403, 72 N.W. 2d 455; *Carrere v. Prunty,* Iowa, 133 N.W. 2d 692, 696; *Finken v. Porter, supra; Kouris v. Lunn, supra,* R.C.P. 344 (f) 15.

Second, Jeanne's will named her husband guardian of her children and if he failed to qualify or ceased to act, named her mother. The parent's wishes are entitled to consideration. *Finken v. Porter, supra.*

Third, the Bannisters are sixty years old. By the time Mark graduates from high school they will be over seventy years old. Care of young children is a strain on grandparents and Mrs. Bannister's letters indicate as much.

We have considered all of these factors and have concluded that Mark's best interest demands that his custody remain with the Bannisters. Mark was five when he came to their home. The evidence clearly shows he was not well adjusted at that time. He did not distinguish fact from fiction and was inclined to tell "tall tales" emphasizing the big "I." He was very aggressive toward smaller children, cruel to animals, not liked by his classmates, and did not seem to know what was acceptable conduct. As stated by one witness: "Mark knew where his freedom was and he didn't know where his boundaries were." In two years he made a great deal of improvement. He now appears to be well disciplined, happy, relatively secure, and popular with his classmates, although still subject to more than normal anxiety.

We place a great deal of reliance on the testimony of Dr. Glenn R. Hawks, a child psychologist. The trial court, in effect, disregarded Dr. Hawks' opinions, stating: "The court has given full consideration to the good doctor's testimony, but cannot accept it at full face value because of exaggerated statements and the witness' attitude on the stand." We, of course, do not have the advantage of viewing the witness' conduct on the stand, but we have carefully reviewed his testimony and find nothing in the written record to justify such a summary dismissal of the opinions of this eminent child psychologist.

Dr. Hawks is head of the Department of Child Development at Iowa State University. However, there is nothing in the record which suggests that his relationship with the Bannisters is such that his professional opinion would be influenced thereby. Child development is his specialty and he has written many articles and a textbook on the subject. He is recognized nationally, having served on the staff of the 1960 White House Conference on Children and Youth and as consultant on a Ford Foundation program concerning youth in India. He is now education consultant on the project "Head Start." He has taught and lectured at many universities and belongs to many professional associations. He works with the Iowa Children's Home Society in placement problems. Further detailing of his qualifications is unnecessary.

Between June 15 and the time of trial, he spent approximately twenty-five hours acquiring information about Mark and the Bannisters, including appropriate testing of and "depth interviews" with Mark. Dr. Hawks' testimony covers seventy pages of the record and it is difficult to pinpoint any bit of testimony that precisely summarizes his opinion. He places great emphasis on the "father figure" and discounts the importance of the "biological father." "The father figure is a figure that the child sees as an authority figure, as a helper, he is a nutrient figure, and one who typifies maleness and stands as maleness as far as the child is concerned."

His investigation revealed: "The strength of the father figure before Mark came to the Bannisters is very unclear. Mark is confused about the father figure prior to his contact with Mr. Bannister." Now, "Mark used Mr. Bannister as his father figure. This is very evident. It shows up in the depth interview, and it shows up in the description of Mark's life given by Mark. He has a very warm feeling for Mr. Bannister."

Dr. Hawks concluded that it was not for Mark's best interest to be removed from the Bannister home. He is criticized for reaching this conclusion without investigating the Painter home or finding out more about Mr. Painter's character. He answered:

I was most concerned about the welfare of the child, not the welfare of Mr. Painter, not the welfare of the Bannisters. Inasmuch as Mark has already made an adjustment and sees the Bannisters as his parental figures in his psychological make-up, to me this is the most critical factor. Disruption at this point, I think, would be detrimental to the child even though Mr. Painter might well be a paragon of virtue. I think this would be a kind of thing which would not be in the best interest of the child. I think knowing something about where the child is at the present time is vital. I think something about where he might go, in my way of thinking is essentially untenable to me, and relatively unimportant. It isn't even helpful. The thing I was most concerned about was Mark's view of his own reality in which he presently lives. If this is destroyed I think it will have rather bad effects on Mark. I think then if one were to make a determination whether it would be to the parents' household, or the McNelly household, or X-household, then I think the further study would be appropriate.

I am appalled at the tremendous task Mr. Painter would have if Mark were to return to him because he has got to build the relationship from scratch. There is essentially nothing on which to build at the present time. Mark is aware Mr. Painter is his father, but he is not very clear about what this means. In his own mind the father figure is Mr. Bannister. I think it would take a very strong person with everything in his favor to build a relationship as Mr. Painter would have to build at this point with Mark.

It was Dr. Hawks' opinion, "the chances are very high [Mark] will go wrong if he is returned to his father." This is based on adoption studies which "establish that the majority of adoptions in children who are changed from ages six to eight will go bad, if they have had a prior history of instability, some history of prior movement. When I refer to instability I am referring to where there has been no attempt to establish a strong relationship." Although this is not an adoption, the analogy seems appropriate, for Mark who had a history of instability would be removed from the only home in which he has a clearly established "father figure" and placed with his natural father about whom his feelings are unclear.

We know more of Mr. Painter's way of life than Dr. Hawks. We have concluded that it does not offer as great a stability or security as the Bannister home. Throughout his testimony he emphasized Mark's need at this critical time is stability. He has it in the Bannister home.

Other items of Dr. Hawks' testimony that have a bearing on our decision follow. He did not consider the Bannisters' age any way disqualifying. He was of the opinion that Mark could adjust to a change more easily later on, if one became necessary, when he would have better control over his environment.

He believes the presence of other children in the home would have a detrimental effect upon Mark's adjustment whether this occurred in the Bannister home or the Painter home.

The trial court does not say which of Dr. Hawks' statements he felt were exaggerated. We were most surprised at the inconsequential position to which he relegated the "biological father." He concedes "child psychologists are less concerned about natural parents than probably other professional groups are." We are not inclined to so lightly value the role of the natural father, but find much reason for his evaluation of this particular case.

Mark has established a father-son relationship with Mr. Bannister, which he apparently had never had with his natural father. He is happy, well adjusted, and progressing nicely in his development. We do not believe it is for Mark's best interest to take him out of this stable atmosphere in the face of warnings of dire consequences from an eminent child psychologist and send him to an uncertain future in his father's home. Regardless of our appreciation of the father's love for his child and his desire to have him with him, we do not believe we have the moral right to gamble with this child's future. He should be encouraged in every way possible to know his father. We are sure there are many ways in which Mr. Painter can enrich Mark's life.

For the reasons stated, we reverse the trial court and remand the case for judgment in accordance herewith.

Reversed and remanded.

All Justices concur except Thornton, J., who concurs in result.

18

The State, Secondary Groups, and the Individual

EMILE DURKHEIM

Is not the state the supreme authority to which the political society as a whole is subordinate? But in fact this term authority is pretty vague and needs definition. Where does the group of officials vested with this authority begin and end, and who constitutes, properly speaking, the state? The question is all the

From *Professional Ethics and Civic Morals,* Cornelia Brookfield, trans. (London: Routledge & Kegan Paul, 1957), pp. 48–50, 60–63. Reprinted by permission of Routledge & Kegan Paul, Ltd.

more called for, since current speech creates much confusion on the subject. Every day we hear that public services are state services; the law, the army, the church (where there is a national church) are held to form part of the state. But we must not confuse with the state itself the secondary organs in the immediate field of its control, which in relation to it are only executive. At very least, the groups or special groups (for the state is complex), to which these secondary groups (called more specifically administrative) are subordinate, must be distinguished from the state. The characteristic feature of the special groups is that they alone are entitled to think and to act instead of representing the society. The representations, like the solutions that are worked out in this special milieu, are inherently and of necessity collective. It is true, there are many representations and many collective decisions beyond those that take shape in this way. In every society there are or have been myths and dogmas, whenever the political society and the church are one and the same, as well as historical and moral traditions: these make the representations common to all members of the society but are not in the special province of any one particular organ.

There exist too at all times social currents wholly unconnected with the state, that draw the collectivity in this or that direction. Frequently it is a case of the state coming under their pressure, rather than itself giving the impulse to them. In this way a whole psychic life is diffused throughout the society. But it is a different one that has a fixed existence in the organ of government. It is here that this other psychic life develops and when in time it begins to have its effect on the rest of the society, it is only in a minor way and by repercussions. When a bill is carried in Parliament, when the government takes a decision within the limits of its competence, both actions, it is true, depend on the general state of social opinion, and on the society. Parliament and the government are in touch with the masses of the nation and the various impressions released by this contact have their effect in deciding them to take this course rather than that. But even if there be this one factor in their decision lying outside themselves, it is none the less true that it is they (Parliament and government) who make this decision and above all it expresses the particular milieu where it has its origin. It often happens, too, that there may even be discord between this milieu and the nation as a whole, and that decisions taken by the government or parliamentary vote may be valid for the whole community and yet do not square with the state of social opinion. So we may say that there is a collective psychic life, but this life is not diffused throughout the entire social body: although collective, it is localized in a specific organ. And this localization does not come about simply through concentration on a given point of a life having its origins outside this point. It is in part at this very point that it has its beginning. When the state takes thought and makes a decision, we must not say that it is the society that thinks and decides through the state, but that the state thinks and decides for it. It is not simply an instrument for canalizing and concentrating. It is, in a certain sense, the organizing center of the secondary groups themselves.

Let us see how the state can be defined. It is a group of officials *sui generis* within which representations and acts of volition involving the collectivity are worked out, although they are not the product of collectivity. It is not accurate to say that the state embodies the collective consciousness, for that goes beyond the state at every point. In the main, that consciousness is diffused: there is at all times a vast number of social sentiments and social states of mind (*etats*) of all kinds, of which the state hears only a faint echo. The state is the center only of a particular kind of consciousness, of one that is limited but higher, clearer, and with a more vivid sense of itself. There is nothing so obscure and so indefinite as these collective representations that are spread throughout all societies: myths, religious or moral legends, and so on. We do not know whence they come nor whither they are tending; we have never had them under examination. The representations that derive from the state are always more conscious of themselves, of their causes and their aims. These have been concerted in a way that is less obscured. The collective agency that plans them realizes better what it is about. There too, it is true, there is often a good deal of obscurity. The state, like the individual, is often mistaken as to the motives underlying its decisions, but whether its decisions be ill motivated or not, the main thing is that they should be motivated to some extent. There is always or at least usually a semblance of deliberation, an understanding of the circumstances as a whole that makes the decision necessary, and it is precisely this inner organ of the state that is called upon to conduct these debates. Hence, we have these councils, these regulations, these assemblies, these debates that make it impossible for these kinds of representation to evolve except at a slow pace. To sum up, we can therefore say that the state is a special organ whose responsibility it is to work out certain representations which hold good for the collectivity. These representations are distinguished from the other collective representations by their higher degree of consciousness and reflection.

• • •

History seems indeed to prove that the state was not created to prevent the individual from being disturbed in the exercise of his natural rights: no, this was not its role alone. Rather, it is the state that creates and organizes and makes a reality of these rights. And indeed, man is man only because he lives in society. Take away from man all that has a social origin and nothing is left but an animal on a par with other animals. It is society that has raised him to this level above physical nature: it has achieved this result because association, by grouping the individual psychic forces, intensifies them. It carried them to a degree of energy and productive capacity immeasurably greater than any they could achieve if they remained isolated one from the other. Thus, a psychic life of a new kind breaks away which is richer by far and more varied than one played out in the single individual alone. Further, the life thus freed pervades the individual who shares in it and so transforms him. While society thus feeds and enriches the individual nature, it tends, on the other hand, at the same time inevitably to subject that nature to itself and for the same reason. It is precisely because the group is a moral force greater to this extent than that of its parts, that it tends of necessity to subordinate these to itself. The parts are unable not to fall under its domination. Here there is a law of moral mechanics at work, which is just as inevitable as the laws of physical mechanics. Any group that exercises authority over its members by coercion strives to model them after its own pattern, to impose on them its ways of thinking and acting and to prevent any dissent.

Every society is despotic, at least if nothing from without supervenes to restrain its despotism. Still, I would not say that there is anything artificial in this despotism: it is natural because it is necessary, and also because, in certain conditions, societies cannot endure without it. Nor do I mean that there is anything intolerable about it: on the contrary, the individual does not feel it any more than we feel the atmosphere that weighs on our shoulders. From the moment the individual has been raised in this way by the collectivity, he will naturally desire what it desires and accept without difficulty the state of subjection to which he finds himself reduced. If he is to be conscious of this and to resist it, individualist aspirations must find an outlet, and that they cannot do in these conditions.

But for it to be otherwise, we may say, would it not be enough for the society to be on a fairly large scale? There is no doubt that when it is small, when it surrounds every individual on all sides and at every moment, it does not allow of his evolving in freedom. If it be always present and always in action, it leaves no room to his initiative. But it is no longer in the same case when it has reached wide enough dimensions. When it is made up of a vast number of individuals, a society can exercise over each a supervision only as close and as vigilant and effective as when the surveillance is concentrated on a small number. A man is far more free in the midst of a throng than in a small coterie. Hence it follows that individual diversities can then more easily have play, that collective tyranny declines and that individualism establishes itself in fact, and that, with time, the fact becomes a right. Things can, however, only have this course on one condition: that is, that inside this society there must be no forming of any secondary groups that enjoy enough autonomy to allow of each becoming in a way a small society within the greater. For then, each of these would behave toward its members as if it stood alone and everything would go on as if the full-scale society did not exist. Each group, tightly enclosing the individuals of which it was made up, would hinder their development; the collective mind would impose itself on conditions applying to the individual. A society made up of adjoining clans or of towns or villages independent in greater or lesser degree, or of a number of professional groups, each one autonomous in relation to the others, would have the effect of being almost as repressive of any individuality as if it were made up of a single clan or town or association. The formation of secondary groups of this kind is bound to occur, for in a great society there are always particular local or professional interests that tend naturally to bring together those people with whom they are concerned. There we have the very stuff of associations of a special kind, of guilds, of coteries of every variety; and if there is nothing to offset or neutralize their activity, each of them will tend to swallow up its members. In any case, just to take the domestic society: we know its capacity to assimilate when left to itself. We see how it keeps within its orbit all those who go to make it up and are under its immediate domination. (At any rate, if secondary groups of this sort are not formed, at least a collective force will establish itself at the head of the society to govern it. And if this collective force itself stands alone, if it has only individuals to deal with, the same law of mechanics will make those individuals fall under its domination.)

In order to prevent this happening, and to provide a certain range for individual development, it is not enough for a society to be on a big scale; the individual must be able to move with some degree of freedom over a wide field of action. He must not be curbed and monopolized by the secondary groups, and these groups must not be able to get a mastery over their members and mold them at will. There must therefore exist above these local, domestic—in a word, secondary—authorities, some overall authority which makes the law for them all: it must remind each of them that it is but a part and not the whole and that it should not keep for itself what rightly belongs to the whole. The only means of averting this collective particularism and all it involves for the individual is to have a special agency with the duty of representing the overall collectivity, its rights and its interests, vis-à-vis these individual collectivities.

These rights and these interests merge with those of the individual. Let us see why and how the main function of the state is to liberate the individual personalities. It is solely because, in holding its constituent societies in check, it prevents them from exerting the repressive influences over the individual that they would otherwise exert. So there is nothing inherently tyrannical about state intervention in the different fields of collective life; on the contrary, it has the object and the effect of alleviating tyrannies that do exist. It will be argued, might not the state in turn become despotic? Undoubtedly, provided there were nothing to counter that trend. In that case, as the sole existing collective force, it produces the effects that any collective force not neutralized by any counterforce of the same kind would have on individuals. The state itself then becomes a leveler and repressive. And its repressiveness becomes even harder to endure than that of small groups, because it is more artificial. The state, in our large-scale society, is so removed from individual interests that it cannot take into account the special or local and other conditions in which they exist. Therefore when it does attempt to regulate them, it succeeds only at the cost of doing violence to them and distorting them. It is, too, not sufficiently in touch with individuals in the mass to be able to mould them inwardly, so that they readily accept its pressure on them. The individual eludes the state to some extent—the state can only be effective in the context of a large-scale society—and individual diversity may not come to light. Hence, all kinds of resistance and distressing conflicts arise. The small groups do not have this drawback. They are close enough to the things that provide their *rai-*

son d'être to be able to adapt their actions exactly and they surround the individuals closely enough to shape them in their own image. The inference to be drawn from this comment, however, is simply that if that collective force, the state, is to be the liberator of the individual, it has itself need of some counterbalance; it must be restrained by other collective forces, that is, by those secondary groups we shall discuss later on. It is not a good thing for the groups to stand alone, nevertheless they have to exist. And it is out of this conflict of social forces that individual liberties are born.

Part II THE SOCIAL BASES OF LAW

Editors' Introduction

Sociologists of law must inevitably concern themselves with the origins of law and the manner in which law fits into the web of social interaction. More specifically, some of the questions that might be raised are: What are the alternatives to law? Under what conditions are they viable? When law is developed, how is it sustained? What is the relation between law and public opinion? Does this vary with the type of law? To what extent is there variation depending on whether we are discussing legislative enactments or judicial pronouncements?

In this section we have attempted to bring together readings that illuminate certain aspects of these issues by concentrating on two roots of law: custom and public opinion. We have selected these two, partly because they are relevant to many of the issues raised in the preceding section on the nature of law and culture conflict; and partly because they tend to express traditional concerns of those who have viewed law as a social phenomenon.

Section Five examines the relation between custom and legal development. Simmel examines custom, law, and morality as normative forms arising under prevailing conditions. He observes that custom represents a stage of undifferentiated normative relations which depend upon a social unity that can be achieved only when the society is very small. As a society grows, law and morality branch out as different directions of normative expression. Morality operates through individual internalization and reworking of societal norms, while law develops a structure through which its contents are enunciated and externally enforced. Simmel's principal concern is with the significance of population size for the development of law. He suggests that large groups offer greater freedom, mobility, and individualization to their membership, and, conversely, that the large group also requires the sort of rigorous and objective norms that are crystallized in a legal order.

Schwartz and Miller examine the process by which societies come to develop the institutions of a fully developed formal legal system. Investigating a range of societies from simple to fairly complex, they discovered that the simplest tend to award damages and to make use of mediators for conflict resolution. Only when considerable technological complexity is present do they find the presence of police and, at a more advanced stage, counsel. Their study is consistent with Simmel's explanation of law as a product of increasing societal complexity.

Schwartz's study of the development of legal controls in two Israeli collective communities may also be viewed as an empirical investigation of theoretical issues raised by Simmel. One of the communities Schwartz studied was entirely collective (the *kvutza*), while in the other (the *moshav*), the family was the unit of production and distribution. In other respects, however, both settlements were essentially similar, and had been founded at about the same time (1921) by Eastern European Jewish settlers imbued with the ideal of building a new life in an agricultural setting.

Schwartz's article traces the development of informal social controls as related to the economic and social structures of the community. In the highly collective community, informal controls are extremely sensitive since they form the basis of a closely integrated group life. The collective community may be viewed as a large family. By contrast, where the community is organized around a group of families, a more contractual system of relationships tends to arise. Thus, the *moshav* developed a judicial authority in the form of a specialized agency that had no counterpart in the entirely collective community.

The *T. J. Hooper* case illustrates one of Simmel's points, that no matter how advanced a society, it may fall back on custom to inform certain of its decisions. This admiralty decision demonstrates that in the allocation of damages, it is often necessary for the courts to observe the customs prevailing in a community but also to counteract custom. This case also illustrates the phenomenon described by H. L. A. Hart as "the open texture of law." [1] Hart asserts that it is impossible to construct rules for the future that could provide in advance for every possibility. He says that it is a feature of the human predicament that we operate under two fundamental and connected handicaps: ignorance of fact and relative indeterminacy of aim.

Eugen Ehrlich, a portion of whose work is reprinted below, would very likely have affirmed Hart's position. Ehrlich, often referred to as the founder of the sociology of law because of his insistence that the center of gravity of legal development lies in social relations rather than in legal propositions, insists that to understand the operation of law one must observe the law in practice, rather than simply the written law. To a sociologist, Ehrlich's contention may by now seem almost self-evident, but there was a time in jurisprudential thinking when Ehrlich was controversial, and to a certain extent, his insistence upon viewing law through societal action still is controversial. In reading Ehrlich's piece, the student should consider whether, from the readings that follow, Ehrlich's discussion of the role of custom in commercial law is accurate.

Kessler and Sharp discuss contract as a form of social control, which is a nontraditional view of the nature of contract. They point out that in the past here has long been an assumption that contract deals with the individual relations of men with each other. In an increasingly large and mechanized society, however, this assumption must give way to the realization that in large sectors of our social and economic life contract is no longer an individual and private affair, but has become a social institution that affects more than the interests of the two contracting parties. Therefore they suggest that contract must be viewed in its broadest sense as a social institution, rather than in its narrow sense as a means of settling or avoiding future disputes between two individual parties.

Stewart Macauley's study of non-contractual relations in business may be viewed as an illustration of the sort of study suggested by Ehrlich. Macauley, whose formal training is in law, indicates that contract is rarely resorted to as a means of settling business disputes in the industry he studied. His findings suggest that in commercial transactions contract may have some importance in setting certain boundaries, but that social-structural and economic factors are more significant in determining the actual outcome of commercial relationships. Such studies as Macauley's invite further investigation in a variety of areas where a large and comprehensive body of law exists, but where informal relations, that is, non-legal relations, may play a more important role in determining behavior.

Section Six is an attempt to set out some of the forces that may influence legislation. The chapter begins with a classic selection on the relations between law and opinion, that of the British political scientist A. V. Dicey. Although Dicey feels that public opinion may control legislation, he is careful to point out conditions under which laws do not result from public opinion. There may be, for example, no opinion existing; or the opinion may not properly be called "public," or there may be lacking a legislative organ for expressing public opinion.

The reading by Harrison suggests that public opinion is not only extremely difficult to assess, but that public opinion may be strongly influenced by the position of leaders. The student may consider how far Harrison's position modifies Dicey, that is, to what extent is there a "real" public opinion, and to what extent, especially in this era of rapid and large-scale communication, public opinion is manipulable through skillful use of mass media?

The study by Frank V. Cantwell, which discusses the relation between public opinion and the reorganization of the Supreme Court, as presented to Congress for consideration by President Roosevelt in 1937, addresses some of these issues as they arise in process. Cantwell's most interesting observations perhaps are on the relationship between leadership and public opinion. It would appear that public opinion is formed more easily by the executive branch of government than by the legislative branch. The latter is less a collator of opinion than a recipient. Are there conditions, however, where that sort of generalization is also open to question?

The selection from Eulau, "The Legislator as Representative," suggests that many legislators feel that it is so difficult to assess the state of public opinion that they cannot in fact operate as delegates but rather as trustees for the public interest as a whole.

The issue of interests and how they affect legislation is discussed in an excerpt from what has by now become a classic work on interest-group politics, David B. Truman's *The Governmental Process*. Truman discusses the important relationship between formal structural arrangements of government and possibilities of access and influence.

Finally, it is worthwhile to note that interest groups may exist within the governmental structure itself as well as outside of government. The commonly held notion that the legislature is a group responding to public interests and pressures may be increasingly challenged with the growth of bureaucracy. As government grows, pressures on the legislature may arise directly from bureaucratic interests, which have the capacity to shape public opinion in a direction that they favor. Howard S. Becker's examination of the development of the marijuana tax act provides an important example of the role that bureaucrats may play in shaping legislation. Underlying the conception of bureaucracy is the idea, as Weber put it, "of control on the basis of knowledge. This is the feature of it which makes it specifically rational." The issue raised by the selection from Becker concerns what happens when a bureaucratic structure that is presumably based on knowledge acts instead on the basis of moral predisposition, and asserts its moral feelings in the form of knowledgeable expertise.

Section Seven addresses the issue of social influences upon judicial decisions. There is a sense in which the very phrasing of the topic might be regarded as both inaccurate and offensive. Judicial decisions, in theory, are supposedly free from outside influence. Judges are often not elected and they presumably do not experience the dilemma of the legislator, who must try to weigh his responsibilities as delegate of a constituency, with his generalized responsibilities as a public official representative of the public interest. The judge is never formally considered to be a delegate or representative. Ostensibly, every case is decided on the merits of that individual decision. At the same time, it is evident that judges are sometimes appointed to offer judicial participation to particular geographical regions or religious or racial groups. Furthermore, it is also evident that judges frequently make decisions in terms of values which they hold, and which are translated into the outcomes of cases they are deciding. The first selection in this chapter by political scientist J. W. Peltason suggests not only that judges have values, but that they may also be responsive to a professional rather than an electoral constituency. Thus, Peltason considers the extent to which judicial decisions are guided by the opinions of the legal profession as expressed, for example, in law review comments, contacts with the bar, and the like.

As discussed by political scientist Samuel Krislov, one important institution for bringing public opinion to bear upon judicial decisions is the *amicus curiae* brief. Krislov argues that this institution has moved from neutrality to partisanship and from "friendship" to advocacy. The brief often serves as a way for groups to endorse the policies or strategies that are being suggested by one of he litigants. The brief may also provide supplementary strategies for the litigants. For example, the brief might suggest certain kinds of social knowledge that would be inappropriate to the development of the legal argument in the main brief. Whatever purpose may be attributed to a particular brief, it is quite clear that the developing institution of *amicus curiae* seriously questions a narrow theory of judicial insulation.

Indeed, in the next selection (by political scientist Robert A. Dahl), the point is made that the Supreme Court cannot for very long fail to be responsive to majority preferences, although the court may in the short run seem to be ruling in the interests of a minority group. Analyzing Supreme Court cases, Dahl concludes that the policy views dominant in the court are never for long out of line with the policy views dominant among popular majorities, as reflected in the Congress of the United States.

Dahl's view is seemingly contested by law professor Alexander M. Bickel. Bickel observes that, while there are various ways of sliding over the gap between majority opinion and judicial decision, some discrepancy between the two is an "ineluctable reality." Nevertheless, the student is invited to question whether the differences between Professors Dahl and Bickel are more apparent than real. Bickel, for example, distinguishes between the countermajoritarian tendencies of the court on specific issues, but acknowledges that in the long run the court affirms basic values. How and to what extent does Bickel's seemingly more traditional conception of the work of the Supreme Court differ from the conception presented by Dahl, who speaks here as a representative of the "behaviorist" approach in political science?

NOTE

1. H. L. A. Hart, *The Concept of Law* (Oxford: The Clarendon Press, 1961), pp. 89–93.

SECTION FIVE   *Custom and Legal Development*

19

Custom, Law, Morality

GEORG SIMMEL

The formal difference in the individual's group behavior, as it is determined by the quantity of his group, is not only of factual but also of normative and moral significance. This is perhaps most clearly evident in the difference between custom and law. Among Aryan peoples, the earliest ties of the individual to a super-individual order of life seem to be rooted in a very general instinct or concept of the normative, the decent, the Ought in general. The Hindu *dharma,* the Greek *themis,* the Latin *fas,* all express this undifferentiated "normative as such." The more special regulations—religious, moral, conventional, legal—are still enfolded in it, are not yet ramified and separated out: the general notion of the normative is their original unity, not a unity abstracted from them in retrospect. In contrast with the opinion according to which morality, custom, and law have developed as supplementations out of this germinal state, it seems to me that this germinal state is perpetuated in what we call custom. And custom, I think, represents a stage of non-differentiation that in different directions sends forth two forms, law and morality.

Morality here concerns us only insofar as it results from the behavior of the individual toward other individuals or groups, that is, insofar as it has essentially the same contents as custom and law. Morality develops in the individual through a second subject that confronts him in himself. By means of the same split through which the ego says to itself "I am"—confronting itself, as a knowing subject, with itself as a known object—it also says to itself "I ought to." The relation of two subjects that appears as an imperative is repeated within the individual himself by virtue of the fundamental capacity of our mind to place itself in contrast to itself,·and to view and treat itself as if it were somebody else. (I do not here answer the question whether this phenomenon represents a transference of the empirically prior inter-individual relation to the elements within the individual, or whether it is a purely spontaneous process originating in these elements.)

On the other hand we find this. Once the normative forms have received particular contents, these contents are emancipated from their original sociological vehicles, and attain an inner and autonomous necessity that deserves the designation of "ideal." At this stage, these contents, which actually are behaviors or states of individuals, are in themselves valuable; they *ought* to be.

From *The Sociology of Georg Simmel,* Kurt H. Wolff, trans. (Glencoe, Ill.: The Free Press, 1950), pp. 99–104. Copyright © 1950 by The Free Press, A Corporation. Reprinted by permission of The Macmillan Company.

Their social nature or significance is no longer alone in giving them their im perative character: at this stage, it rather derives from their objectively idea significance and value. It is true that morality becomes personalized. It is fur thermore true that the three general norms of custom, law, and morality itsel develop into objective and super-social phenomena. But neither fact prevent: our emphasizing here that their contents are socially purposeful, and that those three forms themselves make sure that their contents are actually realizec through the individual.

We deal here with *forms* of the intrinsic and extrinsic relation of the individ ual to his social group. For the same contents of this relation have historically been clothed in different motivations or forms. What at one time or place wa: a custom, elsewhere or later has been a law of the state, or has been left to pri vate morality. What was under the coercion of law has become mere goo custom. What was the matter of individual conscience, later has often enougl been legally enforced by the state. The poles of this continuum are law anc morality, and between them stands custom, out of which both have developed In the legal code and in the executive, law has specialized organs througl which its contents are precisely defined and externally enforced. For thi: reason, law is best limited to the indispensable presuppositions of group life: what the group *can* unconditionally require of the individual is only what i *must* require unconditionally. By contrast, the free morality of the individua knows no other law than that which he autonomously gives himself, and nc other executive power than his own conscience. In practice, therefore, it: jurisdiction has accidental and fluid borderlines that change from case tc case,[1] although in principle it extends to the totality of action.

A group secures the suitable behavior of its members through custom, wher legal coercion is not permissible and individual morality not reliable. Custom thus operates as a supplement of these other two orders, whereas at a time when these more differentiated kinds of norms did not yet exist, or existed only in a germinal form, it was the only regulation of life. This indicates the sociological locus of custom. Custom lies between the largest group, as a mem ber of which the individual is rather subject to law, and absolute individuality, which is the sole vehicle of free morality. In other words, it belongs to smaller groups, intermediate between these two extremes. In fact, almost all custom is custom of estate or class. Its manifestations, as external behavior, fashion, or honor, always characterize only a section of the society, while the whole of this society is dominated by the same law.[2] It is a smaller group, composed of those whom the violation of good custom somehow concerns or who witness it, which reacts to this violation, whereas a breach of the legal order provokes the whole society. Since the only executive organs of custom are public opin ion and certain individual reactions directly related to public opinion, a large group itself cannot administer custom. The everyday experience in which busi ness custom permits and enjoins other things than aristocratic custom, in which the custom of a religious group involves other things than that of a liter-

ry society, suggests that the content of custom consists of the specific condi-
ions necessary for a particular group. For in order to gurantee these
conditions, the group can use neither the coercive power of the state law
nor any reliable autonomous morality of the individual.

The only aspect which these groups share with primitive groups, with which
social history begins for us, is numerical smallness. Life forms that originally
were sufficient for the totality have come to characterize its subdivisions, as
the totality itself has increased. For it is these totalities that now contain the
possibilities of personal relation, the approximately equal level among their
members, and the common interests and ideals, by virtue of which social regu-
ations can be left to such precarious and elastic a norm as custom. But when
the members increase in number and thereby inevitably become more independent, these conditions no longer obtain for the whole group. The peculiar
cohesive power of custom is not enough for the state and too much for the individual, while its *content* is too much for the state and too little for the individual. The state requires surer guarantees; the individual requires greater
freedom. Only in those aspects in which the individual is still a member of
smaller groups is he still governed, socially, by custom.

The fact that the large group both requires and permits the rigorous and objective norm which is crystallized in law is somehow related to the greater
freedom, mobility, and individualization of its members. This process involves
the need for a clearer determination and severer surveillance of socially necessary inhibitions. But on the other hand, the increased restriction is more bear-
able for the individual because, outside of it, he has a sphere of freedom which
is all the greater. The process becomes the more evident, the more law, or a
norm approaching it, is an agency of inhibition and forbiddance. Among Bra-
zilian aborigines, a man is in general not allowed to marry the daughter of his
sister or his brother. This tabu is the more severe the larger the tribe; while in
smaller, more isolated hordes brother and sister frequently live together. The
prohibitive character of the norm—which is more characteristic of law than of
custom—is more indicated in the larger group, because this group compensates
the individual more richly and positively than the small group does. There
is still another aspect which shows that the enlargement of the group favors
the transition of its norms to the form of law. Numerous unifications of
smaller groups into larger ones occurred originally (or are maintained even
permanently) only for the sake of law enforcement; and their unity is founded
exclusively in a pervasive legal order. The county of the New England states
was originally only "an aggregation of towns for judicial purposes."

There are apparent exceptions to this dependence of custom and law on
quantitative differences of groups. The original units of the Germanic tribes,
which resulted in the great Frankish, English, and Swedish realms, were often
able to preserve for long periods their own jurisdictions that became state matters only relatively late. Inversely, in modern international relations there are
many customs that have not yet become fixed as laws. Again, within a particu-

lar state, certain modes of conduct are regulated by law which in relation to the outside, that is, within the ultimate group, must be left to the looser form of custom.

It is simple to account for these apparent exceptions. Obviously, the size of the group requires the law form only to the extent to which its elements form a unity. Where only tenuous common characteristics, rather than a firm centralization, permit the designation of the group as a group, the relative character of this designation becomes clearly evident. "Social unity" is a concept of degree. Variations in unity may be accompanied by changing the forms of group regulations, or by changing group size. Accordingly, a given form of regulation required by a certain group size may be the same as that required by a group of a different size, or it may be different from that required by a group of the same size. The significance of numerical conditions is thus not impaired when we find that a large group, because of its special tasks, may do, or even must do, without the legalization of its norms, something which in general is characteristic only of smaller groups. The cumbersome state forms of Germanic antiquity simply did not yet possess the cohesion of their members which, if it occurs in the large group, is both cause and effect of its legal constitution. By a similar argument we can explain why, in the collective as well as in the individual relations among modern states, certain norms are constituted by mere custom. The reason is the lack of a unity above the parties that would be the vehicle of a legal order. In both smaller and looser groups, this unity is replaced by the immediate interaction among their members, and the regulation that corresponds to this intimate interaction is custom. In other words, the seeming exceptions actually confirm the connection between custom and law, on the one hand, and the quantitative aspects of the group, on the other.

NOTES

1. The fact that law and morality derive (as it were) together from one shift in societal development, is reflected in their teleological functions, which are more closely interrelated than appears on first sight. When strict individual conduct, which is characteristic of a life pervasively regulated by custom, yields to a general legal norm with its much greater distance from all individual matters, the freedom that the individual has thus gained must nevertheless, in the interest of society, not be left to itself. Legal imperatives are supplemented by moral imperatives, and fill the gaps that the disappearance of ubiquitous custom has left in the norms. In comparison with custom moral and legal norms lie much higher above the individual and, at the same time much more deeply within him. For, whatever personal and metaphysical values may be constituted by conscience and autonomous morality, their social value, which alone is in question here, lies in their extraordinary prophylactic efficiency. Law and custom seize the will externally and in its realization; they anticipate and threaten; and, in order to be effective without fear, they usually, though not always, must become part of personal morality. It is personal morality which is at the root of action. It so transforms the innermost aspect of the individual that he automatically does the right deed without the help of the relatively external forces of law and custom. Yet society is not interested in his purely moral perfection. Individual morality is important to society and is bred by it only insofar as it guarantees as much as possible that the individual act in a socially efficient manner. In individual morality, society creates an

organ which is not only more deeply effective than law and custom, but which also saves society the expenditures and labors involved in these institutions. In its tendency to obtain its prerequisites as cheaply as possible, society also makes use of "good conscience." For through his conscience the individual rewards himself for his good deeds; while if he had no conscience, society would probably have to guarantee him this reward somehow by means of law or custom.

2. See the discussion of the sociological form of honor in the chapters on the self-preservation of the group and on the intersection of groups [in the volume from which this reading is selected (Ed.)].

20

Legal Evolution and Societal Complexity

RICHARD D. SCHWARTZ AND
JAMES S. MILLER

. . . Legal evolution [1] provides an opportunity to investigate the relations between law and other major aspects and institutions of society. Thus Main explained the rise of contract in terms of the declining role of kinship as an exclusive basis of social organization.[2] Durkheim saw restitutive sanctions replacing repressive ones as a result of the growth of the division of labor and the corresponding shift from mechanical to organic solidarity.[3] Dicey traced the growth of statutory law-making in terms of the increasing articulateness and power of public opinion.[4] Weber viewed the development of formal legal rationality as an expression of, and pre-condition for, the growth of modern capitalism.[5]

For the most part, these writers were interested in the development of legal norms and not in the evolution of legal organization. The latter subject warrants attention for several reasons. As the mechanism through which substantive law is formulated, invoked, and administered, legal organization is of primary importance for understanding the process by which legal norms are evolved and implemented. Moreover, legal organization seems to develop with a degree of regularity that in itself invites attention and explanation. The present study suggests that elements of legal organization emerge in a sequence, such that each constitutes a necessary condition for the next. A second type of regularity appears in the relationship between changes in legal organization and other aspects of social organization, notably the division of labor.

From *The American Journal of Sociology*, LXX (1964), 159–169. Reprinted by permission of the authors and publisher. Abridged with renumbered notes.

By exploring such regularities intensively, it may be possible to learn more about the dynamics of institutional differentiation. Legal organization is a particularly promising subject from this point of view. It tends toward a unified, easily identifiable structure in any given society. Its form and procedures are likely to be explicitly stated. Its central function, legitimation, promotes cross-culturally recurrent instances of conflict with, and adaptation to, other institutional systems such as religion, polity, economy, and family. Before these relationships can be adequately explored, however, certain gross regularities of development should be noted and it is with these that the present study is primarily concerned.

This study reports preliminary findings from cross-cultural research that show a rather startling consistency in the pattern of legal evolution. In a sample of 51 societies, compensatory damages and mediation of disputes were found in every society having specialized legal counsel. In addition, a large majority (85 per cent) of societies that develop specialized police also employ damages and mediation. These findings suggest a variety of explanations. It may be necessary, for instance, for a society to accept the principles of mediation and compensation before formalized agencies of adjudication and control can be evolved. Alternatively or concurrently, non-legal changes may explain the results. A formalized means of exchange, some degree of specialization, and writing appear almost universally to follow certain of these legal developments and to precede others. If such sequences are inevitable, they suggest theoretically interesting causative relationships and provide a possible basis for assigning priorities in stimulating the evolution of complex legal institutions in the contemporary world.

Method

This research employed a method used by Freeman and Winch in their analysis of societal complexity.[6] Studying a sample of 48 societies, they noted a Guttman-scale relationship among six items associated with the folk-urban continuum. The following items were found to fall in a single dimension ranging, the authors suggest, from simple to complex: a symbolic medium of exchange; punishment of crimes through government action; religious, educational, and government specialization; and writing.[7]

To permit the location of legal characteristics on the Freeman-Winch scale, substantially the same sample was used in this study. Three societies were dropped because of uncertainty as to date and source of description [8] or because of inadequate material on legal characteristics.[9] Six societies were added, three to cover the legally developed societies more adequately [10] and three to permit the inclusion of certain well-described control systems.[11]

Several characteristics of a fully developed legal system were isolated for purposes of study. These included counsel, mediation, and police. These three characteristics, which will constitute the focus of the present study,[12] are defined as follows:

Counsel: regular use of specialized non-kin advocates in the settlement of disputes
Mediation: regular use of non-kin third-party intervention in dispute settlement
Police: specialized armed force used partially or wholly for norm enforcement

These three items, all referring to specialized roles relevant to dispute resolution, were found to fall in a near-perfect Guttman scale. Before the central findings are described and discussed, several methodological limitations should be noted.

First, despite efforts by Murdock [13] and others, no wholly satisfactory method has been devised for obtaining a representative sample of the world's societies. Since the universe of separate societies has not been adequately defined, much less enumerated, the representativeness of the sample cannot be ascertained. Nevertheless, an effort has been made to include societies drawn from the major culture areas and from diverse stages of technological development.

Second, societies have been selected in terms of the availability of adequate ethnographic reports. As a result, a bias may have entered the sample through the selection of societies that were particularly accessible—and hospitable—to anthropological observers. Such societies may differ in their patterns of development from societies that have been less well studied.

Third, despite the selection of relatively well-studied societies, the quality of reports varies widely. Like the preceding limitations, this problem is common to all cross-cultural comparisons. The difficulty is mitigated, however, by the fact that the results of this study are positive. The effect of poor reporting should generally be to randomize the apparent occurrence of the variables studied. Where systematic patterns of relationship emerge, as they do in the present research, it would seem to indicate considerable accuracy in the original reports.[14]

Fourth, this study deals with characteristics whose presence or absence can be determined with relative accuracy. In so doing, it may neglect elements of fundamental importance to the basic inquiry. Thus no effort is made to observe the presence of such important phenomena as respect for law, the use of generalized norms, and the pervasiveness of deviance-induced disturbance. Although all of these should be included in a comprehensive theory of legal evolution, they are omitted here in the interest of observational reliability.[15]

Fifth, the Guttman scale is here pressed into service beyond that for which it was developed. Originally conceived as a technique for the isolation of unidimensional attitudes, it has also been used as a means of studying the interrelationship of behavior patterns. It should be particularly valuable, however, in testing hypotheses concerning developmental sequences, whether in individuals or in societies.[16] Thus, if we hypothesize that A must precede B, supporting data should show three scale types: neither A nor B, A but not B, and A and B. All instances of B occurring without A represent errors that lower the reproducibility of the scale and, by the same token, throw doubt in measurable

TABLE 20-1 *Scale of Legal Characteristics*

Society	Counsel	Police	Mediation	Errors	Legal Scale Type	Freeman-Winch Scale Type
Cambodians	x	x	x	—	3	*
Czechs	x	x	x	—	3	6
Elizabethan English	x	x	x	—	3	6
Imperial Romans	x	x	x	—	3	6
Indonesians	x	x	x	—	3	*
Syrians	x	x	x	—	3	*
Ukrainians	x	x	x	—	3	6
Ashanti	—	x	x	—	2	5
Cheyenne	—	x	x	—	2	*
Creek	—	x	x	—	2	5
Cuna	—	x	x	—	2	4
Crow	—	x	—	1	2	0
Hopi	—	x	x	—	2	5
Iranians	—	x	x	—	2	6
Koreans	—	x	x	—	2	6
Lapps	—	x	x	—	2	6
Maori	—	x	x	—	2	4
Riffians	—	x	x	—	2	6
Thonga	—	x	—	1	2	2
Vietnamese	—	x	x	—	2	6
Andamanese	—	—	x	—	1	0
Azande	—	—	x	—	1	0
Balinese	—	—	x	—	1	4
Cayapa	—	—	x	—	1	2
Chagga	—	—	x	—	1	4
Formosan aborigines	—	—	x	—	1	0
Hottentot	—	—	x	—	1	0
Ifugao	—	—	x	—	1	0
Lakher	—	—	x	—	1	2
Lepcha	—	—	x	—	1	3
Menomini	—	—	x	—	1	0
Mbundu	—	—	x	—	1	3
Navaho	—	—	x	—	1	5
Ossett	—	—	x	—	1	1
Siwans	—	—	x	—	1	1
Trobrianders	—	—	x	—	1	*
Tupinamba	—	—	x	—	1	0
Venda	—	—	x	—	1	5
Woleaians	—	—	x	—	1	0
Yakut	—	—	x	—	1	1
Aranda	—	—	—	—	0	0
Buka	—	—	—	—	0	0
Chukchee	—	—	—	—	0	0
Comanche	—	—	—	—	0	*
Copper Eskimo	—	—	—	—	0	0
Jivaro	—	—	—	—	0	0
Kababish	—	—	—	—	0	1
Kazak	—	—	—	—	0	0
Siriono	—	—	—	—	0	0
Yaruro	—	—	—	—	0	0
Yurok	—	—	—	—	0	1

*Not included in Freeman-Winch sample.

Coefficient of reproducibility = $1 - 2/153$ = .987; coefficient of scalability = $1 - 2/153\text{-}120$ = .94; Kendall's tau = +.68.

degree on the developmental hypothesis.[17] Although the occurrence of developmental sequences ultimately requires verification by the observation of historic changes in given units, substantiating evidence can be derived from the comparative study of units at varying stages of development. The Guttman scale seems an appropriate quantitative instrument for this purpose.

Findings

In the 51 societies studied, as indicated in Table 20–1, four scale types emerged. Eleven societies showed none of the three characteristics; 18 had only mediation; 11 had only mediation and police; and seven had mediation, police, and specialized counsel. Two societies departed from these patterns: the Crow and the Thonga had police, but showed no evidence of mediation. While these deviant cases merit detailed study, they reduce the reproducibility of the scale by less than 2 per cent, leaving the coefficient at the extraordinarily high level of better than .98.[18] Each characteristic of legal organization may now be discussed in terms of the sociolegal conditions in which it is found.

Mediation

Societies that lack mediation, constituting less than a third of the entire sample, appear to be the simplest societies. None of them has writing or any substantial degree of specialization.[19] Only three of the 13 (Yurok, Kababish, and Thonga) use money, whereas almost three-fourths of the societies with mediation have a symbolic means of exchange. We can only speculate at present on the reasons why mediation is absent in these societies. Data on size, using Naroll's definition of the social unit,[20] indicate that the maximum community size of societies without mediation is substantially smaller than that of societies with mediation.[21] Because of their small size, mediationless societies may have fewer disputes and thus have less opportunity to evolve regularized patterns of dispute settlement. Moreover, smaller societies may be better able to develop mores and informal controls that tend to prevent the occurrence of disputes. Also, the usually desperate struggle for existence of such societies may strengthen the common goal of survival and thus produce a lessening of intragroup hostility.

The lack of money and substantial property may also help to explain the absence of mediation in these societies. There is much evidence to support the hypothesis that property provides something to quarrel about. In addition, it seems to provide something to mediate with as well. Where private property is extremely limited, one would be less likely to find a concept of damages, that is, property payments in lieu of other sanctions. The development of a concept of damages should greatly increase the range of alternative settlements. This in turn might be expected to create a place for the mediator as a person charged with locating a settlement point satisfactory to the parties and the society.

This hypothesis derives support from the data in Table 20–2. The concept of damages occurs in all but four of the 38 societies that have mediation and thus appears to be virtually a precondition for mediation. It should be noted, however, that damages are also found in several (seven of thirteen) of the so-

TABLE 20-2   *Damages in Relation to Legal Functionaries*

	No Mediation	Mediation Only	Mediation and Police	Mediation, Police, and Counsel	Total
Damages	7	17	10	7	41
No damages	6*	3	1	0	10
Total	13	20	11	7	51

*Includes Thonga, who have neither mediation nor damages, but have police.

cieties that lack mediation. The relationship that emerges is one of damages as a necessary but not sufficient condition for mediation. At present it is impossible to ascertain whether the absence of mediation in societies having the damage concept results from a simple time lag or whether some other factor, not considered in this study, distinguishes these societies from those that have developed mediation.

Police

Twenty societies in the sample had police—that is, a specialized armed force available for norm enforcement. As noted, all of these but the Crow and Thonga had the concept of damages and some kind of mediation as well. Nevertheless, the occurrence of 20 societies with mediation but without police makes it clear that mediation is not inevitably accompanied by the systematic enforcement of decisions. The separability of these two characteristics is graphically illustrated in ethnographic reports. A striking instance is found among the Albanian tribesmen whose elaborately developed code for settling disputes, Lek's Kanun, was used for centuries as a basis for mediation. But in the absence of mutual agreements by the disputants, feuds often began immediately after adjudication and continued unhampered by any constituted police.[22]

From the data it is possible to determine some of the characteristics of societies that develop police. Eighteen of the 20 in our sample are economically advanced enough to use money. They also have a substantial degree of specialization, with full-time priests and teachers found in all but three (Cheyenne, Thonga, and Crow), and full-time governmental officials, not mere relatives of the chief, present in all but four (Cuna, Maori, Thonga, and Crow).

Superficially at least, these findings seem directly contradictory to Durkheim's major thesis in *The Division of Labor in Society*. He hypothesized that penal law—the effort of the organized society to punish offenses against itself—occurs in societies with the simplest division of labor. As indicated, however, our data show that police are found only in association with a substantial degree of division of labor. Even the practice of governmental punishment for wrongs against the society (as noted by Freeman and Winch) does not appear in simpler societies. By contrast, restitutive sanctions—damages and mediation—which Durkheim believed to be associated with an increasing division of labor, are found in many societies that lack even rudimentary specialization. Thus Durkheim's hypothesis seems the reverse of the empirical situation in the range of societies studied here.[23]

Counsel

Seven societies in the sample employ specialized advocates in the settlement of disputes. As noted, all of these societies also use mediation. There are, however, another 31 societies that have mediation but do not employ specialized counsel. It is a striking feature of the data that damages and mediation are characteristic of the simplest (as well as the most complex) societies, while legal counsel is found only in the most complex. The societies with counsel also have, without exception, not only damages, mediation, and police but, in addition, all of the complexity characteristics identified by Freeman and Winch.

It is not surprising that mediation is not universally associated with counsel. In many mediation systems the parties are expected to speak for themselves. The mediator tends to perform a variety of functions, questioning disputants as well as deciding on the facts and interpreting the law. Such a system is found even in complex societies, such as Imperial China. There the prefect acted as counsel, judge, and jury, using a whip to wring the truth from the parties who were assumed *a priori* to be lying.[24] To serve as counsel in that setting would have been painful as well as superfluous. Even where specialized counsel emerge, their role tends to be ambiguous. In ancient Greece, for instance, counsel acted principally as advisors on strategy. Upon appearance in court they sought to conceal the fact that they were specialists in legal matters, presenting themselves merely as friends of the parties or even on occasion assuming the identity of the parties themselves.[25]

At all events, lawyers are here found only in quite urbanized societies, all of which are based upon fully developed agricultural economies. The data suggest at least two possible explanations. First, all of the sample societies with counsel have a substantial division of labor, including priests, teachers, police, and government officials. This implies an economic base strong enough to support a variety of secondary and tertiary occupations as well as an understanding of the advantages of specialization. Eleven societies in the sample, however, have all of these specialized statuses but lack specialized counsel. What distinguishes the societies that develop counsel? Literacy would seem to be an important factor. Only five of the 12 literate societies in the sample do not have counsel. Writing, of course, makes possible the formulation of a legal code with its advantages of forewarning the violator and promoting uniformity in judicial administration. The need to interpret a legal code provides a niche for specialized counsel, especially where a substantial segment of the population is illiterate.[26]

Conclusions

These data, taken as a whole, lend support to the belief that an evolutionary sequence occurs in the development of legal institutions. Alternative interpretations are, to be sure, not precluded. The scale analysis might fail to discern short-lived occurrences of items. For instance, counsel might regularly develop as a variation in simple societies even before police, only to drop out rapidly enough so that the sample picks up no such instances. Even though this is a possibility in principle, no cases of this kind have come to the authors' attention.

Another and more realistic possibility is that the sequence noted in this sample does not occur in societies in a state of rapid transition. Developing societies undergoing intensive cultural contact might provide an economic and social basis for specialized lawyers, even in the absence of police or dispute mediation. Until such societies are included in the sample, these findings must be limited to relatively isolated, slowly changing societies.

The study also raises but does not answer questions concerning the evolution of an international legal order. It would be foolhardy to generalize from the primitive world directly to the international scene and to assume that the same sequences must occur here as there. There is no certainty that subtribal units can be analogized to nations, because the latter tend to be so much more powerful, independent, and relatively deficient in common culture and interests. In other ways, the individual nations are farther along the path of legal development than subtribal units because all of them have their own domestic systems of mediation, police, and counsel. This state of affairs might well provide a basis for short-circuiting an evolutionary tendency operative in primitive societies. Then too, the emergent world order appears to lack the incentive of common interest against a hostile environment that gave primitive societies a motive for legal control. Even though the survival value of a legal system may be fully as great for today's world as for primitive societies, the existence of multiple units in the latter case permitted selection for survival of those societies that had developed the adaptive characteristic. The same principle cannot be expected to operate where the existence of "one world" permits no opportunity for variation and consequent selection.

Nonetheless, it is worth speculating that some of the same forces may operate in both situations.[27] We have seen that damages and mediation almost always precede police in the primitive world. This sequence could result from the need to build certain cultural foundations in the community before a central regime of control, as reflected in a police force, can develop. Hypothetically, this cultural foundation might include a determination to avoid disputes, an appreciation of the value of third-party intervention, and the development of a set of norms both for preventive purposes and as a basis for allocating blame and punishment when disputes arise. Compensation by damages and the use of mediators might well contribute to the development of such a cultural foundation, as well as reflecting its growth. If so, their occurrence prior to specialized police would be understandable. This raises the question as to whether the same kind of cultural foundation is not a necessary condition for the establishment of an effective world police force and whether, in the interest of that objective, it might not be appropriate to stress the principles of compensatory damages and mediation as preconditions for the growth of a world rule of law.

NOTES

1. The term "evolution" is used here in the minimal sense of a regular sequence of changes over time in a given type of unit, in this case, societies. This usage neither implies nor precludes causal links among the items in the sequence.
2. Sir Henry Maine, *Ancient Law* (London: J. M. Dent, 1917).
3. Emile Durkheim, *The Division of Labor in Society,* George Simpson, trans. (Glencoe, Ill.: The Free Press, 1947).
4. A. V. Dicey, *Lectures on the Relation between Law and Public Opinion in England during the Nineteenth Century* (London: Macmillan Co., 1905).
5. Max Weber, *Law in Economy and Society,* Max Rheinstein ed. (Cambridge, Mass.: Harvard University Press, 1954). For a discussion and development of Weber's thinking on legal evolution, see Talcott Parsons, "Evolutionary Universals in Society," *American Sociological Review,* XXIX (June, 1964), 350–353.
6. Linton C. Freeman and Robert F. Winch, "Societal Complexity: An Empirical Test of a Typology of Societies," *American Journal of Sociology,* LXII (March, 1957), 461–466.
7. This ordering has not been reproduced in other studies that followed similar procedures. Freeman repeated the study on another sample and included four of the six items used in the first study. They scaled in a markedly different order, from simple to complex: government specialization, religious specialization, symbolic medium of exchange, writing. The marked change in position of the first and third items appears attributable to changes in definition for these terms (Linton C. Freeman, "An Empirical Test of Folk-Urbanism," [unpublished Ph.D. dissertation, Northwestern University, 1957], pp. 45, 49–50, 80–83). Young and Young studied all six items in a cross-cultural sample of communities, changing only the definition of punishment. Their ordering is somewhat closer to, but not identical with, that found by Freeman and Winch (*op. cit.*). From simple to complex, the items were ordered as follows: punishment, symbolic medium of exchange, governmental specialization, religious specialization, writing, educational specialization (Frank W. Young and Ruth C. Young, "The Sequence and Direction of Community Growth: A Cross-Cultural Generalization," *Rural Sociology,* XXVII [December, 1962], 374–386, esp. 378–379).

   In the present study, we will rely on the Freeman-Winch ratings and orderings, since the samples overlap so heavily. The reader should bear in mind, however, that the order is tentative and contingent upon the specific definitions used in that study.
8. Southeastern American Negroes and ancient Hebrews.
9. Sanpoil.
10. Three societies—Cambodian, Indonesian, and Syrian—were selected from the Human Relations Area Files to increase the number of societies with counsel. The procedure for selection consisted of a random ordering of the societies in the

Human Relations Area Files until three with counsel were located in geographically separate regions. These were then examined to determine the presence or absence of other legal characteristics. The random search eliminated the possibility of a bias in favor of societies conforming to the scale type.

The three societies were quota-sampled by region to represent a randomly determined three of the following six regions: Asia, Africa, the Middle East, North America, South America, and Oceania. Purposely omitted from the sample were Europe and Russia because they were already represented in the "counsel" type in the Freeman-Winch sample. Selection from different regions was designed to avoid the problem, first noted by Francis Galton, that cross-cultural regularities might be due to diffusion rather than to functional interrelationships. For a discussion of the problem and evidence of the importance of geographical separateness in sampling, see Raoul Naroll, "Two Solutions to Galton's Problem," *Philosophy of Science,* XXVIII (1961), 15–39; Raoul Naroll and Roy G. D'Andrade, "Two Further Solutions to Galton's Problem," *American Anthropologist,* LXV (October, 1963), 1053–1067; and Raoul Naroll, "A Fifth Solution to Galton's Problem," *American Anthropologist,* LXVI (August, 1964) 863–867.

11. These three—Cheyenne, Comanche, and Trobrianders—were selected by James C. Miller before the hypothesis was known to him. Selection of both the Comanche and Cheyenne is subject to some criticism on the grounds that they were prone to diffusion, but this hardly seems a serious difficulty in view of the difference in their scale positions. At all events, the coefficients of reproducibility and scalability would not be seriously lowered by eliminating one of the two.

12. The original study also included damages, imprisonment, and execution. These were dropped from the present analysis, even though this unfortunately limited the scale to three items, to permit focus on statuses rather than sanction. Data on damages will be introduced, however, where relevant to the discussion of restitution.

13. George Peter Murdock, "World Ethnographic Sample," *American Anthropologist,* LIX (August, 1957), 664–687.

14. On this point see Donald T. Campbell, "The Mutual Methodological Relevance of Anthropology and Psychology," in Francis L. K. Hsu, ed., *Psychological Anthropology* (Homewood, Ill.: Dorsey Press, 1961), p. 347. This inference should be treated with caution, however, in light of Raoul Naroll's observation that systematic observer bias can lead to spurious correlations (*Data Quality Control: A New Research Technique* [New York: Free Press of Glencoe, 1962]).

15. Determination of the presence of a characteristic was made after a detailed search by Miller of the materials on each society in the Human Relations Area Files. His search began with a thorough reading for all societies of the material filed under category 18, "total culture." (All categories used are described in detail in George P. Murdock *et al., Outline of Cultural Materials* [4th rev. ed.; New Haven, Conn.: Human Relations Area Files, 1961].) This was followed by a search of the annotated bibliography (category 111) to locate any works specifically dealing with legal or dispute settling processes. When found, works of this kind were examined in detail. In addition, materials filed under the following categories were read: community structure (621), headmen (622), councils (623), police (625), informal in-group justice (627), intercommunity relations (628), territorial hierarchy (631), legal norms (671), liability (672), offenses and sanctions (68), litigation (691), judicial authority (692), legal and judicial personnel (693), initiation of judicial proceedings (694), trial procedure (695), execution of justice (696), prisons and jails (697), and special courts (698). If this search did not reveal the presence of the practice or status under investigation, it was assumed absent. The principal sources relied on for these determinations are given in a mimeographed bibliography which will be supplied by the authors on request.

A reliability check on Miller's judgments was provided by Robert C. Scholl, to whom the writers are indebted. Working independently and without knowledge of the hypotheses, Scholl examined a randomly selected third of the total sample. His judgments agreed with those of Miller 88 per cent, disagreed 4 per cent, and he was unable to reach conclusions on 8 per cent of the items. If the inconclusive judgments are excluded, the reliability reaches the remarkable level of 96 per cent.

The use of a single person to check reliability falls short of the desired standard.

In a more detailed and extensive projected study of the relationships reported here, we plan to use a set of three independent naive judges. For discussion of the problems involved in judging cross-cultural materials see John W. M. Whiting and Irvin L. Child, *Child Training and Personality* (New Haven, Conn.: Yale University Press, 1953), pp. 39–62; and Guy E. Swanson, *The Birth of the Gods* (Ann Arbor: Michigan University Press, 1960), pp. 32–54.

16. The use of the Guttman scale is extensively treated by Robert L. Carneiro in "Scale Analysis as an Instrument for the Study of Cultural Evolution," *Southwestern Journal of Anthropology*, XVIII (1962), 149–169. In a sophisticated critique of the Carneiro paper, Ward L. Goodenough suggests that quasi-scales may be needed for charting general evolutionary trends and for treating the traits that develop and then fail to persist because they are superseded by functional equivalents ("Some Applications of Guttman Scale Analysis to Ethnography and Culture Theory," *Southwestern Journal of Anthropology*, XIX [Autumn, 1963], 235–250). While the quasi-scale is a desirable instrument for analyzing supersedence, Goodenough appears unduly pessimistic about the possible occurrence of approximately perfect scales (see p. 246). Studies that obtained such scales, in addition to the one reported here, include Freeman and Winch, *op. cit.;* Stanley H. Udy, " 'Bureaucratic' Elements in Organizations: Some Research Findings," *American Sociological Review*, XXII (1958), 415–418; Frank W. Young and Ruth C. Young, "Social Integration and Change in Twenty-four Mexican Villages," *Economic Development and Cultural Change*, VIII (July, 1960), 366–377; and Robert L. Carneiro and Stephen L. Tobias, "The Application of Scale Analysis to the Study of Cultural Evolution," *Transactions of the New York Academy of Sciences*, Series II, XXVI (1963), 196–207.

The suggestion that Guttman scales could be used for discovering and testing temporal sequences was made earlier by Norman G. Hawkins and Joan K. Jackson in "Scale Analysis and the Prediction of Life Processes," *American Sociological Review*, XXII (1957), 579–581. Their proposal referred, however, to individuals rather than societies.

17. The developmental inference does not preclude the possibility of reversal of the usual sequence. It merely indicates which item will be added if any is acquired. See S. N. Eisenstadt, "Social Change, Differentiation and Evolution," *American Sociological Review*, XXIX (June, 1964), 378–381. The finding of a scale also does not rule out the possibility that two items may sometimes occur simultaneously, although the existence of all possible scale types indicates that no two items invariably occur simultaneously and that when they occur separately one regularly precedes the other.

18. This coefficient of reproducibility far exceeds the .90 level suggested by Guttman as an "efficient approximation . . . of perfect scales" (Samuel Stouffer, ed., *Measurement and Prediction* [Princeton, N.J.: Princeton University Press, 1950]). The coefficient of scalability, designed by Menzel to take account of extremeness in the distribution of items and individuals, far exceeds the .65 level that he generated from a scalability analysis of Guttman's American Soldier data. Herbert A. Menzel, "A New Coefficient for Scalogram Analysis," *Public Opinion Quarterly*, XVII (Summer, 1953), 268–280, esp. 276. The problem of determining goodness of fit for the Guttman scale has still not been satisfactorily resolved (see W. S. Torgerson, *Theory and Methods of Scaling* [New York: John Wiley & Sons, 1958], esp. p. 324). A method utilizing χ^2 to test the hypothesis that observed scale frequencies deviate from a rectangular distribution no more than would be expected by chance is suggested by Karl F. Schuessler, "A Note on Statistical Significance of Scalogram," *Sociometry*, XXIV (September, 1961), 312–318. Applied to these data, Schuessler's Test II permits the rejection of the chance hypothesis at the .001 level $x^2 = 60.985 \ (7df)$.

19. Statements of this type are based on the ratings in the Freeman-Winch study, as noted in n. 7 above. For societies that did not appear in their sample, we have made our own ratings on the basis of their definitions.

20. Raoul Naroll, "A Preliminary Index of Social Development," *American Anthropologist*, LVIII (August, 1956), 687–720.

21. Data were obtained for 39 of the 51 societies in the sample on the size of their largest settlement. Societies with mediation have a median largest settlement size of

1,000, while those without mediation have a median of 346. Even eliminating the societies with developed cities, the median largest settlement size remains above 500 for societies with mediation.

22. Margaret Hasluck, *The Unwritten Law in Albania* (Cambridge: Cambridge University Press, 1954).

23. A basic difficulty in testing Durkheim's thesis arises from his manner of formulating it. His principal interest, as we understand it, was to show the relationship between division of labor and type of sanction (using type of solidarity as the intervening variable). However, in distinguishing systems of law, he added the criterion of organization. The difficulty is that he was very broad in his criterion of organization required for penal law, but quite narrow in describing the kind of organization needed for non-penal law. For the former, the "assembly of the whole people" sufficed (*op. cit.*, p. 76); for the latter, on the other hand, he suggested the following criteria: "restitutive law creates organs which are more and more specialized: consular tribunals, councils of arbitration, administrative tribunals of every sort. Even in its most general part, that which pertains to civil law, it is exercised only through particular functionaries: magistrates, lawyers, etc., who have become apt in this role because of very special training" (p. 113). In thus suggesting that restitutive law exists only with highly complex organizational forms, Durkheim virtually insured that his thesis would be proven—that restitutive law would be found only in complex societies.

Such a "proof," however, would miss the major point of his argument. In testing the main hypothesis it would seem preferable, therefore, to specify a common and minimal organizational criterion, such as public support. Then the key question might be phrased: Is there a tendency toward restitutive rather than repressive sanctions which develops as an increasing function of the division of labor? Although our present data are not conclusive, the finding of damages and mediation in societies with minimal division of labor implies a negative answer. This suggests that the restitutive principle is not contingent on social heterogeneity or that heterogeneity is not contingent on the division of labor.

24. Sybille van der Sprenkel, *Legal Institutions in Manchu China* (London: Athlone Press, 1962). See also Ch'ü T'ung-tsu, *Law and Society in Traditional China* (Vancouver: Institute of Pacific Relations, 1961).

25. A. H. Chroust, "The Legal Profession in Ancient Athens," *Notre Dame Law Review*, XXIX (Spring, 1954), 339–389.

26. Throughout the discussion, two sets of explanatory factors have been used. The observed pattern could be due to an internal process inherent in legal control systems, or it could be dependent upon the emergence of urban characteristics. It does seem clear, however, that the legal developments coincide to a considerable extent with increased "urbanism" as measured by Freeman and Winch. Evidence for this assertion is to be found in the correlation between the Freeman-Winch data and the legal scale types discerned. For the 45 societies appearing in both samples, the rank correlation coefficient (Kendall's tau) between positions on the legal and urbanism scales is $+ .68$. While this coefficient suggests a close relationship between the two processes, it does not justify the assertion that legal evolution is wholly determined by increasing urbanism. A scatter diagram of the interrelationship reveals that legal characteristics tend to straddle the regression line for five of the seven folk-urban scale positions, omitting only scale types 2 (punishment) and 3 (religious specialization). This suggests that some other factor might emerge upon further analysis that would explain why roughly half of the societies at each stage of urbanism appear to have gone on to the next stage of legal evolution while the others lag behind. A promising candidate for such a factor is the one located by Gouldner and Peterson in their cross-cultural factor analysis of Simmons' data and described by them as "Appollonianism" or "Norm-sending" (Alvin W. Gouldner and Richard A. Peterson, *Technology and the Moral Order* [Indianapolis: Bobbs-Merrill Co., 1962], pp. 30–53).

To test whether the legal sequence has a "dynamic of its own," it would seem necessary to examine the growth of legal systems independent of folk-urban changes, as in subsystems or in societies where the process of urbanization has already occurred. The data covered here do not permit such a test.

27. For an interesting attempt to develop a general theory of legal control, applicable both to discrete societies and to the international order, see Kenneth S. Carlston, *Law and Organization in World Society* (Urbana: University of Illinois Press, 1962).

21

Social Factors in the Development of Legal Control

RICHARD D. SCHWARTZ

The substance of every attempt to state the fundamental principles of the sociology of law [is that] the center of gravity of legal development lies not in legislation, nor in juristic science, nor in judicial decisions, but in society itself.

> Ehrlich, *Fundamental Principles of the Sociology of Law*, Vol. XV (1936).

Legal control is not exercised against all disturbing behavior. Sometimes such behavior never reaches the courts.[1] At other times, it is not dealt with by courts because, we are told, it should be left to the *"interior* forum, as the tribunal of conscience has been aptly called."[2] The effects of non-legal or informal control, whether or not adequately described in terms of "conscience," seem to be an important factor in a court's decision to withhold judgment.

The relationship between legal and informal controls was examined in the cultures of two Israeli communities. One of the differences noted was that the entirely collective community, or *kvutza,* had no distinctly legal institution, whereas the *moshav,* a semi-private property settlement, did. Speculation on the reasons for the difference led to the formulation of a theory of legal control.

• • •

In social groups, two main forms of control may be distinguished: that which is carried out by specialized functionaries who are socially delegated the task of intra-group control, and that which is not so delegated. These will be respectively designated *legal* and *informal* controls. When, as is often the case,

From *The Yale Law Journal,* LXIII (1954), 471–491. Reprinted by permission of The Yale Law Journal Company and Fred B. Rothman & Company. Abridged and revised with renumbered notes.

these two forms of control are in competition, the likelihood of legal control arising at all in a given sphere is a decreasing function of the effectiveness of informal controls. It is the thesis of this article that the presence of legal controls in the *moshav,* the semi-private property settlement, but not in the *kvutza,* the collective settlement, is to be understood primarily in terms of the fact that informal controls did not operate as effectively in the *moshav* as in the *kvutza.*

In most of their superficial characteristics, the two settlements are essentially similar. Both were founded at the same time, 1921, by young settlers who had come from Eastern Europe "to build a new life." Though the *kvutza* was smaller at first, it has grown to a population (just under 500 persons) that is almost identical in size with that of the *moshav.* Both are located on a slope of the Jezreel Valley where they have to deal with the same climate and similar topography. Both have about 2,000 acres of land, which supports a mixed farming economy. Both populations have rejected many of the East European Jewish customs, including traditional religious practices. Though many other Israeli collectives are left-wing socialist, the members of the *kvutza* under consideration resemble those of the *moshav* in adhering to the social-democratic political philosophy represented by the *Mapai* party.

Despite these similarities, the two communities have differed from the outset in their members' ideas about economic organization. In the *kvutza,* members felt they could implement the program, "from each according to his abilities, to each according to his need," as the way to create a "just society." *Moshav* members, many of whom had spent a few years in collectives, decided that the family should be the unit of production and distribution, and that thus a class of small independent farmers could be developed in the *moshav* which would provide a strong agricultural base for the country.

As far as could be ascertained, there were no initial differences in specific ideas concerning legal control. Legal jurisdiction over crimes and civil wrongs is recognized by all to reside in the State of Israel, but very few cases involving members of these settlements have been brought before the state's courts or, earlier, before the courts of the British Mandate. The minimal role of these courts has resulted from an absence of serious crime; the shielding of fellow members from British (and now to a lesser extent even Israeli) "outsiders"; and internal controls which effectively handle existing disturbances. In both settlements, the power to exercise these internal controls stems from the General Assembly, a regularly held meeting of all members in which each one present casts a single vote. This form of government works effectively in both communities, perhaps because they are small enough for everyone to be heard and homogeneous enough so that there is basic agreement on means and ends. While the *kvutza* meetings are more frequent and cover a broader range of issues, *moshav* sessions are held at least bi-weekly and are generally well attended.

In both settlements, the General Assembly delegates responsibility for certain activities to committees whose membership it approves. Committees are, if anything, more active in the *kvutza,* which has separate permanent groups to deal with questions of economic coordination, work assignment, education, social affairs, ceremonies, housing, community planning, and health. The *moshav* also has its committees, but most of these deal with agricultural matters, particularly the dissemination to individual farmers of the kind of scientific information which is handled by managers in the *kvutza.*

The *moshav's* Judicial Committee, however, is a specialized agency for which no counterpart is found in the *kvutza.* This Committee consists of a panel of seven members elected annually by the General Assembly for the purpose of dealing with internal disputes. Complaints by members against members are brought before the Committee either directly or by referral from the General Assembly. A hearing of the complaint is then conducted by a panel of three drawn from the larger Committee. After investigating the circumstances and hearing the direct testimony of both sides, a panel decides whether and how the defendant should bear responsibility. Fines and damages, the major types of punishment, are usually paid upon imposition, but if not, they are enforceable by the secretary of the *moshav.* Though these panels follow simple procedures, there can be no doubt that they have acted as an agency of legal control in the *moshav.*

An example will illustrate the operation of this *moshav* system of legal control. A fifteen-year-old boy took a neighbor's jeep without permission, picked up some of his friends, and went for a joyride outside the village. During the ride, he crashed into a tree and damaged the fender and door of the vehicle. The owner brought a complaint against him which was heard by the panel. When the boy admitted his actions, he was charged for the full cost of repairs. The debt was subsequently discharged by the boy's parents, and the case was considered closed.

By contrast, the *kvutza* has not delegated sanctioning responsibility to any special unit. Even when administrative or legislative action results in gain or loss to an individual, this is not its primary purpose. In the event of a dispute between workers, for example, the Work Assignment Committee or the Economic Council may decide that the interests of production would be better served if one or both of the workers were transferred. But the objective of such action is not punitive; rather it is to insure the smooth functioning of the economy, and the decision is made in much the same manner as any decision relating to production.

In the course of its legislative work, the General Assembly of the *kvutza* also makes decisions that modify the gains and losses of members. Many of these are policy decisions that apply to classes of members, but sometimes an individual's behavior provides the occasion for a policy debate in the Assembly. One young member, for example, received an electric teakettle as a gift from his sister in the city. Though small gifts could be retained as personal property, the kettle represented a substantial item, and one which would draw upon the limited supply of electricity available to the entire settlement. Moreover, the *kvutza* had already decided against supplying each room with a kettle on the grounds that this would be expensive and would encourage socially divisive private get-togethers. By retaining the kettle, therefore, the young man was threatening the principles of material equality and social solidarity on which the *kvutza* is believed to rest. This at any rate was the decision of the Assembly majority following three meetings during which the issue was debated. Confronted with this decision, the owner bowed to the general will by turning his teakettle over to the infirmary where it would be used by those presumed to be in greatest need of it. No organized enforcement of the decision was threatened, but had he disregarded the expressed will of the community, his life in the *kvutza* would have been made intolerable by the antagonism of community opinion.

As will become apparent, it is the powerful force of public opinion that is the major sanction of the entire *kvutza* control system. It may be focused, as in the case of the electric teakettle, by an Assembly decision, or it may, as occurs more commonly, be aroused directly by the behavior it sanctions. In either case, it is an instrument of control that is employed not by any specialized functionaries but by the community as a whole. Since community opinion is the sanction for the entire *kvutza* control system, that system must be considered informal rather than legal. We turn now to a more detailed consideration of the factors which have made this system of control so much more effective in the *kvutza* than in the *moshav*.

• • •

The *kvutza* is in effect a large primary group whose members engaged in continuous face-to-face interaction. Each able-bodied member works eight to ten hours a day, six days a week, at a job that is usually performed wholly or partially in the presence of others. The results of his efforts become known to his associates, the work manager, and the top officials who coordinate the economy. All three meals are eaten in a collective dining hall usually in the company of five other residents who happen to have arrived at the same time. Members of each sex share common washing and shower facilities, and these are used by most members at the same time, during the limited period when hot water is available. Housing is concentrated in one area of the *kvutza* and consists of rows of long houses, each partitioned to make six rooms, with a married couple or two roommates occupying each room. Because most rooms are surrounded by other dwellings, it is easily possible for neighbors to observe entrances and exits and even some behavior within. Child rearing is the primary responsibility of special nurses and teachers, but parents spend about two hours with their children on work days and usually more than this on their days of rest. Much of this relationship is subject to public view as parents and children stroll around the *kvutza*, eat together occasionally in the dining hall, or play in front of their rooms. Other leisure activities are also subject to public observation: participating in Assembly and Committee meetings, celebrating *kvutza* holidays, attending lectures and films, perusing newspapers and periodicals in the *kvutza* reading room, or taking a vacation tour of the country. Even sexual relations, particularly if they are illicit, can become the subject of general public knowledge, although this was the one type of activity excepted by a member when he said, "amongst us, all things except one are done together."

The same conditions of continuous interaction also make it possible to circulate information throughout the entire community. Mealtime and showering are two informal occasions when large numbers of people forgather and find opportunity for conversation. The shower in particular is a forum for the transmission of information where one can hear about anything from fractured ankles to broken hearts. Though "I heard it in the shower" is a *kvutza* equivalent for "take this with a grain of salt," much genuine news is disseminated there. Compared with these informal techniques, the weekly news bulletin and the Assembly meetings run slow supplementary seconds.

Moshav conditions do not permit as great a degree of public observation. Work is typically conducted alone, with other members of the family, or occasionally with the voluntary aid of a friend. As long as the *moshav* farmer maintains a solvent establishment and discharges such community obligations as payment of taxes and correct use of cooperative facilities, he is free to manage his farm as he sees fit. Meals, consisting largely of produce from the farmstead, are prepared by the housewife and eaten in a family dining room that occupies a central place in the home. Houses are small bungalows ranging from three to six rooms, separated from neighboring dwellings by a hundred yards or more, and screened by hedges and fruit trees. Many activities that are publicly performed in the *kvutza* can be, and usually are, carried out in the privacy of the *moshav* home, among them economic husbandry, care of clothing, showering, washing, child rearing, and such recreation as visiting, reading, and listening to the radio. There are, to be sure, places where members come into contact, such as the produce depots, cooperative store, Assembly and committee meetings, and cinema. Though such contacts provide some opportunities for the circulation of information, they are fewer and the information circulated is less complete than in the *kvutza*.

At least partly as a result of these differences, *kvutza* members do in fact learn more about the activities of more of their members than is known in the *moshav*. Less than a week of residence was necessary in the *kvutza* before virtually everyone knew the ostensible purpose of the writer's stay, whereas similar knowledge was not diffused as widely (or accurately) during two months in the *moshav*. Information thus transmitted is not confined to work performance and consumption, though these are of great interest, but ranges over such details as mail received, visitors contacted, time spent with children, and even style of underclothes worn. As a result, it becomes possible to control types of behavior in the *kvutza* which never become public knowledge in the *moshav*.

• • •

Community opinion can be manifested often, swiftly, subtly, and with varying degress of intensity in the *kvutza*. In the course of a day's continual interaction, positive or negative opinion may be communicated by the ways in which members glance at an individual, speak to him, pass him a requested work implement or dish of food, assign him work, give him instructions, sit next to him, and listen to his comments. To an experienced member, these small signs serve to predict more intense reactions of public acclaim or social isolation. They therefore acquire sanctioning power in and of themselves and become able to control the behavior in question before extremes are reached. In the *moshav,* by contrast, there are fewer opportunities to convey public opinion quickly and accurately because there is so much less contact between members in the course of the daily regime. This is an important limitation in the use of public opinion as a means of control in the *moshav.*

In order for public opinion to be effective, it is important not only that changes in it be perceived but that these be capable of providing gain or loss to the sanctionee. If he is indifferent to public opinion, his behavior will not be directly changed by such sanction. If, on the other hand, he is "other-directed," so that modification in public attitude involves relatively greater loss or gain to him, we would expect him to be effectively sanctioned by public opinion. As a whole, the population of the *kvutza* is far more concerned with public opinion than is that of the *moshav.* Several factors appear to have contributed to this characteristic, among them differences in immigration, emigration, child training, and adult experience.

. . . Looking back at their primary reasons for coming, almost three out of four present *kvutza* members refer to socially oriented motives, such as social solidarity, building a just society, changing human nature. Such motives were said to be primary by only one-third of the present *moshav* members. Many of the *moshav* members emphasized economically oriented motives, such as strengthening the country as a whole or their own economic position in particular.

The effect of this self-selection process may have been aided to some extent by a *kvutza* policy of admitting to permanent membership those candidates who receive a majority vote after a trial period ranging from six months to a year. In the early years particularly, potential members were carefully scrutinized for the characteristics that were thought to make good *kvutza* material. For a new person to appear to be a good worker and a harmonious comrade, it was necessary that he respond to public opinion. . . . Oftentimes individuals who fail to meet such tests are subjected to social disapproval that is sufficiently unpleasant to cause their emigration from the settlement. In general the emigration rate has been higher from the *kvutza* than from the *moshav,* and it is presumed that those who have left have been less able to conform to public opinion than those who have remained.

By contrast, no such elaborate procedures are used to determine fitness for *moshav* members. Most of the available farmsteads were taken years ago by the families which still occupy them. Emigration is based primarily on inability to make a success of farming, but it is doubtful whether sensitivity to public opinion enhances or decreases the chances of success. . . .

Kvutza children are raised from infancy in the constant company of other children of their own age with whom they sleep, eat, bathe, dress, play, and later attend school. Though control is at first the task of the nurses, it is increasingly taken over by the children themselves. Their community is organized politically in a manner similar to the adult *kvutza,* with children's public opinion playing a corresponding part. When one child was caught stealing bananas reserved for the babies, the Children's Assembly decided to punish the culprit by abrogating *their own* movie privileges. . . .

Moshav children, brought up in the close-knit farm family under their parents' control, never seem to develop the great respect for public opinion characteristic of the *kvutza.*

Supplementing migration and socialization practices are the day-to-day experiences of adult *kvutza* members. Quick and accurate response to public opinion enables the member to align his behavior with community standards, and thus to enhance his chances of attaining the acceptance and prestige that are needed for even small advantages. In the *kvutza* environment, one is rewarded for responding to the unfavorable reaction of his comrades when he talks too long in the Assembly, does not volunteer for emergency work service, wears inappropriate clothes, or debunks a *kvutza* celebration. Failure to respond has been known to result in serious difficulties, such as that experienced by a teacher who so antagonized public opinion by declining to dig trenches during Israel's War of Independence that he was denied a requested change of job a full year later.

In the *moshav,* this kind of pressure is exerted less frequently and effectively, if for no other reason than that there are fewer gains for which the individual is dependent on the community. Near self-sufficiency in economic affairs makes it difficult for the *moshav* to exert informal control. Primary reliance is placed on sanctions such as fines or, in a few cases of economic failure, expulsion from the settlement.

Thus several factors appear to contribute to the relatively greater power exercised by public opinion in the *kvutza.* It is difficult to estimate the effects of each of these in the absence of accurate knowledge concerning the values of immigrants and emigrants, as well as changes in the values of present residents since their time of settlement. Nevertheless, processes of selection, child training, and adult experience were at work which might well be expected to result in *kvutza* members being more sensitive to community opinion than were *moshav* members.

• • •

If the effects of sanction were confined to the behavior of sanctionees, social control would be very difficult. Because people are able to learn from the experience of others, however, the control process is greatly facilitated. Such experience has been discussed in several disciplines, ranging from psychoanalytic theories on "identification" to jurisprudential discussions of deterrence. A definitive answer has yet to be found to the very important question as to *who* vicariously learns *what* from the observed experience of *whom.*

Our theoretical orientation suggests that vicarious learning depends on the extent to which an observer perceives himself similar to an observed actor. As perceived similarity increases, so also does the likelihood that the observer will have his tendencies increased for behavior that the actor has gainfully performed. At least two factors would thus appear requisite to vicarious learning: the observer must know of the behavior of another and its consequences, and he must perceive that actor as somewhat similar to himself.

In the *kvutza,* both of these conditions for vicarious learning are fulfilled to a very great degree within the informal control system. Intimacy in the *kvutza,* as noted, permits extensive observation of other members' experieinces. Moreover, there is considerable evidence that *kvutza* members perceive themselves as "comrades" in a homogeneous group. Their perception of similarity may well be enhanced by the mere physical resemblance among members. Men are issued the same kind of clothes, and women wear rather similar ones; even their haircuts are given without much variation by one barber who visits the *kvutza.* But such factors only supplement the more basic similarities of life conditions, including work schedule, consumption, and leisure activities. In all of these, members are subject to fairly uniform controls, so that they experience gain when they consider themselves similar enough to their fellow members to learn from their experiences. These factors contribute to a strong "we" feeling, one of whose effects may well be to heighten vicarious learning in the *kvutza.* This feeling is not challenged, as in the *moshav,* by the distinctive customs of individual families.

• • •

The effectiveness of *kvutza* informal controls is enhanced by a system of norms classifying all behavior with reference to desirability. This system is detailed, generally unambiguous, applicable to wide, clearly defined segments of the population, and well known to the members. As a result it provides consistent guides for the application of sanction and at the same time forewarns potential sanctionees of the consequences of their acts. Such norms, found in every sphere of *kvutza* life, are particularly striking in economic matters.

• • •

Moshav norms, by contrast, are far less explicit, uniformly applied, or generally agreed upon. While it is important that a farmer manage his own holdings effectively and be a good neighbor, the exact pattern of actions by which this can be accomplished has never been authoritatively laid down. In most areas, the individual is likely to have his own ideas about the proper behavior in a given circumstance. On particular occasions involving the duty to aid one's sick neighbor, cooperation in the use of machinery, and a member's violation of state ration controls, widespread difference of opinion was discerned among *moshav* members. This difference was partly attributed to the influence on each member of such factors as the effect of the particular behavior on his own economic interest; his relations with the actor in question; and his conception of the responsibility owed to the *moshav* by its members.

Such crucial questions as property relations in the family and between neighbors are still being deliberated and *moshav* members vary widely in their views on such matters. The problem of succession is just beginning to arise with regularity, and its importance and difficulty for a village with limited, indivisible, and inalienable farmsteads may hardly be overestimated. Perhaps a uniform set of norms will be evolved over a period of time to deal with such problems, or perhaps the problems, especially concerning property, defy informal consensus. At any rate, for the present, there is little agreement. It is small wonder, then, that the *moshav* system of informal controls has been supplemented by a specialized group of deliberators able to make norms and to ensure their sanction by legal means.

• • •

Because effective informal control was achieved in the *kvutza,* the tendency for its subsequent use was increased. That this tendency was high is indicated not only by the many successful instances of its use, but perhaps even more by the persistence with which it was employed on the rare ocasions when it failed. Most striking among the illustrations of this is the case of a woman who was considered by the entire *kvutza* to be antisocial. Soon after her arrival she began to behave very aggressively, quarreling with all her fellow workers in the kitchen and even striking them. Though the use of violence against a fellow member was shocking to the other members, only the usual mild sanctions were at first applied. For some reason, however, social disapproval failed to deter the woman. She continued the same course of behavior through seven years, during which she was subjected to more vigorous informal controls and was at the same time denied formal membership. But she was never subjected to force, expulsion, or even to material disadvantage. Only during her eighth year in the *kvutza* was a different type of sanction directed against her: she was given no work assignment and was deprived of the opportunity to work for the *kvutza.* After a year in which her isolation was thus increased, she bowed to the pressure and left the *kvutza.* Whether the new sanction be designated informal or legal, it is clear that it was an alternative to the traditional informal sanctions of public opinion. That it was employed only after seven years of persistent exercise of the traditional sanctions is striking indication of the firmness with which the latter were established.

In the *moshav,* the tendency to exercise informal controls seems much less powerful. This is not surprising in view of previously described conditions that would minimize the effectiveness of such sanctions. Though these conditions are described as existing at the time of the study, they are traceable to the economic structure of the *moshav,* and thus it is reasonable to assume that they also existed at the inauguration of the community. If so, they preceded the rise of legal controls which evolved gradually during the first twenty years of the settlement's history. During this period and subsequently, informal controls have regularly been tried, but have been ineffective presumably because of inadequate information, implementation, sanction magnitude, and norms. In the course of time, members have learned that informal controls are ineffective;

the resultant lowered tendency to invoke these controls, resulting in even less frequent and less vigorous attempts to use them, has further diminished their effectiveness.[3] This attitude toward informal controls was exemplified by *moshav* reaction to the prank of a group of adolescents who raided a melon patch and openly ate the stolen melons. Indignation ran high because the melons had been specially cultivated for the wedding feast to be given in honor of the marriage of the farmer's daughter. Failing action by the Judiciary Committee, the feeling prevailed that there was "nothing at all to do" about it. So on the informal level no serious attempt was undertaken to exert effective control.

NOTES

1. Professor Karl Llewellyn characterizes law as being concerned only with disputes "not otherwise settled." Llewellyn, "Legal Tradition and Social Science Method—A Realist's Critique" in *Essays on Research in the Social Sciences* (Brookings Institute, 1931), pp. 89, 91.
2. *Mills v. Wyman*, 20 Mass. 225, 3 Pick. 207 (1825): "Without doubt there are great interests in society which justify withholding the coercive arm of the law from these duties of imperfect obligation, as they are called; imperfect, not because they are less binding upon the conscience than those which are called perfect, but because the wisdom of the social law does not impose sanctions upon them." 20 Mass. at 228, 3 Pick. at 210–211.
3. This appears to be an instance of what has been described as the "self-fulfilling prophecy," Merton, *Social Theory and Social Structure* (1949), pp. 179–195, although the "prophecy" is here taken not as the independent variable, but simply as a reflection of previous failure and low tendency.

22

The T. J. Hooper

The barges No. 17 and No. 30, belonging to the Northern Barge Company, had lifted cargoes of coal at Norfolk, Virginia, for New York in March, 1928. They were towed by two tugs of the petitioner, the *Montrose* and the *Hooper,* and were lost off the Jersey coast on March 10, in an easterly gale. The cargo owners sued the barges under the contracts of carriage; the owner of the barges sued the tugs under the towing contract, both for its own loss and as

60 F. 2d 737 (1932), U.S. Court of Appeals, Second Circuit, L. Hand, Circuit Judge.

bailee of the cargoes; the owner of the tug filed a petition to limit its liability. All the suits were joined and heard together, and the judge found that all the vessels were unseaworthy; the tugs, because they did not carry radio receiving sets by which they could have seasonably got warnings of a change in the weather that should have caused them to seek shelter in the Delaware Breakwater en route. He therefore entered an interlocutory decree holding each tug and barge jointly liable to each cargo owner, and each tug for half damages for the loss of its barge. The petitioner appealed, and the barge owner appealed and filed assignments of error.

Each tug had three ocean-going coal barges in tow, the lost barge being at the end. The *Montrose,* which had the No. 17, took an outside course; the *Hooper,* with the No. 30, inside. The weather was fair without ominous symptoms, as the tows passed the Delaware Breakwater about midnight of March 8, and the barges did not get into serious trouble until they were about opposite Atlantic City some 60 or 70 miles to the north. The wind began to freshen in the morning of the ninth and rose to a gale before noon; by afternoon the second barge of the *Hooper*'s tow was out of hand and signaled the tug, which found that not only this barge needed help, but that the No. 30 was aleak. Both barges anchored and the crew of the No. 30 rode out the storm until the afternoon of the tenth, when she sank, her crew having been meanwhile taken off. The No. 17 sprang a leak about the same time; she too anchored at the *Montrose*'s command and sank on the next morning after her crew also had been rescued. The cargoes and the tugs maintain that the barges were not fit for their service; the cargoes and the barges that the tugs should have gone into the Delaware Breakwater, and besides, did not handle their tows properly.

The evidence of the condition of the barges was very extensive, the greater part being taken out of court. As to each, the fact remains that she foundered in weather that she was bound to withstand. . . .

A more difficult issue is as to the tugs. We agree with the judge that once conceding the propriety of passing the Breakwater on the night of the eighth, the navigation was good enough. It might have been worse to go back when the storm broke than to keep on. The seas were from the east and southeast, breaking on the starboard quarter of the barges, which if tight and well found should have lived. True they were at the tail and this is the most trying position, but to face the seas in an attempt to return was a doubtful choice; the masters' decision is final unless they made a plain error. The evidence does not justify that conclusion; and so, the case as to them turns upon whether they should have put in at the Breakwater.

The weather bureau at Arlington broadcasts two predictions daily, at ten in the morning and ten in the evening. Apparently there are other reports floating about, which come at uncertain hours but which can also be picked up. The Arlington report of the morning read as follows: "Moderate north, shifting to east and southeast winds, increasing Friday, fair weather tonight." The substance of this, apparently from another source, reached a tow bound north to New York about noon, and, coupled with a falling glass, decided the master to put in to the Delaware Breakwater in the afternoon. The glass had not indeed fallen much and perhaps the tug was overcautious; nevertheless, although the appearances were all fair, he thought discretion the better part of valor. Three other tows followed him, the masters of two of which testified. Their decision was in part determined by example; but they too had received the Arlington report or its equivalent, and though it is doubtful whether alone it would have turned the scale, it is plain that it left them in an indecision which needed little to be resolved on the side of prudence; they preferred to take no chances, and chances they believed there were. Courts have not often such evidence of the opinion of impartial experts, formed in the very circumstances and confirmed by their own conduct at the time.

Moreover, the *Montrose* and the *Hooper* would have had the benefit of the evening report from Arlington had they had proper receiving sets. This predicted worse weather; it read: "Increasing east and southeast winds, becoming fresh to strong, Friday night and increasing cloudiness followed by rain Friday." The bare "increase" of the morning had become "fresh to strong." To be sure this scarcely foretold a gale of from 40 to 50 miles for five hours or more, rising at one time to 56; but if the four tows thought the first report enough, the second ought to have laid any doubts. The master of the *Montrose* himself, when asked what he would have done had he received a substantially similar report, said that he would certainly have put in. The master of the *Hooper* was also asked for his opinion, and said that he would have turned back also, but this admission is somewhat vitiated by the incorporation in the question of the statement that it was a "storm warning," which the witness seized upon in his answer. All this seems to us to support the conclusion of the judge that prudent masters, who had received the second warning, would have found the risk more than the exigency warranted; they would have been amply vindicated by what followed. To be sure the barges would, as we have said, probably have withstood the gale, had they been well found; but a master is not justified in putting his tow to every test which she will survive, if she be fit. There is a zone in which proper caution will avoid putting her capacity to the proof; a coefficient of prudence that he should not disregard. Taking the situation as a whole, it seems to us that these masters would have taken undue chances, had they got the broadcasts.

They did not, because their private radio receiving sets, which were on board, were not in working order. These belonged to them personally, and were partly a toy, partly a part of the equipment, but neither furnished by the owner, nor supervised by it. It is not fair to say that there was a general custom among coastwise carriers so to equip their tugs. One line alone did it; as for the rest, they relied upon their crews, so far as they can be said to have relied at all. An adequate receiving set suitable for a coastwise tug can now be got at small cost and is reasonably reliable if kept up; obviously it is a source of great protection to their tows. Twice every day they can receive these predictions, based upon the widest possible information, available to every vessel within 200–300 miles and more. Such a set is the ears of the tug to catch the spoken word just as the master's binoculars are her eyes to see a storm signal ashore. Whatever may be said as to other vessels, tugs towing heavy coal-laden barges, strung out for half a mile, have little power to maneuver, and do not, as this case proves, expose themselves to weather that would not turn back stauncher craft. They can have at hand protection against dangers of which they can learn in no other way.

Is it then a final answer that the business had not yet generally adopted receiving sets? There are, no doubt, cases where courts seem to make the general practice of the calling the standard of proper diligence; we have indeed given some currency to the notion ourselves. Indeed in most cases reasonable prudence is in fact common prudence; but strictly it is never its measure; a whole calling may have unduly lagged in the adoption of new and available devices. It never may set its own tests, however persuasive be its usages. Courts must in the end say what is required; there are precautions so imperative that even their universal disregard will not excuse their omission. But here there was no custom at all as to receiving sets; some had them, some did not; the most that can be urged is that they had not yet become general. Certainly in such a case we need not pause; when some have thought a device necessary, at least we may say that they were right, and the others too slack. The statute (46 U.S.C.A., §484) does not bear on this situation at all. It prescribes not a receiving, but a transmitting set, and for a very different purpose: to call for help, not to get news. We hold the tugs therefore because had they been properly equipped, they would have got the Arlington reports. The injury was a direct consequence of this unseaworthiness.

Decree affirmed.

23

The Study of the Living Law

EUGEN EHRLICH

The reason why the dominant school of legal science so greatly prefers the legal proposition to all other legal phenomena as an object of investigation is that it tacitly assumes that the whole law is to be found in the legal proposi-

From *Fundamental Principles of the Sociology of Law,* Walter L. Moll, trans. (Cambridge, Mass.: Harvard University Press, 1936), pp. 486–493. Reprinted by permission of Harvard University Press. Copyright © 1936 by the President and Fellows of Harvard College, 1964 by Walter Lewis Moll.

tions. It is assumed furthermore that since, at the present time, all legal propositions are to be found in the statutes, where they are readily accessible to anyone, all that is necessary to get a knowledge of the law of the present time is to
gather the material from the statutes, to ascertain the content of this material
by one's own individual interpretation, and to utilize this interpretation for the
purposes of juristic literature and judicial decision. Occasionally one meets
with the further idea that legal propositions may arise independently of statute.
In Germany the usual belief is that they can be found in juristic literature; in
France, in judicial decisions. "Customary law," on the other hand, in the prevailing view, is so unimportant that no effort is being put forth to ascertain its
content by scientific methods, much less to create methods for its investigation.
Only the teachers of, and writers on, commercial law still concern themselves
with usage, in this case, with business custom. This explains why the efforts of
those who are carrying on research in law at the present time are bent upon
ascertaining the legal propositions of the past, which are not so readily accessible to us as those that are contained in modern statutes. It is believed that the
scientific result of the labor expended upon the study of the law of the past
consists not only in a knowledge of the development of law, which of course
means only the development of legal propositions, but also in an historical understanding of the law of the present; for the law, which is according to the
tacit assumption the legal propositions of the present time, is rooted in the
past. These, I take it, are the lines of thought on which the method of research
in the field of law has hitherto been based.

But the statement that the whole law is not contained in the legal propositions applies to a much greater degree to the law that is in force today than to
the law of the past. For the men who composed the Twelve Tables, the *Lex
Salica,* and the *Sachsenspiegel* actually had a direct personal knowledge of the
law of their own time, and their endeavor was to gather up this law with which
they dealt, and to formulate it in legal propositions. This however does not
apply, even approximately, to the most important part of the legal material
with which the jurists of the present day are concerned: the codes. For in contrast to what once upon a time the jurists had in mind under all circumstances,
vaguely at least, the compilers of the modern codes very often did not have the
slightest intention whatever of stating the law of their own time and of their
own community. They draw their legal material, first, from the compilation of
Justinian, from which, self-evidently, they are likely to obtain reliable information on almost any other subject than the law of their own time, that is of the
eighteenth or of the nineteenth century; second, from older statements of law,
which, even if they met the requirements of their own time, do not meet those
of the time of the legislator; third, from juristic literature, which was chiefly
concerned with the interpretation of older laws and of older codes, and, in any
case, did not belong to the time of the code in question. The truth of this statement appears most clearly in the case of the German Civil Code, the sources
of which have been almost exclusively textbooks of pandect law, earlier German statutes and compilations of law, and foreign codifications. Accordingly
our codes are uniformly adapted to a time much earlier than their own, and

all the juristic technique in the world would be unable to extract the actual law of the present from it, for the simple reason that it is not contained therein. But the territory within which our codes are valid is so vast, the legal relations with which they deal are so incomparably richer, more varied, more subject to changes than they have ever been, that the mere idea of making a complete presentation in a code would be monstrous. To attempt to imprison the law of a time or of a people within the sections of a code is about as reasonable as to attempt to confine a stream within a pond. The water that is put in the pond is no longer a living stream but a stagnant pool, and but little water can be put in the pond. Moreover, if one considers that the living law had already overtaken and grown away from each one of these codes at the very moment the latter were enacted, and is growing away from them more and more every day, one cannot but realize the enormous extent of this as yet unplowed and unfurrowed field of activity which is being pointed out to the modern legal investigator.

It could not be otherwise. The legal propositions are not intended to present a complete picture of the state of the law. The jurist draws them up with a view to existing practical needs, and with a view to what he is interested in for practical reasons. He will not put forth the effort to formulate legal propositions with reference to matters that lie outside of his sphere of interest, perhaps for the sole reason that they are not within the jurisdiction of the courts before which he practices, or because they do not concern his clients. Since commercial law lay outside of the usual sphere of interest of the Roman jurist, we find that the commercial law of the Roman sources is utterly inadequate; and for the very same reason the Romans and, until quite recently, the modern jurists have very little to say about labor law. Even Eyke von Repgow did not deal with the law of cities and with the customs of manors because it lay outside of his immediate sphere of interest.

On the other hand, the attempt to arrive at an understanding of the present through the study of history or of prehistoric times, that is of ethnology, is an error in principle. To explain something, according to a saying of Mach's, is to replace a mystery that one is not accustomed to by a mystery that one is accustomed to. Now the present contains fewer mysteries that we are not accustomed to than does the past. The paleontologist will understand the nature and the functions of the organs of a fossil animal only if he understands the nature and the functions of the organs of living animals. But the zoologist cannot learn the physiology of the animals that he is studying from the paleontologist; he will have recourse to paleontology only for the purpose of getting a picture of the development of the present-day animal kingdom. We arrive at an understanding of the past through the present, and not vice versa. Accordingly the history of law and ethnological legal science will not be of value for the understanding of the existing law but only for the study of the development of law.

As a result of the methods employed by modern legal science, the present state of our law is, in a great measure, actually unknown to us. We often know nothing, not only of things that are remote but also of things that happen before our very eyes. Almost every day brings some juristic surprise that we owe to a lucky accident, to a peculiar lawsuit, or to an article in the daily papers. This surprise may concern the peasant tenants in Schwarzenberg, or puzzling heritable building rights in the heart of the city of Vienna, in the Brigittenau, or peculiar relations involving heritable leases in Berhomet, in Bukowina. But he who observes life with careful attentiveness knows that these are not isolated occurrences. We are groping in the dark everywhere. And we cannot plead the excuse that the legal historian can avail himself of, namely, that a bit of the past has been irrecoverably lost. We need but open our eyes and ears to learn everything that is of significance for the law or our time.

In the part of the Austrian code that deals with matrimonial agreements there are four meager sections, which, according to the marginal heading, deal with the matrimonial regime of community of goods. Anyone who has had opportunity of coming into contact with the German peasantry of Austria knows that they live, almost exclusively, under a matrimonial regime of community of goods. But this matrimonial community of goods, which is the prevailing, freely chosen property regime of the German peasantry in Austria, has nothing in common with the community of goods provided for in the Austrian Civil Code, and the provisions of the Civil Code are never being applied since they are always excluded by a marriage contract formally entered into. What would be the value of a science of law that failed to recognize that the community of goods that the Austrian Civil Code speaks of exists only on paper? What would be the value of a science of law that thinks it is fulfilling its whole task when it ascertains the intent of the lawgiver, which has been expressed in the above four sections, but does not concern itself with the community of goods, which is based on readily accessible legal documents, and according to which practically the entire German peasantry of Austria lives?

Again there is the agricultural usufructuary lease. The few provisions contained in the modern codes on the subject, especially in the Austrian and German codes, were for the most part taken from Roman law, and had arisen on the exhausted soil of Italy in the days of the Roman Empire with its system of extensive *latifundia* and an oppressed peasant class. They would be altogether insufficient today. A glance at life will convince us that they are almost never being applied. Their operation is almost always being excluded and they are being replaced by the provisions of contracts of usufructuary lease such as are suitable to modern social and economic conditions, and are being entered into between the lessor and the lessee in almost every instance. Though they vary according to the region, the nature of the estate which is being let, and the position of the parties, they have, in spite of this limitation, an ever-recurring, typical content. It is apparent, I dare say, in view of this discussion, that a presentation of the law of usufructuary lease of the civil codes, be it ever so careful, cannot reflect the actual state of the German or Austrian law of usufructuary lease. To do this, it would be necessary to set forth the typical content of the leases, and for this purpose it would be necessary to search the archives of the offices of notaries and lawyers, and to make inquiries at the time and place.

Or what information can be gathered from juristic literature as to the system of agriculture in Germany or in Austria? Not even the various methods of cultivation of the soil have been formulated from a juristic point of view, and that would be but a small part of the task that has to be fulfilled. All economic cultivation of the soil is linked with other relations that are of the greatest importance to the jurist. In the first place, the neighborly relations between owners of farms operated for economic purposes and of landed estates. They are being regulated in part by custom, in part by statute. Yet the entire juristic literature has not a single word to say about any of these, except perhaps about the statute. Moreover, agriculture, insofar as it is carried on on a scale larger than the very smallest and most insignificant, presupposes a certain organization of labor, which, in the case of great landed estates, becomes a most artistically interlocking and extraordinarily complicated mechanism. To everyone that takes part in it, there is assigned, partly by custom, partly by contract or statute (regulations for servants), the measure of his powers, rights of supervision, privileges and duties, without a knowledge of which this difficult piece of machinery could be understood neither from the economic, nor technical, nor from the juristic point of view. In case of similar undertakings all these legal relations occur again and again in their typical form throughout the whole region and often throughout the whole realm; and for this reason it is not a difficult task to study them and set them forth.

Note also the law of the family. The first thing that attracts the attention of the observer is the contrast between the actual order of the family and that which the codes decree. I doubt whether there is a country in Europe in which the relation between husband and wife, parents and children, between the family and the outside world, as it actually takes form in life, corresponds to the norms of the positive law; or in which the members of the family, in which there is a semblance of proper family life, would as much as think of attempting to enforce the rights against one another that the letter of the law grants to them. It is evident therefore that in this case, too, the positive law is far from giving a picture of that which actually takes place in life. So much the less must legal science and doctrine confine itself to giving an exposition of the content of the statutes; it must seek to ascertain the actual forms that the family relations assume, which are essentially uniform and typical although they differ in the various classes of society and in the various parts of the country. We shall not discuss in this connection whether the statute has lost its mastery over life or whether it never had it; whether life, in the process of growth, has developed beyond the statute and grown away from it or whether it never corresponded to it. In this connection, too, science fulfills its function as the theory of law and right very poorly if it merely presents that which is prescribed by the statute and fails to tell what actually takes place.

• • •

The only branch of law the juristic science of which is based not merely incidentally, but throughout, on actual usage is commercial law. The latter has been officially received into juristic science in the form of business custom and "usage." The organization of the great landed estate and of the factory, even of the bank, has, to the present day, remained to the jurist a book sealed with seven seals, but the organization of the commercial house he knows, in its main outlines at least, from the Commercial Code. He knows the position of the principal and of the holder of a general power of procuration; [1] of the holder of a mercantile power of agency [2] and of the mercantile employee, of the mercantile agent, [3] of the commercial traveler; he knows the significance of the mercantile trade name (*Handelsfirma*), of the books of account, and of business correspondence. He has a conception of the significance of all of these things not only from the economic but also from the legal point of view. And the contract law of modern commercial law has not been taken over from the *corpus juris;* nor is it a product of the diligent reflection of its authors. What the commercial statutes and the commercial codes have to say about buying and selling, about commissions, about forwarding of goods, about the insurance, the freight, and the banking business, is actually being practiced somewhere even though, possibly, not always to the extent set forth therein. Likewise many commercial institutions, particularly the Exchange, have been properly furrowed and plowed by the jurists. The fact that much hard work remains to be done in every nook and corner is caused less in this sphere than in others by the lack of understanding and appreciation of the actual realities and more by the difficulties inherent in the subject matter and by its extremely rapid development. The gigantic organization of the production of goods which is taking place before our very eyes in trusts and cartels, all the modern achievements of commerce, the numerous new inventions, lead to new formations at every moment, and open new fields of labor for the jurist.

This then is the *living* law in contradistinction to that which is being enforced in the courts and other tribunals. The living law is the law that dominates life itself even though it has not been posited in legal propositions. The source of our knowledge of this law is, first, the modern legal document; second, direct observation of life, of commerce, of customs and usages, and of all associations, not only of those that the law has recognized but also of those that it has overlooked and passed by, indeed even of those that it has disapproved.

NOTES

1. The *Prokura,* or general power of procuration, has been defined by Gareis (*Handelsgesetzbuch,* second edition) in a note to paragraph 48 as a general power of agency that must be registered, that is limited only by statute, that cannot be limited by agreement as to its effect with reference to third persons, and that is designated by a formal designation which is limited to this particular instance.
2. See Commercial Code, § 54.
3. See Commercial Code, I, § 7.

24

Contract as a Principle of Order

FRIEDRICH KESSLER AND
MALCOLM P. SHARP

Even at the risk of oversimplification, the law of contracts may be divided broadly into two sectors governed by principles that are inconsistent with if not diametrically opposed to each other. At one pole is a body of institutions and doctrines that are influenced, if not governed, by the principle of free volition. At the opposite pole, freedom of volition is limited if not suspended by an ever-expanding system of judicial and legislative control. But the two opposing principles of freedom and control have, on an ever-increasing scale, penetrated each other's areas of dominance with the result that the domains in which either principle has pure application are gradually diminishing. Hence there are wide fields in which both principles may be found at work. Nonetheless, in these areas of transition, one of the two principles will be found to dominate, with the other relegated to the role of a counterforce.

The dual nature of contract is reflected in its modern definition. Since the days of Blackstone, if not earlier, contract has been defined as an agreement voluntarily entered into. The attitude of those days was expressed in Leake's classic on contract and exercised a strong influence on subsequent generations of lawyers. Today, as the *Restatement of Contracts* illustrates, the emphasis is no longer on voluntary agreement. According to the definition in Section 1 of the *Restatement,* "A contract is a promise or a set of promises for the breach of which the law gives a remedy, or the performance of which the law in some way recognizes as a duty." Under this modern definition, relations in which the element of consent freely given is difficult to discover, and, indeed, even "contracts by compulsion," can be treated as contracts.

• • •

The predominance of individualism in one sector of the law of contracts may be explained by the fact that this part of contract law is the counterpart, if not the product, of free enterprise capitalism. Contract, in this point of view, is the legal machinery appropriate to an economic system that relies on free exchange rather than tradition and custom or command for the distribution of resources.

From *Contracts: Cases and Materials* (Englewood Cliffs, N.J.: Prentice-Hall, 1953), pp. 2–9. Reprinted by permission of the authors and Little, Brown, and Company. Abridged with renumbered notes.

155

The triumph of capitalism during the eighteenth and nineteenth centuries, with its spectacular increase in the productivity of labor, was possible only because of a constant refinement of the division of labor. This development in turn presupposed that enterprisers could depend on a continuous flow of goods and services exchanged in a free market. And to be able to exploit the factors of production in the most efficient way, enterprisers had (and still have) to be able to bargain for goods and services to be delivered in the future and to rely on promises for future delivery. Thus, it became one of the main functions of our law of contracts to keep this flow running smoothly, making certain that bargains would be kept and that legitimate expectations created by contractual promises would be honored. "The foundation of contract," in the language of Adam Smith, "is the reasonable expectation, which the person who promises raises in the person to whom he binds himself; of which the satisfaction may be extorted by force.[1] In this sense, contract liability is promissory liability. In an industrial and commercial society, where wealth is largely made up of promises, the interest of society as a whole demands protection of the interest of the individual promisee.

Contract, to be really useful to the business enterpriser within the setting of a free enterprise economy, must be a tool of almost unlimited pliability. To accomplish this end, the legal system has to reduce the ceremony necessary to vouch for the deliberate nature of a contractual transaction to the indispensable minimum; it has to give freedom of contract as to form. Furthermore, since the law must keep pace with the constant widening of the market without being able to anticipate the content of an infinite number of transactions into which members of the community may need to enter, parties must be given freedom as to the content of their contractual arrangements. Contract, then, in the sense of a system of free contract, enhances the mobility of factors of production in the interest of the enterpriser who wishes to secure them in the most efficient way, so as to be able rationally to experiment with new methods of satisfying wants. For that matter, it is needed by every member of the community who is desirous of achieving rationality of conduct in the adaptation of means to ends, and who does not want to adhere passively to the compulsory uniformity of behavior imposed by tradition and custom. Thus, its emergence has greatly increased the area and the potentialities of rational conduct.[2]

Within the framework of a free enterprise system the essential prerequisite of contractual liability is volition, that is, consent freely given, and not coercion or status.[3] Contract, in this view, is the "meeting place of the ideas of agreement and obligation." [4] As a matter of historical fact, the rise of contract within Western civilization reflected the erosion of a status-organized society; contract became, at an ever-increasing rate, a tool of change and of growing self-determination and self-assertion. Self-determination during the nineteenth century was regarded as the goal toward which society progressed; the movement of progressive societies, in the words of Sir Henry Maine, is a movement from status to contract. "It is through contract that man attains freedom. Although it appears to be the subordination of one man's will to another, the former gains more than he loses." [5] Contract, in this view, is the principle of order par excellence and the only legitimate means of social integration in a free society. Translated into legal language, this means that in a progressive society all law is ultimately based on contract.[6] And since contract as a social phenomenon is the result of a "coincidence of free choices" on the part of the members of the community, merging their egoistical and altruistic tendencies, a contractual society safeguards its own stability. Contract is an instrument of peace in society. It testifies to the "natural identity of interests" of the members of the community—all the more since, with increasing rationality, man becomes less rather than more egoistic.

The high hopes with regard to the potentialities inherent in the contractual mechanism have found admirable expression in Sidgwick's *Elements of Politics* (1879), p. 82:

In a summary view of the civil order of society, as constituted in accordance with the individualistic ideal, performance of contract presents itself as the chief positive element, protection of life and property being the chief negative element. Withdraw contract—suppose that no one can count upon the fulfillment of any engagement—and the members of a human community are atoms that cannot effectively combine; the complex cooperation and division of employments that are the essential characteristics of modern industry cannot be introduced among such beings. Suppose contracts freely made and effectively sanctioned, and the most elaborate social organization becomes possible, at least in a society of such human beings as the individualistic theory contemplates: gifted with mature reason, and governed by enlightened self-interest. Of such beings it is *prima facie* plausible to say that, when once their respective relations to the surrounding material world have been determined so as to prevent mutual encroachment and secure to each the fruits of his industry, the remainder of their positive mutual rights and obligations ought to depend entirely on that coincidence of their free choices, which we call contract. Thoroughgoing individualists would even include the rights corresponding to governmental services, and the obligations to render services to government, which we shall have to consider later: only in this latter case the contract is tacit.

Thus, a system of free contract did not recommend itself solely for reasons of sheer expediency and utilitarianism; it was deeply rooted in the moral sentiments of the period in which it found strongest expression. The dominant current of belief inspiring nineteenth-century industrial society—an open society —was the deep-felt conviction that individual and cooperative action should be left unrestrained in family, church, and market and that such a system of *laissez faire* would not lessen the freedom and dignity of the individual, but would secure the highest possible social justice.[7] The representatives of this school of thought were firmly convinced, to state it somewhat roughly, of the existence of a natural law according to which, if not in the short run then at least in the long run, the individual serving his own interest was also serving the interest of the community.[8] Profits, under this system, could only be earned by supplying wanted commodities, and freedom of competition would prevent profits from rising unduly. The play of the market, if left to itself, would, therefore, maximize net satisfactions and afford the ideal conditions for the distribution of wealth. Justice within this context has a very definite meaning.[9] It means freedom of property and of contract, of profitmaking and of trade. The "pre-established harmony" of a social system based on freedom of enterprise and perfect competition sees to it that the private autonomy of contracting parties will be kept within bounds and will work out to the benefit of society as a whole. Freedom of contract, within this cultural framework, like all freedom, is not an end in itself; it is only valuable as a means to an end: "the liberation of the powers of all men equally for contributions to a common good." [10]

Small wonder, that freedom of contract, as evolved in the spirit of *laissez faire,* has found repeated expression in Anglo-American case law. "(If) there is one thing which more than another public policy requires," Sir George Jessel, M.R., assures us, "it is that men of full age and competent understanding shall have the utmost liberty of contracting, and that their contracts entered into freely and voluntarily shall be held sacred and shall be enforced by Courts of Justice." [11] True, fraud and force must be ruled out by the courts in the exercise of their function of making sure that the "rules of the game" will be adhered to. But this qualification was thought to be of no great moment, owing to the policing force of the competitive market. Except for according protection against force and fraud, it is not the function of courts to make contracts for the parties or to strike down or tamper with improvident bargains. Courts have only to interpret contracts made by the parties; they do not make them. This attitude is in keeping with liberal social and moral philosophy, according to which it pertains to the dignity of man to lead his own life as a reasonable person and to accept responsibility for his own mistakes.

These pronouncements, however, are representative only of the main current of thought that deeply influenced freedom of contract. They fail to take into account that even during the period that is traditionally called the height of liberalism there was an undertow that gradually increased in strength.

The opposing viewpoint . . . found expression . . . in the dissent of Justice Holmes to the majority opinion in *Lochner v. N. Y.* (The majority had declared a New York statute imposing maximum hours for work in bakeries unconstitutional.) In the words of Justice Holmes:

> This case is decided upon an economic theory which a large part of the country does not entertain. If it were a question whether I agreed with that theory, I should desire to study it further and long before making up my mind. But I do not conceive that to be my duty, because I strongly believe that my agreement or disagreement has nothing to do with the right of a majority to embody their opinions in law. It is settled by various decisions of this court that state constitutions and state laws may regulate life in many ways which we as legislators might think as injudicious or if you like as tyrannical as this, and which equally with this interfere with the liberty to contract. Sunday laws and usury laws are ancient examples. A more modern one is the prohibition of lotteries. The liberty

of the citizen to do as he likes so long as he does not interfere with the liberty of others to do the same, which has been a shibboleth for some well-known writers, is interfered with by school laws, by the Post Office, by every state or municipal institution which takes his money for purposes thought desirable, whether he likes it or not. The Fourteenth Amendment does not enact Mr. Herbert Spencer's *Social Statics*. [12]

It took several decades till the spirit of the Holmes dissent, with its recognition that there may be no greater inequality than the equal treatment of unequals, and that freedom must sometimes be limited in the interest of its own preservation, conquered considerable areas of the law of contracts. The principle of control, which began as a countercurrent in the early days of the dominance of freedom of contract, finally swelled into a main current of thought in these areas. This is particularly true of the field of labor relations, where the constitutionality of social legislation, which might have been struck down as late as 1936, has since been upheld. In addition, under the protective cover of legislation, the bargain for individual terms of employment has been replaced in many fields by master contracts arrived at between labor unions and employers or groups of employers. But the law has not yet reached the state of compulsory arbitration; it requires only collective bargaining on the part of both sides.

Furthermore, to protect the public against the danger of powerful suppliers' dictating the terms of contracts or not contracting at all, statutes frequently prescribe, either wholly or partially, the terms of transactions of great social significance. The field of insurance contracts furnishes excellent illustrations. And public utilities frequently have been required by statute to furnish their services and to comply with conditions and rates approved by public authority. "Compulsory" contracts have thus made their appearance. Furthermore, if businessmen possess what the courts classify as a substantial degree of market power, the antitrust laws have markedly qualified their freedom to select their own customers, and to refuse to deal with prospective customers.

To sum up, the individual member of the community continuously finds himself involved in contractual obligations, the contents of which are often "predetermined for him" by statute, public authority, or group action.[13] The terms and conditions under which he obtains his supply of electricity and gas will in all likelihood be regulated by a public utility commission. So will his fare, should he use a public conveyance going to work. The rent he will have to pay may be fixed by governmental authority. The price of his food will depend partly on the government's farm support program and not solely on the interplay of demand and supply in a free market. No longer will he be able to have the advantages of simple price competition in buying many a standard brand used in daily consumption, since prices may well be fixed by arrangement between producer and distributor under price maintenance requirements with the blessing of statutory approval.[14] The wages he will have to pay or will earn may have been fixed for him beforehand. If he is a businessman, he must also beware of violating the antitrust laws, which since the end of the N.R.A. in 1935 have acquired a new vitality both in doctrine and in enforcement policy. A body of law and of precedent has been established which is having substantial impact on industrial organization and on price policy in many areas of our economy.

Thus, in the evolution of the law of contracts, the basic assumption of the past that contract deals with the individual relations of men with each other has gradually given way to the realization that in large sectors of our social and economic life contract is no longer an individual and private affair, but a social institution affecting more than the interests of the two contracting parties. An analysis, therefore, of present-day contract exclusively in terms of volition and agreement does not do justice to contract as a social institution. Social control has become an integral part of contract itself, and cannot be omitted from any analysis of the modern law of contract.

NOTES

1. *Lectures on Justice, Police, Revenue, and Arms,* Cannan, ed. (1896), p. 7.
2. For a discussion of the significance of "rationality" for modern capitalism, see Max Weber, *Gesammelte Aufsaetze zur Religionssoziologie,* I (1925), 4–12, 30 ff., 437 ff., summarized in Parsons, *The Structure of Social Action* (1949), 503 ff.
3. Freedom of contract thus means that subject to narrow limits the law, in the field of contracts, has delegated legislation to the contracting parties. As far as the parties are concerned, the law of contracts is of their own making; society merely lends its machinery of enforcement to the party injured by the breach. To be sure, society, to accommodate the members of the business community, has placed at their disposal a great variety of typical transactions whose consequences are regulated in advance; it has thus "supplied the short-sightedness of individuals, by doing for them what they would have done for themselves, if their imagination had anticipated the march of nature." Bentham, "A General View of a Complete Code of Laws," *Works,* Bowring, ed., III (1843), 191. Bentham's statement does not do justice to the significance of statutory provisions. They often reflect existing patterns of behavior. But these statutory provisions come into operation only in the absence of an agreement to the contrary.
4. Watt, *The Theory of Contract in Its Social Light* (1897), p. 2.
5. The quotation is taken from Stone, *The Province and Function of the Law* (1946), p. 251.
6. See Parsons, *The Law of Contracts,* I (1855), 3.
7. For the most impressive formulation of the beneficial operation of *laissez faire,* see Marshall, *Principles of Economics* (8th ed., 1938), pp. 246–247: "This doctrine of natural organization contains more truth of the highest importance to humanity than almost any other." See further Moos, "Laissez-faire, Planning, and Ethics," *The Economic Journal,* LV (1947), 17.
8. Adam Smith, *Wealth of Nations,* Cannan, ed. (1937), p. 423. For a more guarded expression of this idea, see Knight, *Freedom and Reform* (1947), pp. 45, 54.
9. Hamilton, "Competition," *Encyclopedia of the Social Sciences,* II, 141–142.
10. Green, "Liberal Legislation and Freedom of Contract," *Works,* III (1888), 365, 372.
11. *Printing and Numerical Registering Co. v. Sampson,* L.R., 19 Eq. Cas. 462, 465 (1875).
12. 198 U.S. 45, 75 (1904). Consult also *Muller v. Oregon,* 206 U.S. 412 (1908) and the dissenting opinions in *Morehead v. New York ex rel. Tipaldo,* 298 U.S. 587 (1936).
13. Eastwood and Wortley, "Administrative Law and the Teaching of the Law of Contracts," *Journal of the Society of Public Teachers of Law* (1938), p. 23.
14. See *infra,* p. 701.

25

Non-Contractual Relations in Business:
A Preliminary Study

STEWART MACAULAY

What good is contract law? Who uses it? When and how? Complete answers would require an investigation of almost every type of transaction between individuals and organizations. In this report, research has been confined to exchanges between businesses, and primarily to manufacturers.[1] Furthermore, this report will be limited to a presentation of the findings concerning when contract is and is not used and to a tentative explanation of these findings.

This research is only the first phase in a scientific study. The primary research technique involved interviewing 68 businessmen and lawyers representing 43 companies and six law firms. The interviews ranged from a 30-minute brush-off where not all questions could be asked of a busy and uninterested sales manager to a six-hour discussion with the general counsel of a large corporation. Detailed notes of the interviews were taken and a complete report of each interview was dictated, usually no later than the evening after the interview. All but two of the companies had plants in Wisconsin; 17 were manufacturers of machinery but none made such items as food products, scientific instruments, textiles or petroleum products. Thus the likelihood of error because of sampling bias may be considerable.[2] However, to a great extent, existing knowledge has been inadequate to permit more rigorous procedures; as yet one cannot formulate many precise questions to be asked a systematically selected sample of "right people." Much time has been spent fishing for relevant questions or answers, or both.

Reciprocity, exchange or contract has long been of interest to sociologists, economists, and lawyers. Yet each discipline has an incomplete view of this kind of conduct. This study represents the effort of a law teacher to draw on sociological ideas and empirical investigation. It stresses, among other things, the functions and dysfunctions of using contract to solve exchange problems and the influence of occupational roles on how one assesses whether the benefits of using contract outweigh the costs.

To discuss when contract is and is not used, the term "contract" must be specified. This term will be used here to refer to devices for conducting exchanges. Contract is not treated as synonymous with an exchange itself, which

From *American Sociological Review*, XXVIII, No. 1 (1963), 55–67. Reprinted by permission of the author and the American Sociological Association. Abridged with renumbered notes.

may or may not be characterized as contractual. Nor is contract used to refer to a writing recording an agreement. Contract, as I use the term here, involves two distinct elements: (a) rational planning of the transaction with careful provision for as many future contingencies as can be foreseen, and (b) the existence or use of actual or potential legal sanctions to induce performance of the exchange or to compensate for non-performance.

These devices for conducting exchanges may be used or may exist in greater or lesser degree, so that transactions can be described relatively as involving a more contractual or a less contractual manner (a) of creating an exchange relationship or (b) of solving problems arising during the course of such a relationship. For example, General Motors might agree to buy all of the Buick Division's requirements of aluminum for ten years from Reynolds Aluminum. Here the two large corporations probably would plan their relationship carefully. The plan probably would include a complex pricing formula designed to meet market fluctuations, an agreement on what would happen if either party suffered a strike or a fire, a definition of Reynolds' responsibility for quality control and for losses caused by defective quality, and many other provisions. As the term contract is used here, this is a more contractual method of creating an exchange relationship than is a homeowner's casual agreement with a real estate broker giving the broker the exclusive right to sell the owner's house which fails to include provisions for the consequences of many easily foreseeable (and perhaps even highly probable) contingencies. In both instances, legally enforceable contracts may or may not have been created, but it must be recognized that the existence of a legal sanction has no necessary relationship to the degree of rational planning by the parties, beyond certain minimal legal requirements of certainty of obligation. General Motors and Reynolds might never sue or even refer to the written record of their agreement to answer questions which come up during their ten-year relationship, while the real estate broker might sue, or at least threaten to sue, the owner of the house. The broker's method of dispute settlement then would be more contractual than that of General Motors and Reynolds, thus reversing the relationship that existed in regard to the "contractualness" of the creation of the exchange relationships.

Tentative Findings

It is difficult to generalize about the use and non-use of contract by manufacturing industry. However, a number of observations can be made with reasonable accuracy at this time. The use and non-use of contract in creating exchange relations and in dispute settling will be taken up in turn.

The Creation of Exchange Relationships. In creating exchange relationships, businessmen may plan to a greater or lesser degree in relation to several types of issues. Before reporting the findings as to practices in creating such relationships, it is necessary to describe what one can plan about in a bargain and the degrees of planning which are possible.

People negotiating a contract can make plans concerning several types of issues: (1) They can plan what each is to do or refrain from doing: S might agree to deliver ten 1963 Studebaker four-door sedan automobiles to B on a certain date in exchange for a specified amount of money. (2) They can plan what effect certain contingencies are to have on their duties: What is to happen to S and B's obligations if S cannot deliver the cars because of a strike at the Studebaker factory? (3) They can plan what is to happen if either of them fails to perform: What is to happen if S delivers nine of the cars two weeks late? (4) They can plan their agreement so that it is a legally enforceable contract: so a legal sanction would be available to provide compensation for injury suffered by B as a result of S's failure to deliver the cars on time.

As to each of these issues, there may be a different degree of planning by the parties. (1) They may carefully and explicitly plan: S may agree to deliver ten 1963 Studebaker four-door sedans that have six cylinder engines, automatic transmissions, and other specified items of optional equipment and which will perform to a specified standard for a certain time. (2) They may have a mutual but tacit understanding about an issue: Although the subject was never mentioned in their negotiations, both S and B may assume that B may cancel his order for the cars before they are delivered if B's taxicab business is so curtailed that B can no longer use ten additional cabs. (3) They may have two inconsistent unexpressed assumptions about an issue: S may assume that if any of the cabs fails to perform to the specified standard for a certain time, all S must do is repair or replace it. B may assume S must also compensate B for the profits B would have made if the cab has been in operation. (4) They may never have thought of the issue: Neither S nor B planned their agreement so that it would be a legally enforceable contract. Of course, the first and fourth degrees of planning listed are the extreme cases and the second and third are intermediate points. Clearly other intermediate points are possible: S and B neglect to specify whether the cabs should have automatic or conventional transmissions. Their planning is not as careful and explicit as that in the example previously given.

Table 25–1 represents the dimensions of creating an exchange relationship just discussed with "X's" representing the example of S and B's contract for ten taxicabs.

TABLE 25-1

	Definition of Performances	Effect of Contingencies	Effect of Defective Performances	Legal Sanctions
Explicit and careful	X			
Tacit agreement		X		
Unilateral assumptions			X	
Unawareness of the issue				X

Most larger companies, and many smaller ones, attempt to plan carefully and completely. Important transactions not in the ordinary course of business are handled by a detailed contract. For example, recently the Empire State Building was sold for $65 million. More than 100 attorneys, representing 34 parties, produced a 400-page contract. Another example is found in the agreement of a major rubber company in the United States to give technical assistance to a Japanese firm. Several million dollars were involved and the contract consisted of 88 provisions on 17 pages. The 12 house counsel—lawyers who work for one corporation rather than many clients—interviewed said that all but the smallest businesses carefully planned most transactions of any significance. Corporations have procedures so that particular types of exchanges will be reviewed by their legal and financial departments.

More routine transactions commonly are handled by what can be called standardized planning. A firm will have a set of terms and conditions for purchases, sales, or both printed on the business documents used in these exchanges. Thus the things to be sold and the price may be planned particularly for each transaction, but standard provisions will further elaborate the performances and cover the other subjects of planning. Typically, these terms and conditions are lengthy and printed in small type on the back of the forms. For example, 24 paragraphs in eight-point type are printed on the back of the purchase order form used by the Allis Chalmers Manufacturing Company. The provisions: (1) describe, in part, the performance required, for example: DO NOT WELD CASTINGS WITHOUT OUR CONSENT; (2) plan for the effect of contingencies, for example: ". . . in the event the seller suffers delay in performance due to an act of God, war, act of the government, priorities or allocations, act of the buyer, fire, flood, strike, sabotage, or other causes beyond seller's control, the time of completion shall be extended a period of time equal to the period of such delay if the seller gives the buyer notice in writing of the cause of any such delay within a reasonable time after the beginning thereof"; (3) plan for the effect of defective performances, for example: "The buyer, without waiving any other legal rights, reserves the right to cancel without charge or to postpone deliveries of any of the articles covered by this order which are not shipped in time reasonably to meet said agreed dates"; (4) plan for a legal sanction, for example, the clause "without waiving any other legal rights," in the example just given.

In larger firms such "boiler plate" provisions are drafted by the house counsel or the firm's outside lawyer. In smaller firms such provisions may be drafted by the industry trade association, may be copied from a competitor, or may be found on forms purchased from a printer. In any event, salesmen and purchasing agents, the operating personnel, typically are unaware of what is said in the fine print on the back of the forms they use. Yet often the normal business patterns will give effect to this standardized planning. For example, purchasing agents may have to use a purchase order form so that all transactions receive a number under the firm's accounting system. Thus, the required accounting record will carry the necessary planning of the exchange relationship printed on its reverse side. If the seller does not object to this planning and accepts the order, the buyer's "fine print" will control. If the seller does object, differences can be settled by negotiation.

This type of standardized planning is very common. Requests for copies of the business documents used in buying and selling were sent to approximately 6,000 manufacturing firms that do business in Wisconsin. Approximately 1,200 replies were received and 850 companies used some type of standardized planning. With only a few exceptions, the firms that did not reply and the 350 that indicated they did not use standardized planning were very small manufacturers such as local bakeries, soft drink bottlers, and sausage makers.

While businessmen can and often do carefully and completely plan, it is clear that not all exchanges are neatly rationalized. Although most businessmen think that a clear description of both the seller's and buyer's performances is obvious common sense, they do not always live up to this ideal. The house counsel and the purchasing agent of a medium-size manufacturer of automobile parts reported that several times their engineers had committed the company to buy expensive machines without adequate specifications. The engineers had drawn careful specifications as to the type of machine and how it was to be made but had neglected to require that the machine produce specified results. An attorney and an auditor both stated that most contract disputes arise because of ambiguity in the specifications.

Businessmen often prefer to rely on "a man's word" in a brief letter, a handshake, or "common honesty and decency," even when the transaction involves exposure to serious risks. Seven lawyers from law firms with business practices were interviewed. Five thought that businessmen often entered contracts with only a minimal degree of advance planning. They complained that businessmen desire to "keep it simple and avoid red tape" even where large amounts of money and significant risks are involved. One stated that he was "sick of being told, 'We can trust old Max,' when the problem is not one of honesty but one of reaching an agreement that both sides understand." Another said that businessmen when bargaining often talk only in pleasant generalities, think they have a contract, but fail to reach agreement on any of the hard, unpleasant questions until forced to do so by a lawyer. Two outside lawyers had different views. One thought that large firms usually planned important exchanges, although he conceded that occasionally matters might be left in a fairly vague state. The other dissenter represents a large utility that commonly buys heavy equipment and buildings. The supplier's employees come on the utility's property to install the equipment or construct the buildings, and they may be injured while there. The utility has been sued by such employees so often that it carefully plans purchases with the assistance of a lawyer so that suppliers take this burden.

Moreover, standardized planning can break down. In the example of such planning previously given, it was assumed that the purchasing agent would use his company's form with its 24 paragraphs printed on the back and that the seller would accept this or object to any provisions he did not like. However, the seller may fail to read the buyer's 24 paragraphs of fine print and may accept the buyer's order on the seller's own acknowledgment-of-order form. Typically this form will have ten to 50 paragraphs favoring the seller, and these provisions are likely to be different from or inconsistent with the buyer's provisions. The seller's acknowledgment form may be received by the buyer and checked by a clerk. She will read the face of the acknowledgment but not the fine print on the back of it because she has neither the time nor ability to analyze the small print on the 100 to 500 forms she must review each day. The face of the acknowledgment—where the goods and the price are specified—is likely to correspond with the face of the purchase order. If it does, the two forms are filed away. At this point, both buyer and seller are likely to assume they have planned an exchange and made a contract. Yet they have done neither, as they are in disagreement about all that appears on the back of their forms. This practice is common enough to have a name. Law teachers call it "the battle of the forms."

Ten of the 12 purchasing agents interviewed said that frequently the provisions on the back of their purchase order and those on the back of a supplier's acknowledgment would differ or be inconsistent. Yet they would assume that the purchase was complete without further action unless one of the supplier's provisions was really objectionable. Moreover, only occasionally would they bother to read the fine print on the back of supplier's forms. On the other hand, one purchasing agent insists that agreement be reached on the fine print provisions, but he represents the utility whose lawyer reported that it exercises great care in planning. The other purchasing agent who said that his company did not face a battle of the forms problem, works for a division of one of the largest manufacturing corporations in the United States. Yet the company may have such a problem without recognizing it. The purchasing agent regularly sends a supplier both a purchase order and another form which the supplier is asked to sign and return. The second form states that the supplier accepts the buyer's terms and conditions. The company has sufficient bargaining power to force suppliers to sign and return the form, and the purchasing agent must show one of his firm's auditors such a signed form for every purchase order issued. Yet suppliers frequently return this buyer's form plus their own acknowledgment form which has conflicting provisions. The purchasing agent throws away the supplier's form and files his own. Of course, in such a case the supplier has not acquiesced to the buyer's provisions. There is no agreement and no contract.

Sixteen sales managers were asked about the battle of the forms. Nine said that frequently no agreement was reached on which set of fine print was to govern, while seven said that there was no problem. Four of the seven worked for companies whose major customers are the large automobile companies or the large manufacturers of paper products. These customers demand that their terms and conditions govern any purchase, are careful generally to see that suppliers acquiesce, and have the bargaining power to have their way. The other three of the seven sales managers who have no battle of the forms problem, work for manufacturers of special industrial machines. Their firms are careful to reach complete agreement with their customers. Two of these men stressed that they could take no chances because such a large part of their firm's capital is tied up in making any one machine. The other sales manager had been influenced by a lawsuit against one of his competitors for over a half million dollars. The suit was brought by a customer when the competitor had been unable to deliver a machine and put it in operation on time. The sales manager interviewed said his firm could not guarantee that its machines would work perfectly by a specified time because they are designed to fit the customer's requirements, which may present difficult engineering problems. As a result, contracts are carefully negotiated.

A large manufacturer of packaging materials audited its records to determine how often it had failed to agree on terms and conditions with its customers or had failed to create legally binding contracts. Such failures cause a risk of loss to this firm since the packaging is printed with the customer's design and cannot be salvaged once this is done. The orders for five days in four different years were reviewed. The percentages of orders where no agreement on terms and conditions was reached or no contract was formed were as follows in Table 25–2.

TABLE 25-2

Year	Per Cent
1953	75.0
1954	69.4
1955	71.5
1956	59.5

It is likely that businessmen pay more attention to describing the performances in an exchange than to planning for contingencies or defective performances or to obtaining legal enforceability of their contracts. Even when a purchase order and acknowledgment have conflicting provisions printed on the back, almost always the buyer and seller will be in agreement on what is to be sold and how much is to be paid for it. The lawyers who said businessmen often commit their firms to significant exchanges too casually, stated that the performances would be defined in the brief letter or telephone call; the lawyers objected that nothing else would be covered. Moreover, it is likely that businessmen are least concerned about planning their transactions so that they are legally enforceable contracts.[3] For example, in Wisconsin, requirements contracts—contracts to supply a firm's requirements of an item rather than a definite quantity—probably are not legally enforceable. Seven persons interviewed reported that their firms regularly used requirements contracts in dealings in Wisconsin. None thought that the lack of legal sanction made any difference. Three of these people were house counsel who knew the Wisconsin law before being interviewed. Another example of a lack of desire for legal sanctions is found in the relationship between automobile manufacturers and their suppliers of parts. The manufacturers draft a carefully planned agreement, but one which is so designed that the supplier will have only minimal, if any, legal rights against the manufacturers. The standard contract used by manufacturers of paper to sell to magazine publishers has a pricing clause which is probably sufficiently vague to make the contract legally unenforceable. The house counsel of one of the largest paper producers said that everyone in the industry is aware of this because of a leading New York case concerning the contract, but that no one cares. Finally, it seems likely that planning for contingencies and defective performances are in-between cases: more likely to occur than planning for a legal sanction, but less likely than a description of performance.

Thus one can conclude that (1) many business exchanges reflect a high degree of planning about the four categories—description, contingencies, defective performances, and legal sanction—but (2) many, if not most, exchanges reflect no planning, or only a minimal amount of it, especially concerning legal sanctions and the effect of defective performances. As a result, the opportunity for good faith disputes during the life of the exchange relationship often is present.

The Adjustment of Exchange Relationships and the Settling of Disputes. While a significant amount of creating business exchanges is done on a fairly non-contractual basis, the creation of exchanges usually is far more contractual than the adjustment of such relationships and the settlement of disputes. Exchanges are adjusted when the obligations of one or both parties are modified by agreement during the life of the relationship. For example, the buyer may be allowed to cancel all or part of the goods he has ordered because he no longer needs them; the seller may be paid more than the contract price by the buyer because of unusual changed circumstances. Dispute settlement involves determining whether or not a party has performed as agreed and, if he has not, doing something about it. For example, a court may have to interpret the meaning of a contract, determine what the alleged defaulting party has done, and determine what, if any, remedy the aggrieved party is entitled to. Or one party may assert that the other is in default, refuse to proceed with performing the contract, and refuse to deal ever again with the alleged defaulter. If the alleged defaulter, who in fact may not be in default, takes no action, the dispute is then "settled."

Business exchanges in non-speculative areas are usually adjusted without dispute. Under the law of contracts, if B orders 1,000 widgets from S at $1.00 each, B must take all 1,000 widgets or be in breach of contract and liable to pay S his expenses up to the time of the breach plus his lost anticipated profit. Yet all ten of the purchasing agents asked about cancellation of orders once placed indicated that they expected to be able to cancel orders freely subject to only an obligation to pay for the seller's major expenses such as scrapped steel.[4] All 17 sales personnel asked reported that they often had to accept cancellation. One said, "You can't ask a man to eat paper (the firm's product) when he has no use for it." A lawyer with many large industrial clients said,

Often businessmen do not feel they have "a contract"; rather they have "an order." They speak of "canceling the order" rather than "breaching our contract." When I began practice I referred to order cancellations as breaches of contract, but my clients objected since they do not think of cancellation as wrong. Most clients, in heavy industry at least, believe that there is a right to cancel as part of the buyer-seller relationship. There is a widespread attitude that one can back out of any deal within some very vague limits. Lawyers are often surprised by this attitude.

Disputes are frequently settled without reference to the contract or potential or actual legal sanctions. There is a hesitancy to speak of legal rights or to threaten to sue in these negotiations. Even where the parties have a detailed and carefully planned agreement that indicates what is to happen if, say, the seller fails to deliver on time, often they will never refer to the agreement but will negotiate a solution when the problem arises apparently as if there had never been any original contract. One purchasing agent expressed a common business attitude when he said,

If something comes up, you get the other man on the telephone and deal with the problem. You don't read legalistic contract clauses at each other if you ever want to do business again. One doesn't run to lawyers if he wants to stay in business because one must behave decently.

Or as one businessman put it, "You can settle any dispute if you keep the lawyers and accountants out of it. They just do not understand the give-and-take needed in business." All of the house counsel interviewed indicated that they are called into the dispute settlement process only after the businessmen have failed to settle matters in their own way. Two indicated that after being called in house counsel at first will only advise the purchasing agent, sales manager, or other official involved; not even the house counsel's letterhead is used on communications with the other side until all hope for a peaceful resolution is gone.

Lawsuits for breach of contract appear to be rare. Only 5 of the 12 purchasing agents had ever been involved in even a negotiation concerning a contract dispute where both sides were represented by lawyers; only 2 of 10 sales managers had ever gone this far. None had been involved in a case that went through trial. A law firm with more than 40 lawyers and a large commercial practice handles in a year only about six trials concerned with contract problems. Less than 10 per cent of the time of this office is devoted to any type of work related to contracts disputes. Corporations big enough to do business in more than one state tend to sue and be sued in the federal courts. Yet only 2,779 out of 58,293 civil actions filed in the United States District Courts in fiscal year 1961 involved private contracts.[5] During the same period only 3,447 of the 61,138 civil cases filed in the principal trial courts of New York State involved private contracts.[6] The same picture emerges from a review of appellate cases.[7] Mentschikoff has suggested that commercial cases are not brought to the courts either in periods of business prosperity (because buyers unjustifiably reject goods only when prices drop and they can get similar goods elsewhere at less than the contract price) or in periods of deep depression (because people are unable to come to court or have insufficient assets to satisfy any judgment that might be obtained). Apparently, she adds, it is necessary to have "a kind of middle-sized depression" to bring large numbers of commercial cases to the courts. However, there is little evidence that in even "a kind of middle-sized depression" today's businessmen would use the courts to settle disputes.[8]

At times relatively contractual methods are used to make adjustments in ongoing transactions and to settle disputes. Demands of one side that are deemed unreasonable by the other occasionally are blocked by reference to the terms of the agreement between the parties. The legal position of the parties can influence negotiations even though legal rights or litigation are never mentioned in their discussions; it makes a difference if one is demanding what both concede to be a right or begging for a favor. Now and then a firm may threaten to turn matters over to its attorneys, threaten to sue, commence a suit, or even litigate and carry an appeal to the highest court that will hear the matter. Thus, legal sanctions, while not an everyday affair, are not unknown in business.

One can conclude that while detailed planning and legal sanctions play a significant role in some exchanges between businesses, in many business exchanges their role is small.

Tentative Explanations

Two questions need to be answered: (A) How can business successfully operate exchange relationships with relatively so little attention to detailed planning or to legal sanctions, and (B) Why does business ever use contract in light of its success without it?

Why are relatively non-contractual practices so common? In most situations contract is not needed.[9] Often its functions are served by other devices. Most problems are avoided without resort to detailed planning or legal sanctions because usually there is little room for honest misunderstandings or good faith differences of opinion about the nature and quality of a seller's performance. Although the parties fail to cover all foreseeable contingencies, they will exercise care to see that both understand the primary obligation on each side. Either products are standardized with an accepted description, or specifications are written calling for production to certain tolerances or results. Those who write and read specifications are experienced professionals who will know the customs of their industry and those of the industries with which they deal. Consequently, these customs can fill gaps in the express agreements of the parties. Finally, most products can be tested to see if they are what was ordered; typically in manufacturing industry we are not dealing with questions of taste or judgment where people can differ in good faith.

When defaults occur they are not likely to be disastrous because of techniques of risk avoidance or risk spreading. One can deal with firms of good reputation or he may be able to get some form of security to guarantee performance. One can insure against many breaches of contract where the risks justify the costs. Sellers set up reserves for bad debts on their books and can sell some of their accounts receivable. Buyers can place orders with two or more suppliers of the same item so that a default by one will not stop the buyer's assembly lines.

Moreover, contract and contract law are often thought unnecessary because there are many effective non-legal sanctions. Two norms are widely accepted. (1) Commitments are to be honored in almost all situations; one does not welsh on a deal. (2) One ought to produce a good product and stand behind it. Then, too, business units are organized to perform commitments, and internal sanctions will induce performance. For example, sales personnel must face angry customers when there has been a late or defective performance. The salesmen do not enjoy this and will put pressure on the production personnel responsible for the default. If the production personnel default too often, they will be fired. At all levels of the two business units personal relationships across the boundaries of the two organizations exert pressures for conformity to expectations. Salesmen often know purchasing agents well. The same two individuals occupying these roles may have dealt with each other from five to twenty-five years. Each has something to give the other. Salesmen have gossip about competitors, shortages, and price increases to give purchasing agents who treat them well. Salesmen take purchasing agents to dinner, and they give purchasing agents Christmas gifts hoping to improve the chances of making a sale. The buyer's engineering staff may work with the seller's engineering staff to solve problems jointly. The seller's engineers may render great assistance, and the buyer's engineers may desire to return the favor by drafting specifications that only the seller can meet. The top executives of the two firms may know each other. They may sit together on government or trade committees. They may know each other socially and even belong to the same country club. The inter-relationships may be more formal. Sellers may hold stock in corporations that are important customers; buyers may hold stock in important suppliers. Both buyer and seller may share common directors on their boards. They may share a common financial institution that has financed both units.

The final type of non-legal sanction is the most obvious. Both business units involved in the exchange desire to continue successfully in business and will avoid conduct that might interfere with attaining this goal. One is concerned with both the reaction of the other party in the particular exchange and with his own general business reputation. Obviously, the buyer gains sanctions insofar as the seller wants the particular exchange to be completed. Buyers can withhold part or all of their payments until sellers have performed to their satisfaction. If a seller has a great deal of money tied up in his performance which he must recover quickly, he will go a long way to please the buyer in order to be paid. Moreover, buyers who are dissatisfied may cancel and cause sellers to lose the cost of what they have done up to cancellation. Furthermore, sellers hope for repeat for orders, and one gets few of these from unhappy customers. Some industrial buyers go so far as to formalize this sanction by issuing "report cards" rating the performance of each supplier. The supplier rating goes to the top management of the seller organization, and these men can apply internal sanctions to salesmen, production supervisors, or product designers if there are too many "D's" or "F's" on the report card.

While it is generally assumed that the customer is always right, the seller may have some counterbalancing sanctions against the buyer. The seller may have obtained a large down payment from the buyer that he will want to protect. The seller may have an exclusive process that the buyer needs. The seller may be one of the few firms that has the skill to make the item to the tolerances set by the buyer's engineers and within the time available. There are costs and delays involved in turning from a supplier one has dealt with in the past to a new supplier. Then, too, market conditions can change so that a buyer is faced with shortages of critical items. The most extreme example is the post World War II gray market conditions when sellers were rationing goods rather than selling them. Buyers must build up some reserve of good will with suppliers if they face the risk of such shortage and desire good treatment when they occur. Finally, there is reciprocity in buying and selling. A buyer cannot push a supplier too far if that supplier also buys significant quantities of the product made by the buyer.

Not only do the particular business units in a given exchange want to deal with each other again, they also want to deal with other business units in the future. And the way one behaves in a particular transaction, or a series of transactions, will color his general business reputation. Blacklisting can be formal or informal. Buyers who fail to pay their bills on time risk a bad report in credit rating services such as Dun and Bradstreet. Sellers who do not satisfy their customers become the subject of discussion in the gossip exchanged by purchasing agents and salesmen, at meetings of purchasing agents' associations and trade associations, or even at country clubs or social gatherings where members of top management meet. The American male's habit of debating the merits of new cars carries over to industrial items. Obviously, a poor reputation does not help a firm make sales and may force it to offer great price discounts or added services to remain in business. Furthermore, the habits of unusually demanding buyers become known, and they tend to get no more than they can coerce out of suppliers who choose to deal with them. Thus often contract is not needed as there are alternatives.

Not only are contract and contract law not needed in many situations, their use may have, or may be thought to have, undesirable consequences. Detailed negotiated contracts can get in the way of creating good exchange relationships between business units. If one side insists on a detailed plan, there will be delay while letters are exchanged as the parties try to agree on what should happen if a remote and unlikely contingency occurs. In some cases they may not be able to agree at all on such matters and as a result a sale may be lost to the seller and the buyer may have to search elsewhere for an acceptable supplier. Many businessmen would react by thinking that had no one raised the series of remote and unlikely contingencies all this wasted effort could have been avoided.

Even where agreement can be reached at the negotiation stage, carefully planned arrangements may create undesirable exchange relationships between business units. Some businessmen object that in such a carefully worked out relationship one gets performance only to the letter of the contract. Such planning indicates a lack of trust and blunts the demands of friendship, turning a cooperative venture into an antagonistic horse trade. Yet the greater danger perceived by some businessmen is that one would have to perform his side of the bargain to its letter and thus lose what is called "flexibility." Businessmen may welcome a measure of vagueness in the obligations they assume so that they may negotiate matters in light of the actual circumstances.

Adjustment of exchange relationships and dispute settlement by litigation or the threat of it also has many costs. The gain anticipated from using this form of coercion often fails to outweigh these costs, which are both monetary and non-monetary. Threatening to turn matters over to an attorney may cost no more money than postage or a telephone call; yet few are so skilled in making such a threat that it will not cost some deterioration of the relationship between the firms. One businessman said that customers had better not rely on legal rights or threaten to bring a breach of contract lawsuit against him since he "would not be treated like a criminal" and would fight back with every means available. Clearly actual litigation is even more costly than making threats. Lawyers demand substantial fees from larger business units. A firm's executives often will have to be transported and maintained in another city during the proceedings if, as often is the case, the trial must be held away from the home office. Top management does not travel by Greyhound and stay at the Y.M.C.A. Moreover, there will be the cost of diverting top management, engineers, and others in the organization from their normal activities. The firm may lose many days' work from several key people. The non-monetary costs may be large too. A breach of contract lawsuit may settle a particular dispute, but such an action often results in a "divorce" ending the "marriage" between the two businesses, since a contract action is likely to carry charges with at least overtones of bad faith. Many executives, moreover, dislike the prospect of being cross-examined in public. Some executives may dislike losing control of a situation by turning the decision-making power over to lawyers. Finally, the law of contract damages may not provide an adequate remedy even if the firm wins the suit; one may get vindication but not much money.

Why Do Relatively Contractual Practices Ever Exist? Although contract is not needed and actually may have negative consequences, businessmen do make some carefully planned contracts, negotiate settlements influenced by their legal rights, and commence and defend some breach of contract lawsuits or arbitration proceedings. In view of the findings and explanation presented to this point, one may ask why. Exchanges are carefully planned when it is thought that planning and a potential legal sanction will have more advantages than disadvantages. Such a judgment may be reached when contract planning serves the internal needs of an organization involved in a business exchange. For example, a fairly detailed contract can serve as a communication device within a large corporation. While the corporation's sales manager and house counsel may work out all the provisions with the customer, its production manager will have to make the product. He must be told what to do and how to handle at least the most obvious contingencies. Moreover, the sales manager may want to remove certain issues from future negotiation by his subordinates. If he puts the matter in the written contract, he may be able to keep his salesmen from making concessions to the customer without first consulting the sales manager. Then the sales manager may be aided in his battles with his firm's financial or engineering departments if the contract calls for certain practices which the sales manager advocates but which the other departments resist. Now the corporation is obligated to a customer to do what the sales manager wants to do; how can the financial or engineering departments insist on anything else?

Also one tends to find a judgment that the gains of contract outweigh the costs where there is a likelihood that significant problems will arise.[10] One factor leading to this conclusion is complexity of the agreed performance over a long period. Another factor is whether or not the degree of injury in case of default is thought to be potentially great. This factor cuts two ways. First, a buyer may want to commit a seller to a detailed and legally binding contract, where the consequences of a default by the seller would seriously injure the buyer. For example, the airlines are subject to lawsuits from the survivors of passengers and to great adverse publicity as a result of crashes. One would expect the airlines to bargain for carefully defined and legally enforceable obligations on the part of the airframe manufacturers when they purchase aircraft. Second, a seller may want to limit his liability for a buyer's damages by a provision in their contract. For example, a manufacturer of air conditioning may deal with motels in the South and Southwest. If this equipment fails in the hot summer months, a motel may lose a great deal of business. The manufacturer may wish to avoid any liability for this type of injury to his customers and may want a contract with a clear disclaimer clause.

Similarly, one uses or threatens to use legal sanctions to settle disputes when other devices will not work and when the gains are thought to outweigh the costs. For example, perhaps the most common type of business contracts case fought all the way through to the appellate courts today is as action for an alleged wrongful termination of a dealer's franchise by a manufacturer. Since the franchise has been terminated, factors such as personal relationships and the desire for future business will have little effect; the cancellation of the franchise indicates they have already failed to maintain the relationship. Nor will a complaining dealer worry about creating a hostile relationship between himself and the manufacturer. Often the dealer has suffered a great financial loss both as to his investment in building and equipment and as to his anticipated future profits. A canceled automobile dealer's lease on his showroom and shop will continue to run, and his tools for servicing, say, Plymouths cannot be used to service other makes of cars. Moreover, he will have no more new Plymouths to sell. Today there is some chance of winning a lawsuit for terminating a franchise in bad faith in many states and in the federal courts. Thus, often the dealer chooses to risk the cost of a lawyer's fee because of the chance that he may recover some compensation for his losses.

An "irrational" factor may exert some influence on the decision to use legal sanctions. The man who controls a firm may feel that he or his organization has been made to appear foolish or has been the victim of fraud or bad faith. The lawsuit may be seen as a vehicle "to get even" although the potential gains, as viewed by an objective observer, are outweighed by the potential costs.

The decision whether or not to use contract—whether the gain exceeds the costs—will be made by the person within the business unit with the power to make it, and it tends to make a difference who he is. People in a sales department oppose contract. Contractual negotiations are just one more hurdle in the way of a sale. Holding a customer to the letter of a contract is bad for "customer relations." Suing a customer who is not bankrupt and might order again is poor strategy. Purchasing agents and their buyers are less hostile to contracts but regard attention devoted to such matters as a waste of time. In contrast, the financial control department—the treasurer, controller, or auditor—leans toward more contractual dealings. Contract is viewed by these people as an organizing tool to control operations in a large organization. It tends to define precisely and to minimize the risks to which the firm is exposed. Outside lawyers—those with many clients—may share this enthusiasm for a more contractual method of dealing. These lawyers are concerned with preventive law: avoiding any possible legal difficulty. They see many unstable and unsuccessful exchange transactions, and so they are aware of, and perhaps overly concerned with, all of the things that can go wrong. Moreover, their job of settling disputes with legal sanctions is much easier if their client has not been overly casual about transaction planning. The inside lawyer, or house counsel, is harder to classify. He is likely to have some sympathy with a more contractual method of dealing. He shares the outside lawyer's "craft urge" to see exchange transactions neat and tidy from a legal standpoint. Since he is more concerned with avoiding and settling disputes than selling goods, he is likely to be less willing to rely on a man's word as the sole sanction than is a salesman. Yet the house counsel is more a part of the organization and more aware of its goals and subject to its internal sanctions. If the potential risks are not too great, he may hesitate to suggest a more contractual procedure to the sales department. He must sell his services to the operating departments, and he must hoard what power he has, expending it on only what he sees as significant issues.

The power to decide that a more contractual method of creating relationships and settling disputes shall be used will be held by different people at different times in different organizations. In most firms the sales department and the purchasing department have a great deal of power to resist contractual procedures or to ignore them if they are formally adopted and to handle disputes their own way. Yet in larger organizations the treasurer and the controller have increasing power to demand both systems and compliance. Occasionally, the house counsel must arbitrate the conflicting positions of these departments; in giving "legal advice" he may make the business judgment necessary regarding the use of contract. At times he may ask for an opinion from an outside law firm to reinforce his own position with the outside firm's prestige.

Obviously, there are other significant variables that influence the degree to which contract is used. One is the relative bargaining power or skill of the two business units. Even if the controller of a small supplier succeeds within the firm and creates a contractual system of dealing, there will be no contract if the firm's large customer prefers not to be bound to anything. Firms that supply General Motors deal as General Motors wants to do business, for the most part. Yet bargaining power is not size or share of the market alone. Even a General Motors may need a particular supplier, at least temporarily. Furthermore, bargaining power may shift as an exchange relationship is first created and then continues. Even a giant firm can find itself bound to a small supplier once production of an essential item begins for there may not be time to turn to another supplier. Also, all of the factors discussed in this essay can be viewed as components of bargaining power. For example, the personal relationship between the presidents of the buyer and the seller firms may give a sales manager great power over a purchasing agent who has been instructed to give the seller "every consideration." Another variable relevant to the use of contract is the influence of third parties. The federal government or a lender of money may insist that a contract be made in a particular transaction or may influence the decision to assert one's legal rights under a contract.

Contract, then, often plays an important role in business, but other factors are significant. To understand the functions of contract the whole system of conducting exchanges must be explored fully. More types of business communities must be studied, contract litigation must be analyzed to see why the non-legal sanctions fail to prevent the use of legal sanctions and all of the variables suggested in this essay must be classified more systematically.

NOTES

1. The reasons for this limitation are that (a) these transactions are important from an economic standpoint, (b) they are frequently said in theoretical discussions to represent a high degree of rational planning, and (c) manufacturing personnel are sufficiently public relations minded to cooperate with a law professor who wants to ask a seemingly endless number of questions. Future research will deal with the building construction industry and other areas.

2. However, the cases have not been selected because they did use contract. There is as much interest in, and effort to obtain, cases of non-use as of use of contract. Thus, one variety of bias has been minimized.

3. Compare the findings of an empirical study of Connecticut business practices in Comment, "The Statute of Frauds and the Business Community: A Re-Appraisal in Light of Prevailing Practices," *Yale Law Journal*, LXVI (1957), 1038–1071.

4. See the case studies on cancellation of contracts in *Harvard Business Review*, II (1923–1924), 238–240, 367–370, 496–502.

5. *Annual Report of the Director of the Administrative Office of the United States Courts* (1961), p. 238.

6. State of New York, The Judicial Conference, Sixth Annual Report (1961), pp. 209–211.

7. My colleague Lawrence M. Friedman has studied the work of the Supreme Court of Wisconsin in contracts cases. He has found that contracts cases reaching that court tend to involve economically marginal business and family economic disputes rather than important commercial transactions. This has been the situation since about the turn of the century. Only during the Civil War period did the court deal with significant numbers of important contracts cases, but this happened against the background of a much simpler and different economic system.

8. New York Law Revision Commission, *Hearings on the Uniform Code Commercial Code*, II (1954), 1391.

9. The explanation that follows emphasizes a considered choice not to plan in detail for all contingencies. However, at times it is clear that businessmen fail to plan because of a lack of sophistication; they simply do not appreciate the risk they are running or they merely follow patterns established in their firm years ago without reexamining these practices in light of current conditions.

10. Even where there is little chance that problems will arise, some businessmen insist that their lawyer review or draft an agreement as a delaying tactic. This gives the businessman time to think about making a commitment if he has doubts about the matter or to look elsewhere for a better deal while still keeping the particular negotiations alive.

SECTION SIX *Social Influences on Legislation*

26

The Relation Between Law
and Public Opinion

A. V. DICEY

. . . We are all of us so accustomed to endow public opinion with a mysterious or almost supernatural power, that we neglect to examine what it is that we mean by public opinion, to measure the true limits of its authority, and to ascertain the mode of its operation. Surprise may indeed be felt, not at the statement that law depends upon opinion, but at this assertion being limited to England, and to England during the last century. The limitation, however, is intentional, and admits of full justification.

True indeed it is that the existence and the alteration of human institutions must, in a sense, always and everywhere depend upon the beliefs or feelings, or, in other words, upon the opinion of the society in which such institutions flourish.

Hume writes:

> As force is always on the side of the governed, the governors have nothing to support them but opinion. It is, therefore, on opinion only that government is founded; and this maxim extends to the most despotic and most military governments, as well as to the most free and most popular. The Soldan of Egypt, or the Emperor of Rome, might drive his harmless subjects, like brute beasts, against their sentiments and inclination; but he must, at least, have led his mamelukes, or praetorian bands, like men, by their opinion.[1]

And so true is this observation that the authority even of a Southern planter over his slaves rested at bottom upon the opinion of the Negroes whom he at his pleasure flogged or killed. Their combined physical force exceeded the planter's own personal strength, and the strength of the few whites who might be expected to stand by him. The blacks obeyed the slave-owner from the opinion, whether well or ill founded, that in the long run they would in a contest with their masters have the worst of the fight; and even more from that habit of submission which, though enforced by the occasional punishment of rebels, was grounded upon a number of complicated sentiments, such, for example, as admiration for superior ability and courage, or gratitude for kindness, which cannot by any fair analysis be reduced to a mere form of fear, but

From *Lectures on the Relation Between Law and Public Opinion in England During the Nineteenth Century* (London: Macmillan and Co., 1905), pp. 1–16.

constitute a kind of prevalent moral atmosphere. The whites, in short, ruled in virtue of the opinion, entertained by their slaves no less than by themselves, that the slave-owners possessed qualities which gave them the might, and even the right, to be masters. With the rightness or wrongness of this conviction we are not here in any way concerned. Its existence is adduced only as a proof that, even in the most extreme case conceivable, Hume's doctrine holds good, and the opinion of the governed is the real foundation of all government.

But, though obedience to law must of necessity be enforced by opinion of some sort, and Hume's paradox thus turns out to be a truism, this statement does not involve the admission that the law of every country is itself the result of what we mean by "public opinion." This term, when used in reference to legislation, is merely a short way of describing the belief or conviction prevalent in a given society that particular laws are beneficial, and therefore ought to be maintained, or that they are harmful, and therefore ought to be modified or repealed. And the assertion that public opinion governs legislation in a particular country means that laws are there maintained or repealed in accordance with the opinion or wishes of its inhabitants. Now this assertion, though it is, if properly understood, true with regard to England at the present day, is clearly not true of all countries, at all times, and indeed has not always been true even of England.

For, in the first place, there exist many communities in which public opinion —if by that term be meant speculative views held by the mass of the people as to the alteration or improvement of their institutions—can hardly be said to have any existence. The members of such societies are influenced by habits rather than by thoughts. Their mode of life is determined by customary rules, which may indeed have originated in the necessities of a given social condition, or even in speculative doctrines entertained by ancient lawgivers, but which, whatever be their origin, assuredly owe their continuance to use and wont. It is, in truth, only under the peculiar conditions of an advanced civilization that opinion dictates legislative change. In many Eastern countries, opinion—which is better described as traditional or instinctive feeling—has for ages been, in general, hostile to change and favorable to the maintenance of inherited habits. There, as in the West, opinion, in a very wide sense of that word, rules; but such aversion to change as for ages keeps a society within the limits of traditional action, is a very different thing from the public opinion which in the England of the nineteenth and twentieth centuries has demanded constant improvements in the law of the land.

It is possible, in the second place, to point to realms where laws and institutions have been altered or revolutionized in deference to opinion, but where the beliefs which have guided legislative reform have not been what we mean in England by "public" opinion. They have been, not ideas entertained by the inhabitants of a country, or by the greater part thereof, but convictions held by a small number of men, or even by a single individual who happened to be placed in a position of commanding authority. We must, indeed, remember that no ruler, however powerful, can stand completely alone, and that the despots who have caused or guided revolutions have been influenced by the opinion, if not of their own country, yet of their generation. But it may be asserted with substantial truth that Peter the Great laid the foundation of Russian power without much deference to the opinion of Russia, and that modern Prussia was created by Frederick the Great, who certainly drew his ideas of good government from other than Prussian sources. It was not, then, the public opinion of the Russian people or the public opinion of the Prussians, but the convictions of a single man which in each case molded the laws and institutions of a powerful country. At this moment legislation in British India is the work of a body of English specialists who follow to a great extent the current of English opinion. They are, indeed, it is to be hoped, guided far more by their own experience and by their practical knowledge of India, than by English sentiment; but Anglo-Indian officials, though they may not always obey the transitory feelings of the English public, certainly do not represent Indian public opinion.

In the third place, the law of a country may fail, for a time, to represent public opinion owing to the lack of any legislative organ which adequately responds to the sentiment of the age. A portion, at least, of that accumulation of abuses, which was the cause or the occasion of the French Revolution, may fairly be ascribed to the want of any legislative body possessing both the power and the will to carry out reforms which had long been demanded by the intelligence of the French nation. Some critics may, it is true, deny that a legislative organ was lacking; a French king held in his hands under the *ancien régime* an authority nearly approaching to sovereign power, and an enlightened despot might, it has been suggested, have conferred upon the country all the benefits promised by the Revolution. But the power of the French Crown was particularly more limited than modern critics always perceive, while the circumstances no less than the character of Louis XV and Louis XVI disqualified these monarchs for performing the part of enlightened despots. The "Parliaments," again, which assuredly possessed some legislative power, might, it has been argued, have reformed the laws and institutions of the country. But the Parliaments were after all courts, not legislatures, and represented the prejudices of lawyers, not the aspirations of reformers; Frenchmen, zealous for the removal of abuses, looked, as a matter of fact, with more hope to the action of the king than to the legislation of Parliaments which represented the antiquated conservatism of a past age. The want, then, of a legislative organ was in France a check upon the influence of public opinion. Nor can it be denied that even in England defective legislative machinery has at times lessened the immediate influence of opinion. The chief cause, no doubt, of the arrest of almost every kind of reform during the latest years of the eighteenth and the earlier part of the nineteenth century, was a state of feeling so hostile to revolution that it forbade the most salutary innovations. But "legislative stagnation," as it has been termed, lasted in England for at least 10 or 20 years beyond the date when it ought naturally to have come to an end; and it can hardly be disputed that this delay in the improvement of English institutions was due in part to the defects of the unreformed Parliament, that is, to the non-existence of a satisfactory legislative organ.

The close and immediate connection then, which in modern England exists between public opinion and legislation, is a very peculiar and noteworthy fact, to which we cannot easily find a parallel. Nowhere have changes in popular convictions or wishes found anything like such rapid and immediate expression in alterations of the law as they have in Great Britain during the nineteenth century, and more especially during the last half thereof. France is the land of revolution, England is renowned for conservatism, but a glance at the legal history of each country suggests the existence of some error in the popular contrast between French mutability and English unchangeableness. In spite of revolutions at Paris, the fundamental provisions of the Code Napoléon have stood to a great extent unaltered since its publication in 1804, and before 1900 the Code had become invested with a sort of legal sanctity which secured it against sudden and sweeping change. In 1804 George the Third was on the throne, and English opinion was then set dead against every legal or political change, yet there is now hardly a part of the English statute book which between 1804 and the present day has not been changed in form or in substance; and the alterations enacted by Parliament have been equalled or exceeded by innovations due to the judge-made laws of the courts. The United States of America, again, have been under the government of a pure democracy, and in no country is the expression of opinion more free; but the whole history of the United States shows that federal legislation, at any rate, does not lend itself easily to large and sudden changes, nor do alterations introduced by state legislation appear to have been on the whole either fundamental or rapid.

This condition of legislative quiescence, it may be objected, is, in the case both of France and of the United States, due to a condition of opinion hostile to legal innovations, and therefore in no way shows that public opinion cannot as easily effect alterations in the law of the land as it can in England, and this suggestion contains a certain amount of truth. The occasional outbreak of revolution has among Frenchmen been unfavorable to that habit of constantly and gradually amending the law, which has become natural to Englishmen, while admiration for American institutions and a certain general satisfaction with things as they are have in the United States created a remarkable kind of legal conservatism. The condition of opinion is, however, not the only reason for the existence of legislative quiescence both in the greatest of European and in the greatest of American republics. In neither country are there wanting critics of the national institutions, but in neither has effective criticism usually led so easily to legislation as in England. The difficulty imposed by many French constitutions on meeting with rapidity the requirements of public opinion has not only been an excuse for revolutionary violence, but has also hindered the gradual amendment of the law of France; nor is it irrelevant to note that the constitution of the Third Republic renders the Parliament a body that responds more easily to the immediate sentiment of the moment than any legislature that has existed in France since the National Assembly of 1789, and that simultaneously with this change, a tendency toward the introduction of amendments into the law of the country has begun to make itself apparent. In the United States the Federal Constitution limits the power both of Congress and of the state legislatures; and the hands of any state legislature, be it noted, are tied by the articles, not only of the Federal Constitution, but also of the state constitution, while throughout the United States there exists a tendency to restrict more and more closely the authority of the state representative assemblies. The constitutionalism, then, of the United States, no less than of France, has told against the promotion of that constant legislative activity that is a characteristic feature of modern English life. From whatever point of view, in short, the matter be regarded, it becomes apparent that during the last 75 years or more public opinion has exercised in England a direct and immediate control over legislation that it does not even now exert in most other civilized countries.

There are, then, to be found three different reasons why we cannot assert of all countries, or of any country at all times, that laws are there the result of public opinion. No "opinion," in the proper sense of that word, with regard to the change of the law may exist; the opinion which does direct the development of the law may not be "public opinion"; and there may be lacking any legislative organ adapted for carrying out the changes of the law demanded by public opinion.

In England, however, the beliefs or sentiments that, during the nineteenth century, have governed the development of the law have in strictness been public opinion, for they have been the wishes and ideas as to legislation held by the people of England, or, to speak with more precision, by the majority of those citizens who have at a given moment taken an effective part in public life.

And here the obvious conclusion suggests itself that the public opinion that governs a country is the opinion of the sovereign, whether the sovereign be a monarch, an aristocracy, or the mass of the people.

This conclusion, however, though roughly true, cannot be accepted without considerable reservation. The sovereign power may hold that a certain kind of legislation is in itself expedient, but may at the same time be unwilling, or even unable, to carry this conviction into effect, and this from the dread of offending the feelings of subjects who, though they in general take no active share in public affairs, may raise an insuperable opposition to laws that disturb their habits or shock their moral sentiment; it is well indeed, thus early in these lectures, to note that the public opinion that finds expression in legislation is a very complex phenomenon, and often takes the form of a compromise resulting from a conflict between the ideas of the government and the feelings or habits of the governed. This holds good in all countries, whatever be their form of government, but is more manifest than elsewhere in a country such as England, where the legislation enacted by Parliament constantly bears traces of the compromise arrived at between enlightenment and prejudice. The failure of Parliament during the eighteenth century to introduce reasonable reforms, for instance, was due far less to the prejudices of members of Parliament, or even of the electorate, than to the deference that statesmen instinctively, and on the whole wisely, paid to the dullness or stupidity of Englishmen, many of whom had no votes, and were certainly not able to dictate by constitutional means to Parliament. Walpole and his Whig associates were utterly free from bigotry, yet Walpole would never consent to relieve Dissenters from the Test Act, though Dissenters were his most strenuous supporters. The Act facilitating the naturalization of Jews was, in obedience to popular clamor, repealed in the next session after it had been passed. Even the amendment of the calendar was found to be a matter of great difficulty; the ignorance of the electors was imposed upon by the phrase that they had been robbed of 11 days. The moderate measure of 1778 for the mitigation of the penal laws against Roman Catholics gave rise in 1780 to an outbreak of revolutionary violence; and the Lord George Gordon Riots explain, if they do not justify, the long delay of Catholic Emancipation. But the Roman Catholic Relief Act of 1829 is itself the most striking monument of legislative compromise. The measure was carried by reformers who desired the removal of all the political disabilities under which the Roman Catholics of the United Kingdom suffered, but it contains stringent provisions on the face of them intended to banish from the United Kingdom "every Jesuit and every member of any other religious order, community, or society of the Church of Rome bound by monastic or religious vows." [2] How does it happen that a law restoring to Roman Catholics the rights of citizenship contained penal laws against Jesuits and monks? The answer lies close at hand. The general scope of the Act represents the enlightenment of a governing class which, by favor of peculiar circumstances, carried through a scheme of religious toleration opposed to the prejudices of the people. Penal enactments threatening Jesuits and monks with a banishment, which have never in a single instance been put in force, are the monument of a concession made by parliamentary statesmanship to vulgar bigotry.[3]

The principle that the development of law depends upon opinion is, however, open to one objection.

Men legislate, it may be urged, not in accordance with their opinion as to what is a good law, but in accordance with their interest, and this, it may be added, is emphatically true of classes as contrasted with individuals, and therefore of a country like England, where classes exert a far more potent control over the making of laws than can any single person.

Now it must at once be granted that in matters of legislation men are guided in the main by their real or apparent interest. So true is this, that from the inspection of the laws of a country it is often possible to conjecture, and this without much hesitation, what is the class that holds, or has held, predominant power at a given time. No man could cast a glance at the laws and institutions of the Middle Ages without seeing that power then went with ownership of land. Wherever agriculturalists are predominant you will find laws favoring the cultivators of the soil, and if you discover laws passed for the special benefit of manufacturers or artisans, you may be certain that these classes, in some way or other, are or were of political weight. Who could look into the statute book of Jamaica or South Carolina without discovering that at one time the whites were despotic masters of the blacks? Who could contrast the English land law with the modern land law of France and fail to perceive that political authority has in England been in the hands of large landowners, and is in the France of today in the hands of small proprietors? The criminal law of the eighteenth century, and also many of its trade laws, bear witness to the growing influence of merchants. The free trade legislation of 1846 and the succeeding years tells us that political authority had come into the hands of manufacturers and traders. Nor would any man, even though he knew not the history of our Parliamentary Reform Acts, hesitate, from the gist of modern statutes, to infer that during the nineteenth century, first the middle classes, then the artisans of our towns, and lastly the country laborers, had obtained an increase of political power. The connection, however, between legislation and the supposed interests of the legislators is so obvious that the topic hardly requires illustration.

The answer to the objection under consideration is, however, easy to find.

"Though men," to use the words of Hume, "be much governed by interest, yet even interest itself, and all human affairs, are entirely governed by *opinion*." [4] Even, therefore, were we to assume that the persons who have power to make law are solely and wholly influenced by the desire to promote their own personal and selfish interests, yet their view of their interest and therefore their legislation must be determined by their opinion; and hence, where the public has influence, the development of the law must of necessity be governed by public opinion.

But though this answer is sufficient, there exists so much misunderstanding as to the connection between men's interests and their beliefs that it is well to pursue the matter a step further. The citizens of a civilized country, such as England, are for the most part not recklessly selfish in the ordinary sense of that word; they wish, no doubt, to promote their own interests, that is, to increase their own pleasures and to diminish their own discomforts, but they certainly do not intend to sacrifice, to their own private advantage or emolument, either the happiness of their neighbors or the welfare of the state. Individuals, indeed, and still more frequently classes, do constantly support laws or institutions that they deem beneficial to themselves, but that certainly are in fact injurious to the rest of the world. But the explanation of this conduct will be found, in nine cases out of ten, to be that men come easily to believe that arrangements agreeable to themselves are beneficial to others. A man's interest gives a bias to his judgment far oftener than it corrupts his heart. The heir of an English landowner is convinced that the law of primogeniture is a blessing to the country, but, if he looks too favorably upon a scheme for the devolution of property, which most Frenchmen consider patently unjust, his "sinister interest" (to use a favorite term of Bentham's) affects him with stupidity rather than with selfishness. He overestimates and keeps constantly before his mind the strength of the arguments in favor of, and underestimates, or never considers at all, the force of the arguments against, the principle of primogeniture which, whatever its evils, confers upon him a large estate and an influential position. English manufacturers were sincere believers in protection as long as they thought it beneficial to trade, and became equally sincere enthusiasts for freedom of trade from the moment they were convinced that free trade in corn would be favorable to commerce and would give additional weight to the manufacturing interest. Landlords and farmers who found their gain in keeping up the price of corn were in general perfectly honest protectionists, and were convinced that protection, by rendering the country self-supporting and extending the sphere of agriculture, was of the greatest benefit to the nation. At this day an artisan who holds that the welfare of working men, in which his own prosperity is included, is promoted by trade unionism, is honestly convinced that there can be little evil in practices which, though they certainly trench upon the personal freedom of individual workmen, enhance the authority of trade unions. It is well to insist upon the true relation between self-interest and belief, because ardent reformers, and notably Bentham and his disciples, have at times misunderstood it, and have used language that implied that every opponent of progress was, if not a fool, then a rogue, who deliberately preferred his own private advantage to the general benefit of mankind, whereas in reality he will be found in most cases to have been an honest man of average ability who has opposed a beneficial change not through exceptional selfishness, but through some intellectual delusion unconsciously created by the bias of a sinister interest. Take the extreme case of American slave-owners. It will not be denied that, at the outbreak of the War of Secession, there were to be found in the South many fervent enthusiasts for slavery (or rather for the social system of which it was a necessary part), just as there were to be found in the North a far greater number of ardent enthusiasts for abolition. Some Southerners at least did undoubtedly hold the *bona fide* belief that slavery was the source of benefit, not only to the planters, but to the slaves, and indirectly to the whole civilized world. Such Southern fanatics were wrong and the Abolitionists were right. The faith in slavery was a delusion; but a delusion, however largely the result of self-interest, is still an intellectual error, and a different thing from callous selfishness. It is at any rate an opinion. In the case, therefore, of Southerners who resisted the passing of any law for the abolition of slavery, as in all similar instances, we are justified in saying that it is at bottom opinion that controls legislation.

NOTES

1. Hume, *Essays,* I, Essay iv, 110.
2. See Roman Catholic Relief Act, 1829, § 28–36. These enactments (which do not apply to religious orders of women, *ibid.* 37) have never been enforced.
3. So the Ecclesiastical Titles Act, 1851, prohibiting the assumption of ecclesiastical titles, is a record of popular panic caused by Papal aggression, whilst the absolute non-enforcement, and the subsequent repeal of the Act in 1871, mark the tolerant spirit of Parliament.
4. Hume, *Essays,* I, Essay vii, 125.

27

What Is Public Opinion?

TOM HARRISON

The phrase "public opinion" has become vague and ambiguous through abuse and misuse. Yet it is a phrase that is of vital importance in any democracy. It is neither pedantic nor academic to attempt an exact analysis of "public opinion."

As a preliminary, it is convenient to distinguish several levels of opinion and behavior. So long as we continue to talk about public opinion as an all-embracing generality, we shall have difficulty in seeing vital problems and possible solutions. First there are the three main levels of behavior: Say—Do—Think. What a person says he will do is often quite different from what he does actually do. What he thinks he will do, or thinks he will say, may also be very different from what he does do or say. There is not space here to go into these distinctions. They are, however, of fundamental importance to the understanding of social and political processes. Their analysis and description in factual terms has not yet been attempted. Here, we are concerned mainly with what people say; within this we must distinguish:

> What a person says to a stranger.
> What a person says to an acquaintance.
> What a person says to a friend.
> What a person says to his wife.
> What a person says to himself.
> What a person says in his sleep.

It is at the level of wife, self, and dream that the most significant, as well as the most difficult, assessment of opinion can be made. This may be termed, provisionally, the level of private opinion. At the top level, the level of stranger (such as an interviewer), is public opinion.

. . .

There are always tensions and changes in private opinion that are likely to emerge quite suddenly into public opinion, and in so doing to take people by surprise. The people taken by surprise are especially likely to be those most interested in the subject, most deeply concerned in it, and therefore least able to appreciate the much duller, more confused, and obscure attitude of the private

From *The Political Quarterly,* XI (1940), 368, 371–373. Reprinted by permission of the publisher.

individuals composing their public. It is clear, for instance, that the majority of Conservative M.P.s are still perfectly happy about their hold on public opinion and their position in public prestige. They will probably get the shock of their lives when and if there is another General Election. Similarly, Mr. Chamberlain evidently thought, right up until the last moment of his resignation, that he had public opinion solidly behind him. And so, in the superficial sense of the word, he had. Public opinion was for him; private opinion against.

The only organization in this country that systematically takes opinion cross-sections, the British Institute of Public Opinion, had shown in its regular Chamberlain polls that his popularity increased after the outbreak of war, from a prewar average figure of under 60 per cent to nearly 70 per cent. But in the privacy of the darkened cinema, our own monthly surveys of audience response showed that applause for Mr. Chamberlain, when he appeared on newsreels, fell steadily from September onward. Similarly, the number of unfavorable comments on him in diaries (kept by our nationwide panel of voluntary informants) steadily increased. Private opinion was gathering against Mr. Chamberlain long before M.P.s were aware of it. Indeed, as we pointed out in a study of the Munich crisis, in private opinion feelings about him were far from approving long ago. To quote from our comment at that time:

> Every big paper, including the *Herald,* filled pages with praises of Chamberlain, and not to be outdone, the Premier gave the people a pat on the back, told how the deliberations of the four politicians at Munich had been influenced, apparently in some mystic way, "by the peoples of the different countries." During one whole week, no outsider reading an English newspaper could have guessed that an increasing proportion of the population were feeling once more increasingly bewildered, fearful, and ashamed. The readers themselves didn't guess it in many cases. That is a very important point. The fact that the papers hang back has a delaying effect on public opinion, because newspapers are so much looked to for social and talk sanction. People's sense of shame about Britain has to be backed up collectively, in order to be positive and recognized, just as much as smoking, football pools, etc. By representing pro-Chamberlain as the universally felt sentiment (when in fact even at its top point he never scored more than 54 per cent), individuals in their homes were temporarily made to feel that being anti-Chamberlain was old, antisocial, or Socialist.

So, *public* opinion polls showed Chamberlain with a big majority in favor. Even at the beginning of April, 1940, there was no external sign of a crack in his universe. Most M.P.s and newspapers continued to proclaim that the country was uniquely united behind the Prime Minister.

So, when there was a terrific explosion against Chamberlain, it all seemed very sudden. But it couldn't have occurred so quickly if there hadn't been a long-standing antagonism. Parliament was for a long time protected against that private opinion antagonism, and hardly realized the extent of its existence, because of the social sanction that delayed dislike for a Premier, the pressure toward "loyalty," respectability. It always tends to be the done thing (for the mass of people) in this country to be loyal to the Government (except on the socially sanctioned occasions for attack, elections); in war this becomes even more marked. Patriotism is at a premium. Party elections are abolished. Violent criticism is frowned upon. There is censorship and suppression. Everyone is supposed to be more than ever for king and country. There is thus, in the present organization of our society, a constant tendency favoring answers supporting the status quo of democratic institutions on major issues of home policy.

An example of the socially done-thing answer (as obtained by direct interviewing) was provided by the British Institute of Public Opinion and published in *News Chronicle*. The day before conscription was announced they completed a survey on attitudes to conscription, with the following results:

> 39 per cent in favor.
> 53 per cent against.
> 8 per cent doubtful.

The week after, with conscription introduced, they repeated a similar survey, with the following results:

> 58 per cent in favor.
> 38 per cent against.
> 4 per cent doubtful.

28

Public Opinion and the Legislative Process

FRANK V. CANTWELL

The role played by public opinion in a democracy, particularly as it affects the legislative process, has long been a subject for speculation by political scientists. The advent of controlled quota sampling permits of the study of this important relationship in measurable terms. The object of the present discussion is to trace the interaction of public opinion and the executive and legislative

From *The American Political Science Review*, LV (1946), 924–935. Reprinted by permission of the publisher.

branches of government as they have dealt with a single public question: reorganization of the Supreme Court, as presented to Congress for consideration by President Roosevelt on February 5, 1937. Enlargement of the Supreme Court from nine to 15 members was the most controversial feature of the general reorganization of the federal judiciary proposed by the President, aimed at speeding up the process of clearing cases through the federal court system, and making the system more "representative" of the wishes of the people.

The debate on enlargement of the Supreme Court provides a useful and interesting case study for several reasons. The case as a public issue has a definite beginning and end, ranging from the proposal of the judiciary reform bill by the President on February 5 to the death of Senator Joseph T. Robinson on July 14, 1937. As it was debated by public and legislators, the issue was a relatively clear-cut one, uncomplicated by side issues or utterly foreign events that might have influenced the course of either legislators or the public. Finally, and of decided importance, the American Institute of Public Opinion made weekly measurements of opinion toward the proposal during the entire period that reorganization of the Court was a public question. This permits the correlation of reliable opinion samplings with events in the debate and the observation of their relationship.

From this observation it is hoped to throw light on several specific questions: (1) What is the general nature of the relationship between the public and its legislators? (2) What are the forces at work which determine the direction that public opinion will take in a debate of this type? (3) Is there a noticeable tendency on the part of legislators to follow the guidance of public opinion, and if so, to what extent do legislators take their lead from the public? (4) To what extent do legislators attempt to swing opinion to their way of thinking? (5) Are there any phases of the relationship between the public and legislators that might be improved so as to make it more effective in approaching the process of deciding public policy?

From accounts of the Court debate as carried in the *New York Times,* the following short outline of leading developments in the debate has been prepared:

Chronological Listing of Events in the Court Debate

February 5—President Roosevelt sends message to Congress recommending reorganization of the federal judiciary, including increasing the membership of the Supreme Court from nine to 15 members. President reported "calm and confident," reflecting his conviction that he has a huge popular mandate for what he is doing. Message creates shock throughout country.

March 1—The Supreme Court upholds Congressional resolution abrogating payments in gold. Decision is of aid to New Deal.

March 4—President Roosevelt, in Democratic Victory Dinner speech, calls for party loyalty on the Supreme Court issue.

March 8—The President, in a fireside chat, assures Americans that in proposing reorganization of the Court he is seeking to protect them from the Court's usurpations.

March 9—Homer Cummings, Attorney-General, opens Administration arguments before Senate Judiciary Committee, saying the bill will restore the governmental machinery to its proper balance.

March 22—Senator Burton K. Wheeler opens opposition arguments before Senate Judiciary Committee and reads a statement from Chief Justice Charles Evans Hughes saying enlargement of the Court is "unnecessary." Statement is said to have the approval of Justices Brandeis and Van Devanter.

March 29—The Supreme Court reverses *Adkins v. Children's Hospital* decision and upholds constitutional minimum wage law of the state of Washington. Adkins case specifically overruled by 5–4 decision. Decision opens way for federal minimum wage legislation.

April 12—In handing down decisions in four specific cases, the Supreme Court upholds the National Labor Relations Act (Wagner Act). Decision in chief case is 5–4.

April 28—Senators Hatch, McCarran, and O'Mahoney, members of the Senate Judiciary Committee previously uncommitted on Supreme Court Bill, announce opposition on basis of testimony offered before the Committee.

May 10—Washington reports say that Justices Brandeis and Van Devanter will retire from Court in June.

May 18—Justice Willis Van Devanter, 78, retires.

May 24—The Supreme Court upholds the Social Security Act in ruling on three cases, two by 5–4 decisions.

June 14—The Senate Judiciary Committee reports unfavorably to the Senate on the Court bill, terming the proposal "a needless, futile, and utterly dangerous abandonment of constitutional principle." Vote is 10–8 against proposal.

July 14—Senator Joseph T. Robinson, majority leader of the Senate, dies suddenly. Supreme Court Bill will be abandoned.

Two questions were asked weekly by the Gallup Poll during the debate. The first question, asked during the period from February 15 to April 5, reads: "Are you in favor of President Roosevelt's proposal regarding the Supreme Court?" The second question, for the period from April 12 to June 7, reads: "Should Congress pass the President's Supreme Court plan?" In both questions, the Supreme Court plan was stated to be "President Roosevelt's." Possibly the use of the President's name might have introduced a bias, although throughout the debate, in the newspapers, on the radio, and in the halls of Congress, the plan was also identified with the President. In view of this very common identification, the possibility of such a bias is minimized. In any event, any tendency toward bias would not affect the validity of the figures as used in this study, since a bias would be constant.

Phase One of the Debate. The initial period in the debate extends from the introduction of the President's proposal on February 5 until the week immediately preceding the two speeches made by the President. In this early period public attitudes toward the proposal divided equally, 45 per cent of the people expressing approval of the proposal, and 45 per cent expressing disapproval, with 10 per cent in the "no opinion" category. These figures are from the Gallup Poll taken during the week of February 15. At approximately the same time, the *New York Times* reported that an informal poll of senators made by *Times* reporters showed that 32 senators were on record as favoring the proposal, 28 as against the proposal, while 35 remained uncommitted. Thus, while 90 per cent of the public had put themselves on record as approving or disapproving of the proposal, only 63 per cent of the senators had taken a definite stand. One week later, on February 17, the *Times* news columns carried this statement from a Washington staff member: "Conservative Democrats . . . especially those in the Senate, gagged at the proposals. . . . Many of them maintained a prudent silence, waiting to see how the cat of public opinion would jump."

In this first stage of the debate, newspapers and radio commentators began to take definite stands on the proposals, and senators and other public figures began to make statements setting forth their positions. Senator Norris declared against the bill; former Governor Alf Landon, who had carried the Republican standard in the presidential election a few months earlier, came out against the proposal; Senator Champ Clark declared against the scheme; and Senators Glass and Wheeler denounced it. The only figure of magnitude to raise his voice in favor of the proposal was Senator La Follette. In the face of this cumulation of official opinion against the proposal, public opinion began to turn against the plan, and by March 1 the Gallup Poll reported that the anti-proposal vote had grown to 48 per cent, while the pro-proposal vote had slumped to 41 per cent, a difference of 7 percentage points. The President and his advisers became aware that public sentiment was turning away from the proposal.

As early as February 15, the *Times* reported that Attorney-General Cummings and Senator Sherman Minton were planning to make appeals for public support of the plan. The *Times* news columns said: "The frank object of all these appeals is to induce the backers of the President to send telegrams and letters to their senators and representatives to offset the thousands received at the Capitol in the last few days in opposition to his sweeping plan for remaking the Supreme Court with more liberal-minded men." On February 19, the *Times* said:

> On the showing of informal polls that the Administration's judiciary reform bill may hang on the decision of less than a dozen senators, President Roosevelt and the forces identified with him, particularly organized labor, intensified their efforts to insure its passage as a prerequisite to further New Deal legislation. . . . The opposition strategists in the Senate . . . were . . . making preparations for one of the stiffest legislative battles of recent years. They were making no particular effort to dig into the dwindling reservoir of unpledged senators, leaving that to the weight of the letters and telegrams still coming in from all parts of the country.

Phase One of the debate may be summarized by saying that the President introduced the proposal with the hope that public opinion, which had given him a handsome victory in November, would provide the pressure necessary to push the proposal through Congress. This public pressure was not forthcoming, and the public had become increasingly hostile. Opposition senators were biding their time as they watched public opinion swing behind them. So far as the Administration was concerned, a counterattack was necessary to win back public favor to the proposal.

Phase Two. The second phase of the debate may be entitled the Administration drive for public support. The outstanding development during this phase was the entry of the President directly into the discussion. With opinion turning away from the proposal, it became obvious that use of the most powerful weapon in the New Deal arsenal was indicated, a personal appeal from the President. Consequently, the President made two speeches to the nation within five days: an address at the Democratic Victory Dinner on March 4 and a fireside chat on March 8. The *New York Times* reported the fireside chat in these words: "He had no intention of packing the Court with 'spineless puppets.' He simply proposed to return the Court to its 'rightful and historic place' and save the Constitution from 'hardening of the arteries.' " On the morning following the fireside chat, Attorney-General Cummings opened the Administration case before the Senate Judiciary Committee, saying that the proposal would restore the governmental machinery to its proper balance. The Gallup Poll for the week of March 1 immediately registered the impact of the President's speeches. The anti-proposal vote fell to 47 per cent and in two weeks dropped precipitately to 41 per cent, the lowest point reached by the "No" vote at any stage of the debate. On the other hand, the pro-proposal vote began a climb that was to last until March 29, rising from 41 to 45 per cent during the month. Success had apparently crowned the effort of the Administration to win the favor of public opinion, for the "Yes" vote now held a slim margin over the "No" vote. However, as will be seen, this margin was to prove far from decisive.

Phase Three. On March 22, the opposition forces swung back into action as Senator Burton Wheeler, chief of the anti-reorganization forces, opened the opposition arguments before the Senate Judiciary Committee. As the first opposition witness, Senator Wheeler read a statement from Chief Justice Hughes saying enlargement of the Court was "unnecessary"; and the statement was said to have the approval of Justices Brandeis and Van Devanter. During that week the "No" vote turned again and began a steady climb upward which was to mount almost steadily until the proposal was finally killed. Evidently, opposition arguments before the Judiciary Committee were sufficiently convincing to solidify the "No" vote, the constant strength of the oppositionists among the public from this date onward is shown.

Phase Four. The turning point in the debate was reached on March 29. On that day, the Supreme Court handed down a decision reversing an earlier decision in the *Adkins v. Children's Hospital* case. The effect was to hold constitutional the minimum wage law of the state of Washington, thus paving the way for federal minimum wage legislation, one of the chief objectives of the New Deal. The effect on public opinion of the switch by the Supreme Court was nothing short of profound. The "Yes" vote, or those in favor of reorganization, began a sharp slump from which it never fully recovered. In terms of percentages, the "Yes" vote dropped from a high of 45 per cent in the week before the reversed decision in the *Adkins* case to a low of 31 per cent on May 17. It is safe to say that the Administration lost its case before the public on the day when the Supreme Court did its famous about-face. It is to be noted, however, that the "Yes" vote which became estranged from the proposal did not shift into the "No" group, but fell into indecision and became allied with the "No Opinion" group. The growth of the "No Opinion" group almost matches, point for point, the decline in the "Yes" group. This phenomenon will be enlarged upon below.

From the beginning of Phase Two onward, the Senate Judiciary Committee had been holding extensive hearings at which educators, farm and labor leaders, women's group leaders, and representatives of almost every special interest group in the nation appeared and presented their case. To what extent the members of the Judiciary Committee were "holding off" from presenting the bill for a formal test on the Senate floor is difficult to tell with exactness. During this period, opinion was in a state of flux, and the Judiciary Committee served a valuable function by permitting opinion to crystallize. Some evidence of political maneuvering to take advantage of a favorable climate of opinion is revealed in a charge made by Senators Wheeler and Van Nuys on April 3, five days after the Supreme Court handed down the decision in the *Adkins* case. The *New York Times* reported the two Senators as charging Attorney-General Cummings with a "gag" attempt, based on reports that Mr. Cummings had hinted that he would like to see the Judiciary Committee bring the hearings to a close. The *Times* reported the Senators as saying: "There is no doubt the Attorney-General would like to close public hearings on this issue. . . . Hundreds of American citizens, holding responsible positions at the bar, in universities, and in the molding of public opinion have asked to be heard . . . it is the duty of the Senate Judiciary Committee to continue these hearings until every cross-section of public opinion has been given an opportunity to present its views." Senator Wheeler was astute enough to realize that the tide of opinion was running against the proposal and that time was playing into the hands of the opposition, just as Mr. Cummings knew that time was playing against the Administration. The two opposition Senators realized the impact of the Supreme Court decision of March 29 on the public and were willing to continue the hearings of the Judiciary Committee until such time as the increased opposition they expected from the public should have an opportunity to register itself through witnesses at the hearings and through senatorial channels of sounding opinion. The Judiciary Committee did continue its hearings, and reports continued to furnish the bulk of newspaper and radio accounts of the reorganization debate. The incident is illustrative of the dependence that both sides placed upon the pressure of public opinion to furnish the force needed to carry the day. Opponents and proponents alike realized that without the backing of public opinion they were lost, and were anxiously trying to win opinion to their side, while waiting for opinion to crystallize sufficiently so that a clear-cut case of public support would be forthcoming.

On April 12 with the "No" vote holding a 6 per cent margin over the "Yes" vote, the Supreme Court handed down a decision upholding the National Labor Relations Act in rulings on four specific cases. In the chief case, the decision was five to four in favor of the act. Strangely enough, the effect of this decision on public opinion was the reverse of that in the Adkins case. The "No" vote went down slightly while the "Yes" vote mounted slightly. This reversal of opinion can be traced to the fact that the Administration immediately made capital of the two successive favorable decisions of the Court, following a series of reverses for the New Deal, maintaining that the two decisions proved the point that the Court was actually composed of human beings who were subject to error and could see the error of their ways. The Administration raised its famous cry that Court decisions rested on whether a Justice came down heads or tails, which indicated the need for a larger Court membership. This argument, although it had an immediate effect, was not powerful enough to change the trend of opinion, and the following week (April 19) the "No" vote rose three percentage points, while the "Yes" vote sank two points.

Phase Five. The next development of note in the debate occurred on May 10, when reports from Washington circled the country to the effect that Justices Brandeis and Van Devanter intended to retire from the Court in June. The effect of this report was to increase public indecision, which had been mounting steadily from the introduction of the proposal, and after the report had gained credence the "No Opinion" group stood at a high of 25 per cent on May 17. It is worth pausing to note the state of opinion at this time.

Table 28–1 shows that the opposition group had held its own, despite sharp dips. The "Yes" group proponents of reorganization had lost a total of 14 percentage points; the "No Opinion" group had risen from 10 per cent to 25 per cent; and the table shows that those who lost faith in their position did not feel powerfully enough affected to jump into the opposite camp, but that their

TABLE 28-1   *Shift in Vote on Court Reorganization,*
February 15-May 17*

	February 15	May 17	Difference
Yes, favor reorganization	45%	31%	−14%
No, oppose reorganization	45%	44%	−1%
No opinion	10%	25%	+15%

*February 15 represents roughly the introduction of the proposal; May 17 is representative of the period following the circulation of the report that Justices Brandeis and Van Devanter would retire in June.

reaction was to fall into a state of indecision. The gain for the "No Opinion" group represents the total defection from both the "Yes" and "No" groups. In other words, the public was still not clear upon a course of action, although the number of "Yes" people who were growing increasingly doubtful of their position was very much larger than the respective "No" group. The importance of this observation lies in the assumption that members of the Senate were idling along, waiting for a popular reaction. This was not to be forthcoming, since the people were becoming increasingly indecisive. But for the next event unfolding on May 18, it is difficult to say how long this deadlock between the people and their legislators, each waiting for the other to act, might have lasted.

Phase Six. The deadlock was broken on the date mentioned with announcement of the retirement from the Supreme Court of Justice Willis Van Devanter at the age of 78. This announcement immediately cleared the atmosphere, and both opponents and proponents of the court reorganization proposal were enabled to make up their minds definitely. Opinion had at last crystallized. The retirement of Justice Van Devanter meant that the President would be able to appoint to the Court a Justice more in sympathy with New Deal objectives. In turn, this appointment, together with the recent "liberalization" of the Court in the *Adkins* and Wagner Act decisions, meant that for all practical purposes the Court had been reorganized. *De facto* reorganization apparently was satisfactory to the public, and the "No" vote rose quickly until on June 7 opponents of court reorganization had 50 per cent of the public behind them, while only 35 per cent favored reorganization. The "No Opinion" vote sank rapidly from 25 per cent on May 17 to 15 per cent on June 7.

TABLE 28-2   *Shift in Vote on Court Reorganization,*
February 15-June 7

	February 5	June 7	Difference
Yes, favor reorganization	45%	35%	−10%
No, oppose reorganization	45%	50%	+5%
No opinion	10%	15%	+5%

Table 28–2 shows that after the retirement of Justice Van Devanter, opinion crystallized more rapidly in the direction of opposition to the proposal than in favor of it. A total defection of 10 per cent of those originally favoring reorganization can be noted, 5 per cent of these people switching their vote into opposition, while 5 per cent were unable to come to a decision and moved into the "No Opinion" group.

This evident satisfaction of the people with the changed court situation came as a great relief to legislators, who were now able to deal with the delicate problem of *de jure* court reorganization. On June 14, with the battle of public opinion decided, and with opinion firmly behind it, the Senate Judiciary Committee reported unfavorably (10–8) to the Senate on the Judiciary Reorganization Bill, terming the measure "a needless, futile, and utterly dangerous abandonment of constitutional principle." Reorganization of the Court was no longer a public issue; and whatever lingering inclination there might have been on the part of the Administration to press for court reform in the face of public opposition was dissipated by the death on July 14 of Senator Joseph T. Robinson, majority leader of the Senate, who had thrown all of his strength into the fray on behalf of the proposal.

Having examined in some detail the interplay between public opinion and events in the court debate, it is now possible to form conclusions as to the general nature of the relationship between the public and its legislators as they deal jointly with a public question. In many respects, the debate on the Court is typical of the problems that present themselves for solution in our democracy. For this reason, the conclusions that follow have been cast in such a form that they may be applied to understanding the nature of any similar debate on a public question. At the same time, it must be borne in mind that so many diverse factors operate while a question runs its public course that these conclusions have applicability only in so far as the phenomena at work in a given situation are taken into consideration. Further study of the type of relationship under consideration will permit the understanding with considerable exactness of how public opinion and the legislative process affect each other. This, in turn, will enable the public and legislators to operate together at full efficiency; for it is undeniable that national questions must be solved by the joint action of the people and their elected legislative representatives.

1. *Legislators display an inclination to "wait on" public opinion to shape itself before dealing formally with questions.* This does not mean that the senators were content merely to follow the lead of public opinion, for many made an effort to mold opinion to their way of thinking through radio addresses and personal appearances. It does mean that the great majority of senators were keenly aware of the existence of public opinion and hesitant to take action so long as its final direction was not absolutely certain. Although many senators committed themselves publicly during the course of the debate, at no time did either side show determination to force a showdown on the floor of the Senate, such hesitation seeming to stem from the uncertain condition of public opinion, which never registered above 50 per cent either for or against the proposal.

The function of the Senate Judiciary Committee as a sounding board is interesting. So long as any doubt remained about public sentiment toward the bill, the committee remained in session, and only when it was perfectly plain that public support for the proposal would not be forthcoming did it make its unfavorable report. During the extended period of public hearings, an amazing array of witnesses appeared before the committee and every possible type of argument for and against the proposal was brought forth. Doubtless this varied array of witnesses gave to the senators valuable clues as to public feeling on the proposal, and it was on the basis of testimony offered before the committee that Senators Hatch, McCarran, and O'Mahoney announced their opposition to the bill. The most useful function of the committee seems to have been to hold in abeyance the necessity of making a formal decision while senators waited in the hope that public opinion would develop in a decisive direction and render unnecessary a decision on the Senate floor.

2. *Events played a more important role than Congress or the President in shaping the direction of public opinion.* The six leading determinates of opinion in the debate were: (1) the President's Victory Dinner speech and fireside chat on March 4 and 8; (2) the opening of the Administration case before the Senate Judiciary Committee on March 9; (3) the opening of opposition arguments against the proposal before the committee on March 22; (4) the decision of the Supreme Court overruling an earlier decision in the *Adkins v. Children's Hospital* case on March 29, which paved the way for federal minimum wage legislation and broke the succession of anti-New Deal decisions handed down by the Court; (5) Washington reports, beginning on May 10, that Justices Brandeis and Van Devanter were planning to retire; and (6) the retirement on May 18 of Justice Van Devanter.

Of these six steps in the downfall of the Court proposal, three were attempts by government officials (the President and senators) to mobilize opinion in a particular direction. The other three were events in the sense of being unanticipated happenings beyond the province of either proponents or opponents of the proposal. While the President's speeches and the arguments given before the Senate Judiciary Committee affected public opinion measurably, they were incapable of affecting it decisively. The major event in opinion-determination was the decision of the Court in the *Adkins* case. From the time of this decision, the public "Yes" vote dropped off steadily, while the "No" vote rose. The second most important step in opinion-determination was the retirement of Justice Van Devanter, with the effect of crystallizing opinion that had been drifting into indecision as the debate wore on. As Cantril has said, "opinion is generally determined more by events than by words unless those words are themselves interpreted as an 'event.' " [1]

3. *Public opinion cannot propose a course of action, and a healthy public opinion requires leadership.* Throughout the course of the debate, as shown by the accompanying data, public opinion was responsive to political moves and events. At no time was there observable any great spontaneous movement of opinion in a direction that would have indicated to legislators the necessity for taking a particular course of action that would have broken the deadlock. It is characteristic of public opinion that it cannot generate a proposal or series of proposals serving to satisfy its needs. Public opinion can indicate very powerfully the general area of its needs, but it remains for an individual or group of individuals to come forward with specific proposals toward which opinion can

display approval or disapproval. We have seen how, during the course of the debate, the public support that fell away from both the "Yes" and "No" sides of the discussion tended to gather in the "No Opinion" category, where it remained in a state of indecision awaiting some new determining factor that would move it once more into the realm of decision. Those legislators who waited in the hope that public opinion would show them the way were waiting in vain. Public opinion in a democracy responds to leadership, and needs the stimulus of leadership to crystallize one way or the other on specific proposals. Legislators are perfectly correct in sounding opinion so that they may determine whether or not they are moving in a direction calculated to meet popular needs. It is completely fallacious for legislators to wait for public opinion to tell them what to do, because public opinion waits on leadership to supply the grist of fact and suggestion so that it can fulfill its function, which is the acceptance or rejection of proposals. In a sentence, when faced with a specific problem, public opinion will respond to proposals, but cannot generate them; generation of proposals is the function of the legislators.

NOTE

1. Hadley Cantril, *Gauging Public Opinion* (Princeton: Princeton University Press, 1944), p. 226.

29

The Legislator as Representative

HEINZ EULAU

Public opinion may affect law through the selection of legislators and by influence exerted on them during their tenure in office. The degree of influence exercised by public opinion is contingent in part on whether legislators define their roles as "delegates," following express or implied instructions from their constituents, or as "trustees," guided by their conscience and an independent judgment of the issues. Edmund Burke formulated the distinction in his "Speech to the Electors of Bristol" in 1774.

From John C. Wahlke, Heinz Eulau, Buchanan, and Ferguson, *The Legislative System: Explorations in Legislative Behavior* (New York: Wiley, 1962), pp. 280–282. Reprinted by permission of the author and publisher. Abridged.

Parliament is not a congress of ambassadors from different and hostile interests; which interests each must maintain, as an agent and advocate against other agents and advocates; but Parliament is a deliberative assembly of one nation, with one interest, that of the whole; where, not local purposes, not local prejudices ought to guide but the general good, resulting from the general reason of the whole.

The following findings suggest that Burke's concept is very much alive, at least in the responses of state legislators to explicit questions on their role orientations. The results are based on interviews, conducted in 1957, with 94 per cent of all state legislators in California, Ohio, New Jersey, and Tennessee. Responses were content-analyzed to categorize the legislators as trustees, delegates, or (a composite of the two) "politicors." . . .

The spell of the Burkean formulation on the interpretation of representation tended to create reactions which, it seems, are almost as arbitrary as Burke's formula itself. In particular, the functional notion, itself quite realistic under modern conditions, that the legislature is an agency for the coordination and integration of diverse social, economic, and political interests makes apparent the simplemindedness of Burke's theory, now as then. . . .

We may, for instance, assume the following: the exigencies of modern government, even on the relatively low level of state government, are exceedingly complex. Taxation and finance, education and public welfare, legal reform, licensing and regulatory problems, transportation, and so on are topics more often than not beyond the comprehension of the average citizen. Unable to understand their problems and helpless to cope with them, people are likely to entrust the affairs of government to the elected representatives who, presumably, are better informed than their constituents. Many of the comments made by trustees about their constituents articulated this set of reasoning. People themselves may pay lip service to the notion that a representative should not use his independent judgment, but in fact they are unlikely to be able, or may not care, to give him instructions as was possibly the case at an earlier time when the tasks of government were comparatively simple. It is likely, therefore, that the representative has become less and less a delegate and more and more a trustee as the business of government has become more and more intricate and technical as well as less locally centered. Rather than being a "pious formula," the role orientation of trustee may be a functional necessity. We might expect, therefore, that it is held by state legislators more frequently today than the role orientation of delegate, with the politico orientation in a middle position.

Comparative analysis of the distribution of representational-role orientations in the four states seems to support these considerations. As Table 29–1 shows, the role orientation of trustee is held by greater proportions of legislators in all four states than either the politico or delegates orientations. Moreover, the politico appears somewhat more often in all four states than the delegate.

TABLE 29-1   *Distribution of Representational-Role Orientations,*
by Per Cent

Role Orientation	California N = 49	New Jersey N = 54	Ohio N = 54	Tennessee N = 78
Trustee	55	61	56	81
Politico	25	22	29	13
Delegate	20	17	15	6
Total	100	100	100	100

The trustee orientation, Table 29–1 indicates, appears more frequently in Tennessee than in the other three states, a fact that seems to contradict the proposition that the orientation of trustee varies with the complexity of governmental affairs. As Tennessee is less urbanized and industrialized than the other states, one might expect Tennessee legislators to be less often trustees and more often delegates than legislators in California, New Jersey, or Ohio. But it may be that "complexity" is a function of perceptions, regardless of the real situation. If so, then to Tennesseeans the relatively less complex character of socio-economic life may appear more complex than it actually is, compared with the other states. The more frequent appearance of the trustee there may only be symptomatic of an even greater feeling of helplessness and inefficacy on the part of people vis-à-vis governmental problems, as it is perceived by their representatives. It may also be a reflection of the lower educational level in Tennessee. In all these cases, the political character of Tennessee constituencies would seem to make it very difficult for a legislator to be a delegate for his constituency, forcing him to act as either a trustee or a politico. But to demonstrate this is beyond the limits of this analysis.[1] But the most surprising feature of Table 29–1 is the very small proportion of legislators in each state subscribing to the role orientation of delegate. If one assumes that the extent to which any role is taken is a function of its difficulty, it would seem that the role orientation of delegate is, indeed, most difficult to hold. We noted in the review of responses regarding different orientations made in the interviews that legislators repeatedly gave as a reason for their taking the role of trustee the fact that it was impossible to find out what people really wanted, and that, therefore, the delegate role was unrealistic.

NOTE

1. As the trustee orientation includes responses stressing traditional moral values, it might be assumed that these virtues—such as following one's conscience or what one feels to be "right"—are more valued in rural Tennessee than in the three more urbanized states. But inspection of the frequency with which this attitude appears in Tennessee as against the other states does not reveal significantly different distributions of relevant responses: California, 18 per cent; New Jersey, 8 per cent; Ohio, 28 per cent; Tennessee, 23 per cent.

30

The Dynamics of Access in the Legislative Process

DAVID B. TRUMAN

"Every opinion," Justice Holmes observed in one of his great dissents, "tends to become a law." [1] In thus adumbrating his conception of the legislative process Holmes pointed to a distinctive feature of modern representative government. Especially in the United States, the legislature, far more than the judiciary or the executive, has been the primary means of effecting changes in the law of the land. In consequence, the legislature traditionally has been the major focus of attention for political interest groups. Though this interest in legislation has not been an exclusive preoccupation, the established importance of group activities in legislatures is reflected in a popular synonym for the political interest group, the word *lobby*. Though for tactical reasons many groups profess slight or no concern with lobbying, legislative activity has been for the layman the distinguishing feature of the political interest group.

It follows that access to the legislature is of crucial importance at one time or another to virtually all such groups. Some groups are far more successful in this pursuit than others. Moreover, access is not a homogeneous commodity. In some forms it provides little more than a chance to be heard; in others it practically assures favorable action. Some groups achieve highly effective access almost automatically, whereas it is denied to others in spite of their most vigorous efforts.

It will be appropriate, therefore, to begin an exploration of the role of groups in the legislative process by examining some of the factors that affect the kind of access that various groups are able to achieve. For the sake of convenience these may be divided into two types: first, a set of formal, structural factors whose importance will be readily apparent; second, a set of informal determinants whose effect is somewhat more subtle but of at least equal significance.

Governmental Structure and Differential Access

The formal institutions of government in the United States do not prescribe all the meanderings of the stream of politics. They do mark some of its limits,

From *The Governmental Process* (New York: Knopf, 1951), pp. 321–332. Copyright © 1945 by Alfred A. Knopf, Inc. Reprinted by permission.

however, and designate certain points through which it must flow whatever un-
charted courses it may follow between these limits. . . . Although the effect
of formal structural arrangements is not always what its designers intended,
these formalities are rarely neutral. They handicap some efforts and favor
others. Debate over proposals to eliminate such a ritualistic bit of procedure as
the electoral college, for example, reveals the fact that, although no one knows
the exact consequences that would follow if it were to be abandoned or modified, a change would affect various segments of the community unequally.
Such, inevitably, is the influence of formal structure.

Access is one of the advantages unequally distributed by such arrangements;
that is, in consequence of the structural peculiarities of our government some
groups have better and more varied opportunities to influence key points of
decision than do others. Take as an example the provision for equal representation of states in the Senate of the United States. This has allowed agricultural interest groups that are predominant in many thinly populated states
more points of access in the Senate than urban groups whose members are
concentrated in a few populous states. Thus, were it not for this structural
provision, the United States would not have been so solicitous for the sugar-
beet or silver-mining interests as it has been over the years. It is obvious, moreover, that a group such as the American Farm Bureau Federation, which
can cover a great many rural states, can gain readier access than urban groups
concerning any matter on which it can achieve a satisfactory measure of cohesion. It is less obvious, but equally important, that an urban group whose interests are such that it can ally with the Farm Bureau derives an advantage in
access over another urban group whose claims are such that it cannot effect an
alliance of this sort. The National Association of Manufacturers and various
trade associations, among others, have been the beneficiaries of such combina-
tions.

Similar advantages, gained from the way in which the boundaries of legislative districts are drawn whether by legislatures or by constitutions, can be observed throughout the governmental system. They are clearly observable in the
House of Representatives, many of whose districts, even in relatively urban
states like Illinois, are defined by state legislatures in which rural groups predominate. The state legislatures, of course, show similar patterns.

The existence of the federal system itself is a source of unequal advantage
in access. Groups that would be rather obscure or weak under a unitary arrangement may hold advantageous positions in the state governments and will
be vigorous in their insistence upon the existing distribution of powers between
states and nation. As the advantage of access shifts through time, moreover,
groups shift from defenders to critics of the existing balance. At the turn of the
century, for example, the insurance companies were active in Washington to
get the federal government to take over the regulation of insurance, despite
the obstacle of an adverse Supreme Court decision handed down shortly after
the Civil War. Since the Court in 1944 altered the prevailing doctrine, the insurance companies have been equally vigorous in the opposite direction, at

least insofar as they have tried to gain exemption from the Sherman Antitrust Act. A somewhat complicated symptom of a similar state of affairs is suggested by the contrast between argument and behavior in connection with the Tydings-Miller Act of 1937. This legislation, sponsored principally by the National Association of Retail Druggists, exempted from the provisions of the Sherman Act contracts fixing resale prices on goods sold in interstate commerce, provided that they were resold in a state which permitted such contracts. Proponents of the measure argued that it was simply a means of permitting the individual states to regulate their own affairs. When the law was passed, however, the N.A.R.D. set up an unofficial *national* board through which uniform contracts between manufacturers and retailers could be approved and administered. The policy was a national one, but the druggists' access to the states was more effective once the federal antitrust hurdle was eliminated.

The separation of powers, especially between the legislature and the executive, and the accompanying system of checks and balances mean that effective access to one part of the government, such as the Congress, does not assure access to another, such as the presidency. For the effective constituencies of the executive and the members of the legislature are not necessarily the same, even when both are represented by men nominally of the same party. These constituencies are different, not simply because the president is elected from the whole country rather than from a particular state or congressional district, although this fact has significance under a system characterized by loose party discipline, but rather because within any state or district, for various reasons, the organized, active elements responsible for the election of a senator or representative are not necessarily the same as those which give the state's or district's support to a candidate for president. This situation is accentuated at the national level by the staggered terms of senators, representatives, and president. A senator elected at the same time as a president must face re-election in an "off" year, and vice versa; a representative must "go it alone" at least every four years. In consequence, as Herring has put it, "Most congressmen are still independent political entrepreneurs." [2] The representative, the senator, and the president each must give ear to groups that one or both of the others frequently can ignore.

An admirable illustration of this situation is the fact that four successive presidents—Harding, Coolidge, Hoover, and Franklin Roosevelt—found it possible to veto veterans' bonus legislation passed by the Congress, although on each occasion approximately four-fifths of the House of Representatives chose to override the veto. Somewhat the same circumstance is indicated by the periodic group demands that reciprocal trade agreements should be submitted to the Senate for ratification as treaties. Such requests imply less effective access to the executive than to the maximum of 33 senators sufficient to reject a treaty.

As the preceding paragraphs suggest, access to points of decision in the government is significantly affected by the structure and cohesion of the political parties considered not just as electioneering devices, but as instruments of governing within the legislature. A single party organization that regularly succeeds in electing an executive and a majority in the legislature will produce one pattern of access to the government. The channels will be predominantly those within the party leadership, and the pattern will be relatively stable and orderly. A quite different pattern will be produced if the party is merely an abstract term referring to an aggregation of relatively independent factions. Then the channels of access will be numerous, and the patterns of influence within the legislature will be diverse, constantly shifting, and more openly in conflict. Party discipline provides the power to govern because it permits stable control of access to the points of policy determination.

It is no novelty to observe that in the United States political parties, particularly on the national scene, correspond more closely to the diffused than to the disciplined type of structure. Because the legislator's tenure in office depends on no over-arching party organization, he is accessible to whatever influences are outstanding in his local constituency almost regardless of more inclusive claims. Whether he carries the label of the majority or the minority party, he finds himself now in the majority and now in the minority on legislative votes. Majorities rarely are composed of the same persons in votes on successive measures. They are likely to be bi-partisan or, more accurately, non-partisan.

The dominant character of access and of influence under the American system is well stated in the remark of a Texas Representative in response to a query concerning his motives in advocating the repeal of federal taxes on oleomargarine: "If I were from the South and were not interested in a market for my people, I would indeed be unworthy to represent my people. Of course I am interested in the right of the cotton farmer to sell his seed." [3] Diffusion of access has its ramifications as well. During the struggle over the McNary-Haugen farm "relief" bill from 1924 through 1928, President Coolidge was hostile both to the measure and to its principal group sponsor, the American Farm Bureau Federation. Vice-President Dawes, however, gave "support and assistance," to quote the words of the group's president, that were "of the utmost importance." [4]

Advantages of access are likely to go to the group that can accentuate and exploit the local preoccupations of the legislator. Many corporations and trade associations have long made use of this tactic although the exact forms have been various. Railroad companies have worked through lawyers and doctors retained in the states and counties in which they practice to reach influential supporters of state and national legislators, as have other corporate enterprises. The Association of Railway Executives, predecessor of the Association of American Railroads, organized such a device in a rather complete form. As outlined by one of its officials:

> I had it in mind putting into effect a plan whereby we would be advised as to who are the influential men behind the several Congressmen, and the further thought that we might be able through personal contact or by the careful distri-

bution of literature to influence in a perfectly proper way the judgment of the men upon whom the several Congressmen rely for support and advice.[5]

Such a system has never been more completely organized than it has been by the Iowa Farm Bureau Federation. Although the group does not openly endorse candidates for election, after the election it sets up committees of five members in each legislative district, whose function it is to capitalize upon local support. The qualifications of the members of these committees, according to Kile, are four in number: (1) they must be "willing to put Farm Bureau policies ahead of any personal interest"; (2) they must be from the same party as the successful candidate; (3) they must be men who "individually helped get the candidate elected"; and (4) they must be "politically potent in the district." [6] A very similar plan of organization to exert local influence has been employed by, among others, the National Association of Retail Druggists. The Federal Trade Commission has described it as "the most important device" used by the association in its efforts to secure passage of desired legislation.[7]

Such is the effect of our disintegrated national party structure upon access. Although this structure may be in process of gradual change in the direction of greater integration and central control, as some competent observers believe,[8] conclusive evidence of this shift is not at hand. We can be sure, however, that an altered party structure will be reflected in an altered pattern of group access to the Congress.

The effects of party structure upon group access to many of the state legislatures are similar to its effects upon access to Congress. The channels of approach for various groups are numerous and varied, as in Congress, except in those cases where an individual party leader or faction has been able to impose a high degree of discipline upon the rank and file. In the heyday of Boss Platt, access to the legislature of New York was available primarily through him, usually at a price. When in 1935 the Governor of Florida established temporary dominance over the state legislature, the Association of Life Insurance Presidents found that it could not even gain admission to legislative committee hearings until it had persuaded the Governor of its point of view. Other states, such as New York and New Jersey, have quite consistently shown a pattern of party government quite different from that at the national level. Where the party structure is integrated and the legislators are under discipline, access is channeled and is more available to those groups upon which the party as a whole, rather than the individual legislator, is dependent.

Once it has established access, by whatever means, a group will exert tremendous efforts to retain the structural arrangements that have given it advantage. An illustration is afforded by the struggle over the adoption of the Twenty-first Amendment repealing the Eighteenth. When the prohibition amendment was submitted, the Anti-Saloon League favored the method of ratification by the state legislatures, since it had built up its access to most of those bodies and could be sure that the weapons at its disposal would assure favorable action by the required number of states. When the repeal proposal was passed by the Congress in 1933, however, the method of ratification by conventions called especially for the purpose was specified for the first time in the history of amendments to the Federal Constitution. This means was employed in order to get around the established access of the league.

All the factors of a structural character that result in the unequal distribution of access among interest groups operating upon a legislature need not be discussed in detail. We must, however, even in this rough sketch, discuss one additional type, closely related to the structure of the party system: the structure of the legislature itself, including legislative procedure and the committee system. Legislative structure and rules of procedure are by no means neutral factors in respect to access. As Schattschneider observed with reference to the Smoot-Hawley Tariff Act of 1930: "Legislation cannot be understood apart from the manner in which it is made." [9]

No legislative assembly of whatever size can, of course, carry on its activities without some internal division of labor, without methods of setting the order of business, or without means of regulating the process of deliberation. The procedures for selecting those to whom the leadership of an assembly is entrusted, for example, have a direct bearing upon the kind of access to the legislature that various groups may be able to achieve. Thus the practice in Congress and most of the states of assigning committee memberships and designating their chairmen on the basis of seniority gives a special advantage to groups having access to members from "safe" constituencies who are likely to look with hostility on the demands of the less established groups. Organizations whose membership is concentrated in "close" districts, where the incidence of change and the consequent demands for adjustment are high, are less easily able to establish access to committee chairmen.

Whoever sets the timetable of a legislature and determines how long debate on a measure shall continue has a significant control upon access. This power, of course, is one of the principal means by which the British Cabinet leads the House of Commons. In American state legislatures a unified party leadership, both legislative and executive, may enjoy similar dominance, and in that case effective access will be through such leadership. In the Congress, and at times in all of the state legislatures, control of the timetable lies with a loosely integrated collection of men belonging to the majority party, sometimes acting in consultation with the minority leaders. In the Senate this scheduling function is performed by the floor leader, his aides, and the chairmen of the standing committees. The party Steering Committee and its Policy Committee are nominally a part of this machinery, but their importance is slight. In the House the timetable is set by the Rules Committee, the floor leader, the Speaker, and the chairmen of standing committees. The Steering Committee is of as little functional significance as in the Senate. Depending on the nature of the legislation to be considered and on the skill of the leadership, the legislators who determine the schedule may work in concert, or they may operate at cross purposes. In the latter case the legislative timetable is a compromise or emerges from a test of strength among these various points of power, a process in which the president, if he is of the same party, may play a significant role. Groups with access to parts of this machinery have a privileged influence upon the legislative program, especially if their objective is to obstruct rather than to promote a particular bill.

Both the power to limit debate and the practice of permitting unlimited debate on a measure have significance for the degree of access that various groups achieve. In the House of Representatives, where limitation on debate is customary, it usually takes the form of adopting a special rule reported by the Rules Committee. Practically all major legislation in the House is handled under this sort of procedure, which sets both the terms and the duration of debate. The Committee is thus in a position either to block or to expedite action on a bill, and access to its membership is a crucial advantage. Such access is likely to go disproportionately to established groups dominant in "safe" constituencies, since the seniority of all members of this committee is high. For example, in the Seventy-seventh Congress, elected in 1940, no member of the Rules Committee had had less than four consecutive terms of service, and the average number of such terms represented on the Committee was just under seven. Thus most of the members came from districts that had made no change in their representation since before the onset of the New Deal. A similar advantage accrues in the Senate to any defensive group that has access to even a small bloc of members. Under that body's practice of unlimited debate, such a minority can "talk a bill to death" through the filibuster, effectively preventing action by the Senate as a whole. In some cases this result has been achieved by one member alone. Although the Senate has had since 1917 a rule permitting closure of debate, it is rarely applied, and the effective veto power of a Senate minority remains virtually unchallenged.

Finally, the enormously complicated and technical rules under which debate is carried on in legislative chambers have an important influence upon relative access. In the first place, the rules themselves are not neutral; witness the heat frequently generated by an attempt to change them. At the beginning of the Eighty-first Congress in January, 1949, a successful effort was made to modify the House rules so that committee chairmen could call up bills that the Rules Committee failed to report out. The significance of such a modification was indicated both by the activity in the House and by the attention given the amendment in the press. But groups gain advantages in access not just from the substance of such procedural regulations. They may derive tremendous advantage if their representatives, whether in or out of the legislative halls, have a mastery of the ins and outs of parliamentary procedure. Like the technicalities of legal procedure in courts of law, procedural arrangements may be used as often to delay and obstruct action as to facilitate it. Thus the ability to command the services of a skillful parliamentary tactician may be the key to effective access to a legislature.

Reference has already been made to legislative committees, and in the next chapter we shall give close attention to their functions. At this point it is necessary, however, to indicate that the place of committees in a legislative body has important effects upon the degree of access that various groups can achieve. It is as accurate today as it was nearly three-quarters of a century ago when Woodrow Wilson published his little classic, *Congressional Government,* to say that, although the Congress as a whole formally legislates, the real policy determination takes place in the standing committees.[10] Both because of the volume and the complexity of the problems coming before a modern legislature and because of the size of such bodies, they have had to leave the most important part of the examination, if not the preparation, of legislation to smaller units. Under the British system this function is performed primarily by the Cabinet, which is strictly speaking a committee of the legislature. Relatively minor use is made of other standing committees. In the Congress of the United States the sifting of legislative projects is pre-eminently the function of the committees, primarily the standing committees. Neither house, with rare exceptions, considers any measure that has not first been acted upon by one of these nominally subordinate bodies. Refusal to report a bill from a committee usually dooms the proposal. But perhaps the most significant feature of the system is that, although many major measures are altered by the Senate or the House after a committee has reported, both houses usually follow closely the recommendations of their committees. Few bills are passed in a form substantially different from that given them at the committee stage.

The effect that this system of committees has upon access stems not only from the relative finality of their actions but also from the comparative independence that they enjoy. These bodies are subject to little or no co-ordinating influence from any source. A committee majority, or even its chairman alone, effectively constitutes a little legislature, especially insofar as it blocks action on a proposal. Therefore access to a committee majority or even to a chairman may give a group effective advantage in the legislature itself, to the virtual exclusion of its competitors.

The role of committees in the state legislatures varies widely. In some their place is roughly similar to that of the congressional committee, whereas in others it is sharply different. One general difference is that, since state legislative sessions are shorter and less frequent and since many state legislators perform their duties on a part-time basis, there is usually less opportunity for prolonged committee consideration in the states. In some states, New Jersey, for instance, the committees are of no significance, except as graveyards for bills, since control by the party leaders is pervasive. Access to the committee under such circumstances is almost meaningless. In other states the committee function appears to be quite similar to that in Congress. Thus a study of several legislative sessions in Maryland and Pennsylvania shows that well over 80 per cent of the committee reports were accepted outright by these legislatures.[11]

This evidence would suggest that committees in Maryland and Pennsylvania were indeed "little legislatures" and that access to them was crucial. Although such undoubtedly was the case in some instances, in these same two states there were other regularities that lay behind the acceptance of committee reports. The legislators followed the committees, to be sure, but the latter were dominated by chairmen who in turn co-operated closely with the governors and other legislative leaders.[12] Similar evidence on the New York legislature indicates that state legislative committees and their chairmen enjoy much less freedom of action than their congressional counterparts. Political management by an informal conference of legislative leaders determines the content of major bills, not the individual committees operating independently.[13] Under such circumstances access to the legislature is not assured merely by establishing relationships with individual committeemen or chairmen. Lines of access tend to be integrated rather than diffused; consequently, the tactics of groups and relative advantage among them can be expected to show a pattern quite different from that characteristic of the Congress.

Aspects of formal structure, therefore, are significant determinants of the channels of access to legislatures, national and state. They afford advantages to some groups and impose handicaps upon the efforts of others to achieve influence in the legislature. Formal structure both reflects and sustains differences in power. It is never neutral.

NOTES

1. *Lochner v. New York,* 198 U.S. 45 (1905).
2. Pendleton Herring, *Presidential Leadership* (New York: Farrar & Rinehart, 1940), p. 27. Copyright by Pendleton Herring and used with the permission of Rinehart & Company, Inc.
3. U.S. House of Representatives, Committee on Agriculture: *Hearings on Repeal of the Oleomargarine Tax,* 80th Cong., 2d Sess. (1948), p. 36.
4. Orville M. Kile, *The Farm Bureau Through Three Decades* (Baltimore: The Waverly Press, 1948), p. 146. Copyright 1948 by and used with the permission of Orville M. Kile.
5. U.S. Senate, Committee on Interstate Commerce: *Senate Report No. 26, 77th Cong.,* 1st Sess. (1941), part 2, pp. 51–53. Cf. Danielian: *A.T.&T.: The Story of Industrial Conquest,* pp. 321–325.
6. Kile, *op. cit., supra* note 4, at 381–382.
7. U.S. Federal Trade Commission: *Report on Resale Price Maintenance* (Government Printing Office, 1945), pp. 64–66.
8. Cf. E. E. Schattschneider, *The Struggle for Party Government* (College Park, Md.: University of Maryland, 1948), pp. 28–29.
9. E. E. Schattschneider, *Politics, Pressures and the Tariff* (Englewood Cliffs, N. J.: Prentice-Hall, Inc., 1935), p. 13.
10. Woodrow Wilson, *Congressional Government* (Boston: Houghton Mifflin Company, 1885), p. 56 and *passim.*
11. C. I. Winslow, *State Legislative Committees: A Study in Procedure* (Baltimore: The Johns Hopkins Press, 1931), pp. 7, 112 ff., 139.
12. *Ibid.,* pp. 118–121, 137. Cf. Robert Luce, *Legislative Procedure* (Boston: Houghton Mifflin Company, 1922), pp. 493–494.
13. Joseph P. Chamberlain, *Legislative Processes, National and State* (New York: D. Appleton-Century Company, 1936), p. 90.

31

The Marijuana Tax Act

HOWARD S. BECKER

It is generally assumed that the practice of smoking marijuana was imported into the United States from Mexico, by way of the southwestern states of Arizona, New Mexico, and Texas, all of which had sizable Spanish-speaking populations. People first began to notice marijuana use in the 1920s but, since it was a new phenomenon and one apparently confined to Mexican immigrants, did not express much concern about it. (The medical compound prepared from the marijuana plant had been known for some time, but was not often prescribed by U.S. physicians.) As late as 1930, only 16 states had passed laws prohibiting the use of marijuana.

In 1937, however, the United States Congress passed the Marijuana Tax Act, designed to stamp out use of the drug. According to the theory outlined above, we should find in the history of this Act the story of an entrepreneur whose initiative and enterprise overcame public apathy and indifference and culminated in the passage of Federal legislation. Before turning to the history of the Act itself, we should perhaps look at the way similar substances had been treated in American law, in order to understand the context in which the attempt to suppress marijuana use proceeded.

The use of alcohol and opium in the United States had a long history, punctuated by attempts at suppression.[1] Three values provided legitimacy for attempts to prevent the use of intoxicants and narcotics. One legitimizing value, a component of what has been called the Protestant Ethic, holds that the individual should exercise complete responsibility for what he does and what happens to him; he should never do anything that might cause loss of self-control. Alcohol and the opiate drugs, in varying degrees and ways, cause people to lose control of themselves; their use, therefore, is evil. A person intoxicated with alcohol often loses control over his physical activity; the centers of judgment in the brain are also affected. Users of opiates are more likely to be anesthetized and thus less likely to commit rash acts. But they become dependent on the drug to prevent withdrawal symptoms and in this sense have lost control of their actions; insofar as it is difficult to obtain the drug, they must subordinate other interests to its pursuit.

Another American value legitimized attempts to suppress the use of alcohol

From *Outsiders* (Glencoe, Ill.: The Free Press, 1963), pp. 135–146. Abridged with renumbered notes. Copyright © 1963 by The Free Press of Glencoe, A Division of The Macmillan Company. Reprinted by permission of the publisher.

and opiates: disapproval of action taken solely to achieve states of ecstasy. Perhaps because of our strong cultural emphases on pragmatism and utilitarianism, Americans usually feel uneasy and ambivalent about ecstatic experiences of any kind. But we do not condemn ecstatic experience when it is the by-product or reward of actions we consider proper in their own right, such as hard work or religious fervor. It is only when people pursue ecstasy for its own sake that we condemn their action as a search for "illicit pleasure," an expression that has real meaning to us.

The third value that provided a basis for attempts at suppression was humanitarianism. Reformers believed that people enslaved by the use of alcohol and opium would benefit from laws making it impossible for them to give in to their weaknesses. The families of drunkards and drug addicts would likewise benefit.

These values provided the basis for specific rules. The Eighteenth Amendment and the Volstead Act forbade the importation of alcoholic beverages into the United States and their manufacture within the country. The Harrison Act in effect prohibited the use of opiate drugs for all but medical purposes.

In formulating these laws, care was taken not to interfere with what were regarded as the legitimate interests of other groups in the society. The Harrison Act, for instance, was so drawn as to allow medical personnel to continue to use morphine and other opium derivatives for the relief of pain and such other medical purposes as seemed to them appropriate. Furthermore, the law was carefully drawn to avoid running afoul of the constitutional provision reserving police powers to the several states. In line with this restriction, the Act was presented as a revenue measure, taxing unlicensed purveyors of opiate drugs at an exorbitant rate while permitting licensed purveyors (primarily physicians, dentists, veterinarians, and pharmacists) to pay a nominal tax. Though it was justified constitutionally as a revenue measure, the Harrison Act was in fact a police measure and was so interpreted by those to whom its enforcement was entrusted. One consequence of the passage of the Act was the establishment, in the Treasury Department, of the Federal Bureau of Narcotics in 1930.

The same values that led to the banning of the use of alcohol and opiates could, of course, be applied to the case of marijuana and it seems logical that this should have been done. Yet what little I have been told, by people familiar with the period, about the use of marijuana in the late '20s and early '30s leads me to believe that there was relatively lax enforcement of the existing local laws. This, after all, was the era of Prohibition and the police had more pressing matters to attend to. Neither the public nor law-enforcement officers, apparently, considered the use of marijuana a serious problem. When they noticed it at all, they probably dismissed it as not warranting major attempts at enforcement. One index of how feebly the laws were enforced is that the price of marijuana is said to have been very much lower prior to the passage of federal legislation. This indicates that there was little danger in selling it and that enforcement was not seriously undertaken.

Even the Treasury Department, in its report on the year 1931, minimized the importance of the problem:

A great deal of public interest has been aroused by newspaper articles appearing from time to time on the evils of the abuse of marijuana, or Indian hemp, and more attention has been focused on specific cases reported of the abuse of the drug than would otherwise have been the case. This publicity tends to magnify the extent of the evil and lends color to an inference that there is an alarming spread of the improper use of the drug, whereas the actual increase in such use may not have been inordinately large.[2]

The Treasury Department's Bureau of Narcotics furnished most of the enterprise that produced the Marijuana Tax Act. While it is, of course, difficult to know what the motives of Bureau officials were, we need assume no more than that they perceived an area of wrongdoing that properly belonged in their jurisdiction and moved to put it there. The personal interest they satisfied in pressing for marijuana legislation was one common to many officials: the interest in successfully accomplishing the task one has been assigned and in acquiring the best tools with which to accomplish it. The Bureau's efforts took two forms: cooperating in the development of state legislation affecting the use of marijuana, and providing facts and figures for journalistic accounts of the problem. These are two important modes of action available to all entrepreneurs seeking the adoption of rules: they can enlist the support of other interested organizations and develop, through the use of the press and other communications media, a favorable public attitude toward the proposed rule. If the efforts are successful, the public becomes aware of a definite problem and the appropriate organizations act in concert to produce the desired rule.

The Federal Bureau of Narcotics cooperated actively with the National Conference of Commissioners on Uniform State Laws in developing uniform laws on narcotics, stressing among other matters the need to control marijuana use.[3] In 1932, the Conference approved a draft law. The Bureau commented:

The present constitutional limitations would seem to require control measures directed against the intrastate traffic in Indian hemp to be adopted by the several state governments rather than by the Federal Government, and the policy has been to urge the state authorities generally to provide the necessary legislation, with supporting enforcement activity, to prohibit the traffic except for bona fide medical purposes. The proposed uniform state narcotic law . . . with optional text applying to the restriction of traffic in Indian hemp, has been recommended as an adequate law to accomplish the desired purposes.[4]

In its report for the year 1936, the Bureau urged its partners in this cooperative effort to exert themselves more strongly and hinted that Federal intervention might perhaps be necessary:

In the absence of additional federal legislation the Bureau of Narcotics can therefore carry on no war of its own against this traffic . . . the drug has come into wide and increasing abuse in many states, and the Bureau of Narcotics has therefore been endeavoring to impress upon the various states the urgent need for vigorous enforcement of local cannabis [marijuana] laws.[5]

The second prong of the Bureau's attack on the marijuana problem consisted of an effort to arouse the public to the danger confronting it by means of "an educational campaign describing the drug, its identification, and evil effects." [6] Apparently hoping that public interest might spur the states and cities to greater efforts, the Bureau said:

In the absence of federal legislation on the subject, the states and cities should rightfully assume the responsibility of providing vigorous measures for the extinction of this lethal weed, and it is therefore hoped that all public-spirited citizens will earnestly enlist in the movement urged by the Treasury Department to adjure intensified enforcement of marijuana laws.[7]

The Bureau did not confine itself to exhortation in departmental reports. Its methods in pursuing desired legislation are described in a passage dealing with the campaign for a uniform state narcotic law:

Articles were prepared in the Federal Bureau of Narcotics, at the request of a number of organizations dealing with this general subject [uniform state laws] for publication by such organizations in magazines and newspapers. An intelligent and sympathetic public interest, helpful to the administration of the narcotic laws, has been aroused and maintained.[8]

As the campaign for federal legislation against marijuana drew to a successful close, the Bureau's efforts to communicate its sense of the urgency of the problem to the public bore plentiful fruit. The number of articles about marijuana that appeared in popular magazines, indicated by the number indexed in the *Reader's Guide,* reached a record high. Seventeen articles appeared in a two-year period, many more than in any similar period before or after.

TABLE 31-1   *Articles on Marijuana Indexed in The Reader's Guide to Periodical Literature*

Time Period	Number of Articles
January, 1925-December, 1928	0
January, 1929-June, 1932	0
July, 1932-June, 1935	0
July, 1935-June, 1937	4
July, 1937-June, 1939	17
July, 1939-June, 1941	4
July, 1941-June, 1943	1
July, 1943-April, 1945	4
May, 1945-April, 1947	6
May, 1947-April, 1949	0
May, 1949-March, 1951	1

Of the 17, ten either explicitly acknowledged the help of the Bureau in furnishing facts and figures or gave implicit evidence of having received help by using facts and figures that had appeared earlier, either in Bureau publications or in testimony before the Congress on the Marijuana Tax Act. (We will consider the Congressional hearings on the bill in a moment.)

One clear indication of Bureau influence in the preparation of journalistic articles can be found in the recurrence of certain atrocity stories first reported by the Bureau. For instance, in an article published in the *American Magazine,* the Commissioner of Narcotics himself related the following incident:

> An entire family was murdered by a youthful [marijuana] addict in Florida. When officers arrived at the home they found the youth staggering about in a human slaughterhouse. With an ax he had killed his father, mother, two brothers, and a sister. He seemed to be in a daze. . . . He had no recollection of having committed the multiple crime. The officers knew him ordinarily as a sane, rather quiet young man; now he was pitifully crazed. They sought the reason. The boy said he had been in the habit of smoking something which youthful friends called "muggles," a childish name for marijuana.[9]

Five of the 17 articles printed during the period repeated this story, and thus showed the influence of the Bureau.

The articles designed to arouse the public to the dangers of marijuana identified use of the drug as a violation of the value of self-control and the prohibition on search for "illicit pleasure," thus legitimizing the drive against marijuana in the eyes of the public. These, of course, were the same values that had been appealed to in the course of the quest for legislation prohibiting use of alcohol and opiates for illicit purposes.

The Federal Bureau of Narcotics, then, provided most of the enterprise that produced public awareness of the problem and coordinated action by other enforcement organizations. Armed with the results of their enterprise, representatives of the Treasury Department went to Congress with a draft of the Marijuana Tax Act and requested its passage. The hearings of the House Committee on Ways and Means, which considered the bill for five days during April and May of 1937, furnish a clear case of the operation of enterprise and of the way it must accomodate other interests.

The Assistant General Counsel of the Treasury Department introduced the bill to the Congressmen with these words: "The leading newspapers of the United States have recognized the seriousness of this problem and many of them have advocated Federal legislation to control the traffic in marijuana." [10] After explaining the constitutional basis of the bill—like the Harrison Act, it was framed as a revenue measure—he reassured them about its possible effects on legitimate businesses:

> The form of the bill is such, however, as not to interfere materially with any industrial, medical, or scientific uses that the plant may have. Since hemp fiber and articles manufactured therefrom [twine and light cordage] are obtained from the

harmless mature stalk of the plant, all such products have been completely eliminated from the purview of the bill by defining the term "marijuana" in the bill so as to exclude from its provisions the mature stalk and its compounds or manufactures. There are also some dealings in marijuana seeds for planting purposes and for use in the manufacture of oil which is ultimately employed by the paint and varnish industry. As the seeds, unlike the mature stalk, contain the drug, the same complete exemption could not be applied in this instance.[11]

He further assured them that the medical profession rarely used the drug, so that its prohibition would work no hardship on them or on the pharmaceutical industry.

The committee members were ready to do what was necessary and, in fact, queried the Commissioner of Narcotics as to why this legislation had been proposed only now. He explained:

Ten years ago we only heard about it throughout the Southwest. It is only in the last few years that it has become a national menace. . . . We have been urging uniform state legislation on the several States, and it was only last month that the last state legislature adopted such legislation.[12]

The commissioner reported that many crimes were committed under the influence of marijuana, and gave examples, including the story of the Florida mass-murderer. He pointed out that the present low prices of the drug made it doubly dangerous, because it was available to anyone who had a dime to spare.

Manufacturers of hempseed oil voiced certain objections to the language of the bill, which was quickly changed to meet their specifications. But a more serious objection came from the birdseed industry, which at that time used some four million pounds of hempseed a year. Its representative apologized to the Congressmen for appearing at the last minute, stating that he and his colleagues had not realized until then that the marijuana plant referred to in the bill was the same plant from which they got an important ingredient of their product. Government witnesses had insisted that the seeds of the plant required prohibition, as well as the flowering tops smokers usually used, because they contained a small amount of the active principle of the drug and might possibly be used for smoking. The birdseed manufacturers contended that inclusion of seed under the provisions of the bill would damage their business.

To justify his request for exemptions, the manufacturers' representative pointed to the beneficial effect of hempseed on pigeons:

[It] is a necessary ingredient in pigeon feed because it contains an oil substance that is a valuable ingredient of pigeon feed, and we have not been able to find any seed that will take its place. If you substitute anything for the hemp, it has a tendency to change the character of the squabs produced.[13]

Congressman Robert L. Doughton of North Carolina inquired: "Does that seed have the same effect on pigeons as the drug has on human beings?" The manufacturers' representative said: "I have never noticed it. It has a tendency to bring back the feathers and improve the birds." [14]

Faced with serious opposition, the Government modified its stern insistence on the seed provision, noting that sterilization of the seeds might render them harmless: "It seems to us that the burden of proof is on the Government there, when we might injure a legitimate industry." [15]

Once these difficulties had been ironed out, the bill had easy sailing. Marijuana smokers, powerless, unorganized, and lacking publicly legitimate grounds for attack, sent no representatives to the hearings and their point of view found no place in the record. Unopposed, the bill passed both the House and Senate the following July. The enterprise of the Bureau had produced a new rule, whose subsequent enforcement would help create a new class of outsiders—marijuana users.

I have given an extended illustration from the field of federal legislation. But the basic parameters of this case should be equally applicable not only to legislation in general, but to the development of rules of a more informal kind. Wherever rules are created and applied, we should be alive to the possible presence of an enterprising individual or group. Their activities can properly be called *moral enterprise,* for what they are enterprising about is the creation of a new fragment of the moral constitution of society, its code of right and wrong.

Wherever rules are created and applied we should expect to find people attempting to enlist the support of coordinate groups and using the available media of communication to develop a favorable climate of opinion. Where they do not develop such support, we may expect to find their enterprise unsuccessful.[16]

And, wherever rules are created and applied, we expect that the processes of enforcement will be shaped by the complexity of the organization, resting on a basis of shared understandings in simpler groups and resulting from political maneuvering and bargaining in complex structures.

NOTES

1. See John Krout, *The Origins of Prohibition* (New York: Columbia University Press, 1928); Charles Terry and Mildred Pellens, *The Opium Problem* (New York: The Committee on Drug Addiction with the Bureau of Social Hygiene, Inc., 1928); and *Drug Addiction: Crime or Disease?*, Interim and Final Reports of the Joint Committee of the American Bar Association and the American Medical Association on Narcotic Drugs (Bloomington: Indiana University Press, 1961).
2. U.S. Treasury Department, *Traffic in Opium and Other Dangerous Drugs for the Year Ended December 31, 1931* (Washington: Government Printing Office, 1932), p. 51.
3. *Ibid.*, pp. 16–17.

4. Bureau of Narcotics, U.S. Treasury Department, *Traffic in Opium and Other Dangerous Drugs for the Year Ended December 31, 1932* (Washington: Government Printing Office, 1933), p. 13.
5. Bureau of Narcotics, U.S. Treasury Department, *Traffic in Opium and Other Dangerous Drugs for the Year Ended December 31, 1936* (Washington: Government Printing Office, 1937), p. 59.
6. *Ibid.*
7. Bureau of Narcotics, U.S. Treasury Department, *Traffic in Opium and Other Dangerous Drugs for the Year Ended December 31, 1935* (Washington: Government Printing Office, 1936), p. 30.
8. Bureau of Narcotics, U.S. Treasury Department, *Traffic in Opium and Other Dangerous Drugs for the Year Ended December 31, 1933* (Washington: Government Printing Office, 1934), p. 61.
9. H. J. Anslinger, with Courtney Ryley Cooper, "Marihuana: Assassin of Youth," *American Magazine,* CXXIV (July, 1937), 19, 150.
10. *Taxation of Marihuana* (Hearings before the Committee on Ways and Means of the House of Representatives, 75th Congress, 1st Session, on H.R. 6385, April 27–30 and May 4, 1937), p. 7.
11. *Ibid.,* p. 8.
12. *Ibid.,* p. 20.
13. *Ibid.,* pp. 73–74.
14. *Ibid.*
15. *Ibid.,* p. 85.
16. Gouldner has described a relevant case in industry, where a new manager's attempt to enforce rules that had not been enforced for a long time (and thus, in effect, create new rules) had as its immediate consequence a disruptive wildcat strike; he had not built support through the manipulation of other groups in the factory and the development of a favorable climate of opinion. See Alvin W. Gouldner, *Wildcat Strike* (Yellow Springs, Ohio: Antioch Press, 1954).

SECTION SEVEN *Social Influences and the Court*

32

Judicial Insulation

J. W. PELTASON

. . . The insulation of judges from outside influence is one of the major distinguishing characteristics between legislative and judicial decision-makers. The very purpose of constitutional provisions, canons, and socially established rules is to minimize numbers, money, patronage, and fear of reprisal as factors influencing judicial interest representation, all factors of recognized importance in the determination of legislative behavior.

One can exaggerate the difference between the insulation of judges and legislators. Numbers do affect how judicial power will be used. Whenever an interest includes the sustained support of a considerable number of voters, it can safely be predicted that this interest will be represented by some judges. Brooks Adams, one of the more astute observers of judicial behavior, put it this way: "In fine, whenever pressure has reached a given intensity, on one pretext or another, courts have enforced or dispensed with constitutional limitations with quite as much facility as have legislatures, and for the same reasons. The only difference has been that the pressure which has operated most directly upon courts has not always been the pressure which has swayed legislatures, though sometimes both influences have combined." [1]

Yet to agree with Adams is not to agree with Mr. Dooley's celebrated dictum that "th' Supreme Coort follows th' iliction returns." On the contrary, as Professor Earl Latham indicates, evidence seems to indicate that the Court defends interests "independent of the desires of new popular majorities as reflected in the election returns or the legislation that their representatives have enacted." [2] Numbers of supporters are of less significance, designedly so, in determining how judicial power will be used than in the case of legislative decisions. Judges have not hesitated to engage in conflict with the legislature, a conflict, however, that judges usually lose. . . .

The insulation of judges is related to the lack of widespread and continuous public concern about judicial activity. Except for spectacular criminal trials and a few Supreme Court decisions, news commentators and reporters who summarize the major debates in Congress and describe the daily business of government normally give less attention to judicial activity. "Inside information" about Congress or the White House is eagerly sought, but a reporter who revealed any judicial secrets might find himself in contempt of court.

From *Federal Courts in the Political Process* (New York: Random House, 1955), pp. 24–26, 27–28. Abridged with renumbered notes. Copyright © 1955 by Random House, Inc. Reprinted by permission of the publisher.

The general public lacks knowledge about the views and values represented by judges, even of those supremely significant policy-makers on the Supreme Court. Many students in college courses on American government can describe the values represented by Senator Bricker, Secretary Benson, or Congressman Taber. Yet they do not know what concepts of public interest, what values, are promoted by Justices Black or Frankfurter. Voting records of legislators are often published. Various organizations rate these records according to the degree to which they represent those organizations' concepts of the public interest. But when a scholar (Professor C. Herman Pritchett) started a vogue of publishing in popular and scholarly magazines the voting records of Supreme Court justices and arranging them according to values supported, he and his followers were criticized. Professor Mark de Wolfe Howe, for example, wrote that he doubted "whether the statistical analysis of Supreme Court opinions can, under any circumstances, be fruitful" since box scores cannot "record the impalpable factors in a process as subtle and complex as that of constitutional adjudication." The *Washington Post* commented: "We hope that Mr. Howe's exposé of this shallow thinking about the judicial process will hasten the relegation of box scores to the sports pages, where they belong." [3] Although the legislative process is as subtle and complex as that of the judicial, few have denied that something can be learned from an analysis of legislators' voting records. But to show the impact of a judge's use of his voting power, stripped of his defense of his vote, is somehow thought to be "misleading."

Although judges are isolated from non-judges and although the public is generally indifferent, there is one group that makes up an important part of the environment in which judges operate. As Jeremy Bentham pointed out, "The law is not made by judge alone, but by judge and company," and of the company, the lawyers are of special significance.

Except for persons who are formal litigants, only lawyers can file briefs and directly address the judges. Great care is taken to exclude from judicial consideration all matters except those which lawyers introduce. Thus the lawyer's skill in argument, his knowledge of other decisions and ability to weave them together, and his proficiency in presenting a well-contained conclusion to the judge are factors in determining how judicial decisions are formulated. The lawyer's briefs often form the threads out of which the judge weaves his decision.

Lawyers are thought to be experts, the elite from which judges are selected, who translate and explain judicial decisions and opinions to the laymen. Lawyers consider themselves, and are frequently considered by others, to have a special responsibility for guiding the public on questions involving the Constitution and the law. The legal elite, so it is argued, serves as a vital and necessary aristocratic check on the majority. It is the lawyers' function to see that law and not men govern. . . .

The law reviews published by law schools, the journals published by bar associations, and professional books do for judicial decisions what the drama critics' reviews do for a Broadway play. "It was the law journals, reversing the decisions of the Supreme Court, which led the fight on the Old Court," remarks Professor Hamilton.[4] Since 1937 the law reviews have anticipated most of the changes in public policy that the Supreme Court has made. Charles Evans Hughes once said, "In confronting any serious problems, a wide-awake and careful judge will at once look to see if the subject has been discussed or the authorities collated and analyzed, in a good law periodical." [5] As Professor Clement Vose has suggested, it may be that the Supreme Court follows not the election returns but the law reviews.[6]

The values represented by the law schools frequently differ from those supported by the bar association journals. Lawyers share a common training, speak the same technical language, owe allegiance to the same canons of conduct. Yet there are many different kinds of lawyers and it is misleading to think that they all represent the same interests. For example, there are the teaching lawyers and the practicing lawyers. Until the end of the nineteenth century, those who taught the law practiced it, but the modern law school brought specialized scholars and teachers who frequently represent interests different from those supported by such organizations as the American Bar Association.

The law reviews published by the law schools tended to be critical of the pre-1937 Supreme Court. On the other hand, the *American Bar Association Journal* tends to support the interests previously represented by the older Supreme Court. During the years 1896 to 1937, for example, the American Bar Association through its resolutions and *Journal* opposed the capital gains tax, campaigned against recall of judges, resolved that injunctions should be available in labor disputes, opposed the Child Labor Amendment, criticized the national government for relying so heavily on the income tax, and protested the growth of bureaucracy.[7] The Association opposed President Roosevelt's court-packing plan, has worked to expand the extent of judicial review of administrative agencies, has supported the Bricker Amendment, and has developed and defended the official theory of judicial power against the legal realists and modern-day skeptics.

Other agencies make up an important part of the judges' company and are major adjuncts to the courts in determining the uses of judicial power. One is the Department of Justice whose decision to invoke judicial power frequently initiates significant interest conflict.[8] Other major participants are the Senate and House Committees on the Judiciary, especially the former, through whose hands pass most legislation dealing with court processes and operations. . . .

NOTES

1. Brooks Adams, *The Theory of Social Revolutions* (New York: Macmillan, 1913), p. 97.
2. Earl Latham, "The Supreme Court and the Supreme People," *The Journal of Politics,* XVI (1954), 209.
3. Both are quoted by H. C. Pritchett, *Civil Liberties and the Vinson Court* (Chicago: University of Chicago Press, 1954), p. 189.
4. *Yale Law Journal,* LVI (1947), 1460.
5. Found in C. E. Vose, "NAACP Strategy in the Covenant Cases," *Western Reserve*

Law Review, VI (1955), 118, from Foreword to *The Yale Law Journal,* L (1941), 737.

6. Clement E. Vose, "The Impact of Pressure Groups on Constitutional Interpretation," paper delivered at annual convention, American Political Science Association, Chicago, Illinois, September 8, 1954; see also article mentioned above.

   In addition to the 1937 constitutional revolution, the law reviews soundly criticized the 1940 *Minersville* decision which was reversed by the Court in 1943 (see Francis H. Heller, "A Turning Point for Religious Liberty," *Virginia Law Review,* XXIX (1943), 450, for evidence of law review disapproval, disapproval that was brought to the Court's attention in the briefs filed in 1943). The law reviews also anticipated and called for *O'Malley v. Woodrough,* 307 U.S. 277 (1938) overruling *Evans v. Gore,* 253 U.S. 245 (1920) and *Girouard v. United States,* 319 U.S. 61 (1946) overruling 1929 and 1931 decisions. The reviews have also led the way in developing doctrines to extend the coverage of federal civil rights legislation and for restricting restrictive covenants and segregation. Other examples could be cited. On the other hand, the Supreme Court represents different values in its decisions interpreting the naturalization laws and rights of persons to counsel in state criminal cases than do the bulk of law review writers.

   However, before any generalizations can be made with any degree of confidence about correlations between law review "decisions" and those of judges, more systematic research is needed.

7. Drawn in large part from James Willard Hurst, *The Growth of American Law* (Boston: Little, Brown and Company, 1950), pp. 363–364.

8. See Simon E. Sobeloff, "Attorney for the Government," *American Bar Association Journal,* XLI (March, 1955), 232, and Homer Cummings and Carl McFarland, *Federal Justice* (New York: Macmillan, 1937).

33

The *Amicus Curiae* Brief: From Friendship to Advocacy

SAMUEL KRISLOV

. . . the institution of the *amicus curiae* brief has moved from neutrality to partisanship, from friendship to advocacy.

However, the change from "impartial friend of the court" to acknowledged adversary has implications that go far beyond a mere shift in the use of the brief from a source of neutral information to a flexible tactical instrument available to litigants and third parties. More significantly, the increased use of the *amicus* brief mirrors the change in tactics and structure of interest articula-

From *The Yale Law Journal,* LXXII (1963), 704–705, 706–714, 717–718, 720–721. Reprinted by permission of the author, The Yale Law Journal Company, and Fred B. Rothman & Company. Abridged with renumbered notes.

tion in American politics as a whole that occurred during the latter quarter of the nineteenth century. As Harold Lasswell has noted,[1] that period saw a transformation of dominant modes of interest activity. The emphasis shifted from personal, face-to-face contacts (including corruption) to impersonal, organized, and systematic, bureaucratically undertaken and oriented activity. This transformation is usually recognized only implicitly by commentators when accounted for in terms of reaction, either to industrialization or bureaucratization—that is, as the product of either the industrial or the organizational revolution.

The advantages that accrue to bureaucratically sophisticated groups in other political arenas became evident in the judicial sphere as well. Involved are such factors as: sensitivity to the possibility of raising new issues (whether for offensive or defensive purposes); the ability to mobilize resources (including human resources), and to bring to bear expertise, memory, or files; and the organizational flexibility to respond quickly and sensitively before policy is set. . . .

One major development that has contributed to the use of the *amicus* brief has been the emergence of administrative agencies. The regulatory agencies enforcing and establishing administrative policies have necessarily been involved with a broad complex of interests. Their policies, in turn, affect a broader skein of interests, both in direct and indirect fashion, than those of the older executive agencies. In short, the activities of these agencies have involved potential interests and actual participants beyond the normal course of individual social and political interaction with governmental agencies. The fact that this has been explicitly recognized has also reinforced the trend. Many administrative agencies, acting by legislative provision or on their own initiative, have broadened the base of official participation in hearings before them. They, thus, have mobilized and alerted groups to issues and stakes involved at a stage prior to judicial litigation. So alerted, groups and individuals have sought means of strengthening favorable policies, both at the administrative level and at the judicial level.

A transitional link between governmental agents acting as interest articulators and private interest group activity in the judicial sphere was the participation of government officials in the guise of organized groups. So, in 1913 the railroad commissions of eight states were conjoined in a single *amicus curiae* brief.[2] The 1916 term of the Court saw the National Association of Attorneys-General participate in cases, as well as groups, of attorneys-general.[3]

Among the private interest groups that were the first to utilize the opportunities of broader access were racial minority groups, securities and insurance interests, railroad interests, and miscellaneous groups under severe attack, notably the liquor interests in the first quarter of this century. Sheer familiarity with the intricacies of the existing system, strong dissatisfaction with it, and relative desperation seemingly can all function as sufficient motives for the seeking out and the finding of new channels of influence for self-protection or aggrandizement.

The first example of minority group activity appears to have been the participation of the Chinese Charitable and Benevolent Association of New York in immigration cases. Beginning in the 1904 case of *Ah How (alias Louis Ah How) v. United States*,[4] Mr. Max J. Kohler was to intervene in such cases, explaining that:

> The peculiar character of these Chinese Exclusion cases, involving arrests or exclusions of Chinese persons, frequently indigent travellers far from their home, and beyond the convenient reach of relatives and friends, as well as of witnesses in their own behalf, has made it desirable for the Chinese persons of the City of New York, and its immediate vicinity, by concerted action and mutual aid, to assist each other . . . and accordingly at or about August 1, 1903, your petitioning corporation did retain Mr. Max Kohler . . . to defend Chinese persons arrested within or prevented from entering the United States. . . .[5]

Moreover, the identification of the NAACP with such briefs is not merely a contemporary one, for that organization has, almost from its inception, participated as *amicus curiae* in litigation. An early case in point is *Guinn v. United States*,[6] the famous Grandfather Clause case, where the NAACP justified its participation on the grounds that "the vital importance of these questions to every citizen of the United States, whether white or colored, seems amply to warrant the submission of this brief." [7]

Highly regulated groups also were early participants. Since before the turn of the century, litigation involving the ICC regulatory powers has involved extensive non-party participation of interest groups (though not necessarily as *amicus curiae*). Following the principle enunciated by Merle Fainsod that interest structure often arises in response to governmental patterns, the transportation industry has continued to be the most highly and intricately organized area of the interest group spectrum. Not only has there been continued representation paralleling the political struggles of the railroad with the trucking interests, of railroad management with laborers, or even individual members with leaders; but also the report of *Noble v. United States* [8] records the appearance on opposite sides of the fence of both the Regular Common Carriers Conference of the American Trucking Association and the Contract Carriers Conference of the ATA.

While stockholders, committees, and rival companies began to participate as third parties in the last quarter of the nineteenth century, organized financial groups and associations became active later, noticeably appearing in the Court after about 1917. *Hamilton v. Kentucky Distil. Co.*,[9] involving the constitutionality of liquor prohibition, saw participation of interested organizations in 1919, as did *Pacific St. Tel. & Tel. Co. v. Oregon* [10] in 1912, with public service and ideologically oriented groups being the principal actors.

The transitional dates tend to cluster closely about the time of Brandeis' effective use of a separate brief on behalf of the National Consumers' League in *Muller v. Oregon* [11] in 1908. It is difficult to assess how strong a causal relationship there was, for Brandeis insisted on appearing for the state of Oregon, and as far as the Court was concerned, there were no indications of his being in reality an *amicus curiae*. Such an arrangement was, for Brandeis, a condition of his participation in that "the status of appearing as an official participant on behalf of the state seemed to him an important element of strength for the defense." [12] However, as early as 1916, Frankfurter called attention to the fact that Brandeis' role was essentially that of *amicus curiae*.[13]

Yet another type of interest was to be heard from. In 1925 the *Myers* case,[14] which tested the limits of legislative control over the power of executive appointment and removal, presented peculiar dilemmas of representation. Legislative interests were presumably to be defended by the plaintiff, and the executive position directly by the Department of Justice. Quite naturally Congress was restive under the arrangement, and the President Pro Tem of the Senate and the Chairman of the House Judiciary Committee were conferring with regard to possible action, when the Court, apparently on its own initiative, appointed George Wharton Pepper as *amicus curiae* to present the congressional point of view. Such legislative representation has been employed periodically since that time, including an extended oral presentation on one occasion by the Chairman of the House Judiciary Committee.[15]

Thus, by the mid 1920's, these major types of political interests had all witnessed at least one major instance of representation before the United States Supreme Court. Throughout the subsequent years the number of cases in which such briefs were filed grew in number, as did the number of such briefs filed in cases. By the 1930's, such briefs were commonplace, and by the late 1940's they were beginning to be regarded by the Court as potential sources of irritation. At the same time they were increasingly of significance to the outcome and were even cited on occasion as justification for the granting of *certiorari*.[16]

While a series of "discrete and insular minorities" of a fiscal and commercial nature early found the *amicus curiae* brief a useful and potent instrument, it was the use of the device by civil rights organizations which drew widespread public attention. The American Civil Liberties Union was most active in this, as in other aspects of fostering minority group activity. In accordance with its standard policy of developing groups so as to encourage self-defense, the ACLU has characteristically contracted its activities as each minority group has become capable of handling its own litigation, participating only by invitation. Thus, numerous organizations that developed under ACLU tutelage are now largely independent in orientation and activities. Despite sharp differentiation in attitudes toward, and methods of, litigation, some lessons of legal strategy have remained a common legacy of the various civil rights groups. They also have retained some minimal cohesion in many of the efforts to affect court rulings, as well as in their political activities, although hardly to the extent sometimes portrayed by opponents.

Vose has shown that by informal and non-systematic cooperation civil rights groups did tend to coordinate their activities in the conduct of litigation, although the vagaries of chance and the actions of legal participants often thwarted any of the vague efforts at coordination.[17] An increased reliance on litigation as a means of vindicating minority rights otherwise difficult to obtain through the political process, however, resulted in civil rights organizations such as the ACLU, and the American Jewish Congress, being among the most active filers of *amicus curiae* briefs over the past few years. In addition, labor organizations have been active, and not only in labor cases.[18] Important civil rights cases such as the desegregation decision or the restrictive covenant cases saw a turnout of large numbers of *amicus curiae* briefs from varying minority group organizations. All of this focused attention and provoked criticism of the *amicus curiae* brief.

Such briefs reached an apex of notoriety and criticism during the last half of the '40's and the early '50's. A previous rise in the number of filings was a major factor in this criticism. In a classic instance, *Lawson v. United States,*[19] the problem of the Hollywood "unfriendly ten" evoked attention through *amicus curiae* briefs from 40 organizations. Left-wing groups were both aggressive and open in their efforts to exploit the increased significance of this avenue to interest participation. The National Lawyers Guild, for example, both was and is a major filer of *amicus curiae* briefs. The relation of the *amicus* brief to standard pressure group tactics has been made even more overt. Thus, the Communist *Daily Worker* has called upon individuals to file "personal" *amicus curiae* briefs by writing letters directly to the justices.[20] Clearly, *amicus* briefs are merely the most formal of a number of lobbying tactics which include other devices such as the picketing utilized during the trial of Communist party leaders under the Smith Act in New York City. Similarly in 1953, petitions were circulated by the National Committee to Secure Justice in the *Rosenberg case.* A campaign of telegrams was part of the effort to save the life of Willie McGee, who had been sentenced to death in Mississippi. Justice Black, who had been generally sympathetic to interest group expression, found this a repugnant development and condemned the "growing practice of sending telegrams to judges in order to have cases decided by pressure." He refused to read them and noted that "counsel in this case has assured me they were not responsible for these telegrams." [21]

The lack of discreetness here—the ignoring of the traditions and practices of the judicial process—has even been demonstrated by attorneys. Wiener characterizes a brief in *Girouard v. United States* as purposely ignoring in its preoccupation with propaganda the decisive issue on which the case turned.[22] Similarly, the American Newspaper Publishers' brief in *Craig v. Harney* [23] evoked from Justice Jackson a strong response indicating that he thought its emphasis on the size and power of the constituent newspapers was neither of legal significance nor an accident but simply intimidation. (In fairness, it should be noted that size and distribution of membership are relevant to any showing of interest in an instant case and even *amicus curiae* briefs are expected to represent a specific rather than a diffuse interest.)

The question of the proper relationship of an *amicus* to the principal party and the principal argument is a complex one. In the modern context of partisan "neutrality" the *amicus'* orientation is a peculiar one and it has been a tenet of proponents of the need for restrictions that the modern *amicus* briefs have lacked a well-defined rule. A simple endorsement of a basic brief adds nothing to the cause except the prestige of the group making the endorsement. This is to invite the charge of political pressure. On the other hand concentrating on purely legal argument has its problems as well. Some *amicus curiae* briefs have, of course, been of great legal guidance to the Court. Justice Frankfurter relied greatly upon the Synagogue Council of America brief in the *McCollum* case, for example.[24] This, however, occurs generally when there is evidence of some weakness in the legal talent arrayed by the principal party, or when the interest of the *amicus curiae* is, in fact, very sharply differentiated from that of the litigant. These cases are not the run-of-the-mill ones. In most instances the situation is less stark and the considerations more complex.[25]

Where there is relatively adequate representation of the basic points of view, the *amicus curiae,* however, may perform a valuable subsidiary role by introducing subtle variations of the basic argument, or emotive and even questionable arguments that might result in a successful verdict, but are too risky to be embraced by the principal litigant. The strategy here is the reverse of that utilized by Brandeis: instead of identifying new techniques with a litigant's official position, it may very well be advantageous to label the new as unofficial so that, if it should be rejected, a minimum of disapprobation attaches to the official cause. Arguments that might anger the Justices, doctrines that have not yet been found legally acceptable, and emotive presentations that have little legal standing can best be utilized in most instances by the *amicus* rather than by the principals. The NAACP, for example, suggested the overruling of *Plessy v. Ferguson* as an *amicus curiae* in *Henderson v. United States.*[26] And sometimes such suggestions bear fruit. For example, the ACLU *amicus curiae* brief was apparently influential in the overturning of *Wolf v. Colorado.*[27]

The considerations involved in such supplementary usages of the *amicus curiae* brief are admirably portrayed in the discussion between Charles Abrams and Newman Levy of the American Jewish Committee in connection with the restrictive covenant cases. When asked his views of a prospective brief to be filed by the American Jewish Committee, Abrams wrote:

> It is an excellent "main brief" written with your fine straight style. But I question the adequacy of its emphasis as a brief *amici.*
>
> I have always viewed the function of the *amici* to take up and emphasize those points which are novel or which, if stressed in the main brief, might dilute or weaken the main forceful arguments.
>
> I never thought there was much cumulative force in the repetition of logic by 18 briefs. Unlike good poetry, repeated it has a tendency to bore. But a weak legal argument, with a moral quality, forcefully presented by an "outsider" will not detract from the force of the main argument. . . .

The *amici* should be providing the arguments that will salvage the judges' consciences or square with their prepossessions should they lean toward holding for us. . . .

Play up what entailment of all land would mean socially. Use the relevant references by Gunnar Myrdal; give the British background for exclusion of nonconformists and their migration to America where the freehold and the fee simple became one of our earliest and greatest traditions. Show how Jefferson and the states immediately after Independence adopted laws excluding primogeniture and entail. . . . May people band together to bar a race from food and clothing? These are a few of the important irrelevancies that occur to me.

Why desert all these rich and adventurous passages to jam the safe waters that should be reserved for the main advocates? [28]

But the strategies for the *amici* may be different from the strategies of those interested merely in winning the case. This is suggested by Newman Levy's reply:

I thoroughly agree with everything you say about the function of an *amicus* brief. So far as the court is concerned I am inclined to think that it is pretty much like an endorsement on a note. Its purpose is to tell the court that we agree with the appellant and we hope it will decide in his favor. . . .

When this brief was first contemplated I discussed it with my legal committee, and they agreed that I should confine myself exclusively to this constitutional question. That was why I omitted the sociological stuff, the United Nations Charter, and the rest of it. You see, if the Supreme Court should happen to mention in its decision that restrictive covenants are illegal upon the authority of *Buchanan v. Warley,* we will be able to say to our members, "Isn't that exactly what we told the court?" [29]

Thus the function of the *amicus* can be viewed as simply one of endorsement, or it can be seen also as part of the supplementary strategies available to the principal litigants.

Whether or not the tactical potential of the *amicus* brief is realized in any given suit will ultimately depend on the rules of the Court governing the filing of *amicus* petitions and the willingness of the Court to permit the filing of any given brief. Prior to 1937, there appears to have been no written rule on the subject of the filing of an *amicus curiae* brief, and leave of the Court was necessary for filing. The specification in that year that litigating parties must give consent to non-governmental *amicus* briefs made no real difference in practice. Prior to the adoption of the rule, it had been standard procedure to request permission from the parties. In the absence of such consent, leave to file was easily obtained from the Court in almost every instance both before and after promulgation of the rule.

The change of 1949, on its face, seemed to liberalize the rules. It recognized the existence of briefs filed by order of the Court without consent of the parties, a procedure that had not been formalized in previous rules. Since such filings had, as we have seen, been standard, the more significant indicator for future practice was the intimation that *amicus* briefs and motions to file would have to be submitted within "a reasonable time" prior to decision, indicating some dissatisfaction with dilatory filing of such briefs in the past. Further, the brief for motion to file was to be a separate document from the brief on the merits, permitting the Justices to avoid wading through the entire argument before deciding whether such a brief was to be permitted their attention. Even more direct and succinct was the Court's reaction to applications to file without consent of the parties: "Such motions are not favored." [30] Although a technical reading of the rules [now Rules 42(1) and 42(2)] indicates disfavor only for motions to file on the jurisdictional question or for petitions for a writ of *certiorari* without party consent and do not extend this disfavor to *amicus curiae* briefs on the merits, in practice it has appeared that the disfavor obtains equally in both instances.[31]

The result was quite marked. In the 1948 term prior to the new rule, 14 briefs were filed without party consent, while the Court denied permission to file only three such briefs. With the new attitude of the Court, the five terms following promulgation of the rule saw denial of leave to file without party consent in 39 instances, while in only 12 instances was permission granted.[32] . . .

The participation of the *amici* need not be at their own initiative. A court may request participation on its own. The Solicitor General of the United States and representatives of other government units are regularly invited to participate and file a brief. From time to time individuals with specialized knowledge have been called upon to offer their expertise in service to the United States Supreme Court. Lower courts have utilized the *amicus* for various special formal assignments, similar to those of a Master or Referee. Such functions include the handling of special problems dealing with juvenile delinquents, and the individuals are sometimes designated by the anglicized title, Friends of the Court, to distinguish this investiture from the less formalized *amicus* function.

Again, a court may call upon members of the bar (or more usually appropriate law officers) to act directly on behalf of the court itself. Here, in a sense, the old private relationship of the lawyer to the court is recreated; the friendship of the officer is most emphatically for the court. Thus in *Universal Oil Products Co. v. Root Refrigerating Co.,*[33] the *amici* had been designated to participate in an inquiry with regard to the possibility of fraud and bribery in the original court order. When dishonesty on the part of a judge was shown, the *amici* who had also been attorneys for affected parties, though not principal litigants, sought to obtain compensation which in effect would have been reimbursement for their employers. The Court rejected such a claim. The role precluded their basically participating in a dual capacity:

> No doubt, a court that undertakes an investigation of fraud upon it may avail itself, as did the court below, of *amici* to represent the public interest in the administration of justice. But compensation is not the normal reward of those who offer such services. . . . Here the *amici* also represented substantial private in-

terests. Their clients were interested in vacating the *Root* judgment though they would not subject themselves to the court's jurisdiction and the hazards of an adverse determination. While the *amici* formally served the court, they were in fact in the pay of private clients. *Amici* selected by the court to vindicate its honor ordinarily ought not to be in the service of those having private interests in the outcome. Certainly it is not consonant with that regard for fastidiousness which should govern a court of equity, to award fees and costs of *amici curiae* who have already been compensated by private clients so that these be reimbursed for what they voluntarily paid.[34]

Thus while vindicating the right to appoint such *amici,* the Supreme Court asserted a special relationship between such *amici* and the court who designates them.

Indeed "friendship" at this point becomes a peculiar sort of advocacy. The *amicus* becomes the spokesman for court interests in a vital and active sense. This is well borne out in the recent cases involving desegregation. The Supreme Court's device of delegating to the district courts the implementation of its desegregation decision has thrust upon the district courts an unusual burden of decision and activity.[35] Where defiance has occurred, the courts have been particularly dependent upon the activities of the executive and have acknowledged this dependency.

So in both the Little Rock, Ark., and the University of Mississippi integration crises the federal district court, on its own initiative, designated the United States Attorney-General and the United States Attorney as *amici* and specifically instructed its designated *amici* to carry out activities on behalf of the court. . . .

The *amicus curiae* brief represents a prime example of a legal institution evolving and developing while maintaining superficial identity with the past. It has been a catch-all device for dealing with some of the difficulties presented by the common law system of adversary proceeding. In the United States, in particular, it has allowed representation of governmental and other complex interests generated by the legal involutions of federalism. In addition, the United States Supreme Court has helped foster its development as a vehicle for broad representation of interests, particularly in disputes where political ramifications are wider than a narrow view of common law litigation might indicate. Groups inherently weak in the political arenas or unequally endowed with resources of wealth or skills have quite naturally been the leaders in the use of the brief. The growth of the regulatory process and the welfare state have played a significant role in fostering group organization and an awareness of policy determination by the judiciary.

On occasion, the *amicus curiae* has been an agent of the court acting as champion of the court's point of view, vigorously pursuing and defending a legal position at the request of the bench itself. In the main, however, the *amicus curiae* has been a means of fostering partisan third-party involvement through the encouragement of group representation by a self-conscious bench. The judges have sought to gain information from political groups as well as to give them a feeling of participation in the process of decision. Access to the legal process on the part of such organizations is a logical extension of realistic awareness of law as a process of social choice and policy-making. Even criticism of the *amicus curiae* brief as "political propaganda," court embarrassment at such criticism, and changes in the rules that have hampered such briefs in the short run have not seriously stemmed the growing reliance upon it.

NOTES

1. Book Review, *University of Pennsylvania Law Review*, CVII (1958), 295.
2. Minnesota Rate Cases, 230 U.S. 352 (1913); Missouri Rate Cases, 230 U.S. 474 (1913).
3. *Cladwell v. Sioux Falls Stock Yards Co.*, 242 U.S. 559 (1917); and *Hall v. Geiger-Jones Co.*, 242 U.S. 539 (1917), where both the National Association of Attorneys-General and the Investment Bankers Association of America filed briefs; and *Utah Power & Light v. United States*, 243 U.S. 389 (1917).
4. 193 U.S. 65 (1904).
5. Brief for the Chinese Charitable and Benevolent Association of New York, as *Amicus Curiae*, p. 2, *Ah How v. United States, supra* note 4.
6. 238 U.S. 347 (1915).
7. Brief for NAACP as *Amicus Curiae*, p. 2, *Guinn v. United States, supra* note 6.
8. 319 U.S. 88, 89 (1943).
9. *Hamilton v. Kentucky Distil.*, 251 U.S. 146 (1919).
10. 223 U.S. 118 (1912). Among others, briefs were filed for The American Bureau of Political Research and the People's Rule League of America.
11. 208 U.S. 412 (1908).
12. Mason, *The Language of Dissent* (1959), p. 248; Vose, "The National Consumers League and the Brandeis Brief," *Midwest Journal of Political Science*, I (1957), 267: Goldmark, *Impatient Crusader* (1953), p. 163.
13. Frankfurter, "Hours of Labor and Realism in Constitutional Law," 29 *Harvard Law Review*, 353, 372 *n.* 63 (1916).
14. *Myers v. United States*, 272 U.S. 52 (1926).
15. See *Jurney v. MacCracken*, 294 U.S. 125, 128 (1935), for presentation by Representative Hatton W. Sumners.
16. See *Pennsylvania v. Nelson*, 350 U.S. 497 (1956), and *Georgia v. Evans*, 316 U.S. 159 (1942).
17. Vose, *Caucasians Only* (1959), chs. 4–8.
18. See, for example, *Shelley v. Kraemer*, 334 U.S. 1 (1948).
19. 176 F. 2d 49 (D.C. Cir. 1949), *cert. denied*, 339 U.S. 934 (1950).
20. Harper and Etherington, "Lobbyists Before the Court," *University of Pennsylvania Law Review*, CI (1954), 1172–1173.
21. Vose, "Litigation as a Form of Pressure Group Activity," *Annals*, CCCXIX, 29 (September, 1958); *New York Times*, March 16, 1951, p. 23.
22. Wiener, "The Supreme Court's New Rules," *Harvard Law Review*, LXVIII (1954), 20, 80 *n.*296.
23. 331 U.S. 367, 397 (1947).
24. *McCollum v. Board of Education*, 333 U.S. 203, 229 *n.*19 (1948).
25. See generally Harper and Etherington, *supra n.* 20.
26. Brief for NAACP as *Amicus Curiae*, *Henderson v. United States*, 314 U.S. 625 (1941).
27. For the role of the *amicus curiae* and of the principal litigant see the dissenting opinion of Justice Harlan, *Mapp v. Ohio*, 367 U.S. 643, 675 *n.* 5 (1961).
28. Vose, *Caucasians Only* (1959), pp. 166–167.
29. *Id.* at 167.

30. *Sup. Ct. Rules* 27:9 (b), 338 U.S. 959 (1949).
31. Comment, "The *Amicus Curiae*," *Northwestern University Law Review,* LV (1960), 469, 475.
32.   Trends in Filing, Granting, and Denial of
                    Briefs *Amicus* and Oral Participation,
                       United States Supreme Court
                            1949–1961 Terms *

	1949	1950	1951	1952	1953	1954	1955	1956	1957	1958	1959	1960	1961
Cases	53	36	30	39	20	47	41	39	43	63	43	57	54
Briefs	118	70	44	64	34	57	74	69	64	85	64	97	107

* Sources of this table include U.S. Reports; Sonnenfeld, *Participation of* Amici Cúriae *by Filing Briefs and Presenting Oral Argument in Decisions of the Supreme Court, 1949–1957* (Michigan State University Governmental Research Bureau, 1958) p. 4, Table 1; and Schubert, *Quantitative Aspects of Judicial Behavior* (1959), pp. 74–75.
33. 328 U.S. 575, 581 (1946).
34. *Id.* at 580–581.
35. See Peltason, *Fifty-Eight Lonely Men* (1961).

34

The Supreme Court as a National Policy-Maker

ROBERT A. DAHL

Every policy dispute can be tested, at least in principle, by the majority criterion, because (again, in principle) the dispute can be analyzed according to the numbers of people for and against the various alternatives at issue, and therefore according to the proportions of the citizens or eligible members who are for and against the alternatives. Logically speaking, except for a trivial case, every conflict within a given society must be a dispute between a majority of those eligible to participate and a minority or minorities; or else it must be a dispute between or among minorities only. Within certain limits, both possibilities are independent of the number of policy alternatives at issue, and

From Robert A. Dahl, "Decision-Making in a Democracy: The Supreme Court as a National Policy-Maker," *The Journal of Public Law,* VI (1957), 281–295. Reprinted by permission of the author and publisher.

since the argument is not significantly affected by the number of alternatives, it is convenient to assume that each policy dispute represents only two alternatives.

If everyone prefers one of two alternatives, then no significant problem arises. But a case will hardly come before the Supreme Court unless at least one person prefers an alternative that is opposed by another person. Strictly speaking, then, no matter how the Court acts in determining the legality or constitutionality of one alternative or the other, the outcome of the Court's decision must either (1) accord with the preferences of a minority of citizens and run counter to the preferences of a majority; (2) accord with the preferences of a majority and run counter to the preferences of a minority; or (3) accord with the preferences of one minority and run counter to the preferences of another minority, the rest being indifferent.

In a democratic system with a more or less representative legislature, it is unnecessary to maintain a special court to secure the second class of outcomes. A case might be made out that the Court protects the rights of national majorities against local interests in federal questions, but so far as I am aware, the role of the Court as a policy-maker is not usually defended in this fashion; in what follows, therefore, I propose to pass over the ticklish question of federalism and deal only with "national" majorities and minorities. The third kind of outcome, although relevant according to other criteria, is hardly relevant to the majority criterion, and may also be passed over for the moment.

One influential view of the Court, however, is that it stands in some special way as a protection of minorities against tyranny by majorities. In the course of its 167 years, in 78 cases, the Court has struck down 86 different provisions of federal law as unconstitutional,[1] and by interpretation it has modified a good many more. It might be argued, then, that in all or in a very large number of these cases the Court was, in fact, defending the rights of some minority against a "tyrannical" majority. There are, however, some exceedingly serious difficulties with this interpretation of the Court's activities.

One problem, which is essentially ideological in character, is the difficulty of reconciling such an interpretation with the existence of a democratic polity, for it is not at all difficult to show by appeals to authorities as various and imposing as Aristotle, Locke, Rousseau, Jefferson, and Lincoln that the term democracy means, among other things, that the power to rule resides in popular majorities and their representatives. Moreover, from entirely reasonable and traditional definitions of popular sovereignty and political equality, the principle of majority rule can be shown to follow by logical necessity.[2] Thus to affirm that the Court supports minority preferences against majorities is to deny that popular sovereignty and political equality, at least in the traditional sense, exist in the United States; and to affirm that the Court *ought* to act in this way is to deny that popular sovereignty and political equality *ought* to prevail in this country. In a country that glories in its democratic tradition, this is not a happy state of affairs for the Court's defenders; and it is no wonder that a great deal of effort has gone into the enterprise of proving that, even if the

Court consistently defends minorities against majorities, nonetheless it is a thoroughly "democratic" institution. But no amount of tampering with democratic theory can conceal the fact that a system in which the policy preferences of minorities prevail over majorities is at odds with the traditional criteria for distinguishing a democracy from other political systems.[3]

Fortunately, however, we do not need to traverse this well-worn ground; for the view of the Court as a protector of the liberties of minorities against the tyranny of majorities is beset with other difficulties that are not so much ideological as matters of fact and logic. If one wishes to be at all rigorous about the question, it is probably impossible to demonstrate that any particular Court decisions have or have not been at odds with the preferences of a "national majority." It is clear that unless one makes *some* assumptions as to the kind of evidence one will require for the existence of a set of minority and majority preferences in the general population, the view under consideration is incapable of being proved at all. In any strict sense, no adequate evidence exists, for scientific opinion polls are of relatively recent origin, and national elections are little more than an indication of the first preferences of a number of citizens—in the United States the number ranges between about 40 and 60 per cent of the adult population—for certain candidates for public office. I do not mean to say that there is no relation between preferences among candidates and preferences among alternative public policies, but the connection is a highly tenuous one, and on the basis of an election it is almost never possible to adduce whether a majority does or does not support one of two or more policy alternatives about which members of the political elite are divided. For the greater part of the Court's history, then, there is simply no way of establishing with any high degree of confidence whether a given alternative was or was not supported by a majority or a minority of adults or even of voters.

In the absence of relatively direct information, we are thrown back on indirect tests. The 86 provisions of federal law that have been declared unconstitutional were, of course, initially passed by majorities of those voting in the Senate and in the House. They also had the president's formal approval. We could, therefore, speak of a majority of those voting in the House and Senate, together with the president, as a "lawmaking majority." It is not easy to determine whether any such constellation of forces within the political elites actually coincides with the preferences of a majority of American adults or even with the preferences of a majority of that half of the adult population which, on the average, votes in congressional elections. Such evidence as we have from opinion polls suggests that Congress is not markedly out of line with public opinion, or at any rate with such public opinion as there is after one discards the answers of people who fall into the category, often large, labeled "no response" or "don't know." If we may, on these somewhat uncertain grounds, take a "lawmaking majority" as equivalent to a "national majority," then it is possible to test the hypothesis that the Supreme Court is shield and buckler for minorities against national majorities.

Under any reasonable assumptions about the nature of the political process, it would appear to be somewhat naïve to assume that the Supreme Court either would or could play the role of Galahad. Over the whole history of the Court, on the average one new justice has been appointed every 22 months. Thus a president can expect to appoint about two new justices during one term of office; and if this were not enough to tip the balance on a normally divided Court, he is almost certain to succeed in two terms, Thus, Hoover had three appointments; Roosevelt, nine; Truman, four; and Eisenhower, so far, has had four. Presidents are not famous for appointing justices hostile to their own views on public policy nor could they expect to secure confirmation of a man whose stance on key questions was flagrantly at odds with that of the dominant majority in the Senate. Justices are typically men who, prior to appointment, have engaged in public life and have committed themselves publicly on the great questions of the day. As Justice Frankfurter has recently reminded us, a surprisingly large proportion of the justices, particularly of the great justices who have left their stamp upon the decisions of the Court, have had little or no prior judicial experience.[4] Nor have the justices—certainly not the great justices—been timid men with a passion for anonymity. Indeed, it is not too much to say that if justices were appointed primarily for their "judicial" qualities without regard to their basic attitudes on fundamental questions of public policy, the Court could not play the influential role in the American political system that it does in reality play.

The fact is, then, that the policy views dominant on the Court are never for long out of line with the policy views dominant among the lawmaking majorities of the United States. Consequently it would be most unrealistic to suppose that the Court would, for more than a few years at most, stand against any major alternatives sought by a lawmaking majority. The judicial agonies of the

TABLE 34-1   *The Interval Between Appointments*
to the Supreme Court*

Interval in Years	Per Cent of Total Appointments	Cumulative Per Cent
Less than 1	21	21
1	34	55
2	18	73
3	9	82
4	8	90
5	7	97
6	2	99
12	1	100

*The table excludes the six appointments made in 1789. Except for the four most recent appointments, it is based on data in the *Encyclopedia of American History*, Morris, ed. (1953), pp. 461-462. It may be slightly inaccurate because the source shows only the year of appointment, not the month. The twelve-year interval was from 1811 to 1823.

New Deal will, of course, quickly come to mind; but Mr. Roosevelt's difficulties with the Court were truly exceptional. Generalizing over the whole history of the Court, the chances are about one out of five that a president will make one appointment to the Court in less than a year, better than one out of two that he will make one within two years, and three out of four that he will make one within three years. Mr. Roosevelt had unusually bad luck: he had to wait four years for his first appointment; the odds against this long an interval are four to one. With average luck, the battle with the Court would never have occurred; even as it was, although the "court-packing" proposal did formally fail, by the end of his second term Mr. Roosevelt had appointed five new justices and by 1941 Justice Roberts was the only remaining holdover from the Hoover era.

It is to be expected, then, that the Court is least likely to be successful in blocking a determined and persistent lawmaking majority on a major policy and most likely to succeed against a "weak" majority: a dead one, a transient one, a fragile one, or one weakly united upon a policy of subordinate importance.

TABLE 34-2 *Percentage of Cases Held Unconstitutional*
Arranged by Time Intervals Between
Legislation and Decision

Number of Years	Per Cent New Deal Legislation	Per Cent Other	Per Cent All Legislation
2 or less	92	19	30
3-4	8	19	18
5-8	0	28	24
9-12	0	13	11
13-16	0	8	6
17-20	0	1	1
21 or more	0	12	10
Total	100	100	100

An examination of the cases in which the Court has held federal legislation unconstitutional confirms, on the whole, our expectations. Over the whole history of the Court, about half the decisions have been rendered more than four years after the legislation was passed.

Of the 24 laws held unconstitutional within two years, 11 were measures enacted in the early years of the New Deal. Indeed, New Deal measures comprise nearly a third of all the legislation that has ever been declared unconstitutional within four years after enactment.

It is illuminating to examine the cases where the Court has acted on legislation within four years after enactment: where the presumption is, that is to say, that the lawmaking majority is not necessarily a dead one. Of the 12 New

Deal cases, two were, from a policy point of view, trivial; and two, although perhaps not trivial, were of minor importance to the New Deal program.[5] A fifth [6] involved the NRA, which was to expire within three weeks of the decision. Insofar as the unconstitutional provisions allowed "codes of fair competition" to be established by industrial groups, it is fair to say that President Roosevelt and his advisers were relieved by the Court's decision of a policy they had come to find increasingly embarrassing. In view of the tenacity with which Mr. Roosevelt held to his major program, there can hardly be any doubt that had he wanted to pursue the major policy objective involved in the NRA codes, as he did, for example, with the labor provisions, he would not have been stopped by the Court's special theory of the Constitution. As to the seven other cases,[7] it is entirely correct to say, I think, that whatever some of the eminent justices might have thought during their fleeting moments of glory, they did not succeed in interposing a barrier to the achievement of the objectives of the legislation; and in a few years most of the constitutional interpretation on which the decisions rested had been unceremoniously swept under the rug.

TABLE 34-3 *Cases Holding Legislation Unconstitutional Within Four Years after Enactment*

Interval in Years	New Deal		Other		Total	
	No.	%	No.	%	No.	%
2 or less	11	29	13	34	24	63
3 to 4	1	3	13	34	14	37
Total	12	32	26	68	38	100

The remainder of the 38 cases where the Court has declared legislation unconstitutional within four years of enactment tend to fall into two rather distinct groups: those involving legislation that could reasonably be regarded as important *from the point of view of lawmaking majority* and those involving minor legislation. Although the one category merges into the other, so that some legislation must be classified rather arbitrarily, probably there will be little disagreement with classifying the specific legislative provisions involved in 11 cases as essentially minor from the point of view of the lawmaking majority (however important they may have been as constitutional interpretations).[8] The specific legislative provisions involved in the remaining 15 cases are by no means of uniform importance, but with one or two possible exceptions it seems reasonable to classify them as major policy issues from the point of view of the lawmaking majority.[9] We would expect that cases involving major legislative policy would be propelled to the Court much more rapidly than cases involving minor policy, and, as the table below shows, this is in fact what happens.

Thus a lawmaking majority with major policy objectives in mind usually has

TABLE 34-4   *Number of Cases Involving Legislative Policy Other Than Those Arising under New Deal Legislation Holding Legislation Unconstitutional Within Four Years after Enactment*

Interval in Years	Major Policy	Minor Policy	Total
2 or less	11	2	13
3 to 4	4	9	13
Total	15	11	26

an opportunity to seek for ways of overcoming the Court's veto. It is an interesting and highly significant fact that Congress and the president do generally succeed in overcoming a hostile Court on major policy issues. It is particularly instructive to examine the cases involving major policy. In two cases involving punitive legislation enacted by Radical Republican Congresses against supporters of the Confederacy during the Civil War, the Court faced a rapidly crumbling majority whose death knell as an effective national force was sounded with the election of 1876.[10] Three cases are difficult to classify and I have labeled them "unclear." Of these, two were decisions made in 1921 involving a 1919 amendment to the Lever Act to control prices.[11] The legislation was important, and the provision in question was clearly struck down, but the Lever Act terminated three days after the decision and Congress did not return to the subject of price control until World War II, when it experienced no constitutional difficulties arising from these cases (which were primarily concerned with the lack of an ascertainable standard of guilt). The third case in this category successfully eliminated stock dividends from the scope of the Sixteenth Amendment, although a year later Congress enacted legislation taxing the actual income from such stock.[12]

The remaining ten cases were ultimately followed by a reversal of the actual policy results of the Court's action, although not necessarily of the specific constitutional interpretation. In four cases,[13] the policy consequences of the Court's decision were overcome in less than a year. The other six required a long struggle. Workmen's compensation for longshoremen and harbor workers was invalidated by the Court in 1920;[14] in 1922 Congress passed a new law which was, in its turn, knocked down by the Court in 1924;[15] in 1927 Congress passed a third law, which was finally upheld in 1932.[16] The notorious income tax cases[17] of 1895 were first somewhat narrowed by the Court itself;[18] the Sixteenth Amendment was recommended by President Taft in 1909 and was ratified in 1913, some 18 years after the Court's decisions. The two child labor cases represent the most effective battle ever waged by the Court against legislative policy-makers. The original legislation outlawing child labor, based on the commerce clause, was passed in 1916 as a part of Wilson's

TABLE 34-5 *Type of Congressional Action Following Supreme Court Decisions Holding Legislation Unconstitutional Within Four Years after Enactment (Other Than New Deal Legislation)*

Congressional Action	Major Policy	Minor Policy	Total
Reverses Court's policy	10*	2§	12
Changes own policy	2†	0	2
None	0	8‖	8
Unclear	3‡	1#	4
Total	15	11	26

Pollock v. Farmers' Loan & Trust Co., 157 U.S. 429 (1895); Employers' Liability Cases, 207 U.S. 463 (1908); *Keller v. United States*, 213 U.S. 138 (1909); *Hammer v. Dagenhart*, 247 U.S. 251 (1918); *Bailey v. Drexel Furniture Co.*, 259 U.S. 20 (1922); *Trusler v. Crooks*, 269 U.S. 475 (1926); *Hill v. Wallace*, 259 U.S. 44 (1922); *Knickerbocker Ice Co. v. Stewart*, 253 U.S. 149 (1920); *Washington v. Dawson & Co.*, 264 U.S. (1924)

†*Ex parte Garland*, 4 Wall. (U.S.) 333 (1867); *United States v. Klein*, 13 Wall. (U.S.) 128 (1872).

‡*United States v. Cohen Grocery Co.*, 255 U.S. 81 (1921); *Weeds, Inc. v. United States* 255 U.S. 109 (1921); *Eisner v. Macomber*, 252 U.S. 189 (1920).

§*Gordon v. United States*, 2 Wall. (U.S.) 561 (1865); *Evans v. Gore*, 253 U.S. 245 (1920).

‖*United States v. Dewitt*, 9 Wall. (U.S.) 41 (1870); *Monongahela Navigation Co. v. United States*, 148 U.S. 312 (1893); *Wong Wing v. United States*, 163 U.S. 228 (1896); *Fairbank v. United States*, 181 U.S. 283 (1901); *Rassmussen v. United States*, 197 U.S. 516 (1905); *Muskrat v. United States*, 219 U.S. 346 (1911); *Choate v. Trapp*, 224 U.S. 665 (1912); *United States v. Lovett*, 328 U.S. 303 (1946).

#*Untermyer v. Anderson*, 276 U.S. 440 (1928).

New Freedom. Like Roosevelt later, Wilson was somewhat unlucky in his Supreme Court appointments; he made only three appointments during his eight years, and one of these was wasted, from a policy point of view, on McReynolds. Had McReynolds voted "right," the subsequent struggle over the problem of child labor need not have occurred, for the decision in 1918 was by a Court divided five to four, McReynolds voting with the majority.[19] Congress moved at once to circumvent the decision by means of the tax power, but in 1922 the Court blocked that approach.[20] In 1924 Congress returned to the engagement with a constitutional amendment that was rapidly endorsed by a number of state legislatures before it began to meet so much resistance in the states remaining that the enterprise miscarried. In 1938, under a second reformist president, new legislation was passed, 22 years after the first; this a chastened Court accepted in 1941,[21] and thereby brought to an end a battle that had lasted a full quarter-century.

The entire record of the duel between the Court and the lawmaking majority, in cases where the Court has held legislation unconstitutional within four years after enactment, is summarized in Table 34–6.

TABLE 34-6 *Type of Congressional Action after Supreme Court Decisions Holding Legislation Unconstitutional Within Four Years after Enactment (Including New Deal Legislation)*

Congressional Action	Major Policy	Minor Policy	Total
Reverses Court's policy	17	2	19
None	0	12	12
Other	6*	1	7
Total	23	15	38

*In addition to the actions in Table 34-5 under "Changes own policy" and "Unclear" this figure includes the NRA legislation affected by the *Schechter Poultry* case.

Thus the application of the majority criterion seems to show the following: First, if the Court did in fact uphold minorities against national majorities, as both its supporters and critics often seem to believe, it would be an extremely anomalous institution from a democratic point of view. Second, the elaborate "democratic" rationalizations of the Court's defenders and the hostility of its "democratic" critics are largely irrelevant, for lawmaking majorities generally have had their way. Third, although the Court seems never to have succeeded in holding out indefinitely, in a very small number of important cases it has delayed the application of policy up to as much as 25 years.

How can we appraise decisions of the third kind just mentioned? Earlier I referred to the criterion of Right or Justice as a norm sometimes invoked to describe the role of the Court. In accordance with this norm, it might be argued that the most important policy function of the Court is to protect rights that are in some sense basic or fundamental. Thus (the argument might run) in a country where basic rights are, on the whole, respected, one should not expect more than a small number of cases where the Court has had to plant itself firmly against a lawmaking majority. But majorities may, on rare occasions, become "tyrannical"; and when they do, the Court intervenes; and although the constitutional issue may, strictly speaking, be technically open, the Constitution assumes an underlying fundamental body of rights and liberties which the Court guarantees by its decisions.

Here again, however, even without examining the actual cases, it would appear, on political grounds, somewhat unrealistic to suppose that a Court whose members are recruited in the fashion of Supreme Court justices would long hold to norms of Right or Justice substantially at odds with the rest of the political elite. Moreover, in an earlier day it was perhaps easier to believe that certain rights are so natural and self-evident that their fundamental validity is as much a matter of definite knowledge, at least to all reasonable creatures, as the color of a ripe apple. To say that this view is unlikely to find many articulate defenders today is, of course, not to disprove it; it is rather to suggest that we do not need to elaborate the case against it in this essay.

In any event the best rebuttal to the view of the Court suggested above will be found in the record of the Court's decisions. Surely the six cases referred to a moment ago, where the policy consequences of the Court's decisions were overcome only after long battles, will not appeal to many contemporary minds as evidence for the proposition under examination. A natural right to employ child labor in mills and mines? To be free of income taxes by the federal government? To employ longshoremen and harbor workers without the protection of workmen's compensation? The Court itself did not rely upon such arguments in these cases, and it would be no credit to their opinions to reconstruct them along such lines.

So far, however, our evidence has been drawn from cases in which the Court has held legislation unconstitutional within four years after enactment. What of the other 40 cases? Do we have evidence in these that the Court has protected fundamental or natural rights and liberties against the dead hand of some past tyranny by the lawmakers? The evidence is not impressive. In the entire history of the Court there is not one case arising under the First Amendment in which the Court has held federal legislation unconstitutional. If we turn from these fundamental liberties of religion, speech, press, and assembly, we do find a handful of cases—something less than ten—arising under Amendments Four to Seven in which the Court has declared acts unconstitutional that might properly be regarded as involving rather basic liberties.[22] An inspection of these cases leaves the impression that, in all of them, the lawmakers and the Court were not very far apart; moreover, it is doubtful that the fundamental conditions of liberty in this country have been altered by more than a hair's breadth as a result of these decisions. However, let us give the Court its due; it is little enough.

Over against these decisions we must put the 15 or so cases in which the Court used the protections of the Fifth, Thirteenth, Fourteenth, and Fifteenth Amendments to preserve the rights and liberties of a relatively privileged group at the expense of the rights and liberties of a submerged group: chiefly slaveholders at the expense of slaves,[23] white people at the expense of colored people,[24] and property holders at the expense of wage earners and other groups.[25] These cases, unlike the relatively innocuous ones of the preceding set, all involved liberties of genuinely fundamental importance, where an opposite policy would have meant thoroughly basic shifts in the distribution of rights, liberties, and opportunities in the United States—where, moreover, the policies sustained by the Court's action have since been repudiated in every civilized nation of the Western world, including our own. Yet, if our earlier argument is correct, it is futile—precisely because the basic distribution of privilege *was* at issue—to suppose that the Court could have possibly acted much differently in these areas of policy from the way in which it did in fact act.

Thus the role of the Court as a policy-making institution is not simple; and it is an error to suppose that its functions can be either described or appraised by means of simple concepts drawn from democratic or moral theory. It is possible, nonetheless, to derive a few general conclusions about the Court's role as a policy-making institution.

National politics in the United States, as in other stable democracies, is dominated by relatively cohesive alliances that endure for long periods of time. One recalls the Jeffersonian alliance, the Jacksonian, the extraordinarily long-lived Republican dominance of the post-Civil War Years, and the New Deal alliance shaped by Franklin Roosevelt. Each is marked by a break with past policies, a period of intense struggle, followed by consolidation, and finally decay and disintegration of the alliance.

Except for short-lived transitional periods when the old alliance is disintegrating and the new one is struggling to take control of political institutions, the Supreme Court is inevitably a part of the dominant national alliance. As an element in the political leadership of the dominant alliance, the Court of course supports the major policies of the alliance. By itself, the Court is almost powerless to affect the course of national policy. In the absence of substantial agreement within the alliance, an attempt by the Court to make national policy is likely to lead to disaster, as the *Dred Scott* decision and the early New Deal cases demonstrate. Conceivably, the cases of the last three decades involving the freedom of Negroes, culminating in the now famous decision on school integration, are exceptions to this generalization; I shall have more to say about them in a moment.

The Supreme Court is not, however, simply an *agent* of the alliance. It is an essential part of the political leadership and possesses some bases of power of its own, the most important of which is the unique legitimacy attributed to its interpretations of the Constitution. This legitimacy the Court jeopardizes if it flagrantly opposes the major policies of the dominant alliance; such a course of action, as we have seen, is one in which the Court will not normally be tempted to engage.

It follows that within the somewhat narrow limits set by the basic policy goals of the dominant alliance, the Court *can* make national policy. Its discretion, then, is not unlike that of a powerful committee chairman in Congress who cannot, generally speaking, nullify the basic policies substantially agreed on by the rest of the dominant leadership, but who can, within these limits, often determine important questions of timing, effectiveness, and subordinate policy. Thus the Court is least effective against a current lawmaking majority —and evidently least inclined to act. It is most effective when it sets the bounds of policy for officials, agencies, state governments, or even regions, a task that has come to occupy a very large part of the Court's business.[26]

Few of the Court's policy decisions can be interpreted sensibly in terms of a "majority" versus a "minority." In this respect the Court is no different from the rest of the political leadership. Generally speaking, policy at the national level is the outcome of conflict, bargaining, and agreement among minorities; the process is neither minority rule nor majority rule but what might better be called *minorities* rule, where one aggregation of minorities achieves policies opposed by another aggregation.

The main objective of presidential leadership is to build a stable and dominant aggregation of minorities with a high probability of winning the presidency and one or both houses of Congress. The main task of the Court is to confer legitimacy on the fundamental policies of the successful coalition. There are times when the coalition is unstable with respect to certain key policies; at very great risk to its legitimacy powers, the Court can intervene in such cases and may even succeed in establishing policy. Probably in such cases it can succeed only if its action conforms to and reinforces a widespread set of explicit or implicit norms held by the political leadership; norms that are not strong enough or are not distributed in such a way as to insure the existence of an effective lawmaking majority but are, nonetheless, sufficiently powerful to prevent any successful attack on the legitimacy powers of the Court. This is probably the explanation for the relatively successful work of the Court in enlarging the freedom of Negroes to vote during the past three decades and in its famous school integration decisions.[27]

Yet the Court is more than this. Considered as a political system, democracy is a set of basic procedures for arriving at decisions. The operation of these procedures presupposes the existence of certain rights, obligations, liberties, and restraints; in short, certain patterns of behavior. The existence of these patterns of behavior in turn presupposes widespread agreement (particularly among the politically active and influential segments of the population) on the validity and propriety of the behavior. Although its record is by no means lacking in serious blemishes, at its best the Court operates to confer legitimacy, not simply on the particular and parochial policies of the dominant political alliance, but upon the basic patterns of behavior required for the operation of a democracy.

NOTES

1. Actually, the matter is somewhat ambiguous. There appear to have been 78 cases in which the Court has held provisions of federal law unconstitutional. Sixty-four different acts in the technical sense have been construed, and 86 different provisions in law have been in some respects invalidated. I rely here on the figures and the table given in Library of Congress, Legislative Reference Service, *Provisions of Federal Law Held Unconstitutional By the Supreme Court of the United States* (1936), pp. 95, 141–147 (1936), to which I have added *United States v. Lovett,* 328 U.S. 303 (1946), and *United States ex rel. Toth v. Quarles,* 350 U.S. 11 (1955). There are some minor discrepancies in totals (not attributable to the differences in publication dates) between this volume and *Acts of Congress Held Unconstitutional in Whole or in Part by the Supreme Court of the United States,* in Library of Congress, Legislative Reference Service, *The Constitution of the United States of Amer-*

ica, Analysis and Interpretation, Corwin, ed. (1953). The difference is a result of classification. The latter document lists 73 acts held unconstitutional (to which *Toth v. Quarles, supra,* should be added) but different sections of the same act are sometimes counted separately.

2. Dahl, *A Preface to Democratic Theory* (1956), ch. 2.
3. Compare Commager, *Majority Rule and Minority Rights* (1943).
4. Frankfurter, "The Supreme Court in the Mirror of Justices," *University of Pennsylvania Law Review,* CV (1957), 782–784.
5. *Booth v. United States,* 291 U.S. 339 (1934), involved a reduction in the pay of retired judges. *Lynch v. United States,* 292 U.S. 571 (1934), repealed laws granting to veterans rights to yearly renewable term insurance; there were only 29 policies outstanding in 1932. *Hopkins Federal Savings & Loan Ass'n v. Cleary,* 296 U.S. 315 (1935), granted permission to state building and loan associations to convert to federal ones on a vote of 51 per cent or more of votes cast at a legal meeting. *Ashton v. Cameron County Water Improvement District,* 298 U.S. 513 (1936), permitting municipalities to petition federal courts for bankruptcy proceedings.
6. *Schechter Poultry Corp. v. United States,* 295 U.S. 495 (1935).
7. *United States v. Butler,* 297 U.S. 1 (1936); *Perry v. United States,* 294 U.S. 330 (1935); *Panama Refining Co. v. Ryan,* 293 U.S. 388 (1935); *Railroad Retirement Board v. Alton R. Co.,* 295 U.S. 330 (1935); *Louisville Joint Stock Land Bank v. Radford,* 295 U.S. 555 (1935); *Rickert Rice Mills v. Fontenot,* 297 U.S. 110 (1936); *Carter v. Carter Coal Co.,* 298 U.S. 238 (1936).
8. *United States v. Dewitt,* 9 Wall. (U.S.) 41 (1870); *Gordon v. United States,* 2 Wall. (U.S.) 561 (1865); *Monongahela Navigation Co. v. United States,* 148 U.S. 312 (1893); *Wong Wing v. United States,* 163 U.S. 228 (1896); *Fairbank v. United States,* 181 U.S. 283 (1901); *Rassmussen v. United States,* 197 U.S. 516 (1905); *Muskrat v. United States,* 219 U.S. 346 (1911); *Choate v. Trapp,* 224 U.S. 665 (1912); *Evans v. Gore,* 253 U.S. 245 (1920); *Untermyer v. Anderson,* 276 U.S. 440 (1928); *United States v. Lovett,* 328 U.S. 303 (1946). Note that although the specific legislative provisions held unconstitutional may have been minor, the basic legislation may have been of major policy importance.
9. *Ex parte Garland,* 4 Wall. (U.S.) 333 (1867); *United States v. Klein,* 13 Wall. (U.S.) 128 (1872); *Pollock v. Farmers' Loan & Trust Co.,* 157 U.S. 429 (1895), rehearing granted 158 U.S. 601 (1895); *Employers' Liability Cases,* 207 U.S. 463 (1908); *Keller v. United States,* 213 U.S. 138 (1909); *Hammer v. Dagenhart,* 247 U.S. 251 (1918); *Eisner v. Macomber,* 252 U.S. 189 (1920); *Knickerbocker Ice Co. v. Stewart,* 253 U.S. 149 (1920); *United States v. Cohen Grocery Co.,* 255 U.S. 81 (1921); *Weeds, Inc. v. United States,* 255 U.S. 109 (1921); *Bailey v. Drexel Furniture Co.,* 259 U.S. 20 (1922); *Hill v. Wallace,* 259 U.S. 44 (1922); *Washington v. Dawson & Co.,* 264 U.S. 219 (1924); *Trusler v. Crooks,* 269 U.S. 475 (1926).
10. *Ex parte Garland,* 4 Wall. (U.S.) 333 (1867); *United States v. Klein,* 13 Wall. (U.S.) 128 (1872).
11. *United States v. Cohen Grocery Co.,* 255 U.S. 81 (1921); *Weeds, Inc. v. United States,* 255 U.S. 109 (1921).
12. *Eisner v Macomber,* 252 U.S. 189 (1920).
13. *Employers' Liability Cases,* 207 U.S. 463 (1908); *Keller v. United States,* 213 U.S. 138 (1909); *Trusler v. Crooks,* 269 U.S. 475 (1926); *Hill v. Wallace,* 259 U.S. 44 (1922).
14. *Knickerbocker Ice Co. v. Stewart,* 253 U.S. 149 (1920).
15. *Washington v. Dawson & Co.,* 264 U.S. 219 (1924).
16. *Crowell v. Benson,* 285 U.S. 22 (1932).
17. *Pollock v. Farmers' Loan & Trust Co.,* 157 U.S. 429 (1895).
18. *Nicol v. Ames,* 173 U.S. 509 (1899); *Knowlton v. Moore,* 178 U.S. 41 (1900); *Patton v. Brady,* 184 U.S. 608 (1902); *Flint v. Stone Tracy Co.,* 220 U.S. 107 (1911).
19. *Hammer v. Dagenhart,* 247 U.S. 251 (1918).
20. *Bailey v. Drexel Furniture Co.,* 259 U.S. 20 (1922).
21. *United States v. Darby,* 312 U.S. 100 (1941).
22. The candidates for this category would appear to be *Boyd v. United States,* 116 U.S. 616 (1886); *Rassmussen v. United States,* 197 U.S. 516 (1905); *Wong Wing v.*

United States, 163 U.S. 228 (1896); *United States v. Moreland,* 258 U.S. 433 (1922); *Kirby v. United States,* 174 U.S. 47 (1899); *United States v. Cohen Grocery Co.,* 255 U.S. 81 (1921); *Weeds, Inc. v. United States,* 255 U.S. 109 (1921); *Justices of the Supreme Court v. United States ex rel. Murray,* 9 Wall. (U.S.) 274 (1870); *United States ex rel. Toth v. Quarles,* 350 U.S. 11 (1955).

23. *Dred Scott v. Sandford,* 19 How. (U.S.) 393 (1857).
24. *United States v. Reese,* 92 U.S. 214 (1876); *United States v. Harris,* 106 U.S. 629 (1883); *United States v. Stanley* (Civil Rights Cases), 109 U.S. 3 (1883); *Baldwin v. Franks,* 120 U.S. 678 (1887); *James v. Bowman,* 190 U.S. 127 (1903); *Hodges v. United States,* 203 U.S. 1 (1906); *Butts v. Merchants & Miners Transportation Co.,* 230 U.S. 126 (1913).
25. *Monongahela Navigation Co. v. United States,* 148 U.S. 312 (1893); *Adair v. United States,* 208 U.S. 161 (1908); *Adkins v. Children's Hospital,* 261 U.S. 525 (1923); *Nichols v. Coolidge,* 274 U.S. 531 (1927); *Untermyer v. Anderson,* 276 U.S. 440 (1928); *Heiner v. Donnan,* 285 U.S. 312 (1932); *Louisville Joint Stock Land Bank v. Radford,* 295 U.S. 555 (1935).
26. "Constitutional law and cases with constitutional undertones are of course still very important, with almost one-fourth of the cases in which written opinions were filed [in the two most recent terms] involving such questions. Review of administrative action . . . constitutes the largest category of the Court's work, comprising one-third of the total cases decided on the merits. The remaining . . . categories of litigation . . . all involve largely public law questions." Frankfurter, *op. cit., supra, n.* 4, at 793.
27. *Rice v. Elmore,* 165 F. 2d 387 (C.A. 4th, 1947), *cert.* denied 333 U.S. 875 (1948); *United States v. Classic,* 313 U.S. 299 (1941); *Smith v. Allwright,* 321 U.S. 649 (1944); *Grovey v. Townsend,* 295 U.S. 45 (1935); *Brown v. Board of Education,* 347 U.S. 483 (1954); *Bolling v. Sharpe,* 347 U.S. 497 (1954).

35

The Counter-Majoritarian Difficulty

ALEXANDER M. BICKEL

The root difficulty is that judicial review is a counter-majoritarian force in our system. There are various ways of sliding over this ineluctable reality. Marshall did so when he spoke of enforcing, in behalf of "the people," the limits that they have ordained for the institutions of a limited government. And it has been done ever since in much the same fashion by all too many commentators. Marshall himself followed Hamilton, who in the 78th *Federalist* denied that judicial review implied a superiority of the judicial over the legislative

From *The Least Dangerous Branch: The Supreme Court at the Bar of Politics* (Indianapolis: Bobbs-Merrill, 1962), pp. 16–33. Copyright © 1962 by The Bobbs-Merrill Company, Inc. Reprinted by permission of the author and the publisher. Abridged with renumbered notes.

power—denied, in other words, that judicial review constituted control by an unrepresentative minority of an elected majority. "It only supposes," Hamilton went on, "that the power of the people is superior to both; and that where the will of the legislature, declared in its statutes, stands in opposition to that of the people, declared in the Constitution, the judges ought to be governed by the latter rather than the former." But the word "people" so used is an abstraction. Not necessarily a meaningless or a pernicious one by any means; always charged with emotion, but non-representational—an abstraction obscuring the reality that when the Supreme Court declares unconstitutional a legislative act or the action of an elected executive, it thwarts the will of representatives of the actual people of the here and now; it exercises control, not in behalf of the prevailing majority, but against it. That, without mystic overtones, is what actually happens. It is an altogether different kettle of fish, and it is the reason the charge can be made that judicial review is undemocratic.

Most assuredly, no democracy operates by taking continuous nose counts on the broad range of daily governmental activities. Representative democracies—that is to say, all working democracies—function by electing certain men for certain periods of time, then passing judgment periodically on their conduct of public office. It is a matter of a laying on of hands, followed in time by a process of holding to account—all through the exercise of the franchise. The elected officials, however, are expected to delegate some of their tasks to men of their own appointment, who are not directly accountable at the polls. The whole operates under public scrutiny and criticism, but not at all times or in all parts. What we mean by democracy, therefore, is much more sophisticated and complex than the making of decisions in town meeting by a show of hands. It is true also that even decisions that have been submitted to the electoral process in some fashion are not continually resubmitted, and they are certainly not continually unmade. Once run through the process, once rendered by "the people" (using the term now in its mystic sense, because the reference is to the people in the past), myriad decisions remain to govern the present and the future despite what may well be fluctuating majorities against them at any given time. A high value is put on stability, and that is also a counter-majoritarian factor. Nevertheless, although democracy does not mean constant reconsideration of decisions once made, it does mean that a representative majority has the power to accomplish a reversal. This power is of the essence, and no less so because it is often merely held in reserve.

I am aware that this timid assault on the complexities of the American democratic system has yet left us with a highly simplistic statement, and I shall briefly rehearse some of the reasons. But nothing in the further complexities and perplexities of the system, which modern political science has explored with admirable and ingenious industry, and some of which it has tended to multiply with a fertility that passes the mere zeal of the discoverer—nothing in these complexities can alter the essential reality that judicial review is a deviant institution in the American democracy.

It is true, of course, that the process of reflecting the will of a popular majority in the legislature is deflected by various inequalities of representation and by all sorts of institutional habits and characteristics, which perhaps tend most often in favor of inertia. Yet it must be remembered that statutes are the product of the legislature and the executive acting in concert, and that the executive represents a very different constituency and thus tends to cure inequities of over- and under-representation. Reflecting a balance of forces in society for purposes of stable and effective government is more intricate and less certain than merely assuring each citizen his equal vote. Moreover, impurities and imperfections, if such they be, in one part of the system are no argument for total departure from the desired norm in another part. A much more important complicating factor—first adumbrated by Madison in the 10th *Federalist* and lately emphasized by Professor David B. Truman and others [1]—is the proliferation and power of what Madison foresaw as "faction," what Mr. Truman calls "groups," and what in popular parlance has always been deprecated as the "interests" or the "pressure groups."

No doubt groups operate forcefully on the electoral process, and no doubt they seek and gain access to and an effective share in the legislative and executive decisional process. Perhaps they constitute also, in some measure, an impurity or imperfection. But no one has claimed that they have been able to capture the governmental process except by combining in some fashion, and thus capturing or constituting (are not the two verbs synonymous?) a majority. They often tend themselves to be majoritarian in composition and to be subject to broader majoritarian influences. And the price of what they sell or buy in the legislature is determined in the biennial or quadrennial electoral marketplace. It may be, as Professor Robert A. Dahl has written, that elections themselves, and the political competition that renders them meaningful, "do not make for government by majorities in any very significant way," for they do not establish a great many policy preferences. However, "they are a crucial device for controlling leaders." And if the control is exercised by "groups of various types and sizes, all seeking in various ways to advance their goals," so that we have "minorities rule" rather than majority rule, it remains true nevertheless that only those minorities rule that can command the votes of a majority of individuals in the legislature who can command the votes of a majority of individuals in the electorate. In one fashion or another, both in the legislative process and at elections, the minorities must coalesce into a majority. Although, as Dahl says, "it is fashionable in some quarters to suggest that everything believed about democratic politics prior to World War I, and perhaps World War II, was nonsense," he makes no bones about his own belief that "the radical democrats who, unlike Madison, insist upon the decisive importance of the election process in the whole grand strategy of democracy are essentially correct." [2]

The insights of Truman and other writers into the role that groups play in our society and our politics have a bearing on judicial review. They indicate that there are other means than the electoral process, though subordinate and subsidiary ones, of making institutions of government responsive to the needs and wishes of the governed. Hence one may infer that judicial review, although not responsible, may have ways of being responsive. But nothing can finally depreciate the central function that is assigned in democratic theory and practice to the electoral process; nor can it be denied that the policy-making power of representative institutions, born of the electoral process, is the distinguishing characteristic of the system. Judicial review works counter to this characteristic.

It therefore does not follow from the complex nature of a democratic system that, because admirals and generals and the members, say, of the Federal Reserve Board or of this or that administrative agency are not electorally responsible, judges who exercise the power of judicial review need not be responsible either, and in neither case is there a serious conflict with democratic theory.[3] For admirals and generals and the like are most often responsible to officials who are themselves elected and through whom the line runs directly to a majority. What is more significant, the policies they make are or should be interstitial or technical only and are reversible by legislative majorities. Thus, so long as there has been a meaningful delegation by the legislature to administrators, which is kept within proper bounds, the essential majority power is there, and it is felt to be there—a fact of great consequence. Nor will it do to liken judicial review to the general lawmaking function of judges. In the latter aspect, judges are indeed something like administrative officials, for their decisions are also reversible by any legislative majority, and not infrequently they are reversed. Judicial review, however, is the power to apply and construe the Constitution, in matters of the greatest moment, against the wishes of a legislative majority, which is, in turn, powerless to affect the judicial decision. The late Judge Learned Hand said:

> For myself, it would be most irksome to be ruled by a bevy of Platonic Guardians, even if I knew how to choose them, which I assuredly do not. If they were in charge, I should miss the stimulus of living in a society where I have, at least theoretically, some part in the direction of public affairs. Of course I know how illusory would be the belief that my vote determined anything; but nevertheless when I go to the polls I have a satisfaction in the sense that we are all engaged in a common venture. If you retort that a sheep in the flock may feel something like it; I reply, following Saint Francis, "My brother, the Sheep." [4]

This suggests not only the democratic value that inheres in obtaining the broad judgment of a majority of the people in the community and thus tending to produce better decisions. Judge Hand, if anything, rather deprecated the notion that the decisions will be better, or are affected at all. Some might think that he deprecated it beyond what is either just or realistic when he said that the belief that his vote determined anything was illusory. Hardly altogether. But the strong emphasis is on the related idea that coherent, stable—*and morally supportable*—government is possible only on the basis of consent, and that the secret of consent is the sense of common venture fostered by institutions that reflect and represent us and that we can call to account.

It has been suggested [5] that the Congress, the president, the states, and the people (in the sense of current majorities) have from the beginning and in each generation acquiesced in, and thus consented to, the exercise of judicial review by the Supreme Court. In the first place, it is said that the Amending Clause of the Constitution has been employed to reverse the work of the Court only twice, perhaps three times; and it has never been used to take away or diminish the Court's power. But the Amending Clause itself incorporates an extreme minority veto. The argument then proceeds to draw on the first Judiciary Act, whose provisions regarding the jurisdiction of the federal courts have been continued in effect to this day. Yet we have seen that the Judiciary Act can be read as a grant of the power to declare federal statutes unconstitutional only on the basis of a previously and independently reached conclusion that such a power must exist. And even if the Judiciary Act did grant this power, as it surely granted the power to declare state actions unconstitutional, it amounted to an expression of the opinion of the first Congress that the Constitution implies judicial review. It is, in fact, extremely likely that the first Congress thought so. That is important; but it merely adds to the historical evidence on the point, which, as we have seen, is in any event quite strong. Future Congresses and future generations can only be said to have acquiesced in the belief of the first Congress that the Constitution implies this power. And they can be said to have become resigned to what follows, which is that the power can be taken away only by constitutional amendment. That is a very far cry from consent to the power on its merits, as a power freely continued by the decision or acquiescence of a majority in each generation. The argument advances not a step toward justification of the power on other than historical grounds.

A further, crucial difficulty must also be faced. Besides being a counter-majoritarian check on the legislature and the executive, judicial review may, in a larger sense, have a tendency over time seriously to weaken the democratic process. Judicial review expresses, of course, a form of distrust of the legislature. James Bradley Thayer wrote at the turn of the century,

> The legislatures are growing accustomed to this distrust and more and more readily inclined to justify it, and to shed the considerations of constitutional restraints—certainly as concerning the exact extent of these restrictions—turning that subject over to the courts; and what is worse, they insensibly fall into a habit of assuming that whatever they could constitutionally do they may do, as if honor and fair dealing and common honesty were not relevant to their inquiries. The people, all this while, become careless as to whom they send to the legislature; too often they cheerfully vote for men whom they would not trust with an important private affair, and when these unfit persons are found to pass foolish and bad laws, and the courts step in and disregard them, the people are glad that these wiser gentlemen on the bench are so ready to protect them against their

more immediate representatives . . . [I]t should be remembered that the exercise of it [the power of judicial review], even when unavoidable, is always attended with a serious evil, namely, that the correction of legislative mistakes comes from the outside, and the people thus lose the political experience, and the moral education and stimulus that comes from fighting the question out in the ordinary way, and correcting their own errors. The tendency of a common and easy resort to this great function, now lamentably too common, is to dwarf the political capacity of the people, and to deaden its sense of moral responsibility. It is no light thing to do that.[6]

To this day, in how many hundreds of occasions does Congress enact a measure that it deems expedient, having essayed consideration of its constitutionality (that is to say, of its acceptability on principle), only to abandon the attempt in the declared confidence that the Court will correct errors of principle, if any? It may well be, as has been suggested,[7] that any lowering of the level of legislative performance is attributable to many factors other than judicial review. Yet there is no doubt that what Thayer observed remains observable. It seemed rather a puzzle, for example, to a scholar who recently compared British and American practices of legislative investigation. Professor Herman Finer wrote, with what might have seemed to Thayer charming ingenuousness:

> Is it not a truly extraordinary phenomenon that in the United States, where Congress is not a sovereign body, but subordinate to a constitution, there appear to be less restraints upon the arbitrary behavior of members in their . . . rough handling of the civil rights of the citizen during investigations . . . ? Though Parliament is sovereign and can legally do anything it likes, its practices are kinder, more restrained, and less invasive of the rights of those who come under its investigative attention. The student is forced to pause and reflect upon this remarkable reversal of demeanor and status.[8]

Finally, another, though related, contention has been put forward. It is that judicial review runs so fundamentally counter to democratic theory that in a society which in all other respects rests on that theory, judicial review cannot ultimately be effective. We pay the price of a grave inner contradiction in the basic principle of our government, which is an inconvenience and a dangerous one; and in the end to no good purpose, for when the great test comes, judicial review will be unequal to it. The most arresting expression of this thought is in a famous passage from a speech of Judge Learned Hand, a passage, Dean Eugene V. Rostow has written, "of Browningesque passion and obscurity," voicing a "gloomy and apocalyptic view." [9] Absent the institution of judicial review, Judge Hand said:

> I do not think that anyone can say what will be left of those [fundamental principles of equity and fair play which our constitutions enshrine]; I do not know whether they will serve only as counsels; but this much I think I do know—that a society so riven that the spirit of moderation is gone, no court *can* save; that a

society where that spirit flourishes, no court *need* save; that in a society that evades its responsibility by thrusting upon the courts the nurture of that spirit, that spirit in the end will perish.[10]

Over a century before Judge Hand spoke, Judge Gibson of Pennsylvania, in his day perhaps the ablest opponent of the establishment of judicial review, wrote: "Once let public opinion be so corrupt as to sanction every misconstruction of the Constitution and abuse of power that the temptation of the moment may dictate, and the party that may happen to be predominant will laugh at the puny efforts of a dependent power to arrest it in its course." [11] And Thayer also believed that "under no system can the power of courts go far to save a people from ruin; our chief protection lies elsewhere." [12]

The Moral Approval of the Lines: Principle

Such, in outline, are the chief doubts that must be met if the doctrine of judicial review is to be justified on principle. Of course, these doubts will apply with lesser or greater force to various forms of the exercise of the power. For the moment the discussion is at wholesale, and we are seeking a justification on principle, quite aside from supports in history and the continuity of practice. The search must be for a function which might (indeed, must) involve the making of policy, yet which differs from the legislative and executive functions; which is peculiarly suited to the capabilities of the courts; which will not likely be performed elsewhere if the courts do not assume it; which can be so exercised as to be acceptable in a society that generally shares Judge Hand's satisfaction in a "sense of common venture"; which will be effective when needed; and whose discharge by the courts will not lower the quality of the other departments' performance by denuding them of the dignity and burden of their own responsibility. It will not be possible fully to meet all that is said against judicial review. Such is not the way with questions of government. We can only fill the other side of the scales with countervailing judgments on the real needs and the actual workings of our society and, of course, with our own portions of faith and hope. Then we may estimate how far the needle has moved.

The point of departure is a truism; perhaps it even rises to the unassailability of a platitude. It is that many actions of government have two aspects: their immediate, necessarily intended, practical effects; and their perhaps unintended or unappreciated bearing on values we hold to have more general and permanent interest. It is a premise we deduce not merely from the fact of a written constitution but from the history of the race, and ultimately as a moral judgment of the good society, that government should serve not only what we conceive from time to time to be our immediate material needs but also certain enduring values. This in part is what is meant by government under law. But such values do not present themselves ready-made. They have a past always, to be sure, but they must be continually derived, enunciated, and seen in relevant application. And it remains to ask which institution of our government—if any single one in particular—should be the pronouncer and guardian of such values.

Men in all walks of public life are able occasionally to perceive this second aspect of public questions. Sometimes they are also able to base their decisions on it; that is one of the things we like to call acting on principle. Often they do not do so, however, particularly when they sit in legislative assemblies. There, when the pressure for immediate results is strong enough and emotions ride high enough, men will ordinarily prefer to act on expediency rather than take the long view. Possibly legislators—everything else being equal—are as capable as other men of following the path of principle, where the path is clear or at any rate discernible. Our system, however, like all secular systems, calls for the evolution of principle in novel circumstances, rather than only for its mechanical application. Not merely respect for the rule of established principles but the creative establishment and renewal of a coherent body of principled rules—that is what our legislatures have proven themselves ill equipped to give us.

Initially, great reliance for principled decision was placed in the senators and the president, who have more extended terms of office and were meant to be elected only indirectly. Yet the Senate and the president were conceived of as less closely tied to, not as divorced from, electoral responsibility and the political marketplace. And so even then the need might have been felt for an institution which stands altogether aside from the current clash of interests, and which, insofar as is humanly possible, is concerned only with principle. We cannot know whether, as Thayer believed, our legislatures are what they are because we have judicial review, or whether we have judicial review and consider it necessary because legislatures are what they are. Yet it is arguable also that the partial separation of the legislative and judicial functions—and it is not meant to be absolute—is beneficial in any event, because it makes it possible for the desires of various groups and interests concerning immediate results to be heard clearly and unrestrainedly in one place. It may be thought fitting that somewhere in government, at some stage in the process of lawmaking, such felt needs should find unambiguous expression. Moreover, and more importantly, courts have certain capacities for dealing with matters of principle that legislatures and executives do not possess. Judges have, or should have, the leisure, the training, and the insulation to follow the ways of the scholar in pursuing the ends of government. This is crucial in sorting out the enduring values of a society, and it is not something that institutions can do well occasionally, while operating for the most part with a different set of gears. It calls for a habit of mind, and for undeviating institutional customs. Another advantage that courts have is that questions of principle never carry the same aspect for them as they did for the legislature or the executive. Statutes, after all, deal typically with abstract or dimly foreseen problems. The courts are concerned with the flesh and blood of an actual case. This tends to modify, perhaps to lengthen, everyone's view. It also provides an extremely salutary proving ground for all abstractions; it is conducive, in a phrase of Holmes, to thinking things, not words, and thus to the evolution of principle by a process that tests as it creates.

Their insulation and the marvelous mystery of time give courts the capacity to appeal to men's better natures, to call forth their aspirations, which may have been forgotten in the moment's hue and cry. This is what Justice Stone called the opportunity for "the sober second thought." [13] Hence it is that the courts, although they may somewhat dampen the people's and the legislatures' efforts to educate themselves, are also a great and highly effective educational institution. Judge Gibson, highly critical as he was, took account of this. "In the business of government," he wrote, "a recurrence to first principles answers the end of an observation at sea with a view to correct the dead reckoning; and, for this purpose, a written constitution is an instrument of inestimable value. It is of inestimable value also, in rendering its principles familiar to the mass of the people. . . ." [14] The educational institution that both takes the observation to correct the dead reckoning and makes it known is the voice of the Constitution: the Supreme Court exercising judicial review. The justices, in Dean Rostow's phrase, "are inevitably teachers in a vital national seminar." [15] No other branch of the American government is nearly so well equipped to conduct one. And such a seminar can do a great deal to keep our society from becoming so riven that no court will be able to save it. Of course, we have never quite been that society in which the spirit of moderation is so richly in flower that no court need save it.

Thus, as Professor Henry M. Hart, Jr., has written, and as surely most of the profession and of informed laity believe; for if not this, what and why?—thus the Court appears "predestined in the long run, not only by the thrilling tradition of Anglo-American law but also by the hard facts of its position in the structure of American institutions, to be a voice of reason, charged with the creative function of discerning afresh and of articulating and developing impersonal and durable principles. . . ." [16] This line of thought may perhaps blunt, if it does not meet, the force of all the arguments on the other side. No doubt full consistency with democratic theory has not been established. The heart of the democratic faith is government by the consent of the governed. The further premise is not incompatible that the good society not only will want to satisfy the immediate needs of the greatest number but also will strive to support and maintain enduring general values. I have followed the view that the elected institutions are ill fitted, or not so well fitted as the courts, to perform the latter task. This rests on the assumption that the people themselves, by direct action at the ballot box, are surely incapable of sustaining a working system of general values specifically applied. But that much we assume throughout, being a representative, deliberative democracy. Matters of expediency are not generally submitted to direct referendum. Nor should matters of principle, which require even more intensive deliberation, be so submitted. Reference of specific policies to the people for initial decision is, with few exceptions, the fallacy of the misplaced mystics, or the way of those who would use the forms of democracy to undemocratic ends. It is not the way in which working democracies live. But democracies do live by the idea, central to the process of gaining the consent of the governed, that the majority has the ultimate power to displace the decision-makers and to reject any part of their policy. With that idea, judicial review must achieve some measure of consonance.

"Democratic government under law." The slogan pulls in two opposed directions, but that does not keep it from being applicable to an operative polity. If it carries the elements of explosion, it doesn't contain a critical mass of them. Yet if the critical mass is not to be reached, there must be an accommodation, a degree of concord between the diverging elements. Having been checked, should the people persist; having been educated, should the people insist, must they not win over every fundamental principle save one, which is the principle that they must win? Are we sufficiently certain of the permanent validity of any other principle to be ready to impose it against a consistent and determined majority, and could we do so for long? Have not the people the right of peaceable revolution, as assuredly, over time, they possess the capacity for a bloody one?

The premise of democracy is egalitarian, and, as Professor Herbert J. Muller has written, every bright sophomore knows how to punch holes in it. Yet, as Mr. Muller goes on to say, there is "no universal standard of superiority," there are no sure scales in which to weigh all the relevant virtues and capacities of men, and many a little man may rightly claim to be a better citizen than the expert or the genius. Moreover, and most significantly, "all men are in fact equal in respect of their common structure and their common destiny." Hence, to repeat the insight of Judge Hand, government must be their common venture. Who will think it moral ultimately to direct the lives of men against the will of the greater number of them? Or wise? "Man's historical experience should sober the revolutionaries who know the certain solution to our problems, and sober as well the traditionalists whose solution is a return to the ancient faiths, which have always failed in the past." [17]

To bring judicial review into concord with such presuppositions requires a closer analysis of the actual operation of the process in various circumstances. The preliminary suggestions may be advanced that the rule of principle imposed by the Court is seldom rigid, that the Court has ways of persuading before it attempts to coerce, and that, over time, sustained opinion running counter to the Court's constitutional law can achieve its nullification, directly or by desuetude. It may further be that if the process is properly carried out, an aspect of the current—not only the timeless, mystic—popular will finds expression in constitutional adjudication. The result may be a tolerable accommodation with the theory and practice of democracy.

The Mystic Function

This inquiry into a general justification of judicial review cannot end without taking account of a most suggestive and perceptive argument recently advanced by Professor Charles L. Black, Jr.[18] It begins by emphasizing that the

Court performs not only a checking function but also a legitimating one, as Mr. Black well calls it. Judicial review means not only that the Court may strike down a legislative action as unconstitutional but also that it may validate it as within constitutionally granted powers and as not violating constitutional limitations. Mr. Black contends, further, that the legitimating function would be impossible of performance if the checking function did not exist as well: what is the good of a declaration of validity from an institution that is by hypothesis required to validate everything that is brought before it? This is plainly so, though it is oddly stated. The picture is accurate, but it is stood on its head. The truth is that the legitimating function is an inescapable, even if unintended, by-product of the checking power. But what follows? What is the nature of this legitimating function, and what the need for it?

With a relish one can readily share, Black cites the story of the French intellectual who, upon arrival in New York harbor, exclaims: "It is wonderful to breathe the sweet air of legitimacy!" He contends essentially that what filled the Frenchman's lungs, what smelled to him so different from the succession of short-lived empires and republics endemic to his homeland, was the sweet odor of the Supreme Court of the United States. But I think it much simpler and nearer the reality of both the American and the French experience to begin with the proposition that legitimacy comes to a regime that is felt to be good and to have proven itself as such to generations past as well as in the present. Such a government must be principled as well as responsible; but it must be felt to be the one without having ceased to be the other, and unless it is responsible it cannot in fact be stable, and is not in my view morally supportable. Quite possibly, there have been governments that were electorally responsible and yet failed to attain stability. But that is not to say that they would have attained it by rendering themselves less responsible—that is, by divorcing the keepers of their principles from the electoral process. Legitimacy, being the stability of a good government over time, is the fruit of consent to specific actions or to the authority to act; the consent to the exercise of authority, whether or not approved in each instance, of as unified a population as possible, but most importantly, of a present majority.

Very probably, the stability of the American Republic is due in large part, as Professor Louis Hartz has eloquently argued, to the remarkable Lockeian consensus of a society that has never known a feudal regime; to a "moral unity" that was seriously broken only once, over the extension of slavery. This unity makes possible a society that accepts its principles from on high, without fighting about them. But the Lockeian consensus is also a limitation on the sort of principles that will be accepted. It is putting the cart before the horse to attribute the American sense of legitimacy to the institution of judicial review. The latter is more nearly the fruit of the former, although the "moral unity" must be made manifest, it must be renewed and sharpened and brought to bear—and this is an office that judicial review can discharge.[19]

No doubt it is in the interest of the majority to obtain the acquiescence of the minority as often and in as great a degree as possible. And no doubt the Court can help bring about acquiescence by assuring those who have lost a political fight that merely momentary interest, not fundamental principle, was in play. Yet is it reasonable to assume that the majority would wish to see itself checked from time to time just to have an institution which, when it chooses to go along with the majority's will, is capable of helping to assuage the defeated minority? That is too much of an indirection. The checking power must find its own justification, particularly in a system which, in a number of important ways (such as the Senate's reflection of the federal structure, practices of legislative apportionment), offers prodigious political safeguards to the minority.

Thus the legitimating function of judicial review cannot be accepted as an independent justification for it. Yet it exists. Not only is the Supreme Court capable of generating consent for hotly controverted legislative or executive measures; it has the subtler power of adding a certain impetus to measures that the majority enacts rather tentatively. There are times when the majority might, because of strong minority feelings, be inclined in the end to deny itself, but when it comes to embrace a measure more firmly, and the minority comes to accept it, because the Court—intending perhaps no such consequence—has declared it consistent with constitutional principle. This tendency touches on Thayer's anxiety that judicial review will "dwarf the political capacity of the people" and "deaden its sense of moral responsibility." We shall return to it as a consideration that should cause the Court to stay its hand from time to time.

But the Supreme Court as a legitimating force in society also casts a less palpable yet larger spell. With us the symbol of nationhood, of continuity, of unity and common purpose, is, of course, the Constitution, without particular reference to what exactly it means in this or that application. The utility of such a symbol is a commonplace. Britain—the United Kingdom, and perhaps even the Commonwealth—is the most potent historical demonstration of the efficaciousness of a symbol, made concrete in the person of the Crown. The president in our system serves the function somewhat, but only very marginally, because the personification of unity must be above the political battle, and no president can fulfill his office while remaining above the battle. The effective presidents have of necessity been men of power, and so it has in large part been left to the Supreme Court to concretize the symbol of the Constitution. Keeping in mind that this is offered as an observation, not as justification, it is surely true that the Court has been able to play the role partly—but only partly—by virtue of its power of judicial review.

The Court is seen as a continuum. It is never, like other institutions, renewed at a single stroke. No one or two changes on the Court, not even if they include the advent of a new chief justice, are apt to be as immediately momentous as a turnover in the presidency. To the extent that they are instruments of decisive change, justices are time bombs, not warheads that explode on impact. There are exceptions, to be sure. In 1870, President Grant made two appointments that promptly resulted in the reversal of a quite crucial recent decision concerning the monetary powers of the federal government.[20] And it may seem that strong new doctrine became ascendant soon after the first of President Roosevelt's appointees, Justice Black, came on the Bench in 1937.

But on the whole, the movements of the Court are not sudden and not suddenly affected by new appointments. Continuity is a chief concern of the Court, as it is the main reason for the Court's place in the hearts of its countrymen.

No doubt, the Court's symbolic—or, if you will, mystic—function would not have been possible, would not have reached the stage at which we now see it, if the Court did not exercise the power of judicial review. It could scarcely personify the Constitution unless it had the authority finally to speak of it. But as the symbol manifests itself today, it seems not always to depend on judicial review. It seems at times to have as much to do with the life tenure of the Court's members and with the fact of the long government service of some of them, not only on the Court; in short, with the total impression of continuity personified. Here the human chain goes back unbroken in a small, intimate group to the earliest beginnings. Take two recent retirements. Justice Minton, who left in October, 1956, was a fire-eating New Deal Senator, and when he retired from the Court men no doubt remembered his stance in the 1930's and thought, perhaps a little self-deprecatingly, of the emotions it had aroused. Justice Reed, who retired early in 1957, had, some 20 years earlier, when he was Solicitor-General, argued a number of celebrated New Deal cases. His was the second of President Franklin Roosevelt's appointments, and he sat with Hughes and Brandeis and McReynolds. When McReynolds went, in 1941, a remembrance of the Wilson era and of trust-busting in the early 1900's went with him. Justice Van Devanter, a contemporary of McReynolds who retired in 1937, had been appointed by Taft, had held office under McKinley, and had sat with appointees of Cleveland and of Hayes. And so on back.

Senior members of the Court are witnesses to the reality and validity of our present—distracted, improbable, illegitimate as it often appears—because in their persons they assure us of its link to the past which they also witnessed and in which they were themselves once the harbingers of something outrageously new. This is true not only of those who are constructive and creative; it is true of justices who oppose all that is not as they knew it. Say what they will, their very existence among us reassures us. When the great Holmes, who was wounded at Ball's Bluff and at Antietam, retired in 1932, being past ninety, the emotional public response was not due wholly to his undoubted greatness. It was also that his years, his years alone, fulfilled one of the functions of the Supreme Court.

NOTES

1. David B. Truman, *The Governmental Process* (New York: Knopf, 1951).
2. Robert A. Dahl, *A Preface to Democratic Theory* (Chicago: University of Chicago Press, 1956), pp. 125, 132.
3. See Eugene V. Rostow, "The Democratic Character of Judicial Review," *Harvard Law Review,* LXVI (1952), 193, 195.
4. L. Hand, *The Bill of Rights* (Cambridge: Harvard University Press, 1958), pp. 73–

74. (Copyright © 1958 by the President and Fellows of Harvard College. Reprinted by permission of the publishers.)

5. See, *e.g.,* C. L. Black, Jr., *The People and the Court* (New York: Macmillan, 1960), pp. 23 *et seq.,* 210 *et seq.*

6. J. B. Thayer, *John Marshall* (Boston: Houghton Mifflin, 1901), pp. 103–104, 106–107.

7. See Rostow, *op. cit. supra n.* 3, at 201.

8. H. Finer, "Congressional Investigations: The British System," *University of Chicago Law Review,* XVIII (1951), 521, 522.

9. Rostow, *op. cit. supra n.* 3, at 205.

10. Learned Hand, "The Contribution of an Independent Judiciary to Civilization," in I. Dilliard, ed., *The Spirit of Liberty* (New York: Knopf, 1953), pp. 155–165.

11. *Eakin v. Raub,* 12 S. & R. 330, 343, 355 (1825).

12. J. B. Thayer, "The Origin and Scope of the American Doctrine of Constitutional Law," in *Legal Essays* (Boston: Boston Book Co., 1908), pp. 1, 39.

13. Harlan F. Stone, "The Common Law in the United States," *Harvard Law Review,* L (1936), 4, 25.

14. *Eakin v. Raub, supra n.* 8, at p. 354.

15. Rostow, *op. cit., supra n.* 3, at 208.

16. Henry M. Hart, Jr., "Foreword: The Time Chart of the Justices," *Harvard Law Review,* LXXIII (1959), 84, 99.

17. Herbert J. Muller, *The Uses of the Past* (New York: Oxford University Press, 1957), pp. 364–365, 367.

18. See Black, *op. cit., supra n.* 5, at pp. 34 *et seq.*

19. See Louis Hartz, *The Liberal Tradition in America* (New York: Harcourt, Brace, 1955), pp. 9 *et seq.;* B. F. Wright, "Editor's Introduction," in *The Federalist,* John Harvard Edition (Cambridge: Harvard University Press, 1961), p. 41.

20. See C. Fairman, "Joseph P. Bradley" in A. Dunham and P. B. Kurland, eds., *Mr. Justice* (Chicago: University of Chicago Press, 1956), pp. 69, 80–82; C. Fairman, "Mr. Justice Bradley's Appointment to the Supreme Court and the Legal Tender Cases," *Harvard Law Review,* IV (1941), 977.

Part III
ORGANIZATION FOR
THE ADMINISTRATION
OF LAW

Editors' Introduction

The first two parts of this reader have addressed themselves largely to questions of the development of substantive law. The readings have discussed, for example, how such phenomena as social values, culture, and public opinion influence the promulgation of various statutes and their interpretation. In the language of science, we have thus far considered law as a dependent variable. This part and the next look at law as a process and as an independent variable. Rather than asking what causes law, we turn now to the organization of law as a social system and go on in Part IV to discuss the consequences of legal arrangements.

In this part, the readings concentrate specifically upon outstanding aspects of legal organization and administration. But the reader should be cautioned against construing these readings as providing a systematic introduction to legal organization. That would be a much more ambitious task than we could undertake. Rather, we have attempted to touch some important segments of legal organization—the legal profession, the jury, and the courts—that have received the attention of sociologists. We have omitted the judiciary, except indirectly, especially as judges are synonymous with courts. We have also omitted studies of administrative agencies, at least under that institutional heading. Section Fourteen, which concentrates on the legal process, does raise some issues about administrative agencies.

Here we begin with the legal profession. A principal theme is the role of the legal profession in society. Thus, for example, in an article prepared for the *International Encyclopedia of the Social Sciences,* Philippe Nonet and Jerome E. Carlin write:

As long as law remains a mere expedient for the settlement of disputes or the accommodation of conflicting interests, the lawyer's trade may hardly distinguish itself from any other occupation: one speaks of a "profession" only in a rudimentary sense. A fuller professional development occurs when law is used as "an embodiment of values," rather than as a sheer social technique. Society then re-

263

quires specialized group energies for the protection of its legal heritage, and may find them in that occupation whose interests are identified with the preservation of legal skills and values. In this process, the legal craftsmen are transformed into a legal elite and assume the critical mission of maintaining the legal order and shaping its development.

The first reading, an excerpt from Erwin O. Smigel's *The Wall Street Lawyer,* emphasizes not so much the legal values that are performed as the conservative political influence that the highest-status lawyers in the legal profession exert. Smigel speaks of this approvingly, but the reader may question whether the conservatism of the Wall Street lawyer is as desirable as Smigel presents it to be.

David T. Bazelon's "Portrait of a Business Generalist" suggests the variety of functions that may be played by an individual who holds himself out as an attorney. The lawyer is not only someone who is skilled in the law itself; in practice, lawyers who specialize in commercial affairs may become incisive analysts of business trends and opportunities and may branch out into a distinctive sort of business role, one that is hardly encompassed in the curriculum of the law school or the ideals of the legal profession as suggested by Carlin and Nonet. Is law a phenomenon that is necessarily associated with business enterprise? Or is there also an important role for the lawyer in non-business settings?

The selection by William Henri Hale describes another type of legal practice, that of the urban Negro lawyer, who is really a lawyer for the poor. One of the questions that is raised by this article and the subsequent ones is the extent to which the legal profession is a unified occupational group. What common functions are performed by these different types of legal counselors? Certain suggestions are contained in the excerpt from the chapter by Edgar S. and Jean C. Cahn. They view the advocacy orientation of the legal profession as a specialized competence which lawyers can use to assist the poor as well as the business community. Is their argument persuasive?

Finally, there is a discussion of how the conditions of work of lawyers affect their capacity to meet their ethical obligations. The excerpt is from Jerome E. Carlin's *Survey of the New York City Bar.* While analyzing the capacity of lawyers to respond to ethical codes, Carlin necessarily addresses the question of whether it is realistic to speak in terms of a single profession.

As developed in our society, the essential elements of the legal system comprise the roles of plaintiff, defendant, and judge. Whether lawyers constitute an essential element of a legal system is open to question. But of all the elements of the legal structure, the jury is surely the most debatable. From the point of view of efficiency, the jury is virtually a total loss. Where a jury sits, a judge sits. Every case could be heard by a judge alone; he would not be obliged to explain rules of law to a jury, citizens would not have to give up valuable time to sit in the jury box, and the whole system would undoubtedly run more smoothly. Why then the jury? First of all, the existence of the jury challenges the idea that efficiency is a major value of legal organization. Second, the existence of the jury suggests that justice and fairness in a legal system depend also upon perspective. Thus, in a posthumously published article, Edmund Cahn distinguishes between the "imperial or official perspective" on law and the "consumer perspective." The official perspective, according to Dr. Cahn, is so called "because it has been largely determined by the dominant interests of rulers, governors, and other officials." In contrast, the consumer perspective reflects the interests and opinion of those on the receiving end of law. It is this perspective, it would seem, that the institution of the jury is supposed to bring to the trial process.

In the first selection of Section Nine, Alexis de Tocqueville analyzes the jury as a political institution. As usual, de Tocqueville is able to see beyond the obvious function served by institutions. He suggests that rather than diminishing the stature and power of judges, the existence of juries tends to heighten their power. The jury, asserts de Tocqueville, is a means by which the judiciary can reach the mass of the people and imbue in them the spirit of the legal profession. Thus, de Tocqueville sees the jury as an important political device for allowing the legal profession to introduce its ideas to the public. Does this suggestion of de Tocqueville mean that the jury cannot serve as a popular institution exerting leverage on judicial authorities?

The article by Fleming James, Jr., professor of law at Yale, provides an excellent introduction into the legal roles that the judge and jury are supposed to play in negligence cases. James acknowledges that the jury does not necessarily always abide by the role accorded to it in legal theory. He points out that the great majority of jury verdicts in accident cases are in favor of the plaintiff who is usually suing an insured defendant.

The most important empirical study of the American jury has been going on for more than a decade at the University of Chicago. The selection from Kalven and Zeisel is a summary of the basic pattern of disagreement between jury and judge in criminal cases. Like James, Kalven and Zeisel find that while there is general agreement between jury and judge (in some 75 per cent of the cases), where there is disagreement, it is massively in one direction and the expected one of greater leniency for the criminal defendant. In light of these findings, how would you evaluate the case of *Fay v. New York* in which Justice Jackson upholds the constitutionality of the special or so-called "blue ribbon jury" as used by state courts in the state and county of New York? The blue ribbon jury is a jury of citizens of higher social standing and education. How persuasive is Justice Jackson's argument that this difference in social status does not deny the defendant due process of law?

The reading by Strodbeck, James, and Hawkins, also a product of the Chicago jury study, offers further evidence on the role of social status and jury deliberations. The study finds that men, in contrast with women—and persons of higher status, in contrast with lower status—tend to have a higher measure of participation, influence, satisfaction, and perceived confidence for service on the jury. Does this mean that juries should be selected from such higher-status occupations? If not, why not?

Section Ten attempts to direct the reader's attention to some of the most fundamental problems of the courts in action, especially trial courts. If we canvass the literature on courts in the metropolis, it becomes apparent that the municipal courts of the United States are beset by two major problems. One of these is the problem of the multiplicity of separate trial courts; the other is the problem of delay. The dangers of court specialization are alluded to in the brief excerpt from Maxine B. Virtue's *Survey of Metropolitan Courts*. The problem of delay and its remedies is carefully analyzed by Zeisel, Kalven, and Buchholz. The problem of delay is put in a more historical perspective by Lawrence M. Friedman. Friedman sees the problem of delay not merely as something to be analyzed within the context of the balances of power and opportunity offered by the legal system as a whole. He conceives of it as a problem of volume and potential volume of legal services. The Zeisel, Kalven, and Buchholz excerpt is largely reformist and programmatic. They are trying to figure out ways to modify the delay problem and to examine the costs of alternative devices. Friedman presents a more systemic view of the problem and its consequences for the capacity of the legal system to meet potential demand for its services. Both styles of viewing the problem, the activistic and the analytic, represent significant trends within the developing field of the sociology of law.

The last two chapters on the courts deal specifically with the criminal courts. The excerpt from the President's Commission on Law Enforcement and Administration of Justice task force report on the courts reveals the disorganization and ineptitude that characterize so many of the lower criminal courts in America. It should raise questions in the mind of the reader about the possibilities of translating legal rules into administrative action when the structures of the institutions that are enforcing the rules are liable to such fundamental criticism.

The article by David Sudnow really addresses two questions. One is how the penal code is used in the context of heavy volume by a public defender's office. The other is an analysis of the function of the public defender in the administration of criminal justice.

The final selection, by Jerome H. Skolnick, also was written in the context of increasing volume in the criminal courts. Skolnick suggests that the model of the adversary system that is posed as an ideal gives way under the strain of heavy volume. Thus, it is not only that legal rules may not operate in practice as in theory but also that the very conception of the system itself tends to be undermined by the administrative problems associated with volume. Skolnick's study also challenges Sudnow's analysis of the public defender, partly by showing that private defense attorneys with a heavy criminal practice behave in much the same fashion as public defenders, and partly by suggesting that Sudnow's analysis fails to analyze variations within the public defender's office. Both Sudnow and Skolnick base their conclusions upon observation of the same public defender's office.

SECTION EIGHT *The Legal Profession*

36
Realities and Possibilities

ERWIN O. SMIGEL

Clearly, the Wall Street lawyers and their law firms play an important role in our society. Their influence pervades most important social arenas; they have affected the law by their legal innovations and by their ability (implemented by the clients' strong financial position) and determination (when advisable) to appeal decisions more readily and in some instances to bring cases all the way to the United States Supreme Court. The very way they practice law—in an organizational structure that provides for a division of labor, in which specialists who band together are able to engage in almost unlimited research—allows them to consult easily with men who are especially competent in their specific fields, and on this basis (plus the big assist from their recruitment and development systems which secures and processes an impressive array of talented lawyers) to produce the model brief. This is not an insignificant fact. Riesman says of these briefs that they are "like the anonymous law review note" which many "judges crib from . . . in 'writing' their opinions."

Competition is keen for both the preferred lawyers and the preferred clients. The Wall Street firms easily win this contest. They get more than their share of the best law school graduates and the largest and wealthiest big-business clients. This has some importance for the practice of law in areas of the country not represented by large law firms, for other law firms and lawyers, and for the various strata comprised in our society. It means that the wealthy and the powerful have access to the best attorneys and that those not so affluent must be satisfied with what is left. This statement is something of an exaggeration, since the Wall Street firms do not take the best candidates from all the law schools and they do not recruit all the candidates from the preferred schools. And, as Riesman points out, law review graduates (whom the large law firms prefer) do not always make the best attorneys. Still, there is a tremendous concentration of talent in Wall Street. The reputation and excellence of their firms help perpetuate an imbalance in the distribution of lawyers throughout the country at the same time that this concentration of lawyers helps recruit and retain big-business clients.

Some Wall Street lawyers have been labeled members of the "power elite" —a significant element in the "establishment"; it is clear that they are favored advisors to high government and business leaders. In this capacity, as history has shown, they influence business and government decisions and help shape policy for these institutions. Primarily they are advisors to big business and in this capacity they sometimes also serve as its conscience. They provide, as Parsons remarks, "a kind of buffer between the illegitimate desires of . . . clients and the social interest." Their main function, however, is to maintain the status quo for their large corporate clients. This they attempt to do, and if speculation is in order (and I believe it is a responsibility of the researcher), they do it in an efficient, quiet, creative, and knowledgeable manner: observers enough to know they are fighting the tides of a shifting economic system; artists enough to advise and provide for cautious change (a position, incidentally, to which many clients object). Thus, these lawyers help give our society continuity. Their cautious use of societal brakes provides the liberal with time and opportunity to seek change in a relatively stable society. The revolutionary is thwarted because the keepers of the status quo do not allow the seeds of deep discontent to flower.

37

Portrait of a Business Generalist

DAVID T. BAZELON

Successful corporate lawyers like to be described these days as "generalists." This new term has a touch of magic for them; it seems to catch the essence of their drastically changed role in shepherding money and men of money through the green pastures of the new American property system. The word is not derived from any military analogy, but comes directly from "general"— meaning not specific or particular. We have come so far along the road of specialization and "expertise" that it is now a new and somehow different thing *not* to be an expert. The role I speak of is really that of a *pseudo*-non-expert, since the lawyer-as-generalist must be quite currently knowledgeable about tax law, corporate law, the securities market, and what's going on around town and in Washington. He is in fact quite expert about the broadest matters affecting the fortunes of men and corporations; but his expertness is not attuned primarily to specificities. So he is a generalist, one of the more significant

From *Commentary*, XXIX (1960), 277–279, 280, 281–286. Reprinted by permission of the author.

forces creating and caring for our managerial system. He kind of manages the managers, with their permission.

The root distinction to be made here (which of course goes far beyond the role of lawyers) is between the manager of actual production and the manager of the *purpose* of production. If we were talking about the Soviet Union, the difference would be easier to describe: in that special society, all the managers who manage the managers are hierarchically organized in the Communist Party; their roles are more easily identified. The production superintendent of a factory in Russia may very possibly be a member of the Communist Party, but if so, he is still under the direction of someone above him in the Party who is charged with managing the purpose of production. In America the distinction is not so clear; and the confusion comes from the fact that no one will admit that he is doing anything other than trying to make a profit. Making a profit means making money, and money is made both in producing and selling goods *and* in orienting a corporation more effectively to the selling of paper. First you produce goods and sell them at a profit; and then, in effect, you sell the profit. The latter is sometimes referred to as selling paper, and managing it is a very different matter from managing the actual production of goods. Here enters the generalist.

Now, among generalists, each individual is special, and can serve only as a rough example of the type. Yet, looking for a real generalist, whose actual career I could portray, I think I've found a good one.

Arnold M. Grant is what one might call a "pure" generalist, who has pursued his role with a creative vengeance, probably because it suits him so neatly in a personal way. A highly trained lawyer who helped build a substantial New York-Los Angeles law firm, he doesn't "practice" law as that term is understood by most other lawyers who do. For example, if there is a federal securities registration to be accomplished as a part of an over-all transaction that he is engineering, he acts like a client and hires a law firm to do it. (But he acts like a lawyer toward the corporate client in coming to the decision that a registration is called for in the first place.) Of course, he also edits the work turned out by the law firm he has seen fit to hire. The generalist's own staff consists largely of himself (with his briefcase) and a harassed secretary. He has relations, however, with more than one leading New York law firm; and on a five o'clock phone call from him, a complement of several men will be put to work for the night, drafting the necessary papers. The generalist certainly offers ordinary legal advice, but quite incidentally. What he actually does, sitting tense and urgent at the corporation president's elbow, is to guide the asset value and earning power—his truest, most important clients—into that reality of realities, After-Tax Money; with this ultimate purpose of production consummated, his work is done—except for the mop-up job of making sure the new values are not lost.

Mr. Grant's own description of his work is somewhat simpler: when asked point-blank, he says that he "merchandises paper" or "packages property."

But most of us need to have the meaning of these laconic phrases spelled out. And to elaborate them is to tell the long, intricate, important story of our entire business system. Most values in our business civilization are represented by various pieces of paper—money, bank deposits, stock certificates, debt instruments, deeds, and other contracts—and the heart of the whole story is how and why the value of a particular piece of paper is established. In our paper economy, merchandising paper and packaging property is the most highly rewarded activity open to men of mind and talent. No wonder, then, that it has become a fine creative art and undergone exquisite development.

Mr. Grant is a tall, trim, high-voltage individual in his early fifties, a man of considerable charm, and a talker to call the wind down. As if to complete the symbol of the special (yet general) career he was to mark out for himself, he got out of law school in 1929—that last-of-the-old-world year. In those woebegone days it was something of a curse to be a lawyer; many young lawyers took it as a favor to work for peanuts or even promises of peanuts, in order to get experience. But litigation was also a bigger thing in those unprosperous days before the New Deal and taxes, and anybody with a license could litigate. Like other determined young men of that time, Arnold Grant amassed a considerable amount of trial experience.

In 1943 he went out to California on behalf of a big electrical outfit in New York to negotiate a contract with the Kaiser shipbuilding interests. This agreement, which covered the construction of 30 C-4 troopships in Richmond, Calif., turned out to be so complicated that Grant was induced to stay out there to interpret its provisions and supervise operations under it. He worked around the clock for nearly six months and learned the lessons of a lifetime. (So often a man gains insight or perspective that amounts almost to a spiritual conversion as a result of an extended and concentrated involvement in something, anything.) Grant dates a major turn in his career from the time of this experience as a production supervisor; he began then to learn his trade as a generalist. The primary insight he derived (with considerable surprise) from this engagement was that you didn't have to be a highly seasoned production man to understand costs or efficiency and make actual contributions to production. Without ever putting on a construction helmet, dealing only with paper and foremen, Grant found that the "general point of view" could be crucially helpful in the building of ships. He discovered, for example, that it had previously been necessary to rip out the electrical installation in a hull, because the sheet metal—or maybe it was the plumbing—had to but hadn't gone in first. You don't have to go to engineering school to solve that problem—just find out who is responsible for initiating installations of electricity, sheet metal, plumbing, or whatever, call them in and introduce them to each other, and procure a statement from each as to what job precedes what other job. The general point of view is not always complicated—but it is always general.

In the course of his California experience, Grant also had the opportunity to appreciate the inner financial workings of the creation of the Kaiser empire, which was one of the first and certainly the most flamboyant in the new context of government procurement together with deadly high taxes. It was his introduction to the overriding importance of public relations, to credit as the true way of business life, and to what he calls "astute" tax thinking.

· · ·

He was, in fact, one of the first to incorporate personal income in Hollywood—to expand the use of the corporate device to translate personal income into appreciation of corporate shares that could be disposed of at capital gains rates. The way this worked—mostly for the very biggest stars—was to set up a corporation which then employed the star, and produced and owned the movie —all this done, however, under elaborate contracts with the studio. These independent companies (in the 1940's, but not today) were little more than tax and bookkeeping forms, since the studio retained control over everything important. But when the movie was completed, and before the corporation began to take in any income, the shares held by the star could be sold to the studio at a price reflecting the appreciated value of the completed film. The gain was taxed at the comfortable 25 per cent rate. It was a wonderful lawful loophole while it lasted. So good, in fact, that the success of Grant and others in its use led to the adoption in the late '40s of the "collapsible corporation" provision of the Internal Revenue Code, which was supposed to make the maneuver impossible, and in fact did make it considerably more difficult.

Once the gorgeous vision of "capital gains" caught on, however, the enthusiasts became irrepressible. Everybody wanted to be a corporation—and in fashionable Hollywood if you were not one, you were just not with it. Although the high-C phase of this song ended in the late 1940's, the deeper music of capital gains has of course lingered on.

But the generalist moves with the times: indeed, he is in a kind of lock step —but a step or two ahead—with the gentlemen in Washington. He is charged with appraising the general situation, meaning the whole situation, and properly relating the different factors thereof. The logic of inversion (the basic logic of psychoanalysis and detective stories) is central to his role: it is incumbent on him to remember what everybody else is forgetting, to look for what isn't there, and to test every proposition by formulating and fooling around with its opposite. Capital gains became such a thing that Grant's biggest problem with non-corporate clients was to get them to take another look at the possibilities of ordinary income, which had been more or less lost sight of in the frantic shuffle. (An entree to this prosaic approach was to remind the client that there had to be actual *gain* along with a good capital gains plan— that some of the latter just looked good on paper.)

· · ·

In 1948, Grant made perhaps the most crucial "generalist" decision of his career. He was at that time a senior partner of a sizable New York-Los Angeles law firm, and making more money than he could spend. But not more than the government could spend; he says he felt like a slave to overhead. So he in effect walked away from it and put himself on what he calls "50 per cent free time"—meaning he is committed to clients of his firm for only half his time, the golden remainder being available to "anything good that comes up." Plenty has.

He has designed, engineered, and executed a substantial number of big deals—including the purchase of the Empire State Building from the Raskob estate, a $50 million private transaction. But of course there are a lot of people around who put deals together—I suppose a Murchison hears from several of them every day. What Grant has done more especially has been to create for himself a role as a kind of total adviser to corporations—a role which, as far as I know, is duplicated only by similar quintessential generalists and by the more imaginative investment bankers. He is usually retained as financial and legal consultant to the board of directors, and frequently goes on the board itself. His generalist purpose is to alter, orient, and organize both the enterprise itself and its appearance to the financial public, so that the inherent values will be recognized and will become marketable. The Wall Street term for this is "merchandising paper."

The kinds of situations and solutions involved in the process of "merchandising paper" are too numerous to tell about, or even to catalogue. I shall content myself with offering two case histories in which Grant played an important role. The first concerns a leading company in the postwar office building boom in the revolutionized urban real estate market, which in New York City alone has transformed the face of midtown Park Avenue and Fifth Avenue in a single decade.

The company I speak of is the Tishman Realty & Construction Co., Inc., a third-generation family enterprise (Julian Tishman began building tenements in 1898), which is currently 53.5 per cent publicly owned. Tishman claims several firsts in the new bonanza market: that the 22-story office building it put up at 445 Park Avenue in 1947 was the first to be erected on that street of streets since the late 1920's (and thus started the fabulous trend); that it was the first fully air-conditioned structure in New York City; and more important still, that it was one of the first to be financed by the "sale-lease-back" method, which perhaps more than anything else distinguishes the current real estate market from the ill-remembered one of the '20s.

Just as people were slow to get into the postwar stock market because of the lingering odor of 1929, although it was a totally different market, so also it took effort and clever merchandising to get across the even greater differences between the two real estate markets. But to tell the complicated story briefly, the difference from which all other differences flow is the present practice of major corporations of signing long-term leases for substantial prime office space, frequently several full floors. (One has only to stroll up Park Avenue from Grand Central to 57th Street to realize that this small stretch is becoming the plush headquarters of the corporate world, comparable to the blocks of Wall Street which for nearly a century have been known as the center of the financial world.) The corporations go for the long-term leases these days probably because they have greater confidence they will be in business 15 or 20 years from now; the government in effect pays half the cost of fancier, fully integrated headquarter offices; there is no good reason any longer (and a number of disadvantages) for leaving the main office in Keokuk where the first plant happened by chance to be located. Business, as distinct from production, is concentrated in the largest cities, with New York first.

A lease for 20 years with the signature of General Motors on it is as good as money—better, in fact, since the new leases include escalator clauses which provide against rising taxes and labor costs, and so contain a built-in hedge against inflation. Before the era of the big lease, the amount of money a builder could borrow on a mortgage was ordinarily two-thirds of the appraised value of the land acquired and the building to be constructed. The additional one-third had to be supplied out of the builder's own pocket (equity capital) or by means of an expensive second mortgage, when that was available. Today, the mortgage lender will take into consideration the value of the long-term leases as well as the land and building, and so is willing to lend more than two-thirds. This of course reduces the builder's investment—and there have been some wonderful instances where, after a brief period, the builder's investment has been reduced to zero by the time construction was completed.

The legal device for effectuating this marvelous maneuver is the "sale-and-lease-back," which substitutes for the conventional mortgage. What happens is that instead of mortgaging the land and building, the builder sells it and simultaneously leases it back from the purchaser, usually an insurance company. Because of the added value of the long-term corporate leases, the insurance company is willing to pay a purchase price of more than two-thirds of the cost of the completed building—on some occasions, the full cost. The rental that the builder is required to pay to the insurance company under the lease-back is sufficiently smaller than the net operating income on the fully rented building to allow for a good profit. The margin of profit on the lease-back is like an owner's equity under conventional mortgage financing. Instead of paying mortgage interest and amortization, the builder—now a lessee—pays rental. This gives him a tax advantage in that he pays deductible rent rather than non-deductible amortization. In a reversal of roles, the insurance company—now an owner—gets the right to depreciate the cost of the building, which is just about as good, taxwise, as amortization of a mortgage. In the year 2000-something, the insurance company ends up owning the land and building free of any leasehold. (Grant himself half believes the big life insurance companies will finally own the better part of Manhattan Island in fee simple in 50 or 100 years.) This whole financial operation is in effect underwritten by major corporate tenants. It's a beautiful thing.

In fact, it's so good that a lot of people who should have known better wouldn't believe it at first. They just couldn't see it: they remember the 1930's as a dreary procession of reorganizations in bankruptcy of almost every major building put up in the 1920's in New York City. Many investors were determined not to be burned again. One consequence of this backwardness was that Tishman's stock was selling for $8 million in 1955 (400,000 shares at $20 a share), although the new proposition had already been proven in practice.

Two years later, when Grant's generalist work was done, the stock sold for $37 million. Recently, 1,900,000 shares were selling at about $25 a share, or better than $47 million. The $29 or $39 million difference is "merchandised paper," and real as rain.

How was it done? On one level, it can be said that the existing values of the business were properly presented. On another, that conventional backwardness was overcome by conventional forwardness. But the heart of the matter was the merchandising of corporate values—bringing certain facts about the operation, and their interrelations, to the attention of the financial public. For example:

1. People were overlooking the highly important fact that substantial cash was being generated by the company under the guise of depeciation charges. Depreciation deductions are taken and allowed for tax purposes on the theory that as each year passes buildings "wear out" and decrease in value—but in the postwar real estate market almost all buildings, including the oldest, have increased in value. Viewed practically rather than conventionally, this depreciation-cash was similar to net profits after taxes and dividends—and on this basis the company had developed over $23 million from 1945 to 1956 which (cash alone) was $15 million more than the stock was selling for.

2. Tishman regularly showed important profit in capital gains on the sale of older properties, but apparently the public discounted this because such profits usually appear on operating statements under the heading "non-recurring gain," which is the conventional accounting designation. It took the financial community a little while to realize that these profitable sales were a recurrent feature of Tishman's business, and that they also indicated a significant upgrading of the company's inventory (that is, the company was replacing not as good old buildings with better new buildings).

3. The better this inventory became, and the more depreciation (really profit) that was taken, the more company's assets were undervalued on its books (balance sheet entries are conventionally set at depreciated cost). With the most successful sale-lease-back deal, no cost at all would appear on the books, because the future profit was based on a lease that entailed no continuing investment, and so would not be an asset at all. Since the balance sheet understated the appreciated value of properties, $29 million of assets actually had a market value of about $70 million.

4. In the real estate market of the '20s the big danger, and what ended up by collapsing the whole endeavor, was that the builder had to hock everything to get the necessary second mortgage and equity money. But in the new market, based on long-term leases and sale-lease-back, lenders have allowed the builder to insulate each transaction in a separate corporation, without any extra guarantees or collateral. So if a particular deal goes sour, other profitable enterprises are not dragged down with it. A very important difference.

The pattern of concealed values was brought out in the open, and the means of trading in the paper representing them were facilitated. First, the annual report to Tishman stockholders was overhauled (the one for 1955 began, unpardonably, with a "Submitted herewith" and went on to the deadly "I am pleased to report" and "It is most gratifying to note") and turned into a potent exposition of the new market and Tishman's position in it. These reports, which are required by the SEC, have come to be recognized as a blessing rather than an imposition, and now are widely used as publicity vehicles. Also, Norman Tishman as president of the company told the new story with considerable effect to the influential New York Society of Security Analysis, and, as usual with addresses to this group, copies were distributed to the market community and through them to the buying public. So the story got around.

Then, the floating supply of stock was too small—only 400,000 shares, well over half of which were held by the Tishman family, employees, and so on—with the result that infrequent trading and erratic price changes marred the market for the stock. So the 400,000 shares, selling at $20 a share in 1955, were split 2-for-1 in December of that year; a 10 per cent stock dividend was declared in January, 1956; another 5 per cent increase in December; a second 2-for-1 split in June, 1957; and another 5 per cent dividend in January, 1958. All this cutting up came to about a 385 per cent increase in paper, better than 1,500,000 additional potential pieces of it—each of which has been selling recently for $23-$25 apiece! During most of this time, the aggregate cash dividend was not noticeably increased, although after a while there were some extras.

(Stock splits—and stock dividends, which have the same effect—are among the weirdest phenomena of the current market. In 1944, there were 22 splits or dividends on the Big Board, six in the popular 2-for-1 range. The movement hit its peak in 1956 when there were 290 in all, including 65 2-for-1'ers. Again and again, the increased aggregate of shares will sell for more after the split, although nothing real has happened except that paper has been cut up. The whole strange phenomenon is supposed to have started big after a 2-for-1 by General Motors in 1950, when it was noticed that twice as many pieces of paper were somehow more valuable. Cheaper stock and more of it increase the floating supply and trading volume generally—you might say it enlarges the game by letting the pikers in. Tradition has always made the round-lot—multiples of 100 shares—somewhat magical, and cheaper stock broadens the base of round-lot trading. So all by itself more paper means greater volume which, in this market, moves the price up.)

So, complicated values inhering in the whirl of modern paper property were coherently presented, and the Tishman Company had an up-to-date coming-out party. This "merchandising" program was not at all hurt, of course, by the fact that 1956–1958 were Tishman's best years for earnings. But there's the whole point, for the business generalist, who knows that earning potential is the heart of paper value. He feels sometimes it is downright wicked to allow innocent stockholders to sell a piece of paper, all unknowing, at a fraction of its value. But you have to get up and *move,* to make it clear to the stockholder.

Grant has a firm belief that property must be made available in the proper "package" to be appreciated—to be taken at its inherent value. This has nothing to do with hustling stock through excessive puff in the selling, or indeed with any of the various elements of a Madison Avenue hard sell. Proper packaging of paper values is comparable, rather, to effective writing: instead of lumping together a miscellany of ideas, moods, and burble, one can, by prior analysis and sensitive use of language, present a rhetorically coherent expression. The analogy to the classical sense of rhetoric is quite apt: by packaging, one creates a rhetorical bridge between the existence of property values and the market for them. (The old word "rhetoric" does not have the same meaning of falsification as the modern word "propaganda": the Greeks understood that it was one thing to discover the truth and something else again to make it known.)

Packaging means—to be academic for a moment—both the legal form property values are given, and the combination of actual values within a legal form. As in the previous real estate example, the legal form would be a conventional mortgage or the newer sale-and-lease-back device; the values within the legal form would be land-bricks-and-mortar alone, or those usual elements along with long-term leases. In one sense, the story of packaging is probably co-equal with the history of property and contract law; but in modern times at least we are becoming much more aware of what this history of our law was all about—especially under the bursting proliferation of corporate and tax forms.

One of Grant's fondest feats of packaging was the "spin-off" of S. Klein Department Stores, Inc., from its parent, Grayson-Robinson Stores, Inc. (A spin-off is more or less the opposite of a merger—an approved device under the Internal Revenue Code for making two companies out of one, in a tax-free transaction.) Klein's is a famous and very profitable low-price store located in New York City's Union Square district. This fast-action department store—which has more than one "discount riot" to its credit—pioneered a number of modern merchandising concepts, including low-overhead self-service, cash-and-carry department store selling, and what came to be known as the discount house operation. It is a cash business that turns over its inventory money 12 times a year, and has a bare minimum of fixed assets.

Grayson-Robinson is a chain of nationwide specialty stores which started out in California and is still concentrated in the West. It runs a good business, but has nothing like the fast profitable turnover of Klein's. Grayson, again unlike its former subsidiary, has a high-asset value—mostly leasehold improvements on its more than 120 stores. The market value of its stock has always been less than its book value (net worth according to the balance sheet). After the spin-off, Grayson sold on the New York Stock Exchange for about one-third of book value. Klein's sold on the American at 13 times book.

Grayson acquired the Union Square store from the estate of the founder in 1946. The new management up-dated and expanded the low-price, mass-selling policies initiated by Samuel Klein decades before in New York's famous working-class area. And they made a lot of money. But the Klein operation was, so to speak, under the lid of the more widely known (outside of New York) and less flamboyant Grayson-Robinson business. Moreover, Klein's profit capacity was seen always in relation to Grayson's heavy asset investment. (Following the usual practice, Klein was carried on Grayson's books at cost; and the management prepared consolidated financial statements which lumped together the operations of the two businesses.)

When he came into the situation, Grant recognized that this was clearly the wrong package. Utilizing one of the generalist's first principles—that two plus two seldom equals an obvious four in financial matters—and being a tax man aware of the spin-off technique, he decided to lift the lid and present Klein in its own true package. It took a year of hard work to accomplish this: the details make interesting lawyer talk, but would probably bore or confuse the lay reader. As an example, there was a large insurance company loan the obligation on which had to be parceled out between the divided companies, and that took months of negotiation. It is much easier to merge two separate companies than to make two out of an existing one.

But it was worth all the work, because Grant's idea about the proper package turned out to be right. From the announcement of the intention to separate the companies to the date of the actual spin-off, when new shares of Klein were distributed share-for-share to Grayson stockholders (and while the lawyer work was going on), the price of Grayson stock went from $7 to better than $20. After the spin-off, Klein sold at $13 while Grayson (without Klein) stayed at $7. There were about 800,000 shares of Grayson outstanding, worth $5.6 million at $7 a share—and when 800,000 shares of Klein emerged, $10.4 million in paper value appeared from "nowhere." Three years after the spin-off, the range of Grayson averaged about $12 and that of Klein about $18, so the whole fresh package went from $5.4 to $24 million.

That's an example of "packaging." (There are many others.) Perhaps the concept can be summed up in this way: never sell a pregnant mare for the price of an ordinary horse. Or: the whole is equal to the sum of its parts—yes, but only for the generalist who ignores the *given* whole, studies the parts carefully, and does his own addition.

Grant is so completely the general expert that he can both enjoy and profit immensely from his nice involvement in our property system, and also stand off and look at it objectively. When in a mellow mood, his favorite image is that in our business system we are playing a "kitty" poker game—the kind he says he played throughout college. In this sort of poker, something from every pot goes into a kitty, and after enough action has been had the kitty is divided up among the losers and you can start playing again. Otherwise, there would be one or two big winners and no more poker game. By the percentage to the kitty, of course, he means to refer to the annual tax bite, which the government in effect distributes to the losers.

But as with a lot of people these days who are perceptive as well as successful, not all of his moods are mellow, and he is both uneasy and discouraged that Americans are continuing the conventional poker game even after the

Russians have challenged us to a much more serious—and exciting—competition for production rather than merely paper profit. (He takes the continuing bull market as proof of our lack of seriousness in meeting this challenge, of our concentration on paper rather than production: and maybe in his musings he also remembers those wartime days back in Richmond, California, and 30 important troopships.) A lifelong liberal Democrat, and active in both of Stevenson's campaigns, he is not one of those in his party who have been lulled or enticed into a spiritual me-too-ism by eight years of Prosperous Nothing. He thinks we're in trouble and that we ought to get busy doing something about it. In the present unusual circumstances, too much business as usual could end up ruining the business system.

38

The Career Development of the Negro Lawyer in Chicago

WILLIAM HENRI HALE

Client Meets Lawyer

Problems don't cast their shadows before themselves, in most instances. The research worker studying the life of the family or the social worker treating its problems may see premonitory symptoms of problems in some instances, but for the most part, to the family at least, they drop like lightning from the sky. Caught in its own worries, bogged down by the exigencies of urban existence, and confused by the changing scene about it, the family knows only that yesterday things seemed to have been going fairly smoothly and today it faces what appears to be a solid wall of trouble. What does the family do under such circumstances? In most cases, the people were confused and bewildered and groped aimlessly about, fair game to "agents" or open to suggestions from those whose opinions in many instances were no sounder than their own. One Negro lawyer put it as follows:

> You can do a great service for our people, if you can help them know how to select their professional men. They just don't know. They listen to police or politi-

From an unpublished Ph.D. dissertation, University of Chicago (1949), pp. 126–149, 96–97, 78–86. Reprinted by permission of the author.

cians or somebody else and don't give it a bit of thought themselves. They've got to learn to pick a dentist or a doctor or a lawyer because he's a specialist in that field. It would be foolish for anybody to come and get me for a personal injury case, just like it would be foolish for them to get some lawyers for a criminal case.

A woman came to me to get her a divorce and I told her, "Madam, I can't take your case because it isn't my specialty and I don't have the time."

She squawked and said, "Oh, you don't want my money?"

I told her to go home and shoot her husband and then come to see me and I'd take her case. That's my business.[1]

Who, then, are these persons from whom the Negro seeks advice, or who volunteer advice in times of trouble? Table 38–1 shows the persons giving advice and the lawyers—Negro or "other"—they recommend.

TABLE 38-1 *Source of Advice for the 71 Families Using a Total of 135 Individual Lawyers by Class Position of Family and Race of Lawyer*

| Source of Advice | Lower-Class Families | | | Middle-Class Families | | | Total |
| | Lawyer Recommended | | | Lawyer Recommended | | | |
	Negro	Other	Total	Negro	Other	Total	
Lawyer known to client	9	1	10	40	12	52	62
Lawyer recommended by:							
Friends or relatives	8	10	18	13	8	21	39
Business and professional men	2	1	3	5	4	9	12
Public officials and public workers	2	2	4	1	3	4	8
Himself or his agent	–	5	5	–	1	1	6
Employers and labor representatives	–	4	4	–	–	–	4
Legal organizations	–	3	3	1	–	1	4
Total	21	26	47	60	28	88	135

The 71 families experienced a total of 165 problems. In nine of these cases, the families sought no advice nor received any assistance, and in seven other instances non-legal assistance was obtained. For the remaining 149 problems, the families used 135 individual lawyers. One notes a tendency on the part of the client to return to a lawyer previously used provided there had been satisfaction with his services, for, of the 14 lower-class and 28 middle-class families who had cause to use a lawyer on more than one occasion, 14 of these (five lower-class and nine middle-class) returned to the same lawyer. In nine instances, the same lawyer was used twice; in four instances, the same lawyer was used three times; while one family used the same lawyer four times. This reveals 20 instances in which a lawyer was used on more than one occasion and raised the total number of times in which the services of a lawyer was used to 155. We now turn to a more detailed description of the factors that brought lawyer and client together.

Lawyer Known to Client. The largest single source of advice was the lawyer who was either a relative, a friend, or one who was known to the client by reputation. It is not surprising that families turned to such persons since they may have been in some measure familiar with the family's problem. It should be noted, however, that this occurred more frequently with the middle-class than with the lower-class family. The common social level of the lawyer and the middle-class client plus this client's greater concern with "respectable" matters, no doubt helps explain this situation. Several of the families had used specific lawyers because they were members of the same church. In these instances the lawyers had plainly played important roles in the life of the church, holding offices, giving financial support, and generally "making their presence felt."

One middle-class woman declared, "We wouldn't think of using anyone other than Mr.————. He's been in the church all his life."

Church membership played a more important part with the middle-class family than with the lower-class family obviously because the lawyer was more frequently a member of the middle-class family's church.

The generally "harmless" character of the middle-class family's problem is to be seen in the fact that while no lower-class family reported ever using a lawyer who was representing others in the case, there were six instances where this was true of the middle-class family. All of these were in cases of buying property.

The Lawyer Recommended by Friends, Relatives, or Acquaintances. The opinions of friends and relatives are always important to the family with a problem. In many instances these people have confronted similar situations and can pass on to the family the benefit of their experiences. They serve, thus, as counsellors as well as confidantes. The impression gained of such advisors is that their advice is spontaneous, resulting from the desire to assist a friend rather than because of any "understanding" that might exist between advisor and lawyer. A person associated with a member of the family in business was a source of advice in five situations. A certain amount of trust in the advisor and respect for his opinion had already developed. It was a logical next step then to seek his advice on the current problem. Landlords and landladies, because of their proximity to the families, were frequently sought out for advice. Here it was perhaps not so much a matter of affection existing between tenant and landlord as it was the family's impression of the worldly wisdom of the person who must, in the course of managing an apartment building, develop valuable contacts.

The Lawyer Recommended by Business or Professional Men. This group included Negro doctors, Negro insurance men, Negro and white druggists, Negro and white lawyers, Negro ministers, Negro real estate men. This group differed as advisors from the above. While the welfare of the family seemed to be the motive behind the advice of friends, relatives, and acquaintances, one frequently detected here an interest in a specific lawyer.

The use of such persons as advisors in 12 instances was not unexpected. One has only to realize the aloneness of many of these families—despite the fact that they have friends and relatives—to understand their grasping at the nearest "authoritative" source of information. To many of these families, these advisors were "authorities" and this authority status carried over into areas outside their specific specialty. They were not only "educated" but had attained position in the community, and the people saw them as guides, counsellors, and sources of strength in time of trouble.

In all of these instances there existed a feeling on the part of the family that some sort of a relationship existed between advisor and lawyer for the sending of clients. One Negro pastor in advising a woman to obtain a white lawyer was met by protestations on the woman's part that she would rather have a Negro lawyer. He concluded the discussion with the remark, "Well, sister, you do as you please, but if I were in your shoes, I would certainly get Mr. _____." Since the woman was not acquainted with any Negro lawyer and since her pastor was so "sold" on the white lawyer, she went to him. She reported that she knew, as an officer of the church, that the white lawyer had frequently "made donations." The pastor had reminded her of that when he suggested the lawyer.

The Lawyer Recommended by Public Officials and Public Workers. Here again is found a group of advisors who have more than the interests of the family at heart. They are the people the family necessarily has to contact in attempting to solve its problems. One must visit the tax office to conduct business. One must visit the city hall, the courts, the jails, the hospitals when one has that kind of problem and one is arrested by a police officer. If the source of advice was seen as a continuum with the client knowing and associating with his lawyer, on one end of the continuum, then these advisors would fall at the opposite end, outranked only by the group of lawyers and their known agents who actively seek business.

The bar itself recognizes the existence of "understandings" between certain lawyers and certain personnel of the system of justice. The *Chicago Bar Record,* a publication of the Chicago Bar Association, takes account of the fact in a recent issue:

Many deputy clerks and bailiffs occupy positions having direct or indirect contact with members of the bar and with the public. It lies within the power of such attachés to delay, annoy, and harass attorneys and litigants, or conversely to prefer and expedite their business in many ways. It would be naive to assume that these employees are unaware of their power, or that the temptation to "make a little on the side" is always resisted. The "approach" may be bold or it may be subtle, but no amount of subtlety can conceal the fact, nor will anyone who knows his way around the court be long in doubt about its meaning.[2]

In most of these instances, the "approach" was not subtle. One woman, who along with her sister had been injured in a taxicab wreck, reported on the activities of the police who appeared at the scene of the accident.

> The police took us to X Hospital and before we got in their car, they were giving us lawyers' cards and telling us not to talk to anybody. But they didn't let us stay in X Hospital because I guess it isn't a cooperative hospital and don't allow these chasers in there. The police came back and got us in a patrol wagon with a stretcher and took us to Y Hospital. They lectured us all the way about, "Don't talk to anybody. Yes, we know you're in the right; everybody saw it. This lawyer will take care of you," and all that kind of stuff.

From certain individuals within the "personnel" group come statements which help to round out the picture. A police officer said:

> Lawyers have hook-ups with policemen who are friendly with them and put them on good cases. If an officer looks up a man for a crime and feels that the fellow has a chance of raising some good money and he has a friend who is a lawyer, he might make contact with him. Sometimes the policeman puts the lawyer in contact with the witnesses and they can be "handled" and if the case isn't too big, the person may not need to go to a lawyer because sometimes the policemen will listen to reason, you know. . . . There are a few Negro lawyers with reputations for being good criminal lawyers and who get good criminal cases. Course in nine out of ten cases, the average Negro criminal will get a white lawyer. They think the white lawyer's better. They don't know that half of it is influence and contact and being able to talk to the prosecutor and the judge and others. These lawyers are not necessarily good criminal lawyers, but it's the contacts they have. How do they get contacts? A lot of them have worked in the State's Attorney's office or have held political jobs where they came in contact with fellows who are now judges. They know them by their first names and can go right into their offices and chambers and lay their cards right on the table.

This police officer thus begins to reveal not only how the client gets in touch with a lawyer, but also how some lawyers win their cases. Another officer contributed to the picture by saying:

> In most cases, a lawyer can make a deal with a policeman. When we arrest a man, we "charge" him according to regulations and "book" him, but we can book him for a lesser or a graver charge. It's like the difference in being charged with manslaughter instead of murder. In both cases you've killed someone, but there's a helluva lot of difference in the punishment. Lawyers often get policemen to book a man on a lesser charge. Then when it gets to court the judge asks the policeman what happened and the way he tells the story may make all the difference in the world.
>   I arrested some fellows for disturbing the peace and one got real nasty and I planned to have him up on an assault charge, which is pretty serious. The next morning a lawyer came to me and said this boy's mother had come to him to get him to go into court with the boy. He told me that he could get me maybe a "fin" ($5) if I'd let things go easy with him.

The professional bondsman is one who also "knows his way around." A part of the legal process, he is familiar with the machinery both as to how lawyers get clients and how they win their cases. The following excerpt is from a statement of a bondsman who pointed out that bondsmen and lawyers work closely together to the mutual benefit of all.

If I go a $500 bond, I'd get $50 out of it and if a lawyer had referred this client to me, I'd be expected to give him $10. On the other hand I frequently refer clients to lawyers and I get a commission, too. Then, too, you've got jail guards in the county jail. They're on their P's and Q's and if they see a fellow come in who looks like he's got some money, they'll call a bondsman or a lawyer in order to get a commission for themselves.

Chicago is a corrupt town and in the courts—especially the Municipal Court —judges are on the "take." In the State's Attorney's office the same thing applies. Most all the municipal courts are corrupt. The judges take money, not directly from the lawyer, but through their bailiffs.

While little doubt exists as to the existence of the foregoing pattern, it is virtually impossible to determine the extent of the system by direct "on the record" evidence of specific situations. The reasons for this seem reasonably clear: it is not to be expected that participants in such a system would care to disclose their roles openly; and others, who might have knowledge of pertinent facts, experience a reluctance to point a finger in public.

The Family Contacted by the Lawyer or His Agent. "The lawyer just happened up" or "a runner came from nowhere" accounted for six instances of lawyer-client contact. In five of these six instances, the family fell in the lower-class group. Personal injury was the type of case each time, and the lawyer was always white while the runner was always a Negro. A man who traces the source of his present affluence to his connection with lawyers as a "representative" described the process of "going out and getting business":

Connections are sometimes more important than just being a lawyer and I know that Negro lawyers just can't get those connections. I used to be with half-a-dozen firms downtown myself and I saw how it worked. I was what you might call a representative. The white lawyer says if you can bring him a dollar, he can afford to give you fifty or seventy-five cents of it back 'cause you'll bring him lots more. The average Negro lawyer wants the whole hog and therefore, he don't get many pigs to cut up. . . .

If I'd get a case of something like a compound fracture for my lawyer, I'd get $75 the minute the contract was signed and 40 per cent of the lawyer's fees when the case was settled. That sounds like a lot of money, but I was making money for them. The insurance adjuster got his; I got mine; and everybody was happy. A case that a Negro lawyer would get $500 out of, we'd get $1,500. My lawyer and the insurance adjuster would make a nice settlement; the lawyer would get a gibber fee, and there would be a kick-back to the insurance adjuster. Negro lawyers just can't get those contacts. He wants it all and they don't trust him; so nobody gets a damned thing. I know a case where a fellow had a colored lawyer and he had been fooling around with it for seven months. Hadn't gotten anything and wasn't going to get anything. We took the case away from him and settled it in nine days for $2,100. We had to pay the lawyer what he would have gotten to get him to release the case, but we still made money.

How did I get my cases? That's easy. I worked with the police. I had connections with the Police Department and I could find out what was happening all over the city through them. I had a press card which would allow me to go into the stations and look at the book where accidents had been reported. You have to have a car because this leg work don't get it and you've got to get there fast. The person who gets to the victim's family first doesn't always get the case, but he's got an advantage 'cause he can tell the people to lock up the house and not let anybody else in. Sometimes it takes two or three days to get the case 'cause the people are looking around, too, to see the best offer, but if they don't see anything better, they'll usually call you and give the case to you 'cause you were first.

The families frequently felt that their share of the settlement was inadequate and that the lawyer had taken the lion's share. Nevertheless, they stated that should a similar incident occur, they would probably return to the lawyer who had previously handled their case. The attitude was always one of "anything is better than nothing." Though these lawyers specialized in personal injury work, it is likely that the families would return for advice on any type of problem. This provides an enormous potential clientele for the lawyer, the decision for the disposal of which rests with him.

The Lawyer Recommended by Employers and Labor Representatives. Employers and labor representatives hold a status position in the opinion of the families not unlike that of the professional man. Each of these four instances were lower-class families who had the image of the southern "boss man" as a source of strength. It is not surprising that one would turn to his employer in time of trouble for advice. That this advice would be acted upon is just as likely since the employer may be called upon for an advance to finance the problem's solution.

The labor representative, too, is seen as a friend who is in position to assist the workers in the solution of many of their problems. The litigation in which unions find themselves increasingly involved makes necessary the retention of a legal staff or at least the effecting of a more or less continuous relationship with lawyers. In each of these instances, the lawyers recommended were white. The fact that Negroes as a group are not employers, plus the point raised by several lawyers to the effect that Negro lawyers are not employed to any great extent by unions, help account for this.

The Lawyer Recommended by Legal Organizations. Four of the cases fall in this group which includes the Chicago Bar Association, the Cook County Bar Association, the Public Defender's Office, and the Legal Aid Bureau. The Cook

County Bar Association, an essentially Negro organization, recommended a middle-class family to a Negro lawyer. The other three organizations recommended lower-class families to white lawyers.

The Public Defender's Office performs the service of defense for those who are unable to secure representation of their own. Individuals exercise little or no choice in getting a specific lawyer as he is appointed to each case by the director of the office. People who are able would be likely to prefer the services of an advocate of their own choosing. Families turned to two Bar Associations because of their lack of knowledge of any lawyer. Rather than "just get anybody," and having great respect for the integrity of the associations, they felt that their interests would best be protected by these agencies.

The Legal Aid Bureau is an agency under the auspices of the United Charities organized in 1919 [3] to provide certain legal services for persons unable to provide these services for themselves. The purpose is given in more detail by the Bureau itself:

> Legal aid work consists of giving legal assistance in negotiation and litigation to poor persons without cost to them, or at a minimum cost which they can afford in matters where no other assistance is available.[4]

The Legal Aid Bureau is essentially a charitable organization. Since families may have some feeling against accepting charity and since the standards for receiving assistance are necessarily stringent, it is probably true that only the poorest people receive such assistance. In terms of its role as a factor in the development of a career for the Negro lawyer, it is interesting to note that the Bureau serves as an unwitting party to the channeling of clients to "other" attorneys. When a prospective client approaches the Legal Aid with a problem, he is carefully interviewed to see if his income falls within the scope of the Bureau which, as we have seen, is designed for the poor. If the client successfully meets the Bureau's standards, his case is accepted and handled free. If, however, he is found to be above the income limit, the client is referred to the Chicago Bar Association. The client is again interviewed by an official of the Chicago Bar Association for a nominal fee, and if he "has a case," is referred to one of the lawyers on the Chicago Bar Association's "lawyers' reference panel."

An official of the Bar Association stated that although the association had a membership of 5,500 attorneys, there were only 500 of the member attorneys on the Lawyer's Reference Panel. He stated further that there were but seven Negro members of the Chicago Bar Association, none of whose names appeared on the reference panel.[5] It is impossible, then, for any of the clients who passed through the Legal Aid Bureau to the Chicago Bar Association to be referred to Negro attorneys. Information on the extent of such business is supplied by the Legal Aid Bureau.

In 1947, the Bureau received a total of 13,487 new cases. Of this number, 3,633 (26.94 per cent) were Negro clients. The Bureau found that 3,045

(22.58 per cent) of the total cases were unable to pass the qualifying test and so were referred to the Chicago Bar Association. Table 38–2 shows by months the racial distribution of clients referred to the Chicago Bar Association by the Legal Aid Bureau.

These figures show that of the 3,045 clients referred to the Chicago Bar Association, 695 (22.82 per cent) were Negroes. An explanation of the smaller percentage of Negroes "referred" as compared with the percentage that applied to the Legal Aid Bureau (26.94 per cent) may be found in the fact of the greater poverty of the Negro group which makes more of their members eligible for the services of the Bureau. Since, as has already been pointed out,

TABLE 38-2 *Monthly Distribution of Clients Referred by Legal Aid Bureau to the Chicago Bar Association, 1947**

Month	Total	Negro	Other
January	222	43	179
February	170	46	124
March	214	36	178
April	180	29	151
May	240	47	193
June	257	60	197
July	288	61	227
August	267	56	211
September	331	77	254
October	341	88	253
November	250	62	188
December	285	90	195
Total	3,045	695	2,350

*From the files of the Legal Aid Bureau.

there is some tendency for the client to return to a lawyer who has previously been of service, it seems reasonable to assume that these 695 cases form only a small part of the Negro business diverted to "other" lawyers through this channel.

Mention was made earlier of the fact that for nine problems the families involved neither sought nor received advice. Three of these problems were of middle-class families and were all personal injury cases. Here the families had reasoned that a more satisfactory settlement could be made directly with the insurance company. The attitude expressed in each of these instances was that it would be unwise to hire a lawyer since he would get the bulk of whatever settlement he negotiated. It is interesting to note that no lower-class family reported personal injury as a problem for which no assistance was sought or accepted. Their problems included being defrauded of a deposit on an apartment, destruction of their property by others, inability to receive payment for labor, and the arrest of children for fighting and stealing. Their inaction in these matters reflects a feeling of resignation to circumstances about which little could be done. "What's the use?" seemed to be the prevailing attitude. Living at a level where such problems are less the exception than the rule, the families accept as their lot the many hardships that come to them. The following statement by a member of one of these families expressed a feeling which all seemed to share. "Nobody cares anything about you. Everybody's out to see what he can get for himself." "Rights" are thus seen to be relative things and the family with a problem may choose to define the situation solely in terms of what it considers the more practical aspects of the situation.

Though the majority of the families sought assistance on their problems, there were seven instances in which they did not reach a lawyer. The persons whose advice assisted the families in solutions of their problems included social service workers, police officers, juvenile probation officers, and politicians. All of these families were in the lower class. Most of these advisors have already been discussed and reasons can be seen for their use as counsellors. Something further needs to be said about politicians, especially since their sub-group accounted for four of the seven cases. Frequently a relationship is developed between politician and prospective voter to the mutual benefit of each party. The individual feels that he can approach this local leader and expect help. This help is not conceived by the client as charity, but as a consideration to which he has a right. The politician, on the other hand, expects the beneficiary of his benevolence to be a loyal worker in good standing with the party. One woman saw the politician as taking the role played in the South by the "influential white friend." She said:

> Down there in the South, it's the white man what gits you out. Up here, it's votes that counts. My stepfather used to be always getting into fights and the politician told him, "If you do anything in my territory, I'll take care of you, but I can't do you no good nowheres else."

In a society so sensitive to political maneuverings, one can expect that people will avail themselves of such sources of help. The politician holds a strategic position in the functions of government, a part of which are the institutions of law and order. He frequently, then, can make the contact and perform for free the service a lawyer would demand payment for. The client may very often feel safer to know that his case is being handled by his politician. He can never know just how vigorously a lawyer will pursue his interests, but he does know that the politician's status among his constituents depends in part on his ability to keep them contented and satisfied with things as they are. This includes, among other things, the bestowal of favors. Thus the politician's success is tied up with his ability to "get things done."

The Race of the Negro Client's Lawyer

It was pointed out earlier that the 71 families used 135 individual lawyers in 155 instances. This section treats with the distribution of the problems between Negro and other attorneys in terms of the types of problems.

The Negro lawyer, perhaps of all people, recognizes that he does not get all the business of the Negro client. He deplores this fact, but heartens himself by observing that the situation is changing. Our data tell nothing of trends either in support or refutation of the view that Negroes are turning more frequently to Negro lawyers. This is a question that should hold some significance for future study, but lies outside the immediate scope of this project. Table 38–3 indicates the pattern of the use of lawyers by the families studied.

The data show that of the 155 instances in which the services of a lawyer were used, 58 (37 per cent) were "other" lawyers. When, however, the two client groups are taken separately, a noticeable thing appears. In the middle-class group, out of a total of 94 problems taken to lawyers, 29 (31 per cent) were given to "other" lawyers, but in the lower-class sample with a total of 61 problems, "other" lawyers resolved 29 (48.0 per cent) of the cases.

TABLE 38-3 *Distribution of the 155 Instances of Legal Services Used; By Race of Lawyer, Type of Problem, and Class Position of Families*

Types of Problems	Lawyers Used by Lower-Class Families		Lawyers Used by Middle-Class Families		Total		
	Negro	Other	Negro	Other	Negro	Other	Total
Personal injury	3	18	7	9	10	27	37
Real estate	3	—	20	7	23	7	30
Domestic relations	4	5	15	4	19	9	28
Estates and wills	4	1	12	5	16	6	22
Criminal and quasi-criminal	9	3	3	2	12	5	17
Breach of contract	2	1	5	1	7	2	9
Financial advice	6	—	—	—	6	—	6
Landlord-tenant relations	1	—	3	1	4	1	5
Labor relations	—	1	—	—	—	1	1
Total	32	29	65	29	97	58	155

Personal injury work is a field in which "other" lawyers have obtained the bulk of the Negro client's business. According to lawyers, such cases are very desirable because of their respectable character, the relative ease with which they might be disposed of, and the satisfactory pecuniary return therefrom. Negro lawyers, as might be expected, are extremely critical of this tendency on the part of the Negro client to select "other" lawyers for personal injury matters. There are various reasons given for this selection. One client who has had considerable experience, but who had never used a Negro lawyer, stated:

> I never thought about colored lawyers 'cause I don't know anything about any colored lawyers. Colored lawyers don't publish themselves so people don't know what they are doing. I know that lawyers aren't supposed to advertise, but you

just don't hear of them much. I'm always seeing something about white lawyers and their cases in the papers, but I don't see nothing about colored lawyers. Maybe I see 'em and don't know 'em 'cause they don't say they're colored. I think colored lawyers should let themselves be known. Other people call us colored, so why can't they say "Negro" lawyers? Colored people make a big noise about things that don't mean much, always getting mad about being called colored, but why should we, we can't help it 'cause that's the way we was made.

There seem to be sounder explanations than this "anonymity" theory. It has already been suggested that personal injury work has developed into a very elaborate and highly systematized branch of the profession with its various contacts with individuals and institutions such as police officers, "ambulance chasers," insurance adjusters, and hospital personnel to mention a few. One Negro lawyer, in speaking of the role of the hospital in channeling cases to such "other" lawyers, stated that his annual contribution to a certain hospital was being discontinued for the reason that the hospital "worked with" such lawyers. A man who had been in the bail bond business for many years made the following comment on the subject. He said:

Jewish lawyers get most of the personal injury work. They hire ambulance chasers and learn about accidents through the accident prevention squads that arrive on the scene. In case the injured party has been taken to a hospital before the squad arrives, the cops get the information from the hospital and get in touch with a lawyer. They give him the patient's name, address, relatives, and all such information, and the lawyer gives them a commission.

Negro lawyers don't get much of this kind of work because they want quick money. The majority want to practice in the criminal court. They want money right away, right now. They don't want to take the time it takes to settle the case, and it sometimes takes months. The Negro lawyers—some of them—have the money necessary to go into that kind of work, but they just don't want to take the chance.

The attorneys who have developed the organizations for handling personal injury cases are said to specialize in such matters almost exclusively. Concentrating on this kind of work, such practitioners build up a volume of business that enables them to take cases on a contingency fee basis, which means that the lawyer's compensation will come when a settlement is made, usually with the lawyer receiving one-third of the settlement. The Negro lawyer, like many non-Negro attorneys, is frequently unwilling or financially unable to take the gamble of waiting until the case is settled to receive his compensation. Additional insights into the pattern of personal injury practice are gained from the following narrative given by a medical doctor who has practiced in the city for a number of years.

Since January 1, 1946, all drivers of cars are required to carry a $10,000 public liability insurance. This has made the personal injury work very desirable for lawyers, for you have the assurance that you will be compensated for your work.

There are certain doctors whose knowledge of fractures makes them especially advantageous to lawyers who specialize in personal injury work. You see, the kinds of reports they make can be very important to the lawyer. I don't know of any group of Negro lawyers who make any special effort to handle personal injury cases. They won't take the risk or chance of waiting and getting a large sum of money, rather than a small sum. There is a group of white lawyers who will even pay hospital bills and advance money to the person. Now that type of service is universally known on the South Side and people avail themselves of it.

At a certain hospital there are what you call runners. If you are taken to the hospital, they look into it and tell you the best man for your case is Attorney A or Attorney B. A doctor of my acquaintance told me that at his hospital, they had tried to get rid of these runners. One of them called him aside and said, "Now look here, Doctor, you're running us out of here and not only do we lose business, but so do you and the hospital. You don't think we just happen here, do you? The police call us and tell us about accidents."

Doctors have been asked not to deal with these people because it's unethical, but suppose I'm called and told by a lawyer that he has a client with a leg broken in an accident, that he will assume all expenses, and will I take the case. I'd say, "Yes."

Two things seem to emerge from this discussion: first, the Negro lawyer does not possess the financial resources necessary for the mobilizing of such an array of workers and second, coming later on the legal scene, he does not yet have the contacts required for the successful pursuit of such a specialty. Clients have stated that Negro attorneys frequently would not accept their cases on contingency bases, but required a fixed amount payable partly in advance. This may not be true of all Negro lawyers who handle such cases, but a similar report was never made about any "other" lawyer by the families.

The investigator was seated one day in the outer office of a Negro attorney and overheard a conversation between the lawyer's secretary and the lawyer's male assistant. The man asked if anything had been heard from a certain prospective client, the victim of a traffic accident, and was told no. The assistant then telephoned the man, and on one side of the conversation was heard, "Hello, Mr. X. We hadn't heard from you about letting us have that case and we're wondering what's wrong. (Pause) Oh, so you don't have the forty dollars. (Pause) Well, when you get it, be sure and get in touch with us."

The Negro lawyer may argue that personal injury work is but one phase of the practice and that he is not interested in that kind of work with the consequent strain that may be placed on his ethics. Such an argument is legitimate, but the specific case is not necessarily within itself all important. An equally if not more important point is the fact that the client, if pleased with the lawyer's services in this instance, may return to him for even other kinds of problems. Over and over again, the families reported that they went to a specific lawyer because he had served them or some friends in a personal injury case.

Real estate matters rank high on the list of problems taken to lawyers, especially with the middle-class family. These problems, like those of estates and wills, financial advice, and landlord-tenant relations, imply property ownership.

The relatively inconsequential nature of such problems, the friendship relationship that exists between lawyers and families at this level, plus the weight of public opinion, operate to send the middle-class client to Negro lawyers.

Divorce is one of the more numerous of the problems of the Negro family and it is also a field where "other" lawyers show considerable activity. Though more difficult of analysis than the personal injury field, there seems to be a mixture of three main reasons why the Negro client seeks the "other" lawyer when his marriage is to be dissolved: (1) when the individual exercises little or no choice, accepting advice from one of the several sources already mentioned, (2) when there are circumstances present that the client doesn't wish revealed to other Negroes, and (3) when the client has much at stake—doesn't want to "take chances" and gets the "best man available."

An example of the desire for anonymity is seen in the following statement:

I didn't want my business all over the South Side. I couldn't afford it. If I'd gotten a Negro lawyer, everyone would have known all about it. I didn't have to appear in court, but it really cost me plenty. This was the best way for me to do it as it had to be under cover.

Divorce is an indication of failure, and failure in our society is not popular. People are reluctant to have their friends and associates learn the "facts" that often lead to divorce. The "other" lawyer, then, fills a need by guaranteeing that the facts will remain hidden since he moves in an entirely different circle of friends. It is highly likely that, in the middle-class group at least, only the pressure of public opinion prevented more people from using "other" lawyers in matters of this kind. Those who did dare to use "other" lawyers always felt the necessity of explaining why. The feeling no doubt existed that the act of employing a white attorney was, in a sense, a betrayal of the Negro group.

People select their lawyers for a variety of reasons. It may be because they know them, know of them, know someone who does know them, or because circumstances, chance or otherwise, provide the lawyer in the client's hour of need. Being little versed in the intricacies of the law, most of these families expected to be "typed" by the lawyer and often when the lawyer may have been living up to the highest standards of his profession, the client thought he detected chicanery and collusion.

One senses that the families expect from the Negro lawyer not only a diligent application of his professional abilities, but a personal concern for the client as well. One lawyer, in speaking to this point, said:

Give your client a lot of personal attention. They want to be coddled and talked to. Regardless of whether you get an adverse decision or not they seem to be satisfied if you've given this personal attention.

This is what the client is referring to when he says that a particular lawyer "doesn't seem to have time to fool with you." The families were more inclined to excuse this lack of personal concern in the "other" attorney than in the

Negro lawyer. The lower-class family is especially alert to any signs of condescension or "airs" on the part of the Negro lawyer and is as likely to remember the way the lawyer spoke as what he was able to do in their case.

Like other Negro professional men, the lawyer is expected to be a model of conduct for the group. His church activities, his public behavior, even his domestic affairs tend to be carefully scrutinized by the people. Notwithstanding the fact that the Negro community includes some 300,000 persons and is spread over a wide area, the compactness of the area plus common interests of the people enable it to retain many of the characteristics of the small community with its intimate face-to-face relations and its gossip. The middle-class Negro, relieved to some extent of the pressures of making a living, has time to discuss and evaluate his professional people. At teas, at bridge parties, dances, in the intimacy of the home, the personal as well as professional activities of these nominal leaders often provide interesting topics for discussion. An upper middle-class woman commented on the personal aspects of the Negro lawyer's life:

> I know all the Negro lawyers and I'm disappointed in many of them. I think they should conduct themselves so that the public will respect them. They should lead fairly clean, wholesome lives and treat their families well. Some of the men I know are anything but what they should be at home. I know one man who is a fairly good lawyer, but I wouldn't be bothered with him, because he was mean to his wife. I know another man who wasn't able to raise his children right and one of them got into a lot of trouble, and it took him considerable money to get her out of it. I don't suppose that should detract from him, but it does.

Such moral evaluations are absent from the Negro families' expectations of the white attorney. They know nothing of his private life and would not be interested in it if they did. On the other hand, they experience vicariously the successes and failures of other Negroes. Anything which tends to indicate that their middle-class professional men are failing to live up to the most rigid demands of middle-class morality is cause for concern. As is frequently true of people, these families often expected higher standards of behavior in others than they themselves maintained. One woman criticized a lawyer for having had several wives, apparently unmindful that she was now married for the third time.

Church participation may affect the Negro lawyer's career development. Lawyers who strike a casual attitude about church relations tend to minimize the importance of such contacts and consider church contacts to be expenses rather than assets.

Some few lawyers, however, have found their church connections to be very important and many families knew of lawyers because of their activities in church. One gathers from these families that the man who takes an active part in the affairs of the church, who serves in whatever capacity he is needed, and yet seemingly does it because of an earnest and sincere interest rather than as a means to an obvious end is apt to realize in a material way the results of his labor.

• • •

The types of problems observed in these 71 families are shown in Table 38-4. There were a total of 165 separate problems experienced by all the families. These problems involved a wide variety of matters, but for convenience, they have been grouped under ten major headings, according to the character of the problems. Lawyers may have other terms by which to distinguish these categories, but it is believed that their nature is better revealed when they are expressed in language more or less familiar to the layman.

TABLE 38-4   *Number and Per Cent of 165 Problems Observed in 71 Families by Types of Problems*

Type of Problem	Number	Per Cent
Personal injury	40	24.2
Domestic relations	28	17.0
Real estate	28	17.0
Criminal and quasi-criminal	24	14.6
Estate matters and wills	19	11.5
Breach of contract	9	5.5
Landlord-tenant relations	6	3.6
Financial advice	6	3.6
Labor relations	3	1.8
Juvenile problems	2	1.2
Total	165	100.0

From this distribution, it is apparent that the majority of the problems of these families is not of the type that would provide the lawyer with maximum satisfaction from the standpoint of professional and financial growth. The great majority of these problems tend to fall in the area of minor civil and criminal work, for the situations that give rise to and initiate these problems are a real part of the living and working experiences of the families studied. Workers, for the most part, they are concerned with making a living and improving their conditions. In the act of pursuing these goals, they frequently meet with situations that take on for them the nature of problems. Firsthand knowledge of these problems revealed that none was in the area of corporation or "big business" work where the "big money is" and where the highest professional status is to be achieved.

• • •

The Professional Practice. In this section, we are interested in inquiring into the kind of legal work that the lawyer does, as well as the manner in which he does it. In accordance with the custom of the lawyers themselves, the professional practice is here classified into two main branches. First, criminal practice, or that type wherein the lawyer is engaged in the defense of one thought to be guilty of the commission of a crime, the penalty for which is a fine or imprisonment, or both. The other type is the civil practice into which is conveniently dumped all matter exclusive of the above. Here are included such matters as corporation work, real estate, personal injury, probate, divorce, tax, labor, landlord-tenant relations, etc. It is immediately apparent that the Negro lawyer is a general practitioner, rather than a specialist, and usually accepts whatever kind of case comes his way. His refusal of a case, then, is usually not so much a refusal of the case as such, as it is a rejection of the client. Even the most established "civil" lawyers confess that they also do criminal work, adding, however, that they do not seek such employment, but do it as a service for friends or regular clients.

Though this matter of general work must be kept in mind, it is possible to classify lawyers into one of the two general types in terms of the matters which they listed as the predominating type of cases handled. Ninety-six (85.7 per cent) of the lawyers studied reported themselves as civil lawyers. The remaining 16 (14.3 per cent) considered themselves as essentially criminal practitioners. Since the majority of men claim the civil law as their field of practice, some consideration must be given to a further delineation of this type. The data show that divorce is the predominant type of work in which the Negro lawyer engages. Thirty-six of the 96 civil lawyers (37.5 per cent) listed divorce as the kind of case handled most frequently. Next came real estate, represented by 23 (23.9 per cent). Eleven lawyers (11.5 per cent) would list no specific subtype, referring to their practice as "general civil." Eight (8.3 per cent) claimed business and corporation work as their main employment; seven (6.3 per cent) dealt in landlord-tenant problems; while the remaining five were distributed in the following order: three in probation of estates; one in labor law; and one in civil liberties. From these figures, it appears that the "civil" practice of the Negro lawyer seldom reaches that high level of the "big money" toward which his training has led him to aspire.

The kind of practice engaged in is, by and large, a function of chance. Lawyers, in their explanations for practicing civil law, emphasize their abhorrence of the criminal practice and the attraction and respectability of civil practice. They point out that civil work is clean, easy, and remunerative and permits the man to exhibit his professional abilities. Criminal law, on the other hand, is declared to be less a matter of practicing law than it is of effecting the proper relationships. One "civil" lawyer in commenting on the matter stated:

> I like civil work. It's clean and it's more dignified than criminal work. You can see your clients in your office, don't have to go to jail houses to see them. In criminal practice there's too much of a division of fees, too much palm-greasing and paying off. Then, too, I don't like the idea of representing criminals, because I cannot conscientiously fight to protect them when I know they're guilty and that I, too, may be the victim of some of their atrocities. In criminal law, it's money that counts. Criminal lawyers have a slogan that the man who has money has no business in jail. Everybody in the criminal court has his hand out—judge, prosecutor, bailiff, police—all are hustling.

Another explanation frequently encountered is that the criminal client does not provide the basis for an on-going relationship. The delinquent who is not a professional frequently will have little further use for a lawyer, since this may be his only criminal act and also since his civil legal needs may be very limited. The civil client, on the other hand, will likely have other civil business as well as friends on the same level who will also have such work. While there is no doubt that much importance is attached to these lawyers' preference for civil work, it would appear that this preference comes after rather than prior to a clientele. It will be shown later how factors other than individual preference effect the Negro in his role as a personal injury lawyer. It seems also true that the practice of criminal law (above the level of "back fence" litigation and disorderly conduct) is a consequence of the organization that is developing in other phases of social life. The significance of this is that the Negro lawyer is frequently not only unwilling to develop the necessary contacts, but may find it exceedingly difficult to effect such relationships.

Civil attorneys sometimes refer rather disparagingly to the criminal lawyer as a "fixer." This implies that the lawyer in question is possessed of little legal ability, but wins his cases by means other than the pure practice of the law. A further implication is that the civil practitioner would not resort to the use of marginal practices in dealing with his client. Fixing in civil cases, however, is not unknown. The lawyer who tells his client to "get some witnesses" when he knows that no witnesses exist is "fixing." This practice is not uncommon. Also lawyers frequently resort to questionable practices in enhancing their fees, as can be seen in the following statement:

> There are ways of getting fees from clients without them knowing it. You're entitled to money for your services and frequently the client can't see it. For instance, I recently handled a $1,000 tax foreclosure deal for an organization. I included my fees and told them that the deal was for $1,400. They never raised a whisper, but they'd have called me a robber if I'd told them my fee was $400. Another way lawyers use to get fees is to take a certain fee for investigating the case and then they tell the client what they will take the case for. Your fee is based on two things: the standard or scale set up by the bar association and what the market will bear. I try to lead a client on and impress him that he's talking to a lawyer now who isn't just out to get his money, especially in little things. Sometimes I take the case for nothing, or charge something that sounds reasonable to the client. Once you get the client's confidence, he will pay you just about whatever you charge. It's purely psychological.

The Negro lawyer, denied access to the big money, must take whatever cases he can get. The majority of these cases seem to fall under the heading of minor civil matters. In obtaining and winning these cases and in receiving his compensation, he develops certain techniques.

The image that most people have of the lawyer is that of a great champion of the underprivileged, of one who presents his stirring appeal before the court and at the crucial moment snatches the accused from the gallows. In spite of the unquestioned human values involved in this concept, the practice of criminal law has nevertheless lost caste if not so much with the layman, certainly with the legal brotherhood. Raymond Moley cites Dean Roscoe Pound, who comments on various stages of emphasis in the practice of law. Dean Pound phrases the transition thus:

> The first stage is marked by the leadership of the trial lawyer. The great achievements of the bar were in the forum and the most conspicuous success was before juries in the trial of criminal cases. . . . In the second stage, leadership passed to the railroad lawyer. The proof of professional success was to represent a railroad company. . . . Criminal law became the almost exclusive field of the lower stratum of the bar.[6]

The problems involved become still more complicated when it is considered that the persons caught in the criminal law as defendants are, for the most part, poor, ignorant, and without helpful friends. While the theory of the law requires that these should stand equal with the others, the fact is that they do not. Some progress has been made through the public defender movement which challenges interest as a means by which the disposition of a criminal case may become rather a cooperative search for corrective and preventive care than a contest of skill.

The criminal branch of the legal profession has become highly specialized. On the whole, it is comparatively unremunerative, since it is impossible to build up a clientele except among professional criminals. This, in spite of the fact that some lawyers of this class are loud in praise of the fascination and "quick money" associated with this type of practice.

In theory, and in tradition, the criminal lawyer is an agent of society to see that justice is done to his client. But the criminal lawyer, like the prosecutor, builds up his reputation by winning cases. Thus, if there is a trial (which is not the garden variety of criminal cases) it is a battle between two men, the lawyer for the defense, whose economic and professional career is involved, and the prosecutor, whose record is waiting for an entry of a conviction. The trial room becomes an arena and the judge frequently merely an umpire. The ordinary criminal case takes on the nature of a "dickering" job with arrangements frequently being made behind the scenes. Because of the odium attached to such practices and because of the important contacts necessary to success, a large part of the lucrative practice of Negro lawyers in the criminal courts goes to a small number of specialists, men who "know their way around." There are perhaps not more than half a dozen of these top criminal lawyers within the Negro group. From the foregoing discussion, it appears that the criminal practice may be divided into two groups on the basis of the degree of seriousness of the case: the police court where cases are handled, such as disorderly conduct, assault and battery, and rather petty criminal matters. Moley [7] describes the activities in settings such as this as follows:

Many of the branches of the Chicago Municipal Court seem to tolerate a condition in connection with attorneys for the defense which is even more serious than a lack of prosecution. . . . Certain privileged characters come to the court daily and solicit business through the assistance of clerks, bailiffs, and assistant prosecutors, and occasionally through the judges themselves. They also mingle freely among the unfortunates who are hailed before the court, and so get business firsthand. The continuous presence of a "permanent" defense lawyer in the courtroom means that pleasant and sometimes profitable relationships are established between him and court attachés. Such lawyers have been known to divide their profits with the kindly officers who throw business to them.

It is just a step from this type of practice to that type who deals with more serious kinds of infractions that carry severe penalties. Here are found practicing that small group of "specialists" who have achieved reputations as top criminal practitioners. There is little doubt that much of the behavior mentioned above is also true of this type; nevertheless, these men seem to possess abilities that are not so widespread. They study the client; they have good relations with the court; and they are rather keen analysts of human nature. The following statement of a criminal lawyer points out certain factors that are helpful in understanding this branch of the profession.

I'd much rather handle a murder case than a pure case of robbery. Contrary to popular belief, a murder case is one of the easiest things in the world to beat. There is one of two defenses: either self-defense or the accused was not there. In self-defense, you can always play on the human nature of the jury 'cause they can imagine themselves in the same fix. Then you can claim the other fellow was trying to hurt you, and if no one else saw it but the dead man, your case is a cinch. In case of murder connected with robbery, however, the thing is different. The best out here is to establish an alibi, show that your man couldn't have done it because he was somewhere else at the time. You see nobody likes a robber, and so a jury will be inclined to be very severe on him. It all boils down to this. In case of murder in self-defense every juror thinks back to incidents in his own life when he felt justified in doing somebody in, but in the case of robbery, even if they felt any kinship with the act, or actor, they would be reluctant to admit it even to themselves.

Living in a subordinated situation, it is only natural that the Negro lawyer would attempt to make the most of his position by "bringing in the race angle." This is a delicate matter, however, and the lawyer must know when and how to do this to obtain best results. Sometimes this is done directly as in the case of one lawyer who objected to a statement made by the prosecution on the grounds that it interposed the matter of the client's race. Again, this is done by showing that the case in question cannot be judged solely in terms of the fact that the client committed the act, but must be seen, too, in light of the social conditions which produced the act. The argument here is that although the client may have committed the act, guilt for it should not rest on him, but upon society. Such a plea is calculated to bring the jurors face to face with their own consciences and make them assume for society some of the guilt which the prosecution is attempting to place on this "poor plaything of fate." The approach may be less direct as in the following excerpt where the lawyer pleads that the client's race not be considered in terms of leniency:

> I like jury work because juries are human and try to be understanding. No juror wants to carry to his own grave the thought that he's sent an innocent man to the chair, so he eagerly listens for things which will aid him in arriving at a favorable decision. I sometimes use the race angle, but I try to do it subtly without appearing to do so. I ask the jury to give us a fair American trial and ask them can they give that. I call on their patriotism and put them on the spot. I never imply that they would be prejudiced. I don't want any breaks, no consideration —only an American trial just as they would want for any one of their acquaintance. Any feeling that they might have had that I was going to call for help on the basis that my client is Negro is gone when I start waving the flag.

Winning the case is the primary interest of the lawyer and his education has not necessarily equipped him for this. It does provide a theoretical framework within which all cases are supposed to fall, but the actual techniques must be learned in a world of competition. These techniques come with long practice and, because of the marginal, insecure position of most Negro lawyers, are seldom shared. To the lawyer who "deals in crime," reliance is frequently placed less on a knowledge of law than on an understanding of the individuals whose job it is to administer that law. The following statement shows something of the importance of knowing these institutional personnel.

> After you've been in this business for a long time, you get to know the judges and their attitude toward certain cases. Some of them hate sex cases, some hate robbery with guns and some other things. Knowing this, you might try to bring your case before another judge or try to bring certain pressures to bear on him. Judges are elected practically for life and you're in front of them dozens of times a year; so you study them and you learn what kind of a case to plead a man guilty on. After you get established as okay, sometimes the clerk of the court or the State's Attorney will suggest what to do. When you're new, though, the State's Attorney will try and take advantage of you until he learns in one way or another that he's got to respect you. I had a case not so long ago and it was a tough one. I asked the young State's Attorney to give us a break and permit my client to plead guilty and take a probationary sentence. The State's Attorney wouldn't hear of this and insisted that he'd settle only for a two-year sentence with no probation or parole. Well, that made me mad, so I pleaded him "not guilty" and won an acquittal. The next time I had a proposition, the State's Attorney was glad to bargain with me.

The preceding discussion has dealt mainly with the lawyer operating in the courts, after an indictment has been brought against an individual. Some consideration must now be given to the coroner's inquest which comes prior to an indictment. One criminal lawyer referred to the coroner's inquest as being "75 per cent of the battle," meaning that in many criminal cases the ultimate fate of the accused is decided at this investigation. The main function of the coroner today is, as it was in the thirteenth century, to pronounce in the case of a homicide that "this man is dead." In England, during the Middle Ages, the coroner was the King's direct representative and protector of the King's interest. When a felon was convicted, his property was forfeited to the King. The lords, however, reluctant to see all this property pass into the King's hands, would frequently, through their friends the sheriffs, get to the felon before the coroner and, for a consideration, disclaim that a crime had been committed. It thus became the duty of the coroner to not only prove that a crime had been committed, but how it had occurred, in order to procure for the King what was deemed rightfully his. Today the coroner is essentially a homicide investigator whose purpose it is to determine whether or not a crime has been committed. The importance of the coroner's investigation may be seen in the fact that it is at this point that the condition of the deceased is said to result from accident or intent, justifiable or unjustifiable.

In one day's observation of three coroner's inquests, the jury was seen to return verdicts of "justifiable homicide" in each case. By this decision, the accused was sent before the felony court where the lawyer would have little difficulty in obtaining a light sentence if not the clear release of his client.

Frequently, the coroner is a doctor rather than a lawyer, but actually performs many of the functions of a judge. He conducts the investigation through impanelling a jury usually composed of six persons. In the case of the specific jury observed, it was learned that the names of the jurors were submitted by a military organization and receive as compensation for their services one dollar per inquest. This figure becomes more important when it is seen that the jury sits on one case after the other and that as many as a dozen might conceivably be disposed of in one day. Lawyers insist that a close relationship exists between coroner and jury. In referring to this connection, one lawyer said, "The coroner and his jury understood each other. Although the American Legion selects the men, I can imagine that if one got out of hand and didn't see things the coroner's way, he wouldn't be on the jury next week." The coroner's jury is not a listening jury only. Each man is theoretically an investigator and has the privilege of asking questions of witnesses themselves—a privilege of which this jury's members never avail themselves. This rather informal session lends itself well to the development of understandings between defense attorney and the coroner's organization. One criminal lawyer pointed up what may happen behind the scenes of a coroner's inquest. He reported:

> This is the most important phase of the whole process. If I can get a verdict of justifiable homicide for my client, that's all there will be to it. Now this coroner is not a lawyer but he's shrewd and knows what the score is. He will hear evidence—that is what he wants to hear—the investigating officer will testify right and everything will come out okay in the end. Justice works beautifully, especially when there's a fee of $1,000 paid in advance. The deceased is dead, every-

body knows that, but life must go on. Negro life is cheap in the city of Chicago. Just think, for a thousand dollars you can kill almost any Negro in Chicago. . . . I always get my fee in advance; I have to. Why, if I waited until after the trial was over, as short as most people's memories are, I'd never get my money. Regardless of how much work I'd put into it, the client would claim there was nothing to it.

The coroner's investigation followed the pattern outlined by the lawyer. It was evident that the lawyer was no stranger to the setting. The respectful manner in which the coroner addressed him, the hearty handshake of other attorneys and personnel bespoke an easy familiarity with this milieu occasioned by a man's violent death. When the arresting officer testified, he subtly told a story aimed at showing the defendant in as good a light as possible. Such remarks as, "He dropped his gun soon as he saw us," and in commenting on one of the eyewitnesses whose testimony was against the defendant, "He appeared to be pretty intoxicated," referring to the witness. The coroner, too, was helpful. Impatient to end the hearing, he frequently consulted his watch and finally said, "We'll hear just one more good eyewitness." This good eyewitness turned out to be a witness for the prosecution. He was shown to have been intoxicated on the night of the homicide and was promptly turned into a mass of stuttering, confused, and bewildered humanity by the defense counsel. The coroner then charged the jury, who filed heavily out to return shortly with the verdict of justifiable homicide that the defense attorney had been led to expect.

NOTES

1. All quoted material is from personal interviews unless otherwise documented.
2. "Report on 'Gratuities' by the Committee on Municipal Court," *Chicago Bar Record*, XXIX, No. 3 (December, 1947), 97–101.
3. *Annual Report of the United Charities Legal Aid Bureau for 1945* (Chicago: Legal Aid Bureau, 1945).
4. Legal Aid Bureau of the United Charities of Chicago, *An Outline of Policies* (Chicago: Legal Aid Bureau, 1938).
5. Personal interview with official in the offices of the Chicago Bar Association, March 15, 1948.
6. Raymond Moley, *Our Criminal Courts* (New York: Minton Balch, 1930), p. 62.
7. *Ibid.*, p. 65.

39

The War on Poverty:
A Civilian Perspective

EDGAR S. CAHN AND JEAN C. CAHN

Implementing the Civilian Perspective—
A Proposal for a Neighborhood Law Firm

If the foregoing analysis is correct, it suggests that there is a need for supplying impoverished communities the means with which to represent the felt needs of its members. The remainder of the article details a proposal for the establishment of one kind of institution—a university-affiliated, neighborhood law firm—which could serve as a vehicle for the "civilian perspective" by placing at the disposal of a community the services of professional advocates and by providing the opportunity, the orientation, and the training experience to stimulate leadership among the community's present inhabitants. Such an institution would include a staff of lawyers, research assistants, and investigators who would represent persons and interests in the community with an eye toward making public officials, private service agencies, and local business interests more responsive to the needs and grievances of the neighborhood.

While there is no claim made to exclusiveness in the performance of the advocacy function (lawyers maintain no monopoly on the arts of criticism, protest, scrutiny, and representation), lawyers are particularly well equipped to deal with the intricacies of social organization. This factor, among others, prompts our proposal.

Such an institution must have ready access to the grievances of the neighborhood. Here, the respectability of seeking a lawyer's services in situations of trouble can be a significant asset. While lawyers are often distrusted as shysters and sophists, there is no self-demeaning implication or taint of helplessness and internal confusion in requesting the services of an attorney. Consequently, lawyers are often presented with problems which call for the services of a psychiatrist, family counsellor, or social worker, but which never would have been brought to such professionals voluntarily.

Besides access to grievances, such an institution must be able to establish rapport and communication. Here, the middle-class status of professional per-

From *The Yale Law Journal*, LXXIII (July, 1964), 1334–1336. Reprinted by permission of the authors, The Yale Law Journal Company, and Fred B. Rothman & Company. Abridged with renumbered notes.

sons often constitutes an impediment to the development of confidence and identification. This problem has been dealt with by various kinds of out-reaching social work carried on by the community organizer, detached worker, and gang or street worker.

The lawyer is not obliged in the same manner to be apologetic about his middle-class background, because the justification for his presence is that he is a professional advocate and that he possesses skills and knowledge not otherwise available. He does not have to pretend to be "one of them" to his clients to fulfill his function and merit their confidence. Middle-class status thus need not be a barrier for the lawyer. This should not be confused with middle-class orientation and values that can be a major barrier to trust unless the lawyer is able to suspend such values in judging his client's case and conduct.

The lawyer's most significant asset, however, is the unique advocacy orientation of his profession—one to which our legal system and the canons of legal ethics commit him. Other professionals such as social workers and educators are institutionally given the role of mediating between their employers and their clients.[1] A lawyer need not be apologetic for being partisan, for identifying.[2] That is his function.

In addition, the lawyer is "case oriented." And in the context of a disorganized neighborhood there are merits to a mode of articulating criticism or protest which stem from a specifically defined situation, an identifiable client, and an articulated demand. Such communities are, by and large, lacking in stable, energetic citizens groups to advance demands. These must be reckoned as middle-class attributes. Thus, in communities unable and unwilling to expend energy for anything other than the most immediate needs and incapable of organizing except around specific short-term grievances, the case and controversy focus of legal activity can provide one possible alternative to middle-class forms of organization and protest. In sum, it may take less time and effort to "import" a lawyer to articulate a concern than to press the same demand by organizing citizens' groups.

Finally, legal expertise in and of itself can be extremely useful. Many of the problems faced by slum dwellers are either legal in nature or have legal dimensions. Divorce, eviction, welfare frauds, coerced confessions, arrest, police brutality, narcotics convictions, installment buying—all involve legal problems, at least by the time a crisis arises. Further, nothing destroys the momentum of a militant community effort more than alleged technicalities of law[3] or the alleged statutory inability of an official to redress a grievance. Lawyers are equipped to circumvent obstacles and to detect specious claims that mask a lack of responsiveness.

Nonetheless, we recognize that a proposal to establish a neighborhood law firm to articulate the "civilian perspective" may seem inappropriate or inadequate, because many of the problems encountered by slum dwellers have economic, psychological, and sociological dimensions with which a lawyer is not professionally equipped to deal. Yet the assumption that the problems that beset the poor are not "legal" is frequently based on an artificially narrow conception of "law." When we say that a grievance calls for the skill of a lawyer, we mean only that there is an official (usually called a judge or administrator) who is empowered to provide redress and remedy when he is presented, in accordance with proper procedures, with legitimate grievance. The lawyer's function is essentially that of presenting a grievance so that those aspects of the complaint which entitle a person to a remedy can be communicated effectively and properly to a person with power to provide a remedy. Slum dwellers have many grievances not thought of as calling for lawyers' skills. Yet the justiciability of such grievances should not be prejudged; they require the scrutiny of a skilled advocate, for it is altogether possible that for many a remedy is available if the grievance is properly presented—even though the decision-maker may be a school board, principal, welfare review board, board of police commissioners, or urban renewal agency.

Thus, there are at least four areas in which legal advocacy and legal analysis may prove useful in implementing the civilian perspective: traditional legal assistance in establishing or asserting clearly defined rights; legal analysis and representation directed toward reform where the law is vague or destructively complex; legal representation where the law appears contrary to the interests of the slum community; and legal representation in contexts which appear to be non-legal and where no judicially cognizable right can be asserted.

NOTES

1. This is not a necessary concomitant of their disciplines. And we would urge that social workers, educators, counsellors, administrators, and placement personnel should think through the possibility of creating within their professions new adversary and grievance-presenting roles. Lawyers have had to do the converse in modifying their pure "adversary" model in the context of administrative law and arbitration.
2. We recognize, of course, that lawyer's duties include broadening his clients' perspectives to enable them to recognize when a demand is self-defeating or unrealistic, and also involve assisting clients to define problems for themselves and to assess and reconsider their initial demands.
3. See Silberman, "Up From Apathy—The Woodlawn Experiment," *Commentary,* (May, 1964), p. 51. Saul D. Alinsky, in organizing the poor, found it necessary to use his own professional staff of city planners and consultants to critique the city's slum clearance plan to counter official designs effectively. *Ibid.*

40

Lawyers' Ethics

JEROME E. CARLIN

We have examined in detail some of the conditions affecting the capacity of metropolitan lawyers to meet their ethical obligations. Let us now summarize the findings and then consider their implications for the administration of justice and for an understanding of the social conditions of deviant behavior.

Summary of Findings

NATURE OF ETHICAL NORMS

Two kinds of ethical standards are found in the bar: those that proscribe behavior considered immoral and unethical by society generally, such as bribery, stealing, and cheating; and those that deal with professional problems, such as relations among colleagues, methods of obtaining business, and conflicts of interest. While the more general standards are accepted by most lawyers in all strata of the bar, the distinctively professional standards are accepted for the most part only by elite lawyers. The limited acceptance of these professional standards is undoubtedly due to the special constraints they impose; they tend to cut off the practitioner "from many immediate opportunities for financial gain . . . legitimately open to the businessman." [1]

Ethical norms of metropolitan lawyers are thus largely indistinguishable from the norms of the lay or business community: they demand conformity only to ordinary standards of honesty and fair dealing. Moreover, these are the standards that are most often enforced by the organized bar.

SOCIAL ORGANIZATION AND ETHICAL CONDUCT

Clientele. The type of clientele a lawyer serves has a profound effect on his ability to conform even to basic ethical standards. Lawyers with low-status clients are subject to far more temptations, opportunities, and client pressures to violate than are lawyers with high-status clients. And given the nature of their practice, these lawyers are far less able to resist. The lower the status of the lawyer's clientele the more precarious and insecure his practice, and the more willing he is, therefore, to violate basic standards of ethical conduct. Because of the instability of his practice, the lawyer with a low-status clientele is

From *Lawyer's Ethics: A Survey of the New York City Bar* (New York: Russell Sage Foundation, 1966), pp. 165–170, 176–182. Abridged with renumbered notes. Reprinted by permission of the author and publisher.

also more vulnerable to opportunities and pressures. Thus, we found that lawyers who have frequent opportunities to exploit clients are most likely to commit violations if they have an expendable clientele; and client pressure is most likely to result in violation for lawyers who become economically dependent upon a few more secure clients in an otherwise unstable clientele.

Institutional Setting. Different levels of the court and agency structure place lawyers under very different types of ethical constraints. Lower courts tend to expose lawyers to corrupting influences and upper courts to benign. The lower the court, the more weight its officials give to extralegal considerations in their decisions, and the more likely they are to initiate (as well as be receptive to) such illegitimate practices as bribery and fraud. Consequently, lawyers who deal with these courts have greater opportunities and are subject to more pressures to violate than are those in contact with upper-level courts. Moreover, at each level a normative climate emerges that reinforces pressures to violate or conform; and the more exposed lawyers are to a particular court setting the more influenced they are by its moral tone.

Work Setting. In theory, colleagueship should provide strong group support for professional goals and norms, making lawyers more resistant to outside pressures. While the office colleague group does affect conformity to ethical standards, it mainly reinforces outside pressures or determines exposure to them.

The form of control exercised by the colleague group depends largely on its structure:

(a) The Peer-Group Office: In peer-group offices (where members are similar in age and type of practice) colleague controls tend to reinforce the influences to which their members are exposed in their client and court-agency contacts. The more socially cohesive the office, the more likely this outcome. Newer offices of this type are characterized by an informal process of seeking and giving support for violation among lawyers facing similar problems. In older, more established peer-group offices, ethical conduct is controlled by the normative climate of the office. The longer a lawyer has been a member of the office, and the more socially cohesive the office, the more likely it is that his behavior will be in line with the attitudes of his colleagues.

(b) The Stratified Law Office: In hierarchically organized offices, the ethical behavior of members is affected by the allocation of work rather than by the office climate or by direct colleague sanctions. An individual's adherence to ethical norms in these offices depends on his rank in the status hierarchy of the firm. Rank determines the kinds of work the lawyer does and, hence, the ethical influences he faces. In peer-group offices the absence of status distinctions facilitates uniformity of behavior in line with the prevailing ethical climate. In stratified offices, status distinctions probably lessen the effect of office climate on ethical behavior, and may even prevent development of a normative consensus.

SOCIAL STRATIFICATION AND THE DISTRIBUTION OF PRESSURES

Situational pressures do not operate independently of one another. Nor are they randomly distributed within the bar. Pressures are systematically "allocated" among different groups of lawyers in accordance with their position in a system of social stratification.

The metropolitan bar is a highly differentiated and highly stratified professional community. There are marked differences in what lawyers do and the kinds of clients they serve. This diversity of practice is, in turn, related to size of the law firm. Lawyers in the larger firms are at the top of the status ladder; individual practitioners and small-firm lawyers are the lowest group; members of medium-sized firms fall between. Large-firm lawyers have the highest average incomes. They represent the most affluent clients and come into contact with the highest levels of government, including the judiciary. Individual practitioners and small-firm lawyers have the lowest incomes. They represent the least affluent clients and deal with the lowest levels of government.

The magnitude of these differences—in clientele, type of practice, and income—brings into focus the caste-like divisions which characterize the metropolitan bar. The striking differences in background between lawyers in the upper and lower strata suggest lasting social entities, capable of replenishing their ranks with lawyers from similar backgrounds. Continuity of status groups is indicated by the tendency of a lawyer to remain in the same stratum in the course of his career. While there is some movement from one level to another, this most often occurs in the early years of practice and follows highly predictable patterns. Finally, there is relatively little contact between the two extremes of the bar; the upper stratum is very largely isolated from the lower in work, in social activities, and in professional associations.

The stratification system determines the pattern of pressures and constraints to which lawyers are exposed. As we have seen, exposure to these pressures depends primarily on type of clientele and level of court and agency structure with which lawyers come into contact; these factors, in turn, are a function of the lawyer's position in the status hierarchy of the bar. As a result, lawyers at the top experience maximum pressure to conform to distinctively professional standards, as well as the more ordinary, ethical norms; at the same time they are insulated from pressures to violate. Conversely, lawyers at the bottom of the status ladder are maximally exposed to pressures to violate, and least subject to pressures to conform.

CAREER LINES AND SOCIAL BACKGROUND

Lawyers are distributed among firms of different sizes by a process of self-selection and recruitment in which religion, parents' social class, quality of college and law school attended, and law school standing all play important parts. The process begins when the future lawyer enters college. His religion and class origin strongly affect his chances of attending a top-quality college and law school. Law school, class standing, *and* religion are the most important determinants of the size of the firm the young lawyer will enter.

As social background and academic training determine the lawyer's status in the bar, so they determine the ethical influences to which he will be exposed in his practice. Social background and professional training, however, have little or no *independent* effect on conformity to ethical standards. Jewish and Catholic lawyers have a lower ethics rating than Protestant lawyers because they are more likely to be exposed to pressures to violate ethical norms. Under similar conditions of practice, Jewish and Catholic lawyers are no more likely to violate norms than Protestant lawyers.

INNER DISPOSITION

The lawyer's inner disposition to conform plays an important role in maintaining or weakening his adherence to ethical standards. The stronger the lawyer's inner disposition to be ethical, the greater his capacity to resist pressures to violate basic standards, and the more positive his response to influences that encourage conformity to distinctively professional standards. A weak inner disposition, on the other hand, reduces the lawyer's capacity to resist pressure.

The lawyer's ethical concern is not markedly influenced by his professional training, his status in the bar, or the vicissitudes of his practice. More important is national origin and generation in the United States, which suggests that early family influence may be decisive in the development of ethical concern.

FORMAL CONTROLS

Very few violators are caught and punished by the formal disciplinary machinery of the bar. We estimate that only about 2 per cent of the lawyers who violate generally accepted ethical norms are processed, and fewer than 0.2 per cent are officially sanctioned. This leads us to question whether the policing function is effective or even important.

A more likely function of these formal controls is the forestalling of public criticism of the legal profession. This interpretation is suggested by our finding that the visibility of the offense is the principal factor accounting for the severity of the official sanction imposed. This may also explain why so few violators are caught and punished. It is not the punishment of all violations, or even of all serious violations, that is crucial for avoiding public criticism and control; only the *highly visible* violations are really important. If only some violations are highly visible, few violators need be caught and punished.

While violations of distinctively professional norms are far more widespread than violations of ordinary, community-wide standards, violators of professional norms are far *less* likely to be officially charged and sanctioned than violators of ordinary standards. This greater commitment to ordinary standards of morality underscores the overriding concern of the organized bar for its public image.

Implications for the Legal Order

The metropolitan bar, over the past 50 to 75 years, has evolved into a highly stratified professional community with a distinct elite consisting of lawyers in the very large firms. This arrangement raises a number of serious problems for the lower levels of the bar, for certain parts of the administration of justice, and for the development of the legal system, including its capacity to meet new demands on it.

Although the elite segment of the bar is able to insulate itself from ethically contaminating influences, lower-status lawyers are forced to bear the brunt of these pressures; in the process they become deprofessionalized. This moral division of labor in the profession is described by Everett Hughes:

> . . . the division of labor among lawyers is as much one of respectability (hence of self-concept and role) as of specialized knowledge and skills. One might even call it a moral division of labor, if one keeps in mind that the term means not simply that some lawyers, or people in the various branches of law work, are more moral than others; but that the very demand for highly scrupulous and respectable lawyers depends in various ways upon the availability of less scrupulous people to attend to the less respectable legal problems of even the best people. I do not mean that the good lawyers all consciously delegate their dirty work to others (although many do). It is rather a game of live and let live.[2]

The system of social stratification in the bar, by undermining the integrity of lower-status lawyers, also tends to weaken the quality and authority of the legal order, particularly at the lower levels of the administration of justice. The insecurity of low-ranking lawyers increases their willingness to influence official decision-makers through such illegitimate means as bribery or the prospect of political favor. Consequently, whatever corrupt tendencies are exhibited by lower-level courts and agencies are unlikely to be countered by the lawyers who characteristically practice before them. Moreover, those attorneys who are capable of resisting such practices rarely appear before these agencies.

Stratification of the bar also has much to do with the highly uneven character of the legal services provided to different classes in our society. The best-trained, most technically skilled, and ethically most responsible lawyers are reserved to the upper reaches of business and society. This leaves the least competent, least well-trained, and least ethical lawyers to the smaller business concerns and lower-income individuals. As a result, the most helpless clients who most need protection are least likely to get it. Lower-status clients are most likely to provide lawyers with opportunities for exploitation and to end up with lawyers who are least capable of resisting temptation.

The uneven character of legal services, moreover, leads to a highly selective development of the law itself. Those areas that reflect the interests of large corporations and wealthy individuals are most likely to be elaborated; law dealing with the poor and other disadvantaged groups, particularly in the consumer, landlord-tenant, welfare, and domestic relations areas, remains largely neglected and underdeveloped.

Whatever efforts have been made by leaders of the profession to cope with these problems have been largely ineffective. Lack of leadership is particularly evident in the failure of the organized bar to seek or support new forms of legal representation that might help in extending legal services to a larger segment of the population. Lower-income individuals are, for all practical purposes, denied access to and effective use of the legal system.[3] In New York City we have seen that fewer than 5 per cent of the lawyers report that the median income of their clients is under $5,000 a year, although half the total families and unrelated individuals have incomes under this amount. Conversely, 70 per cent of the lawyers report that the median income of their clients is in excess of $10,000, though fewer than 10 per cent of New York's families and unrelated individuals receive incomes that high. Furthermore, the traditional substitutes for private lawyers, such as Legal Aid and assigned counsel, have apparently done little to overcome these class differences in legal representation and may even have worked against the interests of the poor by undermining their capacity for asserting legal rights.[4]

The inability of the bar to increase the availability of its services has compelled the Supreme Court of the United States to assume responsibility in this area as in others. Two recent landmark decisions—*Gideon v. Wainwright*[5] and *Brotherhood of Railroad Trainmen v. Virginia*[6]—have critical implications for the traditional organization of the profession. In the *Brotherhood* case the Court guaranteed the right of a private organization to advise its members to obtain legal services and to recommend particular attorneys to handle their cases, including attorneys selected by the organization for such purpose. The *Brotherhood* opinion states in part:

> Virginia undoubtedly has broad powers to regulate the practice of law within its borders; but we have had occasion in the past to recognize that in regulating the practice of law a state cannot ignore the rights of individuals secured by the Constitution. . . . Here what Virginia has sought to halt is not a commercialization of the legal profession that might threaten the moral and ethical fabric of the administration of justice. It is not "ambulance chasing." The railroad workers, by recommending competent lawyers to each other, obviously are not themselves engaging in the practice of law, nor are they or the lawyers whom they select parties to any soliciting of business. . . . A state could not, by invoking the power to regulate the professional conduct of attorneys, infringe in any way the right of individuals and the public to be fairly represented in lawsuits authorized by Congress to effectuate a basic public interest. Laymen cannot be expected to know how to protect their rights when dealing with practiced and carefully counseled adversaries . . . and for them to associate together to help one another to preserve and enforce rights granted them under federal laws cannot be condemned as a threat to legal ethics. The state can no more keep these workers from using their cooperative plan to advise one another than it could use more direct means to bar them from resorting to the courts to vindicate their legal rights.[7]

Shortly after the *Brotherhood* decision was handed down, the Virginia State Bar Association petitioned for a rehearing of the case, and 45 state bar associations and 4 major local bar associations joined with the American Bar Association in an *amicus curiae* brief stating:

> [The opinion] severely and unnecessarily damages the canons of ethics and the rules of law prohibiting unauthorized practices, so as to make future enforcement of the canons almost impossible.[8]

Walter E. Craig, a former president of the American Bar Association, is reported as having "urged the organized bar to stand firmly behind its present position against solicitation of clients despite implications of the recent Supreme Court decision in *Brotherhood of Railroad Trainmen v. Virginia*." [9] And a report of the Committee on Lawyer Referral Service has asserted:

> These decisions strike at the very heart of the traditional standards of the profession, and they open the gates for lay organizations of all kinds to provide legal services to their members with little or no regard for the bar's traditional ethical standards and controls.[10]

Ironically, according to our findings, client solicitation is not a matter of great moment to most lawyers, nor does it show up as an important reason for discipline by the organized bar. More important, broadening the availability of legal services by encouraging new forms of group representation might well serve to increase the financial security of lawyers practicing at the lower levels of the bar, thereby strengthening their capacity to conform to ethical norms.

The response of the organized bar to the *Brotherhood* decision suggests that it may be less concerned with extending legal services than with preserving its monopolistic control over the provision of such services. This orientation is also reflected in the bar's stance with respect to the legal service component of the federal poverty program. The House of Delegates of the American Bar Association in a resolution of February 8, 1965, authorized full cooperation with the Office of Economic Opportunity in the development and implementation of programs for extending the availability of legal services to indigents.[11] As of June, 1965, however, only one-half of one per cent of all applications to the Office of Economic Opportunity for community action programs contained some provision for legal services.[12] A major obstacle seems to be fear of lay control. Thus at a recent National Conference on Law and Poverty the president of the National Legal Aid and Defender Association expressed grave concern over "several dark threats that are looming on the horizon." He went on to say:

> Our apprehension . . . stems from the recent suggestion to the New York Legal Aid Society that, after 90 years of service, it reorganize its board of directors and admit one third of its members from the poor and representatives of the poor. If this occurs, many legal aid societies may withdraw from the program.[13]

Informed, responsible leadership is needed, capable of mobilizing the very considerable talents and resources of the legal profession for bringing about and supporting basic structural reforms. Top priority should be given to expanding and rationalizing the market for legal services. Measures such as government subsidy, prepaid insurance plans, and group legal practice would serve to increase and stabilize the demand for legal services, thereby enhancing the economic security of marginal practitioners. If this requires altering certain canons of ethics, then let it be done, since it would permit a *genuine* improvement of ethical conduct in the bar. The effective extension of legal services is thus entirely consistent with, if not an indispensable condition for, strengthening the moral integrity of the legal profession.

Attention should also be directed to the lower levels of the administration of justice. Improving the quality and character of these institutions will not only enhance the ideals of our legal system, but will also help to remove a major source of ethical contamination affecting the legal profession. Certain changes in the organization of these agencies of law administration will be necessary to provide more effective control over the exercise of official discretion, and to ensure greater independence from political pressure and other corrupting influences. The accomplishment of these tasks may be facilitated by increasing the number of lawyers appearing in these agencies, particularly from the ranks of the more competent and less vulnerable members of the bar. Moreover, reducing the insecurity of lawyers presently practicing before these tribunals may well stiffen their commitment to orderly procedure and reasoned argument.

Isolation of the elite from rank-and-file members of the bar and from lower reaches of the administration of justice partly accounts for the unwillingness of bar leaders to accept responsibility for seeking reform. Elite lawyers, as we have seen, are cut off from meaningful contact with lower-status lawyers. They have little in common with the rank and file in social background and professional training, and the two groups are largely segregated from each other in work, social activities, and participation in professional associations. Under these conditions elite lawyers cannot be expected to have much sensitivity to, or understanding of, the problems faced by their less fortunate colleagues, nor an adequate appreciation of their own role in supporting a viable legal profession. The elite lawyer's isolation from the lower levels of the administration of justice tends to weaken his concern for the problems of these institutions and, more generally, for the capacity of the legal system to enlarge its scope and relevance.

NOTES

1. Talcott Parsons, *The Social System* (Glencoe, Ill.: The Free Press, 1951), p. 464.
2. Everett C. Hughes, *Men and Their Work* (Glencoe, Ill.: The Free Press, 1958), p. 71.
3. See U.S. Department of Health, Education, and Welfare, *The Extension of Legal Services to the Poor* (Washington, 1964); Edgar S. Cahn and Jean C. Cahn, "The War on Poverty: A Civilian Perspective," *Yale Law Journal,* LXXIII (July, 1964),

1317–1352; and "The Availability of Counsel and Group Legal Services: A Symposium," *U.C.L.A. Law Review,* XII (January, 1965), 279–463.

4. Jerome E. Carlin and Jan Howard, "Legal Representation and Class Justice," *U.C.L.A. Law Review,* XII (January, 1965), 432.

5. 372 U.S. 335 (1963).

6. 377 U.S. 1 (1964).

7. *Ibid.,* pp. 6–7.

8. American Bar Association, *American Bar News,* IX (May, 1964), 1.

9. *Loc. cit.*

10. *Loc. cit.*

11. See F. William McCalpin, "The Bar Faces Forward," *American Bar Association Journal,* LI (June, 1965), 548.

12. Noted in remarks presented by Lewis F. Powell, Jr., president of the American Bar Association, at the National Conference on Law and Poverty, Washington, June 25, 1965.

13. "Legal Aid—Current Needs and New Directions," address delivered by Theodore Voorhees, president of the National Legal Aid and Defender Association at the National Conference on Law and Poverty, Washington, June 24, 1965, p. 6.

SECTION NINE *The Jury*

41

Trial by Jury in the United States Considered as a Political Institution

ALEXIS DE TOCQUEVILLE

Since my subject has led me to speak of the administration of justice in the United States, I will not pass over it without referring to the institution of the jury. Trial by jury may be considered from two separate points of view: as a judicial, and as a political institution. If it was my purpose to inquire how far trial by jury, especially in civil cases, insures a good administration of justice, I admit that its utility might be contested. As the jury was first established when society was in its infancy and when courts of justice merely decided simple questions of fact, it is not an easy task to adapt it to the wants of a highly civilized community when the mutual relations of men are multiplied to a surprising extent and have assumed an enlightened and intellectual character.

My present purpose is to consider the jury as a political institution; any other course would divert me from my subject. Of trial by jury considered as a judicial institution I shall here say but little. When the English adopted trial by jury, they were a semi-barbarous people; they have since become one of the most enlightened nations of the earth, and their attachment to this institution seems to have increased with their increasing cultivation. They have emigrated and colonized every part of the habitable globe; some have formed colonies, others independent states; the mother country has maintained its monarchical constitution; many of its offspring have founded powerful republics; but everywhere they have boasted of the privilege of trial by jury. They have established it, or hastened to re-establish it, in all their settlements. A judicial institution which thus obtains the suffrages of a great people for so long a series of ages, which is zealously reproduced at every stage of civilization, in all the climates of the earth, and under every form of human government, cannot be contrary to the spirit of justice.

But to leave this part of the subject. It would be a very narrow view to look upon the jury as a mere judicial institution; for however great its influence may be upon the decisions of the courts, it is still greater on the destinies of society at large. The jury is, above all, a political institution, and it must be regarded in this light in order to be duly appreciated.

By the jury I mean a certain number of citizens chosen by lot and invested

From *Democracy in America,* Phillips Bradley, trans. (New York: Vintage Books, 1960), I, 291–297. Copyright © 1945 by Alfred A. Knopf, Inc. Reprinted by permission of the publisher.

with a temporary right of judging. Trial by jury, as applied to the repression of crime, appears to me an eminently republican element in the government, for the following reasons.

The institution of the jury may be aristocratic or democratic, according to the class from which the jurors are taken; but it always preserves its republican character, in that it places the real direction of society in the hands of the governed, or of a portion of the governed, and not in that of the government. Force is never more than a transient element of success, and after force comes the notion of right. A government able to reach its enemies only upon a field of battle would soon be destroyed. The true sanction of political laws is to be found in penal legislation; and if that sanction is wanting, the law will sooner or later lose its cogency. He who punishes the criminal is therefore the real master of society. Now, the institution of the jury raises the people itself, or at least a class of citizens, to the bench of judges. The institution of the jury consequently invests the people, or that class of citizens, with the direction of society.

In England the jury is selected from the aristocratic portion of the nation; the aristocracy makes the laws, applies the laws, and punishes infractions of the laws; everything is established upon a consistent footing, and England may with truth be said to constitute an aristocratic republic. In the United States the same system is applied to the whole people. Every American citizen is both an eligible and a legally qualified voter. The jury system as it is understood in America appears to me to be as direct and as extreme a consequence of the sovereignty of the people as universal suffrage. They are two instruments of equal power, which contribute to the supremacy of the majority. All the sovereigns who have chosen to govern by their own authority, and to direct society instead of obeying its directions, have destroyed or enfeebled the institution of the jury. The Tudor monarchs sent to prison jurors who refused to convict, and Napoleon caused them to be selected by his agents.

However clear most of these truths may seem to be, they do not command universal assent; and in France, at least, trial by jury is still but imperfectly understood. If the question arises as to the proper qualification of jurors, it is confined to a discussion of the intelligence and knowledge of the citizens who may be returned, as if the jury was merely a judicial institution. This appears to me the least important part of the subject. The jury is pre-eminently a political institution; it should be regarded as one form of the sovereignty of the people; when that sovereignty is repudiated, it must be rejected, or it must be adapted to the laws by which that sovereignty is established. The jury is that portion of the nation to which the execution of the laws is entrusted, as the legislature is that part of the nation which makes the laws; and in order that society may be governed in a fixed and uniform manner, the list of citizens qualified to serve on juries must increase and diminish with the list of electors. This I hold to be the point of view most worthy of the attention of the legislator; all that remains is merely accessory.

I am so entirely convinced that the jury is pre-eminently a political institution that I still consider it in this light when it is applied in civil causes. Laws are always unstable unless they are founded upon the customs of a nation: customs are the only durable and resisting power in a people. When the jury is reserved for criminal offenses, the people witness only its occasional action in particular cases; they become accustomed to do without it in the ordinary course of life, and it is considered as an instrument, but not as the only instrument, of obtaining justice.

When, on the contrary, the jury acts also on civil causes, its application is constantly visible; it affects all the interests of the community; everyone cooperates in its work: it thus penetrates into all the usages of life, it fashions the human mind to its peculiar forms, and is gradually associated with the idea of justice itself.

The institution of the jury, if confined to criminal causes, is always in danger; but when once it is introduced into civil proceedings, it defies the aggressions of time and man. If it had been as easy to remove the jury from the customs as from the laws of England, it would have perished under the Tudors; and the civil jury did in reality at that period save the liberties of England. In whatever manner the jury be applied, it cannot fail to exercise a powerful influence upon the national character; but this influence is prodigiously increased when it is introduced into civil causes. The jury, and more especially the civil jury, serves to communicate the spirit of the judges to the minds of all the citizens; and this spirit, with the habits which attend it, is the soundest preparation for free institutions. It imbues all classes with a respect for the thing judged and with the notion of right. If these two elements be removed, the love of independence becomes a mere destructive passion. It teaches men to practice equity; every man learns to judge his neighbor as he would himself be judged. And this is especially true of the jury in civil causes; for while the number of persons who have reason to apprehend a criminal prosecution is small, everyone is liable to have a lawsuit. The jury teaches every man not to recoil before the responsibility of his own actions and impresses him with that manly confidence without which no political virtue can exist. It invests each citizen with a kind of magistracy; it makes them all feel the duties which they are bound to discharge toward society and the part which they take in its government. By obliging men to turn their attention to other affairs than their own, it rubs off that private selfishness which is the rust of society.

The jury contributes powerfully to form the judgment and to increase the natural intelligence of a people; and this, in my opinion, is its greatest advantage. It may be regarded as a gratuitous public school, ever open, in which every juror learns his rights, enters into daily communication with the most learned and enlightened members of the upper classes, and becomes practically acquainted with the laws, which are brought within the reach of his capacity by the efforts of the bar, the advice of the judge, and even the passions of the parties. I think that the practical intelligence and political good sense of the Americans are mainly attributable to the long use that they have made of the jury in civil causes.

I do not know whether the jury is useful to those who have lawsuits, but I am certain it is highly beneficial to those who judge them; and I look upon it as one of the most efficacious means for the education of the people that society can employ.

What I have said applies to all nations, but the remark I am about to make is peculiar to the Americans and to democratic communities. I have already observed that in democracies the members of the legal profession and the judicial magistrates constitute the only aristocratic body that can moderate the movements of the people. This aristocracy is invested with no physical power; it exercises its conservative influence upon the minds of men; and the most abundant source of its authority is the institution of the civil jury. In criminal causes, when society is contending against a single man, the jury is apt to look upon the judge as the passive instrument of social power and to mistrust his advice. Moreover, criminal causes turn entirely upon simple facts, which common sense can readily appreciate; upon this ground the judge and the jury are equal. Such is not the case, however, in civil causes; then the judge appears as a disinterested arbiter between the conflicting passions of the parties. The jurors look up to him with confidence and listen to him with respect, for in this instance, his intellect entirely governs theirs. It is the judge who sums up the various arguments that have wearied their memory, and who guides them through the devious course of the proceedings; he points their attention to the exact question of fact that they are called upon to decide and tells them how to answer the question of law. His influence over them is almost unlimited.

If I am called upon to explain why I am but little moved by the arguments derived from the ignorance of jurors in civil causes, I reply that in these proceedings, whenever the question to be solved is not a mere question of fact, the jury has only the semblance of a judicial body. The jury only sanctions the decision of the judge; they sanction this decision by the authority of society which they represent, and he by that of reason and of law.

In England and in America the judges exercise an influence upon criminal trials that the French judges have never possessed. The reason for this difference may easily be discovered; the English and American magistrates have established their authority in civil causes and only transfer it afterwards to tribunals of another kind, where it was not first acquired. In some cases, and they are frequently the most important ones, the American judges have the right of deciding causes alone. On these occasions they are accidentally placed in the position that the French judges habitually occupy, but their moral power is much greater; they are still surrounded by the recollection of the jury, and their judgment has almost as much authority as the voice of the community represented by that institution. Their influence extends far beyond the limits of the courts; in the recreations of private life, as well as in the turmoil of public business, in public, and in the legislative assemblies, the American judge is constantly surrounded by men who are accustomed to regard his intelligence as superior to their own; and after having exercised his power in the decision of causes, he continues to influence the habits of thought, and even the characters, of those who acted with him in his official capacity.

The jury, then, which seems to restrict the rights of the judiciary, does in reality consolidate its power; and in no country are the judges so powerful as where the people share their privileges. It is especially by means of the jury in civil causes that the American magistrates imbue even the lower classes of society with the spirit of their profession. Thus the jury, which is the most energetic means of making the people rule, is also the most efficacious means of teaching it how to rule well.

42

Functions of Judge and Jury in Negligence Cases

FLEMING JAMES, JR.

The jury system plays an important part in the administration of accident law. This means that procedural rules and devices that allocate power between court and jury may have great bearing on the way accident law actually works. And it also means that the practical implications of many rules of substantive law can scarcely be appreciated without an understanding of just how the rules affect that allocation of power. This has been pointed out before. But there is a good deal of reason to believe that much of accident law is now in a period of transition from older notions based on individual blame or fault toward some form of social insurance roughly comparable to workmen's compensation. And it is in such a time of flux, when legal theory is apt to be laggard, that the jury is likely to play a particularly significant role—one that calls for frequent re-examination and reappraisal. In trying to analyze the functions of judge and jury, let us first take up the question where in theory the law draws the line of division, then inquire into the ways in which each branch of the tribunal is sought to be kept within its theoretical sphere, and draw some conclusions as to the practical effectiveness of these means. Finally we may be

From *The Yale Law Journal,* LVIII (1949), 667. Reprinted by permission of the author, The Yale Law Journal Company, and Fred B. Rothman & Company. Abridged with renumbered notes.

able to make some generalizations about the practical implications of certain kinds of substantive rules—implications that might not be seen, if their procedural setting should be overlooked.

Theoretical Division of Function

It is a commonplace today that questions of law are for the court and questions of fact for the jury, whatever the historical vicissitudes of this notion may have been. It is just as commonplace, at least in the profession, that this statement has never been fully true in either of its branches, and tells us little or nothing that is helpful. Able analyses of the extent to which it is true and how it must be qualified have been made. But it will be more helpful for our purpose to disregard the statement and see what jobs the tribunal as a whole has to perform in tort cases, then examine the roles that have been assigned by precedent to judge and jury respectively, in connection with performing that job. This will reveal the points at which theory is elastic, and most subject to change.

Determination of Facts

The tribunal's first job is to determine what the parties did and what the circumstances surrounding their conduct were. This we denote as the *facts* of the specific case, as distinguished from an evaluation or interpretation of those facts in terms of their legal consequences. To be sure, any such distinction (here as elsewhere in the law) is somewhat theoretical and by no means clear-cut; but if we keep its limitations in mind and remember its rough character, the distinction will be useful enough for present purposes. The questions whether a pedestrian looked for traffic before stepping off the curb, whether at this time defendant's automobile was 50 feet or 200 feet away, whether the traffic signal was red or green, the speed of the car, the distance in which it could be stopped at that speed, whether the driver saw the pedestrian, whether he sounded a horn, and so on, may conveniently be distinguished from such questions as whether the pedestrian should have looked or should have seen the car, whether he should have proceeded with the traffic light as it was, the reasonableness of the car's speed, the adequacy of brakes that could perform as these could, whether the driver should as a reasonable man have foreseen that the pedestrian would continue into danger, and should have blown his horn.

Now the determination of what the facts of a specific case were, in the sense referred to above, may be called the determination of the very prototype of questions of fact that are to be determined by the jury; and so it is, to the extent that any question is. Yet it is at once apparent that in connection with this very process the court has important roles to play, and opportunity to exercise very real control over the jury. All this stems from the basic notion, now universally accepted, that the jury is limited, in making these determinations, to the evidence produced in court and to matters so commonly known and so beyond dispute, that the principle of judicial notice is applied to them. The notion has this consequence because it is the court that determines what evidence may be received, what the proper limits of judicial notice are, and whether sufficient evidence has been produced to warrant the finding of any given fact.

The Court Limits What the Jury May Consider. The court decides questions of the admissibility of evidence. These are of two kinds: those involving notions of relevancy, and those involving the exclusionary rules. Now the concept of relevancy itself is not a legal one, but one involving principles of logic of general application. That is to say, the question whether a given piece of evidence is relevant in the attempt to prove a proposition and the question of the extent of its probative value, are both referable to general principles of logical reasoning and not to any rules of law. Nevertheless, the decision of questions of relevancy invokes the function of the court in the following ways:

(1) The court determines what the propositions are that need to be proved or which may be proved. Thus the court limits and selects the evidence that will come before the jury for consideration. If, for example, the court rules that the novice and the experienced driver are both held to the same standard of conduct, it will exclude testimony that the defendant was just learning to drive if that evidence is offered as tending to excuse him from taking a given precaution, and if a timely and proper objection is made. Or if a court believes that the standard of care is an objective one which takes no account of a defendant's honest but substandard misjudgment, it will not let the jury hear evidence that tends to show the defendant's good-faith belief that his course of action was the wisest one.

(2) The court determines what degree of relevance or probative value will satisfy the requirements of the law. General reasoning may reveal whether offered evidence has *any* relevancy or probative value and if so how much. But there are infinite degrees of relevancy, and it is the court that determines what degree is requisite for admissibility and whether offered evidence will be so confusing or prejudicial that its probative value is outweighed. Thus the court decides whether a restaurateur may show that his beans were eaten by many patrons without ill effects for the purpose of proving that they were not the cause in fact of plaintiff's sickness.

The limits imposed by the concept of relevancy are not the only ones. Anglo-American law has developed the great exclusionary rules of evidence and these of course are administered by the court. Thus the court determines whether evidence of a conversation is offered for a hearsay purpose and if so whether it comes within any exception to the hearsay rule. Moreover, it is often necessary for the court to make a finding, on conflicting evidence, as to whether a fact exists as a preliminary step in ruling on this kind of question of admissibility.

We have noted that, in addition to the evidence produced in court, the jury may consider whatever is judicially noticeable, and that the court (at least in theory) determines the limits of what may and what must be considered under this head. Thus where there has been no evidence as to whether or not a given trolley car had a gong, it is for the court to decide whether the jury may proceed on the assumption that it did have one. The formula for making this decision is one that gives the courts in practice a good deal of latitude.

The Court Determines the Sufficiency of the Evidence to Show the Existence of a Fact. When there is direct evidence of the existence of a fact in issue, a jury will in most cases be authorized to find the existence of that fact. Thus if plaintiff says he looked before he stepped off the curb, or the defendant's engineer says he blew his whistle for the crossing, or a tenant testifies that he requested the landlord to make certain repairs in the premises six weeks before the accident, it is the jury's province to decide whether to believe the witness. But even here the court has retained some control. In all cases it may find a direct testimonial assertion of a fact insufficient evidence of that fact's existence where under all the circumstances the testimony is not reasonably credible. A witness's story may be so inherently fantastic as to be incredible. Or it may fly in the face of incontrovertible physical facts. Perhaps the commonest instance of this is the case where a motorist says he looked carefully down the track just before crossing it and saw no train, but was struck at the crossing by a train which was in clear view for half a mile. Of course it is the court which decides whether evidence is reasonably credible and the concept under discussion here could theoretically be extended so that the court's judgment was in effect substituted for the jury's. In fact, however, the courts have exercised restraint in using this notion, and if there is any trend it is probably toward even greater restraint. There is another basis on which courts sometimes (but rarely) rule direct evidence of a fact in issue to be insufficient. That is by requiring corroboration. Thus some courts have held that an unusual jerk or jolt of a trolley, car, train, or bus is not sufficiently proven by testimony which simply describes the jolt's severity by appropriate adjectives.

Where the question is one of the sufficiency of circumstantial evidence to prove a fact in issue, the courts have exercised far more control although its extent is partly concealed and not, perhaps, often fully realized. This is true because the test for determining whether an inference (from circumstantial evidence) is a *rational* one is stated in terms of mathematical precision but is one that allows the very greatest latitude in actual application. The test has been expressed thus: "If the plaintiff cannot show the possibility of a conclusion of [the existence of the fact to be proved] by a clear preponderance of its likelihood . . . and excluding other probabilities just as reasonable . . . the plaintiff should not be permitted to go to the jury." Or as it is sometimes put, where from the facts most favorable to plaintiff the non-existence of the fact to be inferred is just as probable as its existence, the conclusion that it exists is a matter of speculation, surmise, and conjecture, and a jury will not be permitted to draw it. Thus the test purports to invoke only the processes of logical reasoning and the mathematics of probability.

Difficulty comes from the fact that anything even remotely adumbrating accurate statistical knowledge about the relative probabilities in even the most commonly recurring situations is completely lacking. Of course some generalizations would command wide, even universal, acceptance. These are the judgments of "common sense." But even here it is not safe to forget how often the science of the morrow makes the common sense of the day seem foolish. Moreover, the area is vast wherein thoughtful men who accept today's common sense would either disagree or refuse to guess on which side of the line the greater probability lies. All that has been said has not, quite properly, prevented the law from constantly coming to conclusions about circumstantial proof. But it does mean that the authoritative language of nice and scientific precision in which such conclusions are cast is after all only the language of delusive exactness. And it does mean that throughout the field of circumstantial proof there is not a little room for considerations of policy and expediency to play a part in choosing between two very fallible and equally undemonstrable generalizations about the balance of probability.[1]

In some jurisdictions the supervisory power of the courts to decide whether the evidence supports a verdict is not limited by the concept of sufficiency of the evidence so far as the granting of new trials is concerned. In them the trial court may set aside a verdict which it feels is against the clear weight of the evidence even though the evidence to support the verdict cannot be rejected as utterly incredible. Of course this rule and the more usual one could be so administered that the tests approached each other in practice. Probably, however, courts actually exercise more supervisory power over verdicts where the rule is stated in terms of "weight of the evidence."

The Court Creates Persumptions and Allocates the Burden of Proof. We have seen how the court determines whether from facts in evidence a rational inference may be drawn of a fact to be proved, and how very much room for discretion in this process lurks behind the false precision of a phrase. But even if such a "purely logical" inference may not be drawn, the court may create a rebuttable presumption on the basis of certain facts that a fact to be proved existed. This may either permit or require a decision that the presumed fact existed, depending on the effect that the court determined the presumption to have, and, on what, if any, evidence has been introduced which tends to show the non-existence of the presumed fact.

Moreover, in all cases the court determines who has the burden of producing evidence in the first place, and at various stages in the trial such as upon the closing of his case by either party. And it is the court which allocates the risk of non-persuasion of the jury.

Determination of Legal Consequences

The other main job confronting the tribunal as a whole in accident cases is to evaluate the conduct of the parties, in the light of the circumstances, in terms of its legal consequences. At one end of this function the exclusive role of the court is clear. It alone determines what the broad rules of substantive law are, and which ones may be applicable to the case at hand. Thus the court decides whether the case is one where liability is absolute or whether it depends on negligence; what, if any, effect contributory negligence will have; how liability will be affected if injury is produced through the intervention of some unforeseeable factor; that negligence consists in conduct involving an unreasonable risk of harm, and the like. But each case also involves a more specific evaluation of the conduct in the concrete situation with which it deals; a determination of specific standards of conduct for the parties under the circumstances of the actual case. It must be decided, for instance, whether *this* driver should have been proceeding more slowly at this intersection, whether he should have blown his horn, whether he should have anticipated that a pedestrian on the sidewalk would continue on to the crosswalk. Now it is perfectly clear that rules of law could be so formulated and so administered as to exclude the jury from making these evaluations. A court could decide, for instance, that under a given set of circumstances a motorist must blow his horn; that under a different set of circumstances he need not do so. Under such a pair of rules, the theoretical function of the jury would be only to decide which set of circumstances existed in the case before them, and whether the horn was blown; the question whether it should have been blown being decided by the court. On the other hand it would be perfectly possible so to formulate the rule that the jury is to decide not only what the circumstances and the conduct were but also whether the horn should have been blown.

On the whole the rules of accident law are so formulated as to give the jury considerable scope in deciding what the parties should have done, in each specific case, as well as what they did do. The cardinal concept is that of the reasonably prudent man under the circumstances: what he would have observed; what dangers he would have perceived; what he would have done, and the like. And as a rule the jury is called upon to determine such questions under broad directions as to what evidence and what kinds of factors they ought to consider in making such decisions. Here again, however (as in the case of what testimonial evidence a jury may believe), the courts set outer limits. A jury will not be permitted to require a party to take a precaution that is clearly unreasonable. Nor may it excuse a party from taking a precaution that all reasonable men would clearly take under the circumstances. Thus, for example, the jury may not require a train to stop before passing over each grade crossing in the country. On the other hand a pedestrian may not be excused from looking at some point when he is about to cross a busy thoroughfare. Since it is the courts that determine what is clearly or undoubtedly reasonable under this rule of limitation, they could so administer it as to leave little or nothing for the jury to decide in this sphere. But here again (also as in the case of what testimonial evidence a jury may believe), the courts have exercised restraint in invoking this limitation, and the trend is probably on the whole toward even greater liberality.

Within these limitations (of what reasonable men could find to be reasonable conduct or its opposite), courts sometimes go further in setting specific standards for the parties in a given case. Where they do, they may derive the standard from any one or more of a number of sources such as from their own notions of what is proper and reasonable; from a prescription of the legislature; from what is customary in a trade, business, or profession; from the opinion of experts, and the like. Thus a court may decide that when coal is piled by an open coal hole in a sidewalk in Boston, no further warning of the situation need be given. It may hold that the jury is not free to exonerate the failure to take a precaution required by statute. It may refuse to let a jury hold a manufacturer or a railroad to the taking of precautions not generally adopted by the industry. It may rule that a case of malpractice may not be maintained against a doctor unless there is expert medical testimony as to what doctors should do under the circumstances of the case. The adoption of any such rule enlarges the function of the court and narrows that of the jury. Here again the tendency has been away from fixed standards and toward enlarging the sphere of the jury.

It should be noted here that matters of presumption and burden of proof may affect the evaluation of conduct as well as the ascertainment of what conduct was. Thus a presumption that there was negligence in the setting of a fire by a locomotive spark covers an assumption of some (here unspecified) standard of care in equipment and operation of the train as well as an assumption of substandard conduct in this case. And in evaluating known conduct as reasonable or the opposite, a jury should find against the party having the risk of non-persuasion if their minds are in equipoise as to whether that conduct is reasonable.

How the Division of Functions Is Implemented; Effectiveness of Various Devices

So much for the theoretical allocation of function to judge or jury. Let us next examine the means by which the law seeks to implement this theory and the effectiveness of these means.

In any given case, some one of these rules, or a combination of them, may so operate that the jury has no theoretical function to perform. Thus it may happen that in one case the only reasonable claim of negligence is failure to blow a horn but that there is no credible evidence of such a failure. In a grade-crossing case the physical facts may demonstrate that if the plaintiff had taken any reasonable precaution there would have been no collision. Or there might be evidence that the decedent, whose body was found along the right of way, was struck by a train that was going too fast, but no basis for an inference that the excess speed had any connection whatever with the death. In such cases the law has ample means to withdraw the case effectively from the jury. The court may direct a verdict, or grant a nonsuit, or order a new trial if an improper verdict is brought in.

Difficulty is encountered, however, in cases where, under the theoretical rules, there is at least one issue for the jury, but where these rules operate to exclude one or more *other* issues from them. This situation is much more common than withdrawal of the whole case. And the difficulty lies in this: if the jury is given the power to decide the case, it is impossible actually to prevent them from deciding it on any basis whatever that appeals to their own minds, tastes, prejudices, or emotions. The effectiveness of the various devices designed to keep the jury within the bounds of their theoretical function in cases where there is some issue within their province must therefore be considered in the light of the fact that the jury may decide the case on bases that they have been expressly told to disregard.

The Rules of Evidence; Judicial Notice. It might be thought simply that whatever is excluded from evidence does not get before the jury for their consideration. In many cases that is true. Where it is, this device is an effective one. Where, for instance, a line of testimony about the safe use of a similar appliance in another factory is offered in the absence of the jury, and excluded, the jury may never know about that line of testimony at all. But often this is not the situation for any one or more of the following reasons:

(1) The jury may in several ways know of the fact though it is excluded from evidence. It may be apparent in court, as would be the approximate age of a party, or the fact that he is a foreigner unaccustomed to the ways of this country; its offer in evidence may be made in the presence of the jury; it may be privately known to one or more jurors.

(2) Under the principle of multiple admissibility, the fact may be before the jury for a limited purpose, but not for the purpose in connection with which its use is sought to be prevented.

(3) The jury may, independently of what is produced in evidence, proceed on their own assumptions about law or fact (whether or not they are correct assumptions) although the thing assumed is not a proper subject of judicial notice.

Instructions to the Jury. Where there is *some* issue for the jury, the law places principal reliance upon the court's instructions to keep the jury within their theoretical bounds. It seeks in this way to guard against the jury's improper use of facts that come under their observation, or of assumptions that are theoretically unwarranted. Thus it may tell the jury (if this is its ruling on the law) to disregard the age of the defendant, or his ignorance of this country's ways, in determining the standard of conduct to which they find he should conform. Or if a prior statement of a witness is admitted for the sole purpose of impeaching him because of its inconsistency with his present testimony, the jury will be told that they may consider it only for such a purpose and not as evidence that the facts were as represented in the prior statement.

The function of instructions is, of course, much broader than this. Primarily it is to tell the jury what the substantive law is and how the jury should "apply" it to the facts of the particular case. It will outline the elements of legal liability, explain the concept of burden of proof (in the sense of risk of non-persuasion), and describe the respective functions of judge and jury. It will "withdraw" from the jury any issue upon which the party having the burden of proof has failed to produce sufficient evidence to call for the jury's consideration. It will lay down the general standard for evaluating conduct and tell the jury whether or not they are at liberty to conclude that it is met by any given combination of facts that may be found from the evidence. Thus the jury may be told that if (from conflicting evidence) they find the facts to be A, B, and C, they must then determine whether or not that constitutes reasonable care under the circumstances; but if they find the facts to be A, Y, and Z, they must conclude that the party concerned was negligent (or the reverse). In the first half of this instruction the court is leaving the evaluation of conduct to the jury; in the second half, it is itself setting a specific standard and, through a "binding instruction," "withdrawing" the question of evaluation of other conduct from the jury.

Now it should be clear in all these situations that *the instruction is an effective device only to the extent that it is actually followed by the jury.* Moreover there is in many jurisdictions no real way (save through the jurors' own consciences) to make a jury follow instructions.

The question then arises whether juries, having the *power* to decide cases in violation of instructions, actually do so in a significant number of instances. A scientific answer to this question probably cannot be had. There is, however, good reason to believe that instructions are not particularly effective in getting the jury to perform their theoretical function and in keeping them within the bounds charted out for them by the rules of law. As Leon Green says:

> The functions of neither judge nor jury can be performed accurately through the general charge and verdict, nor can any workable check on them be devised whereby litigants can be assured that the law has been properly administered to their disputes. The instructions of a judge to a jury normally relate to the law applicable to the possible findings of facts, stated hypothetically, which are supported by the evidence. In any but the simplest cases, they are long and involved, phrased in terms of the nicest distinctions, capable of being understood only by lawyers, and, more frequently than not, inaccurate. No one seriously claims that they are understood by juries or that they assist a jury in reaching a verdict. For the most part they are ritual.[2]

Of course the law has made some efforts to enhance the moral sanction behind instructions. Jurors are everywhere put under oath.[3] And the use of cautionary or hortatory instructions is common. Perhaps the most effective devices, however, are those involving some form of special verdict or interrogatories to which the jury must respond. The special verdict, at common law, was a statement by the jury of their finding upon the facts, leaving for the judge the applications of the law to those facts. To be valid it had to be a "complete finding of all the material facts, disputed and undisputed (and not merely of evidence or conclusions)."[4] It developed in England largely as a means of escape from the rigors of attaint, and it became settled there that it was the jury's option to bring in a special verdict; that it could not be compelled by the court (though this outcome was not reached without a struggle). In most American jurisdictions, on the other hand, the judge may require a special verdict. But in both countries the cumbersome technicalities with which such verdicts became encrusted prevented their widespread use.

Another development, largely American, was the special interrogatory which the judge could compel the jury to answer when they brought in a general verdict. Still a third device, which has received much praise, has grown up in three American states. Leon Green has described this as a "simplified special verdict" [5]; it involves the use of a limited number of simple interrogatories covering all the material issues in the case.

All of these devices are calculated to put psychological pressure on the jury to make them perform (and stay within) their theoretical function. They focus attention on the questions that the jury is supposed to decide and make them at least record a decision on those questions. It is still entirely within the jury's power to come to a conclusion on an improper basis, and then to answer the interrogatories (or state the facts) in the way they know they must to support their verdict, even though such answers do not represent their honest conclusions as to the facts. Thus, if the only possible ground of railroad negligence in a crossing case is failure to blow the whistle, a jury that was determined to hold the defendant could state that they found such failure, when in fact they were convinced that the whistle was blown. Nevertheless, it is probably harder for people generally to do that sort of thing than it is for them to bring a general plaintiff's verdict in the face of an instruction (which they may not have understood) requiring an implied but unrecorded and unexpressed finding to the same effect. Then, of course, there is always the chance that the jury may not perceive the legal effect of any given answer, so that even though they are perfectly willing to fit their answers to meet the end they want, their purpose may be defeated through a mixture of ignorance and unguarded honesty.

There is another aspect of the part instructions play in the present jury system. They furnish the most prolific source of error and reversal by appellate courts. Leon Green has developed the thesis that, partly as an antidote to the relaxation of trial court control of juries under the influence of American democratic notions, the power of appellate courts over both jury and trial court has grown apace.[6] It does seem to be true, at least, that there are so many possible pitfalls for a trial judge in giving instructions to the jury, and at the same time so many procedural rules by which appellate courts can avoid reversal, that there exists here a great deal of room within which such courts are relatively free to exercise control over jury verdicts, within their discretion.

Appraisal of the Jury's Role in Present Day Accident Law

Clearly, a number of devices are available either to expand or contract the jury's function in accident cases. It remains to consider the role that the jury does and probably will play in this field—what its greatest possibilities of usefulness here are. Such considerations will have great bearing on the present and probably future attitude of the courts toward the questions that arise at the various points where the chance for flexibility exists.

One role that the jury is supposed to play in the present system is to bring the common sense wisdom of the layman to bear on the problems of finding facts. Their ability as a fact finding body has been both highly praised and seriously challenged. Holmes said that in his experience he had not found the jury "specially inspired for the discovery of truth." [7] Becker speaks of trial by jury as a method of determining facts as "antiquated, unscientific, and inherently absurd—so much so that no lawyer, judge, scholar, prescription clerk, cook, or mechanic in a garage would ever think for a moment of employing that method for determing the facts in any situation that concerned him." [8] On the other hand, Chalmers finds it a "far better tribunal than a judge for dealing with questions of fact." [9] Another author considers it the "best, safest, and most satisfactory fact finding body there is." [10]

The jury is also, with limits, supposed to bring the common sense wisdom of the layman to bear on the problem of evaluating conduct. The extent to which the jury should set the specific standard of conduct for the circumstances of the case before them has also been the subject of dispute. Holmes, for example, felt that such standards ought increasingly to be fixed by the court so that men should know in advance to the greatest possible extent just what they are supposed to do in any given set of circumstances.[11] This goal could not be attained if in every case the setting of the standard is left to "the featureless generality of a general verdict." [12] But the law has, on the whole, rejected Holmes' view (in this regard) either because of the supposed desirability of the lay judgment on these matters, or because of the strength of the considerations about to be mentioned.

The two roles just discussed are the only ones that strict legal theory assigns to the jury under the present body of accident law. Both roles are (under that theory) supposed to be played so as to determine "fault" in each case. Those who whole-heartedly accept the present system of liability will, therefore, seek to perfect devices for controlling the jury so as to keep it within these functions. There is, however, another role that the jury is actually playing. Holmes has described it thus: "They will introduce into their verdict a certain amount —a very large amount so far as I have observed—of popular prejudice, and thus keep the administration of the law in accord with the wishes and feelings of the community." [13] Probably this role assumes greatest importance when, in any field, the substantive law does not by and large correspond with prevailing (though often inarticulate) popular notions of what the law ought to be in that field. This is often true of periods of transition or impending transition, as in the days when the rules rigorously limiting a master's liability to his servant for work injuries persisted on the surface in spite of the growing undercurrent of popular feeling that culminated in the workmen's compensation acts, with their adoption of the principle of absolute liability and social insurance. Leon Green has described the part played by the jury in this period:

There is only one bright spot. Whenever a case for any reason broke through legal theory and reached the jury it was almost invariably decided against the master and for the servant. And what is more, the judges, both trial and appellate, found themselves so enmeshed in their theories that their only retreat in many cases was found in passing the matter to the jury. The superstructure of theory broke under its own weight. Verdicts were too constant and too overwhelming to be withstood except in the most haphazard fashion. And the jury probably rendered the most important of its scanty service to legal science in civil cases at this juncture. Seemingly, juries saw only the parties before them, and placed the risk where they thought it could best be borne. The judges had been interested in principles; juries were interested in doing justice between the parties. The judges evolved a nice scheme for determining responsibility, the juries gave verdicts which wrecked the scheme. Juries held their ground here until legal theory could catch up with the new order of things that had emerged under the very eyes of the judges without most of them noticing it.[14]

There is much reason to believe that we are today in a very nearly parallel period in most of the rest of accident law, a conclusion that the facts next to be noticed tend to fortify.

No appraisal of the jury's role in the present situation can be complete without pointing out that the great majority of jury verdicts in accident cases today are in favor of the plaintiff. Thus in 1947 plaintiffs in New York State won 60 per cent to 66 per cent of the jury verdicts. In the Massachusetts Superior Court, the plaintiff was successful in 73.5 per cent of the cases tried to the jury. This is especially significant when it is realized that defendants try especially hard to settle cases where they regard liability as clear.

Practical Implications of the Foregoing. A rule in favor of the admissibility of evidence by and large helps plaintiffs, though in any given case its application may help a defendant prove his own due care, or the contributory negligence of plaintiff. This is because it is the plaintiff who has the need of producing a sufficiency of evidence on most issues, and it is he who receives the greatest benefit from getting to the jury upon them. Some courts, for instance, admit an appropriate company rule in evidence as tending to show the standard of care that its employees should observe toward the public. Such a rule may be used in one case to show the company's negligence (where it is coupled with evidence that the rule was violated), in another to show the company's due care (where it is coupled with evidence that the rule was observed). In the first type of situation the rule helps a plaintiff to make out a jury question, by opening up one more possibility of showing negligence. In the second type of situation, the rule does not help defendant to keep the case from the jury, but merely affords him some evidence of due care which the jury may weigh. Since, therefore, juries apparently tend to resolve doubts in favor of liability, the ruling in the first case does the plaintiff more good than the ruling in the second case does him harm. What has just been said would be generally true whether the ruling concerned a matter of relevancy, or one of the exclusionary rules.

A ruling that relaxes the requirements of sufficiency of proof tends on the whole to extend liability since it will mean fewer directed verdicts against the party having the burden of proof and this is usually the plaintiff. This scarcely needs elaboration, and is well understood in the profession. Included here are presumptions and such doctrines as *res ipsa loquitur*.

A ruling by which the court sets the specific standard of conduct to be applied to the case at hand tends to restrict liability. This is true whether the standard is derived from judicial notions of what is reasonable, from statute, from trade practice, or any other source. Sometimes they have been applied as maximum standards, so that one who has taken certain defined precautions cannot be found negligent. But even when they operate as minimum standards so that a party who has not met them is negligent as a matter of law, they generally work in favor of defendants, by taking the issue of contributory negligence away from the jury. As Nixon says:

> . . . for plaintiff's counsel, already enjoying the favor of the jury, the need to obtain a directed verdict based upon a proved deviation from a specific standard is less important than for a defendant's counsel who will strive to wrest the case from the jury by seeking a directed verdict based on the plaintiff's failure to observe such a standard.[15]

What has just been said may be summarized as follows:

Any rule of substantive law or procedure that enlarges the jury's theoretical sphere tends to extend liability, and conversely any rule that restricts the jury's sphere tends to restrict liability. Rules of the latter kind, however, are effective in restricting liability only when they result in a withdrawal of the whole case from the jury, and are not particularly effective when they are reflected only by language in the charge.

Any procedural device that effectively keeps the jury within their theoretical sphere tends to restrict liability and to prevent the jury from performing their possible role of keeping the actual operation of the law more responsive to human needs than an archaic substantive law would permit if it were carried out in letter and spirit. It is not contended here that the jury should play such a role. It is suggested, however, that accident law is in a period of transition wherein the jury's catalytic function in hastening legal change will occupy a central position.

NOTES

1. Fleming James, "Accident Liability: Some Wartime Developments," *Yale Law Journal*, LV (1946), 387–388.
2. Leon Green, *Judge and Jury* (1930), p. 351.
3. See, for example, the Connecticut oath for jurors in civil cases. "You solemnly swear

that you will well and truly try the issue or issues, now to be given you in charge, between the plaintiff and the defendant (or plaintiffs and defendants), according to the evidence given you in court, and the laws of this state, and accordingly a true verdict give; your own counsel, and your fellows', you will duly observe and keep; you will speak nothing, to any one, of the business or matters you have in hand, but among yourselves, nor will you suffer any one to speak to you about the same, but in court; and, when you are agreed upon any verdict, you will keep it secret until you deliver it up in court; so help you God." Conn. Gen. Stat. (1949), § 3576.

4. Green, *op. cit., supra,* at 353; Clementson, *Special Verdicts* 4 (1905) at c.1; Morgan, "A Brief History of Special Verdicts and Special Interrogatories," *Yale Law Journal,* XXXII (1923), 575; Sunderland, "Verdicts, General and Special," *Yale Law Journal,* XXIX (1920), 253, 265; note, *Texas Law Review,* XV (1937), 396.
5. Green, *op. cit., supra,* at 357.
6. Green, *op. cit., supra,* at c. 14.
7. Oliver Wendell Holmes, *Collected Legal Papers,* (1921), pp. 237.
8. Carl Becker, *Freedom and Responsibility in the American Way of Life* (1945), p. 82 ". . . the real task of the jury is to guess, with such aid as it can, by questions, induce the judge to give, which set of attorneys has been the most adroit in confusing the witnesses and clouding the issues." Becker, *op. cit., supra,* at 81.
9. Chalmers, "The County Court System," *Law Quarterly Review,* III (1887), 1, 10.
10. Hyde, "Fact Finding by Special Verdict," *Law Journal American Judiciary Society,* XXIV (1941), 144, 145.
11. Holmes, *The Common Law* (1881), pp. 110–112. See also Holmes' opinions in *Lorenzo v. Worth,* 170 Mass. 596, 49 N.E. (1898), 1010 and *Baltimore and Ohio Railroad Company v. Goodman* 275 U.S. 66 (1927).
12. Holmes, *op. cit., supra,* at 111.
13. Holmes, *Collected Legal Papers, op. cit., supra* n. 7, at 237.
14. Green, *op. cit., supra* at 122–123.
15. Richard Nixon, "Changing Rules of Liability in Automobile Accident Litigation," *Law and Contemporary Problems,* III (1936), 476.

43

The Basic Pattern of Disagreement between Jury and Judge

HARRY KALVEN, JR., AND HANS ZEISEL

This study seeks to answer two basic questions: First, what is the magnitude and direction of the disagreement between judge and jury? And, second, what are the sources and explanations of such disagreement? It is the business of this chapter to give the overall answers to the first question. The remainder of

From *The American Jury* (Boston: Little, Brown, and Company, 1966), pp. 55–59. Reprinted by permission of the authors and publishers.

the book is fundamentally devoted to analyzing and explaining the differences between judge and jury that this chapter reports.

Although any distinctive function of the jury must be found in the possibility of disagreement between judge and jury, there is something curious in the question how much judge and jury agree and disagree. No prior expectations exist either among the legal profession or in legal tradition as to what a proper amount of disagreement between judge and jury should be. We lack a pre-existing context in which to place the measurements. You may find it amusing to make your own private guess and to see whether it overestimates or underestimates the amount of actual disagreement.

Table 43–1 reports for the full sample of 3,576 cases the actual verdict of the jury and the matching hypothetical verdict of the judge. Since the jury may acquit, convict, or hang, where realistically the judge may only acquit or convict, the verdicts distribute in six cells.[1]

Table 43–1 thus furnishes the basic measure of the magnitude of judge-jury disagreement. Reading the two shaded cells first, we obtain the percentage of cases in which judge and jury agree. They agree to acquit in 13.4 per cent of all cases and to convict in 62.0 per cent of all cases, thus yielding a total agreement rate of 75.4 per cent.

Looking next at the four unshaded cells, we see that the total disagreement, 24.6 per cent of all cases, consists of (16.9 + 2.2 =) 19.1 per cent of cases in which judge and jury disagree on guilt, and (1.1 + 4.4 =) 5.5 per cent of cases in which the jury hangs.[2]

It is not easy to know what to make of these figures. To some, no doubt, the fact that judge and jury agree some 75 per cent of the time will be read as a reassuring sign of the competence and stability of the jury system; to others the fact that they disagree 25 per cent of the time will be viewed as a disturb-

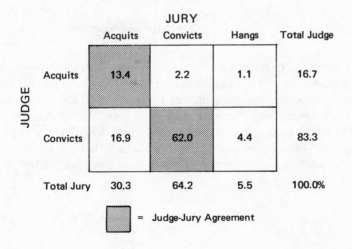

TABLE 43-1   *Verdict of Jury and Judge*
(In Per Cent of All 3,576 Trials)

		JURY			
		Acquits	Convicts	Hangs	Total Judge
JUDGE	Acquits	13.4	2.2	1.1	16.7
	Convicts	16.9	62.0	4.4	83.3
	Total Jury	30.3	64.2	5.5	100.0%

☐ = Judge-Jury Agreement

ing sign of the anarchy and eccentricity of the jury. We would suggest that the significance of these figures for any judgment about the jury must depend on the reasons for these disagreements and must wait upon the detailed examination of those reasons.

The inclusion of hung juries makes Table 43–1 somewhat awkward to handle. At times it will prove useful to employ the following convention in the counting of hung juries: a hung jury will be considered as in effect half an acquittal.[3] Accordingly in Table 43–2, Table 43–1 is rewritten by redistributing the hung juries half to the acquittals and half to the convictions and rounding off to integers.[4]

It is immediately apparent in Table 43–2 that the jury's disagreement with the judge is massively in one direction, and the direction is the expected one. The jury has long been regarded as a bulwark of protection for the criminal defendant, and Table 43–2 can be taken to retell this story. There is some

TABLE 43-2   *Verdict of Jury and Judge —*
Consolidated
(Per Cent of All 3,576 Trials)

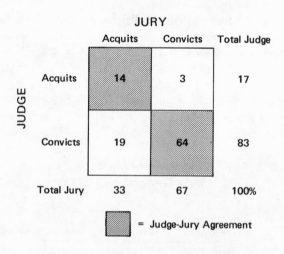

JURY

		Acquits	Convicts	Total Judge
JUDGE	Acquits	14	3	17
	Convicts	19	64	83
	Total Jury	33	67	100%

▨ = Judge-Jury Agreement

puzzle, however, as to how best to state the extent of this imbalance in favor of the defendant. After considerable deliberation over the point, we now conclude that the most meaningful statement is the simplest. The jury is less lenient than the judge in 3 per cent of the cases and more lenient than the judge in 19 per cent of the cases. Thus, the jury trials show on balance a net leniency of 16 per cent. This means that in the cases which the defendant decides to bring before the jury, on balance, he fares better 16 per cent of the time than he would have in a bench trial.

NOTES

1. Though to be precise Table 43–1 is a sixfold table (2 x 3), it can serve to introduce its simpler prototype, the fourfold (2 x 2) contingency table (see Table 43–2). It matches the verdicts of jury and judge by confronting two dichotomies: *jury acquits* or *convicts* with *judge acquits* or *convicts*. Such a matrix is a remarkably economic expositive device. It enables us to see not only what juries and judges do independently (this is reflected in the pair of marginal percentages outside the quadrangle), but simultaneously, what they decide as against each other. See Zeisel, *Say It With Figures* (4th ed., 1957), chs. 8, 9. Table 43–1 has, of course, no provision for judges who "hang," but not surprisingly we had two cases (excluded from the sample) in which the judges stated that they simply could not make up their minds.
2. The figure of 5.5 per cent hung juries conceivably understates somewhat the true frequency of hung juries. Since our instructions to the judges as to what constitutes a reportable jury trial were perhaps imprecise on the point, it is possible that some felt no need to report on what is technically a mistrial. However, the total lack of more reliable data on this point moved us to accept our figure.
3. Before the hung juries are redistributed, it is worth noting that the judge's ratio of acquittals to convictions is roughly the same for cases where the jury reaches a verdict as for cases where the jury does not:

	Jury Hangs	Jury Decides
Judge acquits	1.1%	15.6%
Judge convicts	4.4	78.9
Total	5.5%	94.5%

4. This distribution is predicated on the experience that, as a practical matter, roughly half the hung jury cases end up having the same consequences for the defendant as an acquittal, either because his prosecution is dropped or because he is acquitted in a subsequent trial. This is based on an estimate we were given by an experienced prosecutor. We were unable to obtain reliable statistics on the final disposition of the hung juries. The practice varies according to jurisdiction. The Los Angeles Municipal Court, for instance, considers the final vote, and if a clear majority found the defendant guilty the case is retried. For data on that court, see generally, Holbrook, *A Survey of Metropolitan Trial Courts—Los Angeles Area* (1956). And, of course, some of the retried cases end in acquittal, if not in a second hung jury.

Compare also the English practice: "There is . . . no compulsion upon the Crown to re-indict a man, after a disagreement of the jury, but it is the usual practice to re-indict once, and then, if the jury disagree a second time, to enter a *nolle prosequi* or consent to a directed acquittal. Sometimes, for special reasons, the Crown abandons a case after a single disagreement of the jury." Williams, *The Proof of Guilt* (London, 1955), p. 283.

44

Fay v. New York

Justice Jackson delivered the opinion of the Court.

These cases present the same issue, a challenge to the constitutionality of the special or so-called "blue ribbon" jury as used by state courts in the State and County of New York.

Such a jury found Fay and Bove guilty of conspiracy to extort and of extortion. Bove was Vice-President of the International Hod Carriers, Building, and Common Laborers' Union of America. Fay was Vice-President of the International Union of Operating Engineers.

• • •

The question is whether a warranted conviction by a jury individually accepted as fair and unbiased should be set aside on the ground that the make-up of the panel from which they were drawn unfairly narrows the choice of jurors and denies defendants due process of law or equal protection of the laws in violation of the Fourteenth Amendment to the Federal Constitution. If answered in the affirmative, it means that no conviction by these special juries is constitutionally valid, and all would be set aside if the question had been properly raised at or before trial.

The defendants raise no question as to the constitutionality of the general statutes of New York that prescribe the qualifications, disqualifications, and exemptions for ordinary jury service. Neither is any question raised as to the administration of these general statutes by which the population of New York County, numbering some 1,800,000, is sifted to produce a general jury panel of about 60,000, unless it be that there is discrimination against women. It is from this panel that defendants insist, apart from any objection they may have as to improper exclusion of women even from the general panel, they had a constitutional right to have their trial jury drawn. The statutes advanced as a standard may be roughly summarized:

To qualify as a juror, a person must be an American citizen and a resident of the county; not less than 21 nor more than 70 years old; the owner or spouse of an owner of property of the value of $250; in possession of his or her natural faculties and not infirm or decrepit; not convicted of a felony or a misdemeanor involving moral turpitude; intelligent; of sound mind and good character; well informed; able to read and write the English language under-

Fay v. N.Y., Syllabus, Walter Wyatt Reporter. U.S. Government Printing Office, Washington, D.C., 1948. #377 Certiorari to the Court of Appeals of N.Y.

standingly. From those qualified the following classes are exempt from service: clergymen, physicians, dentists, pharmacists, embalmers, optometrists, attorneys, members of the Army, Navy, or Marine Corps, or of the National Guard or Naval Militia, firemen, policemen, ship's officers, pilots, editors, editorial writers, sub-editors, reporters, and copy readers.

Women are equally qualified with men, but as they also are granted exemption, a woman drawn may serve or not, as she chooses.

The attack is focused upon the statutes and sifting procedures that shrink the general panel to the special or "blue ribbon" panel of about 3,000.

Special jurors are selected from those accepted for the general panel by the county clerk, but only after each has been subpoenaed for personal appearance and has testified under oath as to his qualification and fitness. The statute prescribes standards for their selection by declaring ineligible and directing elimination of these classes: (1) All who have been disqualified or who claim and are allowed exemption from general service. (2) All who have been convicted of a criminal offense, or found guilty of fraud or misconduct by judgment of any civil court. (3) All who possess such conscientious opinions with regard to the death penalty as would preclude their finding a defendant guilty if the crime charged be punishable with death. (4) All who doubt their ability to lay aside an opinion or impression formed from newspaper reading or otherwise, or to render an impartial verdict upon the evidence uninfluenced by any such opinion or impression, or whose opinion of circumstantial evidence is such as would prevent their finding a verdict of guilty upon such evidence, or who avow such a prejudice against any law of the state as would preclude finding a defendant guilty of a violation of such law, or who avow such a prejudice against any particular defense to a criminal charge as would prevent giving a fair and impartial trial upon the merits of such defense, or who avow that they cannot in all cases give to a defendant who fails to testify as a witness in his own behalf the full benefit of the statutory provision that such defendant's neglect or refusal to testify as a witness in his own behalf shall not create any presumption against him.

The special jury panel is not one brought into existence for this particular case nor for any special class of offenses or type of accused. It is part of the regular machinery of trial in counties of one million or more inhabitants. In its sound discretion the court may order trial by special jury on application of either party in a civil action and by either the prosecution or defense in criminal cases. The motion may be granted only on a showing that "by reason of the importance or intricacy of the case, a special jury is required" or "the issue to be tried has been so widely commented upon . . . that an ordinary jury cannot without delay and difficulty be obtained" or that for any other reason "the due, efficient, and impartial administration of justice in the particular case would be advanced by the trial of such an issue by a special jury."

• • •

We fail to perceive on its face any constitutional offense in the statutory standards prescribed for the special panel. The Act does not exclude, or authorize the clerk to exclude, any person or class because of race, creed, color, or occupation. It imposes no qualification of an economic nature beyond that imposed by the concededly valid general panel statute. Each of the grounds of elimination is reasonably and closely related to the juror's suitability for the kind of service the special panel requires or to his fitness to judge the kind of cases for which it is most frequently utilized. Not all of the grounds of elimination would appear relevant to the issues of the present case. But we know of no right of defendants to have a specially constituted panel that would include all persons who might be fitted to hear their particular and unique case. This panel is for service in a wide variety of cases and its eliminations must be judged in that light. We cannot overlook that one of the features that has tended to discredit jury trials is interminable examination and rejection of prospective jurors. In a metropolis with notoriously congested court calendars we cannot find it constitutionally forbidden to set up administrative procedures in advance of trial to eliminate from the panel those who, in a large proportion of cases, would be rejected by the Court after its time had been taken in examination to ascertain the disqualifications. Many of the standards of elimination that the clerk is directed to apply in choice of the panel are those the Court would have to apply to excuse a juror on challenge for cause.

These are matters with which local authority must and does have considerable latitude to cope, for they affect the administration of justice, which is a local responsibility. For example, in this case the time of the trial court and its entire retinue of attendants was taken while 89 prospective jurors were examined. How many more would have been examined if the clerk had not already eliminated those who admit that they would not give defendants benefit of the rule that their neglect or refusal to testify in their own behalf would not create a presumption against them? Neither of these defendants themselves have complained of the exceptional publicity given to the charges in this case. How many more jurors would have been examined if the clerk had not already eliminated those who felt themselves subject to influence by publicity? These are practical matters in administering justice in which we will take care not to hamstring local authority by artificial or doctrinaire requirements.

• • •

The allegations of fact upon which defendants ask us to hold these special panels unconstitutional come to three: (1) That laborers, operatives, craftsmen, foremen, and service employees were systematically, intentionally, and deliberately excluded from the panel. (2) That women were in the same way excluded. (3) That the special panel is so composed as to be more prone to convict than the general panel.

(1) The proof that laborers and such were excluded consists of a tabulation of occupations as listed in the questionnaires filed with the clerk. The table received in evidence is set below. It is said in criticism of this list that it shows the industry in which these persons work rather than whether they are laborers or craftsmen; that is, "mechanics" may be and probably are also laborers;

"bankers" may be clerks. Certainly the tabulation does not show the relation of these jurors to the industry in which they were classified, as, for example, whether they were owners or financially interested, or merely employees. It does not show absence or exclusion of wage earners or of union members, although none listed themselves as "laborers," for several of these classes are obviously of the employee rather than the entrepreneur character. One of petitioners' tables showed that 38 per cent of the special panel were "clerical, sales, and kindred workers." Three of those examined as jurors in this case were members of labor unions. Two were pre-emptorily challenged by the People and one accepted by the prosecution was challenged by the defense.

Table 44–1 was prepared at the request of petitioners' counsel by an attor-

TABLE 44-1

Total number of special jurors on file in New York County Clerk's Office	2,911
Total number with classifiable occupations	2,743
Auditors and accountants	166
Bankers	170
Manufacturers	106
Real estate brokers	117
Retired	62
Architects and engineers	229
Educators, teachers, librarians	27
Executives, managers of industrial enterprises	470
Stock brokers	185
Salesmen, promoters of business enterprises, and advertising men	438
Newspaper men, editorial writers, and others engaged in the dissemination of information	148
Mechanics	5
Insurance men	166
Travel agency men	10
Civil service employees	21
Office clerks	94
Retail merchants	144
Entertainers	26
Building and construction superintendents	70
Chemists and physicists	66
Attorneys	5
Laborers	None
Labor union representatives	1
Housewives	20*

*There are only about 30 women on the entire special jury list.

NOTE: Petitioners' attorneys requested the Bureau of Labor Statistics of the United States Department of Labor to conform the classifications of the above table to the Census classifications. In the table thus prepared, 21 persons are classed as civil service employees and a note cautions that "Some members of this group undoubtedly belong elsewhere, as under service trades, or laborers." One hundred and sixty-five persons are listed as "unclassable" in the Bureau's table.

ney who testified that he "found various occupations listed" and "tried to classify them to groups, making them not too numerous."

It is sought to give significance to this exhibit showing the breakdown into occupations of some 2,700 special jurors, however, by reference to a tabulation of occupations of some 920,000 employees and persons seeking employment in Manhattan. The comparison is said to show a great disparity between the percentage of jurors of each occupation represented on the jury list of 1945 and the occupational distribution of the number of employed persons or experienced persons seeking employment in Manhattan in 1940. This table was not put in evidence but is reproduced here. (See table 44–2.) Apart from the discrepancy of five years in the dates of the data and the differences in classification of occupations, the two tables do not afford statistical proof that the jury percentages are the result of discrimination. Such a conclusion would be justified only if we knew whether the application of the proper jury standards would affect all occupations alike, of which there is no evidence and which we regard as improbable. The percentage of persons employed or seeking employment in each occupation does not establish even an approximate ratio for those of each occupation that should appear in a fairly selected jury panel. The former is not limited, as the latter must be, to those over 21 or under 70 years of age. It is common knowledge that many employed and seekers of employment in New York are not, as jurors must be, citizens of the United States. How many could not meet the property qualifications? How many could not read and write the English language understandingly? It is only after effect is given to these admittedly constitutional requirements that we would have any figures that determined or even suggested the effect of the additional disqualifications imposed on special jurors.

An occupational comparison of the special panel with the general panel might afford some ground for an opinion on the effect of the particular practices complained of in the composition of the special panel. But no such comparison is offered. Petitioners' only statement as to the comparative make-up of the general and special panels is as follows: "While the defect of discrimination against women, particularly those who are not members of so-called 'civic conscious' organizations, permeates both the general and special juries, there is no evidence whatever that laborers, operatives, service employees, craftsmen, and foremen, are excluded from the general jury panel." What is more to the point is that petitioners adduced no evidence whatever that the occupational composition of the general panel is substantially different from that of the special.

• • •

(2) As to the exclusion of women, it will be remembered that the law of New York gives to women the privilege to serve but does not impose service as a duty. It is said to have been found impractical to compel large numbers of women, who have an absolute exemption, to come to the clerk's office for examination since they so generally assert their exemption. Hence, only those

who volunteer or are suggested as willing to serve by other women or by organizations, including the League of Women Voters, are subpoenaed for examination. Some effort is made by the officials also to induce women to volunteer. But the evidence does not show that women are excluded from the special jury.

• • •

(3) A more serious allegation against the special jury panel is that it is more inclined than the general panel to convict. Extensive studies have been made by the New York State Judicial Council, which is under the duty of continuous study of the procedures of the courts and of making recommendations for improvement to the Legislature. It is on studies and criticisms by this official body that petitioners base their charge here that the special jury is a convicting jury in an unconstitutional sense.

In 1937 the Council recommended abolition of struck juries, foreign juries, and special juries. It said, "A well-administered ordinary jury system should produce jurors of as high caliber for every action as the special jury system attempts to provide in exceptional cases." The recommendation was followed by the Legislature except as to special juries. In 1938 the Judicial Council renewed its recommendation as to these. It summarized that its data "indicate that special juries are prone to convict." In a study of certain types of homicide cases, it found that, in 1933 and 1934, special juries convicted in 83 per cent and 82 per cent of the cases while ordinary juries those years convicted in 43 per cent and 37 per cent respectively. It reported: "The Judicial Council believes that every petit jury should be of uniformly high caliber and capable of giving a fair trial in all cases. To attain this goal, the ordinary jury, as now provided, may be in need of improvement. It is, however, unjust and should be unnecessary to select supposedly special juries in specific cases." The Council next year reported that the general panel had not been considered adequate, largely because in its selection the standards of the statute had not been followed, and that a complete re-examination of the general panel was undertaken. From time to time the Council renewed its recommendation. In 1945 it proposed that the special jury "be abolished as unnecessary and undesirable." It said, "It is undisputed that the revised jury system for New York City recommended by the Judicial Council and in operation since 1940 has succeeded in improving the quality of jurors generally by applying to all jurors the high standards that formerly were required only of special jurors. Thus, the necessity for special jurors no longer exists."

While the Judicial Council has pointed out and investigated the different conviction ratios, it has at no time suggested that the special jury has been inclined to convict except where conviction was warranted. New York extends an appeal on law and fact as matter of right. If there were a tendency to convict improperly, the Judicial Council, which includes the Chief Judge of the Court of Appeals and the Presiding Justice of the Appellate Division, which courts review these cases, would know it. Despite the Council's desire to abol-

TABLE 44-2 Occupations of Employed Persons (Except on Public Emergency Work) and of Experienced Workers Seeking Work, Residing in Manhattan in the Week of March 24 to 30, 1940, Compared with Occupations of Special Jurors on File in New York County Clerk's Office, January 31, 1945

Occupation	Experienced Labor Force [a]						Special Jurors
	Total			Males			
	Total	Employed [c]	Seeking work, experienced	Total	Employed [c]	Seeking work, experienced	
	A	B	C	D	E	F	G
Total [b]	921,183	778,202	142,981	589,431	489,618	99,813	2,664
Professional and semiprofessional	111,600	98,343	13,257	61,191	53,416	7,775	501
Proprietors, managers, and officials	85,969	81,234	4,735	73,732	69,509	4,223	1,146
Clerical, sales, and kindred workers	196,037	169,066	26,971	112,316	95,853	16,463	1,012
Craftsmen, foremen, and kindred workers	70,497	54,217	16,280	67,504	51,618	15,886	5
Operatives and kindred workers	156,581	128,253	28,328	98,493	79,562	18,931	—
Service workers	254,595	216,992	37,603	131,112	110,157	20,955	—
Laborers, except farm	45,375	29,869	15,506	44,578	29,293	15,285	—
Farmers, farm managers, farm laborers	529	228	301	505	210	295	—

TABLE 44-2   (continued)

Occupation	Total			Males			Special Jurors
	Total	Employed [c]	Seeking work, experienced	Total	Employed [c]	Seeking work, experienced	
			Percentage				
	A	B	C	D	E	F	G
Total	100.0	100.0	100.0	100.0	100.0	100.0	100.0
Professional and semiprofessional	12.1	12.6	9.3	10.4	10.9	7.8	18.8
Proprietors, managers, and officials	9.3	10.4	3.3	12.5	14.2	4.2	43.0
Clerical, sales, and kindred workers	21.3	21.7	18.9	19.1	19.6	16.5	38.0
Craftsmen, foremen, and kindred workers	7.7	7.0	11.4	11.4	10.5	15.9	0.2
Operatives and kindred workers	17.0	16.5	19.8	16.7	16.2	19.0	—
Service workers	27.6	27.9	26.3	22.2	22.5	21.0	—
Laborers, except farm	4.9	3.8	10.8	7.6	6.0	15.3	—
Farmers, farm managers, farm laborers	0.1	[d]	0.2	0.1	[d]	0.3	—

ish this jury, no such reasons were ever assigned. No statistics are produced to show that special juries have been more often reversed on the facts than ordinary ones. Of course, it would be impossible for us to say, even were we to examine the cases in detail, whether the difference in percentage of convictions indicated a too great readiness to convict on the part of special juries or a too great readiness to acquit on the part of ordinary juries, or whether the disparity reflected a difference between the ordinary case and those selected for special jury trial, rather than a reflection of an attitude on the part of either panel. It may result from the greater attention and better counsel which the prosecution gives to these important cases.

These defendants were convicted March 15, 1945, when the statistics offered here as to relative propensity of the two juries to convict were more than ten years old, and when the conditions which may have produced the discrepancy in ratio of convictions had long since been corrected.

The evidence in support of these objections may well, as the Judicial Council thought, warrant a political or social judgment that this special panel in 1945 was "unnecessary and undesirable" and that the Legislature should abolish it. But it is quite another matter to say that this Federal Court has a mandate from the Constitution to disable the special jury by setting aside its convictions. The great disparity between a legislative policy or a political judgment on the one hand and a constitutional or legal judgment on the other finds striking illustration in the position taken by the highest judicial personages in New York State who joined in the recommendation to abolish the special jury.

Two members of the Council who joined in proposing legislation to abolish the dual system sat in this case and abstained from putting their legislative recommendation into a court decision—they sustained as constitutional the system they would abolish as matter of policy. Our function concerns only constitutionality and we turn to the bearing of federal constitutional provisions on the legal issues.

• • •

Our only source of power or guidance for interfering in this case with the state court jury system is found in the cryptic words of the Fourteenth Amendment, unaided by any word from Congress or any governing precedent in this Court. We consider first the clause that forbids a state to "deny to any person within its jurisdiction the equal protection of the laws." This prohibits prejudicial disparities before the law. Under it a system that might be constitutionally unobjectionable, if applied to all, may be brought within the prohibition if some have more favorable treatment. The inquiry under this clause involves defendants' standing before the law relative to that of others accused.

If it were proved that in 1945 an inequality between the special jury's record of convictions and that of the ordinary jury continued as it was found by the Judicial Council to have prevailed in 1933–1934, some foundation would be laid for a claim of unequal treatment. No defendant has a right to escape an existing mechanism of trial merely on the ground that some other could be devised which would give him a better chance of acquittal. But in this case an alternative system actually was provided by the state to other defendants. A state is not required to try all classes of offenses in the same forum. But a discretion, even if vested in the court, to shunt a defendant before a jury so chosen as greatly to lessen his chances while others accused of a like offense are tried by a jury so drawn as to be more favorable to them would hardly be "equal protection of the laws." Perhaps it could be shown that the difference in percentages of convictions was not due to a difference in attitude of the jurors but to a difference in the cases that were selected for special jury trial, or to a more intensive preparation and effort by the prosecution in cases singled out for such trial. But a ratio of conviction so disparate, if it continued until 1945, might, in absence of explanation, be taken to indicate that the special jury was, in contrast to its alternate, organized to convict. A defendant could complain of this inequality even if it were shown that a special jury court never had convicted any defendant who did not deserve conviction.

But the defendants have failed to show by any evidence whatever that this disparity in ratio of conviction existed in 1945 when they were tried. They show that it ever existed only by the studies and conclusions of the Judicial Council. The same source shows that it was corrected before these defendants were tried. As we have pointed out, this official body challenged the fairness of this dual system as formerly constituted and as early as 1937 declared that "A well-considered jury system will insure an impartial cross-section of the community on every petit jury," and set out means to achieve it. We know of no reason why we should ignore or discredit their assurance that by administrative improvements in the selection of the ordinary juries they became the substantial equivalent of the special jury before these trials took place.

We hold, therefore, that defendants have not carried the burden of showing that the method of their trial denied them equal protection of the law.

The defendants' other objection is grounded on that clause of the Fourteenth Amendment that provides, "nor shall any State deprive any person of life, liberty, and property, without due process of law. . . ." It comprises objections that might be urged against any jury made up as the special jury was, even if it were the only jury in use in the state. It does not depend upon comparison with the jury facilities afforded other defendants.

This Court, however, has never entertained a defendant's objections to exclusions from the jury except when he was a member of the excluded class. *Rawlins v. Georgia,* 201 U.S. 638, 640. Cf. *Strauder v. West Virginia,* 100 U.S. 303. Relief has been held unavailable to a Negro who objected that all white persons were purposely excluded from the grand jury that indicted him. *Haraway v. State,* 203 Ark. 912, 159 S. W. 2d 733. Nevertheless, we need not here decide whether lack of identity with an excluded group would alone defeat an otherwise well-established case under the Amendment.

These defendants rely heavily on arguments drawn from our decisions in *Glasser v. United States,* 315 U.S. 60; *Thiel v. Southern Pacific Co.,* 328 U.S. 217; and *Ballard v. United States,* 329 U.S. 187. The facts in the present case are distinguishable in vital and obvious particulars from those in any of these cases. But those decisions were not constrained by any duty of deference to the authority of the State over local administration of justice. They dealt only with juries in federal courts. Over federal proceedings we may exert a supervisory power with greater freedom to reflect our notions of good policy than we may constitutionally exert over proceedings in state courts, and these expressions of policy are not necessarily embodied in the concept of due process.

The due process clause is one of comprehensive generality, and in reducing it to apply in concrete cases there are different schools of thought. One is that its content on any subject is to be determined by the content of certain relevant other amendments in the Bill of Rights which originally imposed restraints on only the Federal Government but which the Fourteenth Amendment deflected against the states. The other theory is that the clause has an independent content apart from, and in addition to, any and all other amendments. This meaning is derived from the history, evolution, and present nature of our institutions and is to be spelled out from time to time in specific cases by the judiciary.

• • •

Undoubtedly a system of exclusions could be so manipulated as to call a jury before which defendants would have so little chance of a decision on the evidence that it would constitute a denial of due process. A verdict on the evidence, however, is all an accused can claim; he is not entitled to a set-up that will give a chance of escape after he is properly proven guilty. Society also has a right to a fair trial. The defendant's right is a neutral jury. He has no constitutional right to friends on the jury.

To establish the unfairness of this tribunal and the lack of due process afforded to one who is being tried before it, the defendants assert two defects in its composition: first, that it unconstitutionally excluded women, and, second, that it unconstitutionally excluded laborers, craftsmen, service employees, and others of like occupation, amounting in sum to the exclusion of an economic class.

. . . The contention that women should be on the jury is not based on the Constitution, it is based on a changing view of the rights and responsibilities of women in our public life, which has progressed in all phases of life, including jury duty, but has achieved constitutional compulsion on the states only in the grant of the franchise by the Nineteenth Amendment. We may insist on their inclusion on federal juries where by state law they are eligible but woman jury service has not so become a part of the textual or customary law of the land that one convicted of crime must be set free by this Court if his state has lagged behind what we personally may regard as the most desirable practice in recognizing the rights and obligations of womanhood.

The other objection that petitioners urge under the due process clause is that the special jury panel was invalidated by exclusion of an economic group comprising such specified classifications as laborers, craftsmen, and service employees. They argue that the jury panel was chosen "with a purpose to obtain persons of conservative views, persons of the upper economic and social stratum in New York County, persons having a tendency to convict defendants accused of crime, and to exclude those who might understand the point of view of the laboring man." As we have pointed out, there is no proof of exclusion of these. At most, the proof shows lack of proportional representation and there is an utter deficiency of proof that this was the result of a purpose to discriminate against this group as such. The uncontradicted evidence is that no person was excluded because of his occupation or economic status. All were subjected to the same tests of intelligence, citizenship, and understanding of English. The state's right to apply these tests is not open to doubt even though they disqualify, especially in the conditions that prevail in New York, a disproportionate number of manual workers. A fair application of literacy, intelligence, and other tests would hardly act with proportional equality on all levels of life. The most that the evidence does is to raise, rather than answer, the question whether there was an unlawful disproportionate representation of lower-income groups on the special jury.

• • •

There may be special cases where exclusion of laborers would indicate that those sitting were prejudiced against labor defendants, as where a labor leader is on trial on charges growing out of a labor dispute. The situation would be similar to that of a Negro who confronts a jury on which no Negro is allowed to sit. He might very well say that a community that purposely discriminates against all Negroes discriminates against him. But it is quite different if we assume that "persons of conservative views" do predominate on the special jury. Does it follow that "liberals" would be more favorably disposed toward a defense that nominal labor leaders were hiring out to employers to "handle" their labor problems? Does it follow that a jury from the "upper economic and social stratum" would be more disposed to convict those who so undertake to serve two masters than "those who might understand the point of view of the laboring man"? We should think it might be the other way about and the defendants offer nothing but assertion to convince us. Our attention, moreover, is called to federal court records which show that Fay reported a net taxable income of over $65,000 for the years 1940 to 1942, while Bove reported over $39,000 for a similar period, both of them exclusive of the sums received from the contractors and involved in these charges. These earnings do not identify them very closely with the viewpoint of the depressed classes. The group with which they might be most closely identified is organized labor. But it cannot be claimed that union members were excluded from this special panel since three union members were called for examination on this particular jury, two being rejected by the People and one by the defendants themselves. The defendants have shown no intentional and purposeful exclusion of any class, and they have shown none that was prejudicial to them. They have had a fair trial, and no reason appears why they should escape its results.

The function of this Federal Court under the Fourteenth Amendment in reference to state juries is not to prescribe procedures but is essentially to protect the integrity of the trial process by whatever method the state sees fit to employ. No device, whether conventional or newly devised, can be set up by which the judicial process is reduced to a sham and courts are organized to convict. They must be organized to hear, try, and determine on the evidence and the law. But beyond requiring conformity to standards of fundamental fairness that have won legal recognition, this Court always has been careful not so to interpret this Amendment as to impose uniform procedures upon the several states whose legal systems stem from diverse sources of law and reflect different historical influences.

We adhere to this policy of self-restraint and will not use this great centralizing Amendment to standardize administration of justice and stagnate local variations in practice.

. . . The states have had different and constantly changing tests of eligibility for service. Evolution of the jury continues even now, and many experiments are under way that were strange to the common law. Some states have taken measures to restrict its use; others, where jury service is a hardship, diminish the required number of jurors. Some states no longer require the unanimous verdict; others add alternate or substitute jurors to avoid mistrial in case of sickness or death. Some states have abolished the general verdict and require answers to specific questions. Well has it been said of our power to limit state action that "To stay experimentation in things social and economic is a grave responsibility. Denial of the right to experiment may be fraught with serious consequences to the nation. It is one of the happy incidents of the federal system that a single courageous state may, if its citizens choose, serve as a laboratory; and try novel social and economic experiments without risk to the rest of the country" Justice Brandeis, dissenting in *New State Ice Co. v. Liebmann,* 285 U.S. 262, 311.

As there is no violation of a federal statute alleged, the challenge to this judgment under the due process clause must stand or fall on a showing that these defendants have had a trial so unfair as to amount to a taking of their liberty without due process of law. On this record we think that showing has not been made. Affirmed.

Justice Murphy, dissenting.

The equal protection clause of the Fourteenth Amendment prohibits a state from convicting any person by use of a jury which is not impartially drawn from a cross-section of the community. That means that juries must be chosen without systematic and intentional exclusion of any otherwise qualified group of individuals. *Smith v. Texas,* 311 U.S. 128. Only in that way can the democratic traditions of the jury system be preserved. *Thiel v. Southern Pacific Co.,* 328 U.S. 217, 220; *Glasser v. United States,* 315 U.S. 60, 85. It is because I believe that this constitutional standard of jury selection has been ignored in the creation of the so-called "blue ribbon" jury panel in this case that I am forced to dissent.

Preliminarily, it should be noted that legislation by Congress prohibiting the particular kind of inequality here involved is unnecessary to enable us to strike it down under the Constitution. While Congress has the power to enforce by appropriate legislation the provisions of the Fourteenth Amendment, and has done so relative to discrimination in jury selection on the basis of race or color, its failure to legislate as to economic or other discrimination in jury se-lection does not permit us to stand idly by. We have consistently interfered with state procedure and state legislation when we felt that they were incon-sistent with the Fourteenth Amendment or with the federal commerce power despite Congressional silence on the matter involved. See *West Virginia State Board of Education v. Barnette,* 319 U.S. 624; *Nippert v. Richmond,* 327 U.S. 416; *Morgan v. Virginia,* 328 U.S. 373. And so in this case we are enti-tled to judge the action of New York by constitutional standards without re-gard to the absence of relevant federal legislation.

The constitutional vice inherent in the type of "blue ribbon" jury panel here involved is that it rests upon intentional and systematic exclusion of certain classes of people who are admittedly qualified to serve on the general jury panel. Whatever may be the standards erected by jury officials for distinguish-ing between those eligible for such a "blue ribbon" panel and those who are not, the distinction itself is an invalid one. It denies the defendant his constitu-tional right to be tried by a jury fairly drawn from a cross-section of the com-munity. It forces upon him a jury drawn from a panel chosen in a manner which tends to obliterate the representative basis of the jury.

The selection of the "blue ribbon" panel in this case rests upon the "degree of intelligence as revealed by the questionnaire" sent to prospective jurors, augmented by personal interviews. The questionnaire, however, does not pur-port to be a test of native intelligence, nor does it appear to offer any sound basis for distinguishing the intelligence of one person from another. The un-deniable result has been to permit the jury officials to formulate whatever standards they desire, whether in terms of "intelligence" or some other factor, to eliminate persons from the "blue ribbon" panel, even though they admittedly are qualified for general jury service. That fact is strikingly borne out by the statistics compiled in this case as to the personnel of the "blue ribbon" panel. Certain classes of individuals are totally unrepresented on the panel despite their general qualifications and despite the fact that high intelligence is to be found in such classes. Such statistics can only mean that the jury officials have evolved some standard other than that of "intelligence" to exclude certain per-sons from the "blue ribbon" panel. And that standard is apparently of an eco-nomic or social nature, unjustified by the democratic principles of the jury sys-tem.

The Court points out some of the difficulties involved in comparing the per-sonnel of the panel with 1940 census figures. But we are dealing here with a very subtle and sophisticated form of discrimination which does not lend itself to easy or precise proof. The proof here is adequate enough to demonstrate that this panel, like every discriminatorily selected "blue ribbon" panel, suffers from a constitutional infirmity. That infirmity is the denial of equal protection

TABLE 44-3

	Percentage of Total Experienced Labor Forces in Manhattan	Percentage of Representation on "Blue Ribbon" Panel
Professional and semi-professional	12.1	18.8
Proprietors, managers, and officials	9.3	43
Clerical, sales, and kindred workers	21.3	38
Craftsmen, foremen, and kindred workers	7.7	0.2
Operatives and kindred workers	17	0
Service workers	27.6	0
Laborers	4.9	0
Farmers	0.1	0

to those who are tried by a jury drawn from a "blue ribbon" panel. Such a panel is narrower and different from that used in forming juries to try the vast majority of other accused persons. To the extent of that difference, therefore, the persons tried by "blue ribbon" juries receive unequal protection.

In addition, as illustrated in this case, the distinction that is drawn in fact between "blue ribbon" jurors and general jurors is often of such a character as to destroy the representative nature of the "blue ribbon" panel. There is no constitutional right to a jury drawn from a group of uneducated and unintelligent persons. Nor is there any right to a jury chosen solely from those at the lower end of the economic and social scale. But there is a constitutional right to a jury drawn from a group that represents a cross-section of the community. And a cross-section of the community includes persons with varying degrees of training and intelligence and with varying economic and social positions. Under our Constitution, the jury is not to be made the representative of the most intelligent, the most wealthy, or the most successful, nor of the least intelligent, the least wealthy, or the least successful. It is a democratic institution, representative of all qualified classes of people. *Smith v. Texas, supra.* To the extent that a "blue ribbon" panel fails to reflect this democratic principle, it is constitutionally defective.

The Court demonstrates rather convincingly that it is difficult to prove that the particular petitioners were prejudiced by the discrimination practiced in this case. Yet that should not excuse the failure to comply with the constitutional standard of jury selection. We can never measure accurately the prejudice that results from the exclusion of certain types of qualified people from a jury panel. Such prejudice is so subtle, so intangible, that it escapes the ordinary methods of proof. It may be absent in one case and present in another; it may gradually and silently erode the jury system before it becomes evident. But it is no less real or meaningful for our purposes. If the constitutional right to a jury impartially drawn from a cross-section of the community has been violated, we should vindicate that right even though the effect of the violation has not yet put in a tangible appearance. Otherwise that right may be irretrievably lost in a welter of evidentiary rules.

Since this "blue ribbon" panel falls short of the constitutional standard of jury selection, the judgments below should be reversed.

45

Social Status in Jury Deliberations

FRED L. STRODTBECK, RITA M. JAMES, AND CHARLES HAWKINS

For the purposes of the present study, which inquires into the relationships between occupation and selected aspects of role differentiation, it is desirable that the focus of the small-group discussion is not too narrowly circumscribed by status prerogatives. For example, a group of officers and enlisted men discussing military problems or a group of doctors and nurses discussing a medical problem would not provide the circumstances we require. A greater presumption of equality is desired.

In the jury situation not only does the widespread norm assume that group members should act toward one another as equals, but the presumption of equality is reinforced by the requirement that the verdict be unanimous. Equal and responsible participation in the deliberation, therefore, is an institutionalized expectation. If evidence indicates that the status differences of the larger community become manifest during the deliberation, then it may be expected that a similar generalization of status will be found in other situations of interaction where hierarchical considerations are more prominent.

It is essential for our study that wide background differences be present within the juror population. This is assured in metropolitan areas such as Chicago, St. Louis, and Minneapolis where our experimental jury research has been conducted, since jurors are selected here by a random process from voting-registration lists. The resultant jury-pool population compares closely with the expected population computed from census reports, although there are sev-

From E. E. Maccoby, T. M. Newcomb, and E. L. Hartley, eds., *Readings in Social Psychology* (3rd ed; New York: Holt, Rinehart and Winston, 1958), pp. 379, 380–388. Copyright 1947, 1952, © 1957 by Holt, Rinehart and Winston, Inc. Reprinted by permission of Holt, Rinehart and Winston, Inc.

eral known sources of bias. Lawyers, doctors, teachers, policemen, and other local and federal employees, including elected officials, are excused from jury service. Aliens, foreign visitors, recent migrants, and persons under 21 who are not eligible to vote do not appear on the jury lists. Finally, men who operate "one-man" businesses and prospective jurors with pressing personal problems can ordinarily have their jury service deferred or canceled. The net effect is that the professions and very low-education and occupation groups are slightly under-represented.

Occupations are classified in four groups: proprietor, clerical, skilled, and labor. "Proprietor" includes the census category of proprietors, managers, and officials as well as professionals such as architects, accountants, and engineers who are not excluded from service. "Clerical" and "skilled" categories correspond to the census categories and "labor" subsumes the census categories of semi-skilled workers, non-farm laborers, and servants. Farm owners and laborers are absent from our populations, and retired persons have been classified by their occupations prior to retirement. Women are classified by their stated occupations, except that housewives are classified by their husbands' occupations. . . .

Mock jury deliberations were conducted in which the participants were jurors drawn by lot from the regular jury pools of the Chicago and St. Louis courts. The jurors listened to a recorded trial, deliberated, and returned their verdict—all under the customary discipline of bailiffs of the court. The jury deliberations were recorded, fully transcribed, and scored in terms of interaction-process categories.

This essay is based primarily upon 49 deliberations for which interaction-process analysis has been carried out. Although further work is in process on more than 100 additional deliberations that have been collected by the project during the past three years, the present report is final since further interaction-process analysis of the type reported here is not contemplated. Two civil trials were used as the basis for the deliberations. In the first (29 deliberations) the plaintiff, a secretary, sought compensation for injuries incurred in a two-car collision. In the second (20 deliberations) a young child sought compensation for facial disfigurement incurred in a fire alleged to have been caused by a defective vaporizer. A total of 49 by 12, or 588, different jurors were involved. Data on 14 additional vaporizer cases and 28 recent experimental trials are used in other portions of the essay. In total, data from 91 juries are used in the examination of different status effects.

Procedures

Selecting a Foreman. After the jury listened to the case, they were told to select their foreman and begin their deliberation. In more than half of the deliberations, the foreman was nominated by one member and then quickly accepted by the remainder of the group. In about a third of the deliberations the man who opened the discussion and sought either to nominate another, or to focus the group's attention on their responsibility in selecting a foreman, was himself selected foreman. However, in all instances the selection of a foreman was quickly and apparently casually accomplished. There was no instance in which mention of any socio-economic criteria was made, but this is not to say that socio-economic criteria were not involved. For example, Table 45–1 shows that some foremen were selected from all strata, but the incidence was three and a half times as great among proprietors as among laborers. In addition, although the details are not given in the table, tabulations show that only one-fifth as many women were chosen as foreman as would be expected by chance. . . .

TABLE 45-1   *Occupational Status of 49 Jury Foremen*

Occupation	Expected*	Observed	Index
Proprietor	9.73	18	185
Clerical	15.03	15	100
Skilled	9.56	8	84
Labor	14.68	8	54

*Computed under assumption that foremen will be proportional to portion of sample in the given occupation.

Since there were 12 persons in the jury, one-twelfth of the total acts is the pro-rata percentage for each juror's acts. This provides the base line against which the effects of external status may be appraised. The higher the average participation of an occupational group, the greater their relative share of the common resource of time. It may be seen in Table 45–2 that in all occupations males talked more than females and the amount of participation was

TABLE 45-2   *Percentage Rates of Participation in Jury Deliberation by Occupation and Sex of Juror*

Sex	Occupation				
	Proprietor	Clerical	Skilled	Laborer	Combined
Male	12.9 (N = 81)*	10.8 (N = 81)	7.9 (N = 80)	7.5 (N = 107)	9.6 (N = 349)
Female	9.1 (N = 31)	7.8 (N = 92)	4.8 (N = 28)	4.6 (N = 62)	6.6 (N = 213)
Combined	11.8 (N = 112)	9.2 (N = 173)	7.1 (N = 108)	6.4 (N = 169)	8.5 (N = 562)†

*Numbers of jurors are shown in parentheses.
†Twenty-six of 588 jurors from the 49 juries used were not satisfactorily classified by occupation and are omitted.

sharply differentiated between higher than expected values for proprietors and clerical workers, and lower than expected values for skilled and unskilled laborers. . . .

One source of differences in participation within a jury may be attributed to the election of one member to play the role of foreman. The foreman was responsible for approximately one-fourth of the total acts and as shown in Table 45–1 was more frequently selected from the higher-status groups. When foreman scores were eliminated the average-participation values were:

Proprietor	8.9
Clerical	7.0
Skilled	6.3
Labor	5.9

The gap between clerical and skilled workers is narrower but the rank order is unchanged.

The latent premise in the study of participation is that high participation indicates greater ability to influence others. Earlier research supports such an interpretation for *ad hoc* problem-solving groups and for families. Further evidence is available from the present research. Jurors were asked before the deliberation what, if anything, they would award the plaintiff. A detailed examination of individual pre-deliberation decisions with the subsequent group awards in 29 deliberations reveals that the more active jurors shifted their pre-deliberation position less often than less active jurors in the process of reaching a unanimous group verdict. This interpretation of the relation between participation and influence by status level may be documented by comparing the average pre-deliberation award (listed according to occupational group) with the jury verdict. The correlations are:

Proprietor	.50
Clerical	.11
Skilled	.29
Labor	.02

$(p < .05)$

Members from the same occupational group sometimes initially favored different verdicts, and in this case not all the members of this group achieved their desired outcome. Nonetheless, the correlation between the proprietors' average and the jury verdicts is significant. . . .

Perceived Fitness as Jurors. Where is the quality of justice to be found? The Courts-Martial reform, which permitted enlisted men to request other enlisted men for their trial panels, was largely nullified by their preference to leave their cases in the hands of officers. How do jurors react? A departure from random selection might have two possible effects. Given a choice, jurors might tend to over-select people in the higher occupations. . . . Or, taking the class theory as the basis of our prediction, we might assume that the chooser might select more jurors from his own occupation group. How these counter tendencies might be balanced is a question for which we have no theoretical answer and, therefore, must investigate empirically.

In an effort to probe deeper for evidence of class identifications, the following question was asked of 28 juries.

The jury pool is made up of people from all walks of life. However, if a member of your family were on trial and you had your choice, which of the following kinds of people would you prefer to make up the majority of the jurors who would hear your case?

(1) Business and professional people
(2) Clerical and white-collar workers
(3) Skilled workers
(4) Unskilled workers (laborers)

The expected values, determined by assuming that equal preference will be shown for each status group, have been divided into the observed values, and the resultant ratio was multiplied by 100 to give index numbers shown in Table 45–3. All groups, except laborers, would prefer to have a member of their family tried before a jury the majority of whose members were proprietors. Like other groups, laborers were also upwardly oriented in their preferences but their first choice was skilled workers, then proprietors. Clerical and skilled workers chose persons from their own occupation group as their second choice. All groups except laborers ranked laborers last. Laborers placed themselves third and clerks last. It is to be stressed that Table 45–3 represents the choice of jurors in terms of occupational stereotypes. It is what a member of one occupational group perceives in terms of his generalized conception of his own and other occupational groups.

TABLE 45-3   *Choice of Juror if Member of Respondent's Family Were on Trial, Based Upon Occupation Stereotypes (Pro rata expected is 100) ***

Respondent's Occupation		Preferred Occupation			
		Proprietor	Clerical	Skilled	Laborer
Proprietor	(N = 63)	241	95	51	13
Clerical	(N = 107)	206	112	71	11
Skilled	(N = 72)	172	55	139	33
Laborer	(N = 76)	126	42	147	84

*These data were collected from jurors in our 28 most recent experimental juries.

We also asked jurors to choose "four of your fellow jurors whom you would best like to have serve on a jury if you were on trial." This question asks jurors not for generalized conceptions of other occupational groups but for evaluations of particular persons. We wished to know if the selections made on the basis of face-to-face contact were similar or different from stereotype choices. If a prototype of a social system had grown during deliberation, jurors might come to regard one another more in terms of performance in the task at hand than in terms of general social status. It was also possible for the deliberation to reveal status-based ideologies that would open latent schisms. The data suggest that differences were ordinarily not magnified by the deliberation and the jurors came to be convinced that a just job had been done. The special thrust of the question "if a member of your family were on trial" could have sensitized jurors to think in terms of personal interests rather than abstract principles such as competence or justice. Possibly these respondents became so sensitive to their personal interests that they turned away from those jurors who had been the arbiters of consensus in their own deliberations.

Table 45–4 shows a preference for proprietors but at a somewhat lower level. More detailed effects of the face-to-face experience in contrast with the response to occupational categories may best be illustrated by subtracting Table 45–3 from Table 45–4. It is to be noted that while Tables 45–3 and 45–4 are based on different populations, the respondents in both cases are random samples from the population available in successive weeks in the jury pool. When Table 45–3 is subtracted from Table 45–4 (see Table 45–5) a positive value in the matrix represents an increase in index value associated with the face-to-face experience.

TABLE 45-4   *Choice of Juror if Respondent Were on Trial, Based*
             Upon Deliberation Experience
                (Pro rata expected is 100) *

Respondent's Occupation		Preferred Occupation			
		Proprietor	Clerical	Skilled	Laborer
Proprietor	(N = 78)	169	110	119	39
Clerical	(N = 129)	145	100	101	75
Skilled	(N = 74)	147	104	84	73
Laborer	(N = 130)	162	100	112	74

*The expected values used to form the index numbers have been determined by assuming that each person distributes his four choices simultaneously under conditions that give an equal chance of each of the 11 fellow juror's being chosen. For example, for two proprietor, four clerical, two skilled and four labor the expected distribution of the eight proprietor votes would be 2/11(8), 8/11(8), 4/11(8) and 8/11(8). It is assumed that no fellow juror can be chosen twice by the same subject. The expected and observed choices for individuals on one jury are combined by status groups and accumulated for the different juries. Only six randomly selected jurors in the 20 vaporizer cases were asked this form of the question, so the 411 responses come from a potential population of (29 X 12) + (20 X 6), or 468.

TABLE 45-5   *Change in Index Value Associated with Delibera-tion Experience*
(Value of Table 45-3 subtracted from Table 45-4)

Respondent's Occupation	Preferred Occupation			
	Proprietor	Clerical	Skilled	Laborer
Proprietor	−72	15	68	26
Clerical	−61	−12	30	64
Skilled	−35	49	−55	40
Laborer	36	58	−35	−10

The main diagonal shows that "own group" choices were lower at each oc-cupation level, particularly among proprietors and skilled laborers. That is, choices after the deliberation experience are not determined by a narrow "in-terest group." In addition, all values above the main diagonal are positive. That is, face-to-face experience caused lower-status persons to be evaluated more highly! As shown below the main diagonal, proprietors were reduced in the evaluation of clerical and skilled workers and increased in the evaluation of laborers; clerical workers were rated more highly by both skilled workers and laborers; and laborers decreased their former preference for skilled work-ers. The lower range of index values in the face-to-face situation arose in part from the effects of forcing the distribution of four votes among the 11 jurors who were members of the respondent's particular jury. Notwithstanding this flattening effect, it still appears that the face-to-face experience (1) results in fewer proprietor and skilled worker "own group" choices; and (2) brings the choice gradients into smoother conformity with the observed contribution of each status group to the deliberation.

Discussion

Jury deliberations have been used to examine the intersection of occupa-tional status and sex with the typically small-group measures of participation, influence, satisfaction, and perceived competence. The assumption that there is no relation between these modes of classification can be safely rejected. Men, in contrast with women, and persons of higher-status, in contrast with lower-status, occupations have higher participation, influence, satisfaction, and per-ceived competence for the jury task.

The present study does little to explain the cause of this differentiation. In-sofar as selection of the foreman may be taken as a guide to more general expectations concerning desirable attributes for the jury task, it appears that the foreman is expected to be a male, preferably a male of higher occupational status. Although we know of no empirical studies, we assume that the business discipline and related experiences of higher-status occupations involve both substantive knowledge and interactional skills that may be used during the deliberation. Hence, in the competition for the available deliberation time, higher-status males may rise to prominence because their comments are perceived to have greater value. On the other hand, since the cues of status—dress, speech, and casual reference to experiences—are easily read, the differentiation may in part be explained by these expectations instead of actual performance.

Jurors who spoke at greater length were perceived by respondents to be the jurors desired if they were on trial. This finding suggests that whatever the criteria used by the groups to regulate the contributions of their members, these criteria were broadly held. The different distribution of speaking time was achieved without serious violation of developing group norms. Further, choices made after face-to-face experience, in contrast with those based on occupational stereotypes, tended to smooth into a gradient which paralleled both activity rates and status.

SECTION TEN *The Courts*

46

Many Separate Courts in Metropolis

MAXINE B. VIRTUE

With the possible exception of delay, multiplicity of separate trial courts is the court problem identified as typical of metropolitan court systems by virtually all writers. From Archeion through Pound to the Tweed Commission, all have been concerned with the vast confusion of multifarious tribunals serving large population centers.

Typical is a recent comment of The Honorable David W. Peck, former Presiding Judge of the Supreme Court of the State of New York, Appellate Division:

> The historic practice, particularly in the large cities, has been to splinter and parcel out fields of jurisdiction among many courts of limited jurisdiction. The trend for a century has been to create rather than consolidate courts, to narrow rather than broaden jurisdiction, to divide rather than concentrate administrative authority. The result, in many places, is a conglomeration of courts, each autonomous in administration, confined but overlapping in jurisdiction.
>
> In many cities administration of the criminal law has been separated from administration of the civil law. Separate courts have been created for probate and estate proceedings and for domestic relations. There has even been an elaborate stratification of courts in the same legal line. New York City, for example, has three layers of courts in both the civil and criminal lines. The civil courts are divided by monetary limits. The criminal courts are divided by degrees of crime.
>
> Such a fragmented court organization, without flexibility in moving judges and cases about to achieve balance in distribution, and without centralization of administrative authority, lacks the elementary essentials of a court system. It is not a court system.[1]

As noted hereinabove,[2] fact studies conducted for the Section of Judicial Administration by this and other writers have confirmed other data demonstrating the existence of a plethora of autonomous judicial tribunals in most states—with California and New Jersey the notable exceptions—and that this multiplicity is most exaggerated in metropolitan areas.

> Reasons for the costly and inefficient piling up of courts include (1) retention of the outmoded justice of the peace system, (2) population shifts resulting in demand for new courts, and (3) ephemeral local pressures to create a new court

From *Survey of Metropolitan Courts: Final Report* (Ann Arbor: The University of Michigan Press, 1962), pp. 155–158. Reprinted by permission of The University of Michigan Press.

for each specialized set of issues. . . . "Sibling rivalry" among . . . governmental units, and heavy case loads in congested population centers, also contribute to the pressure for more courts.[3]

Examples may be found in *Family Cases in Court*[4] and *Children and Families in the Courts of New York City,*[5] *inter alia,* to indicate proliferation of narrowly specialized courts. It is notable that in most large metropolitan cities, however, the problem of the unreconstructed one-man lay justice court has not persisted. In that area, court reform has been at least nominally successful: in general, the municipal court as such has superseded the original justice courts, within the mother city itself.[6]

The problem of multiplicity within the mother city seems to consist partly of duplicating general trial courts set up to ease congestion, and partly of a piling up of separate highly specialized courts.

We have already noted that the problem of the specialized court wears two faces: to some extent, specialization is an informed recognition of the need for specialized attention to certain types of cases. But its other aspect presents the disadvantages of freezing specialized parts or departments of the general court into aggressively independent autonomies, narrowly specialized and so confirmed in their procedures and provincial in their specialties as to have defeated the original purpose of improving the quality of disposition of cases by segregating certain cases for specialized handling. Instead, at this extreme phase, we have all the disadvantages of multiplicity: waste, inefficiency, bureaucratism, lack of communication with other parts of government, and loss of public confidence.

It is this writer's conclusion, based on total contact with the court research projects, including discussions with lay and legal personnel, that the loss-of-confidence problem is in large part based on inadequate, cavalier, or fumbling attention to specialized cases by overspecialized personnel.[7] It may be significant that this particular aspect of the problem also occurs in the subject areas (small claims, family cases, petty criminal cases, mental cases) where one finds the largest part of the metropolitan caseload and where the services of attorneys are likely not to be a routine part of the court contact.

NOTES

1. Peck, "Court Organization and Procedures to Meet the Needs of Modern Society," *Indiana Law Journal,* XXXIII (1958), 182–183. Reprinted by permission.
2. See pp. 29, 45–47 *supra* and studies there cited. Worth repeating: Lepawsky found 556 autonomous tribunals in Chicago metropolitan area in 1932, 205 in Cook County alone. Virtue found 145 independent judicial tribunals in the Detroit metropolitan area in 1948–50. Compare Holbrook, *Los Angeles Study,* 8–9, having in mind that the major trial courts in California have recently been unified. Jackson notes 20,000 male magistrates and 3,000 women magistrates with over 1,000 courts; and, in addition, 27 police magistrates in the County of London, and eighteen Stipendiary Magistrates. Jackson, *Machinery of Justice in England,* pp. 130, 82–83. See *Bad Housekeeping,* I *et seq.* (over 250 judges in New York City alone); and see this

writer's *Family Cases in Court,* p. 53, Chart II (Court System of Cook County, Illinois); p. 5, Chart I (Court System of California); p. 116, Chart III (Court System of Indianapolis); pp. 175 *et seq.* (narrative description of court structural systems affecting family cases in Milwaukee, Ohio, Michigan); Talbott, *Intergovernmental Relations and the Courts,* a study of Minnesota Courts, especially pp. 23 *et seq.,* 47 *et seq.*

3. Virtue, "Improving the Structure of Courts," *Annals* CCLXXXVII (1953), 141.
4. See, for example, Virtue, *Family Cases,* pp. 178–179.
5. Gellhorn, *Children and Families in the Courts of New York City,* pp. 25 *et seq.*
6. Vanderbilt, *Minimum Standards,* pp. 309 *et. seq.;* and annual reports of the Director of State Committees of the Section of Judicial Administration supplementing Standards. The 1952 edition was published in paperback form as *Improvement of the Administration of Justice.*
7. Examples: the refusal by a juvenile court referee to give to a divorce court investigator any information concerning the existence or nature of juvenile court contact with two boys who were subjects of divorce court concern because of change-of-custody proceedings (Detroit); insistence by a mental division administrative clerk that a dubious commitment proceeding be consummated by immediate transfer of patient to state mental facility, for the reason that the local hospital needed the space (Detroit); a violent tongue-lashing administered by a traffic court judge to a nice elderly lady with a New England accent who had dared to request a court hearing (Los Angeles).

47

Justice Delayed . . .

HANS ZEISEL, HARRY KALVEN, JR., AND BERNARD BUCHHOLZ

Delay in the courts is unqualifiedly bad. It is bad because it deprives citizens of a basic public service; it is bad because the lapse of time frequently causes deterioration of evidence and makes it less likely that justice is done when the case is finally tried; it is bad because delay may cause severe hardship to some parties and may in general affect litigants differentially; and it is bad because it brings to the entire court system a loss of public confidence, respect, and pride. It invites in brief the wisecrack made a few years ago in a magazine editorial: "Okay, blind, but why so slow?" [1]

These are obvious evils and scarcely require a statement. But in addition, a delayed court system brings in its wake many not so obvious secondary evils. It produces an unhealthy emphasis on the desirability of settlement and on the

From *Delay in the Court* (Boston: Little, Brown and Company, 1959), pp. xxii–xxvi, 3–17. Reprinted by permission of the publishers.

impropriety of litigation. It creates a stimulus for major changes in substantive law and procedure, such as the abolition of jury trial in civil cases, or shifting large areas of tort law to compensation schemes analogous to workmen's compensation, or changing the rules as to contributory negligence as defense or payment of interest on tort damages. These proposals, whatever their merits, should not be adopted or rejected simply because of extrinsic pressures from a delayed court system. Again, extended delay may result in, indeed almost compel, departure from legal ethics, as lawyers find it necessary to provide financial support for indigent clients over the long interval between accident and trial. And a delayed calendar creates totally new issues for a court, as it seeks to determine what if any cases should be given preference and tried ahead of the others.[2] As Judge Ulysses S. Schwartz of the Illinois Appellate Court eloquently pointed out in a recent opinion, delay in the law is an old, old evil:

> The law's delay in many lands and throughout history has been the theme of tragedy and comedy. Hamlet summarized the seven burdens of man and put the law's delay fifth on his list. If the meter of his verse had permitted, he would perhaps have put it first. Dickens memorialized it in *Bleak House;* Chekhov, the Russian, and Molière, the Frenchman, have written tragedies based on it. Gilbert and Sullivan have satirized it in song. Thus it is no new problem for the profession, although we doubt that it has ever assumed the proportions that now confront us. "Justice delayed is justice denied," and regardless of the antiquity of the problem and the difficulties it presents, the courts and the bar must do everything possible to solve it.[3]

The trial calendars of the criminal courts are kept up to date because a prompt criminal trial is a constitutional requirement.[4] In civil litigation, however, a prompt trial is merely a desirable objective and the litigants themselves have no means of compelling it. No one intends or desires that there be delay in the disposition of civil litigation and no court system falls behind overnight. It is almost always an imperceptibly slow process, a yielding to many pressures. But once a court system suffers appreciable delay it has proved to be extremely difficult to reverse the process and make the system current again. And, if court delay begins as a pedestrian, homely problem of judicial housekeeping, it can grow to become a central concern of a court system and a political issue of importance.

Yet it is a political issue of curiously low intensity, not one that commandeers persistent political pressure on its behalf.[5] Nor is it difficult to see why this must almost inevitably be so. First, it does not hit an organized segment of the public. The majority of the public have little occasion to use the courts, and when they do it is a once-in-a-lifetime matter. Second, delay—at least in New York, as we shall see—characterizes only a small proportion of all litigation. It does not affect the criminal process or the equity process. And due to the special calendar arrangements in New York, it does not affect litigation other than the personal injury jury trial. And third, due to the fact that the courts of limited jurisdiction are reasonably current, delay in the end affects only a small fraction of personal injury litigation itself. Thus, even where delay has become so famous an issue as in New York, it affects probably not more than 5 or 6 per cent of the civil law trial calendar. Finally, the one group of the public that repeatedly experiences court delay are the corporate defendants and insurers who are persuaded that delay is not hostile to their self-interest. And it is not clear that the plaintiff bar really minds the delayed trial schedule either. It is therefore not surprising that there is no organized lobby agitating the delay issue and that serious concern over it has been left to the professionals, largely the judges themselves.

In any study of court congestion questions of tone are important. Concern with the elimination of delay must not blind us to the distinctive nature of the judicial enterprise. The administration of a court is not simply the administration of a business, judges are not simply employees, and the values of the efficiency expert are not the only ones involved. Thus, a few years back, Judge Learned Hand voiced the appropriate caution in a dissent against the too ready use of the summary judgment procedure:

> I cannot help wondering, whether there is not danger that [summary judgment] may not rather impede, than advance, the administration of justice. It is an easy way for a court with crowded dockets to dispose of them and the habit of recourse to it readily becomes a denial of that thorough, though dilatory, examination of the facts, on which justice depends even more than upon a studious examination of the law; for a mistake of law can always be reviewed. Speed and hurry ought to be antipodes of judicial behavior.

And yet deference to the subtle values involved should not make it inadmissible to recognize that the administration of justice too involves problems of management and efficiency. Judge Peck has come as close as perhaps one can to striking a balance between the competing concerns.

> The administration of justice is not a business in the sense of marketing—the machine-made and mass-produced; but it is a business in the very real sense of being affected in the quality, quantity, cost, and delivery of its product by the same factors that make any business a success or a failure.

• • •

The Approach

It is tempting to look for the causes of delay and to propose their removal as the solution to delay. Why is there court congestion? Whose fault is it? In the simplest terms, delay is a problem of supply and demand. If there is delay it must be because the demand for judge time has outrun the supply. At first blush, therefore, we would expect a study of delay to tell us that the court's business has increased more rapidly than its judge manpower, or that some factor has intruded that has slowed down the process of disposition which now takes more time than previously, or that judges work less than they used to, and so forth.

This report, however, has a quite different stance. It is, we have come to believe, an error in perspective to look for the causes of delay, especially where as in New York the court has been delayed for over half a century. Delay does not arise dramatically overnight so that it can be traced meaningfully to a set of specific causes. It is rather the result of a slow accretion of pressures, and by the time it has grown sufficiently to be a practical problem it seems no longer profitable to trace historically how it came about. To be sure, anything that might aggravate delay can be said to be a cause of it. It is fashionable to talk, for example, of the concentration of the trial bar as a cause; and, as we shall see, there is something to the point that conflicting trial commitments of busy counsel may produce gaps in the scheduling of trials and a loss of court time. Hence one may be tempted to blame the bar for the delay. But in this sense there are innumerable other causes of delay. Jury trials, as we shall see, do take somewhat longer than bench trials, and the use of impartial medical experts may facilitate settlement. But it is clearly a misuse of language to say that the jury trial and the adversary medical expert system are to blame for delay. One might equally say that the negligence law itself is a cause because it produces difficult and involved issues of liability for trial. In brief, we think the profitable concern is not with the allocation of blame but simply with an evaluation of the relative strength of the various proposals designed to remedy delay.

The emphasis on remedies carries with it one further emphasis. The one certain remedy for delay in any court system is the creation of a sufficient number of additional judgeships and it needs no special study to tell us that. But the question that deserves careful study is what can be done about court congestion apart from asking for additional judges. The creation of new judgeships raises complex political issues and is persuasive only as a last alternative. Only if there are no other avenues left for reducing delay is the case for additional judges compelling, since the maintenance of prompt justice for its citizens is a fundamental cost that society must bear. This study is primarily devoted to a systematic examination of remedies other than the ultimate one of additional judges.

Three Basic Possibilities

Any discussion of remedies must recognize a basic fact about the pattern of disposition of lawsuits.

To a startling degree the costs that matter are the costs of the cases that reach trial. The point here is that the majority of suits filed are settled voluntarily before trial and that relatively little court time is required for their disposition. To state this quantitatively for the New York Court: some 71 per cent of all suits are settled without trial, and the disposition of these cases requires only 16.2 per cent of the total court time. The problem of remedies for delay therefore is the problem of affecting that minority of cases that takes up the overwhelming majority of judge time. In the large, there are only three ways of doing this and thereby reducing delay: the time required for the disposition of cases can be shortened; the number of cases requiring official disposition can be reduced by affecting the settlement ratio; or the amount of available judge time can be increased, either by directly adding judges or by increasing somehow the efficiency with which the current judge power is now used.

It is true that if there were some way of reducing the number of controversies that arise between citizens, as for example by reducing the number of auto accidents, this would be a fourth avenue. But this seems to be so wholly beyond the powers of the court to affect that we put it aside.

Two simple but important conclusions follow. First, any effective remedy for delay must operate through one or more of these three basic channels. For example, a change in the rules as to the payment of interest on tort damages must, to affect delay, affect it by having an impact on the settlement ratio; proposals for comparative negligence must operate by affecting the jury waiver ratio, thus increasing the relative frequency of the speedier bench trial; proposals for reducing the concentration of the bar must operate by affecting gaps in trial scheduling, thus making more efficient use of the court's time. Second, unless a court system with a stable or growing delay applies one or more of these three basic remedies, it will continue to have delay.

The organization of the study is thus readily apparent. Part I is devoted to the first basic step, measuring the magnitude of the delay. The next three parts are devoted to the second basic step, evaluating the power of the various remedies: Part II deals with the remedies designed to speed up the trial process; Part III with the remedies designed to affect the settlement ratio; and Part IV with the remedies designed to increase the judge power available. The study concludes in Part V with a look at more general, related matters such as claim consciousness, legal experiments, and forecasting the future workload of a court. Only the first four parts are summarized in this chapter.

If this then is the basic approach and structure of the study, what are its principal conclusions?

The Magnitude of Delay: How Long a Wait?

First, as to measuring the magnitude of delay. There are a variety of possible measures—the size of the backlog of pending cases, the age of cases tried in regular order, the average age both of cases tried in regular order and of those given preferment. The size of the backlog, although frequently used in popular discussion, is, we are persuaded, wholly misleading; delay in regular order, although a useful, if rough, predictor for the litigant, fails to show the true efficiency of the court and overstates the magnitude of the delay; thus the average delay of both regular order and preferred cases emerges as the best time index of the magnitude of delay.

If we turn for the moment to the preferred case category, several interesting points come to light. A busy and hard-pressed metropolitan court, suffering delay, is likely to use the preference category for reducing the social costs of delay by giving the most urgent cases a reasonably prompt trial. But the result is to pose a new and difficult policy issue for the court allocating the bonus of a prompt trial. And in New York it is a striking characteristic of the system that not only individual cases but entire types of actions are granted preference. The New York Court has chosen to concentrate all of the delay on the personal injury jury calendar and to keep its other three trial law calendars up to date. The result is to grant blanket preferment to all commercial cases, whether jury or non-jury, and to all non-jury personal inquiry cases as well.

The costs of delay in New York are thus borne very differently by different types of litigants. And perhaps most important, the decision to delay only the personal injury jury calendar has resulted in the widespread misconception that the personal injury jury case is somehow the villain. This is, of course, an illusion created by the separate calendar arrangements. Had the Court elected to delay instead only the commercial case calendars or those for red-headed plaintiffs, it would equally appear that it was the commercial case or the red-headed plaintiff, that was the cause of it all.

If we now translate these comments into statistics, it appears that as of November, 1956, the main cutoff date for this study,[6] delay in regular order of personal injury jury cases was 39 months, a formidable figure; all other categories of cases were approximately current. Yet some 40 per cent of the cases within the personal injury jury calendar were given some preferment and for this group the average waiting period was only 16 months. If the two groups are averaged to reflect the efficiency of the Court, the overall delay on this calendar is 30 months. Finally if we average the delay across all four law trial calendars, the figure drops to about ten months. Thus, most measures used for delay tend to give a partial view and greatly exaggerate its magnitude. In New York this exaggeration is the difference between the 39-month and the ten-month figure.

The Magnitude of Delay: How Big a Job?

We have spoken thus far of the measurement of delay in the time dimension. However, if we are interested in finding out how much of an effort is required to remove delay another measure proves more useful. The time-measure of delay must be translated into a statement of the additional judge effort that would be needed to dispose of the accumulated backlog of cases. This poses, as we shall see, an interesting problem in forecasting and admits of a fairly exact estimate. For the New York Court the requirement is 11.7 judge years; this is the cardinal fact of the study and the pivotal figure for the subsequent discussion of remedies. (The "judge year" means the average workload of one judge during one court year.)

This figure immediately places the problem in perspective. Making available two more judges to the Court, for example, would eliminate the delay in under six years. Since the New York Court uses approximately 17 judges per year for its law trial functions, two judges mean an increase of about 12 per cent of the Court's judge power in its law division.

What emerges then from a systematic effort to measure the magnitude of delay is the simple but overriding conclusion that in New York—and we would guess in any delayed metropolitan court—delay properly measured reveals itself to be within the reach of practical solution. In this instance measurement has the benevolent consequence of cutting the problem down to size.

While study is indispensable for disclosing the exact additional judge power needed to cure delay, it needs no ghost come from the grave to tell us that delay can be cured by adding more judges. The main burden of this study, we repeat, is with the complex and interesting question: how much can be accomplished by using means other than the addition of judges?

Speeding up the Trial Process

To what extent can the trial process itself be speeded up? The most obvious and widely discussed possibility is a shift from jury to bench trial. The difference in length between jury and bench trial of the same case turns out to be a surprisingly difficult point to measure because no case, of course, is ever tried both ways. But a reasonable estimate by various procedures is that a bench trial is on the average about 40 per cent less time-consuming than a jury trial. If the extreme remedy of total abolition of jury trial in personal injury cases were adopted, the saving in the New York Court would be the equivalent of about 1.6 judges per year: and the delay would be removed in five to seven years, depending on whether the abolition of jury trial were made retroactive to pending cases.

These figures can be read in two ways, depending upon one's viewpoint as to the values of jury trial itself. They may impress some with the fact that jury trial is expensive in court time and that the abolition of jury trial offers an effective remedy for delay. Or they may be read, as we ourselves would incline to read them, as a price tag for the jury system. On this view, what is impressive is that the addition of only 1.6 judges per year would net the same impact on delay as the abolition of a basic institution. It may be added, though, that this figure, for reasons which will appear later, is particularly small for the New York Court, and will be relatively larger for most others.

In any event, the abolition of personal injury jury trials is a remedy not lightly to be adopted whatever the dimensions of court congestion. Inquiry therefore turns to the possibilities of inducing voluntary shift from jury to bench trial, that is, of increasing the jury waiver ratio. We conclude that in general little can be expected along this line. Under existing law either party can compel a jury trial if he wants one. Whether at least one party elects a jury trial depends to a substantial degree on whether juries are thought to, and in fact do, decide cases the same way judges would. On the best available evidence, it appears that they do not, and that the bar recognizes they do not. And this is particularly true with respect to damage issues in the personal injury field. Ingenious efforts such as the proposal for use of the comparative negligence formula in bench trials may reduce somewhat the anticipated difference between judge and jury trial, but it is most unlikely that by any such means these differences can be fully removed. And until they are, it will continue frequently to be to the advantage of one party to demand a jury trial. Hence, the decisive difficulty with remedies designed to increase the waiver ratio is that the consumer won't buy them.

It is true, of course, that remedies can be devised which would price the jury trial out of the market, as for example sharply raised fees and costs. But such remedies, since they involve penalizing those who wish a jury trial, are really coercive and but a short step away from compulsory abolition. Ironically the one method of increasing waiver that has worked is delay itself. In the New York Court, unlike in most other jurisdictions, the jury waiver ratio in personal injury cases is substantial, approximately 45 per cent; and this seems to be largely the result of the deliberate policy of giving trial preferences to non-jury personal injury suits.

It can thus be predicted that if the personal injury jury calendar were brought up to date, there would be a noticeable decrease in jury waiver. To the 11.7 judge years needed to remove the backlog, another 0.6 judge years annually must be added. This represents the time cost by which henceforth the reduction in the waiver ratio would increase the Court's annual workload.

The possibility of speeding up the jury trial itself has received far less attention than it merits. Several lines of evidence point to a considerable potential here. In New Jersey, roughly comparable cases are tried to a jury in approximately 40 per cent less time than in New York. The savings come not so much from differences in the obvious jury time costs, such as *voir dire* and instructions, as from differences in the internal trial process itself. This may in part result from the efficiency of the New Jersey pre-trial in narrowing issues for trial, although we have no evidence for this. Perhaps the single most surprising finding of the study is that this difference between jury trial in New York and in New Jersey is as large as the much advertised general difference between bench and jury trial. The inviting conclusion, therefore, is that the remedy for delay is not to abolish the jury trial but to speed it up.

Increasing the Settlement Ratio

So much then for the first of the three basic remedies. What about the second? To what extent can the settlement ratio be increased? The behavior underlying the settlement process is complex and warrants substantial further study. But several basic findings emerge from the work done thus far. Small changes in the settlement ratio would mean substantial changes in the Court's workload. We have seen that only 29 per cent of all suits filed reach trial, and that these require over 80 per cent of the judge time.

There is first an issue analogous to that noted with respect to waiver as to the effect of delay. Does delay itself increase settlement? Available evidence tends to support the conclusion that delay, unless it is of extreme magnitude, does not affect the settlement ratio. Hence, in New York at least, we need not fear that the reduction of delay will have an offsetting cost and bring an increasing number of trials into court. This does not mean that delay has no effect on settlement. It is self-evident that a delayed court permits the defendant to delay performance. Hence it will tend either to reduce the amount of settlement or to delay its date. Yet the proportion of claims settled eventually before they reach trial will not necessarily change.

One promising approach to the reduction of trials has been the introduction of the impartial medical expert, a procedure in which New York has in recent years pioneered. The procedure, by narrowing conflicting estimates of the medical facts in personal injury cases, should improve chances for settlement. And what evidence there is thus far lends support to this conclusion. It remains the more puzzling why some New York judges seem to be hesitant in using this trial saving procedure.

Another remedy designed to affect settlement has been the proposal to change the damage rules so as to allow interest in personal injury cases prior to the date of judgment. Here the expectation is that the threat of paying interest will make defendants more willing to settle. There is virtually no empirical evidence on this point at present. But it does permit of theoretical economic analysis. On the basis of such analysis we conclude with considerable confidence that changes in the interest rules will serve simply to change the amount of the settlement, but will not affect its frequency.

Undoubtedly the most widely discussed and widely used method for effecting settlement has been pre-trial. Judges who have had direct experience with it tend to be convinced that pre-trial is an important agency for bringing about settlement, and they point to the great number of cases that are settled at pre-trial. The exact impact of pre-trial on settlement, however, turns out to be an intricate puzzle that perhaps can be solved satisfactorily only by recourse to an official experiment. In brief, two considerations must be raised in any such evaluation of pre-trial. First, does pre-trial in fact bring about the settlement of cases that would otherwise not be settled? We know that the majority of cases are settled voluntarily before they reach the trial stage, and the apparent settlement effect of pre-trial might simply be a reflection of this basic settlement phenomenon. Various lines of evidence, however, persuade us that pre-trial does have some tendency to increase the settlement ratio.

The second consideration is more stubborn: pre-trial uses judge power that could otherwise be used directly in the trial of cases. The decisive question therefore is whether a judge at pre-trial can settle more cases (beyond those that would have been settled anyway) than he could have tried were he not engaged in pre-trial. If he cannot, it will be more profitable for a delayed court to devote this manpower to trial rather than to pre-trial. On the basis of the evidence available we are not yet prepared to say that pre-trial is effective enough in this respect to overcome the offsetting loss of direct judge trial time. In any event, it is clear that a system can rely too heavily on pre-trial and devote an unprofitable amount of judge power to it in a quest for settlement.

Four other points of interest about pre-trial emerge. First, pre-trial undoubtedly has the socially useful consequence of accelerating the settlement of cases that without it would have been settled later, though still before trial. Second, New York, although committed to the view that pre-trial is effective, uses it only on personal injury jury cases and not on cases on the other three calendars. This is perhaps another instance of the separate calendar arrangement leading to an illusion that only personal injury jury cases need special treatment because only they are delayed. Third, the settlement ratios at pre-trial vary greatly for individual judges. This in turn suggests that the format of pre-trial varies greatly not only by jurisdiction, as for example between the formal procedure in New Jersey and the informal procedure in New York and elsewhere, but even within a jurisdiction, depending on the skill and interest and viewpoint of the individual pre-trial judge. And fourth, there is a widespread feeling that the pressures of delay have deflected pre-trial from its original procedural purposes into little more than a bargaining session between opposing counsel and the judge.

Finally a word about the certificate of readiness, a procedure introduced in New York in 1956, following the example of the Federal District Court for the Southern District of New York. The procedure requires that several preliminary steps, including the discussion of settlement, take place before a suit is officially filed. It was hoped that this procedure would produce a "firmer" calendar by accelerating the settlement of cases that would have been settled later, thus eliminating last-minute adjournments. There was also some expectation that it might affect the settlement ratio itself. The full story on it is not yet in as we write but some conclusions have begun to emerge.

The certificate's impact on personal injury suits seems to have been a temporary one. After a sharp drop in filings, an equally sharp increase has kept their overall level unchanged. But its impact on the cases on the general calendar has been, it seems, a permanent one. It brought about a reduction in the number of filings and, more important, also in the number of cases that required trial. By this indirect route, then, more trial time became available for the disposition of the personal injury cases at which the certificate originally aimed. In this unexpected way, the certificate proved a successful remedy against delay. Why the certificate should affect contract cases but not personal injury cases is a subject for interesting speculation and possibly further research.

In general, though, the policy of increasing settlements must have its limits. At present, not quite five out of every 100 personal injury claims ever reach the trial stage, and not quite two are ever tried to completion. One may well wonder whether, if the proportion of trials be further reduced, cases would be settled and compromised which, in the interest of a living law, ought rather to be tried.

More Effective Use of Judge Time

We come to the last of the three generic remedies for delay: more effective use of judge time.

The most interesting and most delicate topic in this general area is whether judges could put in somewhat more time than they now do. It is realized that judges are not ordinary employees and that the problem, if the judiciary is to retain its dignity and independence, is not simply one of time-clock efficiency. From the records kept by the New York Court, however, it has been possible to make certain assessments of how much time is now lost. If we look first at the loss of whole trial days, it appears that the New York Court averaged 170 days out of a possible 196 or a loss ratio of about 13.4 per cent. As might be expected, the figures for individual judges vary substantially, suggesting that this time loss arises from factors personal to the judge as well as from scheduling gaps over which the individual judge would have little control.

A similar analysis can be made of the loss of hours per trial day. Here too the data vary by individual judges, indicating again that the loss results both from factors personal to the judge and from outside factors. The average judicial trial day for New York is 4.1 hours, and if all judges could be brought up to this average there would be a net increase of about 7 per cent in available judge time.

In many ways the most relevant comparison is to New Jersey, which can be taken as a yardstick of the most that might realistically be expected from more centralized and intensive judicial administration. The loss of trial days in New Jersey is 6.3 per cent as contrasted to 13.4 per cent for New York; the number of hours per trial day is 4.5 for New Jersey, as compared to the 4.1 figure for New York. If we combine both factors, it appears that New Jersey gets from its judges about 19 per cent more time than does New York, or the equivalent of three judges annually in terms of the New York Court. This does indicate that modest help could come from this quarter.

Another important possibility has already been noted. If all trial judges were to concentrate on personal injury jury cases until that calendar was no more delayed than the other three calendars, delay could be leveled across all calendars at a figure of about ten months. This "remedy" rests on nothing more than sharing judge time evenly for all categories of cases, but it raises a difficult issue of policy as to whether the preference given to commercial cases should be abandoned.

Much has been made of the concentration of the trial bar as a factor. The concentration of the bar is indeed an economic fact. A small minority of firms file a substantial fraction of all personal injury suits and a smaller minority actually handle a substantial fraction of all personal injury cases that go to trial. In the New York Court the busiest 1 per cent of the bar makes 6.4 per cent of the trial appearances, and some 5 per cent of the bar make over 20 per cent. But this economic concentration, whatever its significance for other issues, has less impact on court congestion than is popularly supposed. It can only affect delay insofar as it causes gaps in the trial scheduling process and we know from the study of judge time in the New York Court that such gaps cannot exceed a 19 per cent loss. Further, although the busiest part of the trial bar is relatively very busy, its trial commitments fall well below the limits of lawyer capacity. Thus even for the top 5 per cent, the trial burden in the New York Court is less than two cases per month. This does not mean, however, that concentration is not significant for delay. First, the impressions from the New York Court are misleading if taken alone. The same lawyers service several other courts in the New York area, and it appears that the New York County Supreme Court enjoys a preferred position among lawyers in the competition between courts. Second, the concentration is heavy enough at the top to multiply greatly the chances of conflicting trial commitments and thus seriously aggravate the problems of scheduling. In the end, the preferred solution appears to rest not on a direct attack on bar concentration but on two judicial policies: first, scheduling procedures that explicitly recognize the concentration as a fact and seek insofar as possible to accommodate it, and second, greater firmness in refusing continuances, thus placing back on the law firm the responsibility for being adequately manned.

In the course of the study we treat more briefly such other important possibilities as shifting cases from more busy to less busy courts, a procedure which in New York centers on keeping smaller cases in the courts of limited jurisdiction, and the alternative of shifting judges from less busy areas to more busy areas. These moves are facilitated by a centralized administrative control, but it appears that New York makes poor use of the power it already has. We discuss also the possibilities tried in Massachusetts, Pennsylvania, and Oklahoma, of adding judge power by creating temporary substitute judges in the form of auditors, arbitrators, or masters. Since these substitute judge schemes involve a direct adding of manpower to the adjudicating function, they are effective in reducing delay for the same simple reason the appointment of new judges is. Their appeal lies in the fact that they provide judicial machinery in a more flexible and temporary form and at lower cost. But they raise troublesome issues of basic policy. They smack of second-class justice; they involve self-abdication by the courts, and in any event bargain-rate justice is not the objective of the legal system.

Finally, we note that the summer session in 1956 was quite successful. With a burden of two weeks of extra time per individual judge over the summer, the session dispensed the equivalent of 1.5 judge years. The use of comparable summer sessions alone would eliminate delay in about 8 years. As a matter of magnitude, it is as effective a potential remedy for delay as would be the abolition of personal injury jury trials. But it appears that whatever the theoretical potential of this remedy, the customs and traditions of both bar and bench stand seriously in its way. New Jersey, when faced with an increased case load, increased the judges' daily working hours temporarily rather than resort to a summer session. Reducing the court's summer recess, incidentally, is the only congestion remedy tried in antiquity of which we have a record. But even then, in the year 43 A.D., the Emperor Claudius was unable to perpetuate the measure beyond one year's effort.

NOTES

1. *Colliers'* (June 14, 1952), p. 129.
2. In addition delay may contribute to the so-called "litigation neurosis" and impair the rate of recovery of the injured party.
3. *Gray v. Gray*, 6 Ill. App. 2d, 571, 578–579, 128 N.E. 2d 602, 606 (1955). We might add to Judge Schwartz's roster the report of the law's most distinguished poet laureate on what must have been easily the world's most delayed court. Goethe, after having received his *doctor juris* degree, practiced law for a while before the *Reichskammer* Court in Wetzlar, about which he writes in the twelfth chapter of his autobiography: "An immense mountain of swollen files lay there growing every year, since the 17 assessors were not even able to handle the current workload. Twenty thousand cases had piled up, 60 could be disposed of every year, while twice as many were added." It was not unusual for a case to remain on the docket for more than a hundred years. One, for instance, involving the city of Gelnhausen, began in 1459 and was in 1734 still waiting for the court's decision. A dispute between the city of Nuremberg and the electorate of Brandenberg had begun in 1526 and remained forever undecided when in 1806 the court was dissolved. The piteous state of the court created the unique profession of "solicitants" whose sole job it was to secure preferments for their clients. This custom resulted eventually in the jailing of its leading practitioner and in the removal of three judges from the court because of bribery.

   The effects of this delayed court on Goethe were profound and in the end salutary. It made him lose whatever taste he had for the law, gave him sufficient leisure (the court had 174 holidays annually) to fall into desperate love with Charlotte Buff, the heroine of *Werther,* the novel that was to catapult him firmly into world fame.
4. This study has not devoted attention to criminal procedures. However, it might well prove useful to survey the techniques used to keep the criminal courts current; see the remarks of Judge Laws, *Proceedings of the Attorney-General's Conference on Court Congestion and Delay in Litigation,* May 21–22, 1956, pp. 118–122 (hereinafter cited as *Attorney General's Conference.*)
5. The pattern appears to be to always appoint another committee to look into the problem and make recommendations. See Nims, "New York's Hundred Years Struggle for Better Civil Justice," *New York State Bar Bulletin,* XXV (1953), 83, summarizing the 25 commissions and committees that have reported some 30,000 pages on court reform over the century.
6. Many data in this study, however, are as recent as 1958.

48

Judicial Rules and the Volume of Business

LAWRENCE M. FRIEDMAN

Institutions have normal expectations with regard to their work load. They expect to meet with certain kinds of problems in the course of a day: they expect a certain amount of work, and no more. The number of employees, the equipment available, the organizational structure are all based on these expectations. If radically new problems arise, the institution may find it hard to adapt. Equally, if too many problems of a familiar kind arise, the institution faces a crisis.

An increase in volume is not necessarily trouble. For a department store, more business—up to a point—is a blessing. The store may hire more workers, open new branches, and add on to its buildings; however, if there were a severe labor shortage, or if floor space could not be added at a given location, then customers might be alienated by unpleasantness, crowds, poor service, and parking troubles.

The American judicial system is in the position of the department store that cannot hire new staff easily or expand its plant. It cannot, in other words, react to increased demand simply by giving additional service. This characteristic is generally true of *all* American courts, from the United States Supreme Court to the lowest trial court. The court system responds to new demands at a tortoise-like pace. For one thing, control over personnel is not vested in the courts themselves. The labor force is relatively fixed; a court cannot reproduce; it cannot expand out of "profits." Those who control the statute books and the purse strings have allowed court systems to grow only slowly over the years and have not allowed them to grow at all to meet the total *potential* demand for adjudication of disputes.

In the long run it is at least theoretically possible to multiply courts to keep up with changing demand. In the short run the difficulties are immense. The process of creating a new federal judgeship is laborious and delicate; it takes formal or informal action by the President, the Senate, the Senators of the proposed judge's state, and (in recent years) a committee of the American Bar Association. Sometimes a nomination is blocked or a new seat left vacant because of political quarrels not easily resolved. Even if all goes well, pressure on the docket is only slowly translated into new jobs.[1] State court capacity is

From "Legal Rules and the Process of Social Change," *Stanford Law Review*, XIX, No. 4 (April, 1967), 798–810. Copyright © 1967 by the Board of Trustees of the Leland Stanford Junior University. Reprinted by permission of the author and publishers.

generally as difficult to expand as federal court capacity. An increase in the number of judges may require authorization from the legislature, a good deal of political jockeying, new elections, and sometimes even a constitutional change. Moreover, judgeships are typically local in their jurisdiction, and there is no bureaucratic, rational management of the work load and the staff. If the docket in a rural county is virtually empty, what could be more logical than to shift the local judge, at least part-time, to the big city, where there is tremendous congestion in the courtroom? Yet, well into the second half of the twentieth century such responses were the exception rather than the rule; until recently no state was willing to create any central coordinating body to do this.[2]

Since the number of workers (judges and clerks) is fixed, in the short run at least, courts do not have defenses against sharply rising demands. They cannot expand and contract automatically in response to the ebb and flow of litigation. Nor has there been any significant technological improvement to help the courts handle classic kinds of cases in mass. The legal system has therefore had to evolve devices and strategies to prevent a crisis in numbers.

Costs of Litigation

It is worth dwelling on gross historical changes in the character of court dockets in order to illustrate the means of meeting excessive demands for judicial services. A century ago commercial litigation made up much of the ordinary work of both trial and appellate courts. The tremendous growth in population, wealth, and commercial-industrial activities that occurred from 1850 on created such a potential for overburdening the courts that one of the following events had to happen: (1) expansion of the court system; (2) routinization and mass handling of commercial matters in the courts; (3) routinization and mass handling of commercial matters *outside* the courtroom; (4) use or expansion of a policy in favor of settlements to control the volume of litigation; (5) development of efficient dispute-settling mechanisms external to the judicial system; (6) adoption by courts or the imposition upon courts of substantive rules whose effect would be to discourage litigants from using the courts; or (7) increases in the costs of litigation sufficient to reduce its volume.

The first alternative was never adopted. No radical expansion of the court system occurred. The second was adopted where appropriate (in garnishment and collection actions, for example).[3] The third alternative was in some ways the dominant response of the business world—the rationalization of business practices through the development of standard forms and patterns of doing business. The permissive attitude of the courts toward these devices made good sense ideologically, economically, and institutionally.

The effective use of the fourth alternative is difficult to measure. Its existence is evidenced, however, by the constantly enunciated proposition that the law favors settlement rather than litigation and by the fact that it is an unethical—even criminal—act to stir up lawsuits.[4] It is somewhat paradoxical for an institution to declare so emphatically that public policy favors avoiding its use.

There are many reasons other than case-load reasons why non-coerced settlements are preferable to trials. Yet it is also true that if no cases were settled out of court the judicial system as presently constituted could not sustain its share of the dispute-settling business.

The fifth solution, development of extrajudicial mechanisms for settling disputes, is exemplified by the rise of commercial arbitration.[5] The sixth solution, adoption of "hostile" substantive rules, is far more difficult to attest. The seventh, increases in the cost of litigation, is often overlooked, but its institutional impact has been very great. Yet the trend toward judicial substitutes, and the acceptance by the courts of commercial routinization and extrajudicial settlement, is not related to this final factor, the rise in the cost of litigation.

In 1851 the Wisconsin Supreme Court heard a case in which a laborer sued to collect a wage of $6.25.[6] Even then, the case was something of an anomaly; it would be quite unthinkable today, except as a spite case or a test case. In the twentieth century the cost of using the judicial process, especially if an appeal is made, is so high that it acts as a significant barrier against litigation that does not measure its outcome in the thousands of dollars.

The major commercial and industrial interests can afford some recourse to litigation, but they avoid the courts as much as they can. Litigation is expensive in more than dollars spent on lawyers, witness fees, court costs, and the like. It is expensive in business good will and disruptive of ongoing business relationships.[7] These undesirable effects led to the decline of commercial litigation even for those who were not deterred by the costs of actual litigation. Thus, though the tremendous expansion of business could have led to an appetite for litigation far beyond the capacities of the courts, the rising price of going to court has prevented this from happening.

With the decline of commercial litigation, the slack in the dockets was more than taken up with tort cases. In the late nineteenth century industrial accidents became a major producer of litigation. Cases of injury, death, or permanent disability were often settled, but the absence of a continuing relationship between the parties made for a situation in which a combination of costs of litigation and various, restrictive rules (such as the fellow-servant rule) did not choke off the total volume of litigation as efficiently as had been the case for commercial litigation. Jury freedom and the contingent-fee system neutralized the costs of litigation and the severity of common-law tort rules often enough to guarantee an enormous case load.[8] The volume and acrimony of accident litigation came to be perceived as a problem by capital and labor alike.

Industrial accident law was unsatisfactory to the courts as well. First, existing law did not ration justice efficiently enough to avoid a problem of volume. Second, that law did not attain (in the view of more and more judges) equitable substantive ends. Therefore, the system imposed upon the courts a task which they could not and did not perform well, and any such task is a threat to an institution which the institution must avoid, delegate, or remove. The eventual solution (slow to develop because of the conflict of interest between business and labor) was a workmen's compensation system—a relatively stable compromise between the needs of capital and labor and a rough solution as well to the institutional problem of the courts. The first of these statutes was enacted in the United States about 1910; [9] the last state (Mississippi) passed its law in 1948.[10] Workmen's compensation attempted to solve the problem of volume by delegating adjudication and fact-finding to a commission of experts, fully staffed and unhampered by the conventions of court law, and by reducing liability and the amount of recovery to amounts automatically determinable, thus making routinization of the work load possible.[11] Litigation remaining in the courts has turned out to be heavier than hoped; nonetheless, it is less absolutely and proportionately than at the turn of the century.

In the twentieth century, cases arising out of automobile accidents came to dominate the civil dockets. Here too the quantity of litigation is imperfectly routinized and imperfectly controlled by high litigation costs, and progress toward a "solution" (institutionally speaking) is slow, perhaps because there is neither real agreement on the proper substitute nor a strong, organized movement toward one goal.[12] On the trial level, dockets are crowded with accident cases, and the delay between docketing and trial can run into years in some large cities.[13] Although the congestion and delay in the courts have been widely criticized, the problem seems manageable in the short run. Of course, many pending cases are settled before they ever come to trial. It is especially apparent in accidental-injury cases, where the litigant rarely has an interest in the "principles" of law involved, that the economic man would rather settle for ten dollars than sue for 15 dollars, bearing in mind how much it will cost him in time and money to see the matter through the courts. The very fact of congestion is an element of cost—sometimes cruel and unjust. Thus congestion itself encourages settlements and prevents congestion from becoming even worse.

That certain phenomena serve a rationing function in the legal system does not mean that they are ethically "correct," except in the special, narrow sense that they avoid or postpone radical institutional adjustments. One major drawback of allowing the price of litigation to reduce the volume of business is that it rations resources along class lines as well as along lines of preference. If everybody had equal resources at his disposal, a rise in the price of legal remedies would merely eliminate litigation of marginal value to the litigants. A high price for opera tickets will induce some people who could "afford" the opera to go to ball games and musical comedies instead, or to stay home with a book. But in a society with inequality of resources, some people will be unable to go to the opera, no matter how strong their desires. In the legal system, the high price of litigation means that litigation is not a practical method of resolving disputes for the average man.

This state of affairs is not necessarily a major problem for every society. A society may organize its legal system in such a way that different institutions for settling disputes are available for different ethnic groups, occupational groups, or social classes. The medieval common law, for example, was in essence composed of rules and institutions by, for, and of the upper class. The lower classes, indeed, were quite outside the royal common law; its rules did not apply to their affairs, and its institutions were beyond their grasp and their pocketbooks. Not that life below the top was lawless. Quite the contrary. There was an important system of minor local courts, some of them highly informal, which deserved the title of courts of law just as much as the royal courts that usurped the name and the attention.[14] But these local institutions did not apply the same system of rules. Just as a single, unitary nation-state is the product of more or less recent times, so is the growth of a single, unitary legal system that is relatively classless in the sense that rules do not *explicitly* distinguish between litigants on the basis of their income and station in life.

It is true and will perhaps always remain true that most affairs of life are governed by sanctions that operate automatically or without the use of formal institutions of enforcement. But the development of a single, middle-class system of law and legal institutions (rigorously controlled by a cost-rationing device) means that some social goods that are conditioned upon use of the legal process (a divorce, for example) may be beyond the reach of many members of society. Thus the high price of litigation carries its own high price: the denial, in some areas, of justice to the poor. A middle-class democratic society may consider such a situation inherently evil. To avoid this result, many forms of subsidy have been devised—legal aid, public defenders, and small claims courts, among others. Some have successfully broadened access to the legal system; some have not.[15] The recent growth of interest in improving and widening these subsidies is a recognition that some minimum of legal care should be available to the whole population, regardless of price.

The problem of defining a minimum is not peculiar to legal services; all products considered socially important and yet rationed by price (for example, medical care) present similar problems. Free vaccinations—but usually not free psychoanalysis—are provided by the state to those who cannot afford or are unwilling to buy medical care. The movement to provide legal services for the poor man faces the difficult task of deciding what kinds of legal service must be subsidized, and to what degree. There is wide agreement that a poor man arrested for murder needs and should have a good lawyer.[16] Whether a poor man needs or deserves a free divorce, a free civil action against his landlord, or a free claim for damages for invasion of privacy is more difficult to decide and to justify.

The price device has on the whole been useful, however. The price of the law is a factor which, along with the formal and technical structure of the legal system, tends to keep legal and social change relatively even-paced, orderly, and free from caprice. In addition, the cost of litigation has tended to increase the predictability of the consequences that will flow from the acts of private parties.

A legal rule, of course, does not change automatically; it must be challenged, or at least an occasion must be presented at which an authoritative agency has an opportunity to change the rule, even if the rule itself is not directly challenged. Many judge-made and statutory rules, however, are never brought before courts for interpretation or review. It is, in the main, the cost of litigation that shields these rules from change. Otherwise, the inherent uncertainties in the conduct of American trials would expose these rules to challenge. Even where the outcome of a case is quite clear in terms of legal theory, a litigant must reckon with a number of intangibles that affect his actual probabilities of success. The judge and his personality, the jury and its quirks, the possibility that the other party or his witnesses will commit perjury in a persuasive manner, the ineptness of one's own attorney, accidents and miscalculations at the trial are all risks of litigation. The same uncertainties apply to evidentiary facts that before trial appear quite certain. In a legal system where courts and lawyers were free and available to all it might be worthwhile to sue for relatively trivial sums or (what is more important here) on the basis of causes of action with slim probabilities. Of course, even in such a system, powerful informal sanctions would prevent the overwhelming majority of potential suits. Friends would not sue each other for the small damages occasioned by an accidental nudge in the ribs, even if the nudge amounted to a technical assault. Many defendants might plead guilty to avoid the shame, degradation, and risk of open trial. Businessmen in profitable relationships would not sue each other for small deviations from precise contractual duties. But, clearly, in such a system many actions would be brought that would not be brought under the present system, and hence the number of opportunities of upsetting established rules would be greater.

One may look upon a rule of law as a potential command to certain subjects, a command that may be obeyed, ignored, or disputed. But to challenge the rule is costly, especially if the challenge includes litigation. A simple rule of the road—like the rule requiring drivers to keep to the right on a highway—is formally clear-cut. One does not challenge this rule of the road because the likelihood of overturning it or of modifying its meaning is simply too slight to be worth the effort. Some rules equally clear-cut in form are unclear in operation or effect, because of a judicial gloss added in the course of repeated litigation. This encourages challenges to the validity and scope of the rule. Such a fate, for example, has overtaken the Statute of Frauds.

On the other hand, if litigants, for whatever reason, feel strongly enough about an issue to challenge the averages, then the outcome of the suit does take on an element of uncertainty. But the cause of this uncertainty resides not only in the inherent uncertainty of lawsuits, but in the very *fact* that somebody bothers to sue. If the plaintiff is an isolated eccentric, he will almost surely lose his suit, and the rule at issue will remain unchanged. But if enough people hammer away at a rule which (in theory) is "well settled," they stand a good chance of unsettling the rule, for we would then have to ask: Why are so many people hammering away at this "settled" rule? Either they or their lawyers sense a possible change in the direction of the law, or the matter is so vital to the litigants that they cannot or will not face "reality." Pioneers in civil rights cases and reapportionment cases—or in any case in which litigants have persistently challenged "settled" rules—show something of this intensity. And in the cases mentioned, there were indeed powerful forces seeking legal change. The costs of access to the legal system support the legal status quo, but they do not shut off all avenues of evolution. These costs act as a conservative force, or, more accurately, a channeling force; they limit access to the courts only to recognized causes of action and to unrecognized causes of action that have many or unusually intense adherents.

In many trial court cases, of course, only facts are at issue, not doctrine. Here too, a litigant must assess his probability of success, in relation to the stakes. A fact, like a rule, is real and certain to the extent it goes unchallenged. Some "facts" are more certain than others in the sense that the evidence supporting them is convincing. But the strength of the evidence is only one influence on the likelihood that a fact will go unchallenged. Even a "fact" certain beyond any reasonable doubt will be challenged if the stakes are high enough. A man charged with first-degree murder is highly likely to plead not guilty and ask for a jury trial. The stakes are high for him—perhaps even life itself. The costs, pains, and uncertainties of a lawsuit may be outweighed by the chance —however small—of saving his neck.

A related effect of the costliness of the American legal system is the development of what we might call networks of *reciprocal immunities,* which help define and stabilize many common, continuing relationships. For example, the formal legal relationships of a landlord and his tenant are spelled out in their lease. Minor infractions of duty on either side may amount to breaches of the lease, but *both* parties are protected—and given wide freedom of action in fact if not in theory—by the costliness, in money and disruption, of claiming one's "rights." So the tenant can play his radio late at night, keep a dog, and perhaps even move out a month before his lease expires without lawsuit or threat of lawsuit. And the landlord can delay small repairs or shut down the heat while the boiler is fixed without losing a tenant or suffering a lawsuit. This network of reciprocal immunities is beneficial to both parties.

Not all such networks are necessarily mutually advantageous. For example, a relationship may be so one-sided in power or authority that adverse social consequences flow from it, or many people may feel that enforcement of law or rule must be undertaken for social reasons regardless of the wishes of the immediate parties. Thus, the law of landlord and tenant is often said to be unfair to the poor tenant. The reciprocal immunities of landlord and tenant, together with the operation of a vigorously effective real estate market, permit patterns of fairly smooth and equitable transactions for middle-class and upper-class tenants (except perhaps during periods of critical imbalance in housing production). The main reason why the law is unfair to poor tenants is because, being poor, they cannot bring leverage to bear against their landlords. The call for subsidy of tenants' rights is a call for means to break through the wall of immunities—just as the criminal law is a subsidization of sanctions so that (among other things) strangers are not free to steal slightly from each other, protected from punishment or redress by a wall of cost or social relations.[17] Although the system of reciprocal immunities may operate to the detriment of some segments of society, its virtue lies in the fact that it allows for a reservoir of potentially valuable rights. Those rights can be enforced whenever there are high stakes or high intensity of desire for enforcement among bearers of the rights. Otherwise they remain below the threshold of that enforcement rate that would seriously disturb social relations among parties.

Jurisdictional and Procedural Rules

Up to this point, we have discussed how increases in the price of litigation are related to the specific institutional problem of volume of business. Jurisdictional and procedural rules also control the volume of business in courts. Procedural formality adds to the cost of litigation by making lawyers necessary and by requiring time-consuming effort on the part of litigants. A trial of an issue in court results in the risk of public condemnation as well as the chance of public vindication. Procedural technicality increases the difficulty of winning a lawsuit, adds an element of chance to litigation, and in turn increases the uncertainty of outcome, which is a critical element in cost. Procedural technicality as a cost-producing device characterized English royal law in the medieval period. It is much less tolerated in modern law, which has an ideological commitment to rationality and efficiency.

Jurisdictional rules are widely used to control directly the volume of upper-court business. The United States Supreme Court keeps its work load within bounds through its power over its docket. Since 1925 the case load of the Court has been almost completely discretionary.[18] The Court may turn down cases which it deems too trivial, as well as those it deems too controversial to handle at the moment. The Court's right to refuse to hear controversial cases is the right to prevent substantive institutional crisis; the right to refuse to hear vast numbers of trivial cases is the right to prevent a crisis in volume.

The Supreme Court's freedom to choose its cases is unusual, corresponding to the unusual demands that potentially might be made upon the Court. In some states, statutes define which types of cases appellate courts *must* hear and which are discretionary. The lower the court, the less in general its leeway. As we have mentioned, courts (high and low) have been relatively inflexible institutions; they have been unable to increase productivity or staff. Limitations on the docket, or discretionary control of the docket, have allowed upper courts to retain their classic style of weighty deliberation and reasoned opinions. Lower courts, lacking the freedom of their appellate brothers and more vulnerable to the pressures of excess business, have had to countenance more and more informal processes, which—whatever other virtues they may have—succeed in limiting the docket to manageable size.

Of course, judicial institutions are not inherently incapable of handling great quantities of "cases." Mass-handling techniques can indeed be used for some kinds of business. If the social interest in rapid, efficient processing is superior to the social interest in carefully individuated justice, it is certainly possible to devise mass-production legal methods. The traffic courts, for example, handle a tremendous flow of business. Their work is mostly quite routine. The "trial" has been reduced to a formula, a vestige. Parking tickets can be paid by mail in many cities. Other lower courts handle garnishments, debt collections, and wage assignments in fantastic numbers. Probate judges in urban centers sign hundreds of routine orders and forms each session; simple hearings on heirships and intermediate accounts are delegated to clerks or assistants.

The procedures used by courts in "trials" of this kind resemble more the procedures of record-handling and processing offices than the procedures of a court handling a murder trial or a large antitrust suit. The traffic ticket is processed on as perfunctory a basis as the recording of a deed in a county recorder's office. That one task is handled by a "court" and the other by an "office" is not often a fact of much functional importance. If one defines a court as an institution that weighs evidence, hears disputes, and renders carefully reasoned judgments, perhaps traffic and probate courts are not courts at all, but the epigones of courts, retaining from a more vital day their titles and customs. If so, then these "courts" represent not so much an adaption of judicial institutions to mass processing of routine matters, but rather an abandonment of the judicial system. The difference depends solely upon one's definition of a court.

Abandonment of the judicial system, or at least of traditional judicial procedures, has indeed been historically one major social response to the pressures of increasing business. Some work has been transferred to private institutions of conciliation; some to different agencies of government. The boards and commissions that handle industrial accident or social security claims, for example, are dealing with matters that at one time were handled, if at all, through litigation initiated by private parties. In most cases of removal of jurisdiction to administrative bodies, the courts retain a right of review—prestigious, but relatively powerless. Of course, a shift in institutional focus is more than a matter of jurisdiction. As industrial accident law shifted from court to commission, the substantive content of the rules changed too. Indeed, that was one point of the transfer. But the new rules were such that the courts would have been hard pressed to administer them without severe distortion of their classic structure.

Courts also have the power to shut off litigation by adopting a *rule of refusal* —that is, a rule refusing to acknowledge as valid a particular cause of action. Frequently, judges defend a particular rule by arguing that to abandon it would bring on an unmanageable flood of new cases.[19] This argument can be and no doubt often is nothing more than a rationalization disguising some judicial policy choice that remains unarticulated, but it is heard so frequently that it must be at least sometimes honestly put forth. At least *sometimes* courts must deliberately adopt a rule of refusal precisely because they fear being "overwhelmed." The unspoken premise is that society will suffer if the courts are overwhelmed. A further premise is that society will be unable to rescue the courts from suffocation. Yet society certainly has the power to create an unlimited number of bypass institutions. What the courts may mean (even if they do not say so) is that a rule of refusal will preserve the institutional integrity of the courts as they now exist.

To a limited degree, such fears are justified. Rules of refusal may be needed to keep the flow of work through courts in a manageable state. Whether society benefits is another question; perhaps it is good, in some instances, to avoid short-run dislocations and institutional imbalance. Conversely, rules of refusal are harmful if the court's perception of the volume of potential business is wrong, if the claim that has been refused is otherwise justified, and if other institutions are incapable of meeting the demand in the short run. Thus, the Supreme Court might have made a dangerous mistake had it adopted a rule of refusal in the school segregation cases, fearful of the institutional consequences of so grave a decision. The Justices probably believed in their hearts that segregation was morally wrong and constitutionally unsupportable; civil rights groups had failed to get satisfaction in the legislatures; and the Court in fact weathered the crisis. Of course, it is easy to see now that 12 years have passed that the Court survived the crisis stronger than ever. It was not so easy to predict at the time.

Brown v. Board of Education [20] is an excellent example of the impact of a rule of *reception* (as opposed to *refusal*) on litigation. Since the Court in effect opened up a whole new area of law, it invited Negro organizations and individual Negro plaintiffs to use litigation for an attack on this or that aspect of segregation. Such litigation had already been frequent, but the frequency now increased. Federal dockets, particularly in the South, were materially affected by many complicated, controversial cases on segregation in schools, parks, and other public facilities. It can truthfully be said that the result of the rule of reception was to create an additional demand for court services. We must be careful, however, not to overemphasize the word "create." Demand is created, not by the courts, but by society. Certainly, a Supreme Court decision that puts in question the validity of certain kinds of criminal convictions will induce numbers of petitions for redress on the strength of the new doctrine, but the basic desire of prisoners for release was not created by the Court's decision. Nor is the Court to be praised or blamed for such important social events as the rise of Negro protest movements or the sexual frankness of the modern novel. Obviously, specific Supreme Court and state court decisions strongly influenced some strategies taken by the Negro protest movement, and others encouraged bold publishers to print increasingly erotic works. Obviously, too, specific court actions play a role in social movements by sharpening public perception of problems and solutions and by directing attention to the subjects of particular litigation. But the underlying drives come to and not from the courts.

In an important—even vital—sense, a court does not control its potential docket, simply because it does not control its society. It is a member-institution in society, but not the guiding one. To do its job a court must walk a tightrope. It must be able to cope with crises or to avoid them, but it must not evade and avoid so ruthlessly as to diminish its reason for survival and lapse into ceremonial triviality (like the English sovereign). Nor must it grapple with crises in such a way as to arouse forces powerful enough to destroy it. The United States Supreme Court is in a particularly delicate position compared to other courts. It has controlled its volume of work to the point that ordinary litigation no longer reaches it. Its normal docket consists of extraordinary cases, and the necessity for striking a balance between too much avoidance and too much boldness is all the more delicate.

NOTES

1. See generally J. Grossman, *Lawyers and Judges* (New York: John Wiley and Sons, Inc., 1965).
2. See A. Vanderbilt, *Minimum Standards of Judicial Administration* (The Law Center of N.Y.U. for the National Conference of Judicial Counsels, 1949), pp. 32–64. Over the last century or so American law has in general resisted taking steps to make the role of a judge more like that of a civil servant (an employee and subordinate of the state) than that of an independent, free professional whose career lines and prestige derive from his relation to the bar, rather than to the state. See Friedman, "An American Tragedy: The Trial of Jack Ruby," *Wisconsin Law Review* (1966), p. 1188.
3. See Brunn, "Wage Garnishment in California," *California Law Review* LIII (1965), 1214.
4. For example, California Penal Code § § 158–159 (West, 1956): punishing "the practice of exciting groundless judicial proceedings;" American Bar Association canon 28; H. Drinker, *Legal Ethics* (1953), pp. 63–66.
5. On the advantages of commercial arbitration, see M. Domke, *Commercial Arbitration* (1965), pp. 8–12.
6. *Martin v. Martin,* 3 Pin. 272 (Wis., 1851).
7. See Macaulay, "Non-Contractual Relations in Business: A Preliminary Study," *American Sociological Review,* XXVIII (1963), 55.
8. See Friedman and Ladinsky, "Social Change and the Law of Industrial Accidents," *Columbia Law Review,* LXVII (1967), 50.
9. N.Y. Sess. Laws 1910, ch. 674 (declared invalid in *Ives v. South Buffalo Ry.,* 20 N.Y. 271, 94 N.E. 431 (1911)); N.Y. Sess. Laws 1913, ch. 816.
10. Miss. Laws 1948, ch. 354, §§ 1–53.
11. See W. Dodd, *Administration of Workmen's Compensation* (1936), pp. 16–26.
12. See W. Blum and H. Kalven, *Public Law Perspectives on a Private Law Problem— Auto Compensation Plans* (1965); Franklin, Chanin and Mark, "Accidents, Money, and the Law: A Study of the Economics of Personal Injury Litigation," *Columbia Law Review,* LXI (1961) 1.
13. See A. Levin and E. Woolley, *Dispatch and Delay* (1961); H. Zeisel, H. Kalven, and B. Buchholz, *Delay in the Court* (1959).
14. See the materials printed in Maitland and Baildon, eds., *The Court Baron* (1891); Maitland, ed., *Select Pleas in Manorial and Other Seignorial Courts* (1889).
15. The small claims court finds its heaviest use not by the poor, but in small claims against the poor. For documentation of the heavy use of small claims court by unsecured creditors such as doctors and grocers, see Rapson, "The Dane County Small Claims Court" (Unpublished thesis in the University of Wisconsin Library, 1961).
16. See *Gideon v. Wainwright,* 372 U.S. 335, 344 (1963); Black, J.: "[T]he widespread belief that lawyers in criminal courts are necessities, not luxuries." See Carlin, Howard, and Messinger, "Civil Justice and the Poor: Issues of Sociological Research," *Law and Society Review,* I (1966).
17. Note that some instances of petty theft, particularly by juveniles or neighbors, or

DAVID SUDNOW | 389

the children of neighbors, will probably be forgiven; and employers ignore the fact that white-collar employees take home pencils, pads, and other inexpensive items of office equipment.

18. Act of Feb. 13, 1925, ch. 229, 43 Stat. 936, as amended, 28 U.S.C. § 1254 (1964). On the history of Court's jurisdiction, see F. Frankfurter and J. Landis, *The Business of the Supreme Court* (1928).

19. The argument is generally combined with substantive arguments. Thus, in *Pavlinko's Will,* 394 Pa. 564, 148 A.2d 528 (1959), Justice Bell announced that "[o]nce a Court starts to ignore or alter or rewrite or make exceptions to clear . . . provisions of the Wills Act in order to accomplish equity and justice in that particular case, the Wills Act will become a meaningless, although well intentioned, scrap of paper, and the door will be opened wide to countless fraudulent claims which the Act successfully bars." The court denied probate of the will of Vasil Pavlinko, who signed his wife's will (essentially identical to his) by mistake. A contrary decision, of course, would hardly have been an invitation to "countless fraudulent claims."

20. 347 U.S. 483 (1954).

49

The Public Defender

DAVID SUDNOW

Recently, in many communities, the burden of securing counsel has been taken from the defendant.[1] As the accused is, by law, entitled to the aid of counsel, and as his pocketbook is often empty, numerous cities have felt obliged to establish a public defender system. There has been little resistance to this development by private attorneys among whom it is widely felt that the less time they need spend in the criminal courts, where practice is least prestigeful and lucrative, the better.[2]

Whatever the reasons for its development, we now find, in many urban places, a public defender (P.D.) occupying a place alongside judge and prosecutor as a regular court employee. In the county studied, the P.D. mans a daily station, like the public prosecutor, and "defends" all who come before him. He appears in court when court begins and his "clientele," composed without regard for his preferences, consists of that residual category of persons who cannot afford to bring their own spokesmen to court. In this county, the "residual" category approximates 65 per cent of the total number of criminal cases. In a given year, the 12 attorneys who comprise the P.D. Office "repre-

From "Normal Crimes: Sociological Features of the Penal Code in a Public Defender Office," *Social Problems,* XII, No. 3 (Winter, 1965), 255–276. Reprinted by permission of the author and publisher.

sent" about 3,000 defendants in the municipal and superior courts of the county.

While the courtroom encounters of private attorneys are brief, businesslike, and circumscribed, interactionally and temporally, by the particular cases that bring them there, the P.D. attends to the courtroom as his regular work place and conveys in his demeanor his place as a member of its core personnel.

While private attorneys come and leave court with their clients (who are generally "on bail"), the P.D. arrives in court each morning at nine, takes his station at the defense table, and deposits there the batch of files that he will refer to during the day. When, during morning "calendar," [3] a private attorney's case is called, the P.D. steps back from the defense table, leaving his belongings in place there, and temporarily relinquishes his station. No private attorney has enough defendants in a given court on a given day to claim a right to make a desk of the defense table. If the P.D. needs some information from his central office, he uses the clerk's telephone, a privilege that few private lawyers feel at home enough to take. In the course of calendar work, a lawyer will often have occasion to request a delay or "continuance" of several days until the next stage of his client's proceedings. The private attorney addresses the prosecutor via the judge to request such an alteration; the P.D. talks directly over to the D.A.:

> PRIV. ATTY.: "If the prosecutor finds it convenient your Honor, my client would prefer to have his preliminary hearing on Monday, the 24th."
> JUDGE: "Is that date suitable to the district attorney?"
> PROS.: "Yes, your honor."
> PRIV. ATTY.: "Thank you, your Honor."
>
> P.D.: "Bob (D.A.), how about moving Smith's prelim up to the 16th?"
> PROS.: "Well, Jim, we've got Jones on that afternoon."
> P.D.: "Let's see, how's the 22nd?"
> PROS.: "That's fine, Jim, the 22nd."

If, during the course of a proceeding, the P.D. has some minor matter to tend to with the D.A., he uses the time when a private attorney is addressing the bench to walk over to the prosecutor's table and whisper his requests, suggestions, or questions. The P.D. uses the prosecutor's master calendar to check on an upcoming court date; so does the D.A. with the P.D.'s. The D.A. and P.D. are on a first name basis and throughout the course of a routine day interact as a team of co-workers.

While the central focus of the private attorney's attention is his client, the courtroom and affairs of court constitute the locus of involvements for the P.D. The public defender and public prosecutor, each representatives of their respective offices, jointly handle the greatest bulk of the court's daily activity.

The P.D. office, rather than assign its attorneys to clients, employs the arrangement of stationing attorneys in different courts to "represent" all those who come before that station. As defendants are moved about from courtroom to courtroom throughout the course of their proceedings (both from municipal to superior courtrooms for felony cases, and from one municipal courtroom to another when there is a specialization of courts, such as jury, non-jury, arraignment, and so on), the P.D. sees defendants only at those places in their paths when they appear in the court he is manning. A given defendant may be "represented" by one P.D. at arraignment, another at preliminary hearing, a third at trial and a fourth when sentenced.

At the first interview with a client (initial interviews occur in the jail where attorneys go, *en masse,* to "pick up new defendants" in the afternoons), a file is prepared on the defendant. In each file is recorded the charge brought against the defendant and, among other things, his next court date. Each evening attorneys return new files to the central office where secretaries prepare court books for each courtroom that list the defendants due to appear in a given court on a given day. In the mornings, attorneys take the court books from the office and remove from the central file the files of those defendants due to appear in "their court" that day.

There is little communication between P.D. and client. After the first interview, the defendant's encounters with the P.D. are primarily in court. Only under special circumstances (to be discussed below) are there contacts between lawyers and defendants in the jail before and after appearances in court. The bulk of "preparation for court" (either trials or non-trial matters) occurs at the first interview. The attorney on station, the "attending attorney," is thus a stranger to "his client," and vice versa. Over the course of his proceedings, a defendant will have several attorneys (in one instance a man was "represented" by eight P.D.'s on a charge of simple assault). Defendants who come to court find a lawyer they don't know conducting their trials, entering their motions, making their pleas, and the rest. Often there is no introduction of P.D. to defendant; defendants are prepared to expect a strange face:

> Don't be surprised when you see another P.D. in court with you on Tuesday. You just do what he tells you to. He'll know all about your case.

P.D.s seldom talk about particular defendants among themselves. When they converse about trials, the facts of cases, etc., they do so not so much for briefing, as "This is what I think you should do when you 'get him,'" but rather as small talk, as "What have you got going today." The P.D. does not rely on the information about a case he receives from a previous attending attorney to know how to manage his "representation." Rather, the file is relied upon to furnish all the information essential for making an "appearance." These appearances range from morning calendar work (such as arraignments, motions, continuances, etc.) to trials on offenses from drunkenness to assault with a deadly weapon. In the course of a routine day, the P.D. will receive his batch of files in the morning and, seeing them for the first time that day, conduct numerous trials, preliminary hearings, calendar appearances, sentencing proceedings, etc. They do not study files overnight. Attorneys will often only look over a file a half hour or so before the jury trial begins.

The First Interview

As the first interview is often the only interview and as the file prepared there is central for the continuing "representation" of the defendant by other attorneys, it is important to examine these interviews and the file's contents. From the outset, the P.D. attends to establishing the typical character of the case before him and thereby instituting routinely employed reduction arrangements. The defendant's appearance—his race, demeanor, age, style of talk, way of attending to the occasion of his incarceration—provides the P.D. with an initial sense of his place in the social structure. Knowing only that the defendant is charged with section 459 (Burglary) of the penal code, the P.D. employs his conception of typical burglars against which the character of the present defendant is assessed.

> . . . he had me fooled for a while. With that accent of his and those Parliaments he was smoking I thought something was strange. It turned out to be just another burglary. You heard him about New York and the way he had a hold on him there that he was running away from. I just guess N.Y. is a funny place, you can never tell what kind of people get involved in crimes there.

The initial fact of the defendant's "putting in a request to see the P.D." establishes his lower position in the class structure of the community:

> We just never get wealthier people here. They usually don't stay in jail overnight and then they call a private attorney. The P.D. gets everything at the bottom of the pile.

Searching over the criminal history (past convictions and arrests) that the defendant provides when preliminary face-sheet data is recorded in the file, the P.D. gets a sense of the man's typical pattern of criminal activity. It is not the particular offenses for which he is charged that are crucial, but the constellation of prior offenses and the sequential pattern they take:

> I could tell as soon as he told me he had four prior drunk charges that he was just another of these skid row bums. You could look at him and tell.
>
> When you see a whole string of forgery counts in the past you pretty much know what kind of case you're dealing with. You either get those who commit an occasional forgery, or those that do nothing but. . . . With a whole bunch of prior checks (prior forgery convictions) you can bet that he cashes little ones. I didn't even have to ask for the amount you know. I seldom come across one over a hundred bucks.
>
> From the looks of him and the way he said "I wasn't doing anything, just playing with her," you know, it's the usual kind of thing, just a little diddling or something. We can try to get it out on a simple assault.

When a P.D. puts questions to the defendant he is less concerned with recording nuances of the instant event (how many feet from the bar were you when the cops came in, did you break into the back gate or the front door), than with establishing its similarity with "events of this sort." That similarity is established, not by discovering statutorily relevant events of the present case, but by locating the event in a sociologically constructed class of "such cases." The first questions directed to the defendant are of the character that answers to them either confirm or throw into question the assumed typicality. First questions with ADWs (Assault with a Deadly Weapon) are of the order: "How long had you been drinking before this all started?"; with "child molestation cases": "How long were you hanging around before this began?"; with "forgery" cases: "Was this the second or third check you cashed in the same place?"

We shall present three short excerpts from three first interviews. They all begin with the first question asked after preliminary background data is gathered. The first is with a 288 (child molestation), the second with a 459 (burglary) and the last with a 11530 (possession of marijuana). Each interview was conducted by a different Public Defender. In each case the P.D. had no information about the defendant or this particular crime other than that provided by the penal code number:

288

P.D.: O.K., why don't you start out by telling me how this thing got started?

DEF.: Well, I was at the park and all I did was to ask this little girl if she wanted to sit on my lap for awhile and you know, just sit on my lap. Well, about 20 minutes later I'm walkin' down the street about a block away from the park and this cop pulls up and there the same little girl is, you know, sitting in the back seat with some dame. The cop asks me to stick my head in the back seat and he asks the kid if I was the one and she says yes. So he puts me in the car and takes a statement from me and here I am in the joint. All I was doin' was playin' with her a little. . . .

P.D.: (interrupting) . . . O.K. I get the story, let's see what we can do. If I can get this charge reduced to a misdemeanor then I would advise you to plead guilty, particularly since you have a record and that wouldn't look too well in court with a jury.

(The interview proceeded for another two or three minutes and the decision to plead guilty was made.)

459

P.D.: Why don't you start by telling me where this place was that you broke into?

DEF.: I don't know for sure . . . I think it was on 13th Street or something like that.

P.D.: Had you ever been there before?

DEF.: I hang around that neighborhood, you know, so I guess I've been in the place before, yeah.

P.D.: What were you going after?

DEF.: I don't know, whatever there was so's I could get a little cash. Man, I was pretty broke that night.

P.D.: Was anyone with you?

DEF.: No, I was by myself.

P.D.: How much did you break up the place?

DEF.: I didn't do nothing. The back window was open a little bit see and I just put my hand in there and opened the door. I was just walking in when I heard police comin' so I turn around and start to run. And they saw me down the block and that was that.

P.D.: Were you drunk at the time?

DEF.: I wasn't drunk, no, I maybe had a drink or two that evening but I wasn't drunk or anything like that.

11530

P.D.: Well, Smith, why don't you tell me where they found it (the marijuana)?

DEF.: I was driving home from the drugstore with my friend and this cop car pulls me up to the side. Two guys get out, one of them was wearing a uniform and the other was a plainclothes man. They told us to get out of the car and then they searched me and then my friend. Then this guy without the uniform, he looked over into the car and picked up this thing from the back floor and said something to the other one. Then he asked me if I had any more of the stuff and I said I didn't know what he was talking about. So he wrote something down on a piece of paper and made me sign it. Then he told my friend to go home and they took me down here to the station and booked me on possession of marijuana. I swear I didn't have no marijuana.

P.D.: You told me you were convicted of possession in 1959.

DEF.: Yeah, but I haven't touched any of the stuff since then. I don't know what it was doing in my car, but I haven't touched the stuff since that last time.

P.D.: You ought to know it doesn't make any difference whether or not they catch you using, just so as they find it on your possession or in a car, or your house, or something.

DEF.: Man, I swear I don't know how it got there. Somebody must have planted it there.

P.D.: Look, you know as well as I do that with your prior conviction and this charge now that you could go away from here for five years or so. So just calm down a minute and let's look at this thing reasonably. If you go to trial and lose the trial, you're stuck. You'll be in the joint until you're 28 years old. If you plead to this one charge without the priors then we can get you into jail maybe, for a year or two at the most in the joint. If you wait until the preliminary hearing and then they charge the priors, boy, you've had it, it's too late.

DEF.: Well how about a trial?

(After ten minutes, the defendant decided to plead guilty to one charge of possession before the date of the preliminary hearing.)

Let us consider, in light of the previous discussion, some of the features of these interviews.

1. In each case the information sought is not "data" for organizing the particular facts of the case for deciding proper penal code designations (or with a view toward undermining the assignment of a designation in an anticipated trial). In the 288 instance, the P.D. interrupted when he had enough information to confirm his sense of the case's typicality and construct a typifying por-

trayal of the present defendant. The character of the information supplied by the defendant was such that it was specifically lacking detail about the particular occurrences, for example, the time, place, what was said to the girl, what precisely did the defendant do or not do, his "state of mind," etc. The defendant's appearance and prior record (in this case the defendant was a 55-year-old white, unemployed, unskilled laborer, with about ten prior drunk arrests, seven convictions, and two prior sex offense violations) was relied upon to provide the sense of the present occasion. The P.D. straightforwardly approached the D.A. and arranged for a "contributing to the delinquency of a minor" reduction. In the burglary case, the question, "Had you ever been there before?", was intended to elicit what was received, namely, that the place was a familiar one to the defendant. Knowing that the place was in the defendant's neighborhood establishes its character as a skid row area business; that the First Federal Bank was not entered has been confirmed. "What were you going after?", also irrelevant to the 459 section of the penal code, provides him with information that there was no special motive for entering this establishment. The question, "Was anyone with you?", when answered negatively, placed the event in the typical class of "burglaries" as solitary, non-coordinated activities. The remaining questions were directed as well to confirming the typical character of the event, and the adequacy of the defendant's account is not decided by whether or not the P.D. can now decide whether the statutory definition of the contemplated reduction or the original charge is satisfied. Its adequacy is determined by the ability with which the P.D. can detect its normal character. The accounts provided thus may have the character of anecdotes, sketches, phrases, etc. In the first instance, with the 288, the prior record and the defendant's appearance, demeanor, and style of talking about the event were enough to warrant his typical treatment.

2. The most important feature of the P.D.'s questioning is the presupposition of guilt that makes his proposed questions legitimate and answerable at the outset. To pose the question, "Why don't you start by telling where this place was that you broke into?" as a lead question, the P.D. takes it that the defendant is guilty of a crime and that the crime for which he is charged probably describes what essentially occurred.

The P.D.'s activity is seldom geared to securing acquittals for clients. He and the D.A., as co-workers in the same courts, take it for granted that the persons who come before the courts are guilty of crimes and are to be treated accordingly:

> Most of them have records as you can see. Almost all of them have been through our courts before. And the police just don't make mistakes in this town. That's one thing about————, we've got the best police force in the state.

As we shall argue below, the way defendants are "represented" (the station manning rather than assignment of counselors to clients), the way trials are conducted, the way interviews are held, and the penal code employed—all of the P.D.'s work is premised on the supposition that people charged with crimes have committed crimes.

This presupposition makes such first questions as "Why don't you start by telling me where this place was . . ." reasonable questions. When the answer comes: "What place? I don't know what you are talking about," the defendant is taken to be a phony, making an "innocent pitch." The conceivable first question: "Did you do it?", is not asked because it is felt that this gives the defendant the notion that he can try an "innocent pitch":

> I never ask them, "Did you do it?", because on one hand I know they did and mainly because then they think that they can play games with us. We can always check their records and usually they have a string of offenses. You don't have to, though, because in a day or two they change their story and plead guilty. Except for the stubborn ones.

Of the possible answers to an opening question, bewilderment, the inability to answer or silence are taken to indicate that the defendant is putting the P.D. on. For defendants who refuse to admit anything, the P.D. threatens:

> Look, if you don't want to talk, that's your business. I can't help you. All I can say is that if you go to trial on this beef you're going to spend a long time in the joint. When you get ready to tell me the story straight, then we can see what can be done.

If the puzzlement comes because the wrong question is asked, "There wasn't any fight—that's not the way it happened," the defendant will start to fill in the story. The P.D. awaits to see if, how far, and in what ways the instant case is deviant. If the defendant is charged with burglary and a middle-class establishment was burglarized, windows shattered, a large payroll sought after and a gun used, then the reduction to petty theft, generally employed for "normal burglaries," would be more difficult to arrange.

Generally, the P.D. doesn't have to discover the atypical kinds of cases through questioning. Rather, the D.A., in writing the original complaint, provides the P.D. with clues that the typical recipe, given the way the event occurred, will not be allowable. Where the way it occurs is such that it does not resemble normal burglaries and the routinely used penalty would reduce it too far commensurate with the way the crime occurred, the D.A. frequently charges various situationally included offenses, indicating to the P.D. that the procedure to employ here is to suggest "dropping" some of the charges, leaving the originally charged greatest offense as it stands.

In the general case he doesn't charge all those offenses that he legally might. He might charge "child molesting" and "loitering around a schoolyard" but typically only the greater charge is made. The D.A. does so so as to provide for a later reduction that will appear particularly lenient in that it seemingly involves a change in the charge. Were he to charge both molesting and loitering, he would be obliged, moreover, should the case come to trial, to introduce evidence for both offenses. The D.A. is thus always constrained not to set overly high charges or not situationally included multiple offenses by the possibility that the defendant will not plead guilty to a lesser offense and the case will go to trial. Of primary importance is that he doesn't charge multiple offenses so that the P.D. will be in the best position vis-à-vis the defendant. He thus charges the first complaint so as to provide for a "setup."

The alteration of charges must be made in open court. The P.D. requests to have a new plea entered:

> P.D.: Your honor, in the interests of justice, my client would like to change his plea of not guilty to the charge of burglary and enter a plea of guilty to the charge of petty theft.
> JUDGE: Is this new plea acceptable to the prosecution?
> D.A.: Yes, your honor.

The prosecutor knows beforehand that the request will be made, and has agreed in advance to allow it.

I asked a P.D. how they felt about making such requests in open court, that is, asking for a reduction from one offense to another when the latter is obviously not necessarily included and often (as is the case in burglary-to-petty theft) not situationally included. He summarized the office's feeling:

> . . . in the old days, ten or so years ago, we didn't like to do it in front of the judge. What we used to do when we made a deal was that the D.A. would dismiss the original charge and write up a new complaint altogether. That took a lot of time. We had to re-arraign him all over again back in the muni court and everything. Besides, in the same courtroom, everyone used to know what was going on anyway. Now, we just ask for a change of plea to the lesser charge regardless of whether it's included or not. Nobody thinks twice about asking for petty theft on burglary, or drunkenness on car theft, or something like that. It's just the way it's done.

Some restrictions are felt. Assaultive crimes (ADW, simple assault, attempted murder, etc.) will not be reduced to or from "money offenses" (burglary, robbery, theft) unless the latter involve weapons or some violence. Also, victimless crimes (narcotics, drunkenness) are not reduced to or from assaultive or "money offenses," unless there is some factual relation, for example, drunkenness with a fight might turn out to be simple assault reduced to drunkenness.

For most cases that come before their courts, the P.D. and D.A. are able to employ reductions that are formulated for handling typical cases. While some burglaries, rapes, narcotics violations, and petty thefts are instigated in strange ways and involve atypical facts, some manipulation in the way the initial charge is made can be used to set up a procedure to replace the simple charge-alteration form of reducing.

Recalcitrant Defendants

Most of P.D.'s cases that "have to go to trial" are those where the P.D. is not able to sell the defendant on the "bargain." These are cases for which reductions are available, reductions that are constructed on the basis of the typicality of the offense and allowable by the D.A. These are normal crimes committed by "stubborn" defendants.

So-called "stubborn" defendants will be distinguished from a second class of offenders, those who commit crimes that are atypical in their character (for this community, at this time, etc.) or who commit crimes which while typical (recurrent for this community, time, etc.) are committed atypically. The manner in which the P.D. and D.A. must conduct the representation and prosecution of these defendants is radically different. To characterize the special problems the P.D. has with each class of defendants, it is first necessary to point out a general feature of the P.D.'s orientation to the work of the courts that has hitherto not been made explicit. This orientation will be merely sketched here.

As we noticed, the defendant's guilt is not attended to. That is to say, the presupposition of guilt, as a *presupposition,* does not say "You are guilty" with a pointing accusatory finger, but "You are guilty, you know it, I know it, so let's get down to the business of deciding what to do with you." When a defendant agrees to plead guilty, he is not *admitting* his guilt; when asked to plead guilty, he is not being asked, "Come on, admit it, you know you were wrong," but rather, "Why don't you be sensible about this thing?" What is sought is not a confession, but reasonableness.

The presupposition of guilt as a way of attending to the treatment of defendants has its counterpart in the way the P.D. attends to the entire court process, prosecuting machinery, law enforcement techniques, and the community.

For P.D. and D.A. it is a routinely encountered phenomenon that persons in the community regularly commit criminal offenses, are regularly brought before the courts, and are regularly transported to the state and county penal institutions. To confront a "criminal" is, for D.A. and P.D., no special experience, nothing to tell their wives about, nothing to record as outstanding in the happenings of the day. Before "their court" scores of "criminals" pass each day.

The morality of the courts is taken for granted. The P.D. assumes that the D.A., the police, judge, the narcotics agents, and others, all conduct their business as it must be conducted and in a proper fashion. That the police may hide out to deceive petty violators; that narcotics agents may regularly employ illicit entrapment procedures to find suspects; that investigators may routinely arrest suspects before they have sufficient grounds and only later uncover warrantable evidence for a formal booking; that the police may beat suspects; that judges may be "tough" because they are looking to support for higher-office elections; that some laws may be specifically prejudicial against certain classes of persons—whatever may be the actual course of charging and convicting defendants—all of this is taken, as one P.D. put it, "as part of the system and the way it has to be." And the P.D. is part of the team.

While it is common to overhear private attorneys call judges "bastards," policemen "hoodlums," and prosecutors "sadists," the P.D., in the presence of such talk, remains silent. When the P.D. "loses" a case—and we shall see that *losing* is an adequate description only for some circumstances—he is likely to say "I knew *he* couldn't win." Private attorneys, on the other hand, will not hesitate to remark, as one did in a recent case, "You haven't got a fucking chance in front of that son-of-a-bitch dictator." In the P.D. office, there is a total absence of such condemnation.

The P.D. takes it for granted and attends to the courts in accord with the view that "what goes on in this business is what goes on and what goes on is the way it should be." It is rare to hear a public defender voice protest against a particular law, procedure, or official. One of the attorneys mentioned that he felt the new narcotics law (which makes it mandatory that a high minimum sentence be served for "possession or sale of narcotics") wasn't too severe "considering that they wanted to give them the chair." Another indicated that the more rigid statute "will probably cure a lot of them because they'll be in for so long." One P.D. feels that wiretapping would be a useful adjunct to police procedure. It is generally said, by everyone in the office, that "——— is one of the best cities in the state when it comes to police."

In the P.D.'s interviews, the defendant's guilt only becomes a topic when the defendant himself attempts to direct attention to his innocence. Such attempts are never taken seriously by the P.D. but are seen as "innocent pitches," as "being wise," as "not knowing what is good for him." Defendants who make "innocent pitches" often find themselves able to convince the P.D. to have trials. The P.D. is in a professional and organizational bind in that he requires that his "clients" agree with whatever action he takes "on their behalf":

> Can you imagine what might happen if we went straight to the D.A. with a deal to which the client later refused to agree? Can you see him in court screaming how the P.D. sold him out? As it is, we get plenty of letters purporting to show why we don't do our job. Judges are swamped with letters condemning the P.D. Plenty of appeals get started this way.

Some defendants don't buy the offer of less time as constituting sufficient grounds for avoiding a trial. To others, it appears that "copping out" is worse than having a trial regardless of the consequences for the length of sentence. The following remarks, taken from P.D. files, illustrate the terms in which such "stubborn" defendants are conceived:

> Def wants a trial, but he is dead. In lieu of a possible 995. D.A. agreed to put note in his file recommending a deal. This should be explored and encouraged as big break for Def.

Chance of successful defense negligible. Def realizes this but says he ain't going to cop to no strong-arm. See if we can set him straight.

Dead case. Too many witnesses and —————— used in two of the transactions. However, Def is a very squirmy jailhouse lawyer and refuses to face facts.

Possibly the DA in Sup/Ct could be persuaded into cutting her loose if she took the 211 and one of the narco counts. If not, the Def, who is somewhat recalcitrant and stubborn, will probably demand a JT (jury trial).

The routine trial, generated as it is by the defendant's refusal to make a lesser plea, is the "defendant's fault":

What the hell are we supposed to do with them? If they can't listen to good reason and take a bargain, then it's their tough luck. If they go to prison, well, they're the ones who are losing the trials, not us.

When the P.D. enters the courtroom, he takes it that he is going to lose, that the defendant is going to prison. When he "prepares" for trial, he doesn't prepare to "win." There is no attention given to "how am I going to construct a defense so that I can get this defendant free of the charges against him?" In fact, he doesn't "prepare for trial" in any "ordinary" sense. (I use the term *ordinary* with hesitation; what *preparation for trial* might in fact involve with other than P.D. lawyers has not, to my knowledge, been investigated.)

For the P.D., "preparation for trial" involves, essentially, learning what "burglary cases" are like, what "rape cases" are like, what "assaults" are like. The P.D.'s main concern is to conduct his part of the proceedings in accord with complete respect for proper legal procedure. He raises objections to improper testimony; introduces motions whenever they seem called for; demands his "client's rights" to access to the prosecution's evidence before trial (through so-called "discovery proceedings"); cross-examines all witnesses; does not introduce evidence that he expects will not be allowable; asks all those questions of all those people that he must in order to have addressed himself to the task of insuring that the *corpus delicti* has been established; carefully summarizes the evidence that has been presented in making a closing argument. Throughout, at every point, he conducts his "defense" in such a manner that no one can say of him "He has been negligent, there are grounds for appeal here." He systematically provides, in accord with the prescriptions of due process and the Fourteenth Amendment, a completely proper, "adequate legal representation."

At the same time, the district attorney, and the county which employs them both, can rely on the P.D. not to attempt to morally degrade police officers in cross-examination; not to impeach the state's witnesses by trickery; not to attempt an exposition of the entrapment methods of narcotics agents; not to condemn the community for the "racial prejudice that produces our criminals" (the phrase of a private attorney during closing argument); not to challenge the prosecution of "these women who are trying to raise a family without a husband" (the statement of another private attorney during closing argument on a welfare fraud case); in sum, not to make an issue of the moral character of the administrative machinery of the local courts, the community, or the police. He will not cause any serious trouble for the routine motion of the court conviction process. Laws will not be challenged, cases will not be tried to test the constitutionality of procedures and statutes, judges will not be personally degraded, police will be free from scrutiny to decide the legitimacy of their operations, and the community will not be condemned for its segregative practices against Negroes. The P.D.'s defense is completely proper, in accord with correct legal procedure, and specifically amoral in its import, manner of delivery, and perceived implications for the propriety of the prosecution enterprise.

In "return" for all this, the district attorney treats the defendant's guilt in a matter-of-fact fashion, doesn't get hostile in the course of the proceedings, doesn't insist that the jury or judge "throw the book," but rather "puts on a trial" (in their way of referring to their daily tasks) in order to, with a minimum of strain, properly place the defendant behind bars. Both prosecutor and public defender thus protect the moral character of the other's charges from exposure. Should the P.D. attend to demonstrating the innocence of his client by attempting to undermine the legitimate character of police operations, the prosecutor might feel obliged in return to employ devices to degrade the moral character of the P.D.'s client. Should the D.A. attack defendants in court, by pointing to the specifically immoral character of their activities, the P.D. might feel obligated, in response, to raise into relief the moral texture of the D.A.'s and police's and community's operations. Wherever possible, each holds the other in check. But the "check" need not be continuously held in place, or even attended to self-consciously, for both P.D. and D.A. trust one another implicitly. The D.A. knows, with certainty, that the P.D. will not make a closing argument that resembles the following by a private attorney, from which I have paraphrased key excerpts:

> If it hadn't been for all the publicity that this case had in our wonderful local newspapers, you wouldn't want to throw the book at these men.
>
> If you'd clear up your problems with the Negro in ——— maybe you wouldn't have cases like this in your courts.
>
> (After sentence was pronounced) Your Honor, I just would like to say one thing —that I've never heard or seen such a display of injustice as I've seen here in this court today. It's a sad commentary on the state of our community if people like yourself pay more attention to the local political machines than to the lives of our defendants. I think you are guilty of that, your Honor.

(At this last statement, one of the P.D.s who was in the courtroom turned to me and said, "He sure is looking for a contempt charge.")

The P.D. knows how to conduct his trials because he knows how to conduct "assault with deadly weapons" trials, "burglary" trials, "rape" trials, and the rest. The *corpus delicti* here provides him with a basis for asking "proper questions," making the "proper" cross-examinations, and pointing out the "proper" things to jurors about "reasonable doubt." He need not extensively gather information about the specific facts of the instant case. Whatever is needed in the way of "facts of the case" arise in the course of the D.A.'s presentation. He employs the "strategy" of directing the same questions to the witness as were put by the D.A. with added emphasis on the question mark, or an inserted "Did you really see ———?" His "defense" consists of attempting to "bring out" slightly variant aspects of the D.A.'s story by questioning his own witnesses (whom he seldom interviews before beginning trial but who are interviewed by the office's two "investigators") and the defendant.

With little variation the same questions are put to all defendants charged with the same crimes. The P.D. learns with experience what to expect as the "facts of the case." These facts, in their general structure, portray social circumstances that he can anticipate by virtue of his knowledge of the normal features of offense categories and types of offenders. The "details" of the instant case are "discovered" over the course of hearing them in court. In this regard, the "information" that "comes out" is often as new to him as to the jury.

Employing a common-sense conception of what criminal lawyers behave like in cross-examination and argument, and the popular portrayal of their demeanor and style of addressing adversary witnesses, the onlooker comes away with the sense of having witnessed not a trial at all, but a set of motions, a perfunctorily carried-off event. . . .

NOTES

1. For general histories of indigent defender systems in the United States, see The Association of the Bar of the City of New York, *Equal Justice for the Accused* (Garden City, N.Y.: 1959); and E. A. Brownell, *Legal Aid in the United States* (Rochester, N.Y.: The Lawyers Cooperative Publishing Co., 1951).
2. The experience of the public defender system is distinctly different in this regard from that of the Legal Aid Societies, which, I am told, have continually met very strong opposition to their establishment by local bar associations.
3. "Calendar part" consists of that portion of the court day, typically in the mornings, when all matters other than trials are heard, such as arraignments, motions, continuances, sentencing, probation reports, and so on.

50
The Lower Courts

No findings of this Commission are more disquieting than those relating to the condition of the lower criminal courts. These courts are lower only in the sense that they are the courts before which millions of arrested persons are first brought, either for trial of misdemeanors or petty offenses or for preliminary hearing on felony charges. Although the offenses that are the business of the lower courts may be "petty" in respect to the amount of damage that they do and the fear that they inspire, the work of the lower courts has great implications. Insofar as the citizen experiences contact with the criminal court, the lower criminal court is usually the court of last resort. While public attention focuses on sensational felony cases and on the conduct of trials in the prestigious felony courts, 90 per cent of the Nation's criminal cases are heard in the lower courts.

The importance of the lower courts was emphasized almost 50 years ago in Charles Evans Hughes' admonition to the New York State Bar Association:

> The Supreme Court of the United States and the Court of Appeals will take care of themselves. Look after the courts of the poor, who stand most in need of justice. The security of the Republic will be found in the treatment of the poor and ignorant; in indifference to their misery and helplessness lies disaster.[1]

In 1922 the Cleveland Foundation Survey of the Administration of Criminal Justice concluded that

> [T]he office of the municipal prosecutor and the Municipal Court are the points of contact with the administration of justice of the overwhelming majority of the inhabitants who come into any contact with courts and court officials. There the great bulk of the population receives its impressions regarding the speed, certainty, fairness, and incorruptibility of justice as administered. For law to be effective there must not only be justice, but also the appearance of justice. . . . As a deterrent of crime, the Municipal Court is more important than any other of our institutions with the possible exception of the police force.[2]

The significance of these courts to the administration of criminal justice lies not only in sheer numbers of defendants who pass through them but also in

From The President's Commission on Law Enforcement and Administration of Justice, Task Force Report: *The Courts* (Washington, 1967) pp. 29–34.

their jurisdiction over many of the offenses that are most visible to the public. Most convicted felons have prior misdemeanor convictions, and although the likelihood of diverting an offender from a career of crime is greatest at the time of his first brush with the law, the lower courts do not deal effectively with those who have come before them. The Baltimore Criminal Justice Commission noted in 1923:

> Although it is almost invariably true that the serious offender has a long career in the minor courts, we wait until he graduates from such a career into a full-fledged burglar or highwayman before paying serious attention to his conduct.[3]

Nearly a decade later the National Commission on Law Observance and Enforcement (the Wickersham Commission) concluded that the lower courts were the most important in the criminal justice system and yet were the most neglected. In the following years numerous studies have echoed these findings.[4]

It is distressing to report that these warnings have gone largely unheeded. The Commission has gathered available studies and statistical data, and the staff has made brief field studies of the lower courts in several large cities. The inescapable conclusion is that the conditions of inequity, indignity, and ineffectiveness previously deplored continue to be widespread.

Burgeoning population and increasing urbanization have aggravated rather than ameliorated these problems. These courts still operate with the most meager facilities, with the least trained personnel, and with the most oppressive workload. Practices by judges, prosecutors, and defense counsel that would be condemned in the higher courts may still be found in these courts. The most dedicated persons working there are frustrated by huge caseloads, and they lack opportunity to screen and prepare cases carefully or to deal with the problems posed by individuals brought to the bar of justice.

No program of crime prevention will be effective without a massive overhaul of the lower criminal courts. The many persons who encounter these courts each year can hardly fail to interpret that experience as an expression of indifference to their situations and to the ideals of fairness, equality, and rehabilitation professed in theory, yet frequently denied in practice. The result may be a hardening of antisocial attitudes in many defendants and the creation of obstacles to the successful adjustment of others.

The disturbing condition of the lower criminal courts is not without noteworthy exceptions. In many courts conscientious judges, prosecutors, and lawyers have done much to alleviate some of the problems. While their work shows that reforms are practicable, only sweeping changes will successfully raise the quality of justice in the lower criminal courts.

A general description of the lower criminal court system in the United States is complicated by the fact that there is no single system. Within each state, courts and procedures vary from city to city and from rural area to urban area. In most states, the lower courts are separate entities having different judges, court personnel, and procedures from other criminal courts, but in some places an integrated criminal court handles all phases of all criminal cases, with an administrative subdivision or branch for petty offenses. Generally the lower courts process felony cases up to the point of preliminary hearing and misdemeanor and petty offense cases through trial and ultimate disposition. But the categories of offenses classified as misdemeanors and felonies vary, and an offense that is a felony in one state may be a misdemeanor in another.

Despite variations in organization, studies of practice and procedure in the lower criminal courts have exposed critical deficiencies common to most systems. No single system manifests every defect described, but the defects are so widespread that the problem clearly demands attention and action across the country.

The Urban Courts

PRACTICES AND PROCEDURES OF THE LOWER COURTS

Every day in the courthouses of metropolitan areas the inadequacies of the lower criminal courts may be observed. There is little in the process which is likely to instill respect for the system of criminal justice in defendants, witnesses, or observers. Some representative observations are set forth below.

Initial Presentment. Following arrest, the defendant is initially presented in court, often after many hours and sometimes several days of detention. In theory the judge's duty is to advise the defendant of the charges against him and of his rights to remain silent, to be admitted to bail, to retain counsel or to have counsel appointed, and to have a preliminary hearing. But in some cities the defendant may not be advised of his right to remain silent or to have counsel assigned. In others he may be one of a large group herded before the bench as a judge or clerk rushes through a ritualistic recitation of phrases, making little or no effort to ascertain whether the defendants understand their rights or the nature of the proceedings. In many jurisdictions counsel are not assigned in misdemeanor cases; even where lawyers are appointed, it may not be made clear to the defendant that if he is without funds he may have free representation. One Commission staff report notes:

> In the cases observed no defendant was told that he had a right to remain silent or that the court would appoint a lawyer to represent him if he were indigent, notwithstanding the court rule that counsel will be assigned whenever a defendant may be sentenced to more than six months or fined more than $500. We were told that at least one judge takes great care to advise defendants fully, but the three judges we observed did not.[5]

The judges have little time to give detailed consideration to the question of bail. Little is known about the defendant other than the charge and his prior criminal record. The result is that bail is based on the charge instead of on the circumstances of each case; high money bonds are almost invariably set by established patterns, and large numbers of defendants are detained.

Disposition. The initial appearance is also the final appearance for most defendants charged with misdemeanors or petty offenses. While those who can afford to retain counsel are released on bond to prepare for trial at a later date or to negotiate a disposition, a majority of defendants plead guilty immediately, many without advice of counsel. Pleas are entered so rapidly that they cannot be well considered. The defendant is often made aware that if he seeks more time, his case will be adjourned for a week or two and he will be returned to jail.

> Most of the defendants . . . pleaded guilty and were sentenced immediately, without any opportunity for allocution. When they tried to say something in their own behalf, they were silenced by the judge and led off by the bailiff. . . .[6]

Trial. An observer in the lower criminal courts ordinarily sees a trial bearing little resemblance to those carried out under traditional notions of due process. There is usually no court reporter unless the defendant can afford to pay one. One result is an informality in the proceedings that would not be tolerated in a felony trial. Rules of evidence are largely ignored. Speed is the watchword. Trials in misdemeanor cases may be over in a matter of 5, 10, or 15 minutes; they rarely last an hour even in relatively complicated cases. Traditional safeguards honored in felony cases lose their meaning in such proceedings; yet there is still the possibility of lengthy imprisonment or heavy fine.

In some cities trials are conducted without counsel for either side; the case is prosecuted by a police officer and defended by the accused himself. Staff observations in one city were summed up as follows:

> A few defendants went to trial, but the great majority of them did so without counsel. In these cases the judge made no effort to explain the proceedings to the defendants or to tell them of their right to cross-examine the prosecution's witnesses or of their right to remain silent. After the policeman delivered his testimony, the judge did not appear to make any evaluation of the sufficiency of the evidence but turned immediately to the defendant and asked, "What do you have to say for yourself?" Where counsel appeared at a trial, the procedure was slightly more formal, but the judge conducted most of the questioning himself.[7]

Sentence. Most defendants convicted in the lower criminal courts are sentenced promptly. Usually there are no probation services or presentence investigations. Unless the defendant has an attorney who has taken time to inquire into his background, little will be known about him. Sentence may be based on the charge, the defendant's appearance, and the defendant's response to such questions as the judge may put to him in the few moments allotted to sentencing. In the lower courts of one State the availability of violator's records is the exception rather than the rule. Even in the larger cities when the judge wishes to see the record of individual defendants he must send for the record and then delay the trial until it arrives. Delay and inconvenience so caused often lead to a situation where the judge merely asks the defendant what his record is and relies upon his word for its accuracy. . . .[8]

Short jail sentences of one, two, or three months are commonly imposed on an assembly line basis. A defendant's situation can hardly be considered individually. When a defendant is fined but is unable to pay, he may be required to work the penalty off at the rate of $1 to $5 for each day spent in jail.[9]

Petty Offenses. The conditions described above are found in more aggravated form in lower courts that handle petty offenses. Each day in large cities hundreds of persons arrested for drunkenness or disorderly conduct, for vagrancy or petty gambling, or for prostitution are led before a judge. Among the defendants are slum dwellers who drink in public and young men who "loiter" on street corners or "fail to move on" when ordered to do so. Typically, they have no private place to go, no money to spend, and no family or lawyer to lend them support.

Judges sometimes seem annoyed at being required to preside in these courts. Defendants are treated with contempt, berated, laughed at, embarrassed, and sentenced to serve their time or work off their fines.[10] Observers have sometimes reported difficulty in determining what offense is being tried in a given case,[11] and instances have come to light in which the disposition bears little relationship to the original charge. A trial of a defendant charged by police with drunkenness consisted of this exchange:

MAGISTRATE: "Where do you live?"
DEFENDANT: "Norfolk."
MAGISTRATE: "What are you doing in Philadelphia?"
DEFENDANT: "Well, I didn't have any work down there, so I came up here to see if I could find . . ."
MAGISTRATE (who had been shaking his head): "That story's not good enough for me. I'm going to have you investigated. You're a vagrant. Three months in the House of Correction." [12]

The offender subjected to this process emerges punished but unchanged. He returns to the streets, and it is likely that the cycle soon will be repeated in all its futility.

CAUSES OF THE PROBLEMS OF THE LOWER COURTS

The Volume of Cases. More than in any other courts in the system the problems of the lower courts center around the volume of cases. It is estimated that in 1962 more than four million misdemeanor cases were brought to the lower courts of the United States. The crux of the problem is that there is a great disparity between the number of cases and the number of judges.

Data from various cities illustrate this disparity. For example, until legislation last year increased the number of judges, the District of Columbia Court of General Sessions had four judges to process the preliminary stages of more than 1,500 felony cases, and to hear and determine 7,500 serious misdemeanor cases, 38,000 petty offenses and an equal number of traffic offenses per year.[13] In Detroit, more than 20,000 misdemeanor and non-traffic petty offense cases must be handled by the single judge sitting in the Early Sessions Division.[14] In Atlanta in 1964 three judges of the Municipal Court disposed of more than 70,000 cases.[15]

It is not only judges who are in short supply. There are not enough prosecutors, defense counsel, and probation officers even in those courts where some of them are available. The deluge of cases is reflected in every aspect of the courts' work, from overcrowded corridors and courtrooms to the long calendars that do not allow more than cursory consideration of individual cases.

There are other less visible consequences of volume problems. In the lower courts the agencies administering criminal justice sometimes become preoccupied simply with moving the cases. Clearing the dockets becomes a primary objective of all concerned, and cases are dismissed, guilty pleas are entered, and bargains are struck with that end as the dominant consideration. Inadequate attention tends to be given to the individual defendant, whether in protecting his rights, in carefully sifting the facts at trial, or in determining the social risk he presents and how he should be dealt with after conviction. A former municipal court judge summed up his experiences in these words:

> The tremendous volume of cases that must pass through these arraignment courts in a given period of time necessarily limits the opportunity of the judge, city attorney, and the defendant or his attorney to give more than perfunctory attention to any individual case. Frequently, it is physically impossible for the deputy city attorney to know anything about the details of the charge, the background of the defendant, or his record. As a result, both the quality of law enforcement and the rights of the defendants are made to suffer. Police officers and complaining witnesses often feel that their case has not received proper attention. . . . Under such conditions, remedial or beneficial results to the community or the defendant are only incidental.[16]

The heavier the volume, the greater the delay between arrest and disposition for many defendants. This delay weakens the deterrent effect of the criminal process. It can cause the collapse of the prosecutor's case as witnesses tire and fail to appear and as memories fade. In addition, continuing cases time and again needlessly expends witnesses' time, including that of a large number of police witnesses. From the point of view of the defendant delay increases the length of pre-trial detention for those who cannot afford to post bail.

The Quality of Personnel. It is clear that the lower courts are generally manned by less competent personnel than the courts of general jurisdiction. There are judges, attorneys, and other officers in the lower courts who are as capable in every respect as their counterparts in more prestigious courts, but the lower courts regularly do not attract such persons.

In almost every city, judges in courts of general jurisdiction are better paid, are more prominent members of the community, and are better qualified than their lower court counterparts. In some cities lower court judges are not required to be lawyers. The conduct of some judges reveals inaptitude and a lack of familiarity with rules of evidence or developments in case law.

In jurisdictions in which the State is represented by a district attorney, the most inexperienced members of the staff are usually assigned to the lower courts. As they gain experience, the more able assistants are moved to the felony courts to handle more "important" cases, a move commonly regarded as a substantial career advance. For example, in the District of Columbia, five members of the U.S. Attorney's office were transferred from the lower court to the felony court in a four-month period in 1965.[17] In some cities prosecutors are part time and police officers serve as prosecutors.

As has been noted, in many lower courts defense counsel are not provided for defendants without funds. In those places where counsel are assigned, frequently he is not compensated and often his performance is poor. A community gets the kind of legal service it pays for, and typically it pays little or nothing for defense counsel in its lower court.

Attorneys operating regularly in these courts rarely appear in other courts. Often they seem to be more concerned with extracting a fee from their clients than with defending them. They operate on a mass production basis, relying on the plea of guilty to dispose of cases quickly. Frequently these lawyers are unprepared, make little contact with their clients, fail to investigate their backgrounds, and make little effort aside from the plea bargaining session to protect their interests or to secure a favorable disposition. For all the shortcomings of these attorneys who regularly operate in the lower courts, however, probably most defendants are better off with them than without any lawyer at all.

Probation services in the lower courts frequently are not available. More than one-third of the sample counties in the Commission's national survey of corrections had no probation services for misdemeanants. In jurisdictions where probation departments are attached to the lower courts, the probation services are markedly inferior, with few exceptions, to those available in the felony courts. Salary schedules for misdemeanant probation officers are generally too low to attract competent personnel, and in some counties the position of probation officer is filled by persons of limited qualifications who must rely on a part-time job to supplement their inadequate salary.

However, the greatest obstacle to effective probation services in the lower courts is the insufficient number of probation officers. The corrections survey estimated a national average of 114 misdemeanant cases per probation officer, an average that is far in excess of the minimum standards recommended in chapter 6 of the Commission's General Report. Under such heavy caseloads probation is at best a checking rather than a counseling or assisting function.

The result is that lower court judges are unable to make the fullest appropriate use of probation, and pre-sentence reports, when possible at all, are likely to lack sufficient information for effective sentencing.

Administrative Problems. The lower courts usually have separate personnel, facilities, and budgets from courts of general jurisdiction, but they generally manifest the same administrative deficiencies. The problems of lack of co-ordination among judges of a single court and of burdening judges with administrative chores that are found in many court systems are discussed in chapter 7. However, it should be noted that the effects of these problems are greater in the lower courts because of the greater volume of business that must be processed. Moreover, such attention as is directed to problems of court administration tends to be focused on the higher courts, in which more prominent judges and more experienced prosecutors are far more likely to take the initiative than their counterparts in the lower courts. The absence of defense counsel in many lower courts, apart from the "regulars" in the courthouse who often have vested interests in the status quo, also eliminates a source of initiative for reform.

Commission staff research revealed a pervasive lack of statistical data necessary for any attempt to improve the operations of the lower courts. In the District of Columbia Court of General Sessions, for example,

> there is nothing that approaches a comprehensive profile of the offender, . . . [but] the problems are far more basic. There is no agreement among the agencies even as to the volume of business of the court. . . . There are no statistics on the rate or length of pre-trial detention. The incidence of indigency at the court is unknown. There is no comprehensive analysis of the manner in which cases are charged, broken down, or disposed of by the prosecutor. There is no description of sentencing patterns or of the workloads, of individual judges. And there are no reliable statistics on recidivism.[18]

In most cities cases are listed in terms of charges rather than defendants, and there is no way to determine how many persons entered the system. Quite often inconsistencies appear between statistics kept by the police and those kept by the court. In the District of Columbia, for example, some 5,000 defendants shown on police records to have reached court do not appear on court records at all.[19] The lack of data makes it difficult to pinpoint critical areas of need, renders comprehensive assessment of the performance of the court impossible, and restricts sound management control over court business.

UNIFICATION OF THE CRIMINAL COURTS

Division of the criminal courts has produced lower standards of judicial, prosecutorial, and defense performance in the misdemeanor and petty offense courts. Procedural regularity has been a prime casualty. The function performed by these courts, ultimate disposition of misdemeanors and petty offenses only, has meant that community attention is directed to the higher courts where felony cases are processed.

When community resources are committed to criminal justice, the lower courts, largely lacking in articulate spokesmen, are commonly ignored. The result has been the development of two separate court systems of strikingly disparate quality. The distinction between felonies on the one hand and misdemeanors and petty offenses on the other may be useful in fixing the range of punishment and the collateral effects of conviction, but it certainly does not justify the present dual court system. In many respects the distinction between felonies and misdemeanors is an artificial one. Misdemeanants are sometimes liable to lengthy imprisonment, and a large percentage of these offenders were initially charged with felonies that were reduced to misdemeanors as a result of plea bargaining; they may represent the same danger to society and the same need for rehabilitative measures as those processed through the felony courts.

It is hard to see why a defendant charged with a felony should be accorded so many more of the elements of due process than his counterpart charged with a less serious offense in a misdemeanor court: better representation, more care in disposition, and better facilities for rehabilitation.

The community and the offender both suffer when the offender is processed through the lower courts, for he often receives a lighter sentence than is appropriate, and he is denied access to the rehabilitative facilities of the higher courts. The hardened offender does not develop overnight; generally he has a history of repeated misdemeanor and petty offense violations. At the initial stage of a criminal career there should be reason to hope for successful rehabilitative efforts. Yet at just that crucial phase the community's resources fail to be effective. The disturbing rate of recidivism among offenders processed through the lower courts alone is reason enough to try another approach.

The problems of the lower courts can best be met by unification of the criminal courts and abolition of the lower courts as presently constituted. The National Commission on Law Observance and Enforcement reached this conclusion more than 30 years ago. Conditions in the lower courts today have not improved, and increases in caseloads have multiplied the problems. The experience of this century suggests that the lower courts will remain a neglected segment of our criminal justice system unless sweeping reforms are instituted.

All criminal prosecutions should be conducted in a single court manned by judges who are authorized to try all offenses. All judges should be of equal status. Unification of the courts will not change the grading of offenses, the punishment, or the rights to indictment by grand jury and trial by jury. But all criminal cases should be processed under generally comparable procedures, with stress on procedural regularity and careful consideration of dispositions.

Complete unification of the criminal courts would entail central administration which may take a number of forms. The logistics may be handled by a court's chief judge, by a small administrative committee of judges, or by an administrative judge, an office established in the New York Criminal Court and in other cities. The services of professional court administrators to assist the judges charged with administrative duties will be needed for the larger courts, and the use of business management techniques, including the use of data-processing equipment, should be developed.[20] It is in the lower court, with a higher volume of routine cases than the felony court, that mechanical and electronic equipment would have the greatest impact.

In addition to unification of the courts, centralization of the prosecutive function in a single office responsible for all criminal prosecutions and operating on a county level or on a citywide basis in major cities would result in more efficient use of manpower and a higher level of prosecution. The often found systems of special prosecutors, city prosecutors, part-time employees, and police prosecutors should be eliminated.

Two improvements may be anticipated in a unified court system. Such facilities as probation services and pre-sentence investigations, currently of limited availability in most jurisdictions, would be available for all criminal cases, and all defendants would be entitled to assigned counsel to the extent suggested in chapter 5. High-volume courts present the opportunity for experimentation with ways of providing counsel to the poor, including variations of the familiar assigned counsel and defender approaches.

The precise form unification should take in each jurisdiction will have to be considered in light of local conditions. An initial question is whether the civil courts should be included in the unified court structure or whether separate civil and criminal courts should be maintained. The merits and demerits of specialization by judges, and the effects of the several approaches on the administration of the courts and the quality of court personnel must be weighed. Procedural and administrative differences in the processing of petty offenses may lead some jurisdictions to follow the pattern set by Detroit, where an integrated court handles all phases of criminal cases but a special branch of that court deals with petty offenses. At first there will be problems of housekeeping and of the use of the courthouse and other facilities of the merged courts, but the recent accomplishments of court integration efforts in a number of states have demonstrated that these problems can be met.

Unification of the criminal courts may place additional burdens on judges, prosecutors, and lawyers, and additional personnel may be required. More time and attention must be devoted to misdemeanor and petty offense cases by all participants in the administration of criminal justice. But the efficiency that will follow use of modern court administration and management techniques should help to meet some of these burdens. And implementation of proposals to reduce the volume of cases entering the criminal justice system by eliminating drunkenness and other offenses from the criminal law should also result in significant relief.

Inauguration of procedures to screen cases, for early diversion from the criminal process, and for referral to the appropriate social, medical, and psychiatric community services would free substantial resources now processing such cases through the criminal justice system. Other proposals of the Commission concerning court procedures should facilitate the processing of cases within a unified court system. Early assignment of counsel holds the promise of quantitative improvement in the disposition of offenders of the lower court: greater deliberation, more attention to procedural regularity, and careful sifting of evidence and of sentencing information.

Plea negotiations at as early a stage as possible in the proceedings and adoption of procedures for pre-charge conferences would focus the parties' attention on dispositional decisions at an early stage. Court business would be facilitated by scheduling more than one session each day for the initial appearance of defendants. This reform would enable the prompt arraignment of defendants, would permit the court's business to be spread over a longer period of the day with more time for each case, and would substantially reduce time lost for police witnesses. In most medium- and large-size cities the caseloads justify at least three sessions each day for initial appearances, one of which should be at night.

Communities may wish to experiment with the use of laymen to facilitate the initial processing of cases. Many arrested persons need information and advice on a variety of subjects—how to obtain a lawyer, what the charges are, and what the next steps in the proceeding are. These functions could be performed by a defendants' aide, a layman trained to provide basic information and advice and assigned to each precinct or a central detention point. This same person could be given the broader functions of conducting bail and indigency investigations. He might be an employee of a legal aid or public defender's office, or of a community social service agency or bail project. The services of a defendant's aide could help to speed the flow of cases through the courts by reducing the time required to process requests for assignment of counsel and to set the conditions of pre-trial release.

NOTES

1. Address by Charles Evans Hughes, N.Y. State Bar Association 42d Annual Meeting, in *1919 Proceedings of the N.Y. State Bar Association* (1919), pp. 224, 240–241.
2. Pound and Frankfurter, eds., *Criminal Justice in Cleveland* (Cleveland Foundation, 1922), p. 38.
3. *Baltimore Criminal Justice Commission Annual Report* (1923), p. 17.
4. See Sheridan, *Urban Justice* (1964); Subin, *Criminal Justice in a Metropolitan Court* (1966); American Bar Foundation, *The Administration of Criminal Justice in the United States—Pilot Project Report* (mimeo. 1957), pp. 1–7; Pennsylvania Attorney-General, *Report on the Investigation of the Magisterial System* (1965); Dash, "Cracks in the Foundation of Justice," *Illinois Law Review*, XLVI (1951), 385; Foote, "Vagrancy-Type Law and Its Administration," *University of Pennsylvania Law Review*, CIV (1956), 603; Note, "Metropolitan Criminal Courts of First Instance," *Harvard Law Review*, LXX (1956), 320.

    Even before the turn of the century a Philadelphia judge remarked that "complaints of the rapacity of the local magistrates have come down to us, continuously, from the earliest periods." *Commonwealth v. Alderman Hagan,* 9 Phila. Rep. 574 (1872), quoted in Pennsylvania Attorney-General, *supra* at 1.
5. Staff Study, *Administration of Justice in the Municipal Court of Baltimore.*

6. Staff Study, *Administration of Justice in the Recorder's Court of Detroit.*
7. *Ibid.*
8. Sheridan, *op. cit. supra* note 4, at 41.
9. See chapter 2 *supra.*
10. See Sheridan, *op. cit. supra* note 4, at 72–78.
11. Foote, *supra* note 4, at 610–611.
12. *Id.* at 611.
13. President's Commission on Crime in the District of Columbia, *Report 272* (1966) (table 23).
14. Staff Study, *Administration of Justice in the Recorder's Court of Detroit.*
15. Atlanta Commission on Crime and Juvenile Delinquency, *Opportunity for Urban Excellence* (1966), p. 184.
16. Nutter, "The Quality of Justice in Misdemeanor Arraignment Courts," *Journal of Criminal Law, Criminology, and Political Science,* LIII (1962), 215.
17. Subin, *op. cit. supra* note 4, at 25 n.2.
18. *Id.* at 155.
19. *Id.* at 156.
20. See chapter 7 *infra,* and the Report of the Science and Technology Task Force of this Commission.

51

In Defense of Public Defenders

JEROME H. SKOLNICK

. . . We will attempt to show, first, that differences in demeanor and attitude between P.D. and "regular" or "successful" private defense attorneys have been exaggerated by critics of the P.D.; and second, to offer reasons, based upon the character of the P.D.'s clientele, for the criticisms to have arisen. Particular consideration will be given to examining P.D.-private defense attorney differences regarding "client control," an issue that is fundamental to social control in the adversary system. The main argument of the remaining portion of the article will be that, given the prevailing system of prosecutorial discretion, the public defender operates on much the same principles as the private defense attorney, and that perceived differences can be largely explained by the character of the public defender's clientele.

From "Social Control in the Adversary System," *Journal of Conflict Resolution,* XI, No. 1 (1967), 59–67. Reprinted by permission of the publisher. Abridged with renumbered notes.

Similarities Between the P.D. and the Private Defense Attorney

To analyze similarities between the public defender and the private defense attorney, it is instructive to consider the statements of two critics of the P.D. The noted defense attorney, Edward Bennett Williams, has said that:

> . . . the public defender and the prosecutor are trying cases against each other every day. They begin to look at their work like two wrestlers who wrestle with each other in a different city every night and in time get to be good friends. The biggest concern of the wrestlers is to be sure they do not hurt each other too much. They don't want to get hurt. They just want to make a living. Apply that to the public defender and prosecutor situation and it is not a good thing in a system of justice that is based upon the adversary system [in McDonald, 1962, p. 10].

Similarly, David Sudnow, a sociologist who studied a P.D.'s office, writes:

> He [the Public Defender] will not cause any serious trouble for the routine motion of the court conviction process. Laws will not be challenged, cases will not be tried to test the constitutionality of procedures and statutes, judges will not be personally degraded, police will be free from scrutiny to decide the legitimacy of their operations, and the community will not be condemned for its segregative practices against Negroes. The P.D.'s defense is completely proper, in accord with correct legal procedure, and specifically amoral in its import, manner of delivery, and perceived implications for the propriety of the prosecution enterprise.
>
> In "return" for all this, the district attorney treats the defendant's guilt in a matter-of-fact fashion, doesn't get hostile in the course of the proceedings, doesn't insist that the jury or judge "throw the book" but rather "puts on a trial" (in their way of referring to their daily tasks) in order to, with a minimum of strain, properly place the defendant behind bars. Both prosecutor and public defender thus protect the moral character of the other's charges from exposure. . . .[1]

There is a degree of truth in the observations of Williams and Sudnow, especially regarding the "teamwork" conception of D.A.-P.D. relations. Each, however, tends to draw conclusions that are partly false or misleading, because of a fundamental flaw in the assumptions underlying their analysis. This consists in taking given institutional categories—such as "public defender"—at face value. A better understanding of the system is achieved, however, by considering the P.D. to represent a more general phenomenon, that of the "cooperative" defense attorney. Indeed, one of the pitfalls of studying the administration of criminal law from the point of view of only one of the institutional participants is that the analyst may fail to see the possibilities of reconceptualization. To the prosecutor, it matters not so much whether a defendant is being represented by a P.D. as whether the defense attorney, regardless of his institutional base, can be counted upon as a "cooperative" defense attorney, a category that usually includes leading private defense attorneys and only some of the members of the P.D.'s office.

In the county studied, for example, of the six leading private defense attorneys, five report that they settle a greater percentage of their cases by plea of guilty than does the public defender. The one exception settles approximately half his cases in this manner, as compared with upward of 90 per cent for the remainder of the private defense attorney community. There are, however, characteristics distinguishing him from the other leading private defense attorneys. As the leading Negro defense attorney in the area, he represents a predominantly Negro clientele. Some of his clients are small-time "professional" criminals for whom it is difficult to make attractive deals because of prior records. In addition, he is an exceptional courtroom advocate, likely the most articulate in the community, and therefore fares well in the courtroom. Furthermore, his clients generally expect a posture of challenge and defiance, and would mistrust an attorney who appeared to cooperate too closely with the prosecutor and the police. Finally, he tends himself to share the disestablishmentarian view of his clientele, and argues with other defense attorneys over the wisdom of their cooperative tactics. Since he is reinforced in his beliefs by client opinion, he maintains a more challenging posture than the leading white defense attorneys.

A similar report of cooperation, however, was made to the writer by a leading criminal defense firm in an eastern city (employing Negro as well as white lawyers). Each of the other private defense attorneys interviewed made statements *vis-à-vis* relations with the prosecutor that were similar to each other's and also to statements made by the members of the public defender's office. One such statement will suffice to illustrate:

> You have to know the law to practice criminal law, but you also have to know the ropes. Our office is on very good terms with the prosecutor's office, because they trust us. We never misrepresent to them, and we don't degrade them, or the police or their witnesses. But don't get the idea that we don't represent our clients well. If we didn't do that we wouldn't get all the criminal business that we now have—and we could treble our criminal practice if we were to charge smaller fees. When we settle cases, we get a reduction of the original charge in virtually every case. Not only that, but our clients are treated better by the police, and as a result, the prosecutor often has a weaker case against them than he might have. Whenever we can, we have our client bailed out as soon as possible, and instruct the police that we don't want them talking to the client. We're on very good terms with the police. Of course [one of his partners chimed in], we've handled civil matters for a lot of detectives, and we give them a break on the fee.

Every leading white defense attorney interviewed insisted that the layman's notion of adversariness was not in the interests of their clients, and that their clients did better as a result of a "cooperative" posture. It should also be noted, of course, that "cooperation" is in the interests of the defense attorney as well as the prosecutor. Usually, defense attorneys charge a set fee for a defense regardless of whether a trial takes place, although in civil cases it is customary to charge by the hour. Thus it may be to the economic advantage of the private defense attorney to plead his client guilty. Indeed, in this respect, the P.D. enjoys greater flexibility to maintain an adversarial posture than the private defense attorney. One judge interviewed, critical of the practices of some private attorneys, suggested that the fee sometimes deters private defense attorneys from pleading their client guilty. "They often find it hard to collect a fee after their client has been convicted. While a defendant is out on bail, he tries to raise his legal fees, sometimes in illegal activities."

As for the question of testing the constitutionality of procedures and statutes, defense attorneys generally regard this as a naive view of the practice of criminal law in the routine criminal case. There is a great deal of publicity given to constitutional decisions, but appellate courts overturn relatively few decisions of trial courts, although the publicity given to such cases tends to create an appearance of review and instability. It is rare, however, for the average local defense attorney to base his strategy of defense on procedural error in the routine case, whether he is a private attorney or a P.D.

Most private defense attorneys usually operate on a theory of defense similar to that of the public defender, and "bargain" as willingly as he. This theory presupposes the guilt of the client, as a general matter, and the fact that pleas of guilty are so common tends to reinforce the presumption of guilt throughout the system. It is a theory that stresses administrative regularity over challenge, and emphasizes decisions most likely to maximize gain and minimize loss in the negatively valued commodity of penal "time." As a leading private defense attorney writes:

> The public image of a criminal lawyer, as well as that of a general practitioner, is of a trial gladiator eloquently arguing for the acquittal of his client. But it has long been clear to the criminal law specialist, and should be to the general practitioner, that at some points the criminal process is moving away from a strictly adversary proceeding, and the district attorney as well as the criminal defense lawyer is interested in arriving at a settlement or compromising the matter in a way that will bring substantial justice to the defendant and to society. . . .
>
> Although under our system of law a defendant is presumed innocent, and it is the lawyer's duty to present every defense the law permits, whether or not he believes his client to be guilty, it is nonetheless important to understand the dynamics of negotiation and bargaining in the criminal law. An attorney cannot properly communicate with his client unless the attorney understands this changing role of the criminal lawyer. It may be necessary in the opening interview to explain to the defendant that you are less an adversary than an officer of the court who will ensure that he will be given fair treatment and permitted to return to society as a productive human being [Golde, 1964, p. 118].

By law, judges are usually responsible for calculating the sentence. It sometimes happens that the defense attorney will ask the judge for an indication of sentence prior to a plea of guilty. Some defense attorneys are on close enough personal terms with some judges that they may speak to them "off the cuff." In most cases, however, when the defense attorney approaches the judge he seeks to implement an agreement already worked out with the prosecutor. Since the judge is also under administrative pressure, he rarely rejects a plea of guilty, and also rarely fails to cooperate with the defense attorney and prosecutor who have worked out a "deal." Thus a typical plea bargain encompasses a reduction of charges, a limitation of the potential sentence, and an agreement from the prosecutor to urge the judge to sentence in accord with an agreement between defense attorney and prosecutor.

In such negotiations, a norm of "rationality" or "reasonableness" prevails; the defense attorney is expected to accept a sentence that would be in the "interests" of the community as well as his client. While the adversary system contemplates an aggressive defense, the "cooperative" system alters the nature of the services that the defense attorney is capable of performing for his client. He may often act less as an advocate than as a "coach," preparing his client to meet the behavioral and attitudinal standards acceptable to criminal law officialdom. For example, one case was observed in which a young man had been convicted of stealing a purse from an 85-year-old woman. When his attorney asked what he would say to the parole officer, the youth replied with an answer that was exculpatory and defensive, "Well, I needed the money. Anyhow, all we did was take her purse, we didn't hurt her." The attorney instructed the youth that he must not defend his action. Through a series of questions and answers the youth finally understood how to make a "pitch" that was apologetic and repentant: "It was a very bad thing to do; I don't know why I did it." With such a response on the pre-sentence report, the attorney is then in a position to argue for a lighter sentence, and the judge is in a better position to grant it. Thus "cooperation" implies an understanding of the requirements of the other functionaries in the system, "ability" implies the capacity to fulfill those needs, and "rationality" or "reasonableness" suggests the acceptance of prevailing assumptions.

Not only does the public defender tend to follow a theory of his role similar to that of most private defense attorneys, but he is, in some respects, better equipped to carry it out. First, given the administrative concerns of the prosecutor's office, the public defender, as an office, ultimately enjoys a greater capacity to frustrate, precisely because he controls so many cases. To be sure, he also requires the "cooperation" of the prosecutor, but then, the prosecutor also needs the cooperation of the public defender. It is a nice question as to which actually exerts more leverage, and very difficult to measure. Nevertheless, in the course of the study, members of both offices indicated an awareness of and respect for the other's potential to impede the administrative concerns of each. Further, regardless of whether the prosecutor has more leverage over the public defender than the P.D. has over the D.A., as a result of the cases it controls, the P.D.'s office is in a structurally advantageous position when compared to the individual private defense attorney. Thus, contrary to the argument that the social structure necessarily imposes cooperation in D.A.-P.D. relations and, by implication, makes the private attorney a more adversarial agent in comparison, the structure of the situation would appear to give the P.D. relatively greater organizational leverage over the D.A.

It is also not necessarily true, as suggested by Edward Bennett Williams, that in time the prosecutor and the public defender "get to be good friends." The situation is more complicated than that, and its complications are instructive. In the offices studied, several members of the prosecution were asked informally, after the writer had become well known to them, which defense attorneys in the community they thought best of professionally, and whom they liked best. The best liked, and best thought of, was a private defense attorney who reported that he deals out almost all of his cases. As one member of the D.A.'s staff put it:

> We like C.F. because he's smart and he's reasonable. He almost always pleads his clients guilty, but not until he's really worked us over to get the charge reduced or our promise to ask for a minimal sentence. Also we've learned to trust him. He pretty nearly always discloses his case and we ours. Many times he has convinced us that his client is innocent. When he does, we drop the charges, if it's possible to do so, that is, if there isn't too much heat in the case. Most of the men in the office will tell you that Charlie gets better deals from us, on the whole, than any other attorney, and his practice reflects that.

Furthermore, C.F. was observed by the writer to be one of the few defense attorneys in the community who could make deals directly with the police, especially with the vice control squad. In six months spent observing the vice control squad, four occasions were noted when C.F. visited the offices of the vice control squad, went out with the "boys" for coffee, and discussed his client's situation with the police. During this period a member of the public defender's staff was seen in vice control quarters only once, and several were on quite hostile personal terms with police.

Again, it must be remembered that the public defender is not an individual, but, like the district attorney, a staff of individuals and that this also makes for a more complicated set of relations. Each office had men on its staff who were characterized by men on the other staff as "hatchet-men," as unreasonably and aggressively anti-defendant or pro-defendant, depending on the office from which the characterization arose. In general, the calendar men from each office usually maintained friendly relations with the calendar men from the other office, and also seemed to be selected in line with their diplomatic skills. Even the quietly diplomatic ones might, however, privately express feelings of hostility toward members of the other office.

Sudnow (1965, p. 273) claims that the P.D. will "not cause any serious trouble for the routine motion of the court conviction process." Several instances were observed to the contrary, one involving the same attorney that Sudnow used to illustrate "cooperativeness." Following the death penalty phase of a trial in which this attorney represented the P.D.'s office, two of the more "diplomatic" members of the prosecutor's office were interviewed. Each felt that this attorney had exceeded the bounds of propriety in defending his client. One became angry and called the attorney a prostitute; he said that "just because he's against the death penalty, he has no business making a mockery of the courtroom." My point here is simply that not all members of the public defender's office work as a "team" with the prosecutor; and the same man can sometimes appear "cooperative" and sometimes "hostile." Thus the notion of "teamwork," while generally true, breaks down often enough to be notable, and, probably, more often regarding the P.D. than leading private defense attorneys.

Public Defender–Private Attorney Differences

It is impossible to make a systematic comparison between the private defense attorney and the public defender because lawyers do not become attached to clients on a random basis. Even with full cooperation of authorities, such an experiment could not be constructed, since the very act of assignment would create an important set of conditions. It is instructive, nevertheless, to compare some of the factors distinguishing the clientele of the private defense attorney from that of the public defender, to understand how distinctions in the character of clientele might generate such criticisms of the public defender as suggested by Williams and Sudnow. Thus, the principal argument of this section will be that the "public–private" distinction is confounded by the economic class of the clientele represented by the public defender. The following pages will attempt to analyze, first, the consequences of poverty in the administration of criminal justice even when the accused is offered counsel by the state; and second, some of the consequences of a system of *assignment* of attorneys.

In the county studied, the defendant's inability to make bail was taken as evidence of indigence. Thus the public defender has a clientele of defendants who typically cannot make bail. Inability to make bail, in turn, can hamper the defendant in several ways. Most directly, he is required to spend the time awaiting trial in the county jail. Judges may or may not take such time into account in sentencing. Those who do not do this usually justify themselves on the theory that, had the defendant cared to shorten his sentence, he could have pleaded guilty immediately and not have awaited trial. Such "time," known as "deadtime" around the criminal courts, adds pressure on the public defender to have his client plead guilty early.

Inability to make bail not only may result in a longer period of imprisonment—it also impairs the capacity of the defendant to prepare his defense. While on bail, a defendant may be able to locate witnesses whom he remembers in only a vague way, and cannot instruct his middle-class lawyer on how to locate. Furthermore, there is usually a difference in manner and appearance of defendants who make bail and those who do not. The man in jail enters the courtroom under guard, from the jail entrance. His hair has been cut by a jail barber, and he often wears the clothes he was arrested in. By contrast, the "civilian" defendant usually makes a neat appearance, and enters the court from the spectator's seats, emerging from the ranks of the public. Several studies have demonstrated that, for the same charges, defendants who make bail generally are more successful in countering accusations of criminality than those who do not.[2] Thus, the public defender has, as a general matter, the task of defending a class of defendants who are relatively poorly equipped to contribute to their own defense.

"Client Control" and Adversariness

If game theory is reviewed, we learn that models are typically based on an assumption of two sets of interests. The adversary system, as described, is clearly a "mixed-motive" game, that is, "one in which the goals of the players are partly coincident and partly in conflict" (Gallo and McClintock, 1965, p. 68), if we consider the defense attorney and the prosecutor as the players. In addition to the problem of deciding strategy vis-à-vis the prosecutor, however, the defense attorney also experiences the problem of maintaining decisional authority within the context of a normative system of *representation*. Thus the notion that an attorney "represents" a client is not altogether clear. It might mean that he accepts his client's view of the strategy of the case, and offers the client his technical knowledge of various branches of law to implement the client's strategy. In practice, however, this does not seem to be the accepted definition. On the contrary, the defense attorneys typically understand the idea of representation to suggest that the attorney is responsible both for strategy and tactics, that is, that the attorney is the "player." His task is understood as explaining to the client the legal consequences of the facts of the case, and to advise both strategy and tactics on the basis of his interpretation of the facts. His client, however, may not be disposed to accept such an interpretation of the attorney's role. When that occurs, the attorney feels that his reputation may be damaged, since it rests upon a consistent achievement of outcomes over a period of time. Thus, as between attorney and client, there is also a mixed-motive game.

Among the attorneys studied, this game is typically referred to as "client control." It is a problem experienced by all defense attorneys, but is exaggerated in relations between the public defender and his client. A special problem of "client control" exists for the public defender because he has not been selected by his client. For example, a private attorney might inform his client that if he insists on going to trial, against the attorney's advice, the attorney will withdraw from the case. Or he might advise his client that he will take the case to trial if the client insists, but that a trial will be costly. As between public defender and client, however, a different relationship obtains.

It is not so much that "when the defendant himself attempts to direct attention to his innocence . . . such attempts are never taken seriously by the P.D. but are seen as 'innocent pitches,' as 'being wise,' as 'not knowing what is good for him' " (Sudnow, 1965, p. 272). It is rather that when the defendant declares his innocence, the public defender does not accept such declarations at face value, and in effect cross-examines his client. Such a course of action is, however, a standard practice for defense attorneys in general. There is an axiom of legal practice that the lawyer attempts to learn the truth from his client, in the interest of his client. To do otherwise would be to abrogate his responsibility to construct the strategy of the defense, since he cannot successfully construct such a strategy without being able to anticipate the strength of the prosecution's case. It is true that the private cross-examination of one's own defendant is an art, and that some members of the P.D.'s office have not cultivated it as well as others. The art consists in separating the client's illegal behavior from his general moral character, just as a medical doctor segregates the patient's illness from his total self-conception. Thus, the discussion centers around legally related facts, inviting not a confession of immorality as much as a disclosure of reality.

The P.D. does not, however, "require," as Sudnow writes (1965, p. 272), "that his 'clients' agree with whatever action he takes 'on their behalf.' " Sudnow's own quotation indicates just the opposite. He quotes the public defender as stating:

> Can you imagine what might happen if we went straight to the D.A. with a deal to which the client later refused to agree? Can you see him in court screaming how the P.D. sold him out? As it is we get plenty of letters purporting to show why we don't do our job. Judges are swamped with letters condemning the P.D. Plenty of appeals are started this way.

Thus, it is not simply that the P.D. requires his clients to agree with his actions, but rather that the P.D. fears his clients or, at least, is fearful of a charge that he misled his client. He is sensitive to his vulnerability arising out of the situation of assignment rather than selection.

It is true, however, as Sudnow suggests, that when the defendant "refuses to face the facts" the P.D. understands he will lose when he enters the courtroom. Such a trial is referred to by Sudnow as a "routine trial," and is referred to in the system as a "slow plea of guilty" or a "second degree" trial. It is, indeed, a "fixed" trial, since the presumed antagonists merely put on a show. They have already decided what the outcome will be, on the basis of their knowledge of the facts. But two further implications drawn by Sudnow are not true. One is the suggestion that all trials conducted by the P.D. are "fixed." The other is that "slow pleas of guilty" are unknown to private defense attorneys.

Reliable statistics on fixed trials are, of course, impossible to obtain, and prudence prevents an observer from even speculating on the proportions of such trials. Nevertheless it is probable, in terms of the social structure of the system, that the P.D. goes to "routine trial" with proportionately greater frequency than does the private defense attorney, precisely because of his exceptional problems of client control. We have indicated that the P.D. does not command the sanctions of client control that the private defense attorney does. Furthermore, it is difficult for the P.D. to establish a situation of trust between himself and his client. It was not possible to interview privately more than six clients of the public defender,[3] but of those six, three expressed the idea that since the P.D. is a public official, he must have a "tic-in" with the police and the D.A. Several defendants also complained that they felt that nobody in the public defender's office was taking a personal interest in the case.

Clients of the public defender tend, in fact, to be treated as "files" or "cases," although in important cases they may be given considerable attention. It is fair to observe, however, that the "treatment" given to a client is usually more analogous to that given by an efficient hospital clinic than to that offered by an outstanding private physician. Whether the society can afford to give more is presently beside the point. Relevant here is the fact that the P.D. probably serves a more mistrustful, suspicious class of clients than private defense attorneys even if the stated basis of mistrust—that the P.D. is paid out of the same pocket as the D.A. while private defense attorneys are not—is mistaken. The mistrust, however, seems to lead to an incapacity to control clients, and to a measure of prophetic self-fulfillment regarding "routine trials." Since the P.D. cannot exert the sanctions on the client that are available to the private defense attorney, it is likely that he goes to "second degree" trial with proportionately greater frequency and less apparent adversariness than his private counterpart.

NOTES

1. D. Sudnow, "Normal Crimes: Sociological Features of the Penal Code in a Public Defender Office," *Social Problems,* XII (1965), 273. Sudnow offers one example of a private defense attorney who "degraded" the courts in one case, but it is generally unrepresentative. Even in the specific case, there were three private defense attorneys, only one of whom acted in the fashion described by Sudnow for private defense attorneys in general.
2. The studies most clearly showing such effects were initiated at the University of Pennsylvania by Caleb Foote, and in New York by the Vera Foundation. See Foote (1954; 1958); Ares, Rankin, and Sturz (1963).
3. The P.D. withdrew permission to interview after it had been granted. Members of his staff feared that defendants awaiting trial, who had been instructed not to talk about their case to anyone, would be confused if they were to talk to an interviewer. Hence the small number of interviews.

Part IV THE CAPACITY OF LAW TO AFFECT SOCIAL BEHAVIOR

Editors' Introduction

This final section addresses itself to the capacity of law and its limitations as a means of ordering human behavior. It gathers together material from selected areas of social life where such attempts have been made.

In Section Eleven the readings concentrate upon legal attempts to enforce conventional morality. The controversy regarding the use of law to enforce morals goes back to John Stuart Mill's "very simple principle" on the power of the state to regulate individual behavior. Mill wrote that "the sole end for which mankind is warranted, individually or collectively, in interfering with the liberty of action of any of their number, is self-protection. That the only purpose for which power can be rightfully exercised over any member of a civilized community, against his will, is to prevent harm to others. His own good, either physical or moral, is not sufficient warrant."

Mill believed that a man is entitled to live his life in his own way without the state making decisions for him as to what is right and good. Mill's position has been strongly criticized by Sir Patrick Devlin, a distinguished contemporary jurist. Devlin accepts Mill's anti-paternalistic philosophy, but argues that society is nevertheless entitled to prevent the harm that would be done to it by the "weakness or vice" of too many of its members. Devlin acknowledges that while Mill did not overlook the problem of societal harm, he overrode it in the interests of individual freedom.

The Mill-Devlin controversy articulates the dilemma faced by society in this area of the utilization of state power to prevent or reduce immorality. Thus Devlin writes, concerning the use of alcoholic beverages in society:

> While a few people getting drunk in private causes no problem at all, widespread drunkenness, whether in private or in public, would create a social problem. The line between drunkenness that creates a social problem of sufficient magnitude to justify the intervention of a law and that which does not, cannot be drawn on the distinction between private indulgence and public sobriety. It is a practical one based on an estimate of what can safely be tolerated whether in public or in private and shifting from time to time as circumstances change.

425

If there is a principled difference between Mill and Devlin, it is only of emphasis. Mill recognizes the right of society to institute laws for self-protection; Devlin acknowledges that each citizen is entitled to the greatest measure of personal freedom. Given the "balancing" standard, however, it is still difficult to know what we are balancing, to be able to measure it, to analyze the assumptions underlying our measures, and to make predictions or postulations on the basis of these measures.

This section attempts to bring both analyses and empirical findings to the understanding of this issue. Herbert L. Packer of Stanford Law School argues that despite what we think we are doing when we attempt to enforce conventional morality through law, what we are in fact promoting is a crime tariff. Relying upon economic theories for his analysis, Professor Packer points out that laws created to enforce conventional morality also create a protective economic tariff for the sale of prohibited goods and services, since the demand for them may be relatively inelastic.

Following Packer's analysis, the case of *People v. Cahan* demonstrates yet another facet of the problem of enforcement. In crimes of conventional morality there is usually no citizen complainant. As a result, police themselves must seek out the perpetrators of the crime, and in so doing are frequently tempted to skirt or to violate constitutional restrictions on search and seizure. *People v. Cahan* was the first state case to make illegally seized evidence inadmissible in court. Behind the decision there is an empirical theory. The notion is that by excluding such evidence, police will be dissuaded from violating constitutional restrictions.

Jerome H. Skolnick investigated the effect of the "theory" as embodied in the California "exclusionary rule" by working in a police department as a detective, and observing police responses to legal rules. As part of the same study, Skolnick and J. Richard Woodworth investigated the problem of the enforcement of statutory rape as a criminal offense. Their article explores yet another problem arising from the enforcement of conventional morality. This is the intrusion upon privacy and organizational values that may result from a combination of strict enforcement plus an increasing capacity to discover, record, and transfer information.

In the final reading of this section we return to another study written by Herbert L. Packer. Packer's argument is that the courts are not a very efficient agency for controlling illegal police behavior. The basic issue here is the relation between the substantive criminal law and the procedures that are used by legal officials to enforce these laws. So long as legislatures require the enforcement of conventional morality, police will be tempted to violate constitutional restrictions. Thus, the underlying issue posed by this section is whether or not we have been placing undue demands upon our criminal law as an instrument of social control.

Section Twelve introduces one of the most controversial and significant areas in which the law has attempted to alter social attitudes and behavior. The case of *Brown v. the Board of Education of Topeka,* decided in 1954, signaled the emergence of the civil rights movement in the United States. This was the famous school segregation case in which the Supreme Court decided unanimously that segregation is inherently unequal.

Jack Greenberg, council for the NAACP, analyzes the effectiveness of law in bringing racial justice and equality to the American Negro. Greenberg broadens the question by not assuming that the law is a method equally workable at all times and under all circumstances. He points out that there will be considerable variation in the capacity of the law to affect social change in this area.

The selections that follow Greenberg's offer three examples, two by sociologists and one by an economist. Herbert H. Hyman and Paul B. Sheatsley offer evidence to show that the Supreme Court school segregation decisions have affected attitudes concerning the propriety of segregation. On the other hand, Morris Davis, Robert Seibert, and Warren Breed, who examined the effects of a Federal Court order to desegregate busses, indicate the strength of customary segregation practices. The third article, by Ray Marshall, analyzes the problem of reducing discrimination against Negroes within labor unions. This is, perhaps, the most interesting and complicated area of the attempt to achieve equality through law. What is at stake here is a conflict of "liberal" values. Unions, through strikes, protests, demonstrations, and other forms of militant action, won important rights of self-government. The attempt to introduce equality into labor unions often conflicts with narrowly held conceptions of the meanings of these rights, especially as these are interpreted by old-line labor unions. Richard D. Schwartz discusses the frustrations arising from the attempt of Negroes to achieve, through conventional legal processes, the kind of large-scale change needed to alter their underprivileged position in society. Tactical objectives, such as school integration, are often blocked by political and judicial conservatism. Even when obtained, such goals seem to contribute little to the achievement of genuine opportunity and human dignity. When, in despair, black militants turn to direct action often involving violations of the law, the capacity of the legal system to respond effectively is problematic. Jerome H. Skolnick's statement to the American Civil Liberties Union examines the traditional civil libertarian position by showing its inadequacy from the perspective of black militants. His essay makes a case for basic change in legal orientation in a society facing an era of rapid social change and widespread discontent.

Section Thirteen enlarges the scope of the discussion of the influence of law. It brings together several studies dealing with a variety of life conditions in which the law has either attempted to have some effect, or in which lawmakers seem unaware of the effect they may be having.

Harry V. Ball, a sociologist, examines the impact of rent-control restrictions upon landlord practices. Ball concludes that the anticipation by landlords of even more stringent controls overcame their widespread opposition to rent control and their belief that they were being treated unfairly, even though they continued to hold these ideas.

H. Frank Way, Jr., a political scientist, surveyed the effect of the Supreme Court's prayer and Bible reading decisions on actual practices within the schools. Way found that the decision did indeed have a considerable effect and analyzes the factors leading to compliance and non-compliance with the decision.

George F. Break, an economist, investigated the effect of high and steeply progressive income taxes upon incentives to work. Contrary to the writings of many so-called financial experts and journalists, Break found that British accountants did not reduce their working hours with a rise in taxation. On the contrary, their work motivation seemed to stem primarily from professional obligations, sometimes enhanced by the anticipation of heavy taxes.

Vilhelm Aubert, a Norwegian sociologist, examined the impact of legislation intended to change the relationship between employer and employee where the employees are housemaids. Aubert's research suggests that long-standing patterns of relationships are difficult to erase with legislation. Break and Aubert seem to indicate that patterns of work relationships are so deeply embedded that they are extremely difficult to influence through legislation, though the law may work some unintended mischief on these relationships.

Finally, Schwartz and Skolnick conducted an experiment and a survey comparing the effects of legal stigma on two occupational groups. They found that the impact of such stigmata varies considerably depending upon the occupational status of the individual so labeled.

The studies in this section suggest that there is no simple answer to the question of how law will affect attitudes and behavior. What appears to be required is a detailed and careful examination of the conditions under which legally initiated attempts to modify human behavior will be responded to by the community at large.

The final section addresses a more general issue—the potential of law for realizing social values. Law is here not perceived simply as a set of rules. It also encompasses procedures and institutions for implementing these rules. The section concentrates on the capacity of law to develop and respond to claims of right in such a way as to achieve fairness and justice. In this section, perhaps more than in any other, we perceive some of the basic dilemmas of the legal process.

The discussion is begun with Lon L. Fuller's article "On the Nature and Limits of Adjudication." In the context of labor arbitration, Fuller describes the limits of the judicial role that may impede the direct resolution of the issues that are in dispute.

Jerome E. Carlin, Jan Howard, and Sheldon Messinger shift our attention to another requirement to be met if the judicial process is to implement social values. They stress the need for "legal competence" of citizens. The legally competent person not only is willing and able to assert his own legal rights but is also increasingly aware of the consequences of his own actions for the rights of others. The authors analyze the ways in which poverty impedes the legal system by disabling a portion of the population from developing into legally competent citizens.

Charles Reich, of the Yale Law School, develops this notion even further by pointing out that property is not a natural right but a deliberate construction by society. Accordingly, he sees a "new property" in the form of benefits, services, contracts, franchises, licenses, and employment. Thus, as Americans become increasingly dependent on government largesse, Reich perceives in the welfare state the need to develop new claims of right and new demands for a rule of law in the adjudication of such claims.

A similar issue is raised for the educational sphere by sociologist Terry F. Lunsford who, in his examination of the "free speech" controversy at Berkeley, perceives in it a number of fundamental issues relating to the scope and basis of administrative discretion and due process in the university. Lunsford's work represents an increasing interest on the part of sociolegal scholars in the area of quasi-legal systems. The question here is the extent to which certain principles of public governance and participation, and rights of individuals that have been granted by the Constitution, can and ought to be encompassed in the ordering of large, private organizations, such as universities and corporations.

Joel F. Handler, of the Wisconsin Law School, is critical of Reich, and by implication, of Lunsford. Handler contends that the protections that Reich sees as operating in government regulation of business (the old property) do not operate as Reich suggests. Furthermore, Handler argues that the costs of such reforms may well outweigh their benefits. He feels that formal procedural requirements (of having lawyers, of having judicial decisions) will possibly result in more, rather than less, lawless behavior on the part of administrative officials. He also suggests that the sort of position taken by Reich will lead to an undesirable formality in administrative proceedings that will interfere with the capacity of administrative organizations to fulfill the social values for which they were created.

Perhaps the most considered empirical study of these issues is to be found in Philippe Nonet's study on the Industrial Accident Commission of California. He discusses here both the advantages and liabilities of the development of the industrial accident commission from an administrative to a more judicialized body, involving adjudicative proceedings and the assertion of claims of right by the injured worker.

Finally, the selection by Ronald Dworkin stresses the function of the legal process in locating and promoting normative consensus for the society. While every effort should be made to appraise the specific impact of the law, its indispensable task is to develop agreement among the diverse groups in contemporary society on the fundamental principles of a just social order.

SECTION ELEVEN *To Enforce Conventional Morality*

52

Crime Tariffs

HERBERT L. PACKER

There is an important economic dimension to the criminal sanction that can be illustrated by invoking the analogy of a protective tariff. The dictionary defines a tariff as "a schedule, system, or scheme of duties imposed by a government on goods imported or exported." If a tariff imposed "for the artificial fostering of home industries," it is what we call a protective tariff.

Economists tell us that protective tariffs are uneconomic because they get in the way of the optimal allocation of resources that a free market is supposed to bring about. Protective tariffs have a bad name but they continue to flourish, mainly because claims advanced in their behalf have considerable appeal to lawmakers. Some say that the appeal is essentially one of money and votes: the high-minded (or the committed) say that it is the health of the internal economy or, more fashionably these days, the demands of national defense. Whatever the basis really is, the protection of textiles, bicycles, watches, cheese, or what-have-you is always justified by the claim that it is desirable public policy to protect the commodity in question from the rigors of competition. Competition is good, but cheese is better, especially if it comes from Wisconsin.

Cheese is better, perhaps so. But are narcotics better? Is gambling better? Are abortions performed by terrified amateurs better? We do not ordinarily think of these blights as commodities protected by a tariff but it is easy to demonstrate that they are just that. The tariff in question is the criminal law or, more precisely, the particular criminal statutes that make it illegal to do such things as traffic in narcotics, run a gambling enterprise, or perform abortions on pregnant women who don't want to have children. Of course, no one designed criminal enactments such as these to operate as a tariff. The object is not to enhance the profits of entrepreneurs in these particular lines of commerce by protecting them from competition. In fact, we rarely think of these activities as involving commerce because our emotionalism about crime gets in the way of our seeing that they are. We treat conduct as criminal and back the declaration up by threatening and, occasionally, inflicting punishment to prevent or at least reduce their incidence. That is far from providing a protective tariff; just the opposite, or so we think. But there is a common feature of some oddly disparate kinds of conduct covered by our criminal law that produces quite a different effect from that intended. It is very simply that the conduct in question, whatever else it may be and however heinous we may think it, is traffic in a line of commerce.

Commerce involves transactions between willing buyers and willing sellers, each of whom gets what he wants from the deal. By making conduct that answers to this description criminal, what we are in effect doing is limiting the supply of the commodity in question by increasing the risk to the seller, thereby driving up the price of what he sells. It may be suggested that driving up the price is just what we want to do: make it so expensive to buy narcotics, for example, that people will stop buying them. As we know from current experience, it doesn't work that way. People go on buying narcotics, even if they have to steal money to pay the price. Economic theory explains this phenomenon by introducing the concept of elasticity of demand. It is only when the demand is quite elastic that increases in price will reduce the amount demanded. People who are willing to pay $2,000 for a car will not ordinarily want the same car if its price is suddenly doubled. But the demand is inelastic when the commodity is something that people want so badly that they don't think much about price: something like salt, or medicine, or narcotics. And if the sale of the commodity in question happens to be illegal, the crime tariff goes into operation. Regardless of what we think we are trying to do, if we make it illegal to traffic commodities for which there is an inelastic demand, the effect is to secure a kind of monopoly profit to the entrepreneur who is willing to break the law. In effect, we say to him: "We will set up a barrier to entry into this line of commerce by making it illegal and, therefore, risky; if you are willing to take the risk you will be sheltered from the competition of those who are unwilling to do so. Of course, if we catch you, you may possibly (although not necessarily) be put out of business; but meanwhile you are free to gather the fruits that grow in the hothouse atmosphere we are providing for you."

Prohibition was a classic example of the operation of the crime tariff. Traffic in liquor became the monopoly of the lawbreakers, who proceeded to earn enormous monopoly profits and, behind the protective wall of the crime tariff on liquor, to build criminal organizations that could rapidly take advantage of any other crime tariffs with which we were willing to oblige them. With the disappearance of the crime tariff on liquor, a similarly profitable traffic in narcotics developed. The tariff is very high; we make it so hard on narcotics offenders that only the boldest venture into the field. It is far from clear that we have appreciably reduced the total supply of narcotics coming into the country. What we have done is to channel the business into fewer and fewer hands (if the Narcotics Bureau and the F.B.I. are to be believed) and driven the price of the commodity to giddy new heights.

Opinions vary on what the effects would be if all controls on the sale of narcotics were removed overnight (a step, be it said, that lies outside the realm of the politically possible). One highly placed policeman of my acquaintance asserts that the addiction rate would show an immediate increase. A psychiatrist retorts that if narcotics become easily procurable, addiction will lose much of its allure. Who is to say which of them is right? By contrast, the economic effect of such a change is clearly predictable, if economics has anything to teach us at all. With the disappearance of controls the price of narcotics would plummet and the financial ruin of the present illegal suppliers would quickly ensue.

The case of narcotics is not unique. Consider, for example, the problem of abortions. By and large, it is illegal to perform an abortion in this country unless continuation of the pregnancy would be fatal to the mother. Comparatively few abortions are openly performed by reputable doctors in reputable hospitals on that ground or on the ground that the woman's mental health will be gravely impaired if she is forced to bear and raise a child. A much larger number of abortions—estimates range as high as one million per year—are performed clandestinely, with the knowledge that if they come to the attention of the police, arrest, conviction, and imprisonment will very likely follow. Not many do come to the attention of the police, of course. It is doubtful whether the arrest rate is as high as one per thousand abortions performed. Aside from sporadic police activity, the main threat to the abortionist is that something will go wrong and the patient (or her survivor) will complain to the authorities. But the threat is there; and it causes the crime tariff to operate. The case is plainly one of a highly inelastic demand. Women (and their husbands and lovers) who want an abortion do not care what the market price is; if they can possibly raise the money they want the commodity regardless of price. Here the anti-competitive effect of the crime tariff operates not only on price but also on service. Since women cannot generally get abortions from those who are in the best position to supply a satisfactory product, the members of the medical profession, they are driven to accept a product of inferior grade and quality from the hole-in-corner abortionist. They buy injury and even death from sellers who would be driven out of the market overnight if they did not have the protection of the crime tariff.

So far, we have treated the crime tariff from the buyer's standpoint. It can also be analyzed for its economic effect on the seller. Deterrence theory in one aspect is essentially economic in nature, although it has rarely been so described. In its Benthamite aspect, it views human conduct as involving the same kind of rational pursuit of satisfactions implicit in the concept of economic man. On that view, the risk of punishment becomes an offsetting factor that the intending criminal must weigh against the gain he hopes to realize from his criminal conduct. By reducing the potential gain, we hope and expect to reduce the incentive to engage in criminal activity. Deterrence works, however, if the potential gain remains the same when the criminal is successful; the risk of loss diminishes the attraction of the gain, which is a constant. We do not make bank robbery more attractive by punishing the bank robbers whom we manage to catch. The potential gain is unaffected by the offsetting risk of punishment. If murdering one's rich aunt to inherit a million dollars from her were legal, we would not increase the potential gain by making it illegal. The stake would still be the same million dollars. Or, to take a more realistic example, if a certain kind of sophisticated stock swindle happens to be legal, making it illegal will not increase the potential gain; the new risk of punishment will make the same old gain seem less attractive than it used to be. Swindlers will be, in a word, deterred.

But this assumption of a constant in potential gain, upon which the successful operation of deterrence depends, does not hold for the category of "transactions" we have been examining. Because we are dealing with voluntary commerce in a commodity whose buyers are willing to submit to price increases, every increase in risk increases the potential gain to the seller. The harder we work to make the sale of abortions risky, the higher we drive the price that makes the risk worthwhile. The calculus of pleasure and pain, to put it in Jeremy Bentham's terms, produces an equilibrium at a higher level of price. The theory of deterrence, however useful it may be in the ordinary run of crimes, breaks down. In its place, we get a crime tariff, which operates like any other protective tariff.

Should we have crime tariffs? The question is not one that we are likely to answer by focusing on economic factors alone. This is simply one of several undesirable side effects that must be taken into account in deciding when it is wise to use the criminal sanction. Few are swayed by economic considerations alone. Just as debates about the tariff on cheese are unlikely to be resolved by economic arguments about the desirability of free competition in cheese, so is it improbable that any demonstration, however persuasive, that abortions cost more than they need to will carry the day for free competition in abortions.

The argument against the crime tariff is strongest when the proposal is to apply it to a hitherto unprotected commodity. So far, the discussion of legal restrictions on cigarette sales hasn't focused on using the criminal sanction. And not many communities are likely to follow the example of the Texas town that recently made it a crime to sell cigarettes within the municipal limits. But there is a real danger that the lessons that we have had many chances to learn about the crime tariff have not really been learned. Witness, for example, current proposals to extend the same kind of criminal sanctions to traffic in so-called "dangerous drugs"—amphetamines, barbiturates, and the like—that we presently employ for narcotics. Whatever the solution to the vexing problems posed by the crime tariffs we now have, it would be the sheerest folly to create new ones.

While it seems clear that proposals for new crime tariffs should be viewed with the greatest skepticism, the question of what to do with the ones we have now is more baffling. It would be a hardy legislator who would vote to repeal even the most innocuous of criminal enactments, let alone such emotion-freighted bans as those on narcotics, abortions, and (to a lesser extent, because the door is already slightly ajar) gambling. If we could write on a clean slate. . . . But we cannot with the crime tariff any more than with the tariff on cheese, on bicycles, or on watches.

Tariff elimination may be impossibly utopian; tariff reduction is not. Even if we are not prepared to make narcotics freely available to addicts, we should seek intermediate solutions that reduce our unwise reliance on the criminal sanction. Even if we are not prepared to confide the abortion problem to the good judgment of the medical profession, we should expand the grounds on which abortions may be performed. Even if we are not prepared to give up our futile efforts to keep people from gambling, we should be receptive to proposals, like those current in New York, to legalize forms of gambling that cannot be rationally distinguished from forms that are presently legal (the fresh air at racetracks isn't all that good). Measures such as these would all tend to lower crime tariffs. That may not be thought by all to be enough to validate such proposals; it should be enough to get them a fairer hearing than they usually get.

53

People v. Cahan

TRAYNOR, J.—Defendant and 15 other persons were charged with conspiring to engage in horse-race bookmaking and related offenses in violation of section 337a of the Penal Code. Six of the defendants pleaded guilty. After a trial without a jury, the Court found one defendant not guilty and each of the other defendants guilty as charged. Charles H. Cahan, one of the defendants found guilty, was granted probation for a period of five years on the condition that he spend the first 90 days of his probationary period in the county jail and pay a $2,000 fine. He appealed from the order granting him probation and the order denying his motion for a new trial.

Most of the incriminatory evidence introduced at the trial was obtained by officers of the Los Angeles Police Department in flagrant violation of the United States Constitution (Fourth and Fourteenth Amendments), the California Constitution (art. I, §19), and state and federal statutes. Gerald Wooters,

Supreme Court of California, 44 Cal. 2d 434; 282 P. 2d 905 (1955).

an officer attached to the intelligence unit of that department testified that after securing the permission of the chief of police to make microphone installations [1] at two places occupied by defendants, he, Sergeant Keeler, and Officer Phillips one night at about 8:45 entered one "house through the side window of the first floor," and that he "directed the officers to place a listening device under a chest of drawers." Another officer made recordings and transcriptions of the conversations that came over wires from the listening device to receiving equipment installed in a nearby garage. About a month later, at Officer Wooters' direction, a similar device was surreptitiously installed in another house, and receiving equipment was also set up in a nearby garage. Such methods of getting evidence have been caustically censured by the United States Supreme Court: "That officers of the law would break and enter a home, secrete such a device, even in a bedroom, and listen to the conversations of the occupants for more than a month would be almost incredible if it were not admitted. Few police measures have come to our attention that more flagrantly, deliberately and persistently violate the fundamental principle declared by the Fourth Amendment. . . ." (*Irvine v. California,* 347 U.S. 128, 132 [74 S. Ct. 381, 98 L.Ed. 561].)

Section 653h of the Penal Code does not and could not authorize violations of the Constitution, and the proviso under which the officers purported to act at most prevents their conduct from constituting a violation of that section itself.

The evidence obtained from the microphones was not the only unconstitutionally obtained evidence introduced at the trial over defendants' objection. In addition there was a mass of evidence obtained by numerous forcible entries and seizures without search warrants.

The forcible entries and seizures were candidly admitted by the various officers. For example, Officer Fosnocht identified the evidence that he seized, and testified as to his means of entry: ". . . and how did you gain entrance to the particular place?" "I forced entry through the front door and Officer Farquarson through the rear door." "You say you forced the front door?". . . "Yes." "And how?" "I kicked it open with my foot." Officer Schlocker testified that he entered the place where he seized evidence "through a window located I believe it was west of the front door. . . ." "[W]hen you tried to force entry in other words, you tried to knock it [the door] down, is that right?" "We tried to knock it down, yes, sir." "What with?" "A shoe, foot." "Kick it?" "Tried to kick it in, yes." "And then you moved over and broke the window to gain entrance, is that right?" "We did." Officer Scherrer testified that he gained entry into one of the places where he seized evidence by kicking the front door in. He also entered another place, accompanied by Officers Hilton and Horral, by breaking through a window. Officer Harris "just walked up and kicked the door in" to gain entry to the place assigned to him.

Thus, without fear of criminal punishment or other discipline, law enforcement officers, sworn to support the Constitution of the United States and the

Constitution of California, frankly admit their deliberate, flagrant acts in violation of both Constitutions and the laws enacted thereunder. It is clearly apparent from their testimony that they casually regard such acts as nothing more than the performance of their ordinary duties for which the city employs and pays them.

· · ·

Both the United States Constitution and the California Constitution make it emphatically clear that important as efficient law enforcement may be, it is more important that the right of privacy guaranteed by these constitutional provisions be respected.

Since in *no* case shall the right of the people to be secure against unreasonable searches and seizures be violated, the contention that unreasonable searches and seizures are justified by the necessity of bringing criminals to justice cannot be accepted. It was rejected when the constitutional provisions were adopted and the choice was made that all the people, guilty and innocent alike, should be secure from unreasonable police intrusions, even though some criminals should escape.[2]

Moreover, the constitutional provisions made no distinction between the guilty and the innocent, and it would be manifestly impossible to protect the rights of the innocent if the police were permitted to justify unreasonable searches and seizures on the ground that they assumed their victims were criminals. Thus, when consideration is directed to the question of the admissibility of evidence obtained in violation of the constitutional provisions, it bears emphasis that the court is not concerned solely with the rights of the defendant before it, however guilty he may appear, but with the constitutional right of all of the people to be secure in their homes, persons, and effects.

· · ·

The rule admitting the evidence has been strongly supported by both scholars and judges.[3] Their arguments may be briefly summarized as follows:

The rules of evidence are designed to enable courts to reach the truth and, in criminal cases, to secure a fair trial to those accused of crime. Evidence obtained by an illegal search and seizure is ordinarily just as true and reliable as evidence lawfully obtained. The court needs all reliable evidence material to the issue before it, the guilt or innocence of the accused, and how such evidence is obtained is immaterial to that issue. It should not be excluded unless strong considerations of public policy demand it. There are no such considerations.

Exclusion of the evidence cannot be justified as affording protection or recompense to the defendant or punishment to the officers for the illegal search and seizure. It does not protect the defendant from the search and seizure, since that illegal act has already occurred. If he is innocent or if there is ample evidence to convict him without the illegally obtained evidence, exclusion of the evidence gives him no remedy at all. Thus the only defendants who benefit by the exclusionary rule are those criminals who could not be convicted without the illegally obtained evidence. Allowing such criminals to escape punishment is not appropriate recompense for the invasion of their constitutional rights; it does not punish the officers who violated the constitutional provisions; and it fails to protect society from known criminals who should not be left at large. For his crime the defendant should be punished. For his violation of the constitutional provisions the offending officer should be punished. As the exclusionary rule operates, however, the defendant's crime and the officer's flouting of constitutional guarantees both go unpunished. "The criminal is to go free because the constable has blundered" (Cardozo, J., in *People v. Defore, supra,* 242 N.Y. 13, 21), and "Society is deprived of its remedy against one lawbreaker, because he has been pursued by another." (Jackson, J., in *Irvine v. California, supra,* 347 U.S. 128, at 136; see also Wigmore on Evidence [3d ed.], §VIII, 2184, 40.)

Opponents of the exclusionary rule also point out that it is inconsistent with the rule allowing private litigants to use illegally obtained evidence, and that as applied in the federal courts, it is capricious in its operation, either going too far or not far enough. "So many exceptions to [the exclusionary] rule have been granted the judicial blessing as largely to destroy any value it might otherwise have had. Instead of adding to the security of legitimate individual rights, its principal contribution has been to add further technicalities to the law of criminal procedure. A district attorney who is willing to pay the price may easily circumvent its limitations. And the price to be paid is by no means high." (Grant, "Circumventing the Fourth Amendment" *Southern California Law Review,* XIV, 359.) Thus, the rule as applied in the federal courts has been held to protect only defendants whose own rights have been invaded by federal officers. If the illegal search and seizure have been conducted by a state officer or a private person not acting in cooperation with federal officers, or if the property seized is not defendant's, the rule does not apply.

Finally it has been pointed out that there is no convincing evidence that the exclusionary rule actually tends to prevent unreasonable searches and seizures and that the "disciplinary or educational effect of the court's releasing the defendant for police misbehavior is so indirect as to be no more than a mild deterrent at best." (Jackson, J., in *Irvine v. California,* 347 U.S. 128, at pp. 136–37 [78 S.Ct. 381, 98 L.Ed. 561].)

Despite the persuasive force of the foregoing arguments, we have concluded, as Justice Carter and Justice Schauer have consistently maintained,[4] that evidence obtained in violation of the constitutional guarantees is inadmissible, and the cases based thereon are therefore overruled.[5] We have been compelled to reach that conclusion because other remedies have completely failed to secure compliance with the constitutional provisions on the part of police officers with the attendant result that the courts under the old rule have been constantly required to participate in, and in effect condone, the lawless activities of law enforcement officers.

When, as in the present case, the very purpose of an illegal search and seizure is to get evidence to introduce at a trial, the success of the lawless venture depends entirely on the court's lending its aid by allowing the evidence to be introduced. It is no answer to say that a distinction should be drawn between the government acting as law enforcer and the gatherer of evidence and the government acting as judge. "[N]o distinction can be taken between the Government as prosecutor and the Government as judge. If the existing code does not permit district attorneys to have a hand in such dirty business it does not permit the judge to allow such iniquities to succeed." Out of regard for its own dignity as an agency of justice and custodian of liberty, the court should not have a hand in such "dirty business." Courts refuse their aid in civil cases to prevent the consummation of illegal schemes of private litigants; *a fortiori,* they should not extend that aid and thereby permit the consummation of illegal schemes of the state itself. It is morally incongruous for the state to flout constitutional rights and at the same time demand that its citizens observe the law. The end that the state seeks may be a laudable one, but it no more justifies unlawful acts than a laudable end justifies unlawful action by any member of the public. Moreover, any process of law that sanctions the imposition of penalties upon an individual through the use of the fruits of official lawlessness tends to the destruction of the whole system of restraints on the exercise of the public force that are inherent in the "concept of ordered liberty." (See Allen, "The Wolf Case," *Illinois Law Review,* XLV, 1, 20.) "Decency, security, and liberty alike demand that government officials shall be subjected to the same rules of conduct that are commands to the citizen. In a government of laws, existence of the government will be imperiled if it fails to observe the law scrupulously. Our Government is the potent, the omnipresent teacher. For good or for ill, it teaches the whole people by its example. Crime is contagious. If the Government becomes a law-breaker, it breeds contempt for law, it invites every man to become a law unto himself; it invites anarchy. To declare that in the administration of the criminal law the end justifies the means—to declare that the Government may commit crimes to secure the conviction of a private criminal—would bring terrible retribution. Against that pernicious doctrine this Court should resolutely set its face."

If the unconstitutional conduct of the law enforcement officers were more flagrant or more closely connected with the conduct of the trial, it is clear that the foregoing principles would compel the reversal of any conviction based thereon. Thus, no matter how guilty a defendant might be or how outrageous his crime, he must not be deprived of a fair trial, and any action, official or otherwise, that would have that effect would not be tolerated. Similarly, he may not be convicted on the basis of evidence obtained by the use of the rack or the screw or other brutal means no matter how reliable the evidence obtained may be. (*Rochin v. California, supra* 342 U.S. 165.) Today one of the foremost public concerns is the police state, and recent history has demonstrated all too clearly how short the step is from lawless although efficient enforcement of the law to the stamping out of human rights. This peril has been recognized and dealt with when its challenge has been obvious; it cannot be forgotten when it strikes further from the courtroom by invading the privacy of homes.

If the unconstitutional guarantees against unreasonable searches and seizures are to have significance they must be enforced, and if courts are to discharge their duty to support the state and federal Constitutions they must be willing to aid in their enforcement. If those guarantees were being effectively enforced by other means than excluding evidence obtained by their violation, a different problem would be presented. If such were the case there would be more force to the argument that a particular criminal should not be redressed for a past violation of his rights by excluding the evidence against him. Experience has demonstrated, however, that neither administrative, criminal, nor civil remedies are effective in suppressing lawless searches and seizures. The innocent suffer with the guilty, and we cannot close our eyes to the effect the rule we adopt will have on the rights of those not before the court. "Alternatives [to the exclusionary rule] are deceptive. Their very statement conveys the impression that one possibility is as effective as the next. For there is but one alternative to the rule of exclusion. That is no sanction at all." (Murphy, J., dissenting in *Wolf v. Colorado, supra* 338 U.S. 25, 41; see also *Weeks v. United States,* 232 U.S. 383, 393 [34 S. Cit. 341, 58 L.Ed. 652, L.R.A. 1915B 834].) "The difficulty with [other remedies] is in part due to the failure of interested parties to inform of the offense. No matter what an illegal raid turns up, police are unlikely to inform on themselves or each other. If it turns up nothing incriminating, the innocent victim usually does not care to take steps that will air the fact that he has been under suspicion." (Jackson, J., in *Irvine v. California, supra* 347 U.S. 128, 137.) Moreover, even when it becomes generally known that the police conduct illegal searches and seizures, public opinion is not aroused as it is in the case of other violations of constitutional rights. Illegal searches and seizures lack the obvious brutality of coerced confessions and the third degree, and do not so clearly strike at the very basis of our civil liberties as do unfair trials or the lynching of even an admitted murderer. "Freedom of speech, of the press, of religion, easily summon powerful support against encroachment. The prohibition against unreasonable search and seizure is normally invoked by those accused of crime, and criminals have few friends." (Frankfurter, J., dissenting in *Harris v. United States,* 331 U.S. 145, 156 [67 S. Ct. 1098, 91 L.Ed. 1399].) There is thus all the more necessity for courts to be vigilant in protecting these constitutional rights if they are to be protected at all. *People v. Mayen,* 188 Cal. 237 [205 P. 435, 24 A.L.R. 1383], was decided over thirty years ago. Since then case after case has appeared in our appellate reports describing unlawful searches and seizures against the defendant on trial, and those cases undoubtedly reflect only a small fraction of the violations of the constitutional provisions that have actually occurred. On the other hand, reported cases involving civil actions against police officers are rare, and those involving successful prosecutions against officers are non-existent. In short, the constitutional provisions are not being enforced.

Granted that the adoption of the exclusionary rule will not prevent all illegal searches and seizures, it will discourage them. Police officers and prosecuting officials are primarily interested in convicting criminals. Given the exclusionary rule and a choice between securing evidence by legal rather than illegal means, officers will be impelled to obey the law themselves since not to do so will jeopardize their objectives.

NOTES

1. Section 653h of the Penal Code provides: "Any person who, without consent of the owner, lessee, or occupant, installs or attempts to install or use a dictograph in any house, room, apartment, tenement, office, shop, warehouse, store, mill, barn, stable, or other building, tent, vessel, railroad car, vehicle, mine, or any underground portion thereof, is guilty of a misdemeanor; provided, that nothing herein shall prevent the use and installation of dictographs by a regular salaried police officer expressly authorized thereto by the head of his office or department or by a district attorney when such use and installation are necessary in the performance of their duties in detecting crime and in the apprehension of criminals."
2. "Of course, this like each of our constitutional guarantees often may afford a shelter for criminals. But the forefathers thought this was not too great a price to pay for that decent privacy of home, papers, and effects which is indispensable to the individual dignity and self-respect. They may have overvalued privacy, but I am not disposed to set their command at naught." (Jackson, J., dissenting in *Harris v. United States*, 331 U.S. 145, 197, 198 [67 S.Ct. 1098, 91 L.Ed 1399]; see also *United States v. Di Re*, 332 U.S. 581, 595 [68 S.Ct. 222, 92 L.Ed 210].)
3. See *Wigmore on Evidence* [3d ed.] VIII, § 2184; Waite, "Police Regulations by Rules of Evidence," *Michigan Law Review*, XLII, 679; Harno, "Evidence Obtained by Illegal Search and Seizure," *Illinois Law Review*, XIX, 303; Grant, "Circumventing the Fourth Amendment," *Southern California Law Review*, XIV, 359; Grant, "Illegally Seized Evidence," *id.*, XV, 60; Grant, "Search and Seizure in California," XV, 139; Plumb, "Illegal Enforcement of the Law," *Cornell Law Quarterly*, XXIV, 337; Judge Cardozo's opinion in *People v. Defore*, 242 N.Y. 13 [150 N.E. 585, 44 A.L.R. 510], is perhaps the best judicial defense of this position.
4. See dissenting opinions in *People v. Gonzales*, 20 Cal. 2d 165 [124 P.2d 44]; *People v. Kelley*, 22 Cal. 2d 169 [137 P.2d 1]; *People v. Rochin*, 101 Cal. App. 2d 140, 143, 149 [225 P.2d 1, 913]; reversed by United States Supreme Court, *Rochin v. California*, 342 U.S. 165 [72 S. Ct. 205, 96 L.Ed. 183, 25 A.L.R.2d 1396]); *In re Dixon*, 41 Cal. 2d 756, 764 [264 P.2d 513].
5. "[S]ince experience is of all teachers the most dependable, and since experience also is a continuous process, it follows that a rule of evidence at one time thought necessary to the ascertainment of truth should yield to the experience of a succeeding generation whenever that experience has clearly demonstrated the fallacy or unwisdom of the old rule." (Sutherland J., in *Funk v. United States*, 290 U.S. 371, 381 [54 S.Ct. 212, 78 L.Ed 369, 93 A.L.R. 1136].)

54

Conventional Morality, Judicial Control, and Police Conduct

JEROME H. SKOLNICK

The Exclusionary Rule

The most celebrated device for enforcing police lawfulness is the "exclusionary rule" of evidence. The rule is simple to present in its broadest form:

> Upon appropriate motion by the defendant in a criminal prosecution, evidence obtained from the defendant in violation of his constitutional rights to be free from unreasonable searches and seizures will be suppressed by order of the court.[1]

The rule originated in the federal courts with the cases of *Boyd v. United States*[2] and *Weeks v. United States*,[3] decided by the Supreme Court of the United States in 1886 and 1914, respectively. In 1955, the California court in *People v. Cahan*[4] overturned its long established law and adopted the exclusionary rule. Between 1914, when the Supreme Court of the United States decided *Weeks*, and 1960, when it decided *Mapp v. Ohio*,[5] only half of the American states had adopted the exclusionary rule. Of these, 20 appeared to have adopted the rule without substantial qualification. Although these states included many of the most populous jurisdictions, New York State was not among them. As a result of the *Mapp v. Ohio* decision, announced on the last day of the 1960 term, all states are now required, by reason of the due process clause of the Fourteenth Amendment, to exclude from state criminal trials evidence illegally seized by state officers.

The assumption behind the rule as a control device was stated in fullest clarity by Judge Traynor in *People v. Cahan:*

> Granted that the adoption of the exclusionary rule will not prevent all illegal searches and seizures, it will discourage them. Police officers and prosecuting officials are primarily interested in convicting criminals. Given the exclusionary rule and a choice between securing evidence by legal rather than illegal means, officers will be impelled to obey the law themselves since not to do so will jeopardize their objectives.[6]

From *Justice Without Trial: Law Enforcement in a Democratic Society* (New York: Wiley, 1966), pp. 211–227. Reprinted by permission of the publisher.

Thus, the adoption of the exclusionary rule in California was based on an assumed relation between judicial sanctions and the behavior of policing authorities. This assumption would be difficult to "test" rigorously. I believe, however, that the following materials, plus some of those already presented, shed light on the issue. These materials are based upon actual observation of the working of the rule, and more precisely, the working under it. While the rule, of course, applies to all classes of crime, it is pertinent in fact mainly to cases involving conventional morality, or "victimless crimes," those cases falling principally under the jurisdiction of the vice control squad, especially the narcotics detail.

Briefly stated, the exclusionary rule rejects illegally seized evidence. The question, then, is, what constitutes "illegal seizure"? If the rules of search and seizure permitted police to do anything they wanted at any time, for example, to kick in a door on pure hunch, then evidence seized as a result of such entry would still be admissible under an exclusionary rule. The rule excludes only *illegally* seized evidence. Consequently, once an exclusionary rule has been adopted nationally, the question becomes one of defining the legality of search-and-seizure practices.[7] To my knowledge, there has not been any actual observation of police behavior under the exclusionary rule, nor any firsthand discussion of the conditions under which this rule has force. This chapter will discuss the meaning of the exclusionary rule to the policeman, the perspective of the police about the rule, and arrangements leading to greater or lesser compliance with arrest rules.

The Policeman's View of the Exclusionary Rule

Under the exclusionary rule, there are two consecutive problems facing the policeman. Initially, he must consider what behavior constitutes a legal search, or, more precisely, a legal arrest, since most searches are made "incident" to an arrest without a warrant. Second, the policeman must develop a strategy to make his behavior take on the appearance of legality, if not the reality. The police understand the need to create "probable cause" for an arrest to be able lawfully to search the suspect's premises. Since the circumstances, however, do not always offer sufficient time to locate a magistrate who will affirm a warrant for the suspect's arrest, the police may fall back on another arrangement developed for just such emergencies. A working agreement between a parole officer and the vice control police can be reached, for instance, by which the parole officer informally delegates arresting authority to the police. The police, however, do not prefer such arrangements even though they are party to them. In their opinion, the law of arrest is improperly interpreted by the courts and they would much prefer a different context—one not putting them in the position, as they see it, of being required to find ways to avoid restrictions of arrest laws. From the police point of view, the whole problem could be resolved if the courts were to revise their stand on the legality of arrest.

This issue has been much discussed by legal scholars. At the heart of the controversy is the question of whether the courts should continue to focus upon the legality of the arrest rather than the reasonableness of the search and seizure in determining whether to reject evidence on the basis of the exclusionary rule.[8] To the lay reader, the distinction may appear without substance, but it is crucial in the law of arrests, searches, and seizures. When the courts focus on the legality of the arrest, police actions are more closely constrained, at least legally. By contrast, if the focus were on the reasonableness of the search, the police would have considerably greater latitude.

This point requires further explanation. The present standard for a policeman making an arrest is that he have "reasonable cause" to do so. If the police have "reasonable cause" to make an arrest, they also have the right to search, provided the search relates to (is "incident" to) the arrest. In behavioral terms, the issue is whether the police are required to have enough evidence for an arrest *before* they are permitted to search a man's person or home and seize his property, or whether they can search him first, to seize evidence that can be used *afterward* to justify the arrest.

The issue of precedence is of considerable practical consequence. A policeman observes an individual behaving "suspiciously," but not enough to constitute "probable cause" for an arrest. The policeman would like to search the suspicious individual to determine whether something of a criminal nature, for example, a marijuana cigarette, is in the man's pocket. In turn, the finding of the marijuana cigarette would provide the policeman with "probable cause" to make an arrest. The commonly voiced objection to delegating the police the right to search before arrest is, of course, that the police would abuse the privilege by searching indiscriminately, until they discovered evidence sufficient to constitute "probable cause." By contrast, the police maintain that they are able craftsmen who can determine with high accuracy whether a suspect "merits" a search.

It is often difficult for police to draw a line between what, on the one hand, constitutes suspicious behavior, and on the other, provides sufficient evidence to infer "reasonable or probable cause" for an arrest—even under present standards allowing search only as incident to an arrest. No simple formula can determine reasonable cause, since many factors must be taken into account. Those discussed in California cases include:

> . . . nature of information, character of informant, delay which might enable a guilty person to escape, details of description, time of day, flight, furtive conduct, presence at the scene of the crime, results of consent to search, results of reasonable investigatory search, admissions by the person being questioned, criminal record of the arrested person, criminal record of associates, reputation of the premises, and recent crimes in the neighborhood.[9]

The policeman's problem is therefore shared to a degree by the courts, who are called on in numerous cases, each with a different factual situation, to decide under what conditions police have legal cause for arrest and, therefore, grounds to search and seize. Given the frequency of decision, legal requirements about a novel factual situation may be unclear.

The policeman typically feels that courts have provided insufficiently clear standards for routine decisions. Where the policeman perceives the line between legality and illegality as hazy, he usually handles the situation in the interest justifying a contention of legality, irrespective of the actual circumstances. He therefore operates as one whose aim is to legitimize the evidence pertaining to the case, rather than as a jurist whose goal is to analyze the sufficiency of the evidence based on case law.

Bearing in mind the obligation to fulfill the search-and-seizure requirements, his strategy is to try to locate as many congeries of events as appear to fulfill their mandate. Thus, the policeman perceives his job not simply as requiring that he arrest where he finds probable cause. In addition, he sees the need to be able to reconstruct a set of complex happenings in such a way that, subsequent to the arrest, probable cause can be found according to appellate court standards. In this way, as one district attorney expressed it, "the policeman fabricates probable cause." By saying this, he did not mean to assert that the policeman is a liar, but rather that he finds it necessary to construct an *ex post facto* description of the preceding events so that these conform to legal arrest requirements, whether in fact the events actually did so or not at the time of the arrest. Thus, the policeman respects the necessity for "complying" with the arrest laws. His "compliance," however, may take the form of *post hoc* manipulation of the facts rather than before-the-fact behavior. Again, this generalization does not apply in all cases. Where the policeman feels capable of literal compliance (as in the conditions provided by the "big case"), he does comply. But when he sees the case law as a hindrance to his primary task of apprehending criminals, he usually attempts to construct the appearance of compliance, rather than allow the offender to escape apprehension.

Police Work under the Exclusionary Rule

In practice, it may be equally difficult to characterize the precise nature of specific events upon which the *inference* of probable cause may be based as to define the concept itself. For instance, there is in practice nothing clear about a concept like "furtive conduct," a set of behaviors establishing probable cause for an arrest. An incident observed one evening illustrates this point:

I was accompanying a couple of narcotics policemen (one state, one Westville) in an unmarked car. The driver, a Westville policeman, made a slow but wide right turn, said "oh-oh," and beckoned to a tall Negro man standing on the street, perpendicular to a straight line drawn from the driver's seat.

I saw the man glance left and right, and move slightly, with a jerky motion, less pronounced, but akin to that of the first-base runner trying to bluff a pitcher into making a throw. The driver jumped out of the car, began talking to the man, who backed up against the trunk. A few seconds later, I heard scuffling noises, and the state agent jumped out of the car to assist the driver. I jumped out also. By the time I got to the rear of the car, the man had been pushed down on the trunk by the driver, who had one hand on the man's throat and the other on his arm, pinning him down. In the meantime, the state agent had grabbed the other arm and was trying to extract something from the man's mouth.

What had happened was this: the man had made what the policeman later described as a "furtive" movement. A known addict, he was, to the officer's trained eyes, trying to dispose of an item of incriminating evidence that the policeman thought the suspect had dropped onto the pavement. When approached, however, the suspect turned around and backed off to the police car, with his left hand closed. The officer asked the man to open his fist. Instead, the man quickly brought his hand to his mouth, popped a marijuana cigarette into it, and tried to swallow. The policeman immediately grabbed the man's throat to cut off his air supply, and prevent him from swallowing. Incredibly, the suspect was able to swallow the cigarette despite the choking administered by the policeman.[10]

Even if the suspect had not managed to swallow the "joint," however, it might have been difficult for the policeman to have convinced a magistrate that "reasonable cause" was present for an arrest and incidental search. As the policeman said:

It's awfully hard to explain to a judge what I mean when I testify that I saw a furtive movement. I'm glad you were along to see this because you can see what we're up against. . . . I can testify as to the character of the neighborhood, my knowledge that the man was an addict and all that stuff, but what I mean is that when I see a hype move the way that guy moved, I *know* he's trying to get rid of something.

I asked the policeman if he had ever been wrong in this kind of judgment and he replied that he had, but felt that he was right often enough to justify a search, even when lacking evidence to arrest the suspect.

Thus, as a matter of principle, the police would like to have greater freedom to make searches *not* "incident" to an arrest. That is, they would like to be able to search first and then arrest on the basis of incriminating evidence disclosed by the search. Generally, however, constitutional interpretation has not accorded this liberty to the police:

In the law of arrest and by long constitutional history, "reasonable" has been interpreted as the equivalent of probable cause. An officer acts reasonably if, on the facts before him, it would appear that the suspect has probably committed a specific crime. This is the context in which the word is used in the Fourth Amendment and in most state arrest laws. Our cases sharply distinguish the reasonableness of an arrest on probable cause from unreasonable apprehension grounded on "mere" suspicion.[11]

Understandably, the police oppose the continuation of such a "strict" interpretation of the Constitution. They claim to have special skills enabling them to detect criminal activity, or its potential, and thus the privilege of prior search would not be abused. In addition, police and their spokesmen typically argue that a judicial standard based on the reasonableness of the search would not only *not* interfere with the rights of the average citizen, but would, on the positive side, protect him against the ravages of criminal behavior. Thus, one leading opponent of the exclusionary rule takes the position that the " 'turn 'em loose' court decisions" placing limitations on the right of police to search and seize have had the effect of "actually facilitating" the activities of "the criminal element" and asserts that these decisions have caused some of the increase in crime over the ten-year period starting in 1950.[12] While admitting that "in any democratic society police efficiency must necessarily incur a considerable measure of sacrifice in deference to the rights and liberties of the individual," this same critic contends that "some sacrifice of individual rights and liberties has to be made in order to achieve and maintain a safe, stable society in which the individual may exercise those rights and liberties." [13]

The validity of the argument that the rights of the average citizen would be enhanced by a judicial standard of reasonableness of search and seizure varies, however, with the type of citizen about whom one is expressing concern. One of the unanticipated consequences of the policeman's standard of "reasonableness" is that it adversely affects many honest citizens living in high-crime areas. To a degree, all persons residing in such areas are "symbolic assailants." A "symbolic assailant," the reader will recall, need not in fact be a criminal, but needs merely to conform to the stereotype. By this standard, Negroes who live in black ghettos are especially prone to being searched according to a "reasonableness of the search" [14] standard. Furthermore, given the cognitive disposition of the police described earlier, they tend to polarize the population between respectable people and criminals—who, in their eyes, may include otherwise respectable citizens not conforming to the policeman's portrait of respectability, as, for instance, bearded college students.

The most serious difficulty with the "reasonableness of the search" standard for police conduct—indeed, with "reasonableness" in general as a justifying norm for official behavior—applies to all judgments made on a probability basis. If an honest citizen resides in a neighborhood heavily populated by criminals, just as the chances are high that he might be one, so too are the chances high that he might be mistaken for one. The probabilities, from the point of view of the individual, are always the same—either he is or is not culpable. Thus, behavior that seems "reasonable" to the police because of the character of the neighborhood is seen by the honest citizen in it as irresponsible and unreasonable. About *him,* more errors will necessarily be made under a "reasonableness" standard. Indeed, the fewer the honest citizens in such an area, the more the police will be perceived by them as "brutal," "offensive," "unreasonable"; and justifiably so, because the chances are in fact greater that the police will treat honest citizens as criminals. It would also seem to follow that, to the extent the police treat honest citizens living in high-crime areas as criminals, the police inadvertently encourage them to take on the behavior patterns of their more criminal neighbors. For them, the inevitable message is the futility of honesty.[15] Whether police behavior is or is not truly "reasonable" depends on who is judging it: the police doing their job in a high-crime zone, or the honest citizen living in such an area.

In a private communication, Professor Edward Barrett commented upon this section of the manuscript as follows:

> The central legal notion is that official interference with person or property should be discriminate. . . . Inherent in the notion (and inevitable in any enforcement process) is the fact that innocent persons will from time to time be subjected to the process. Is the problem significantly different when it is the innocent person in the high crime area and the innocent person in another area who meets a description or who is carrying a bundle late at night? I suppose the difference mainly is, as you point out, the likelihood that the same innocent person will be subjected to frequent police contacts because he is usually in the suspicious area. And he may not be free for a variety of reasons to move out of the area. But still what is the solution? Does not a furtive movement in one part of town constitute probable cause where the same movement would not in another? Would not police reaction in one part of town be discriminate and in another indiscriminate? Can we afford to structure the system to protect persons living in ambiguous situations?

These pointed and practical questions illuminate the difficulties of reform of criminal procedural rules. All too often writers on the subject fail to give sufficient consideration to the simple notion that legal practices must have a differential impact in a stratified and racially constructed society. As we see here, the negative consequences of the norm of reasonableness are intensified in the highest-crime areas, which also tend to be the most highly "ghettoized."

Police Culture and Legal Rules

Arguments about legal standards are usually unrealistic, whether they come from civil liberties advocates or law enforcement spokesmen. Each group assumes the behavioral efficacy of legally formulated restraints. The civil libertarian typically feels that tighter strictures ought to be placed on police, and that if they were, police would feel obliged to conform. The law enforcement spokesman makes a matching behavioral assumption when he argues that restraints on police behavior are already too severe. My observations suggest, in contrast to both these positions, that norms located within police organization are more powerful than court decisions in shaping police behavior, and that actually the process of interaction between the two accounts ultimately for how police behave.[16] This interpretation does not deny that legal rules have an effect, but it suggests that the language of courts is given meaning through a process mediated by the organizational structure and perspectives of the police. In the following paragraphs, I intend briefly to analyze aspects of the policeman's situation shaping the process by which he develops a set of behaviors and attitudes about the exclusionary rule.

It is instructive to begin this discussion by considering a situation where a narcotics officer observes a known addict make a subtle body movement, indicating to the policeman that the man is carrying some narcotic or drug in violation of a law forbidding the possession of narcotics. The policeman would prefer to have any seizure he makes be accepted as evidence in court under the exclusionary rule. Whether it is or not, however, will not determine his decision to search the suspect. His reasons for selecting arrest criteria are numerous.

Above all, the policeman sees his job as ferreting out crime. The idea that the policeman should be "alert," "vigilant," "on his toes" to the possibility of crime seems the fundamental craft requirement of the policeman. He may try later to figure out what the suspect did which might have justified a search. But the policeman would ordinarily feel embarrassed to report to a superior or to a colleague, for example, that he had hesitated to search an addict on the street because he had first to meditate upon the addict's legal rights, and that, because of his hesitation, the addict had in the meantime escaped, or had disposed of the incriminating evidence. It is part of the policeman's job to locate and confiscate illegal substances. Thus, even if a search revealing possession of an unlawful weapon or an unlawful narcotic was conducted not as "incident" to an arrest, the policeman would have done part of his job simply through the act of retrieval. By failing to make the putatively "unreasonable" search, the policeman would not only have failed to gain a conviction, but would also have missed collecting objects or substances regarded as dangerous. In the policeman's view, only good can come of a search legally defined as "unreasonable," provided the search jibes with the normative assumptions of the police organization about reasonableness.

Arthur Train, writing in an earlier part of the century, implies that police rules have long been conflicting and confusing, and sympathizes with the dilemma faced by the policeman.

It is easy while sitting on the piazza with your cigar to recognize the rights of your fellow-men, you may assert most vigorously the right of the citizen to immunity from arrest without legal cause, but if you saw a seedy character sneaking down a side street at three o'clock in the morning, his pockets bulging with jewelry and silver, would you have the policeman on post insist on the fact that a burglary had been committed being established beyond peradventure before arresting the suspect, who in the meantime would undoubtedly escape? Of course, the worthy officer sometimes does this, but his conduct in that case becomes the subject of an investigation on the part of his superiors. In fact, the rules of the New York police department require him to arrest all persons carrying bags in the small hours who cannot give a satisfactory account of themselves. Yet there is no such thing under the laws of the state as a right "to arrest on suspicion." No citizen may be arrested under the statutes unless a crime has actually been committed. Thus, the police regulations deliberately compel every officer either to violate the law or to be made the object of charges for dereliction of duty. A confusing state of things, truly, to a man who wants to do his duty by himself and by his fellow-citizens! [17]

Of course, a policeman cannot walk up to a man in broad daylight and demand that he stand facing a wall with hands raised, simply because the policeman has decided that to search every tenth citizen on Main Street would be an effective mode of enforcing criminal law. But if a policeman can give some reason to his organizational superiors (including the district attorney) for conducting a search, in practice the worst punishment he can suffer is loss of a conviction. If a search yields no incriminating evidence, those who are illegally searched are usually pleased to drop the matter.

On the other hand, if something is found, the moral burden immediately shifts to the suspect. The illegality of a search is likely to be tempered—even in the eyes of the judiciary—by the discovery of incriminating evidence on the suspect. For example, when a suspect turns out actually to possess narcotics, the perception of surrounding facts and circumstances about the reasonableness of the arrest can shift in only one direction—against the defendant and in favor of the propriety of the search—even if the facts might have appeared differently had no incriminating evidence been discovered.

The case of *Ker v. California* [18] offers an interesting illustration of the tendency to affirm what is later found to be correct. In this case, reasonable cause was not at issue, but the affirmative tendency is expressed in a related area. The salient facts are: an informer's tip, plus some police observations, connected Ker with specific illegal activities involving a known marijuana seller named Murphy. Police officers observed Ker and Murphy conversing, but the officers could not tell whether anything had been exchanged between them. As Ker drove away, however, they recorded his license plate numbers. A check with the Department of Motor Vehicles revealed Ker's address. Officers were dispatched to his residence. "They then went to the office of the building manager and obtained from him a pass key to the apartment. Officer Berman unlocked and opened the door, proceeding quietly, he testified, in order to prevent the destruction of evidence, and found petitioner George Ker sitting in the living room."

The means of entry was upheld, by a 5-4 decision of the court. The dissenters (Justice Brennan, the Chief Justice, Justice Douglas, Justice Goldberg) argued:

Even if probable cause exists for the arrest of a person within, the Fourth Amendment is violated by an unannounced police intrusion into a private home, with or without an arrest warrant, except (1) where the persons within already know of the officers' authority and purposes or (2) where the officers are justified in the belief that persons within are in imminent peril of bodily harm, or (3) where those within, made aware of the presence of someone outside (because, for example, there has been a knock at the door), are then engaged in activity which justifies the officers in the belief that an escape or the destruction of evidence is being attempted.[19]

The dissenters' objections were answered by Justice Clark's opinion for the court, as follows:

> Here justification for the officer's failure to give notice is uniquely present. In addition to the officer's belief that Ker was in possession of narcotics, which could be quickly and easily destroyed, Ker's further furtive conduct in eluding them shortly before the arrest was ground for belief that he might well have been expecting the police. We therefore hold that in the particular circumstances of this case the officer's method of entry, sanctioned by the law of California, was not unreasonable under the standards of the Fourth Amendment as applied to the states through the Fourteenth Amendment.[20]

If one looks at the world primarily through practical lenses, the exclusionary rule is difficult to defend, since it frequently denies the introduction of what would otherwise constitute perfectly acceptable evidence. In my opinion the *Ker* case may also be read as an illustration of the persuasiveness of factual guilt and administrative efficiency over the principle of excluding illegally obtained evidence. I do not doubt the "principled" intentions or moral character of the majority of the Supreme Court. Nevertheless, the language used may be interpreted as a general tendency to give weight to fact, irrespective of how it has been obtained. Thus, I am suggesting that the court itself might have voted differently in a laboratory situation that held all the preceding circumstances constant, but which showed the marijuana not to be present.

If such tendencies are present in the court, they are even more pronounced early in the case, where the police are involved. Here, the onus typically shifts to the suspect if he is found to have incriminating evidence in his possession. The policeman has an upper hand under such conditions, even when his legal position is questionable. Especially in the "small pinch," the policeman is not usually interested in arresting the man with a "joint" or two of marijuana, but in using him to "turn" his supplier. In that situation, the exclusionary rule may not appear salient to the defendant.

That incriminating evidence is found is a fact not lost on the defense attorney, either. For him, too, operating in a context of "reasonableness," as understood in the administrative sense, the defendant comes to represent a less defensible client. The attorney may decide to fight the case energetically on a search-and-seizure point, and he may even win an acquittal for his client. In the routine minor case, however, evidence may influence the defense attorney to persuade his client to plead guilty. This tendency is pronounced when, as so often happens, the reasonableness of the arrest is a borderline judgment. Under such circumstances, the case will not go to trial, and the exclusionary rule issue will consequently not be invoked.

The worst that can happen to the individual policeman for an illegal search is loss of a conviction as a result of the exclusionary rule. Superiors within the police organization will, however, be in sympathy with an officer, provided the search was administratively reasonable, even if the officer did not have legal "reasonable" cause to make an arrest. The officers who search an addict's room, for instance, would certainly not be prosecuted by the district attorney for trespassing, were they caught. Besides, as discussed above, an addict would never make a complaint against the police, just because he is an addict. Moreover, civil suits for false arrest are difficult to prove.[21]

Finally, the case of *Ker v. California* illustrates that the problematic character of legality encourages the police to test the meaning of due process of law. Suppose, for instance, we were to try to construct a model entirely in consonance with the rule of law for the conduct of a police force. Surely, if this were to be a practical model, we would have to take into account the latitude afforded the police by *Ker v. California.* There are presently any number of practices used by the police that a dedicated civil libertarian would not regard as conforming to the rule of law. On the other hand, it would not be at all unreasonable for law enforcement officials to feel, as regards these same practices, that "justification . . . is uniquely present," to cite the words of Justice Clark. Thus, every court ruling based upon the practical needs of the police as a working organization tends to reinforce—in the sense of the term as used by experimental psychologists—the tendency to continue every questionable practice that can be justified in the name of expediency, unless expressly forbidden.

Consequently, all these reasons—the norm of police alertness; the requirement that police confiscate illegal substances; the tendency toward a presumption of the legality of the search once the illegal substance is found; the fact that in a "small pinch" the policeman is usually not interested in an arrest but in creating an informant; the fact that the defense will be impressed by the presence of incriminating evidence; the sympathy of police superiors so long as policemen act in conformity with administrative norms of police organization; the difficulty of proving civil suits for false arrest; the denial of fact by the exclusionary rule; and the problematic character of what behavior is permitted when justification may appear to a court to be "uniquely present"—militate against the effectiveness of the exclusionary rule. In short, the norms of the police are fundamentally pragmatic. Since the policeman has everything to gain and little to lose when he uses the "reasonableness of the search and seizure" standard in small cases, he does so, even though this is not the prevailing legal standard.

To make these observations, however, is not to deny the possible effectiveness of sanctions on police behavior as a way of insuring compliance with procedural roles. I do not wish to be understood as implying that the legal structure under which the police work has no effect, but rather as stating the conditions under which its effects may be perceived. The policeman is more likely to take seriously the more rigorous standard—"search incident to an arrest"—the better the anticipated pinch. Or, put another way, the exclusionary principle puts pressure on the police to work within the rules in those cases where prosecution is contemplated.

At the beginning of a case, or in general patrolling activities, police are only slightly deterred by the prospect of loss of a conviction, because they are still exploring. Thus, the police thought it "reasonable" to search Archie's room beforehand even though the search was illegal, partly because they really had little to lose at that point. Similarly, they have little hesitancy about "frisking" a suspect against whom they have no reasonable cause to make an arrest. Once their explorations have borne fruit, however, they are apt to pay greater attention to the formalities of the rules of search and seizure. When these explorations indicate that a "big case" is in the making, then conditions have been provided under which court injunctions can be taken most seriously. The big case affords time to establish probable cause, to obtain a warrant, and most important, to use a police-informant rather than an addict-informant whose criminal status needs to be protected. Thus, the rule seems to control police almost in direct relation to the gravity of the crime of the suspect.[22]

Police Attitudes Toward the Judiciary

The practical concerns of police do not enter the thinking of the judiciary on the problem of how policemen should act in carrying out their duties. This is not because the policeman's domain of concerns is wider than that of the judge, but rather because their concerns are different, although somewhat overlapping. The police, for example, perceive such informal arrangements as the informer system as necessities if they are to perform their duties adequately. Judges do not—and cannot without abdicating responsibility to evaluate the policeman's work—take such arrangements into full account. The policeman and the judge consequently measure the quality of the policeman's work against inharmonious standards derived from the different responsibilities of each. Or, stated another way, while the policeman and the judge are part of the same system, they are not connected with the same organizations.

One often hears policemen criticizing the "reasonableness" and "intelligence" of judges, sometimes expressing wonderment at how such wrongheaded men could rise to high positions of authority. Implicitly, and sometimes explicitly, there is an invidious contrast drawn between the supervisory policeman, for instance, the captain or chief, and the judge. When the supervisory policeman, however, evaluates the patrolman's behavior toward a suspect, his frame of reference encompasses all the obligations a policeman has. Indeed, the supervisory policeman may be a more severe taskmaster than the judge. The judge may care only whether the policeman complies with the law of arrest and confession, while supervisory law enforcers are likely to be concerned that the policeman "shape up" in a number of behavioral and attitudinal sectors—his ability to cooperate with his associates, his punctuality, his discipline within the organization, and his physical presentability. Thus, the greater "understanding" that the officer may attribute to the supervisor can be located in the similarity between the supervisory policeman's frame of reference about the arresting process, and the arresting officer's. Consequently, the supervisory policeman is able to temper demands in one area of police behavior with an understanding of the arresting officer's obligations in another, for example, his commitment to the informer system. By contrast, the judge need not find it a necessary part of his job to inquire into the consequences of his ruling for police organization and efficiency.

Pleased by the understanding shown by their superiors, policemen generally find it hard to understand why a judge should have so much "say" over their work, especially as supervisory policemen become increasingly "professional." What law enforcement personnel neglect to take into account, however, is not only the obligations of judges to a wider community of interests than the police; they also fail to analyze further consequences. Suppose supervisory police were to be given greater authority. At least in the police force studied, the principal effect might be reduction of cohesion and morale in the police organization itself.

Supervisory police are already attentive to opinions expressed by the general community. Like administrators of various large organizations, including some universities, their inclination is to mollify the concerns of various interests in the larger community, while turning a relatively deaf ear to the constituency over which they wield authority. A student spokesman at the recent University of California "free speech" crisis expressed a general problem of large-scale organizations when he said: "They (the administrators) haven't been interested in finding out what we want—they care only about what they can give to keep us quiet." The same sort of problem is heightened in large police departments, where the norms of military-like obedience camouflage resentments that might otherwise be publicly expressed. Thus, if supervisory police were, for instance, to rule on warrants and probable cause, they would be in the position of sometimes having to invoke a wider perspective and rule against the behavior of their own men. At the same time, they would also be in the position of supporting the same behaviors in their role as leaders of the agency. Either they would begin to take on the perspective of the judge, in which case police demands might remain unsatisfied; or they would maintain the police perspective. If so, the police would be a self-regulating agency, there being in the system no provision for a position esteeming legality over agency requirements. This presently seems to be the situation desired by police officials.

NOTES

1. Francis A. Allen, "The Exclusionary Rule in the American Law of Search and Seizure," in Claude R. Sowle, ed., *Police Power and Individual Freedom* (Chicago: Aldine Publishing Co., 1962), p. 77.
2. 116 U.S. 616 (1886).
3. 232 U.S. 383 (1914).
4. 44 Cal. 2d 434, 282 P. 2d 905 (1955).
5. 81 S. Ct. 1684 (1961).
6. 44 Cal. 2d 434, 448.
7. The *Mapp* case did not affect the State of California, since it had already adopted the rule and was developing case law on the legality of arrest procedures. See Rex A. Collings, "Toward Workable Rules of Search and Seizure—An *Amicus Curiae*

Brief," *California Law Review,* L (1962), 421–458. Following the *Mapp* case, however, the issue remained as to whether states should be permitted to develop their own precedents, as California had, or should be required to follow the decisions of the federal courts with respect to the legality of a particular kind of search or seizure. On June 10, 1963, with its decision in *Ker v. California* (374 U.S. 23), a California case, the Supreme Court of the United States decided the question in favor of federal standards. At the time, however, it was not clear whether federal standards would afford the police greater or lesser latitude than the line of California cases had contemplated. Certainly, a close reading of the *Ker* decision (affirming the conviction of the petitioner) shows the police as having considerable freedom, especially regarding arrest without warrant and surprise entry in narcotics cases.

8. Cf. Edward Barrett, "Personal Rights, Property Rights and the Fourth Amendment," *Supreme Court Review* (1960), pp. 46–74.

9. Collings, *op. cit.,* p. 439.

10. It is worth noting that the choking of this man was the only instance of so-called police "brutality" I ever witnessed, although it should also be noted that the possible use of physical force by police is an important *structural* factor, one which the suspect must take into account regardless of its low frequency. Had I not been along, the man might have been handled more roughly after the arrest. I cannot say. An important point, however, is that the man's behavior was interpreted as *disrespectful.* As one officer said to him, while he was being questioned at the stationhouse (and complaining of the choking), "Goddammit, you'd better learn that when an officer of the law tells you to open up your mouth and spit out what you've got in there, you'd better open up."

11. Caleb Foote, "The Fourth Amendment: Obstacle or Necessity in the Law of Arrest?" in Claude R. Sowle, ed., *Police Power and Individual Freedom: The Quest for Balance* (Chicago: Aldine Publishing Co., 1962), p. 29.

12. Fred E. Inbau, "Public Safety v. Individual Civil Liberties: The Prosecutor's Stand," *Journal of Criminal Law, Criminology, and Police Science,* LIII (March, 1962), 86.

13. Inbau, "More About Public Safety v. Individual Civil Liberties," *ibid.,* LIII (September, 1962), 329. Other presentations of the law enforcement point of view regarding arrests and the exclusionary rule are made by Collings, *op. cit.;* Frank J. McGarr, "The Exclusionary Rule: An Ill Conceived and Ineffective Remedy," in Sowle, ed., *op. cit.,* pp. 99–103; O. W. Wilson, "Police Arrest Privileges in a Free Society: A Plea for Modernization," *ibid.,* pp. 21–28; and Chief William Parker, *Parker on Police* (Springfield: Charles C Thomas, 1957), pp. 113–123 *et passim.*

14. Barrett, *op. cit.,* p. 15.

15. On the point of "secondary deviance" which this discussion raises, see Edwin Lemert, *Social Pathology* (New York: McGraw-Hill, 1951), pp. 75–76. "When a person begins to employ his deviant behavior or a role based upon it as a means of defense, attack, or adjustment to the overt and covert problems created by the consequent societal reaction to him, his deviation is secondary."

16. Arthur L. Stinchcombe, "Institutions of Privacy in the Determination of Police Administrative Practice," *American Journal of Sociology,* LXIX (September, 1963), 18. As Stinchcombe puts it, "Presumably there is a long chain of events on a large scale, structuring rewards and constraints in police practice . . . with respect to the norms established and continually enforced in a few court cases."

17. Arthur Train, *Courts and Criminals* (New York: Charles Scribner's Sons, 1921), pp. 6–7.

18. 374 U.S. 23 (1963).

19. 374 U.S. 23, 40–41.

20. 374 U.S. 23, 47.

21. Caleb Foote, "Tort Remedies for Police Violations of Individual Rights," *Minnesota Law Review,* XXXIX (1955), 493.

22. It would be interesting to observe the operation of the rule within a police force where corruption prevailed. Against such a background, the exclusionary rule is helpless to improve the performance of police. Indeed, I have heard it alleged that the exclusionary rule has been used as a means of sustaining a corrupt system. In such instances, police arrest their collaborators in ways which violate rules of search and seizure, thereby effectively barring prosecution. At the same time, an appearance of zealous law enforcement can be maintained.

55

Bureaucracy, Information, and Social Control: A Study of a Morals Detail

JEROME H. SKOLNICK AND
J. RICHARD WOODWORTH

Awareness of infraction is the foundation of any social control system. Whatever the system of normative standards, whether these be folkways or mores, crimes or rules, a transgression must somehow be observed and reported before sanctions can be applied. The potential efficiency of such a control system therefore varies directly with its capacity to observe or receive reports of transgression. For example, socialization at its most primitive level demands the visibility of the asocial act. If the norm requires that two shoes or no shoes be worn, depending upon whether one is being presented at Court or lying in bed, the socializing agent must be in a position to observe any normative breach. The child who wears shoes to bed must be seen wearing them before he can be told that this act affects "civilized" sensibilities.

Similarly, when an assault takes place, knowledge of its happening must somehow be communicated to authorities who are charged with enforcing the system or rules. If two men fight one another in private and do not report the occurrence of the fight, authorities cannot sanction either man, even if the behavior of each violated legal rules. Many rule violations are, of course, socially managed in this fashion, the disputants preferring to settle matters privately rather than bringing them to the attention of authority. If, however, knowledge of the dispute becomes public—if the fight is noisy, if one of the disputants is injured—authorities must then decide whether or not to invoke the sanctioning process. It is clear, nevertheless, that before legal controls can be invoked, there must first be official knowledge of the criminal act.

This idea may seem extremely obvious, yet without exploring it and without analyzing the empirical relation between awareness and control, we shall fail to examine some of the more serious problems and hidden consequences of control systems. Imagine as an example, a social system where criminality could be accused only if a citizen complained that a law was being violated. Awareness of criminal violation would be the responsibility of the citizen, and

From "Morality Enforcement and Totalitarian Potential" in M. Levitt and B. Rubenstein, eds., *Orthopsychiatry and the Law: A Symposium* (Detroit: The Wayne State University Press, 1968), pp. 175–182. Reprinted by permission of the publisher.

the police would be unconcerned with increasing their capacity to become aware of infractions.

In fact, of course, much energy of the police as an organization is devoted to mobilizing resources for recognition of transgression. We are all familiar with signs warning that a section of highway is being patrolled with radar equipment, a warning intended to caution and restrain potential violators by suggesting an extensive ambit of police awareness. Most citizens are less familiar with other technological and structural devices employed by police to learn of transgression. Crimes of vice, for example, typically have no citizen complainants. The man who uses heroin, or smokes marijuana, or bets on a football game, or patronizes a prostitute, does not complain to the police that someone has sold him narcotics, taken his bet, or has offered to go to bed with him for a fee. In order to enforce these laws the police must develop an information system.

The key to an information system is the *creation of motives* in those aware of transgressions to offer this information to legally constituted authority. There is an exchange for information, sometimes of money, but more typically of a reduction or elimination of criminal charges against the informer. Policemen learn how to create commodities or the appearance of commodities for such an exchange. Under such circumstances, technological advances become significant. Observing and recording devices, such as hidden microphones, wiretaps, and high-power binoculars become increasingly relevant. To the extent that such practices come to the attention of appellate courts, a body of case law is developed to regulate the conditions under which informants, wiretaps, and the like may legitimately be utilized for extending police awareness.

As one observes the information-creating activities of police, its totalitarian potential becomes increasingly apparent. Totalitarianism implies tight socialization. Its conception of man is relatively fixed and inflexible, and its symmetry and conventionalism imply a mandate for developing instrumentalities to enforce conformity. We are not referring here only to such totalitarian social orders as Hitlerism or Stalinism. We are discussing the idea of a totalitarian *potential* inhering in any society, even the most constitutionally protected and democratic, as, bit by bit, legal definitions standardize the conception of moral man and as the apparatus for control becomes increasingly refined.

Improvements in discovery apparatus heighten the totalitarian potential in proportion to a society's use of law as an instrument for achieving conventional morality. It does not matter very much if criminal law forbids various erotic activities, so long as it is impossible to see through walls. When such vision becomes possible, however, the totalitarian potential is enormous because, constitutional standards of search and seizure notwithstanding, the surveillance potential of those performing police functions will be extraordinary.

Our experience observing police has indicated to us that they desire to have as much information as possible, even if these findings are inadmissible as evidence in court. As an agency charged with enforcing a broad spectrum of rules, the police simply cannot know in advance whether stray bits of information will prove useful. Even if enforcement conformed to the citizen complainant model pictured above, the police would continue to utilize an intelligence system, although not so frequently as when they are required to enforce crimes lacking in citizen complainants.

Furthermore, our legal ideals demand that all laws shall be equally and fairly enforced regardless of the personal preferences of officials. Of course, in practice, priorities do exist. Depending on the police force, these may be more or less articulated. Nevertheless, their very existence is a source of embarrassment. Only with hesitancy does a police official admit that he is not attending to the enforcement of certain laws. The ideal of law enforcement is universal enforcement, and even if the norm is not always complied with, as it almost never can be, its presence urges the police to enforce all laws. For this reason, therefore, the police are pressed to use their increased capacity to discover crime, even if they should find themselves in personal disagreement with the statute they are legally bound to execute.

The remainder of this study will be concerned with the enforcement apparatus surrounding statutory rape, a violation for which there are few citizen complainants, and which is therefore difficult to discover. The question, put in practical terms, is this: How do police "discover" that an adolescent girl—one under the age of 18—has had sexual intercourse? Does she herself come to the police department and "complain" that although she gave her consent, that although no force was involved, she was—to use a euphemism instead of the more forceful Anglo-Saxon term—"sexually invaded"? Or do the girl's parents usually make the complaint?

In order to find out, all statutory rapes reported to the Westville Police Department—Westville is a city of approximately 350,000—between January, 1962, and October, 1963, a total of 235 cases, were analyzed from police, probation and court records. For purposes of comparison, all cases for nearby Mountain City, a city of 750,000, were examined for the year 1961. It turns out that in Westville, the source reporting the complaint to the police was neither the girl herself, nor her relatives. Rather, the single most important source of information was the family support division of the prosecutor's office. In general, the overwhelming majority of cases were "non-voluntary" in the sense that the facts were brought to the Westville police as the result of information held by other agencies. The adolescent girl applying for maternity assistance is routinely sent to the police department where she is urged, and often cajoled, into making a complaint.

The consequences of such a policy of information sharing become evident when a comparison is made between Westville and Mountain City. Despite the fact that Mountain City's population outnumbers Westville's by more than two to one, during 1961 there were in absolute numbers 40 fewer cases of statutory rape reported to the Mountain City Police. The Mountain City Family Support Division does not systematically report the violations it discovers while taking welfare applications; it is to this difference in policy that the different outcome—that is, 40 fewer cases—is largely attributable. (Ironically, of the two Mountain City reports that identifiably resulted from welfare application, one was a referral from the Westville Family Support Division.) Consequently, several of the features of the Westville cases are lacking in Mountain City: fewer persons in Mountain City wait until they are certain that the girl is pregnant before reporting the offense (67 per cent compared to 22 per cent); offenses are reported more quickly in Mountain City (44 per cent within one day of the offense, compared to Westville's 13 per cent); and Negroes are involved in far fewer of the Mountain City cases (35 per cent compared to 78 per cent).

Since the proportion of Negroes in Westville is more than two times that in Mountain City, this last finding would not seem to be directly attributable to the welfare policy of sharing information with the morals detail. However, as percentages approach 100 per cent, they cannot be expected to rise at the same rate. This ceiling effect is expressed in the formula, percentage change $=$

$\dfrac{P_2 - P_1}{100 - P_1}$, where P_1 is the initial percentage (proportion in population Negro)

and P_2 is the final percentage (Negroes in morals detail caseload).[1] Using this formula, the percentage increase in Negroes in the morals detail caseload over those in the population is 70 per cent in Westville and 28 per cent in Mountain City.

Westville also receives more reports of offenses from public agencies other than the Family Support Division. Excluding welfare-originated reports, 70 per cent of Westville reports compared with 41 per cent of the Mountain City reports came from these other public agencies. To put the matter another way, if all cases discovered by public agencies (including welfare) were removed from the Westville total, there would be, in the two cities, a similar rate of statutory rape cases per hundred thousand population. It is the addition of cases originating in welfare and in other public agencies that produces the extraordinarily high proportion of Negroes involved in the Westville statutory rape caseload.

These differences in the composition of the statutory rape caseload are reflected in police investigation procedures. In Westville, the encounter between police and suspect appears less adversary, since the caseload contained a greater percentage of cases where the participants themselves felt their behavior to be socially acceptable. The Westville police make use of subjective feelings to incriminate. They *invite* the suspect in to talk with them, and he is likely to comply. By contrast, the Mountain City police usually must arrest the male, and then interrogate him, thereby arousing his suspicions. Consequently, a lower percentage of the Mountain City males confess to the crime, and greater effort must be extended to discover other factual evidence to ready the case for prosecution.

Over all, the Westville Morals Detail is a far more effective agency of legal control with regard to this offense than is the Mountain City detail. Yet it is well to ask about the consequences of increased competence. The great obstacle to repressive dictatorships has always been the limited competence of the rulers. But, as pointed out by Philip Selznick, this poses a conflict between the value of equal justice and the threat of despotism:

> The ideal of equal justice seems to require that all offenders be treated alike. Yet there is evidence that the police routinely attempt to distinguish, especially among juveniles, the apparently casual offender from the committed delinquent. Lawyers and other social scientists may see in this a violation of even-handed justice. And indeed, this is so, especially where racial and class bias are operative.
>
> I am concerned that we do not respond too eagerly and too well to the apparent need for more effective mechanisms of social control. In the administration of justice, if anywhere, we need to guard *human* values and forestall the creation of mindless machines for handling cases according to set routines. Here vigilance consists in careful study of actual operations so that we may know what will be lost or gained when administrative changes are proposed.[2]

Selznick's concern seems especially relevant where increased police efficiency is used to reinforce conventional morality. We should like in closing to examine briefly the possible long-range consequences of the administrative changes whose beginnings have been described.

Eventually most record systems—school, census, income tax, employment, military, criminal, welfare, recreation, etc.—will be computerized and centralized. It is strongly possible that access to records will be granted to those groups that can present socially legitimized needs for such availability. Justifications are already in existence. The police and the district attorney may say that they are charged with enforcing the law and that certain law violations come to light in the records, say, of the welfare department. "We are either serious about enforcing the law or we are not," they can say. "If we are serious, then inform us whenever a violation is uncovered." We found in our research that information is already shared between welfare and the police; the rationale is exactly that stated above.

Consider those public agencies that maintain rehabilitative, therapeutic, and even preventative ideals—this would include welfare, probation, the courts. "We are concerned with the whole individual in his social milieu," they may say, "and unless we can consider all available information, we cannot adequately fulfill our socially approved purpose." Education similarly considers itself the guardian of the whole child. These claims are hard to deny precisely because they make true assessments of need. But *approval* of these claims takes the selection and shaping of his roles from the individual's hands. This destroys the ability of the individual to insulate his various roles. Among those sectors of officialdom that have pooled their data, the individual has no secrets. And as the capacity for secrecy is reduced, so too is the capacity for individual freedom.

A cry of alarm is perhaps not yet warranted, for opposing tendencies do exist. Modern governments operate through a multitude of agencies with frequently conflicting goals and means. (In California you need only think of the

Department of Highways and the Department of Beaches and Parks.) Just how far such agencies are controlled by central policies and finances and how far their concerns are directed by their specialized task is not clear. Moreover, the accepted doctrines of privacy and privileged communication (or the organizational equivalent, confidentiality of records) operate against widespread sharing. Finally, we may put some confidence in the protections afforded by the "natural" inefficiency of bureaucracy. That a system based upon the "ideal type" of rational administration posited by Weber is not truly efficient is an increasingly general theme of sociologists of organization. Nevertheless, our data have shown that the Westville Morals Detail is significantly more successful than its Mountain City counterpart simply because it taps welfare records. Although its efficiency could be heightened by adopting the techniques of other police units, its "success" is mainly attributable to a policy of routinely pooling information rather than to a streamlined administration, per se. Ultimately, therefore, we are faced with the issue Selznick poses: "If the law is administered with prudence, does this not require some differential treatment at the point of contact and not only after judgment, when ultimate disposition is made? Do we need or want agencies of control so efficient and so impartial that every actual offender has an equal chance of being known and processed?"

NOTES

1. See Carl I. Hovland et al., in P. F. Lazarsfeld and S. Rosenberg, eds., *The Language of Social Research* (Glencoe: The Free Press, 1955), pp. 77–82.
2. Philip Selznick, "Legal Institutions and Social Controls," *Vanderbilt Law Review*, XVII (December, 1963), 84.

56

Who Can Police the Police?

HERBERT L. PACKER

What may the police do to persons whom they suspect of committing crimes? What may be done to the police if they do what they are not supposed to do? The range of discourse implicated in these simple-sounding questions is broad,

From *The New York Review*, September 3, 1966, pp. 10–13. Reprinted with permission from *The New York Review of Books*. Copyright © 1966 by The New York Review.

running as it does from the nicest technicalities of lawyers' law to the most impalpable speculations about the uses of coercion in a free society. The pressure for answers has never been more strongly felt than it is being felt just now. And the competition to provide the answers, drawing into the pit institutions as diverse as the Supreme Court and the Patrolmen's Benevolent Association, has never been more savage. Many people find the controversy deeply disturbing: They find in it evidence, depending upon their predilections, that our society is dangerously authoritarian or dangerously permissive or dangerously divided. I find in it evidence of a different proposition: that our society is becoming increasingly self-conscious about the paradoxes of coercion. This seems to me a good thing, because it focuses attention upon prime questions that political thought has tended lately to ignore. In the commonplace ugliness of the criminal process there is concealed the starkest example of a dilemma as old as political thought: *quis ipsos custodes custodiet?* Who will watch the watchers?

The problem of the police is given added poignance by our discovery of the urban poor who, by an interesting coincidence, turn out to be the principal objects of police attention. The War on Poverty, that odd by-blow of the civil rights movement, has forced us to confront what was there for the seeing all along: One of the most significant deprivations to which the poor are subject is their inability to cope when confronted with the demands of administrative bureaucracy. And we are being reluctantly forced to face the fact that the principal administrative bureaucracy of this kind is the police, as they go about the manifold jobs we have insisted upon entrusting to them. As I shall try to suggest later in this essay, the trouble that the police and the rest of us are now in is largely the result of our improvident reliance on the criminal sanction to perform a lot of messy social tasks for which it is not especially suited.

Two important events that have occurred during the past few months illustrate, both separately and in their interaction, some of the dimensions of the police problem. One is the American Law Institute's ambitious attempt to draft a model code of police practices. The other is the Supreme Court's decision in *Miranda v. Arizona,* sharply limiting the circumstances under which the police may interrogate arrested persons and, incidentally, substantially thwarting the interrogation provisions of the American Law Institute's model code. Because the interrogation problem is at once the most visible and the most controversial aspect of police practices (although not, in my view, the most significant), we may as well start with it.

What the Supreme Court held in *Miranda* is that the police may not interrogate a person in custody until he has been advised that he has a right to remain silent and to consult a lawyer; that if he indicates a desire to remain silent the interrogation must cease; that if he indicates a desire to consult a lawyer the interrogation must be suspended until his lawyer appears or, in the case of a person unable to retain a lawyer, until a lawyer has been supplied for him; and that if interrogation does continue without the presence of a lawyer and a statement is taken, "a heavy burden rests on the Government to demonstrate that the defendant knowingly and intelligently waived" the rights thus conferred upon him. There is no doubt that these new standards will interfere to some extent with police efficiency in criminal investigation. Some arrestees —no one knows how many—who would previously have talked will now remain silent.

In so holding, the Court not only laid down far more restrictive standards for police conduct than have so far prevailed; it also made a final break with its exercise of the traditional judicial role in confession cases. That role has simply been to determine, on a case-by-case basis, whether the defendant's statement, taken in the police station and later introduced into evidence at his trial, was "involuntary" and hence excludable under the Fourteenth Amendment. Why did the Court abandon its traditional approach for a set of external criteria having little if anything to do with the individual case? It is true that law enforcement officials had voiced deep dissatisfaction with the old approach, which involved the application of a somewhat nebulous standard— "involuntariness"—to the highly particularistic facts of a series of different cases, and therefore lacked predictive value. (Most law enforcement people would now give their eye teeth for a return to the old approach.) But that is not what troubled the Court. What troubled it, as is apparent from a reading of *Miranda* and its precursor, *Escobedo,* was the lack of any evidence that the police were getting the message. As the cases kept coming up from the state courts in ever-increasing numbers, it became apparent that reversing a few (or even a substantial number) of state criminal convictions each year was not having a conditioning effect on police practices. Furthermore, the amount of time and effort involved in determining the impalpable issue of "involuntariness," often in the face of almost impossible tangles of argument about what really happened, came to seem more and more formidable.

One may well ask what business the Supreme Court has trying to educate (or discipline) the police. Is its function any more than to right wrongs in the particular cases that come before it? A powerful argument can be made that the Court ought to stick to that last. Certainly it functions better when it does, for reasons which we will have to explore. But the Court has chosen a different and broader role in the handling of criminal cases. And it has not done so for indefensible reasons. The plain fact is that the Court is in the business of policing the police because nobody else is and because in a society that likes to think of itself as "free" and "open" someone has to do the job.

Who else could? The police themselves might, but they have not. The great leap forward in police administration during the past generation has been the rationalizing and professionalizing of police work along classic Weberian lines. Corruption has been eliminated or sharpy reduced, efficiency has been increased. These are admirable achievements but they are irrelevant to current concerns. The revolution in expectations among urban minority groups and the due process revolution in the courts will not be satisfied with efficiency. Indeed, the dictates of efficiency—assemblyline arrest and screening processes, swift and thorough searches of private premises, psychologically sophisticated interrogations, electronically advanced eavesdropping—frequently clash with the very values of human autonomy to which the critics of the police wish to see more attention paid.

That is not to say that the enlightened self-interest of the police might not be served by more attention to these efficiency-impairing values—I think they would—but simply that the attention has not so far been forthcoming. Indeed, the leading apostles of police professionalization—the J. Edgar Hoovers, the William Parkers, the Orlando Wilsons—are also the leading opponents of what the courts have been doing. There is no evidence that they would do it themselves. And that is not too surprising. Who ever supposed that the watchers would watch themselves if otherwise unwatched?

Who else, then? The legislature? That seems more plausible. As compared with the Supreme Court, the legislature (by which I mean generically the Congress and the legislative bodies of the states) has far greater institutional competence to deal with the intricate problems of laying down rules for the governance of the police and sanctions for their breach. The legislature has fact-finding facilities that the courts do not have. A court is not a programmatic institution; its mission is to decide cases according to law. And in the area of criminal procedure, the only source of law for the courts to apply is the Constitution, whose spacious imperatives can hardly be mistaken for a detailed code of criminal procedure. Most significantly, the legislature is in a far better position to do two things that lie at or near the heart of the police problem: to adjust the extent of powers given to the magnitude of the interests protected by the criminal law; and to devise adequate sanctions for breach of whatever rules it chooses to lay down for the governance of the police.

We will need to take a more detailed look at these two areas of legislative superiority when we come to assess the achievement of the American Law Institute's model code. It is perhaps enough for the moment to point out why in these two respects the legislature is a preferable forum to the courts for resolving problems of the sort typified by the confession issue. Imagine two men accused of crime. One is charged with murder; the other with, let us say, taking illegal bets. Let us suppose that for some reason the police want to interrogate both of them, and the question is, under what conditions and subject to what restraints should they be entitled to do so? It hardly requires argument that a relevant consideration (I do not say necessarily the decisive one) is the seriousness of the conduct with which our two arrestees are charged, the magnitude of the social interest that each has allegedly invaded, the gravity of the danger that each may be thought to pose. A legislature, making a typical legislative compromise, might well conclude that more latitude should be given the police in investigating crimes that pose serious threats to the most basic of social interests than to nuisance offenses like gambling. Such a conclusion would not be open to the Supreme Court as it goes about its business of interpreting the Constitution. In the absence of a legislative judgment to the contrary, either the privilege against self-incrimination and the right to counsel secure all arrestees against interrogation in the absence of counsel or they secure no arrestees. Justice Jackson, in one of those flashes of unjudicial candor that make his opinions such a joy to read, once remarked that he would be much more willing to allow the police to set up a roadblock to catch a kidnapper and save his victim than to trap a bootlegger and salvage a few bottles of bourbon. He meant: if I were a legislator rather than a judge. A judge interpreting the Constitution cannot, or at least cannot overtly, make discriminations of that kind. The "constitutionalizing" of the rules of criminal procedure militates against that kind of adjustment, as the rules laid down in the *Miranda* case show. So far as police interrogation is concerned, kidnapping and bootlegging are now on a par.

Even graver is the flaw in the Court's sanction-fashioning power. If the Court does not like the way the police have behaved in extracting a confession, it cannot discipline the offending policeman; it can only reverse the defendant's conviction because of the error in admitting the improper confession. That isn't much of a sanction, if what the Court is interested in doing is affecting police conduct. By contrast, the legislature can devise, ordain, and finance an elaborate disciplinary structure, create a claim against the public treasury on behalf of people subjected to illegal police procedures, or do any of a variety of other things directly and specifically adapted for the purpose at hand: seeing to it that the police have some incentive for obeying the rules laid down for their guidance.

Why, then, has the Court not wisely left the problem of policing the police where it so obviously belongs, in the hands of the lawmakers? For the simple reason, of course, that the legislature has utterly abdicated its responsibility. Courts have to decide cases; legislatures do not have to pass bills. And the priority accorded to criminal law reform is very low indeed, except of course for creating new crimes and increasing the penalties for old ones. There is not on the books of a single American jurisdiction a comprehensive code of criminal procedure, regulating the intricate interrelations of the component parts of the criminal process and providing a sensible series of sanctions for breach of the rules thus laid down. And, to make matters worse, state courts have utterly failed to put any teeth in the few legislative enactments that bear on the problem, such as statutes requiring prompt arraignment after arrest and access to one's retained lawyer. That is the law-making and law-enforcing vacuum into which the Supreme Court has seen itself as having to move. *Quis ipsos custodes custodiet?* If not the Court, then nobody.

The Court's performance in the criminal procedure area has been, in my view, an increasingly unsatisfactory one as its constitutional dictates have become more legislative in tone. *Miranda* and its companion cases are particularly disturbing in this regard. Having created by fiat a brand-new constitutional absolute, the application of the privilege against self-incrimination in the police station, the Court has discouraged rational inquiry into how important to the criminal process the interrogation of suspects actually is and what measures can be devised to insure that suspects are apprised of their rights and enabled to exercise them without destroying whatever justifiable interest society may have in the use of interrogation. It happens that we know next to nothing in a systematic way about the facts on which such value judgments ought to be premised. We don't really know whether rules like the ones the Court has just laid down will substantially impair the interrogation process or whether other forms of investigative work can take up the slack. The new rules will presumably have less drastic impact in cities like Detroit, where the police have for some time been advising arrestees of their rights, than in more backward places. And the absence of effective legal aid for the indigent suspect that continues to characterize much of the South will make adjustment to the dictates of *Miranda* acutely painful. All of which underlines the difficulty of generalizing about the facts, the complexity of the problem facing the Court, and the simplistic character of its solution.

The Court, it hardly needs to be said in this age of the knowing smirk, is not impervious to political influences. Indeed, its performance in the confession cases is in one respect—its treatment of the retroactivity problem—so nakedly political as to make congressional log-rolling over the Rivers and Harbors Bill seem positively high-minded. The new constitutional interrogation rules would, under normal judicial procedure, apply to all cases now pending before the courts on appeal. Consider the situation of the thousands of criminal defendants who were convicted on the basis of confessions obtained by police interrogation that did not conform to the new rules and whose convictions were still pending on appeal at the time the Supreme Court decided *Miranda* and its three companion cases. What distinguishes their cases from *Miranda?* Nothing but the fortuity that the four cases selected by the Court as the vehicle for announcing its new rules were not their cases. Indeed, as to approximately 110 such defendants, there was not even the tenuous distinction that they had not sought review in the Supreme Court, for that number of petitions seeking review on the same ground as *Miranda* and the other three had been filed and were awaiting the Court's decision whether to consider them on the merits. Even-handed justice clearly required that the new rules apply with the same force to all pending cases as to the cases of the lucky four.

What even-handed justice required the Court was unwilling to do. The week after *Miranda,* the Court decided in *Johnson v. New Jersey* that the new rules should apply only to cases in which the trial commenced after June 13, 1966, the date on which the decision in *Miranda* was announced. Simultaneously, it denied review of the approximately 110 cases pending on its docket which raised the same question, thereby leaving the convictions standing. This is legislation with a vengeance. What legislature, enacting a new set of rules for the conduct of police interrogations, would have the temerity to say: Our new rules apply only after June 13, 1966, unless your name happens to be Miranda, Vignera, Westover, or Stewart?

There is, of course, no mystery about why the Court acted as it did. The decision in *Johnson* is based on the proposition that retroactive application "would seriously disrupt the administration of our criminal laws." Or to put it less euphemistically: We are in trouble if we turn all these criminals loose.

The Court, in sum, managed to come up with a little something for everyone: for the libertarians, a shiny new set of rules designed to make life tougher for the police; for the police, absolution for past sins; for the lower courts, relief from a potentially oppressive workload. Lyndon Johnson, in his great days of legislative wheeling and dealing, could have done no better.

Among other things, the Court's ruling in *Miranda* has temporarily jarred the American Law Institute's attempt to frame a comprehensive code of pre-arraignment procedure as a model for legislative reform of the police phase of the criminal process. The American Law Institute, or ALI as it is generally known, is a small group of distinguished lawyers, judges, and legal scholars dedicated to making improvements in the law. Its Director is Herbert Wechsler, one of the half-dozen most distinguished legal scholars in this country. Its Council includes Henry Friendly, Erwin Griswold, Edward H. Levi, Carl McGowan, Roger Traynor, and Harrison Tweed. This is the Legal Establishment, the kind of Establishment that made the late Senator McCarthy madder than almost anything else: conservative, powerful, aristocratic, high-minded. No group is more likely to unite two necessary but discordant characteristics: the intellectual capacity to formulate rational proposals for reform and the prestige to get them accepted.

The ALI began its Model Code of Pre-Arraignment Procedure in 1963, although work in earnest did not get under way until November, 1964. As is the custom when a project of this sort is started, the drafting was entrusted to a small group of "Reporters," in this case four professors of law headed by James Vorenberg of Harvard, who subsequently became Executive Secretary of the President's Commission on Law Enforcement and Administration of Justice while continuing his work as Reporter for the ALI project. An advisory committee of 40, mostly judges and law professors, but with a substantial infusion of law enforcement experts, assisted the Reporters in their work. The Reporters did not undertake or commission any independent factual inquiry into aspects of the police process, although the available empiric data are, to put it mildly, thin. Instead, they relied on personal knowledge, conversations with people thought to be knowledgeable, and, above all, on their own feel for the situation.

The professed aim of the ALI code in proposing a set of legislative solutions to the problems of police conduct was "to treat the process from first police contact until arraignment in a systematic and consistent manner." And there is little doubt that their first tentative draft, published in March of this year and discussed at the annual ALI meeting in May, does just that. This code, with its detailed provisions on the investigation of crime arrest, disposition of arrested persons and interrogation during custody represents an enormous improvement over the chaotic, archaic, and largely unarticulated fragments of law that govern the police process at present. Unfortunately, two circumstances—one external, the other internal—combined to damage this promising effort.

The external circumstance was the realization, which overhung the project from the start, that the Supreme Court was rapidly evolving its own set of standards for the important problem of police interrogation and that the Court was likely to foreclose or at least severely restrict any comprehensive legislative effort by its own work. The draftsmen of the ALI Code had their own ideas about how the interrogation problem should be handled. They agreed that an arrestee should be informed of his right to remain silent and to have a lawyer. They also agreed that his lawyer should be able to have access to him on his request, but did not think that interrogation should be absolutely barred before the arrival of counsel. And on the issue of central practical importance, they did not think that the state should have an affirmative obligation to supply a lawyer to a person who wished to have one but was financially unable to retain one.

It seems fair to say that the ALI draftsmen saw the interrogation problem as crucial, and that they were consequently preoccupied with the problem of getting their views on record before the Supreme Court acted. To an outside observer, it appeared that they perceived themselves as being involved in a race to the courthouse, designed to persuade the Court that there was a reasonable alternative to "constitutionalizing" the whole problem of police interrogation. In retrospect, this tactic appears to have been a mistake. A few caustic remarks from the bench during the argument of the *Miranda* group of cases indicated that the very justices to whom this appeal for restraint was addressed were not much disposed to pay any attention to it. And, as we have seen, the eventual disposition of these cases put the ALI draftsmen in the embarrassing position of having advanced proposals that the Supreme Court immediately thereafter branded as in some respects unconstitutional.

Not only did the draftsmen fail to convince the Supreme Court, they also failed to convince the membership of the ALI. That the *Miranda* cases were pending at the time of the annual meeting in May pretty much aborted any discussion of the proposals on the merits. More subtly, the failure of this race to the courthouse may have infected the draftsmen with a sense of bitterness and frustration, which now seems to be expressing itself in an exaggerated notion of how badly the entire enterprise has been damaged by their having come off second-best in this skirmish with the Supreme Court. One can only hope that this mood will not prevail, for there is much useful work that remains to be done.

Obscured though they are by the constitutional fireworks over the interrogation issue, there remain nonetheless problems of the greatest importance about the governance of the police which should be, but have not been, faced by the ALI project. These issues are centered on the two areas of legislative superiority that I have mentioned earlier: the ability to distinguish between serious and trivial crimes in deciding what powers the police should have, and the ability to devise an adequate set of sanctions to deter police conduct in breach of the rules. Both of these potentialities for achieving decent legislative solutions were badly neglected in the ALI draft. The problem is best illustrated not by the glamorous confessions issue but rather by the more humdrum but far more basic question of the circumstances under which the police may stop and question people on the street without actually arresting them.

The prevalent dogma on this issue is summed up by Dicey in his *Introduction to the Study of the Laws of the Constitution.* Writing in 1885 with an ineffable air of Britannic self-congratulation, he said:

> That anybody should suffer physical restraint is in England *prima facie* illegal, and can be justified (speaking in very general terms) on two grounds only, that is to say, either because the prisoner or person suffering restraint is accused of some offense and must be brought before the courts to stand his trial, or because he has been duly convicted of some offense and must suffer punishment for it. Now personal freedom in this sense of the term is secured in England by the strict maintenance of the principle that no man can be arrested or imprisoned except in due course of law, that is (speaking again in very general terms indeed) under some legal warrant or authority, and, what is of far more consequence, it is secured by the provision of adequate legal means for the enforcement of this principle.

It is inherently improbable that this statement was true when made, if indeed it is to be taken as embodying an assertion of fact rather than value. Whatever the historical fact may be, Dicey's dictum is clearly flouted several times a day on the streets of London, New York, and every other large city in the English-speaking world (to mention only those parts of the globe in which Anglo-American ideals of personal liberty are paid lip service). It is flouted for the simple reason that the police have to flout it in order to determine whether the orthodox grounds for arrest—reasonable cause to believe that the person has committed an offense—exist. And it is flouted as well for more dubious reasons: to prevent people from committing offenses when the police think they may be disposed to do so; to harass people whom the police wish to discourage even though they have not, on the specific occasion in question, committed an offense. Consider the ALI draftsmen's favorite example: A policeman sees a man running with a heavy package in a deserted business district at 2 A.M. The policeman may suspect that something is amiss but he certainly does not have reasonable cause to believe that the person has committed an offense. What is he to do? What he does is to stop the man, ask him to identify himself, ask what is in the package and where he got it, and keep the man, by persuasion or by force, from departing until the officer has satisfied himself that nothing sinister is going on. Or consider this example, not cited by the ALI draftsmen (very little on-the-street detention takes place late at night in deserted business districts): The police spot a woman whom they know is a prostitute lounging on the street corner. They engage her in conversation, address a few insulting epithets to her, ask her for information about who has been pushing narcotics in the area, and finally tell her to move along if she doesn't want to get arrested. In both cases, Dicey's dogma has been flouted, but few (one hopes) would argue that it was anything but right to do so in the first case and anything but wrong to do so in the second.

The plain fact is that the realities of crime control require that there be some middle ground between complete immunity from police interference with freedom of movement on the one hand and arrest, in the orthodox sense of being taken into custody to answer to a charge of crime, on the other. The problem of determining what that middle ground should be presents a neat paradigm of the problem of coercion in a free society. The ALI solution to the problem is a reasonable one, as far as it goes. It is to provide for a 20-minute "investigative stop," on the street or in any other place in which the police may be lawfully present, during which the police may stop, question, and search for dangerous weapons any person who either is thought to have knowledge about a crime that has been committed or is observed in circumstances that suggest that he either has committed or will commit an offense. If nothing turns up that would justify an arrest, the police must tell the person so detained that he is free to go at the expiration of the 20-minute period. A very few minor offenses are excluded from the crimes for which this investigative stop may be used: misdemeanors punishable by less than 30 days' imprisonment, vagrancy, and loitering. Otherwise its spectrum is as broad as the criminal law itself.

Now, as I have suggested, this kind of authority is necessary, and therefore should be openly rather than covertly exercised, in the investigation of possible serious offenses against person and property: murder, robbery, rape, burglary, and the like. It is quite another matter whether this kind of authority should be legitimated in the investigation of nuisance offenses: gambling, prostitution, narcotics addiction. For one thing, the social interests threatened by nuisance conduct are hardly so paramount as to require that the police have more power than the orthodox law of arrest confers upon them. For another, it is precisely with respect to offenses of this sort that the power to stop and question is most likely to be exercised sweepingly, indiscriminately, and abusively. As anyone familiar with police practices in urban areas, particularly in Negro slums, is well aware, a substantial part of law enforcement activity is directed not toward arrest and prosecution for nuisance offenses but rather toward harassment. The commission of these offenses is so clandestine and the surrounding circumstances so ambiguous that vast numbers of people in the streets of Harlem or of Watts may every day be "observed in circumstances that suggest" that they are "about to commit a felony or misdemeanor." Is it wise to give the police such sweeping powers to stop and question? May not the regard of minority groups for the police be raised if the police are forced to restrict this kind of aggressive intervention into the daily life of the community to circumstances in which they are seen as protectors rather than as alien intruders?

All of this presupposes, of course, that the police are doing no more than they are authorized to do under the ALI's proposals. They detain people politely, they question them no more than is necessary to elicit the specific information they seek, they do not search for weapons routinely but only when there is a sense of imminent danger, they release promptly at the end of the

20-minute period. *Sed quis ipsos custodes custodiet?* The draftsmen of the ALI Code tell us that they intend to put "principal reliance" on the exclusionary rule as a sanctioning device. That is to say: if an "investigative stop" turns up evidence of crime, and if the person is tried for the crime, and if that evidence is sought to be introduced against him at the trial, and if it turns out that the "investigative stop" did not conform to legal requirements, then the evidence so obtained must be excluded from the trial. Very comforting, in the perhaps one out of a thousand illegal stops in which the end result is a criminal prosecution based on evidence produced by the illegal police activity. The sanction of the exclusionary rule is of course the sanction that has been there for the courts to use right along. It is not a very effective use of the resources of legislation to rely on the only sanction that a court can apply without the help of legislation, any more than it is a very effective use of legislation to ignore the differences in gravity among various crimes in deciding what powers to give to the police.

The problem of sanctions is not an easy one. But it is in a very real sense the basic one. Unless means can be devised to bring the powerful machinery of the police process under some sort of effective outside scrutiny, our urban slums will continue to be miniature police states and the urban poor will continue to see the police as enemies. I do not suggest that they can easily be brought to see the police as friends. Not friends, perhaps, but inhabitants of the same society? There is much evidence that the police are not seen that way now.

How can the police be made responsive to the demands of libertarian values? The most obvious and most effective way is by changing the police: better education, better recruitment policies, better pay. One cannot reproach the ALI draftsmen for failing to legislate these. But one can reproach them for failing to take a few interim precautions pending the millennium when every policeman is a combination of Earl Warren, Benjamin Spock, and Martin Luther King. The need is to develop a few useful models of sanctioning devices that will help to promote a greater degree of police accountability than now exists. In the absence of the carrot, we must place our uncertain reliance on the stick.

Two kinds of sticks immediately suggest themselves. (I do not say that they exhaust the possibilities of human ingenuity.) One is some kind of right to file suit against the governmental unit that employs the policeman, accompanied by provisions for recovery of minimum or fixed damages, counsel fees, and the like. These provisions would be designed to reduce the present deterrents to lawsuits by victims of illegal police action. The strategy underlying this kind of device is to build respect for due process into the policeman's model of efficiency. The policeman who persistently violates the norms costs his employers money and is therefore seen as inefficient. The other line of attack that immediately suggests itself is to create an administrative complaint and review structure designed to make the internal process of police discipline more responsive to values other than efficiency in police terms. The "civilian review board" provides a crude model of what might be designed, although one suspects that an imaginative social engineer could learn a good deal from Mayor Lindsay's travail. Nor does it seem to me utopian to suggest that the ALI draftsmen, with the prestige and authority that they can muster, could make a start at convincing police organizations (although perhaps not Mr. John J. Cassese and his spiritual adviser, Mr. William F. Buckley, Jr.) that their present opposition to proposals designed to pry open the para-military system of police discipline is a case of a sinking ship firing on its rescuers.

Now, none of this—and particularly the designing of better sanctioning devices—is the sort of thing that comes naturally to the ALI, as is evidenced by their failure so far to come to grips with it. But it doesn't at the moment seem to come naturally to anyone else who is in a position to do anything about it. The Supreme Court has not foreclosed the effort. All it has said to the ALI draftsmen in the *Miranda* opinion is that if a choice has to be made between all-or-nothing solutions to the interrogation problem (and inferentially, to other problems of police power), the Court prefers its all-or-nothing solution to the ALI's. If the draftsmen will get back to the drawing board with some attention to possible compromise solutions, all may not be lost. The effort does need to be made. If it is not, we are headed for very deep trouble indeed.

In the end, our salvation may lie in our willingness to see, and to act on the perception, that the tensions inherent in the police situation are exacerbated by the undue demands that we make on the criminal law. So long as we use that most coercive of legal weapons to cope with everything that we, or some of us, find disagreeable in our environment—with narcotics addiction, with gambling, with prostitution, with homosexuality, and now with the flight into the psychedelic universe—so long will we be condemned to endure the nastiness that is, in a large measure, the gist of "efficient" police work. It is no accident that all or almost all of the spectacular cases of unconstitutional searches and seizures, of entrapment and of electronic eavesdropping occur in the pursuit of criminals whose crimes do no visible injury and therefore evoke no complaints: the narcotics peddler, the numbers runner, the prostitute. One need not wait, as the ALI draftsmen seem to prefer, for the elimination of these offenses to question whether, even if they are to remain on the books, their prosecution justifies resort to measures as repulsive as those they evoke. The police are not to blame. They are only doing their job. The blame lies with those who have the responsibility to tell them what their job is and what tools they may use in doing it.

SECTION TWELVE *To Influence*
Race Relations

57

Brown v. the Board of Education of Topeka

Chief Justice Warren delivered the opinion of the Court.

These cases come to us from the States of Kansas, South Carolina, Virginia, and Delaware. They are premised on different facts and different local conditions, but a common legal question justifies their consideration together in this consolidated opinion.

In each of the cases, minors of the Negro race, through their legal representatives, seek the aid of the courts in obtaining admission to the public schools of their community on a non-segregated basis. In each instance, they had been denied admission to schools attended by white children under laws requiring or permitting segregation according to race. This segregation was alleged to deprive the plaintiffs of the equal protection of the laws under the Fourteenth Amendment. In each of the cases other than the Delaware case, a three-judge Federal District Court denied relief to the plaintiffs on the so-called "separate but equal" doctrine announced by this Court in *Plessy v. Ferguson,* 163 U.S. 537. Under that doctrine, equality of treatment is accorded when the races are provided substantially equal facilities, even though these facilities be separate. In the Delaware case, the Supreme Court of Delaware adhered to that doctrine, but ordered that the plaintiffs be admitted to the white schools because of their superiority to the Negro schools.

The plaintiffs contend that segregated public schools are not "equal" and cannot be made "equal," and that hence they are deprived of the equal protection of the laws. Because of the obvious importance of the question presented, the Court took jurisdiction. Argument was heard in the 1952 Term, and re-argument was heard this Term on certain questions propounded by the Court.

Re-argument was largely devoted to the circumstances surrounding the adoption of the Fourteenth Amendment in 1868. It covered exhaustively consideration of the Amendment in Congress, ratification by the states, then existing practices in racial segregation, and the views of proponents and opponents of the Amendment. This discussion and our own investigation convince us that, although these sources cast some light, it is not enough to resolve the problem with which we are faced. At best, they are inconclusive. The most avid proponents of the post-war Amendments undoubtedly intended them to remove all legal distinctions among "all persons born or naturalized in the United States." Their opponents, just as certainly, were antagonistic to both

---

347 U.S. 483 (1953).

the letter and the spirit of the Amendments and wished them to have the most limited effect. What others in Congress and the state legislatures had in mind cannot be determined with any degree of certainty.

An additional reason for the inconclusive nature of the Amendment's history, with respect to segregated schools, is the status of public education at that time. In the South, the movement toward free common schools, supported by general taxation, had not yet taken hold. Education of white children was largely in the hands of private groups. Education of Negroes was almost nonexistent, and practically all of the race were illiterate. In fact, any education of Negroes was forbidden by law in some states. Today, in contrast, many Negroes have achieved outstanding success in the arts and sciences as well as in the business and professional world. It is true that public school education at the time of the Amendment had advanced further in the North, but the effect of the Amendment on Northern States was generally ignored in the congressional debates. Even in the North, the conditions of public education did not approximate those existing today. The curriculum was usually rudimentary; ungraded schools were common in rural areas; the school term was but three months a year in many states; and compulsory school attendance was virtually unknown. As a consequence, it is not surprising that there should be so little in the history of the Fourteenth Amendment relating to its intended effect on public education.

In the first cases in this Court construing the Fourteenth Amendment, decided shortly after its adoption, the Court interpreted it as proscribing all state-imposed discriminations against the Negro race. The doctrine of "separate but equal" did not make its appearance in this Court until 1896 in the case of *Plessy v. Ferguson, supra,* involving not education but transportation. American courts have since labored with the doctrine for over half a century. In this Court there have been six cases involving the "separate but equal" doctrine in the field of public education. In *Cumming v. County Board of Education,* 175 U.S. 528, and *Gong Lum v. Rice,* 275 U.S. 78, the validity of the doctrine itself was not challenged. In more recent cases, all on the graduate school level, inequality was found in that specific benefits enjoyed by white students were denied to Negro students of the same educational qualifications. *Missouri ex rel. Gaines v. Canada,* 305 U.S. 337; *Sipuel v. University of Oklahoma,* 332 U.S. 631; *Sweatt v. Painter,* 339 U.S. 629; *McLaurin v. Oklahoma State Regents,* 339 U.S. 637. In none of these cases was it necessary to re-examine the doctrine to grant relief to the Negro plaintiff. And in *Sweatt v. Painter, supra,* the Court expressly reserved decision on the question whether *Plessy v. Ferguson* should be held inapplicable to public education.

In the instant cases, that question is directly presented. Here, unlike *Sweatt v. Painter,* there are findings below that the Negro and white schools involved have been equalized, or are being equalized, with respect to buildings, curricula, qualifications and salaries of teachers, and other "tangible" factors.[1] Our decision, therefore, cannot turn on merely a comparison of these tangible factors in the Negro and white schools involved in each of the cases. We must look to the effect of segregation itself on public education.

In approaching this problem, we cannot turn the clock back to 1868 when the Amendment was adopted, or even to 1896 when *Plessy v. Ferguson* was written. We must consider public education in the light of its full development and its present place in American life throughout the Nation. Only in this way can it be determined if segregation in public schools deprives these plaintiffs of the equal protection of the laws.

Today, education is perhaps the most important function of state and local governments. Compulsory school attendance laws and the great expenditures for education both demonstrate our recognition of the importance of education to our democratic society. It is required in the performance of our most basic public responsibilities, even service in the armed forces. It is the very foundation of good citizenship. Today it is a principal instrument in awakening the child to cultural values, in preparing him for later professional training, and in helping him to adjust normally to his environment. In these days, it is doubtful that any child may reasonably be expected to succeed in life if he is denied the opportunity of an education. Such an opportunity, where the state has undertaken to provide it, is a right which must be made available to all on equal terms.

We come then to the question presented: Does segregation of children in public schools solely on the basis of race, even though the physical facilities and other "tangible" factors may be equal, deprive the children of the minority group of equal education opportunities? We believe that it does.

In *Sweatt v. Painter, supra,* in finding that a segregated law school for Negroes could not provide them equal educational opportunities, this Court relied in large part on "those qualities which are incapable of objective measurement but which make for greatness in a law school." In *McLaurin v. Oklahoma State Regents, supra,* the Court, in requiring that a Negro admitted to a white graduate school be treated like all other students, again resorted to intangible considerations: ". . . his ability to study, to engage in discussions and exchange views with other students, and, in general, to learn his profession." Such considerations apply with added force to children in grade and high schools. To separate them from others of similar age and qualifications solely because of their race generates a feeling of inferiority as to their status in the community that may affect their hearts and minds in a way unlikely ever to be undone. The effect of this separation on their educational opportunities was well stated by a finding in the Kansas case by a court which nevertheless felt compelled to rule against the Negro plaintiffs:

> Segregation of white and colored children in public schools has a detrimental effect upon the colored children. The impact is greater when it has the sanction of the law; for the policy of separating the races is usually interpreted as denoting the inferiority of the Negro group. A sense of inferiority affects the motivation of a child to learn. Segregation with the sanction of law, therefore, has a tend-

ency to [retard] the educational and mental development of Negro children and to deprive them of some of the benefits they would receive in a racial[ly] integrated school system.[2]

Whatever may have been the extent of psychological knowledge at the time of *Plessy v. Ferguson,* this finding is amply supported by modern authority.[3] Any language in *Plessy v. Ferguson* contrary to this finding is rejected.

We conclude that in the field of public education the doctrine of "separate but equal" has no place. Separate educational facilities are inherently unequal. Therefore, we hold that the plaintiffs and others similarly situated for whom the actions have been brought are, by reason of the segregation complained of, deprived of the equal protection of the laws guaranteed by the Fourteenth Amendment. This disposition makes unnecessary any discussion whether such segregation also violates the Due Process Clause of the Fourteenth Amendment.

Because these are class actions, because of the wide applicability of this decision, and because of the great variety of local conditions, the formulation of decrees in these cases presents problems of considerable complexity. On re-argument, the consideration of appropriate relief was necessarily subordinated to the primary question—the constitutionality of segregation in public education. We have now announced that such segregation is a denial of the equal protection of the laws.

NOTES

1. In the Kansas case, the court below found substantial equality as to all such factors. 98 F. Supp. 797, 798. In the South Carolina case, the court below found that the defendants were proceeding "promptly and in good faith to comply with the court's decree." 103 F. Supp. 920, 921. In the Virginia case, the court below noted that the equalization program was already "afoot and progressing" 103 F. Supp. 337, 341; since then, we have been advised, in the Virginia Attorney General's brief on re-argument, that the program has now been completed. In the Delaware case, the court below similarly noted that the state's equalization program was well under way. 91 A. 2d 137, 139.
2. A similar finding was made in the Delaware case: "I conclude from the testimony that in our Delaware society, state-imposed segregation in education itself results in the Negro children, as a class, receiving educational opportunities which are substantially inferior to those available to white children otherwise similarly situated." 87 A. 2d 862, 865.
3. Clark, "Effect of Prejudice and Discrimination on Personality Development" (Midcentury White House Conference on Children and Youth, 1950); Witmer and Kotinsky, *Personality in the Making* (1952), ch. 6; Deutscher and Chein, "The Psychological Effects of Enforced Segregation: A Survey of Social Science Opinion," *Journal of Psychology,* XXVI (1948), 259; Chein, "What Are the Psychological Effects of Segregation Under Conditions of Equal Facilities?," *International Journal of Opinion and Attitude Research,* III (1949), 229; Brameld, "Educational Costs," in MacIver, ed., *Discrimination and National Welfare* (1949), pp. 44–48; Frazier, *The Negro in the United States* (1949), pp. 674–681. And see generally Myrdal, *An American Dilemma* (1944).

58

The Capacity of Law to
Affect Race Relations

JACK GREENBERG

A number of rules can slow the law's application to race relations. Of primary importance, no suit can be commenced without a plaintiff, as we have previously remarked. And the order in which plaintiffs appear and the relief they seek may bear no relationship to systematic legal development. To some extent a civil rights association can select among the cases it chooses to support in an effort to build precedent step by step. But if this factor were entirely controllable, it seems likely that after the graduate and professional school cases were decided by the Supreme Court, civil rights lawyers would have brought college cases before proceeding to what became the *School Segregation Cases*. The fact is that after the *Sweatt* and *McLaurin* decisions (indeed, while they were pending), complaints continued to mount about Negro elementary and high schools, while at the higher level, where conditions were no better, there were for a time no great efforts to seek legal redress.

Sometimes, notwithstanding the existence of an equalitarian rule of law, no plaintiff may appear to claim its benefits. Social factors often discourage some persons from participating in lawsuits. Outright intimidation and legal harassment may keep others out of court. Even in the North, potential plaintiffs may take the path of least resistance and fill their needs where they can be assured of no rebuff or embarrassment. Negroes are not likely to apply for whites-only jobs, or they will make few attempts to use accommodations that bar them. This is why antidiscrimination commissions seek the power to start cases on their own initiative. Civil rights organizations have thus been important in educating minorities concerning their rights and in supporting legal action to secure them.

In addition, discrimination must be proved. In the early days of civil rights law this was relatively easy, since the statutes often discriminated by their very terms, and since, where discrimination was effected by custom or practice, the administrators were not ashamed to admit it. Today in the North few who discriminate will concede it; they will try to attribute the rebuff to some non-racial factor. Restrictive covenants now do not expressly bar Negroes; they speak in Aesopian terms about compatibility of neighbors and give discretion to, for example, board of directors to bar sales to "undesirables" for any rea-

From *Race Relations and American Law* (New York: Columbia University Press, 1959), pp. 18–25. Reprinted by permission of the publisher.

son they choose. The first report on the administration of New York City's fair housing law emphasizes these evasive tactics. Although the chairman announced a significant degree of compliance, he also said that "there appeared to be a trend away from open discrimination . . . there was no expressed opposition to the law, and . . . most of those charged with discrimination denied it." [1]

In more and more Southern racial cases it is becoming necessary to prove every inconsequential fact as well as the main one, discrimination. For example, nowadays there rarely is a flat rule excluding Negroes from juries in biased courts. Indeed, sometimes a token few are deliberately chosen to confound the defendant. They may later be peremptorily challenged by the prosecutor. Some pupil assignment laws designed to avert or minimize school desegregation have refrained from mentioning race but speak of health factors, mental adjustment, and a host of vague standards that can cover up a racial selection. The Tallahassee bus ordinance treats of weight and balance as bases upon which the drivers are to assign seats. Perhaps we can devise a formula to describe the situation: As rules against discrimination become more clear, proof of discrimination becomes more difficult.

A striking example of evasion involves a South Carolina law that barred members of the NAACP from state employment. When this was attacked in the courts by school teachers, in *Bryan v. Austin* (1957), and it became obvious that the statute could not be sustained, it was repealed. The case, therefore, was declared moot. In place of the first statute a law was substituted which merely required that state employees list the organizations to which they belong. The state may have believed that local school boards would fire known NAACP members without giving a reason connected with membership in the association. Proof of discrimination would be difficult in such instances, and besides, the legislators may have thought that the mere existence of the new statute would deter individuals from joining the association.

There are also the delays of appeal and further appeal, fresh problems presented by fresh legislation, administrative hearings, and innumerable devices not yet even tried out. The key to the effectiveness of these tactics is the stay of execution. Few informed persons seriously believe that the substantive arguments offered by segregationists during these protracted proceedings are a legal bar to desegregation. Yet if stays of execution can be freely obtained, time can be bought almost indefinitely while litigation goes on. There has been some indication that the courts may begin to stop granting stays. Already in a few cases judgments to admit plaintiffs to schools have been placed in effect, leaving defendants to spin out their theories while desegregation is a reality. Preliminary injunctions or temporary restraining orders, summary dismissals of appeals as frivolous, and assessment of damages for unwarranted appeals are other devices that may cut litigation short.

Finally, a decree against one school district or park is enforceable against it alone. If others will not comply voluntarily, they must be sued separately, permitting the use of the same delaying tactics all over again.

The antidiscrimination commissions of some Northern jurisdictions that enforce civil rights laws exemplify the best means of overcoming the problems of legal inefficiency. Most of them may commence proceedings on their own, and they are equipped to ferret out the proof and to implement broad, flexible standards, substantive and procedural, asserting the initiative and absorbing the cost and trouble which would ordinarily be the plaintiff's burden. Their findings, like those of other administrative bodies, are sustained if supported by evidence. Most important, a policy of vigorous enforcement by such a commission, or indeed by any enforcement official, may have an educational effect and help to dissolve so-called "apathy." On the federal level, the proposed Part III of the Civil Rights Act of 1957, which was not enacted but became part of the Civil Rights Bill of 1958 (affording the government administrative and injunctive modes of securing civil rights), could, if firmly applied, pitch implementation at its most effective level.

The Minority Community

Among other factors contributing to the enforcement of desegregation may be determinants in the Negro community itself. In a legal system in which court orders can be obtained only at the suit of an aggrieved plaintiff or on complaint to the government, most change has come about through Negroes' initiative. To the extent that law operates other than through the judiciary, basically it still has been the Negro who has regulated the pace by lobbying, petitioning, and pressuring.

Negro political power is perhaps the most important factor within the minority group helping to set the viewpoint of those who implement the law: governors, mayors, local judges, police, school boards, administrators, and the public generally. For example, it appears that sentencing in the criminal courts often tends to be fairer where there is a substantial Negro vote. The attitude of executive authorities and the police determines whether agitators will succeed in stemming desegregation. The mood of administrators such as school authorities may decide the spirit and course of racial change.

However, urban Negro political organizations—the strongest Negroes have —are up against the fact that rural segregationists who dominate some state governments can use that power as a lever to incite city opposition to desegregation. In Virginia, for example, Norfolk probably would have taken steps toward desegregation if not for massive resistance on the state level; perhaps Richmond, too, would have moved in that direction but for the same reason. Shortly after the school decisions Greensboro would have commenced to change over, but was stopped by the state. Miami and Atlanta, to take only two more examples, would probably show a good deal of desegregation in various activities but for restraint from the state level. The disproportionate power of rural counties is a national political issue, and not one in race relations alone. As urban areas grow more powerful and tend to incorporate some country sections, the imbalance will probably be somewhat lessened. The situation may also change if the 1957 Civil Rights Act is able to increase rural Negro votes. But both alleviatives will probably come only over the long run.

Once more, it should not be forgotten that political power is important for civil rights in the North too. In Northern communities Negro political power has helped to get civil rights laws enacted and to pitch the vigor of their enforcement.

The Negro Lawyer

Another factor related to legal change—and one generally ignored—is the Negro lawyer. The position of leadership which de Tocqueville ascribed to American lawyers generally is probably even more true of the Negro lawyer in his relationship to the Negro community. Not until Howard University in the '30s began graduating numbers of Negro lawyers trained in civil rights did the race relations picture begin to change (of course, other circumstances were involved, and there long have been some Negro lawyers in the South educated at Northern schools; but the role of the Howard law alumni has been crucial in civil rights cases). The Howard graduates have in recent years been joined by those from Southern state law schools desegregated under the law. In Arkansas, Maryland, North Carolina, Texas, and elsewhere Negroes who have attended state schools now appear in civil rights cases. The Negro lawyer handles 99 per cent of the Southern antidiscrimination litigation, and most of it in the North; he plays an important role in legislative campaigns; and he provides community leadership. The Southern white attorney who will handle a desegregation case is almost unique. Yet many large Negro centers and even some important cities in the South still have no Negro lawyer or but a few. Some Negro attorneys, like some white ones, are not well trained; some prefer to devote all their time to earning a living. The economic resources of the Negroes in a locale may decide whether there is to be a Negro lawyer there or not, for unless there is enough legal business in a place to support a lawyer he cannot very well settle there.

Leadership and Community Organization

In some places Negro insurance executives, bankers, doctors, teachers, and other business and professional persons with education, status, and leisure also provide guidance, both where there are Negro lawyers and where there are none. But unpredictably, persons of other stations in life—housewives, government workers, laborers, farmers—may have the ability and perhaps the "personal magic" to guide a change. The Reverend Martin Luther King of Montgomery, among the most striking personalities of the new stewardship, symbolizes and has stimulated the spread of church leadership, although the Negro churches themselves have long been important meeting places for the NAACP and other civic groups.

Group activity is the medium through which the most effective civil rights leadership works. The United States, as Arthur Schlesinger, Sr., has pointed out, is a nation of joiners and Americans work for social change through groups. Litigation on questions of public importance is often group-supported, lobbying is almost invariably an organized activity, and groups aid in policing and law enforcement. There are the NAACP, the Urban League, the Southern Regional Council, the American Civil Liberties Union, and various lay religious associations, as well as civic, labor, fraternal, and church groups generally, all working against discrimination. Sometimes a grouping may arise spontaneously as in the case of the Montgomery boycott, out of which grew the now permanent Montgomery Improvement Association. The MIA, in turn, has given rise to the Southern Christian Leadership Conference. The many Southern state laws and other devices to outlaw the NAACP indicate recognition of its effectiveness.

Group activity has been particularly efficacious in local transportation changeovers because a disproportionately high number of local bus riders are colored, and alternatives to public transportation can be arranged readily. Under this pressure bus lines in a score of cities complied when the Supreme Court held local travel segregation unconstitutional. The Montgomery boycott did not achieve its aim, however, until after the courts had outlawed the Montgomery regulations. The Montgomery bus company and others elsewhere were able to use the legal ruling as a shield against local segregationists.

Some institutions, particularly universities, not only provide leadership or organization but sometimes help to influence attitudes in favor of civil rights. Atlanta University is a major liberal force in that city. The fact that Knoxville College and the University of Tennessee are situated in Knoxville is said to have contributed to the easy move away from transportation segregation there. The site of the University of Arkansas, Fayetteville, is said to be the community fairest in the administration of justice in that state. At times, of course, liberal sentiment in some university towns may be outweighed by other forces. Prosegregationists have worked to suppress campus freedom, so that many Southern faculty members have been or can easily be persuaded to leave for Northern campuses.

The Minority's Responsiveness to Available Rights

An antidiscrimination rule of law and community forces favorable to its enforcement do not settle the extent to which a minority will become integrated into the community. The quickness of Negroes to respond to available rights also helps to decide whether those rights will play a real role in life relationships or remain abstract rules. Not only must cases be filed at the behest of plaintiffs, or legislation pushed in the assemblies, but once suits are won or laws enacted, the rights they confer must be exercised; otherwise they mean nothing. There are school districts where the board has agreed to cease segregating but few or no Negroes have applied for transfer. In some communities carriers have abolished Jim Crow seating, yet most Negroes continue to sit in the rear. There are no restrictions on voting in many Southern counties, but Negro registration is well under that for whites. In some Northern places where public accommodations laws are obeyed, there is little Negro patronage.

A long history of segregation and discrimination directly limits the number of Negroes who can exercise the new freedoms. Of those who have had inferior high school and college educations, not many can qualify for new graduate school opportunities. Those who have never been trained cannot accept new openings in engineering and other specialties. Those without adequate incomes cannot take advantage of a law like New York City's that forbids racial restriction in private housing. The better "white" restaurants in cities may be inconveniently located to Negro housing and proportionately more Negroes may be unable to pay their prices. But in some instances (such as voting, travel, and public recreation) the barrier is hardly so clear-cut and external, so some have called this failure to respond "apathy." The term, however, is misleading unless it is understood to incorporate reference to generations of segregation and thus enforced lack of aspiration of all sorts. And, obviously, it is not necessarily apathetic to retreat or stand pat, as some do, under fire or threat of economic or physical reprisal. The local transportation example underlines the importance of the minority's response. Here a shift can be made fairly easily, and it is the younger Negro passengers, on whom the time-worn patterns have been less firmly pressed, who are more likely to sit in front in the once-white section, while old-timers usually continue to occupy Jim Crow seats. As time goes on, of course, those taking advantage of the new opportunities appear to be multiplying. In Baltimore, where any child may attend virtually any school, Negro registration in formerly white schools has grown from 4,601 in 1955 to 14,826 in 1957, although 80 per cent of the colored children still attend all-colored schools. "Apathy" is decreasing there while housing segregation is becoming the main cause of all-colored schools.

The Elasticity of the Institution to Be Changed

Given a legal rule, assuming obedience and the minority's responsiveness, still other factors must be counted in figuring whether law can change race relations. How elastic is the institution on which law is operating? A rule ending Jim Crow higher learning is limited in realization if colleges are overcrowded. To step back one level, the extent to which the college rule is realized will reflect the capacity of high schools to prepare once-segregated Negro pupils for higher education. Removing bias from hiring signifies little in a depression or a tight job market. But during prosperity, as antibias rules open apprenticeship training and technical education, qualified applicants can begin to fill openings and can commence to accumulate seniority. Ending exclusion from housing does not count for much if there are few homes or apartments available; it can mean more with plentiful housing. Abolishing distinctions in the armed forces when the number of personnel decreases and the need for skill increases may not have much significance for desegregation; it cannot equip Negroes for enlistment or retention in the same ratio as whites nor give them the background training to qualify for higher positions. At an earlier time when the armed forces were larger and there were relatively fewer skilled posts, Negroes entered and advanced more easily. In each case the rule means less if the institution to be changed does not have sufficient play in its joints to shift readily from a bi-racial to a non-racial system.

NOTE

1. *New York Times,* July 21, 1958, p. 23.

59

Attitudes Toward Desegregation

HERBERT H. HYMAN AND
PAUL B. SHEATSLEY

Before we discuss our findings we shall briefly describe how the surveys were made. Each survey was designed to include a representative sample of the nation's adult white population and for that purpose involved interviews with 1,200 to 1,500 individuals. The interviewers were white people trained for the task and living in the sample areas. Each interview resulted in a punched card containing the answers and pertinent information about the person interviewed: age, sex, education, place of residence, and so on. In this way the National Opinion Research Center was able to compare the opinions of various groups, such as the elderly and the youthful, the highly educated and the poorly educated, and many others.

In discussing the findings we shall use the terms "South" and "North." "South" refers to three regions as defined by the Bureau of the Census: the South Atlantic region (Delaware, Maryland, the District of Columbia, Virginia, West Virginia, North Carolina, South Carolina, Georgia, and Florida), the East South Central region (Kentucky, Tennessee, Alabama, and Mississippi) and the West South Central region (Arkansas, Louisiana, Oklahoma,

From *Scientific American,* CCXI (July, 1964), 16–18, 19–23. Reprinted by permission of the authors and publisher. Copyright © 1964 by Scientific American, Inc. All rights reserved.

and Texas). "North" refers to the rest of the country except for Alaska and Hawaii, where no interviews were conducted. Finally, we wish to emphasize that what we have sought to investigate over these 22 years is the trend of white opinion on racial integration. That is why the findings we shall discuss pertain only to the opinions of white adults and do not include the views of the more than 10 million Negro adults in the nation.

The dramatic changes throughout the nation are illustrated by the findings about school segregation, based on the question "Do you think white students and Negro students should go to the same schools or to separate schools?" In 1942 fewer than a third of all whites favored the integration of schools. The attitudes of southern whites at that time were about as close to unanimity as one ever comes in surveys of the U.S. public: only 2 per cent expressed support for integration. Among northerners in that period integration also represented a minority view, endorsed by only 40 per cent of white adults.

By 1956, two years after the Supreme Court decision against racial segregation in public schools, national approval of integrated schools had risen to approximately half of the total white population; in the North it had become the majority view, endorsed by three out of five white adults. Even the South was far from immune to the changing situation. Earlier only one person in 50 had favored school integration; in 1956 the proportion was one in seven. The most recent figures now show not only that the long-term trend has continued but also that in the South it has accelerated. Today [in 1964] a substantial majority of all white Americans endorse school integration. In the North the figure has continued its steady climb and now stands at approximately three out of every four adults. But whereas in the 14 years from 1942 to 1956 the proportion of southern whites who accepted this principle rose only from 2 per cent to 14 per cent, the proportion has now risen to 30 per cent in just seven years since that time.

That these are real changes rather than accidental results reflecting unreliability of the sampling method is indicated by other findings. In spite of the errors inherent in all sampling procedures, which may run as high as three or four percentage points in samples of the size used in these surveys, the figures for the total white population, in three separate surveys in 1956 and in three other separate surveys last year, did not vary by more than one percentage point. Even the findings for the separate regions, based on smaller numbers and therefore subject to an even larger sampling error, are highly stable.

The surveys repeated in 1956 and 1963 also establish that the changes in national opinion on this question represent long-term trends that are not easily modified by specific—even by highly dramatic—events. The survey of November, 1963, was conducted within a week after the assassination of President Kennedy, but the national findings remained unchanged in spite of any soul-searching that may have been occurring in the North or the South. In 1956, between the June and September surveys, the attention of the nation had been focused on the first violent crises over school integration in a number of small towns in the border states and in Texas. Again the figures showed no change.

The overall picture is thus one of a massive trend, unbroken by the particular news events of the day.

What accounts for the steady and strong rise in support for school integration? One important factor would seem to be the conversion of segregationists. The size of the "Don't know" vote in opinion surveys can be taken as a crude but fair measure of the intensity of the public's views. If large numbers report themselves as undecided, the opinions of the remainder are often lightly held. Conversely, if almost everybody has an opinion on the issue, it is probable that opinions are strong.

It could have been expected that in 1942—12 years before the Supreme Court decision and long before the great ferment in civil rights—a considerable number of Americans would have been undecided on the question of school integration. On most issues put to the American public in surveys it is common to find that 10 per cent or more of those interviewed are undecided. Yet in 1942 the "Don't know" group on the question of school integration amounted to no more than 4 per cent of the total.

That group has remained at about 4 per cent since 1942. Therefore the increased support for school integration cannot have come significantly from the ranks of the undecided, leaving the number of staunch segregationists virtually unchanged; nor can it be argued that a number of segregationists have become doubtful of their position and have moved into the ranks of the undecided. The greatly increased support for integration must have come mainly from segregationists who switched to the opposite camp.

There are other indications of the public's strong involvement in the issue of race relations. In the December, 1963, survey, prior to any specific questions about integration, respondents were asked: "What, in your opinion, are some of the most important problems facing the United States today?" More people mentioned civil rights and race relations than mentioned any other problem. Similarly, when respondents were asked to rate their degree of interest in a number of public issues, there were more people reporting themselves "very interested" in Negro-white relations than in Cuba or the forthcoming presidential election.

In sum, the long-term trend toward school integration seems to be moving with considerable force. It has not been reversed even by highly dramatic events. Moreover, integration has been achieving its gains by converting persons with strongly held opposing views.

• • •

That the demonstrated decline in support of segregation reflects changes in fundamental beliefs is suggested by the long-term trend in white opinion about the inherent intelligence and educability of Negroes. On several occasions since 1942 the National Opinion Research Center has asked the question: "In general, do you think that Negroes are as intelligent as white people—that is, can they learn things just as well if they are given the same education and training?" In the responses to that question there has been a striking change. In 1942 only 50 per cent of northern whites answered "Yes." Today the figure has risen to 80 per cent. In the South today a substantial majority (59 per cent) credits Negroes with equal intelligence, in contrast with only 21 per cent in 1942.

This revolutionary change in belief goes far to explain the increased acceptance of school integration over the past two decades. It has undermined one of the most stubborn arguments formerly offered by whites for segregated schools. Table 59–1 shows the relation between belief in the educability of Negroes and the support of integrated schools in the 1956 and 1963 surveys. As one might expect, those who regard the Negro's intelligence as equal to the

TABLE 59-1

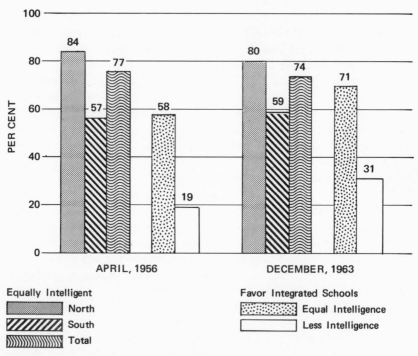

Correlation between belief in the comparability of Negro and white intelligence and support for integrated schools is indicated.

white's are much more likely to favor integrated schools than those who regard the Negro as inferior in intelligence. There is more than this, however, to be said. Belief in the equal intelligence of Negroes, after rising steadily for 14 years, leveled off in 1956 and has remained stable since then. Support of integrated schools, however, has continued to rise. Plainly there are forces at work in the growing support for the integration of schools other than belief in the educability of Negroes.

Attitudes on school integration vary according to the degree of integration existing in a given area. This becomes apparent when one looks at particular southern areas instead of regarding "the South" as a homogeneous region, as we have in this discussion up to now. The occurrence of racial crises in some southern communities but not in others and the varying degrees of official compliance with federal law suggest that there are large differences within the region. Our surveys bear this out. We divided our sample of southern localities into three groups according to the amount of integration in the public schools: those with considerable integration, those with token integration, and those that remain completely segregated. Since few southern communities fall into the first classification, respondents living in those areas constitute a tiny fraction of the total, and the sampling error of this particular statistic could be substantial. To give greater strength to the findings we have pooled the results of the surveys in June and December, 1963, and as another check we have compared responses made when the Gallup Poll, at our request, asked southern whites the question on school integration in June, 1963.

In southern districts where considerable integration of schools has taken place 54 per cent of white adults favor integration; in districts where token integration has occurred, 38 per cent express favorable attitudes, and in segregated districts 28 per cent favor integration. There is obviously some parallel between public opinion and official action, but which came first? In the desegregated areas did integration come about in response to a more favorable public opinion or did the more favorable public opinion develop only after the official act of desegregation?

Close analysis of the current findings, compared with those of the 1956 surveys, leads us to the conclusion that in those parts of the South where some measure of school integration has taken place official action has *preceded* public sentiment, and public sentiment has then attempted to accommodate itself to the new situation.

In the 1956 surveys of those southern districts that had already achieved some integration of schools only 31 per cent of white adults expressed approval of the idea. By 1963 the number of such communities had been increased by those districts that only belatedly and reluctantly accepted a measure of integration; in our current sample more than half of the southern respondents living in communities now classified as integrated to any degree experienced such integration only within the past year, and none of those in areas of considerable integration were exposed to such a level of integration before 1962. One might expect as a result that the proportion approving integration would be even lower than it was seven years ago. Instead approval of integration has risen in such areas from less than a third in 1956 to more than half of their white population today.

Similarly, it was found in 1956 that only 4 per cent of white adults in southern segregated districts favored the integration of schools. Since then some of these communities have reluctantly adopted a measure of integration, so that the segregated districts that remain might be described as the hard core of segregation. Within this hard core, however, approval of school integration has now risen to 28 per cent of the white public. Thus even in the extreme segregationist areas of the South the tides of opinion are moving toward integration, and in the more progressive areas it seems that official action in itself is contributing to the speed and magnitude of popular change.

In this connection it is relevant to cite the results of the following question, asked repeatedly over the years by the Gallup Poll and included in the National Opinion Research Center survey of June, 1963: "Do you think the day will ever come in the South when whites and Negroes will be going to the same schools, eating in the same restaurants, and generally sharing the same public accommodations?" In South and North alike, whether the community has segregated or integrated schools, more than three-quarters of the white adults believed that integration was bound to come. In contrast, only 53 per cent of the respondents felt that way in 1957. Apparently the pattern is that as official action works to bury what is already regarded as a lost cause, public acceptance of integration increases because opinions are readjusted to the inevitable reality.

Data from the 1963 surveys also enable us to compare opinions in northern communities that vary in the extent to which Negro and white children attend the same schools. As we have noted, such segregation in the North stems largely from patterns of residential housing rather than from law, but the comparisons with the South are nonetheless of interest. Again we find greater support for integration where integration actually exists and greater support for segregation where there is no integration. In both types of community, however, the overall level of support is much greater in the North than in the South. Among northern whites living in districts that have segregated schools 65 per cent favor integration; in northern areas where schools are considerably integrated 83 per cent favor the policy.

A similar pattern of support for integration growing with exposure to integrated situations appears to the findings about people who have moved between North and South. Table 59–2 compares the opinions of four groups: northerners who have never lived in the South; northerners who once lived in the South; southerners who have never lived in the North; and southerners who did at one time live in the North. From the comparison it is apparent that northerners who once lived in the South differ very little in their views from northerners who have never been exposed to southern life. They are only slightly less favorable to integration. In striking contrast, those southerners who have previously lived in the North differ greatly from those who have always lived in the South. Except on the issue of school integration, the attitudes of southerners with a history of earlier residence in the North are much closer to those of northerners than to those of their fellow southerners. Even on school integration the difference is substantial.

The influence of geographical mobility on southern opinion may well account for a considerable part of the gross change in southern attitudes over the recent decades. Although the rate of movement from South to North exceeds the rate from North to South, the southern migrants represent a relatively small proportion of the northern population, whereas among southerners today a considerably larger proportion have had some northern exposure.

TABLE 59-2

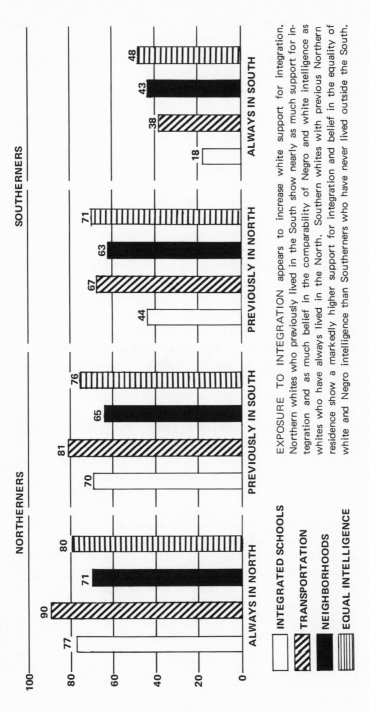

EXPOSURE TO INTEGRATION appears to increase white support for integration. Northern whites who previously lived in the South show nearly as much support for integration and as much belief in the comparability of Negro and white intelligence as whites who have always lived in the North. Southern whites with previous Northern residence show a markedly higher support for integration and belief in the equality of white and Negro intelligence than Southerners who have never lived outside the South.

Thus the net effect of migration is to strengthen support for integration.

As for the relation between amount of education and support of integration, both the 1956 and the 1963 surveys showed that the better-educated groups, North and South, were more favorable to integration of schools and public transportation than people of less education were. Between the two surveys, however, all subgroups have become more favorable to integration. Since the number of cases in the South is small, and since the subgroup estimates are subject to a larger sampling error, we have pooled the two recent surveys.

The most dramatic change of opinion has occurred in the best-educated segment of the southern white population, where the proportion in favor of integration has increased from only about a fourth to almost half. Lest formal education appear to be a decisive factor, however, note that in 1963 the best-educated white southerners were not as favorably inclined to integration as the least-educated white northerners, and that by 1963 those southerners had not yet reached the level of opinion already exhibited in 1956 by poorly-educated northerners.

In 1956 it was found that the segment of the white population represented by people 65 and older, in both the North and the South, was least favorable to integration, and the same finding is documented in the recent surveys. One would expect this result on the basis of education alone; inasmuch as the expansion of educational opportunity is a development of recent decades, the oldest adults are less likely than the younger ones to have had advanced schooling. Indeed, some of the long-term trends in attitudes toward segregation may simply represent the passing of the oldest generation and its replacement in the population by younger individuals of greater tolerance. The persistence of the difference in attitudes between the oldest group and younger groups would help to account for the further changes in public opinion in more recent years and would augur still more change in the future.

Since the analysis of differences between age groups is so relevant to an understanding of long-term opinion trends, the sample in last December's survey was designed to double the number of interviews with the youngest adults—those from 21 to 24. These extra interviews were not included in the tabulations except for this particular analysis, but by using them here we can place greater confidence in our findings for this age group, which otherwise would account for only a small portion of the national sample. In this way we are able to provide more evidence for a new finding that appeared in the survey of June, 1963, but then could be regarded only as suggestive. The finding, which is reflected in the illustration on this page (not shown), is that whereas in 1956 the youngest adults were the most favorable to school integration, by 1963 the pattern—at least for the South—seemed to have changed. Although they were never as prosegregationist as the older age groups, the 21-to-24-year-olds appeared in the recent surveys to be less favorable to the integration of schools than the adults aged 25 to 44. The difference is admittedly small and could conceivably be due to sample variation. But the finding appeared in all of last year's surveys; unless it is disproved by subsequent studies one must accept as valid the evidence that the youngest adults are relatively less tolerant than formerly, in spite of the fact that on the average they are more highly ed-ucated.

The members of the youngest group in 1956 have, of course, now aged suf-ficiently to be included in the present 25-to-44 group and have added their earlier quantum of tolerance to that older group's attitudes. Those who are now in the 21-to-24 group were still children in 1956 and so were not in-cluded in the surveys of that time. But why, having arrived at the status of young adults, do they not exhibit the larger measure of tolerance characteristic of the equivalent age group in earlier years?

That the phenomenon is clearly evident only in the South suggests an expla-nation, because this newest group of young southern adults has lived through experiences quite different from those of the generation of young adults stud-ied in 1956. They have spent their high school and college years in the stormy decade since the Supreme Court decision, and it is they who have been most closely associated with the crises and dislocations that have accompanied the transition to integration in various communities. Actually few of them appear to have suffered directly from these events. They were asked "In what ways have you or any members of your family been affected by integration?" More than four-fifths reported no effects. It is noteworthy, however, that not a single southerner of this age group spontaneously reported any kind of favorable ef-fect, whereas among northerners of the same age 5 per cent volunteered an answer describing the personal effects of integration in favorable terms.

Plainly the conflicts of integration have had a great immediacy for the young southerners. The issue of civil rights is more salient for them than for the older groups in our southern sample. More of them spontaneously mention race relations as the biggest problem facing the country today. The youngest southerners are more likely than the next older group to express themselves as believing the Negro protest movement is "violent" rather than "peaceful" and to voice the opinion that demonstrations and protests have "hurt the cause" of Negroes.

Other questions substantiate the likelihood that a change of attitude has oc-curred among young southern adults. When asked if their views have remained the same in recent years or have become more favorable or less favorable to integration, it is this youngest group that is more likely than others to report both a change in attitude and a shift away from a favorable opinion. For ex-ample, the youngest adults in the South say they have shifted almost two to one against integration in recent years. The older groups report less change of attitude, and when it occurs, the shifts are about equal in both directions.

Apart from this tendency, about the extent or permanence of which we can-not yet be sure, it appears that the attitudes of white Americans of both the North and the South are continuing to shift toward greater acceptance of inte-gration. We cannot be certain that future events will not reverse the course. But the unbroken trend of the past 20 years, and particularly its acceleration in the past decade of intensified controversy, suggests that integration will not be easily halted. In the minds and hearts of the majority of Americans the principle of integration seems already to have been won. The issues that remain are how soon and in what ways the principle is to be implemented.

60

Interracial Seating Patterns on New Orleans Public Transit

MORRIS DAVIS, ROBERT SEIBERT, AND WARREN BREED

As the result of a federal court order, legally enforceable segregation on New Orleans public transit ended on May 31, 1958. Prior to that time no Negro had been permitted to sit forward of any white on NOPSI [1] buses. While in many respects the patterns of practice had not required maximum racial separation—whites and Negroes rode the same buses, entered and exited by the same doors, and occupied a single, physically undivided compartment—they had resulted in a perfect racial ordering of seated passengers.[2] To the extent, then, that whites continued to sit in front of Negroes even after the court order went into effect, legal desegregation would have failed to bring about full *de facto* integration. Indeed, a particular bus could be ranked along the dimension segregation-integration according to the prevalence of interracial mixing by its passengers.

An attempt was made during April and May, 1964, to assess the degree of actual integration on NOPSI vehicles by charting the seating arrays on a sample of bus cross-sections and adducing certain indices from these data. Three graduate students rode buses on 11 of the 39 transit lines during both morning and afternoon peak periods. Routes were selected so as to include a variety of lines passing through different kinds of neighborhoods.[3] At 12-minute intervals during a given run seating patterns were recorded on mimeographed charts. Two of the students (and occasionally all three) would ride the same bus, one sitting in front and one further back, their overlapping observations providing a reliability check.[4]

Three variables were coded: race, dichotomized into "Negro" and "All Others" (the latter being overwhelmingly white and so referred to hereinafter); sex; and age, trichotomized as "Under 16 years," "17 to 45," and "Over 45."

From *Social Problems,* XIII, No. 3 (Winter, 1966), 298–306, journal of The Society for the Study of Social Problems. Reprinted by permission of the authors and publisher.

The last characteristic was, of course, most open to estimation errors. Attempts to record other theoretically interesting kinds of data—for example, type of clothing as an indicator of class—were abandoned during a pre-test as unreliable. No interviewing was conducted.

Eighty-seven vehicle cross-sections were charted during the test period.[5] Each diagram showed the exact placement of every seated passenger at the time of sampling, and specified his race, sex, and estimated age. Time, date, name of line, and weather condition were also noted, though these do not figure in this study. From the diagrammed data we have computed the extent of *de facto* integration (or segregation) on New Orleans public transit, its variations as a bus becomes more crowded or as its racial composition becomes more one-sided, and finally the age and sex characteristics of those whites and Negroes who are sitting in what may be considered an integrated position and who, therefore, may also be considered agents of social change.

These computations should not be thought of as proceeding automatically from the data. For while it is clear that an absolutely segregated bus would at the least have all whites sitting ahead of all Negroes [6] and that an absolutely integrated bus would be one on which information about race would be of no help in predicting seating patterns, it is not obvious how one can measure degrees of segregation-integration on a bus or compare the amount on one vehicle to that on another. One reason for the difficulty is that there are no physical barriers that separate a "white compartment" from a "Negro compartment." There are no vestigial dividing lines either. If some Negroes sit in front of (or beside) some whites, just who has entered whose "section"? An analyst who wishes to partition the bus conceptually must introduce his own cutting lines, and there is no ultimately satisfactory way for him to do that.

A second problem derives from the fact that even among adjacent persons degrees of interaction may differ. Sitting side by side seems behaviorally unlike sitting front to back, diagonally tangent, or across the aisle; and sitting side by side on transverse seats is probably different from the same relation on lengthwise seats. Furthermore, passengers do not always sit immediately next to each other, especially on relatively empty buses. Vacant seats, it would appear, somewhat reduce the impact of integration.[7] One is tempted, of course, to suggest some sort of weighting for these various interpersonal relationships (see note 12), but it is doubtful whether the participants' ratings would agree with ours.

Since it is not obvious how one is to assess degrees of segregation-integration, we have tried some four different summarizing measures. Each of them computes the number of persons who violate the old pattern of white precedence over Negroes. A "perfectly integrated" bus is then defined as one on which half the seated passengers are precedence violators.[8] The measures may be labeled and defined as follows:

Method 1. The Traditional Definition. Starting from the front of the bus, all whites and the first Negro follow the old style of precedence, but any whites seated further back than the first seated Negro are precedence violators.

Method 2. The Split Half. Any Negroes seated in the front half of the bus and any whites in the back half are precedence violators.

Method 3. The Proportional Break. The percentage of seated passengers who are white is calculated. Any Negroes seated in that proportion of seats from the front and any whites in the remaining seats are precedence violators.

Method 4. The Perfect Rank Order. The number of seated whites is tabulated. Any Negroes who are seated among that number of passengers from the front and any whites beyond that number are precedence violators.[9]

All four methods have shortcomings. Findings under Method 1 can be massively affected by the behavior of a single individual. A solitary Negro on the first seat can be the difference between a bus that totally follows or totally violates precedence. Method 2 is imperfect since it overestimates the amount of apparent precedence violation on any crowded bus in which the racial balance departs from unity. A bus on which all seats were occupied, Negroes comprised three-quarters of the passengers, and all whites sat ahead of all Negroes, would under this method supposedly have one out of each four riders violating precedence. Method 3 suffers from a similar, though oppositely caused, defect. On a lightly patronized bus in which Negroes sat behind whites but all persons sat relatively near the front, the extent of precedence violation would again be severely over-reported.[10] Even Method 4, the measure we think is both simplest to compute and conceptually most justifiable, particularly because it does not require "sectioning" of the buses, has at least two partial faults. First, it results in double counting: every Negro who sits in front of a white causes one of the last whites also to be considered a precedence violator. Second, if a Negro sits adjacent to a white at the front of the bus, it is not that white but another further back who is deemed to violate precedence. Neither of these faults, however, seems to damage Method 4 as markedly as their various flaws do the first three methods.[11]

The four methods [12] yield the distributions of segregation-integration on bus cross-sections by per cent of precedence violating passengers given in Table 60-1.

TABLE 60-1 *Segregation-Integration on Bus Cross Sections by Percentage of*
Precedence-Violating Passengers
(Four Methods) *

	Percentage of Passengers Violating Precedence in Cross-Sections						
Method	0	.01-19	20-39	40-59	60-79	80-100	Total
1	17	40	22	7	1	0	87
2	1	29	32	22	3	0	87
3	7	40	27	10	3	0	87
4	14	49	20	4	0	0	87

*Figures in the cells of Tables 60-1, 60-2, and 60-3 refer to bus cross sections, not to individual passengers. Row 1, column 3, for example, shows that 22 of the 87 cross sections observed had between 20 and 40 per cent of their passengers violating precedence according to the rationale of Method 1.

As mentioned above, on a single "perfectly integrated" bus only 50 per cent of the riders should be precedence violators. If the figure were 100 per cent, then perfect reverse segregation would have occurred.[13] Over a series of buses, however, passenger distributions might well depart from the midpoint for various idiosyncratic reasons, the array of cross-sections perhaps assuming a bell curve. The series itself could still be considered perfectly integrated so long as the curve were not markedly skewed to the left. Such "statistical integration" clearly does not obtain with our data, otherwise the number of cross-sections within the 80 to 100 per cent range of precedence violation would approximate that within the 0 to 19 per cent range. Comparing column 6 to columns 1 and 2, one may see that no cross-section shows any extreme reverse segregation, while (depending on the method employed) somewhere between 30 and 63 out of the 87 exhibit high degrees of the usual brand. And as column 4 indicates, relatively few buses (between 4 and 22) individually approach an integrated condition. Any assertions about the precise amount of segregation-integration depend, of course, on which measure one deems most adequate; but as a scanning of Table 60–1 would show, Methods 1 and 4, the vernacular notion and the methodologically most defensible index, yield rather similar results.[14]

We had expected that the "true degree" of integration on NOPSI buses would be greatest as they were most equally balanced racially, and that as they became more exclusively white or Negro, marked segregation would rapidly develop. Further, we imagined that high segregation would be more characteristic of a bus in which whites were relatively few in number than where they predominated. The grounds for our reasoning were these: that as a race becomes a smaller and smaller minority on a vehicle, it is placed in an increasingly more "threatening" situation; that the average threat per bus is least when the two races are evenly balanced; and that minorities of whites see themselves more threatened than similar minorities of Negroes.

Table 60–2, which cross-tabulates the distributions in Table 60–1 (Methods 1 and 4 only) by the percentage of passengers who are white, confirms this interpretation. The data take a general wedge shape, with evenly balanced buses showing the most integration, mono-racially dominated buses the least, and buses with few whites exhibiting rather more segregation than those with few Negroes. (See columns 3 and 4 especially.) Methods 1 and 4 differ slightly, but both demonstrate these phenomena clearly.[15]

We had also thought that, as buses became more crowded and sorting out was more troublesome, the observance of segregated patterns would tend to break down. Table 60–3, which cross-tabulates the data in Table 60–1 by the degree of crowding, does not, however, confirm these suppositions. The degree of integration changes only slightly as the bus population increases, the trend from low to medium being particularly ambiguous. It is our *post hoc* guess that these results stem from two opposite sorts of motives; and that as a bus becomes more crowded and segregation is more difficult to keep in operation, it also becomes more important to uphold segregation, since a crowded bus provides a more "threatening" environment. Integration on crowded public

TABLE 60-2 *Segregation-Integration on Bus Cross Sections by Percentages of Precedence-Violating and of White Passengers (Methods 1 and 4 Only)*

	Per Cent White	Percentage of Passengers Violating Precedence in Cross Sections						
		0	.01-19	20-39	40-59	60-79	80-100	Total
Method 1	80-100	7	6	2	2	0	0	17
	60-79	4	8	8	1	1	0	22
	40-59	2	9	9	4	0	0	24
	20-39	2	11	3	0	0	0	16
	0-19	2	6	0	0	0	0	8
	Total	17	40	22	7	1	0	87
Method 4	80-100	7	8	2	0	0	0	17
	60-79	3	9	8	2	0	0	22
	40-59	1	13	8	2	0	0	24
	20-39	1	13	2	0	0	0	16
	0-19	2	6	0	0	0	0	8
	Total	14	49	20	4	0	0	87

TABLE 60-3 *Segregation-Integration on Bus Cross Sections by Percentage of Precedence-Violating Passengers and Degree of Crowding (Methods 1 and 4 Only)*

	Degree of Crowding	Percentage of Passengers Violating Precedence in Cross Sections						
		0	.01-19	20-39	40-59	60-79	80-100	Total
Method 1	High*	2	12	6	3	0	0	23
	Medium	9	22	9	2	1	0	43
	Low	6	6	7	2	0	0	21
	Total	17	40	22	7	1	0	87
Method 4	High	2	18	3	0	0	0	23
	Medium	7	24	11	1	0	0	43
	Low	5	7	6	3	0	0	21
	Total	14	49	20	4	0	0	87

*"High" means from 35 to 51 seated passengers; "medium," from 18 to 34; and "low", less than 18. Most buses have 51 seats.

transit means adjacent seating, shoulder to shoulder and hip to hip, rather than just occupying a seat in the vicinity of the other race, and it means performing that act before a larger audience. Ease and threat, thus, would work in contrary directions on NOPSI buses, their effects tending to wash out in the observed data.

Those persons who violate precedence may be considered agents of social change, since it is they who are breaking with tradition. Table 60–4 gives the number of white and Negro males and females for each of our three age divi-

TABLE 60-4   *Seated Passengers, Violators and Nonviolators of Precedence, by Race, Sex, and Age*

N = 2,074

Total	Violators of Precedence		Nonviolators of Precedence	Total	
White males	76	(16.2)*	394	470	
Age 1-16	6	(16.2)	31		37
17-45	44	(19.4)	202		246
46+	26	(13.9)	161		187
White females	53	(9.1)	532	585	
Age 1-16	21	(15.2)	117		138
17-45	22	(7.7)	265		287
46+	10	(6.2)	150		160
All whites	129	(12.2)	926	1,055	
Negro males	45	(11.6)	344	389	
Age 1-16	6	(27.3)	16		22
17-45	32	(11.7)	242		274
46+	7	(7.5)	86		93
Negro females	138	(21.9)	492	630	
Age 1-16	26	(38.8)	41		67
17-45	83	(20.5)	322		405
46+	29	(18.3)	129		158
All Negroes	183	(17.9)	836	1,019	
Total	312	(15.0)	1,762	2,074	

*Figures in parentheses give the percentages violating precedence in each row.

sions who did and did not violate precedence.[16] Among the whites it was the males, and among Negroes the females, who did so most frequently. Older persons, both white and Negro, violated precedence less than others of their sex and race, while the contrary tended to be true for the younger riders. The gap between youths and elders was particularly wide among the Negroes.

On the face of it, the data in Table 60–4 seem to "make sense." The fact that the legal rules had changed only six years earlier would account for the greater propensity of youths to integrate and the more uniformly traditional behavior of their elders. The rate reversal by sex between whites and Negroes was also to be expected, if only that in many aspects of southern life it has long been easiest and least stressful for white males and Negro females to perform in somewhat less-than-caste-like roles. That Negroes exhibited greater ranges of precedence violation than whites might have been foreseen, too, since among legally disadvantaged Negroes some subsections (like youths) felt able to exercise their new prerogatives, while others (like grown men) would still practice their traditional reticence.

NOTES

1. Almost all intra-city public transit in New Orleans is provided by New Orleans Public Service, Inc. (NOPSI), a utility that also furnishes both gas and electricity within the city. NOPSI is a wholly owned subsidiary of Middle South Utilities, a New York-based holding company.

2. During the spring of 1957 students in an undergraduate sociology course had ridden the buses, observing behavior under legally segregated seating, and engaging passengers in conversations about possible desegregation. At no time did a student observe a Negro sitting ahead of a white. A few moderating activities were encountered—a white passenger moving forward the sign that demarked the limits of the white and Negro "sections" so that Negro standees could sit, or a Negro arguing with a bus driver—but in general segregated seating seemed to have been accepted by both races among the transit riders.

3. The lines studied were Freret and Magazine (trolley buses); Canal and St. Charles (streetcars); and Tchoupitoulas, Broad, Metairie, Hayne, Esplanade, and Claiborne (gasoline and diesel buses).

4. The students were Miss Gay Brannon, Mr. Muhammed Tayyarah, and Mr. Seibert. Standees were omitted. The ratio of passengers to seats varied between .05 and 1.32 at the times of observation.

5. There is some slight lack of independence among some pairs of these 87 cross-sections. A typical bus line (all of those sampled except Broad, Metairie, and Hayne) runs from the outskirts of New Orleans to downtown Canal Street where it loops, has a virtually complete turnover of passengers, and returns to its starting point. The observers, who remained on the bus during its entire inbound-outbound run, usually charted four cross-sections on a given trip, two going toward and two away from downtown. While the inbound recordings may be considered totally independent from the outbound ones, those taken in the same direction on the same vehicle would involve some redundancy in passengers. There was, however, a surprising amount of turnover even along a route, probably to be accounted for by the low fare (10 cents) and frequent service of the buses. It was not uncommon, in fact, for a bus to have taken in on its way to or from town more than twice as many fares as its average passenger load. Though the cross-sections were not totally independent, then, they were sufficiently so for the purposes to which they are put here.

6. At the most, in traditional New Orleans terms, it would mean that whites would sit from the front and Negroes from the back, and that no whites would be standing. Had white patronage of buses declined precipitously after the court order, the NOPSI system itself would have become segregated in the sense of being virtually a Negro mode of transportation. As Table 60–4 shows, however, whites and Negroes each composed about half the total complement of transit users. Negroes are obviously over-represented (they comprised only about 37 per cent of the city's population in 1960), but income level could easily explain the difference. More crucially, whites are still major utilizers of the buses. And while revenue passengers did decline 23 per cent from 1957 to 1963 on NOPSI lines, that is not too dissimilar from the 17 per cent decline in the United States generally. Buses that service predominantly white (or Negro) neighborhoods tend, of course, to have predominantly white (or Negro) passenger loads; but this is an obvious function of their routes. (The statement needs modifying because of checkerboard patterning, the movement of maids to and from white districts, and so on, but the trend is clear enough.) For that reason our concept of segregation of buses relates not to the proportion of whites or Negroes riding but to their configuration. Fortunately, as the text remarks, this was also the traditional meaning of transit segregation in the New Orleans community.

7. They do not rob the concept of all meaning, however, for under the old rules a Negro could not sit in front of a white no matter how much space separated them.

8. This definition and the reason for employing the term "precedence violators" are explained further in our discussion of Table 60–1.

9. For all four methods any person who is ambiguous is not considered a precedence violator. For example, a white in the same cross row as the first Negro is considered under Method 1 not to be violating precedence.

10. The difficulties in Methods 2 and 3 would not be obviated by employing any derivative ratios, such as the Duncans' index of difference. See Otis D. Duncan and Beverly Duncan, "Residential Distribution and Occupational Stratification," *American Journal of Sociology*, LX (March, 1955), 494. For as crowded buses became mono-racial, their index would tend to decline with a middle cutting point; and, of course, no index *per se* can solve the problem of how to establish consistent cutting points from one relatively empty bus to another. Analogous comments apply to the transactional indices employed by Karl Deutsch and James V. Toscano in their studies of intra- and inter-community flow patterns: see Philip E. Jacob and Toscano, *The Integration of Political Communities* (Philadelphia: Lippincott, 1964), chs. 3 and 4.

11. One could even justify the anomalies. After all, Negroes sitting in front of whites do implicate at least some whites as well as themselves in the violation of precedence, yet the white person sat beside seems less an agent of change than its object.

12. We also attempted a fifth method (cluster analysis) in which the total number of bi-racial and mono-racial adjacencies were measured and compared. Weightings were made in accordance with our *a priori* assumptions about the meanings of such interactions. Thus, sitting beside someone on a crosswise double seat was weighted 3; sitting beside someone on a lengthwise seat was weighted 2; sitting front to back, 2; sitting diagonally tangent, 1; and aisles and the center doorway were deemed to obliterate any interactions that crossed them. This mode of analysis was dropped after a 25 per cent computation sample, however, largely because its results were grossly affected by empty seats.

13. This explains why we have used the awkward phrase "precedence violators" to refer to individual passengers. As inelegant as the term is, it at least keeps us from the apparent paradox of stating that a perfectly integrated bus has only 50 per cent of its passengers integrated.

14. Rank order correlations (Spearman's rho) are as follows. Methods 1 and 2 = .44; 1 and 3 = .52; 1 and 4 = .76; 2 and 3 = .47; 2 and 4 = .53; 3 and 4 = .75.

15. Methods 2 and 3 are omitted from this table, and from the next also, since their findings are contaminated either by racial dominance or by degree of crowding, the very dimensions we are examining here.

16. The white and Negro totals in Column 1 differ solely because more of the former tended to be in ambiguous situations. See note 9. Only those persons who are considered precedence violators under Method 4 are included in this table.

61

State Fair-Employment Practice Laws

RAY MARSHALL

Introduction

Since World War II enforceable fair-employment practice (FEP) laws have been passed in 24 states and many municipalities. By 1964 these laws covered virtually the entire non-white population outside the South and prohibited discrimination by employers and employment agencies as well as unions. The laws are usually administered by commissioners, who are part-time officials in every state except New York. The powers relating to the adjustment of complaints are fairly uniform and include: (1) the power to receive, investigate, and pass upon complaints alleging discrimination in employment; (2) where investigation reveals probable cause for crediting the allegations, the duty to eliminate these practices by conference, conciliation, and persuasion; (3) the power to conduct public hearings, subpoena witnesses, compel their attendance, administer oaths, take testimony of any person under oath, and to require the production of any books or papers relating to matters before the commissions; (4) the power to seek court orders enforcing subpoenas and cease and desist orders; (5) the power to undertake studies of discrimination and publish the results.

The commissions' budgets and staffs are much less uniform than the provisions of the laws under which they operate. Observers generally agree that New York is the best financed of the state agencies. Considered relative to population, the only other fair-employment commission approaching the budget and staff of New York is the Philadelphia Commission on Human Relations.

Aside from some details, there is likewise much uniformity of procedure among the commissions. Except in Ohio, Rhode Island, and Philadelphia, complaints of discrimination must be restricted to discrimination against the persons filing the complaints. Since New York's law has been the model for other agencies, the complaint procedures in that state are typical of others. In New York, after the complaint has been duly registered with the Commission, it is investigated by a field representative, who submits a written report to an investigating commissioner assigned to the case. If the commissioner determines that probable cause exists to warrant an allegation, he is required to "immediately endeavor to eliminate the unlawful discriminatory practice com-

From *The Negro and Organized Labor* (New York: Wiley, 1965), pp. 274–279, 294–295. Reprinted by permission of the publisher. Abridged.

plained of by conference, conciliation, and persuasion." The commissioner utilizes this conciliation conference to work out an agreement eliminating patterns of discrimination even when the specific charge cannot be proved. If the case is settled at this stage, a stipulation is signed by the parties. There will probably be periodic reviews by field representatives, however, to see if discriminatory practices have been corrected. The great majority of cases are settled by conciliation; if not, they are ordered to public hearing before the other commissioners where the entire case is reviewed. If cases are not settled during the public hearing, the Commission can issue cease and desist orders enforceable in state courts. That the New York Commission has used the public hearing only sparingly is indicated by the fact that it ordered only 29 cases to public hearing of over 3,000 cases in which "probable cause" was found between 1945 and 1960. However, other cases were settled only after a threat of public hearing. Most respondents seemed very reluctant to sustain the unfavorable publicity involved in public hearings. In New York the Commission does not have the power to initiate complaints, but does conduct "informal investigations" and studies of employment patterns where there are suggestions of discrimination. It is also possible, moreover, for the New York attorney-general to file complaints with the Commission.

Experience with Unions

Before examining the various commissions' efforts to eliminate racial discrimination by unions, we should note that labor organizations have played a prominent role in the legislative effort that resulted in the passage of fair-employment laws. In almost every state, unions were prominent in the passage of these laws, and in states like California, Michigan, Pennsylvania, and New York the unions were probably the decisive forces causing the laws to be passed. And union leaders have actively served on the commissions in several states (Michigan, Pennsylvania, and Washington, for example). Furthermore, in keeping with its equalitarian civil rights policies, the AFL-CIO strongly favored the passage of the 1964 Civil Rights Act, which President George Meany publicly stated was needed to help organized labor eliminate racial discrimination in its own ranks.

In view of this record of support by organized labor, it may seem paradoxical that some of the most intransigent respondents before the state commissions have been unions. This paradox is more apparent than real, however, because the cases of hostile discrimination have been restricted to a relatively small proportion of the total labor movement. The unions that have actively supported fair-employment legislation are primarily politically oriented organizations, with a large stake in winning Negro support for their political objectives. And the union leaders who are encouraging and participating in the commissions' activities are mainly industrial union or federation leaders whose organizations rarely exclude Negroes from membership.

Unions have provided the commissions with some of their most difficult cases, but there have been relatively few cases against unions—generally less than 10 per cent of all compliance activity. Table 61–1 gives the complaints filed with the New York Commission between 1945 and 1962; it will be noted that complaints against unions constituted just over 8 per cent of the total, and from a quantitative standpoint the New York experience is typical.

There are a number of reasons for the relative paucity of cases against unions. The fewness of discriminating unions in the North where the laws exist

TABLE 61-1   *Complaints Filed by Alleged Discriminatory Act, New York, 1945-1962*

Act	1962		1945-1962	
	Number	Per Cent	Number	Per Cent
Total	1,171	100.0	9,733	100.0
Employment				
Refusal to employ	235	20.0	3,365	34.6
Dismissal from employment	154	13.2	1,732	17.8
Forced retirement	—	0.0	9	0.1
Conditions of employment	113	9.6	1,054	10.8
Employment agency referral	48	4.1	493	5.1
Union membership withheld	5	0.4	138	1.4
Conditions of union membership	39	3.3	504	5.2
Other union discrimination	2	0.2	101	1.0
Unlawful inquiry or specification	4	0.3	207	2.1
Abetting discrimination	11	0.9	122	1.3
Total	611	52.2	7,725	79.4
Public Accommodations				
Total	141	12.0	899	9.2
Other				
Education	2	0.2	27	0.3
Obstructing political nomination	—	—	8	0.1
Total	2	0.2	35	0.4

Source: New York State Commission for Human Rights, *Annual Report* (1962), p. 13.

is surely an important factor. Moreover, those who have the strongest cases frequently will not file complaints for reasons of apathy, fear of retaliation, or desire to avoid embarrassment. In addition, most agencies, in processing complaints against discriminating unions, have displayed a marked reluctance to undertake vigorous and sustained compliance efforts in such cases because the structure of the unions is such as to make it difficult for union leaders to compel compliance by their members. Thus, achieving compliance is inherently more difficult with discriminatory unions than with employers, where only management's acquiescence is necessary to effect compliance. Because they deal directly with the public, employers are also probably more vulnerable than unions to adverse publicity.

The Railroad Unions

In view of the long history of discrimination by railroad unions, it is not surprising that the case which tested the constitutionality of the first FEP law involved a railroad union. The union, the Railway Mail Association (RMA), successfully defended its right to bar Negroes from membership (on the grounds that it was a voluntary association) when that organization was prosecuted under a 1940 New York State law prohibiting racial discrimination by collective-bargaining organizations. The RMA attempted to use the same defense for its discriminatory practices before the New York Commission Against Discrimination (SCAD, established in 1945), but this time the U.S. Supreme Court could see "no constitutional basis for the contention that a state cannot protect workers from exclusion solely on the basis of race, color, or creed by an organization, functioning under the protection of the state, which holds itself out to represent the general business needs of employees."

SCAD also took action against several railroad unions with racial bars in their constitutions and caused them to either eliminate their formal racial restrictions or make them inoperative in New York. After being investigated by SCAD, the following unions removed their color bars on the dates indicated: Maintenance of Way Employees, 1946; Railway Yardmasters of North America, 1946; Railway and Steamship Clerks, 1947; Switchmen's Union of North America, 1947; Airline Dispatchers Association, 1946; Blacksmiths and Boilermakers, 1947; and the International Association of Machinists, 1948. SCAD investigated the Airline Pilots Association and the Wire Weavers Protective Association, but both of these organizations had dropped their restrictive provisions before the New York law was passed. The following organizations made their discriminatory clauses inoperative in New York: the Brotherhood of Locomotive Firemen and Enginemen; National Rural Letter Carriers Association; Brotherhood of Locomotive Engineers; Order of Railroad Telegraphers; Brotherhood of Railway Carmen; Order of Railway Conductors; Railway Mail Association; National Association of Letter Carriers.

The most obstinate of these organizations was the BLE, whose Grand Chief Engineer wrote SCAD on February 11, 1946:

> This organization stands on its constitutional rights to determine by its rules and laws enacted by delegates to a constituted convention who have authority under the laws governing its membership and to determine for itself whom it shall accept for membership.

On October 10, 1947, a month before he used his authority to waive the race bar in New York, the Grand Chief told SCAD:

> We are of the opinion that your Commission does not understand that whether a person is admitted depends upon the will of the members in the respective subdivisions to which such a person makes application. And, it may interest you to

know that included among members of the BLE are full-blooded Indians, Mexicans, half-breeds, etc.

Furthermore, the section of our laws to which your Commission objects has been in our Statutes for many, many years and we do not have any official record of any person having been denied membership because of race, religion, creed, or color.

SCAD reported on January 13, 1948, that "progress has been made in wiping out discriminatory practices in more than 30 unions with a total membership of 750,000" and that only the BLE had refused to cooperate with the Commission.

Despite these formal changes, however, Negroes apparently continued to be barred from the railroads in New York and New Jersey. A joint study by SCAD and the New Jersey Division Against Discrimination (DAD) in 1957 found that there were very few employment opportunities for Negroes in those states; according to the study, "By the irony of history, Negroes in the South had greater opportunities for employment in operating departments of the railroads than those in the North." The DAD also had a number of complaints that railroad locals excluded Negroes.

Conclusions on FEP Experience with Unions

1. The commissions have succeeded in changing the formal racial practices of a number of unions, especially on the railroads, and have succeeded in directly obtaining admission of hundreds of workers who were formerly excluded from membership in labor organizations. Moreover, the commissions have aided in the regularization of many referral systems, making it more difficult for these to be used as vehicles for discrimination. In addition, the FEP laws undoubtedly have been used by some union leaders as excuses to make equalitarian changes that were not considered politically feasible before the laws were passed. The FEP laws are important symbols registering prevailing moral sentiment, so forces within a union favoring equalitarian racial policies are strengthened considerably by having a law on their side. Moreover, the commissions have found that the labor movement's formal equalitarian policies help them enforce the law. One New York SCAD commissioner told the writer:

> We have not always had the cooperation of local union officers, who are much more likely than employers to tell us to go to Hell, but we have always had the cooperation of state federation leaders and international union officers in dealing with their affiliates. This is easily accomplished when we can say to top officials, "because of your unions policy on this matter I am asking your help in overcoming this violation not only of state law but of trade union law."

2. In spite of these positive accomplishments, however, the evidence suggests that the commissions have not changed the basic employment patterns in

most unionized industries. There are many reasons for this. In dealing with unions, the commissions rely heavily on conciliation, persuasion, and the threat of public hearing, though it is generally conceded that recalcitrant local unions are less responsive to these tactics than employers. However, there were other factors complicating the commissions' operations, including internal union politics, nepotism, amicism, the natural intractability of employment patterns, declining economic opportunities in many of the industries where Negroes are concentrated or where they are attempting to get jobs, the natural slowness of the case method in proving racial discrimination, the fewness of verifiable complaints against unions in most of the states, the complicated hiring arrangements in most of the casual occupations, and the autonomy of many local unions.

3. Finally, the FEP cases raise a number of difficult questions for public policy. (a) Effective collective bargaining requires that the parties should be given as much freedom as possible to make their own rules. At a time of declining employment opportunities in many industries, it is particularly important that unions and employers be encouraged to make arrangements to stabilize and regularize employment. But when these arrangements also have the effect of freezing the existing racial employment patterns, as in the brewery and longshore cases, should they be permitted? (b) Although unions have been given the right to make their own internal rules, should they be allowed to exclude Negroes from membership through such internal procedures as blackballing an applicant for membership? (c) It is recognized that unions have a legitimate interest in regularizing employment in an industry, but should those unions that have a vested interest in reducing the labor supply be permitted to determine the number of workers to be trained in an industry, or should such control in fact be vested in a tripartite agency? (d) These cases also raise the question of who is legally responsible for employment when a union hiring hall is used. The commissions' experience demonstrates that the effective way to eliminate "buckpassing" is to jointly charge both the employer and the union.

62

Law, Violence, and Civil Rights

RICHARD D. SCHWARTZ

Anyone inclined to see law as a solution for all social disturbances ought to have done some rethinking of his premises during the past summer. The violence that erupted in inner cities around the country wrote in blood and fire the message that law had been weighed in the balance and been found wanting.

Where the courts entered the picture, it was often as not to obstruct the integrative objectives of the legislature. In Illinois, for instance, the State Supreme Court nullified the Armstrong Act which authorized, if it did not command, school boards to promote public school integration. Where plans for integration succeeded, typically in smaller cities, the objective was reached largely through pressures brought directly on school boards and public officials. The one major attempt to alter *de facto* segregation through court action—Judge Skelly Wright's decision in *Hobson v. Hansen*—was useless where it could be enforced, in virtually all-black Washington, and unenforceable where it might have been useful, in the greater metropolitan area.

The conclusion that courts must sometimes yield to the political process is neither new nor disturbing in itself. These two subsystems have long shared responsibility for adapting to change while retaining order and continuity. As long as the task is adequately handled between them, societal equilibrium can be maintained. The interplay of courts and legislatures becomes an interesting topic for the scholar and an issue for debate (activism v. self-restraint) among judges and other political actors.

It is when disturbance spills beyond the two subsystems into violent action in the streets that nice middle-class people, scholars and officials alike, lose their cool. Explanations increase in diversity, intensity, and futility: We have been moving too fast, too slowly, in the wrong direction. Such responses rarely extend beyond the foolishness of conventional wisdom, because unfortunately we don't have much more than that to rely on.

It is plausible to assume a direct relationship between the frustrations of legal-political action and the increasing violence of the civil rights movement. These frustrations are multiple. The legal-political system tends to focus attention on a limited number of issues which can be framed as justiciable or statutory questions. Legal and political decisions take a long time, execution takes

From *Law and Society Review*, II (November, 1967), 7–10. Reprinted by permission of the publisher. Abridged.

even longer. In securing such decisions, a small and privileged group of leaders pre-empt the action. Defeats arise unpredictably in the legislatures and courts, rationalized by doctrines that use the language of equality and justice but seem to many to produce opposite results.

Even when victories are won, they are not necessarily satisfying. In the struggle for legal or political success, the civil rights forces tend to line up on the side that will best express their resentment at the whole pattern of discrimination that is their major grievance. In practice, however, this may lead them to fight for outcomes which if achieved might well detract from the main objective.

This is well illustrated in the struggle for school integration, an issue so defined that victory may be self-defeating. If integration were achieved through political or legal action, would it help to eliminate racial inequality? If we rely on the Coleman report, the evidence seems to say that it would. That conclusion depends, however, on extrapolation from the few integrated systems that have emerged spontaneously, to the many that would be achieved through conflict. It does not consider the possibility that forced integration in the large cities would expedite the departure of white families to the suburbs. If the central cities become overwhelmingly black, would integration become a meaningless policy?

Alternatively, the achievement of integration may be far less satisfactory a method of promoting educational achievement for Negroes than compensatory education. Recently, black power proponents have increasingly advocated the creation of segregated schools of very high quality. In the absence of empirical instances of this kind, it is currently impossible to compare such schools with those that are integrated. It seems plausible, nevertheless, to suppose that such schools might provide the most effective means of developing the educational techniques and the morale necessary to provide optimal learning conditions for Negroes.

Whether or not these speculations are correct, the legal-political apparatus has in some ways inhibited their exploration. In the adversary context, symbolic victory for Negroes tends to be phrased in terms of winning the right of Negroes to be treated as others are, rather—perhaps—than in the way that would benefit them most. Thus the channels open in the political-legal system seem to have focused on too narrow a range of issues and led to the expenditure of vast energies on potentially self-defeating objectives.

Does this mean that law is inevitably incapable of coping with this kind of problem? Perhaps not, if we think through the nature of the problem and re-examine legal institutions creatively.

What is the nature of the problem? It is that the entire social position of a group in the population is unsatisfactory. Inchoately, it demands a redefinition of the rules of the game. At present, it faces the alternatives of issue-focused action through law, politics, or perhaps economic pressure, on the one hand, and violence on the other. The violence of the summer suggests that the former techniques are unsatisfactory. Is there a third way?

I do not know the answer. I am struck by the fact that alienated groups in society have sometimes achieved a change in the rules of the game so that their grievous demands were more readily met. In the nineteenth century, industrial strikers were criminally liable for conspiracy. Eventually the legitimacy of their interests was recognized and a procedure set up for an orderly test of strength between them and their adversaries. Their organizations, formed according to a regular procedure, were then called unions instead of conspiracies. Other examples of the legitimization of protesting groups come to mind: the official position of professional associations in this country, the religious communities (*Gemeinde*) in Germany, the resistance movement in South Arabia. What form might be appropriate for institutionalizing and legitimizing the range of interests of the Negroes or the poor? I do not know. Nor am I certain that such an approach would be wise. Given the unsatisfactory nature of our present handling of the problem, however, we seem to need some alternatives. Perhaps the law can help if its functions and possible techniques are more broadly considered than usual. At any rate, we need to think of something.

In the meantime, it should be noted that the legal process has played a not unimportant part in furthering the civil rights movement. It provided an initial legitimatization of the grievances of the Negroes. Specifically, it contributed a normative slogan, recognized by the dominant white community, under the phrase "equal protection." It has provided a forum in which the realities of life in the slums could be brought dramatically to the attention of men of conscience in the intelligentsia and middle classes, white and black. It has spotlighted the role of law itself in maintaining inequality under our system of "justice," both in the criminal and civil spheres.

Not that all of these functions were capable of being performed unaided by the courts, legislatures, or administrators. Without assistance from scholars and critics at the margin, these insights might not have been achieved. [Their] critiques are being taken seriously by government (in its neighborhood legal assistance offices), professional associations (for example, ABA resolutions supporting the legal operations of OEO, ABF studies of representation of the indigent), and the law schools (for example, courses and law review articles on race relations and the law of poverty).

It may be true, as William Styron suggests in *The Confessions of Nat Turner* (1968), that "justice" can perpetuate slavery for a thousand years. But it may also be true that the legal system, properly analyzed, can reveal the hidden assumption and devious control devices of the society. Properly used by an aroused minority and an appalled segment of the majority, it may contribute to the conversion of "equal justice under law" from a cruel shibboleth to a vibrant reality. The probable alternative is not very appealing: Violence may be, in Rap Brown's phrase, as American as cherry pie, but who would choose either as a steady diet?

63

Black Separation and Civil Liberties

JEROME H. SKOLNICK

A transformation in perspective similar to that which revolutionized our think-ing about crime and deviance has taken hold in the black communities of America. Perhaps I can make the point most dramatically by suggesting that the very wording of the topic suggests the sensitivity of white liberals to the fact that there is a black movement in America, that "black" means something other than Negro. The term "Negro" is coming to have a revised meaning—it suggests a man with a "black" skin who clings to and supports "white" values. A black man is one who is striving to define and to achieve a sense of positive identity with other black men and women in this country and throughout the world.

The very concept of black "separatism," however, is ambiguous if not ques-tionable. If a historian were asked to give an illustration of a separatist move-ment, he would probably select sectarian religious movements. For example, when Wesley broke off from the established Church of England to form the Methodist Church, that was a separatist movement. When the Disciples of Christ broke off from the Methodists to form their own discipline, that was a "separatist" movement. Once having been joined, that is, "integrated," one group separates from the other for evangelical and social reasons.

The phenomenon we are discussing in this chapter is quite different. It is hardly to be described as black "separatism" but rather as a black response to *de facto* white separatism. Blacks were never integrated into the white commu-nities of America, except as slaves and later as servants. Nor has segregation been limited in America as a whole to blacks who occupy lower social and economic positions. Despite some notable individual exceptions, black people have been discriminated against in suburban housing as well as urban, in high-priced services as well as low-priced ones, and in the honored professions of medicine and law. "Black separatism" is a misnomer for a highly complex phenomenon that might better be termed "black dignity."

The movement to achieve black dignity has stressed the importance of black culture, black history, and black power. The development of a distinctive black culture requires a sense of separation from whites. This, because of the obvious fact that white culture, white values, and white definitions have domi-nated the black communities of America. There is a widely quoted phrase in

"Black Separation and Civil Liberties," *Chicago Today*, V, No. 2 (Summer, 1968) 15–21. Reprinted by permission of the University of Chicago.

the Kerner Commission Report that is exactly to the point. "What white Americans," the Commission said, "have never fully understood—but what the Negro can never forget—is that white society is deeply implicated in the ghetto. White institutions created it, white institutions maintain it, and white society condones it." Thus, the distinctive characteristics of a black culture tend to develop through legitimizing the alien character of white symbols and values.

The separatist black cultural thrust is especially difficult for white liberals to accept, partly because it violates the generalized humanitarian ideals of liberals, and partly because it has created a new ethnic stereotype, the "whitey" or the "honky," the cultural equivalents of "Negro" and "nigger." It is the black equivalent of *epater le bourgeoisie,* of sticking pins in cherished white values, to tear away and reveal such prized traditions as freedom and liberty as white traditions of slight relevance for the history of the black man. History is therefore the main instrument for developing a black culture because cultural transformations of paradigmatic proportion are made possible through new historical interpretation. If black revisionist history is successful, educated men will no longer be able to write, as Joseph Bishop of Yale Law School did in a *Harper's* article:

> The function of the Bill of Rights, which in the English-speaking countries ended the alternating persecutions of temporary minorities by temporary majorities, is to set bounds to the power of the majority to coerce the minority—and, as the price of this protection, to delimit the outer boundaries of the minority's freedom to disobey with impunity the majority's laws. I will defend the proposition that it is the best governor ever invented for the democratic engine and that, indeed, it is the principal reason why our democratic engine has lasted nearly 200 years.

This is an eloquently written illustration of the sort of celebrationist statement that we have all been exposed to countless times in our lives and usually registered without question. It supports the traditional "liberal" world view. But the traditional liberal world view has been revealed as a white liberal world view. To a man with a sense of the history of black men in the English-speaking world, such a statement is ridiculous on its face. Where was the Bill of Rights for slaves? Has the Bill of Rights significantly protected the interests of black citizens after slavery? Frederick Douglass offered a black man's version of America in a Fourth of July oration delivered in 1852:

> What to the American slave is your Fourth of July? I answer: a day that reveals to him, more than all other days of the year, the gross injustice and cruelty to which he is the constant victim. To him your celebration is a sham; your boasted liberty, an unholy license: your national greatness, swelling vanity; your sounds of rejoicing are empty and heartless; your denunciation of tyrants, brass-fronted impudence; your shouts of liberty and equality, hollow mockery; your prayers and hymns, your sermons and thanksgivings, with all your religious parade and

solemnity, are, to him, mere bombast, fraud, deception, impiety, and hypocrisy —a thin veil to cover up crimes that would disgrace a nation of savages.

You invite to your shores fugitives of oppression from abroad, honor them with banquets, greet them with ovations, cheer them, toast them, salute them, protect them, and pour out your money to them like water; but the fugitive from your own land you advertise, hunt, arrest, shoot, and kill. You glory in your refinement and your universal education: yet you maintain a system as barbarous and dreadful as ever stained the character of a nation—a system begun in avarice, supported in pride, and perpetuated in cruelty.

You shed tears over fallen Hungary, and make the sad story of her wrongs the theme of your poets, statesmen, and orators, till your gallant sons are ready to fly to arms to vindicate her cause against the oppressor; but, in regard to the ten thousand wrongs of the American slave, you would enforce the strictest silence, and would hail him as an enemy of the nation who dares to make these wrongs the subject of public discourse!

The works and life of Frederick Douglass form an important component of new courses and curriculum in American history precisely because they are still so relevant. A revisionist history not only rewrites the past—if successful, it also enlightens the meaning of the present.

Power, or the capacity to influence decisions, especially those that shape the course of one's own life, is a necessary condition for dignity. How do people come by power? One important means, surely, is through control of an economy. Black people presently hold only a paltry share of American economic power. Another means of gaining power is to be in the position of an exploited proletariat, capable of organizing and withholding labor, thereby disrupting the economy. Black people are not a proletariat because they have been discriminated against by American labor as much as by American corporate enterprise.

Given this general situation, and I think it a fair overall statement, what are black people to do, how are they to respond to improve their social situation? There are, it seems to me, two complementary strategies, each of which is being pursued. One strategy requires a consciousness of identity. For example, labor organizing traditionally hammered home to workers the theme that they were not part of the company, that their identity was with other workers. And this was often a difficult message to get across, as any oldtime labor organizer will tell you. Just as the unions adopted a rhetoric of brotherhood, so do blacks, and so does any group that is attempting to develop itself to improve its power and dignity.

A second is to locate some force comparable to controlling the economy or the withholding of labor. The force that the black community has located and exploited is the capacity to disrupt social stability. Gandhi, of course, was the first to understand and implement this force politically through large-scale civil disobedience. In America, the black community has relied upon both non-violent and violent tactics to implement stability disruption as a resource for achieving economic and social equality.

It is commonly regarded as impolitic to write that force or violence has been an essential component of the black strategy, but I believe it to be true and fairly obvious. The non-violent protester implicitly threatens violence and is able to produce it *without overt conspiracy* only through a common sense of black identity. If the draftsmen of our conspiracy laws had attended to the dynamics of class consciousness, they would have understood how futile these laws are in a revolutionary situation. What is important, and what the black leadership has come to understand at all levels, is that a conscious sense of black identity will produce, without specific communication, a black-oriented rather than a white-oriented response in a conflict situation. And a black culture, stressing black values, needs, and definitions of objects and events, enlarges this capacity within the black community. Given the strategy of stability disruption, blacks have a need to share common understandings, even more than workers.

Stability Disruption, Crime, and the Civil Libertarian

When stability disruption becomes part of a larger strategy for achieving power, it becomes increasingly difficult for a social analyst to draw a line between crime and political activity. This is not to suggest that legal authorities cannot draw such a line. A young black man who sets fire to a Vietnamese hut is lawfully considered to be serving his country. A young black man who sets fire to a downtown department store is engaged in an act of arson, or an act of revolutionary heroism, depending upon his view of constituted authority. The meaning of the concept of crime is under continuous revision, and when that happens the related concepts, "political action" and "civil liberties," receive associated shock waves.

Revolutionary situations pose a terrible dilemma for the civil libertarian when he finds himself in sympathy with the motives of the revolutionaries, deplores violent means, and at the same time recognizes that an emphasis upon order may impede necessary and desirable social change. The dilemma is particularly agonizing when he finds himself increasingly unable to distinguish between contemporary morality and immorality. Which is preferable, the violent revolutionary act or the severe social sanctions that slowly, sometimes negligently, impinge upon masses of human beings on the basis of racial or ethnic characteristics?

In this perspective, what should be the response to the black struggle? Principally, we must recognize that the needs and concerns of black people in our society are different from those of the comfortably situated white liberal. The black man living in the inner city is not so concerned with freedom of expression as an abstract ideal, not in drawing fine distinctions between expression and action. He has real and immediate legal concerns that are not presently being satisfactorily attended to by institutions in the legal order. For example, after Dr. King's murder, disorders occurred in several cities, notably Chicago and Washington, D.C. Observers found serious deficiencies in the arrest and processing procedures. I myself saw bail proceedings in Chicago where the judge questioned the accused as to guilt or innocence before setting bail, and the public defender stood by and listened without objecting. (Under the circumstances, he may have had no other choice.) Even when arrestees could make bail, there was no one to collect it. In Washington, D.C., David Ginsburg reports that a study (by Ronald Goldfarb) found serious deficiencies in procedure: some prisoners were "lost" or unnecessarily detained for days; detention facilities were overcrowded; transportation was inadequate; and paper work was unbearably burdensome. Most significantly, curfew and arrest policies were ambiguous. Mass arrests almost invariably will depend upon who is available to be arrested.

In the administration of criminal justice the poor man, black or white, is faced with a paucity of defense attorneys. A landmark Supreme Court decision like *Gideon,* requiring that every accused felon be accorded a defense attorney, is not so progressive a step as it initially appears. The function of the defense attorney in our adversary system is to provide, as stated by Dean Francis Allen, ". . . a constant, searching, and creative questioning of official decisions and assertions of authority at all stages of the process." In fact, however, we do not have an adversary system of criminal justice, but an overcrowded administrative system that depends upon the close-knit assistance of all functionaries, defense attorneys included. Our lower courts, especially, are a disgrace, with administrative concerns prevailing over concerns for justice.

In general, we do not have enough competition in the criminal law system, and we do not have enough competent lawyers. As a result, the right to counsel may not be, to the man faced with a criminal charge, what it appears.

The black man in the inner city is often faced with and by the example of police corruption in our urban centers—a subject, incidentally, not considered by the Kerner Commission. Police corruption, precisely because of its wider ramifications, is a more politically sensitive issue than police brutality and police harassment. These latter problems are not limited to interactions with white policemen only. In fact, Negro policemen have been known to be even more brutal than white, and the black man has often even less of an opportunity sustaining a case of victimization against the Negro cop. Our inner-city black communities sometimes appear to be occupied countries, colonial outposts, with colonial police, black and white, living off graft, keeping an eye on the natives, and putting them in their place. We must, therefore, describe and analyze the social reality of our cities, outside the ghetto as well as in it, and address our creative energies to changing that reality.

SECTION THIRTEEN *To Affect Other Life Conditions*

64

Social Structure and Rent-Control Violation

HARRY V. BALL

Legal institutions have offered and continue to offer to the social scientist a vast quantity of relatively well-documented social actions that offer numerous possibilities for the development and testing of general sociological hypotheses. There is the problem, of course, that one cannot tell before beginning the analysis of a given sphere of legal arrangements precisely what behavioral hypotheses may be tested. But the possibilities are numerous, and the obstacle here is no greater than in other areas of sociology.

This study is focused upon the legal controls of residential rents, their differential impressions of fairness upon the landlords, and the relationships between these and violations of rent ceilings in Honolulu in 1952.

Beginning prior to the establishment of Hawaii as a Territory of the United States, the rental housing business in Honolulu operated under what Friedrich has called "the normal law of landlord and tenant."

Dwellings are let according to the rules of property and contract. The landlord as owner of the dwelling can fix the rent of his property at whatever figure he chooses. If a tenant does not pay his rent, the landlord has such remedies as distress and eviction. Upon the expiration of the lease, the landlord can take possession of the property, refusing to renew the lease for any or no reason. The competition between landlords is supposed to protect the tenant against the charge of extortionate rents.[1]

When the United States became involved in World War II, statutory rent control was introduced in Honolulu by local city-county ordinance under the emergency powers granted that government unit by the legislature of Hawaii earlier that year, 1941.[2] The stated intent of this ordinance was to prevent speculative and manipulative practices by landlords while allowing the landlords a fair return on the value of their property. For the period of wartime martial law in Hawaii, 1942–1945, the ordinance was in effect by command of the military governor, after which it continued under its original civil jurisdiction. (At no time between 1941 and 1952 did Honolulu operate directly under the rent-control authorized by the federal Congress and established through the Office of Price Administration [OPA] and its successor agencies.)

From *The American Journal of Sociology,* LXV (1960), 598–604. Copyright © 1960 by the University of Chicago Press. Reprinted by permission of the author and The University of Chicago Press.

When direct control of consumer prices was generally abolished in 1947, modified control of residential rent was retained by the federal Congress. Landlords at that time were thus differentiated from most other kinds of businessmen in the regulation of their businesses. However, the independence of the Honolulu controls permitted variations to be introduced between them and the controls operating in the rest of the nation. Whereas most newly constructed rental housing units were exempted by post-1947 legislation from regulation by statutory-administrative law of the Federal Government, *all* privately owned housing in Honolulu continued under statutory control even after 1947. As a result, the landlords of all the private rental housing units in the city were under the general legal rule not to charge more than the legally established maximum rent. Any person who wilfully violated this rule was subject, upon conviction, to penal sanctions consisting of a fine up to $1,000 or imprisonment up to a period of one year.[3]

The inclusiveness of the Honolulu ordinance did *not* mean, however, that the legal maximum rent of every unit in 1952 had been determined by a single standard, by the application of a single criterion or set of criteria. When the ordinance was initiated in December, 1941, it specified May 27, 1941, as the "freeze" or "fair-rent" date: for all units rented on May 27, 1941, the rent and services in effect on that date were declared to constitute the "maximum-rent" and "minimum-service" standards for each unit, regardless of subsequent changes in ownership, tenancy, or landlord-tenant agreements. For units that had not been rented on the fair-rent date but which had been rented sometime between May 27, 1940 and May 26, 1941, inclusive, the ordinance specified that the ceiling and service standards were to be those which had *last* existed during that specified year. Thus the statute embodied the principle that "fair rents" are those rents generally prevailing in a "normal market," and, in effect, it defined the state of the housing market of May 27, 1941, as "normal." [4]

Another provision applied to all units not rented between May 27, 1940, and May 27, 1941, but rented subsequently. The ceilings of this class of rental accommodations were to be determined by the Rent Control Commission upon the basis of the rent and services "generally prevailing for comparable housing accommodations" on the fair-rent date. The power to decide matters of "comparability" was vested entirely in the commission.

The ordinance did provide for raising the legal maximum rent of particular units under these ceilings to compensate for "substantial" increases in taxes or other operating and maintenance costs or "substantial capital improvements or alterations." But there could be no raising of the ceiling on the ground of increased market value, even if the housing accommodation had been sold to a new landlord at a cost much greater than the owner's original investment on the fair-rent date. In short, for housing rented between May 27, 1940, and May 27, 1941, or existing then but only subsequently rented there was no provision in the ordinance for explicit specific application of the concept of a "fair return upon investment" to individual accommodations.[5]

In 1945 the Board of Supervisors intervened in a dispute between the local Rent Control Commission and the Federal Housing Administration (FHA) and amended the ordinance, directing the commission to accept the rent ceilings on new construction provided by the FHA or other authorized federal agencies.[6] According to the rent-control administrator, these FHA ceilings provided the landlord a gross return of about 16 per cent on the cost of construction and land and were considerably higher than the ceilings then being established by the commission upon the basis of comparability. When, in 1947, the federal Congress exempted most new construction from federal rent control, the board again amended this section to authorize the commission to employ its discretion in accepting or rejecting the bases of the ceilings set by federal agencies.[7]

In this situation the commission did not attempt to "roll back" the ceilings on new construction which had been established between 1945 and 1947 by the FHA. Rather, it adopted (or retained) as the major determinant of the ceilings on subsequent new construction the federal agency's concept of 1947 of a net return of 6.5 per cent of the total of the original cost of construction plus the assessed value of the land.

In the light of the permanence of this special treatment for newly constructed housing, the rent-control administrator and his investigators tended to give comparable considerations to older housing entering the rental market for the first time since May 27, 1940. It became a prevalent practice to establish ceilings on these older units also upon the basis of a 6.5 per cent net return. However, the net return in this instance was based upon an estimate of the original cost of construction rather than the current or replacement cost. Thus it did not constitute the clear-cut "return on investment" for the current landlord that the net return formula represented for landlords of newly constructed accommodations. Rather it constituted a third class of determinations of legal maximum rent.

Thus, while the general rule that no landlord may charge a rent in excess of the legally established maximum applied to all landlords, a number of subclasses of landlords existed by 1952 on the basis of the methods of determining ceilings. The ordinance, the "law in books," had established two substatuses initially, and then it shifted to one mandatory and one optional status. The operations of the commission and its staff, the "law in action," had established three substatuses. Three classes of landlords were created by the three ceilings, and one individual, of course, could belong in more than one class simultaneously:

1. *Landlords with fair-rent-date ceilings.* The landlord of a unit constructed prior to 1945 which had been given an initial ceiling prior to 1947 according to the last rent charged between May 27, 1940, and May 27, 1941, or the rent levels generally prevailing for comparable housing accommodations on May 27, 1941.

2. *Landlords with fair-return ceilings.* The landlord of a unit constructed

prior to 1945 which had received its initial ceiling in 1947 or later. The ceiling determination provided for roughly a 6.5 per cent return on the estimated original cost of construction plus the assessed value of the land.

3. *Landlords with new-construction ceilings.* The landlord of a unit constructed in 1945 or later. For the most part, these ceilings were established to provide a 6.5 per cent return on the cost of construction plus the assessed value of the land. This approximated a net return upon investment formula.

The original expressed intent of the rent-control ordinance was to produce rents that would be fair to both landlords and tenants. But in 1952 new-construction ceilings took considerable account of the general postwar inflation, fair-return ceilings in many instances took some account of this inflation, and fair-rent-date ceilings took account of the inflation only with respect to substantial increases in direct operating costs. Thus the evidence was substantial that these differential treatments would endow the general norm not to violate ceilings with a different meaning for each subclass of landlords.

Let us turn now to a consideration of the other side of this institutional arrangement—the landlords and that part of their conduct which the legal rules regulated. The best estimates are that in Honolulu in 1952 there were about 36,000 private rental units and about 10,000 landlords. The vast majority of the landlords were small investors, described by Grebler as follows:

He sometimes originated rental housing; more often, rental housing of certain types was built by contractors or operative builders for the purposes of immediate sale to the small investor. The structures have usually been two- to four-family dwellings, one of which is typically occupied by the owner who also frequently performs the simple management functions. The motivation of this kind of investor often is to have the net rental income carry his own housing costs. Small, non-professional investors have also entered the field of rental housing without this motivation, attracted by the social distinction of real estate ownership and expectations of above average net returns on invested capital or of capital appreciation.[8]

In Honolulu these small investors very frequently held only one or two units for rent.

The large long-term investors among landlords in Honolulu usually tended to be relatively small by Mainland standards and to be more interested in above-average returns than some large Mainland institutions. It was very rare to find a landlord who held more than 50 units, and the large operators often controlled only one apartment building or one collection of single-family units.[9] The large estates in Hawaii had specialized in land leases rather than in housing operations.

A few speculative sponsors had emerged in postwar Honolulu. Most of their operations centered around large apartment houses in the vicinity of Waikiki; many picked up some windfall profits, and virtually all their units had new-construction ceilings. The operative house-builder was not yet significant in the rental market of Honolulu in 1952.[10]

Thus, as a group, the individuals who had entered the rental housing business had usually done so for one or more of the following reasons: the social distinctions attached to landlordism, which were particularly significant in Honolulu; expectations of above-average net returns on investment or of above-average capital appreciation; or a belief that it was a safe, inflation-proof provision for retirement and a business which could be operated by relatively inexperienced survivors. Against these expectations, landlords found themselves singled out for price regulation in 1952, restricted to prices that in most instances took little or no account of inflation, and operating far more complicated businesses than anticipated.

Forty-two landlords of units with fair-rent-date ceilings and eight landlords with new-construction ceilings were interviewed to ascertain what factors they believed should be taken into account in establishing "fair rents." The landlords with the new-construction ceilings, especially the speculative sponsors, gave greatest prominence in their replies to the idea of providing a proper margin of profit, although they were consistently vague about the precise meaning of "proper."

On the other hand, the landlords with fair-rent-date ceilings, who were much more typical of Honolulu landlords, viewed the problem as a personal, complex, and relative matter. What stood out in their replies were: (1) the rents other landlords were believed to be getting for "comparable units" (with considerable variation in the criteria for "comparable"); (2) the amount by which the landlord believed other prices and incomes had generally risen or fallen since the rent in question was established; (3) the original expectations of the landlord in terms of purchasing power—what he had specifically hoped to accomplish with his rent income; and (4) the difficulty in renting a unit at a given price. It was in terms of the last three generally, but especially (2) and (3), that these landlords often volunteered information about the unfairness, as they saw it, of rent control.

It could be concluded that this examination of landlordism, with respect to its special motivation as an occupation and the techniques of determining "fair rent," corroborated the findings produced by the analysis of the legal structure. The multiple modes of legal maximum-rent determination did seem to constitute a gradation of restrictions upon the opportunities of landlords to establish what they considered to be "fair rents."

But were these apparent consequences actually demonstrable for individual landlords? Were individual landlords with fair-rent-date ceilings more likely to feel restricted or deprived than individual landlords with new-construction ceilings? The hypothesis was formed that the proportion of landlords who believed their legal maximum rent to be unfair would be greatest for those with fair-rent-date ceilings, and least for those with new-construction ceilings.

This hypothesis was tested against data collected from a 5 per cent sample of all rental units within the city of Honolulu that were then registered with the Rent Control Commission.[11] A questionnaire had been mailed to the landlords of each of the 1,522 rental accommodations (in the original sample) that had been established by means of a tenant interview as still in the rental market.[12] A total of 1,068 questionnaires, about 70 per cent, were available for this analysis.[13] One item in the questionnaire asked each landlord to state precisely what rent he believed would provide him a fair return. The responses to this question were classified according to (a) the kind of ceiling determination of the unit in question and (b) whether the landlord's own estimate of a fair rent was above or below the legal maximum rent, as indicated by the record for that unit in the commission's files.

The legal maximum rent was evaluated as unfair in 70.4 per cent of the responses under fair-rent-date ceilings, in 53.6 per cent of the responses under fair-return ceilings, and in 40.3 per cent of the responses under new-construction ceilings—differences statistically significant at the .01 level by the *chi*-square test. The null hypothesis that they had been produced by chance was rejected. The evaluations by the individual landlords of the unfairness of their ceiling rents did vary consistently with the hypothesized relative deprivations involved in the modes of determining maximum rent.

Since the differential treatments under the law did tend to provide the affected individuals with different meanings for the general norm against violating ceilings, did they also tend to produce differing rates of violation of this general norm? Inkeles has pointed out that "the need for a theory of personality is perhaps most evident in the study of those 'rates' that represent the summary or end product of thousands or millions of individual decisions and acts, yet which are of distinctive size for different societies or cultures. To illustrate . . . suicide and delinquency rates." [14] Our problem here is analogous to his, but one major qualification should be introduced. This is that different dimensions or components of personality, even different theories of personality, have varying relevance to different sets of institutional arrangements and the actions they are intended to induce or inhibit.

Now one may assume that, insofar as a landlord has a concept of a fair rent that exceeded the legal maximum for some accommodation, he is persistently motivated to seek to reduce the discrepancy. Perhaps this is not sufficient in itself to induce a landlord to violate his ceiling. But it would certainly enter the mind of any landlord who, for whatever reasons, "needs" more money, or serve as reason enough for any landlord who simply "wants" his "fair return" or whatever he originally anticipated from his rental business.

There are thus two problems: first, what the relationship was between the individual violations of ceilings and the individual evaluations of their fairness or unfairness and, second, what the final relationship was between the legal structure, as expressed in the three methods of determining ceilings and the fact of control itself, and the rates of violations of the ceilings.

To answer these questions, data on the violations among the 1,522 units in the housing sample were required. As indicated previously, the legal maximum-rent and minimum-service standards for each of these units had been obtained from the files of the commission. At the same time, at lease one adult tenant of each rental unit was interviewed to determine the rent actually paid and the services actually provided. These two sets of data were compared for each accommodation, and each was accordingly categorized as a "violation" or "non-violation."

Table 64–1 presents these categories of violation and non-violation cross-tabulated by the landlords' evaluations of the fairness or unfairness of their ceilings for their 1,050 responses.[15] The most striking finding was that *not one* fair response was located in the violation category. This is strong evidence for the hypothesis that having a concept of a fair rent in excess of one's legal maximum rent was a prominent component in motivating the landlord to violate his ceiling. And it was previously shown that the frequency of occurrence of this was related to the kind of determination of the ceiling involved. On the

TABLE 64-1   *Percentage Distributions of Ceiling Violations and Non-Violations by Landlord Evaluations*

Evaluation of Ceiling	Violations	Non-Violations	Total
Fair	—	34.0	26.4
Don't know	—	4.2	3.3
Unfair	92.5	54.6	63.0
No response	7.5	7.2	7.3
Total	100.0	100.0	100.0
No	232	818	1,050

other hand, 54.6 per cent of the non-violations also involved an evaluation of an unfair ceiling. Thus, in 67.5 per cent of the instances of declared unfairness, this, while important, was not *sufficient* to induce an act of violation.

With respect to the second question, the results of the cross-tabulation of violations by mode of ceilings determination were as expected. The proportion of violations was 29.2 per cent for fair-rent-date ceilings, 14.9 per cent for fair-return ceilings, and only 7.3 per cent for new-construction ceilings.[16] The legal structure did appear to exert more pressure on some persons than on others to engage in non-conformist rather than conformist behavior.[17] And a substantial contribution to the understanding of the "how" was made by the intervening analyses of the differential perceptions and concomitant motivation.

It has been suggested that the real differences with regard to violations lay in opposition to rent control and that the evaluation of unfairness by many violators may have been merely a post-violation rationalization. In other words, opposition to rent control might indicate the extent to which the violations represented an "acting out" by individuals strongly hostile to authority in general.

Two analyses were made which tested the significance of opposition to rent control and which may be considered at least a partial test of this idea. In the

questionnaire each landlord was asked, "Do you believe rent control is necessary in Honolulu at the present time?" He was asked to indicate his answer:
"Yes," "Yes, but with changes in the ordinance (law)," or "No." A few respondents wrote "Don't know," or refused to answer at all.

The violation rate for those landlords who indicated rent control was not
necessary was 23.2 per cent; for all others, it was 21.2 per cent. The *t*-test did
not indicate statistical significance, and neither did a *chi*-square test with four
degrees of freedom performed on the entire array of their responses respecting
the necessity of rent control.

Finally, this hypothesis was tested: If a landlord defined his ceiling to be unfair *and* was opposed to rent control, he violated his ceiling. For reasons of
sample size, this test was limited to units with fair-rent-date ceilings whose
landlords had defined the ceilings to be unfair. Of the 179 violation cases in
this class, 54.2 per cent of the landlord responses indicated that rent control
was not necessary. Of the 321 non-violation cases, 55.1 per cent so indicated.
The difference was not statistically significant, and the null hypothesis was accepted.

In short, opposition to legal rent control, as such, did not appear to play
any systematic role in the act of ceiling violation by landlords in Honolulu in
1952. On the other hand, the legal restrictions placed upon previously legitimate methods for achieving still legitimate aspirations, especially that for
more money, seems to have been of considerable importance. The persistent
anticipation that rent control would soon be eliminated prevented any major
movement from rental to other business. And the tendency to perceive one's
treatment under the law to be unfair and thus to be tempted to violate the law
appeared directly related to the law's severity. It only remains to stress that 77
per cent of the rental units in the city in 1952 were operated in compliance
with these legal rules, in spite of widespread opposition to rent control and an
overwhelming belief among landlords generally that they were being treated
unfairly.

NOTES

1. A. A. Friedrich, "Rent Regulation," *Encyclopedia of the Social Sciences* (New
   York: Macmillan Co., 1933), XIII, 293.
2. Ordinance No. 941, City and County of Honolulu, December 13, 1941, and Act
   No. 91, November 5, 1941. This act further amended secs. 2833 and 3201 of the
   Revised Laws of Hawaii, 1935, as amended.
3. Ordinance No. 941, sec. 10.
4. A short time after the adoption of Ordinance No. 941, to take account of some
   particularly low rentals in an otherwise "normal" market, Ordinance No. 952, April
   19, 1942, was passed to amend Ordinance No. 941. Thus if, on the fair-rent date,
   some rent was "substantially" below that "generally prevailing for comparable
   housing accommodations" due to "peculiar circumstances," such as family relationships or unusually long tenancy, it could be raised to the "generally prevailing level"
   of the fair-rent date. The City-County Board of Supervisors eventually reduced the

grounds simply to the existence of a rent substantially lower than that generally prevailing for comparable units.

5. The Supreme Court of Hawaii held that it was "not . . . an obligation of the Commission . . . to fix for individual properties a rental which in its opinion will yield a reasonable return upon their value." *In re Cosmopolitan Hotel,* 31 Hawaii 611 (1947). One year after this study was initiated, the ordinance was amended so that, in effect, it raised ceilings generally 20 per cent above the May 27, 1941, level. This increase was described by the board as "fair and equitable" (Ordinance No. 1366, City and County of Honolulu, November 10, 1953).

6. Ordinance No. 1026, City and County of Honolulu, June 16, 1945.

7. Ordinance No. 1077, City and County of Honolulu, August 7, 1947.

8. Leo Grebler, *Production of Housing* (New York: Social Science Research Council, 1950), p. 120.

9. It was largely from this group that the leaders of the organized opposition to rent control were drawn. For a detailed discussion of the social history of rent control in Honolulu see Harry V. Ball, "A Sociological Study of Rent Control and Rent Control Violations" (Ph.D. dissertation, University of Minnesota, 1956), pp. 534–837.

10. For a more detailed discussion of these types and their places in Honolulu in 1952 as well as of the materials presented in the next three paragraphs see *ibid.,* pp. 840–853.

11. The city proper was defined as Census Tracts 1 through 29 of the island of Oahu. The sample was obtained by selecting every twentieth unit in the files of the commission.

12. Of the units retained, 67.9 per cent had fair-rent-date ceilings, 17.7 per cent had fair-return ceilings, and 14.4 per cent had new-construction ceilings.

13. About 66 per cent of the questionnaires were returned by mail. A 10 per cent sample of the non-residents was interviewed. Between respondents and non-respondents few differences were found, and those that were statistically significant were small in magnitude. For detailed comparisons see Ball, *op. cit.,* pp. 70–77.

14. Alex Inkeles, "Personality and Social Structure," in R. K. Merton, L. Broom, and L. S. Cottrell, Jr., eds., *Sociology Today: Problems and Prospects* (New York: Basic Books, 1959), p. 251. In my paper on rents, I have taken, as a matter of strategy, the position that one should not employ a broader theory or number of ideas about personality than is required by the immediate task at hand.

15. The differences were statistically significant at the .01 level.

16. The differences were statistically significant at the .01 level.

17. Robert K. Merton, *Social Theory and Social Structure* (Glencoe, Ill.: Free Press, 1949), pp. 125–126.

65

The Impact of Supreme Court Decisions on Religious Practices in Public Schools

H. FRANK WAY, JR.

One of the stories circulating among congressional staffs during 1964 involved an elementary teacher who entered a classroom and was shocked to see four boys kneeling on the floor in a corner. The teacher quickly asked the boys what they were doing and the boys replied that they were shooting craps. The teacher heaved a sigh of relief and said, "Oh, that is fine. I thought you were praying."

The story itself may well be indicative of the true level of congressional response to the Supreme Court's prayer and Bible-reading decisions.[1] The public reaction of Congress was more alarmist and strident. One southern congressman remarked of the Court "They have taken God out of the schools and put the Negroes in." A plethora of bills were introduced to reverse the decisions banning prayers and Bible readings by amending the Constitution. The Court had not come under such heavy attack since its desegregation decision, but this time the outcry was not regional. Some churchmen rose to the defense of the Court but in general the national reaction was negative.

Even among the friends of the Court there was talk that the justices had unnecessarily opened up an attack on the Court at a time when the Court was fighting more important battles.[2] The Court was broadly engaged in the civil rights movement, and was at the center of the struggle for legislative reapportionment and the improvement of state criminal procedures. To some critics, these engagements were of greater importance than whether public schools continued their traditional religious exercises.

Given the nature of the public reception of the decisions and the position of religion in America, one could have concluded in 1962–1963 that here was but another instance where the Court's decisions would have little impact beyond the immediate litigants. If this proved to be correct then the Court was the double loser. Its public image had suffered at the time of the decisions and now it would face the prospect of having those decisions ignored.

Yet the Court may well have been the better forecaster of its impact. The results of a national survey of elementary school teachers indicates that the Court has been able to effect a change in classroom religious practices. The re-

From *Western Political Quarterly,* XXI, No. 2 (1968), 189–194. Abridged with renumbered notes. Copyright © 1968 by the University of Utah. Reprinted by permission of the author and publisher.

mainder of this essay will present the results of the author's national survey conducted during the school year 1964–1965.[3]

. . .

The survey was a national random sample of 2,320 public elementary school teachers. It was arbitrarily decided that five teachers per school would be sampled. This meant 464 schools would be in the sample. . . . The return rate was 74 per cent or 1,712 replies.

. . .

The average teacher in the survey did feel the impact of the Supreme Court's decisions. As the following figures indicate there has been a noticeable shift in actual classroom practices in regard to prayers and Bible readings. Prayers were said in over 60 per cent of the classrooms of teachers responding to the questionnaire and who were teaching at the time the Court decisions were announced. Within this group the practice was overwhelmingly a daily one. By the academic year 1964–1965 the situation had changed from the pre-1962 figure of 60 per cent of the classrooms saying prayers at some time to only 28 per cent.[4]

TABLE 65-1 *Morning Prayers Before 1962*

	Daily	Weekly	Less Than Weekly	Not at All
Before 1962	720	33	19	498
1964-1965	321	24	29	946

While classroom prayers were common before 1962, classroom Bible readings were somewhat less common. Forty-eight per cent of the respondents teaching before 1962 indicated that Bible selections were read in their classrooms on a daily to less than weekly basis. Again, this situation changed radically after the Court decisions. By the academic year 1964–1965 only 22 per cent of the respondents indicated Bible selections were being read in their classes.

TABLE 65-2 *Bible Readings*

	Daily	Weekly	Less Than Weekly	Not at All
Before 1962	512	72	106	745
1964-1965	208	43	103	1261

Church Attendance

In a survey concerned with a religious issue one would expect that the frequency of a teacher's attendance at religious services might well influence her attitudes and practices in the public classroom.[5] The results were as expected. The more frequently a teacher attended church the more likely she was to have prayers and Bible readings in her classroom before the Court decisions and to continue them after the decisions were announced. This same trend is noted in the results on opinions about religion in the public classroom. The three sets of percentages which merit the closest attention are those reporting current practices on morning prayers, Bible readings, and grace. Here infrequency of church attendance appears to have had its most pronounced influence.

•   •   •

TABLE 65-3   *Relationship Between Teacher-Church Attendance and Classroom Practices and Attitudes (in percentages)* *

	Church Attendance				
	Never-Rarely Attend	Attend Monthly	Attend Weekly	Attend More Than Weekly	Significance Level
Opinions about Religion in Public Schools					
Prayer and Bible readings decisions					
interfere with teacher freedom	36	61	65	74	p < 1%
Devotional services have no place					
in the public school	69	41	31	20	p < 1%
Released time programs interfere					
with class schedules	68	58	46	36	p < 1%
Don't stop prayers and Bible readings					
because of a few	51	77	83	92	p < 1%
Bible readings and prayers are					
beneficial to students	68	83	90	95	p < 1%
Public school not proper place to					
develop religious values	78	58	48	55	p < 1%
Classroom Religious Practices					
Bible readings, pre-1962	32	44	49	63	p < 1%
Bible readings, 1964-1965	7	16	25	38	p < 1%
Morning prayers, pre-1962	42	60	59	67	p < 1%
Morning prayers, 1964-1965	12	23	30	42	p < 1%
Religious precepts, 1964-1965	71	79	81	86	p < 1%
Grace, pre-1962	30	57	59	67	p < 1%
Grace, 1964-1965	17	31	35	47	p < 1%

*The chi-square test of the significance of differences of two independent samples was used.

NOTES

1. *Engel v. Vitale,* 370 U.S. 421 (1962) and *School District of Abington v. Schempp,* 374 U.S. 203 (1963).
2. See Erwin Griswold's "Absolute Is in the Dark: A Discussion of the Approach of the Supreme Court to Constitutional Questions," *Utah Law Review* (Summer, 1963).
3. This section is from an earlier manuscript and has been reprinted here with the author's permission.
4. It should be noted, however, that there was an increase in 1964–1965 in the practice of "silent meditation" in the classroom. This rose from 178 before 1962 to 294 during 1964–1965.
5. The following is a breakdown of number of respondents in each attendance level:

Never-rarely	271
Monthly	360
Weekly	761
More than weekly	308
	1,700

66

On Legal Sanctions

RICHARD D. SCHWARTZ AND SONYA ORLEANS

If we take seriously the task of developing a model to predict the effects of law, one of our first jobs must be to study closely the impact of sanctions on legal compliance. Accordingly, we need to examine such questions as: (1) Does the threat of punishment deter? (2) How and when does it accomplish its effects? (3) What side effects does it have? and (4) How does it compare with alternative reactions?

In order to approach these issues empirically, it was proposed some years ago that a field experiment be conducted on motivational factors affecting compliance with federal income tax laws.[1] Recently it has become possible to carry out such a study.

Tax compliance was selected for several reasons: (1) The payment of taxes is one of the most widespread of all serious legal obligations in American society. More than a third of the total population is required by law to file fed-

From *University of Chicago Law Review,* XXXIV, No. 2 (Winter, 1967), 283–300. Reprinted by permission of the publisher. Abridged with renumbered notes.

eral income tax returns. Of those obligated, the overwhelming majority do so. As a result, it is possible to sample diverse groups in the population to examine the effect on compliance of various background characteristics. (2) Taxpaying is required at least annually, so that changes over time may be sequentially observed. (3) Compliance with tax law varies from full or even excessive compliance to serious evasion. It has been established that at least one-fourth of all taxpayers evade taxes to some degree. Frequency of violation has practical and methodological implications. In policy terms, it means a serious loss of revenue. According to the IRS sample audit of 1948, $1.4 billion were lost in that year because of underestimations on personal returns of taxes owed to the Government.[2] If the present study reveals legitimate and practical devices for increasing tax compliance, the government's gain could be substantial. Reduction in evasion may, furthermore, serve to distribute the tax burden more equitably and add to the sense of legitimacy on which the legal order presumably rests. From a methodological point of view, the pervasiveness of violations creates an opportunity for study. It means that, in principle at least, violators can be compared with those who comply, to determine the differences between them. It also opens up the possibility, exploited in this study, of examining the efficacy of different motivations through exposing taxpayers to various stimuli and observing the increases toward full compliance which result. (4) Taxpaying is behavior that can be described in detail by quantitative indices. As a result, increases in taxpaying can be rigorously described, and they can be related through powerful statistical tests to the independent variables. (5) Because income taxation is practiced in many countries and in localities within the United States, results of this study can be replicated for comparative purposes in other settings.

The tax project was explicitly designed to study theoretically significant variables. The primary objective was to determine the effect of sanction threats and to compare them with appeals to conscience as determinants of legal compliance.

The technique here employed for examining tax compliance was the field experiment. This method, more widely praised than used in the social sciences, is designed to bring to natural situations some of the precision of the laboratory. In pure form, it includes the full application of the classic experimental model. This means differential application of one or more independent variables to experimental groups and the non-application of these variables to one or more control groups. The experimental and control groups are selected in such a way as to be initially comparable with each other in every way. The experimental groups are then subjected to stimuli which constitute the independent variables. The observer must be in a position to observe changes in the behavior of all groups, so as to be able to appraise the effects of each of the independent variables.

The field experiment differs from laboratory procedure, however, in that it is carried out in a situation that exists without instigation by the experimenter. Subjects are studied in a natural context where they would have been even if no study had been conducted. Care is taken, moreover, to avoid any awareness on the subjects' part that they are participants in an experiment. To the extent that these conditions can be maintained, it is thought that this procedure avoids a major source of distortion, and therefore permits results to be generalized with greater confidence to the "real world."

The key to this experiment lay in obtaining data on the actual taxpaying behavior of those studied. With the cooperation of the Internal Revenue Service, we obtained figures for groups of taxpayers. These groups comprise the experimental treatment groups and the controls. By giving us distributions for entire groups, the IRS complied with the statutory provision that no individual returns be disclosed.

Assignment to experimental groups followed conventional techniques. Subjects were matched individually for precision control using residential criteria from census tracts. The sample was drawn from areas where income was generally above $10,000 to minimize the number of subjects whose compliance was assured by full withholding and short form filing. While this criterion prevented coverage of lower income families, it increased the chances of obtaining differential effects from the varying treatments. Subjects were then assigned to experimental or control groups on a random basis. Treatment groups consisted of 92 taxpayers in the placebo, 92 in the conscience, and 89 in the sanction group. They were interviewed during the month prior to filing their returns on their attitudes toward political and civic issues, with particular emphasis placed on tax policy.

In each of the experimental groups, questions were included that were intended to accentuate certain motives for tax payment. The "sanction-treated" group was asked questions such as the following: "A jail sentence of three years could be imposed for willful failure to pay tax on interest. Under what conditions do you think the Government should impose a jail sentence?" [3] A series of similar questions emphasized the severity of sanctions available to the government and the likelihood that tax violators would be apprehended. The "conscience" group, on the other hand, was exposed to questions accentuating moral reasons for compliance with tax law. These included questions such as: "Would you consider a citizen's willful failure to pay tax on interest an indication that he is unwilling to do something for the country as a whole?" [4] Similar questions posed to this group emphasized non-controversial uses for which tax money is employed, citizen obligation to government, and the value of personal integrity.

In addition to the two treatment groups, a placebo group was selected by the same technique of precision control and random assignment. This group was given the same basic interview without any accentuation questions.[5] A fourth group served as an untreated control. Its purpose was to determine whether the basic interview, with or without accentuation, affects taxpaying behavior.

Two kinds of data may be reported at present: interview responses and actual tax returns. The first is derived from an internal analysis of the interviews themselves. Toward the close of the interview, after the experimental treatment was given, all three groups were asked an open-ended question: "What reasons do you think taxpayers might have for reporting all the interest they earn on their tax returns?" Answers to this question were content-analyzed to determine whether normative reasons were the first given. The results of this analysis indicate that several social variables affect the manner in which taxpayers are oriented toward paying taxes and the manner in which they respond to different motivational appeals.

The first of these variables is social class or socio-economic status. Using the Hollingshead two-factor index of occupation and education,[6] we found no relationship between initial normative orientation, as inferred from responses in the placebo interview group, and social class (Table 66–1, column 1). The success of conscience appeals did not vary systematically by the dimension of social class, being greater in classes II and IV than in classes I and III (Table 66–1, column 2). There was, however, a direct relation between social class and the capacity of sanction threats to elicit normative content. Column 3, Table 66–1, shows a remarkable regularity in the relationship between normative responses after sanction threat and socio-economic status. Comparing columns 1 and 3 in Table 66–1, we find an increase of 26 per cent in normative orientation following the sanction threat for class I as against 7 per cent, 3 per cent and −3 per cent in classes II, III, and IV respectively.

This is the first instance of a phenomenon that occurs repeatedly in the data. For class I, it appears that, while direct appeals to duty do not create a greatly increased sense of obligation, threat of sanction does. This may well indicate a major mechanism of social control. Sanctions may be most effective in preventing violations where they are converted into a sense of moral obligation. Whether this "induced morality" actually increases compliance, however, will only become apparent when it is related to behavior such as the actual taxpaying of the subjects.

TABLE 66-1   *Socio-Economic Status and Normative Orientation Toward Taxpaying (percentage giving primary normative response)*

Class	Placebo		Conscience		Sanction	
	%	N*	%	N	%	N
I (highest)	56	13/23	71	17/24	82	22/27
II	60	15/25	87	13/15	67	16/24
III	56	15/27	71	25/35	59	16/27
IV (lowest)†	53	9/17	88	14/16	50	5/10
Total	57	52/92	75	69/92	67	59/88

*The N column shows the number giving the primary normative response over total respondents in the category. Numbers in the three groups vary slightly in each table because those who did not answer are omitted.

†Hollingshead's lowest socio-economic category was unrepresented in the sample because of a restriction to persons filing long form returns.

Another point of interest emerges from the normative reactions of class IV as seen in Table 66–1, row 4. Respondents in class IV show the highest gain in normative content following the conscience appeal (35 per cent). By contrast, however, they show a slight decline following threat. In effect, they will go along with reminders of the obligation to pay taxes but will not be pushed into that position by warnings of potential punishment. The response to conscience appeals in the working class group suggests a combination of patriotism and an appreciation of the benefits provided by a welfare state. Indifference to sanctions in this stratum may relate to the reality of tax enforcement policy; that is, the probability of tax investigation is, in fact, an increasing function of income. In addition, the working class may be somewhat more prone to view the world as dominated by luck and fate, and thus not expect a close relationship between conduct and consequence.

If such differences affect actual compliance, the practical implications for tax policy may be extremely important. Accentuation of threat, through publicized prosecutions and the like, would be called for against the rich but not against the working class. For the latter, educational campaigns emphasizing patriotic considerations appear to be more promising.

These differences by social class are consistent with reactions by educational background. Initial differences in normative content, as shown in the placebo group (Table 66–2, column 1) are not significant, though slightly higher for college than high school educated. Under the treatments, however, the least educated show a marked response to conscience appeals (36 per cent increase), but no increase at all under sanction threat. College graduates, by contrast, show some evidence of threat-induced conscience (10 per cent), even though this increase is less than the 18 per cent produced by conscience appeals.

TABLE 66-2 *Education and Normative Orientation Toward Taxpaying*

	Placebo		Conscience		Sanction	
	%	N	%	N	%	N
College graduate	60	28/47	78	29/37	70	35/50
College attendance	59	10/17	75	15/20	71	12/17
High school graduate	50	7/14	68	13/19	58	7/12
High school not completed	50	7/14	86	12/14	50	5/10

Taking the two variables of class and education together, what possible explanations of these findings emerge? Less educated, working class people may be more prone to respond to conscience appeals because of greater piety or naïveté, or because of a conviction that government action is needed for the solution of social problems. Alternatively, the better educated, upper class respondents may already have been exposed to such reasons for taxpaying and either accepted them—as the slightly higher proportion of normative responses for upper against lower categories in the placebo in Tables 66–1 and 66–2 suggests—or be resistant to attitude change when it is implicitly urged on them. In regard to sanction, less educated, working class individuals may be inclined to discount the prospect of prosecution being directed against them, be less worried about the experience if it should occur, and be less likely to convert the fear of sanction into normative reasons for acquiescence.

Another factor which relates to the impact of given motivation is the individual's employment status. As seen in Table 66–3, the self-employed were

TABLE 66-3   *Self-Employment and Normative Orientation Toward Taxpaying*

	Placebo		Conscience		Sanction	
	%	N	%	N	%	N
Self-employed	59	34/58	71	42/59	68	39/57
Employed by others	52	16/31	90	27/30	64	18/28

slightly more normative in the placebo condition than those working for others. Subjected to conscience appeals, however, the non-self-employed showed a 38 per cent increase in normative content, whereas the self-employed were only moderately moved (12 per cent). The effects of the conscience appeal on those working for others overshadow the limited effects of sanction threat on either group. The explanation of this finding is not immediately apparent. Perhaps those who are employed in an organization become accustomed to responding to exhortations that they comply for the good of the organization, and they extend this to the government when urged. Whatever the explanation, the phenomenon is intrinsically interesting. It suggests that the increasing pervasiveness of corporations as a source of employment helps to explain tax compliance, if not the fulfillment of the general obligation of citizenship, in complex societies. Along the same lines, it may help to explain the resistance to taxation among small businessmen and farmers, as in the Poujadist movement.

Religion also emerges as a correlate of taxpaying orientation. In the placebo group, Catholics showed the most frequent normative orientation, followed by Protestants and Jews (Table 66–4, column 1). Subjected to the experimental interviews, however, Catholics showed little normative reaction to sanction threat (2 per cent) and actually declined slightly (3 per cent) in these re-

TABLE 66-4   *Religious Affiliation and Normative Orientation Toward Taxpaying*

	Placebo		Conscience		Sanction	
	%	N	%	N	%	N
Catholics	67	16/24	64	14/22	69	18/28
Protestants	52	22/42	83	34/41	67	20/30
Jews	48	10/21	76	19/25	67	20/30

sponses upon being confronted with considerations of conscience. Perhaps their normative orientation is so well set by initial training or so exclusively related to an authoritative church that they do not respond to appeals or threats from other sources. By contrast, Protestants and Jews increased their normative statements to a point exceeding the Catholics under conscience appeals. Protestants showed an increase of 31 per cent in normative content under conscience appeals, and Jews were almost equally responsive to the conscience appeal (28 per cent). Jews showed a slightly greater normative reaction (19 per cent) than Protestants (15 per cent) to sanction threat, the effects of which brought Jews and Protestants virtually up to the position of the Catholics.

These diverse reactions to motivational appeals must be viewed with caution. They are based on relatively small groups that were selected from relatively well-to-do segments of the population. The correlations reported, moreover, have not, because of small numbers, been subjected to multivariate analysis to check the independence of effects. Nevertheless, the marginal analysis which has been done suggests some definite variations in initial orientation to taxpaying and in responsiveness to various motivational appeals. At a minimum, the findings suggest the following relationships:

1. Cultural and social structural factors correlate with legally relevant attitudes.

2. Conscience appeals often have a greater effect on groups with low initial normative orientations than on those who are initially high in normative orientation.

3. Sanction threat has a mixed effect on normative orientations, being capable of "inducing morality" among several categories.

It remains to be seen how these reactions relate to tax compliance. At this point, we are unable to report changes in payment in relation to social characteristics or attitudinal responses. We have received preliminary data, however, for changes in tax payments for the gross experimental and control groups. These data permit comparisons of the two experimental groups with the control group in regard to changes in tax payment on returns filed before the interview (for fiscal 1961) and after the interview (for fiscal 1962). Since the groups were randomly assigned (after matching by residence), differences in increase of taxpaying are presumably attributable to the experimental treatments.

A caveat must be entered at this point. The results obtained from the experiment are not of a magnitude that uniformly produces statistically significant differences. Some of the results reported, especially if taken separately, could well be attributed to chance. This could be the consequence of small samples, weakness of the experimental treatments, a limited amount of cheating relative to the large base of compliance, or the fluctuation of income found in all groups.

Nevertheless, the results do fall into a pattern which is highly suggestive. As

TABLE 66-5   Differences Between 1961 and 1962 in Reported Adjusted Gross Income Deductions, and Income Taxes after Credit

Group	Number	I. Adjusted Gross Income		II. Total Deductions		III. Income Tax after Credits	
		a. Mean of 1961-62 differences	b. Standard deviation of the observed differences	a. Mean of 1961-62 differences	b. Standard deviation of the observed differences	a. Mean of 1961-62 differences	b. Standard deviation of the observed differences
A Sanction threat	87	$181	$3,481	$273	$853	$ 11	$ 956
B Conscience appeal	88	804	4,007	177	535	243	1,189
C Placebo control	88	−87	2,858	132	571	−40	751
D Untreated control	111*	−13	3,510	320	820	−57	965

Comparison of increase, 1961-62, t Test†

		t		t		t	
Sanction(A) v. Conscience(B)		1.09(N.S.)		.88(N.S.)		1.35(.10) B > A	
Sanction(A) v. Placebo(C)		.55(N.S.)		1.30(.10) A > C		.39(N.S.)	
Conscience(B) v. Placebo(C)		1.68(.05) B > C		.53(N.S.)		1.87(.05) B > C	
Placebo(C) v. Untreated control(D)		.14(N.S.)		1.81(.05) D > C		.14(N.S.)	

*Adjusted gross income tabulations are based on 110 taxpayer returns. Data for one taxpayer showing a very large decrease in adjusted gross income were excluded by the Revenue Service from the tabulations to avoid possible identification.
†Brunk, *An Introduction to Mathematical Statics* (1960), p. 246.

indicated in Table 66–5, column 1a, those threatened with sanction declared a mean increase in adjusted gross income of $181 as compared with a mean decrease of $87 for the placebo control (and a mean decrease of $13 for the untreated control). It should also be noted, as seen in Table 66–5, column 3a, that income tax after credit shows a mean increase for the sanction-threatened group, compared with a decrease for the two controls.

If we look at the *number* of individuals in the sanction group who increased their adjusted gross income, this pattern is repeated. In the sanction-treated group, as shown in Table 66–6, 49 of 87 taxpayers, or 56 per cent, exceeded the median dividing line set by the placebo group. The number of sanction-threatened individuals also slightly exceeded the placebo median on income tax paid.

It is equally important to note that the *conscience* appeal had a stronger effect on income reported than did the threat of sanction. Adjusted gross income (AGI) reported by the conscience-appeal group showed a mean increase of $804 compared with $181 for those threatened with sanction (Table 66–5, column 1a). The mean increase in AGI in the conscience group is statistically significant when compared with the placebo. Income tax payments for this group are also appreciably higher than for the sanction group or the controls. The number of conscience group members who exceeded the placebo median on adjusted gross income reported is 56 of 88 or 64 per cent (Table 66–6, column 1). From this it may be inferred that more than one-fourth of the conscience group who would—in the absence of the appeal—have been below the median, were moved above it on AGI reporting. (The number of individuals who increased their taxes—Table 66–6, column 3—also exceeded the median, although this effect is slight and statistically not significant.) These results tend to confirm the proposition that conscience appeals can be more effective than sanction threats.

Various interpretations of these results are possible. Despite efforts to avoid threats, some implication of punishment may have been conveyed in the conscience interview. If so, the greater reporting of income by this group might have resulted from a subjective summation of threat and conscience motivations. Moreover, threats conveyed under the guise of an appeal to conscience may have led to much greater compliance because of the mechanism of threat-induced moralism noted in the interview results. On the other hand, it is possible that the subjects of these interviews were simply more responsive to appeals to conscience than to the kind of threats which apparently made at least some sanction group members dig in their heels.

There is additional evidence that suggests that some who are induced to comply by threat find ways of expressing their resentment. Deductions taken by the sanction-threatened group showed a mean increase as compared with those who were given the conscience appeal. As shown in column IIa of Table 66–5, those threatened with sanction had a mean increase in deductions of $273, compared with $177 for the normative group. It is tempting to interpret this difference as meaning that the threatened group said: "You may beat me

TABLE 66-6 Numbers of Taxpayers in Each Experimental Group Exceeding Median Increase, 1961-62, of Control Groups in Various Elements of Tax Reporting: Sign Test for Significance*

Comparison	I. Adjusted Gross Income				II. Total Deductions				III. Income Tax after Credits			
	N	N > Median of C(144)	%	P	N	N > Median of C(97)	%	P	N	N > Median of C(34)	%	P
Sanction threat(A) v. Placebo(C)	87	49	56	.17	87	31	35	.0026	87	46	52	.334
Conscience appeal(B) v. Placebo(C)	88	56	64	.0073	88	39	44	.0838	88	49	56	.169
Combined experimental (A + B) v. Placebo (C)†	175	105	60	.0071	175	70	40	.0034	175	95	54	.1469

*Brownlee, *Statistical Theory and Methodology in Science and Engineering* (1960), pp. 180-184. This test uses the placebo to establish a median and then computes the probability of at least the number which exceeds that median doing so by chance.

†A sign test of the placebo against the medians of the untreated control shows that the two groups are very similar on AGI (P = .54, median of D = 114), but very different for deductions (P = .000002, median of D = 233) and somewhat so for tax (P = .084, median of D = −63). These observations reinforce the conclusion, indicated earlier, that the untreated control is not dependable in the absence of further data. In substance, this means that the bias resulting from dropouts or the interview made a difference, particularly in deductions. The similarity of AGI's of the placebo and the untreated control strongly suggests that the smaller deductions in the two experimental and the placebo groups resulted from the interview rather than from dropout bias.

into admitting higher income, but I'll find a way of getting it back." One might also infer that the conscience-appeal group kept its deductions low in recognition of the importance of tax payments for the welfare of the country.

These interpretations lose force, however, from the position of the two control groups on deductions. For one thing, the placebo control shows an even lower mean increase in deductions than the conscience group, a result that is not attributable to induced motivations. A second confounding fact is that the untreated control shows even higher deductions than the sanction treated group. A third point to be noted is that a minority of members of both experimental groups increased their deductions over the median provided by the placebo (Table 66–6). This shows that the increase in aggregate deductions by the experimental groups is attributable to a minority of the members of each group, the minority being even smaller in the sanction than in the conscience group. If there is a heel-dragging effect, then, it is found in a relatively small group. It remains to be seen whether this group can be identified as having distinctive social characteristics and attitudes.

These three findings make it prudent to interpret the suggestive differences between the two experimental groups with considerable caution. The results, nevertheless, give some evidence to support the following propositions:

1. Compliance can be increased by threat of punishment.
2. Appeals to conscience can be a more effective instrument than sanction threat for securing compliance.

Further analysis is needed to determine how these experimentally induced motives affected subgroups whose verbal reactions to the interviews varied so widely. Those results are now being prepared by the Internal Revenue Service. When completed, it is hoped that they will contribute to a fuller understanding of the motivations affecting legal compliance.

Conclusion

This essay has reviewed some widely held assumptions concerning the operation of legal sanctions. These were then subjected to empirical examination. The study reported was a field experiment aimed at determining the effectiveness of sanction, as compared with an appeal to conscience and with a placebo control, in increasing normative sentiments about compliance and in heightening actual compliance in the payment of federal income taxes. The findings indicate that motivations of various kinds make a difference in taxpaying. They suggest that the two types of appeal affect normative orientation differently according to the status of those subjected to the appeals. Sanction threat increases normative orientation most markedly among the upper class, the better educated, and non-Catholics. Appeals to conscience change attitudes toward tax compliance most among the best and least well educated, those employed by others, and Protestants and Jews. As to actual changes in tax compliance, returns currently available for the gross treatment groups suggest that conscience appeals are more effective than sanction threats, though both have some effect. The conscience appeal appears, moreover, to produce less loss through resistance, an effect implied by the increase in aggregate deductions noted in the sanction-treated group.

These results must, of course, be viewed with caution. They were obtained from a population in a given geographical area, by a novel (that is, otherwise untested) method, in an examination of a largely well-to-do population. The behavior examined, moreover, may be atypically sensitive to conscience considerations, particularly in the American urban setting. Before these results can be confidently used as a girder in the construction of a theory of legal compliance, they must be joined with studies of the same problem which use different methods, populations, and types of legal compliance. To build an adequate theory of legal compliance, much more work is needed both at the drawing board and in the field.

Nevertheless, the results of the study carry several implications for a theory of sanction. They suggest that the threat of sanction can deter people from violating the law, perhaps in important part by inducing a moralistic attitude toward compliance. This mechanism seems particularly significant when those subject to sanction threat are not trained by, and associated with, an authoritative institution other than the state. The threat of punishment appears, however, to produce some resistance to compliance. Such resistance can be minimized through alternative techniques of securing compliance, such as the utilization of appeals to conscience and to a sense of civic responsibility, motives that can be more powerful than sanction threat in increasing compliance with the law.

NOTES

1. Schwartz, "Field Experimentation in Socio-legal Research," *Journal of Legal Education,* XIII (1961), 401.
2. Farioletti, "Some Results from the First Year's Audit Control Program of the Bureau of Internal Revenue," *National Tax Journal,* V (1925), 656; see also Bittker, *Federal Income Estate and Gift Taxation* (3rd ed. 1964), p. 899.
3. The questions aimed at inducing sanction threat are given below. Italicized portions comprise instructions to the interviewer. The interviews were carried out by a professional research firm, the Research Guild, using ten experienced interviewers who were randomly assigned. We are grateful to Hugh Edwards of the Research Guild for the adroit execution of an unusually complex field operation.

SANCTION QUESTIONS

One important area of government which is of concern to many people is the Federal Income Tax. We would like to know how people like you feel about the way the Government goes about enforcing the income tax.

1. First of all, we are interested in experiences people may have had with the Internal Revenue Service. Has your return ever come up for investigation?
If No, Go On To 2.
If So: 1a. Briefly, do you recall what happened in the investigation?
1b. How did you feel about the experience? (*PROBE. For example, did you*

feel that you were treated fairly, was the experience anxiety producing?)
2. In the last session of Congress a bill was passed which requires banks and other savings institutions to report the names of people who have interest payments of $10 or more. Do you feel that it is right for the government to have this kind of information about people?
    2a. Why do you feel this way?
3. The Internal Revenue Service is installing high-speed computers like Univac. Do you think that these electronic computers should be used to check up on whether people report all their interest?
4. These computers together with the information from the banks would make it possible for the Internal Revenue Service to check up on as much as 70 per cent or more of the people who have interest, with little effort and expense. Do you think the government should investigate the reported income from interest of so many people?
    4a. Why do you feel that way?
5. Would you be in favor of the Internal Revenue Service making public the names of people who wilfully did not report the full amount of their interest?
    5a. Why do you feel that way?
6. Failure to report all interest would involve "subscribing to a false tax return." The fine for such an offense is $5,000. Do you think this fine is set so high to deter people from evading their tax on interest, or to make up for the money lost due to tax evasion, or for some other reason?
7. A jail sentence of three years could be imposed for wilful failure to pay tax on interest. Under what conditions do you think the Government should impose a jail sentence?
8. Would you approve of a plan to investigate the previous returns of individuals who did not report their interest on this year's return?
    8a. Why is that?
9. What do you think are the chances that the Internal Revenue Service will examine your return to find out whether you reported all of your interest?
    It's a sure thing
    Chances are 50-50
    Unlikely
    Very unlikely
    No chance
Last year there was a lot of talk about the reporting of income from interest. Many of the questions to follow are concerned with enforcement of tax on income from interest.
10. Apparently, a lot of people have not been reporting all the interest they earned. Do you think the Internal Revenue Service should stiffen punishment and increase their auditing procedures to get people to report and pay tax on interest?
    10a. Why do you feel this way?
11. About how much money do you think should be involved in tax evasion before a large fine or jail sentence is imposed?
4. The set of questions intended to induce a conscience effect were designed to arouse motives for taxpaying ranging from guilt at violation to a patriotic desire to support the government in its most valued activities:

CONSCIENCE QUESTIONS

In this portion of the interview we want to explore how people like yourself evaluate the citizen's obligation to pay income tax. No one likes to pay taxes, but there are many obligations people have which they do not want or like. Paying income tax is one of these and little is known about how people really feel about their obligation to obey the tax laws.

Most of these questions will focus on the law stating that people must pay the tax they owe on interest income. This particular item was chosen because it was talked about in the news a good deal in the past year.
1. The Treasury Department has indicated that hundreds of millions of dollars are not available for programs of great importance to the country because some of the people

have not paid the full amount of tax on their interest income. Do you think it would be a good idea for the government to engage in a campaign to inform the people of their responsibilities and obligations to pay the tax they owe on their interest?

1a. Why do you feel that way?

2. If the government should have a program to educate citizens about their responsibilities and obligations to pay the tax they owe on their interest, what points should be stressed, in your opinion?

3. Some people say that it is all right to use illegal means to get out of paying taxes, like not reporting their interest, because taxes are too high. Do you think they are justified?

3a. Why do you feel that way?

4. Which of the following activities do you think should be given additional Federal Government support if everyone paid the tax they owe on their interest? Choose as many as you like.

1. Financing the building of hospitals
2. Scholarships to medical students
3. Government sponsored research on mental illness
4. Scholarships to needy college students
5. Loans to small business
6. Basic research in nuclear physics
7. Development of modern weapons systems
8. Civil defense
9. The space program
10. The Peace Corps
11. The foreign aid program
12. Building roads and highways
13. Area redevelopment
14. Flood control projects
15. Urban renewal programs
16. National recreation areas
17. Other

5. Some people think that it is "fair game" to swindle the United States Government, by not reporting all their income from interest, for example. What is your opinion of such an attitude?

5a. Do you think this kind of attitude (that is, fair game to swindle the government) indicates weakened respect for law?

5b. Why do you feel that way?

5c. Do you feel that such an attitude indicates disrespect for the government?

5d. Why do you feel that way?

6. It has been suggested that there is not much difference between draft-dodging and tax evasion.

6a. Do you think that failure to pay tax on interest and draft-dodging both indicate that evaders and dodgers put their own self-interest above the interest of others?

6b. Do you think that failure to pay tax on interest and draft-dodging are similar in that both indicate a failure to take seriously the responsibilities of citizenship?

6c. Why do you feel that way?

6d. When you consider all relevant factors, including the number of people involved, do you think that the people who fail to pay all the tax they owe on interest hurt the country about as much as, more, or less than, the men who illegally evade the draft?

6e. Why do you feel that way?

7. How guilty do you think a person should feel who knowingly does not pay his tax on the interest which he earned?

5. The interviewed or placebo control group was provided to rule out a number of threats to validity. This group was initially as similar to the two experimental groups as random assignment could make it. It was subjected to an interview that was the same as that received by the experimental groups, except, of course, for those questions which constituted the two experimental treatments. The history and

motivation of all three groups after the interview and prior to their payment of taxes were presumably the same, except insofar as the treatments made the experimental groups behave differently. The effects on taxpaying behavior were determined by the same measurements, and the impact of these observations was minimized by virtue of the subjects' lack of awareness that changes in taxpaying conduct were under scrutiny. Regression effects were constant, since all three groups were drawn at random from the same initial segment of the population. Dropout rate following the initial interview was constant and below 5 per cent for all three groups. All of these considerations lead to the conclusion that the differences between the groups were internally valid; that is, that the experimental treatments did in fact account for the observed differences among the treatment groups and the interviewed, or placebo, control. For a detailed authoritative discussion of these threats to validity, see Campbell and Stanley, "Experimental and Quasi-Experimental Designs for Research," in *Handbook of Research in Teaching* (Gage ed. 1963), p. 171 (also available as a 1966 monograph).

6. The Hollingshead Index of Social Position identifies five classes, of which four are represented in our sample. These four classes range from the top executives and professionals of class I through the upper middle class II, middle and lower middle class III, to working or upper lower class IV. Only the unskilled lower class are unrepresented in this sample. For a detailed description of the characteristics of these classes as described for New Haven (where the scale was validated), see Hollingshead and Redlich, *Social Class and Mental Illness* (1958), pp. 66–136. The techniques for generating and validating the scale are described *id.* at pp. 387–407.

67

Income Taxes and Incentives to Work: An Empirical Study

GEORGE F. BREAK

The question of how incentives to work are affected by high and steeply progressive income taxes has long been approached with caution by tax economists, whose answers have been full of tantalizing ambiguities. It has encountered no such reticence, however, on the part of the great bulk of financial experts and journalists who with ready clarity on the point have had no difficulty convincing the public of the truth of the axiom that high taxes inevitably mean a reduction in the aggregate work supply. This has frequently been cited as one of the major causes of Great Britain's present economic tribulations and has been held up as a warning to our lawmakers to beware bringing the same fate on this country.

From *American Economic Review*, XLVII (1957), 529–543. Reprinted by permission of the author and publisher.

In the face of such overwhelming public opinion, the specialist who goes into the relevant economic theory in detail finds himself able to maintain with assurance only that the matter is not so simple. Whereas taxation certainly does tend to impair incentives by reducing the net monetary reward to be earned by an extra hour's work, it also exerts a quite opposite effect in that it lowers the taxpayer's disposable income and hence increases the pressure on him to earn more. Indeed, to the extent that a family has committed itself to a high level of living expenses, incurring obligations such as mortgage payments, life insurance premiums, installment buying contracts, school and college fees for the children, and so forth, higher income taxes may virtually force the income earner to work harder to make ends meet. On theoretical grounds alone, therefore, it can no more be proven that taxation necessarily has a disincentive effect than that it has an incentive one.

The problem, it would seem clear, is one that must be resolved by empirical study. Theory, nonetheless, provides the guidance for designing such a study by suggesting the groups of people who are likely to be particularly sensitive to tax disincentives. It is evident from the beginning that those who are subject to firm institutional rigidities in their working lives are not so free to respond to incentive or disincentive pressures as are those who are self-employed or who have income-earning opportunities available to them outside their regular jobs. Where a choice is possible, disincentives will be found to prevail among those who respond more strongly to the attraction of the lower price for leisure resulting from higher marginal tax rates than they do to the wish to maintain given levels of disposable income in the face of rising taxes. Confronted with a tax increase of given extent, a person's reaction to it will depend upon how rapidly the marginal utility of income increases as income itself decreases: the more rapid the increase the more likely is the person to respond by working harder. People who are induced by higher income taxes to work less, then, are those who are not highly committed to their pre-tax levels of consumption and saving and they are most likely to be found among the upper-income groups, among older people who have already built up a reasonably satisfactory stock of consumer durables and investment assets, and among those in any age or income group who have few dependents, low indebtedness, and relatively modest needs both currently and in the foreseeable future.

The lack of empirical information about the interrelationships between factors of this sort and tax incentives and disincentives led the author during the first half of 1956 to undertake a sample survey in the most vulnerable area possible—Great Britain, where income tax rates rise considerably more steeply than they do in the United States. At that time, for example, English married couples with two children and with incomes after allowable deductions falling in a range equivalent to that of $5,000 to $10,000 faced marginal tax rates of between 33.5 and 60 per cent; in the United States the corresponding tax rates were either 20 or 22 per cent. The groups selected for the survey—solicitors and accountants who were either partners or in business on their own—fall in the tax-sensitive category not only because they were all self-employed but also because, with their practices bringing them in continuous contact with tax problems, they were typically very much aware of the marginal rate at which they themselves were paying taxes. In addition, being as a group somewhat older than the working-force average and belonging in large proportion to the middle- and upper-income categories, they should be particularly prone to tax disincentives. For example, 63 per cent of them faced marginal tax rates greater than 50 per cent.

I. The Sample Studied

Limitations of time confined the study to England, where 306 solicitors and accountants were personally interviewed by the author in London, its suburbs, and in six provincial areas, predominantly rural and agricultural in character and scattered geographically. This design enabled coverage of a wide variety of practices, both urban and country.

For the London sample 87 accountants were selected by taking every thirtieth name, with a random start, from the list for that area of practicing members of the Institute of Chartered Accountants (this list was used because the Institute's membership contains by far the largest proportion of self-employed accountants in the country). The choice of solicitors was slightly more complicated, since the Law Society's list separated the individual suburbs from central London. Accordingly, every fortieth name, from a random start, was taken from the metropolitan list, making 126 in all. Then 20 suburban solicitors were selected by first choosing four suburbs with probabilities proportional to size and then taking names by systematic selection from each one. (The overall sampling fraction for this group was also 1 in 40.)

The country sample, consisting of 122 solicitors and accountants, was taken by systematic selection from six areas in Gloucestershire, Somerset, Warwickshire, Shropshire, Lincolnshire, and Cambridgeshire. The towns from which the selections were made varied in size from a few hundred to 80,000. The sampling fractions ranged from one in five to one in nine.

Of the total sample of 355 names, 28 were found to be no longer practicing in the sampled areas as a result of death, retirement, or other causes. Since by definition these people were not part of the sampled population, the sample was thereby reduced to 327 names. Of these, three of the London list could not be located even after extensive searching, seven country practitioners were out of town during the periods of interviewing in their areas, and 11 in all refused to be interviewed. The total failure rate, therefore, came to $21/327 = .064$, and the refusal rate, among those approached, to $11/317 = .035$.

The very low refusal rate may be attributed in no small degree to the willingness of both the Law Society and the Institute of Chartered Accountants to provide general letters of introduction, which were used in requesting the interviews. There is no doubt that this not only increased the coverage of the samples themselves but encouraged a significant number of those interviewed to answer the questions more freely and thoroughly than they would otherwise have done. The consuming interest of the British taxpayer in matters of taxation could not, of course, be capitalized on in requesting interviews, since any mention of taxation on the part of the interviewer before the appropriate time would have destroyed the important *tabula rasa* effect which he was at pains to preserve. The letter mentioned only the interest of the interview in the "economic position" of the professions in England, and a mimeographed explanatory statement that was presented to the prospective respondent at the same time as the letter was similarly careful, in describing the general nature of the project, to avoid anticipating or prejudicing his answers in any way.

The questionnaire, which was used in all interviews, was divided into several main parts. First, some simple questions were asked about the size of the firm, the number of staff employed, and the vital statistics of the respondent's own professional career. Next he was asked how long a vacation and how many extra "days off" he was accustomed to take each year, and how many hours he customarily worked in a week. Any changes he had made in this program in recent years were explored, and if the respondent had been in practice before the war his pre-war working schedule was compared. The main part of the interview then turned to a discussion of his reasons for doing as much or as little work as he was doing, specifically as they involved his decisions to accept or reject new work for the firm, to take on income-earning opportunities for himself outside the firm, and to promote the expansion of his practice. If the respondent was over 45 years of age, he was also questioned about any retirement plans he might have made. At each stage of the discussion he was encouraged to name the main factors that had led him to the decisions he had made.

Throughout the interview so far the influence of taxation on the respondent's incentives to work entered the discussion only if he introduced it himself. Leading questions were avoided until he had had full opportunity to express himself concerning his reasons for doing the amount of work he was doing. Those who had not mentioned taxation on their own initiative were then asked directly whether this had been a factor in any of their decisions to take on or refuse work; whatever positive reactions they then indicated were explored in as much detail as possible. Those who had already mentioned tax influences were also questioned further about them, earlier statements being clarified and the not infrequent inconsistencies probed.

A few more questions followed, about the size of the respondent's family and the number of his dependents. Finally, he was handed a card on which 14 income classes had been indicated, and he was asked to specify the one or ones in which his professional income before taxes and also his total taxable income fell. This request encountered surprisingly little resistance: of the 306 interviewed only six refused to give the top marginal tax rates to which they were subject and eight to disclose their professional earnings.

With one exception ("If more work had been offered to you last year, do you think that you would have taken it on?") the questions asked only for information about actual past behavior or definite plans for retirement, hypothetical situations not being posed or possible action explored for the reason that a high degree of reliability was desired. A few internal checks to test consistency and reliability were provided in the questionnaire and proved useful as guides in evaluating the evidence obtained. The assertion of one ebullient Irishman, for example, that he was subject to a tax disincentive appeared far less convincing when compared with his statement at another point in the interview that he was working 80 hours a week because he liked to work hard and build up a practice. Even with certain checks and with a maximum of simplicity maintained throughout the questionnaire, however, the evidence yielded by the 306 interviews was a complex of varied reactions open to considerable diversity of interpretation. Such is the raw stuff of the social sciences.

II. Tax Incentive and Disincentive Ratios

A. UNADJUSTED RATIOS

Slightly more than 40 per cent of the solicitors and accountants interviewed, or 128 in all, indicated that taxation had, or was going to have, some influence on their working lives. The most frequent response, given by more than half of those asked (see Table 67–1), was that taxation forced postponement of retirement by preventing a person from saving enough to provide for his future support. Short-term incentives, however, meaning day-to-day and week-to-week longer hours and harder work were indicated by only 6 per cent of the respondents. Disincentives, on the other hand, were distributed in reverse fashion. There were no retirement disincentives reported—that is, earlier retire-

TABLE 67-1 *Unadjusted Tax Incentive and Disincentive Ratios (Combined Samples)*

Type of Tax Effect	Proportion of Respondents Reporting Effect
1. Short-period tax disincentive	54/306 = .18
2. Short-period tax incentive	18/306 = .06
3. Incentive influence at retirement*	78/150 = .52
4. Total tax incentive	96/306 = .31
5. Some kind of tax influence†	128/306 = .42

*Only those over 45 years of age were asked about their retirement plans.

†As indicated by the relation between the numerators on the first three lines and that on the fifth line, 22 respondents reported more than one kind of tax influence.

ments as a result of high tax rates—whereas nearly one-fifth of the people interviewed cited taxation as a factor tending to decrease the amount of work they did on a short-term basis.

These ratios are, of course, only crude first approximations to the true influence of taxation on work incentives. Included in the 128 respondents (row 5 of Table 67–1) there are many who expected the tax influence mentioned to have an actual effect on their working habits only at some rather distant future date, some who themselves rated taxation as a possible though highly doubtful influence on their behavior, and some who had experienced tax influences on only one or two isolated and relatively unimportant occasions in the past. In the next four sections we shall first separate these people from those for whom taxation was a more important and definite factor and then reassess the influence of taxation in the light of these distinctions.

B. QUESTIONABLE TAX INFLUENCES

Least weight must be given to those cases for which the tax effect had not yet occurred and was expected to do so only at some rather distant time or under certain hypothetical conditions. Reactions such as these are not without significance, but there are too many contingencies to make them comparable to those that have already been experienced.

Many of the retirement incentives fall in this questionable category, since for them the date of the expected retirement was by no means imminent. Of the 78 respondents mentioning retirement postponement, 62 were under 61 years of age, and 50 of them were under 55. Their evidence is obviously rather tentative and must be considered to be of less consequence than that of 11 respondents who said that high taxation had already caused their retirement to be delayed, or of five others who said that they would have planned to retire in a year or so but for the demands of the Exchequer.

Three of the short-period incentive cases were of doubtful validity, their vagueness being summed up by one of their number when he said simply that "with more money as a result of tax reductions I might well take more leisure time." The "might well" school was liberally represented, too, in the disincentive category. Nine respondents who had not altered their work loads in any way in the past stated variously that they would very probably ease off somewhat in the future if taxes remained high. Three of them, all solicitors, were thinking of hiring additional staff to take over some of their work because the work was yielding them such a small financial return after taxes. None, however, was definite about when, if ever, he would carry out these plans. Two others said that unless taxes were reduced they would definitely limit their work when their incomes reached certain given levels, but for both the ceilings specified were substantially above their current earnings. The possibility that their aspirations would rise once the more opulent levels were reached and the accompanying satisfactions tasted was not probed. Five other disincentive cases offer similarly weak evidence. These respondents suggested that, on a few isolated occasions in the past when they had turned down work, taxation

TABLE 67-2 *Adjusted Tax Incentive and Disincentive Ratios (Combined Samples): Elimination of Cases Involving Highly Questionable Evidence*

Type of Tax Effect	Disincentive	Incentive
1. Reported, regardless of reliability (Table 67-1, lines 1 and 4)	54/306 = .18	96/306 = .31
Less:		
2. All cases involving highly questionable evidence	14	65
Equals:		
3. Definite tax influences	40/306 = .13	31/306 = .10

might have had some bearing on these decisions; at best, however, they felt that this had been only a minor factor, if one at all.

Table 67–2 gathers together these cases characterized by questionable evidence and eliminates them from the unadjusted incentive and disincentive ratios of Table 67–1. This leaves us with all those respondents whose incentives to work seem definitely to have been affected in some way by taxation. (As will be seen from line 3 disincentives now predominate slightly.) Even these ratios, however, must be subjected to further analysis before the real effects of taxes on the labor supplies of the respondents can be ascertained.

C. DEFINITE TAX DISINCENTIVES

Forty respondents declared definitely that they were under some disincentive pressure from taxation. Since these pressures made themselves felt in different ways and were by no means of equal force, our next step is to classify them according to their economic effect and then to evaluate them according to their strength and importance. Three patterns emerge.

The first type of effect was reported by 19 respondents who said that taxation had been a definite factor in their decisions to turn down work offered to them at various times in the past. The importance of the tax influence may be evaluated on the following grounds: (1) the extent to which the lessening of effort seemed to be a conscious, tax-induced policy on the part of the respondent, as judged by his mentioning it on his own initiative rather than advancing it only after the tax disincentive had been suggested by the interviewer; (2) the number of times in the recent past that the tax disincentive had been experienced; (3) the respondent's own estimate of the importance of the tax factor, that is, whether he himself rated taxation as the chief reason for declining the work, or as one among several equally important considerations, or as a distinctly secondary concern. The details of this analysis need not be given here, but the result is a ranking of the 19 respondents according to three different magnitudes, or orders of significance:

(a) Six respondents are of primary consequence here. All of them rated taxation as the crucial factor in their decisions to do less work, and they offered this evidence entirely on their own initiative. The tax effect had, moreover, occurred frequently enough in the past to warrant its being regarded as important from an economic point of view. All six faced marginal tax rates of 60 per cent or more, and two of them were at the 85 per cent level or above. One said that he turned down work frequently, one that he did it every day, and two others that they declined many outside opportunities of earning income as well as some legal cases (although they took on all work brought to them by established clients and any new clients recommended by them). A fifth had left a partnership and set up an independent firm of his own because he felt he had been working too hard as a partner in relation to his income net of taxes and was freer as a sole owner to cut down his work to his own requirements. The sixth, a sole proprietor 68 years old, had worked hard until 1951, earning a pretax income of between £6,000 and £7,000 a year, and as a result had injured his health, been under a doctor's care for two years, and upon returning to work had eased up considerably because the gain from sustainedly hard effort was not, after taxes, worth risking his health for a second time; his 1955 pretax income was a little less than £2,000.

(b) By contrast with the preceding group, three other respondents belong in the bottom significance bracket, since for them the tax issue was by no means paramount. One rated taxation as a definite but secondary factor in his relatively infrequent decisions to decline work (thereby raising the speculation that a small tax reduction would not affect his behavior at all, although a larger decrease might presumably induce him to do more work). The other two had turned down work on just one occasion apiece, partly because of taxation, partly because the work would have involved a good deal of travel, and (in view of these considerations) partly because the work was not for an established client.

(c) The remaining ten respondents form a somewhat diffuse middle group. Among them there is considerable variation as to the strength of the evidence and the importance of the tax effect, but it is doubtful that a finer classification would be very fruitful.

A second pattern is formed by a group of ten respondents on whom taxation exerted a different type of disincentive pressure. They took on all work that came their way, either for the firm or on the outside, but they were less active in seeking new business than they would have been under lower tax rates. Most significant here are three individuals who said that high tax rates had prompted them deliberately to curtail the promotional efforts (largely participation in social and professional activities) that normally serve to attract new clients. One of them summarized their general reaction as follows: "If taxes were lower I would display more energy in trying to increase business. One is not prepared to drive oneself really hard and perhaps endanger one's health under present tax rates." These three could give no estimate of the extent to which their efforts had been reduced or of the total effect on their practices, but they were conscious of the tax influence, as is shown by their promptness in mentioning it on their own initiative. Six others reported the same type of tax effect, but their evidence must be considered of less significance for our purposes since it came out only in response to the direct tax questions. The tenth respondent occupies the place of least importance in this pattern, since taxes were for him only one among several factors which at one time had led him to decide against expanding the scope of his practice. The fact that he was, even so, working more than 80 hours a week suggests that lower taxes would be unlikely to induce much increase in the supply of his professional services.

Pattern number three has to do with disincentives of a special type and contains only two significance classes. These disincentives took the form of shifting work loads within individual firms. Eleven respondents had, because of their own high tax rates, turned over work to partners or to staff hired for that purpose. The total volume of business handled by the firm was not reduced, therefore, but individual members were doing different amounts of it, the economic rewards being adjusted accordingly.

One interesting aspect of this type of tax effect is that the work re-allocation tended to circumvent several of the institutional rigidities noted in the professions studied, such as the moral obligation not to refuse a client's request for assistance, the professional pride in the firm, and the "expand or perish" maxim, which calls into serious question a firm's ability to maintain the level of work it wants if it acquires a reputation for turning clients away. By taking in new partners and expanding staff a firm is able to accept all work offered to it, and even increase its volume, at the same time that certain members (usually the higher-paid ones) who find their incentives sapped by taxation can take more leisure. In this way there is no risk of sacrificing valuable goodwill.

The fact that none of the 11 respondents subject to this kind of disincentive brought it up on his own, but only in answer to the direct tax questions, is not surprising, nor does it in this case make the evidence less convincing. The particular effect involved was not in the direct line of inquiry up to that point, since none of the preceding questions had given the respondents any opportunity to discuss the factors affecting decisions to take on more staff or additional partners. Since, then, the late appearance of the tax evidence does not necessarily imply low reliability, the 11 cases have been ranked entirely on the basis of the strength of the tax factor and the importance of the changes induced. Ten of the people involved cited taxation as the sole or most important cause of the work shift, and the magnitude of the effect was considerable in each case. Seven among them had been induced to hire additional staff, and all seven had a staff-partner ratio of five or greater, whereas less than one-half of those who reported no tax effect on the size of their staffs had such a high ratio. These ten therefore rate the top significance level, a lower ranking being given to the eleventh case, in which taxation was only one among several motivating factors.

TABLE 67-3   *Respondents Reporting a Definite Tax Disincentive Classified According to the Type of Disincentive and Its Economic Significance*

	Economic Significance Rating		
Type of Tax Disincentive	Greatest	Middle	Least
1. Refusal of work offered to the respondent	6	10	3
2. Reduced incentives to seek new clients	3	6	1
3. Shift of work load within the firm	10	1	0
4. All effects	19	17	4

Table 67–3 assembles the results of the preceding classifications and shows the 40 definite tax disincentives ranged according to the type of effect experienced and its economic significance.

D. DEFINITE TAX INCENTIVES

The 31 respondents reporting definite tax incentives may be classified in a similar way. Of the 17 who said that taxation was preventing them from retiring as soon as they would have liked, 15 belong to the first order of significance. These introduced the tax influence on their own, cited it as the chief reason for their delayed retirement, and were either close to or past the age at which they would have preferred to retire. The other two respondents in this category gave both taxation and a strong interest in their work as reasons for delaying their retirement, and hence have been allocated to the middle-significance level.

The remaining 14 incentive cases felt themselves forced by taxation to work harder on a day-to-day basis than they would have if they had been able to retain more of their earnings. These incentives took a variety of forms. Six said that high taxes kept them from hiring as large a staff as they otherwise would have maintained, with the result that they had to do more work themselves. Typical here is the following comment, made by one of the group: "I am doing work that I am not trained to do, because of taxation. I cannot afford to hire the help needed to do the work for me." One man was able to give a prewar comparison; he was definitely working harder than he had before the war because he could no longer afford such a large staff and now had to do many menial jobs formerly done by them. The problem of how much this situation was due to taxation and how much to higher wage rates for staff complicates the picture, but comparisons with the staff-partner ratios of the firms of respondents who reported no tax effect tend to substantiate the assurances of the six that taxes were the main reason for their staff cuts. Five of them (that is, 83 per cent) had fewer than five staff members for each partner in the firm; among respondents reporting no tax effect on the size of their staffs, only 52 per cent had a staff-partner ratio of less than five.

The other eight in this short-period incentive group were simply taking on all the work they could handle, sacrificing the leisure that they would have taken with less pressure from taxation. Seven of them stated that they would definitely take on more work if it were offered to them; the eighth said that he couldn't because he was already greatly overworked.

All 14 were unequivocal that taxes were the goad, although this was not typically brought out until the tax questions were asked. In deciding whether the late appearance of this evidence reduces its validity it is important to take into consideration a psychological phenomenon which the survey clearly bore out—the propensity of the average person, although quite aware of the disincentive potentialities of taxation, to overlook its possible incentive effects. This fact, combined with the respondents' inability in most cases to estimate the extent of the incentive influence to which they were subject, makes it very difficult to draw an exact comparison between the incentive cases and the disincentive ones; the same criteria do not apply in equal measure. The significance classification for row 2 of Table 67–4 has been based primarily on the cer-

TABLE 67-4 *Respondents Reporting a Definite Tax Incentive Classified According to the Type of Incentive and Its Economic Significance*

Type of Tax Incentive	Economic Significance Rating		
	Greatest	Middle	Least
1. Postponed retirement	15	2	0
2. More work on a day-to-day basis	8	5	1
3. All types	23	7	1

tainty of the respondent that taxation was the main factor leading him to work as hard as he was working and on the warmth of his desire to expand the size of his practice (as indicated by the answer he gave to a question asked early in the interview, before the direct tax questions).

E. ADJUSTED TAX INCENTIVE
AND DISINCENTIVE RATIOS AND THEIR INTERPRETATION

Weighted according to the reliability, frequency, and importance of the tax effect, our evidence is reassembled and presented in its most highly refined form in Table 67–5. On the first line the ratios are given for the incentive and disincentive groups to which only the greatest significance is attached; on each subsequent line one group of progressively less significance is added in, until on the fourth line all the tax effects that were reported, regardless of certainty, are included.

One's final estimate of the extent to which the work incentives of the 306 solicitors and accountants interviewed during the course of this survey were affected by the income tax depends upon the strictness with which he interprets their evidence. The most conservative evaluation would include only line 1 of

TABLE 67-5   *Adjusted Tax Incentive and Disincentive Ratios*
(Combined samples)

Significance Rating	Disincentives	Incentives
1. Greatest	19/306 = .06	23/306 = .08
2. Greatest/Middle	36/306 = .12	30/306 = .10
3. Greatest/Middle/Least		
(All definite tax effects)	40/306 = .13	31/306 = .10
4. All tax effects, definite/questionable	54/306 = .18	96/306 = .31

Sources: Line 1. First column of Tables 67-3 and 67-4.
Line 2. Sum of first two columns of Tables 67-3 and 67-4.
Line 3. Sum of all columns of Tables 67-3 and 67-4. Also Line 3, Table 67-2.
Line 4. Line 1, Table 67-2.

Table 67–5 and allow that less than 15 per cent of the sample were to an important extent impelled to increase or decrease their labor supplies, the incentives prevailing slightly over the disincentives. A less narrow estimate, on the other hand, or one that could be called a moderately conservative view, would hold that just over 20 per cent of the entire group were adjusting their working lives to the pressures of taxation, with a little more than half of them cutting down on work and a few less than half working harder. If our standards of judgment are relaxed so as to include all those who indicated even the rather distant future likelihood of some tax influence, we find nearly 20 per cent reporting an impairment of incentives due to taxation and over 30 per cent evidencing the opposite effect.

A number of the tax effects shown in Table 67–5 are not simple, unidirectional effects and illustrate further the complexity involved in interpreting the evidence. The 71 definite tax effects shown in line 3 of Table 67–5 were in fact reported by only 66 individuals, since five of the respondents gave evidence of both an incentive and a disincentive influence from taxes. All five had reacted to high post-war taxation by working less hard on a day-to-day basis and then later had found it necessary to postpone their retirement because taxes had made it impossible for them to put aside sufficient savings. They were, in effect, averaging their incomes over a longer working lifetime. As might be expected, none of them was able to say whether the net effect was in the incentive or the disincentive direction, and the further question remains as to whether, for each individual, the services withdrawn were of the same quality as those added to the total labor supply. Some, because of increased knowledge and skill, would be able to render better services in their more advanced years than they would have under lower taxes earlier in their working lives; others would undoubtedly have been more vigorous and effective in the earlier stages of their careers.

Even if the figures shown in Table 67–5 were simpler and easier to interpret, however, the net effect of income taxation would not be shown by a straight subtraction of the incentive and disincentive percentages. At best only a rough estimate of the magnitude of the tax influence could be made in each case, and many of the respondents reporting an incentive effect could be no more specific than to state merely that they were working harder because of taxation. Even if it could be demonstrated that the work hours sacrificed by the 6 per cent who were subject to a definite and important tax disincentive were exactly made up by the 8 per cent who felt a significant tax incentive, it cannot be assumed that services of equal quality would be obtained in the exchange. The only evidence that could be obtained relevant to this point indicates that the services withdrawn because of taxation might well be of a higher average quality than the additional services offered by those forced to work harder. This would suggest that there might be some net disincentive effect from taxation on the accountants and solicitors interviewed. The fact that neither the qualitative nor the quantitative dimension of the problem can be measured with any precision, however, means that this conclusion, like any estimate of the magnitude of the net effect, is almost purely speculative. It can be stated with considerable certainty, nonetheless, that this net effect, be it disincentive or incentive, is not large enough to be of great economic or sociological significance.

68

The Housemaid—An Occupational Role in Crisis

VILHELM AUBERT

This chapter is an incidental product of a survey of the impact of labor legislation upon the working conditions of housemaids in Oslo.[1] It is intended as a contribution to the sociology of occupations. Its main thesis is this: The occupational relationship and the role expectations between a family and its domestic servants were patterned throughout a long tradition in a society with a preponderance of *Gemeinschaft*-characteristics. In Sir Henry Maine's terms, it was for a very long time a status-relationship and not one based upon contract. The *Gesellschaft*-characteristics that today dominate in most other occupations of industrial society have not left the same marks on this time-honored relationship. But neither do present conditions permit a continuation of a rela-

From *Acta Sociologica*, I (1955–1956), 149–158. Reprinted by permission of the publisher.

tionship on a genuine *Gemeinschaft*-basis. While the role of the housemaid is wavering between these two occupational models, its incumbents are escaping from the field as statistics show beyond any doubt. Attempts to restore the balance in the relationship through legislation has not been very successful in reversing this trend.

The significance of our problem is twofold. It is based upon the assumption that the employer and employee are not "free" to arrange their relationship in any way they want. There is certainly room for great variation, and the personalities of the parties have a determining influence on the success and satisfaction in the relationship, probably more so than in most occupational relationships. But the arrangements made have repercussions and premises that go way beyond the factors controlled by the housemaid and her employer. They are both caught in the web of role-expectations that are traditionally given or imposed by present economic and material conditions, legislation, etc. These expectations may be more or less psychologically compatible seen from the individual's point of view. Our main thesis implies that the psychological compatibility is doubtful in the case of the modern housemaid. Certain elements in her role encourage her to wish for avenues of satisfaction that other elements in her role deny her. Although a psychological problem, it can probably not be satisfactorily solved without modifications on the social level. That is one reason why a "structural" sociological analysis seems called for.

On the other hand, an analysis of a microcosmic social system like that of employer-housemaid has general sociological implications. It follows from the above that the concrete arrangements and conflicts to be observed in this microcosmos mirror far-reaching structural features of society at large. Without any claims to representativeness, we nevertheless felt during the analysis of the housemaid's role that we were studying something more general. To put this problem in its most abstract form we have felt that we were in touch with the general way in which our existing social institutions deal with the task of keeping some kind of a motivational balance between "work" and "private life."

First of all this task consists in securing some motivation both for "work" and "living." That is not so hard. But how does "society" solve the problem of encouraging people to invest in work that kind of motivation that can be satisfied in work and to invest in private life that kind of motivation that can best be satisfied in private life? The concrete solution of this problem in each individual is very much a question of personality. But not altogether. The individual is guided by the clues given, that is, by the occupational culture. These clues, both as they appear from the outside to the new recruit and as they appear from the inside of the role to the veteran, may, by their consistency or inconsistency, encourage realistic or unrealistic attachments of needs to environmental situations.

A few examples of culturally determined displacement of motivation might clarify the nature of the problem. Around the occupational role of the seaman have risen a number of myths that must be assumed to play their part in the recruitment to the occupation. Among these myths are several that are heavily loaded with "private" motives. A sailor has a girl in every harbor, it is often said. No doubt this aspect of the role as seen from the outside gets attached to the need for sexual and intimate contact in the motivation of quite a few novices who go to sea. There is good reason to believe that this motivation in most cases is tragically misplaced. The occupational culture induces a disturbance in the motivational balance between work and private life. A parallel disturbance, which has to do with certain expectations to a family role, a role in private life, can be found among housewives. Many housewives, deprived of any opportunity to seek work outside their homes, develop a certain professional attitude toward their housework. That is to say, they attribute autonomous value to objective standards of performance in cleaning, cooking, and mending, irrespective of the emotional implications in their relationships to husband and children. No doubt, many elements in the role of the housewife and current expectations encourage her to pursue a kind of professional ambition within this role. At the same time the role makes demands upon her which conflict with a professional attitude. This conflict indicates a disturbance in the motivational balance between work and private life.

Against the general background outlined above, it will probably be seen that a study of the role of the housemaid, with its marginal character, may offer new insights into problems of general significance. As tools of analysis I shall use in a liberal way some of the concepts developed by Talcott Parsons in his scheme of "pattern variables." [2] In this scheme the value-orientations characterized as affectivity, diffuseness, particularism, and ascription seem to have an affinity to private life. Work seems in our society to be more connected with affective neutrality, functional specificity, universalism, and achievement.

The modern housemaid is a species of the genus "servant." To trace the historical development of the specific occupational role of the housemaid it will be useful to throw a glance at the position of servants in general in Norwegian society from the Middle Ages until this century. Few occupations have a longer tradition, and in few do more traditional patterns survive. A historical approach to this occupational role would therefore of necessity be misleading.

The role of the free servant displaced the role of the serf when serfdom was abolished toward the end of the twelfth century. Since then, the legislative authorities have been constantly occupied by the problem of how to secure an adequate supply of servants and agricultural workers. A general prescription was issued in 1291 making it a legal duty for all able-bodied men and women, under threat of penalties, to seek employment in the service of others. This duty is clearly reaffirmed in the law of Christian V of 1687. It states that servants who leave their service, together with vagrants, are to be caught and sentenced to forced labor for as long a period as they have shirked the job. A prescription from 1754 made it a duty for all unmarried sons and daughters of farmers, who didn't themselves run a farm (as owner or tenant), to seek employment for the duration of at least one year. This prescription remained in force until 1854. Parallel to these prescriptions ran statutory determination of the days of notice twice a year, the so-called hiring days.

These various legal enactments show very clearly that the occupational role of the servant was largely based upon an ascribed status. It was not, even in principle, a matter of achievement and free choice to become a servant. "Servant" was more or less a born characteristic of the person. In this respect the role of servant was more closely related to some of the family roles than to modern occupational roles. This kinship with family roles is clearly acknowledged in Blackstone's *Commentaries,* where he makes this illuminating statement: "The three great relations in private life are . . . of master and servant . . . husband and wife . . . parent and child." [3] In Norwegian jurisprudence from the middle of the nineteenth century, the legal status of servants is treated as part of the Law of Parsons.[4] To be a servant was a lasting quality ascribed to a person irrespective of his free choice. His relationship to the master was, as already mentioned, one based predominantly upon status and not upon contract.[5]

The kinship between the occupational role of the servant and the family roles is not, however, limited to the pattern variable achievement-ascription. It is also evident in relation to the patterns of universalism and particularism. Modern occupational roles of the service kind, such as doctor, lawyer,[6] dance-musician,[7] are based upon criteria of performance that are relatively independent of the recipient of the service. The incumbent's duties are not to any great extent dependent upon the particular relationship to this or that client. Not so with the role of the servant in nineteenth-century Norway or earlier. The strong particularistic element is brought out in the treatment of a leading legal authority of the servant's duty to obey the master.[8] Only under two conditions may the servant decline to obey an order. To define the duties negatively in this way is in itself the clearest indication that we deal with a particularistic relationship. There are no set objective standards of performance in which the servant can legitimately refuse to obey unreasonable orders. The two exceptions to the rule of unconditional obedience bring this out even more clearly. A master cannot prevent his servant from performing legal duties to the state, such as doing military service, and a servant may refuse to obey an order to do something that is obviously unlawful. That the legality is doubtful is not sufficient ground for refusal. A servant cannot demand permission to exercise his rights as a citizen, such as by casting his vote, if it collides with his duties as a servant. The master had, until 1891, a legal right to punish his servants just as he could punish his children. The particularistic element in the master-servant relationship is very one-sidedly expressed in the legislation. There is reason to believe, however, that the good servant had a moral, if not legal, right to expect a particularistic attachment on the part of his master, too.

The nature of the domestic servant's work was functionally diffuse. This was partly contingent upon the nature of the task itself. Neither in terms of time limitations nor with regard to qualitative differentiation is it easy to limit the duties along lines of functional specificity. This was particularly true in relatively small households without specialized cooks, chambermaids, or the like. Practically unlimited duty to obey the Master was in itself also an indication that the relationship would be functionally diffuse.

One implication of the preceding analysis is that the servant was exposed to a constant threat of invasion of his or her "private life." The role arrangements made no solid safeguards against complete domination of the servant's private life by his or her occupational role. First of all, the ascription pattern made it impossible, not only economically difficult, to keep out of the occupation even if it clashed with the most important "private needs." Once in the role, the particularistic pattern made it impossible to legitimate a defense of the private sphere by the claim that the job is done according to generally accepted objective standards of occupational performance. The diffuseness of the role had similar repercussions. Under such conditions the basic question is not to secure a motivational balance between work and private life. The two are not sufficiently differentiated for that. Rather, the problem is how the occupational situation in itself may, if necessary, give satisfaction to needs that belong to the private sphere, since "private life" is something that does not exist for everyone.

The saving grace in such an occupational situation must be sought in a certain emotional security and opportunity for affective expression. From literary and biographical evidence we know that servants were often "members of the family" in this sense. Particularly the relationship to the children offered avenues of immediate emotional gratification; avenues that in certain periods in certain strata were less open to the parents themselves. Whether the patterns of affectivity also comprised security valves for release of aggressive emotions is more doubtful. The nature of the affective element in the role is poignantly expressed in the following quotation from a book, *For Housemaids,* from the middle of the nineteenth century. It was widely read and we can interpret this "Bible of the housemaids" as an authoritative expression of the ethos of this occupational role in the nineteenth century. The quotation weaves together the patterns of ascription, particularism, diffuseness, and affectivity in a convincing total picture.

The master and mistress must, if they want to obey the word of the Lord, look out for their servants' welfare, care for them in case of sickness and other accidents, warn them when they see them on off-paths, and on the whole show an affectionate disposition toward them and set a good example, and not load them with more work than their strength permits them to carry.

The housemaids must obey their master and mistress both for their own and for the sake of the Lord, who commands servants to love and to obey their masters and mistresses. They (the housemaids) should in all things look for what is best for their masters, and must have a loving and pliable disposition toward them like a good and obedient child has toward strict but honorable parents.

You ought never to sulk if unexpected or unpleasant business turns up, and this may infringe a little on your spare time. A good mistress knows how to make up for this on another occasion and she does it so much the more when you serve her without hesitancy in busy moments.

Your position in life implies much exertion and self-denial. But you ought not to be dissatisfied therewith because you can rest assured that the Lord has put every one of us in the position best suited for trying us and leading us to His Kingdom.[9]

What prevented the role of the housemaid from becoming part of the social system of an individual family in spite of its close affinity to family roles was the status differential. The role of the servant is essentially a feudal role, developed during a period of rigid social stratification, a *Ständer*-society. Characteristic of such a society is the possibility of close physical, even emotional proximity, without minimization of status differentials. Not only the status of the servant was ascribed, but also that of the master and his family. They belonged normally by birth to the "conditioned" class of the privileged landowners, the class that set the pattern for the housemaid role. Nothing that the housemaid could observe through her intimate contact with the family was highly relevant to its social status. Human frailties, ignorance, laziness, even poverty were irrelevant from the point of view of status, although they might be important in other respects. This ascriptive status pattern is brought out in the Norwegian novelist, Trygve Andersen's book *I kansellirådens dager*. It describes the relationship between the state officials and other members of the "conditioned" class on the one hand, and the farmers on the other about the year 1800 in Hedemarken. Among other sociological characteristics of this interesting period in our history, it communicates some very perceptive insights into the relationship between servants and their masters. In some ways it was a close relationship and it certainly gave the servants ample opportunity to observe the human frailties, alcoholism, dishonesty, laziness, etc., among some of their unhappy and culturally isolated masters. This did not, however, change the status of the master. However close the relationship, the status difference and the concomitant element of distance remained unaltered. This particular status system, still heavily dominated by ascription patterns, made it possible to keep the housemaid in a role dominated by the ethos of the family role and yet not running any risk of assimilating her into the social system of any one family. Concrete evidence of this might sometimes be difficult to trace when the household was functioning as a group. But as soon as the household ceased functioning and went into a latency phase, the evidence would be striking. The family members would move into social groupings that tended to reaffirm the values, interests, and "culture" they had in common with the other members of their family. The servants, however, would move into social interaction within their social stratum, being constantly reminded of the gap between their "culture" and that of their master.

From the preceding analysis it can be surmised that the role of the housemaid entered into a state of very precarious balance when status criteria were increasingly perceived in achievement terms, of the individual's toil, ability, and performance. We can read the uneasiness of the situation out of the various abortive attempts around the turn of the century to restore balance through legislation. The housewives' organization suggested legislation and made recommendations that, on a very minor scale, would introduce a contractual pattern resembling other occupational roles.

In the official publications from around 1900 we can perceive an interest in introducing achievement, universalism, and functional specificity as patterns governing the housemaid's role. Achievement patterns were expressed in the emphasis upon the freedom of contract, functional specificity in the limitation of work hours and time off, universalism in the emphasis upon education, and objective standards of performance. Paradoxically the strong emphasis upon that particular pattern of achievement that is called "freedom of contract" prevented the legislators from furthering the goals of universalism and functional specificity. Under the impact of other occupational models and the scarcity of supply of housemaids, these patterns became nevertheless more prevalent from 1900 onward, and were given legal sanction in 1948 and even more explicit recognition in the preamble of the law.

Today the role of the housemaid is in acute crisis. Between 1930 and 1952 the statistics show a decline in the number of housemaids from 115,000 to 49,000 for all of Norway. In Oslo the decline seems to have been even sharper. The same trend is apparent in the increasing average age of the housemaids. Between 1938 and 1950 it seems to have increased by close to ten years. According to certain statistics from 1938, 76 per cent of the housemaids were under 30 years old. In our investigation, which is not strictly comparable, only 45 per cent were under 30. Another symptom of the precarious position of this occupational role became apparent in this survey, which was conducted with a representative sample of housewives and housemaids in Oslo. Questioned whether there was any other kind of job they would rather have, 61 per cent answered yes, and 50 per cent even mentioned a specific job which they would prefer to their present one. We might also mention as a similar symptom that only 1 per cent of our samples were organized in the housemaids' union, which is generally known to have very weak support.

As mentioned already, the new law on working conditions for housemaids attempts to narrow the gap between this occupational role and the more "advanced" ones (in industry). The survey did, however, reveal that realities are lagging behind the legislative attempts. In spite of the law and the general economic and social development, the working conditions of many housemaids have preserved many important traits from the old *Gemeinschaft*-pattern. Others have gone quite far in approaching the work-models from industry, with important modifications. We shall attempt to analyze some aspects of this empirical material in terms of the pattern variables already applied to the historical material from the study.

Recruitment to the housemaid role is no longer a matter of ascription as it was according to the old prescriptions. It is a matter of "free choice" to become a domestic servant. The legislators also debated how to secure a new kind of recruitment and selection through formal education in domestic work. There was a general agreement that it would be highly desirable to have more education for housemaids, but also that this problem could not be solved by this law. In our sample of housemaids only 17 per cent had attended school in domestic work. If we go beyond the question of how these occupational roles are filled we must say that the enactment of a law regulating domestic work has introduced a new element of ascription. Given that a certain work-relationship is established, certain rights and duties for the parties involved flow from the law irrespective of the choice, agreements, or achievements of these. This contrasts with the period immediately preceding the law. As Karl Renner put it in his general analysis of employer-employee relations: ". . . the labor relationship has now developed into a 'position,' just as property has developed into public utility. If a person occupies a 'position,' this means that his rights and duties are closely circumscribed, and the position has become a legal institution in character much like the fee of feudal times." [10] In this respect, however, the housemaid's role is no different from other labor roles, except in the frequency of deviations from this pattern of legal ascription. There is in our material ample evidence on the widespread ignorance of the law and the rights and duties established by the law. Hardly more than 10–15 per cent of all the surveyed work-relationships are in full conformity with the law.

We have also evidence of an ascriptive element in the housemaid role from a different and negative point of view. The law has attempted to institute more formalized contracts in the area of domestic work. According to Section 2 in the law, both parties have a right to demand a written contract. Forty-one per cent of the housemaids claim, however, that they do not have any contract at all. Barely 3 per cent of the work-relationships surveyed are based upon a written contract. Nevertheless, 82 per cent of the housemaids and 70 per cent of the housewives believe that the parties are free to arrange their relationship the way they want.

The minimum rights of the housemaids are defined in the new law in universalistic terms. That is, irrespective of their particular relationships there are certain demands they can make according to objective, universally applicable criteria. As already mentioned, we find frequent, and sometimes gross, deviations from these universalistic norms. In cases where the deviations are striking, we are also least likely to find a contractual agreement that might set up an alternative norm. What then determines the rights of the housemaids in such cases? It is difficult to escape the conclusion that the parties are strongly oriented toward the peculiarities of their particular relationship. Whether this particularism should be viewed as institutionalized or just as deviations from a universalistic norm is debatable.

The question of functional specificity is vital in any analysis of occupational roles. As we have pointed out before, the role of the servant has traditionally been defined as diffuse in its orientation. This involved both the dimensions of time and space and dimension of work content. Even today we find that 92 per cent of the housemaids in Oslo live with the family in which they are employed.[11] Their place of work is not separated on the basis of function from their own homes. This is, no doubt, a sociological fact with considerable psychological importance, tying the occupation to old work models.

How pressing this problem of diffuseness along the space-dimension has been is borne out by Section 5 of the law. It states that the housemaid should have her own bed, that it should be possible for her to lock her room, and that she cannot be ordered to sleep in the same room as the children. This is obviously intended as a defense against symbiosis between work and private life as far as space is concerned.

The major aim of the present legislation has been to introduce functional specificity along the dimension of time. The housemaid has a right to demand a limitation of her working hours that will give her an opportunity to spend some of her own time awake. In this area, however, we find frequent, and sometimes very marked deviations from the rules of the law. Ten per cent of the housemaids claim they work 12 hours a day or more, which is pretty much the same as saying that the working day has no specific limits. Nearly half of the relationships examined exhibited a break of the law that puts a 10 hour limit on housework. A sizeable group of employers violated the rules about free days or about limitation of overtime. It is, in other words, still difficult for many housemaids to protect their private life by referring to universalistic standards concerning the nature of the work. Although such universalistic standards are to be found in the law, they are still insufficiently institutionalized or internalized in the actual interaction between housewives and housemaids.

The results of our study indicate that there is a move in the direction of more universalism and more of our study indicates that there is a move in the direction of more universalism and more specificity also on the level of internalized norms for interpersonal behavior. The younger housemaids and the younger housewives show more conformity with legal norms than do the older ones. In one respect, however, this trend toward "occupationalization" will probably not emerge for a long time to come. The housemaid who wants to avoid emotional conflicts has to do the job the way her particular mistress wants her to do it, irrespective of which one of the two is better from an occupational point of view. Under present conditions, the problem is hard to settle. Its ultimate settlement may depend upon the future solution of another problem: How far should one go toward making the *housewife's* role an occupational role? This involves very intricate emotional problems.

In a nutshell, the situation of the housemaid seems to be this: she will in many cases find it difficult or impossible to evaluate her own work in terms of recognizable objective standards of performance. Although the work may have other satisfying features, she often lacks this essential source of self-esteem. Concomitant with this comes her lack of informal emotional contact with colleagues at the place of work. She cannot satisfy her craving for companionship in this way and she does not have a role in a work group as a possible substitute for direct work satisfaction.

At the same time as the housemaid is bound to be frustrated by these aspects of her work situation, she is constantly encouraged by the peculiarities of this situation to invest some of her "private" emotions in the family with which she works. Both the content of her work, the proximity of her employer, and the uncertain boundaries (in many cases) between work hours and time off operate in this direction. Since there are obvious dangers for the housemaid in getting too emotionally involved with the family, she may solve her problem by creating internal barriers against such involvement.

NOTES

1. V. Aubert, T. Eckhoff, and K. Sveri, *"En lov i sokelyset"* ("A Law in the Searchlight"), *Akademisk Forlag,* Oslo, 1952.
2. *The Social System* (Glencoe, Ill.: Free Press, 1951), pp. 58 ff.
3. William Blackstone, *Commentaries of the Laws of England* (1st ed. 1765), I, 422. (Here quoted from 15th ed., London, 1809.)
4. P. J. Collett, *Foreloesninger over Personretten* (Christiania, 1865), I, 331 ff.
5. Sir Henry Sumner Maine, *Ancient Law* (London, 1861).
6. Parsons, *supra,* pp. 428 ff.
7. Howard S. Becker, "The Professional Dance Musician and His Audience," *American Journal of Sociology,* LVII (1951–1952), 136 ff.
8. Collett, *l. c.,* pp. 337–338.
9. Hanna Winsnes, *For Tjenestepiger* (2d ed., Christiania, 1868).
10. Karl Renner, *The Institutions of Private Law and Their Social Functions* (London, 1949), p. 121.
11. Our sample excluded, in accordance with the law, the increasingly numerous groups of housemaids who work less than three days a week with one family and who do not live at their place of work. Actually, the development of this type of household may afford the best solution to many of the emotional problems inherent in the more traditional housemaid role.

69

Two Studies of Legal Stigma

RICHARD D. SCHWARTZ AND
JEROME H. SKOLNICK

Legal thinking has moved increasingly toward a sociologically meaningful view of the legal system. Sanctions, in particular, have come to be regarded in func-

From *Social Problems,* X, No. 2 (1962), 133–142, the journal of The Society for the Study of Social Problems. Reprinted by permission of the publisher.

tional terms.[1] In criminal law, for instance, sanctions are said to be designed to prevent recidivism by rehabilitating, restraining, or executing the offender. They are also said to be intended to deter others from the performance of similar acts and, sometimes, to provide a channel for the expression of retaliatory motives. In such civil actions as tort or contract, monetary awards may be intended as retributive and deterrent, as in the use of punitive damages, or may be regarded as a *quid pro quo* to compensate the plaintiff for his wrongful loss.

While these goals comprise an integral part of the rationale of law, little is known about the extent to which they are fulfilled in practice. Lawmen do not as a rule make such studies, because their traditions and techniques are not designed for a systematic examination of the operation of the legal system in action, especially outside the courtroom. Thus, when extra-legal consequences —such as the social stigma of a prison sentence—are taken into account at all, it is through the discretionary actions of police, prosecutor, judge, and jury. Systematic information on a variety of unanticipated outcomes, those that benefit the accused as well as those that hurt him, might help to inform these decision makers and perhaps lead to changes in substantive law as well. The present essay is an attempt to study the consequences of stigma associated with legal accusation.

From a sociological viewpoint, there are several types of indirect consequences of legal sanctions that can be distinguished. These include differential deterrence, effects on the sanctionee's associates, and variations in the degree of deprivation that sanction imposes on the recipient himself.

First, the imposition of sanction, while intended as a matter of overt policy to deter the public at large, probably will vary in its effectiveness as a deterrent, depending upon the extent to which potential offenders perceive themselves as similar to the sanctionee. Such "differential deterrence" would occur if white collar antitrust violators were restrained by the conviction of General Electric executives, but not by invocation of the Sherman Act against union leaders.

The imposition of a sanction may even provide an unintended incentive to violate the law. A study of factors affecting compliance with federal income tax laws provides some evidence of this effect. Some respondents reported that they began to cheat on their tax returns only *after* convictions for tax evasion had been obtained against others in their jurisdiction. They explained this surprising behavior by noting that the prosecutions had always been conducted against blatant violators and not against the kind of moderate offenders that they then became. These respondents were, therefore, unintentionally educated to the possibility of supposedly "safe" violations.

Second, deprivations or benefits may accrue to non-sanctioned individuals by virtue of the web of affiliations that join them to the defendant. The wife and family of a convicted man may, for instance, suffer from his arrest as much as the man himself. On the other hand, they may be relieved by his absence if the family relationship has been an unhappy one. Similarly, whole groups of persons may be affected by sanctions to an individual, as when discriminatory practices increase because of a highly publicized crime attributed to a member of a given minority group.

Finally, the social position of the defendant himself will serve to aggravate or alleviate the effects of any given sanction. Although all three indirect consequences may be interrelated, it is the third with which this *essay* will be primarily concerned.

Findings

The subjects studied to examine the effects of legal accusation on occupational positions represented two extremes: lower-class unskilled workers charged with assault, and medical doctors accused of malpractice. The first project lent itself to a field experiment, while the second required a survey design. Because of differences in method and substance, the studies cannot be used as formal controls for each other. Taken together, however, they do suggest that the indirect effects of sanctions can be powerful, that they can produce unintended harm or unexpected benefit, and that the results are related to officially unemphasized aspects of the social context in which the sanctions are administered. Accordingly, the two studies will be discussed together, as bearing on one another. Strictly speaking, however, each can, and properly should, stand alone as a separate examination of the unanticipated consequences of legal sanctions.

STUDY I. THE EFFECTS OF A CRIMINAL COURT RECORD ON THE
EMPLOYMENT OPPORTUNITIES OF UNSKILLED WORKERS

In the field experiment, four employment folders were prepared, the same in all respects except for the criminal court record of the applicant. In all of the folders he was described as a 32-year-old single male of unspecified race, with a high school training in mechanical trades, and a record of successive short-term jobs as a kitchen helper, maintenance worker, and handyman. These characteristics are roughly typical of applicants for unskilled hotel jobs in the Catskill resort area of New York State where employment opportunities were tested.[2]

The four folders differed only in the applicant's reported record of criminal court involvement. The first folder indicated that the applicant had been convicted and sentenced for assault; the second, that he had been tried for assault and acquitted; the third, also tried for assault and acquitted, but with a letter from the judge certifying the finding of not guilty and reaffirming the legal presumption of innocence. The fourth folder made no mention of any criminal record.

A sample of 100 employers was used. Each employer was assigned to one of four "treatment" groups.[3] To each employer only one folder was shown; this folder was one of the four kinds mentioned above, the selection of the folder being determined by the treatment group to which the potential employer was assigned. The employer was asked whether he could "use" the man described in the folder. To preserve the reality of the situation and make it a true field experiment, employers were never given any indication that they were participating in an experiment. So far as they knew, a legitimate offer to work was being made in each showing of the folder by the "employment agent."

The experiment was designed to determine what employers would do in fact if confronted with an employment applicant with a criminal record. The questionnaire approached used in earlier studies [4] seemed ill adapted to the problem, since respondents confronted with hypothetical situations might be particularly prone to answer in what they considered a socially acceptable manner. The second alternative—studying job opportunities of individuals who had been involved with the law—would have made it very difficult to find comparable groups of applicants and potential employers. For these reasons, the field experiment reported here was used.

Some deception was involved in the study. The "employment agent"—the same individual in all hundred cases—was in fact a law student who was working in the Catskills during the summer of 1959 as an insurance adjuster. In representing himself as being both an adjuster and an employment agent, he was assuming a combination of roles that is not uncommon there. The adjuster role gave him an opportunity to introduce a single application for employment casually and naturally. To the extent that the experiment worked, however, it was inevitable that some employers should be led to believe that they had immediate prospects of filling a job opening. In those instances where an offer to hire was made, the "agent" called a few hours later to say that the applicant had taken another job. The field experimenter attempted in such instances to locate a satisfactory replacement by calling an employment agency in the area. Because this procedure was used and since the jobs involved were of relatively minor consequence, we believe that the deception caused little economic harm.

As mentioned, each treatment group of 25 employers was approached with one type of folder. Responses were dichotomized: those who expressed a willingness to consider the applicant in any way were termed positive; those who made no response or who explicitly refused to consider the candidate were termed negative. Our results consist of comparisons between positive and negative responses, thus defined, for the treatment groups.

Of the 25 employers shown the "no record" folder, nine gave positive responses. Subject to reservations arising from chance variations in sampling, we take this as indicative of the "ceiling" of jobs available for this kind of applicant under the given field conditions. Positive responses by these employers may be compared with those in the other treatment groups to obtain an indication of job opportunities lost because of the various legal records.

Of the 25 employers approached with the "convict" folder, only one expressed interest in the applicant. This is a rather graphic indication of the effect which a criminal record may have on job opportunities. Care must be exercised, of course, in generalizing the conclusions to other settings. In this context, however, the criminal record made a major difference.

From a theoretical point of view, the finding leads toward the conclusion that conviction constitutes a powerful form of "status degradation" [5] that continues to operate after the time when, according to the generalized theory of justice underlying punishment in our society, the individual's "debt" has been paid. A record of conviction produces a durable if not permanent loss of status. For purposes of effective social control, this state of affairs may heighten the deterrent effect of conviction, though that remains to be established. Any such contribution to social control, however, must be balanced against the barriers imposed upon rehabilitation of the convict. If the ex-prisoner finds difficulty in securing menial kinds of legitimate work, further crime may become an increasingly attractive alternative.[6]

Another important finding of this study concerns the small number of positive responses elicited by the "accused but acquitted" applicant. Of the 25 employers approached with this folder, three offered jobs. Thus, the individual accused but acquitted of assault has almost as much trouble finding even an unskilled job as the one who was not only accused of the same offense, but also convicted.

From a theoretical point of view, this result indicates that permanent lowering of status is not limited to those explicitly singled out by being convicted of a crime. As an ideal outcome of American justice, criminal procedure is supposed to distinguish between the "guilty" and those who have been acquitted. Legally controlled consequences that follow the judgment are consistent with this purpose. Thus, the "guilty" are subject to fine and imprisonment, while those who are acquitted are immune from these sanctions. But deprivations may be imposed on the acquitted, both before and after victory in court. Before trial, legal rules either permit or require arrest and detention. The suspect may be faced with the expense of an attorney and a bail bond if he is to mitigate these limitations on his privacy and freedom. In addition, some pre-trial deprivations are imposed without formal legal permission. These may include coercive questioning, use of violence, and stigmatization. And, as this study indicates, some deprivations not under the direct control of the legal process may develop or persist after an official decision of acquittal has been made.

Thus two legal principles conflict in practice. On the one hand, "a man is innocent until proven guilty." On the other, the accused is systematically treated as guilty under the administration of criminal law until a functionary or official body—police, magistrate, prosecuting attorney, or trial judge or jury —decides that he is entitled to be free. Even then, the results of treating him as guilty persist and may lead to serious consequences.

The conflict could be eased by measures aimed at reducing the deprivations imposed on the accused, before and after acquittal. Some legal attention has been focused on pre-trial deprivations. The provision of bail and counsel, the availability of *habeas corpus,* limitations on the admissibility of coerced confessions, and civil actions for false arrest are examples of measures aimed at protecting the rights of the accused before trial. Although these are often limited in effectiveness, especially for individuals of lower socio-economic status, they at least represent some concern with implementing the presumption of innocence at the pre-trial stage.

By contrast, the courts have done little toward alleviating the post-acquittal consequences of legal accusation. One effort along these lines has been employed in the federal courts, however. Where an individual has been accused and exonerated of a crime, he may petition the federal courts for a "Certificate of Innocence" certifying this fact.[7] Possession of such a document might be expected to alleviate post-acquittal deprivations.

Some indication of the effectiveness of such a measure is found in the responses of the final treatment group. Their folder, it will be recalled, contained information on the accusation and acquittal of the applicant, but also included a letter from a judge addressed "To whom it may concern" certifying the applicant's acquittal and reminding the reader of the presumption of innocence. Such a letter might have had a boomerang effect, by re-emphasizing the legal involvement of the applicant. It was important, therefore, to determine empirically whether such a communication would improve or harm the chances of employment. Our findings indicate that it increased employment opportunities, since the letter folder elicited six positive responses. Even though this fell short of the nine responses to the "no record" folder, it doubled the number for the "accused but acquitted" and created a significantly greater number of job offers than those elicited by the convicted record. This suggests that the procedure merits consideration as a means of offsetting the occupational loss resulting from accusation. It should be noted, however, that repeated use of this device might reduce its effectiveness.

TABLE 69-1 *Effect of Four Types of Legal Folder on Job Opportunities (In Per Cent)*

	No Record	Acquitted with Letter	Acquitted Without Letter	Convicted	Total
	(N = 25)	(N = 25)	(N = 25)	(N = 25)	(N = 100)
Positve response	36	24	12	4	19
Negative response	64	76	88	96	81
Total	100	100	100	100	100

The results of the experiment are summarized in Table 69–1. The differences in outcome found there indicate that various types of legal records are systematically related to job opportunities. It seems fair to infer also that the trend of job losses corresponds with the apparent punitive intent of the authorities. Where the man is convicted, that intent is presumably greatest. It is less where he is accused but acquitted and still less where the court makes an effort to emphasize the absence of a finding of guilt. Nevertheless, where the difference in punitive intent is ideally greatest, between conviction and acquittal, the difference in occupational harm is very slight. A similar blurring of this distinction shows up in a different way in the next study.

STUDY II. THE EFFECTS ON DEFENDANTS OF SUITS
FOR MEDICAL MALPRACTICE

As indicated earlier, the second study differed from the first in a number of ways: method of research, social class of accused, relationship between the accused and his "employer," social support available to accused, type of offense and its possible relevance to occupational adequacy. Because the two studies differ in so many ways, the reader is again cautioned to avoid thinking of them as providing a rigorous comparative examination. They are presented together only to demonstrate that legal accusation can produce unanticipated deprivations, as in the case of Study I, or unanticipated benefits, as in the research now to be presented. In the discussion to follow, some of the possible reasons for the different outcomes will be suggested.

The extra-legal effects of a malpractice suit were studied by obtaining the records of Connecticut's leading carrier of malpractice insurance. According to these records, a total of 69 doctors in the State had been sued in 64 suits during the post World War II period covered by the study, September, 1945, to September, 1959.[8] Some suits were instituted against more than one doctor, and four physicians had been sued twice. Of the total of 69 physicians, 58 were questioned. Interviews were conducted with the approval of the Connecticut Medical Association by Robert Wyckoff, whose extraordinary qualifications for the work included possession of both the M.D. and LL.B. degrees. Dr. Wyckoff was able to secure detailed response to his inquiries from all doctors contacted.

Twenty of the respondents were questioned by personal interview, 28 by telephone, and the remainder by mail. Forty-three of those reached practiced principally in cities, 11 in suburbs, and four in rural areas. Seventeen were engaged in general practice and 41 were specialists. The sample proved comparable to the doctors in the State as a whole in age, experience, and professional qualifications.[9] The range was from the lowest professional stratum to chiefs of staff and services in the State's most highly regarded hospitals.

Of the 57 malpractice cases reported, doctors clearly won 38; 19 of these were dropped by the plaintiff and an equal number were won in court by the defendant doctor. Of the remaining 19 suits, 11 were settled out of court for a nominal amount, four for approximately the amount the plaintiff claimed and four resulted in judgment for the plaintiff in court.

The malpractice survey did not reveal widespread occupational harm to the physicians involved. Of the 58 respondents, 52 reported no negative effects of the suit on their practice, and five of the remaining six, all specialists, reported that their practice *improved* after the suit. The heaviest loser in court (a radiologist) reported the largest gain. He commented, "I guess all the doctors in town felt sorry for me because new patients started coming in from doctors who had not sent me patients previously." Only one doctor reported adverse consequences to his practice. A winner in court, this man suffered physical and emotional stress symptoms that hampered his later effectiveness in surgical work. The temporary drop in his practice appears to have been produced by neurotic symptoms and is therefore only indirectly traceable to the malpractice suit. Seventeen other doctors reported varying degrees of personal dissatisfaction and anxiety during and after the suit, but none of them reported impairment of practice. No significant relationship was found between outcome of the suit and expressed dissatisfaction.

A protective institutional environment helps to explain these results. No cases were found in which a doctor's hospital privileges were reduced following the suit. Neither was any physician unable later to obtain malpractice insurance, although a handful found it necessary to pay higher rates. The State Licensing Commission, which is headed by a doctor, did not intervene in any instance. Local medical societies generally investigated charges through their ethics and grievance committees, but where they took any action, it was almost always to recommend or assist in legal defense against the suit.

Discussion

Accusation has different outcomes for unskilled workers and doctors in the two studies. How may these be explained? First, they might be nothing more than artifacts of research method. In the field experiment, it was possible to see behavior directly and to determine how employers act when confronted with what appears to them to be a realistic opportunity to hire. Responses are therefore not distorted by the memory of the respondent. By contrast, the memory of the doctors might have been consciously or unconsciously shaped by the wish to create the impression that the public had not taken seriously the accusation leveled against them. The motive for such a distortion might be either to protect the respondent's self-esteem or to preserve an image of public acceptance in the eyes of the interviewer, the profession, and the public. Efforts of the interviewer to assure his subjects of anonymity—intended to offset these effects—may have succeeded or may, on the contrary, have accentuated an awareness of the danger. A related type of distortion might have stemmed from a desire by doctors to affect public attitudes toward malpractice. Two conflicting motives might have been expected to enter here. The doctor might have tended to exaggerate the harm caused by an accusation, especially if followed by acquittal, in order to turn public opinion toward legal policies that would limit malpractice liability. On the other hand, he might tend to underplay extra-legal harm caused by a legally insufficient accusation to discourage potential plaintiffs from instituting suits aimed at securing remunerative settlements or revenge for grievances. Whether these diverse motives operated to distort doctors' reports and, if so, which of them produced the greater degree of distortion is a matter for speculation. It is only suggested here that the interview method is more subject to certain types of distortion than the direct behavioral observations of the field experiment.

Even if such distortion did not occur, the results may be attributable to differences in research design. In the field experiment, a direct comparison is made between the occupational position of an accused and an identical individual not accused at a single point in time. In the medical study, effects were inferred through retrospective judgment, although checks on actual income would have no doubt confirmed these judgments. Granted that income had increased, many other explanations are available to account for it. An improvement in practice after a malpractice suit may have resulted from factors extraneous to the suit. The passage of time in the community and increased experience may have led to a larger practice and may even have masked negative effects of the suit. There may have been a general increase in practice for the kinds of doctors involved in these suits, even greater for doctors not sued than for doctors in the sample. Whether interviews with a control sample could have yielded sufficiently precise data to rule out these possibilities is problematic. Unfortunately, the resources available for the study did not enable such data to be obtained.

A third difference in the two designs may affect the results. In the field experiment, full information concerning the legal record is provided to all of the relevant decision makers: the employers. In the medical study, by contrast, the results depend on decisions of actual patients to consult a given doctor. It may be assumed that such decisions are often based on imperfect information, some patients knowing little or nothing about the malpractice suit. To ascertain how much information employers usually have concerning the legal record of the employee and then supply that amount would have been a desirable refinement, but a difficult one. The alternative approach would involve turning the medical study into an experiment in which full information concerning malpractice (for example, liable, accused but acquitted, no record of accusation) was supplied to potential patients. This would have permitted a comparison of the effects of legal accusation in two instances where information concerning the accusation is constant. To carry out such an experiment in a field situation would require an unlikely degree of cooperation, for instance by a medical clinic that might ask patients to choose their doctor on the basis of information given them. It is difficult to conceive of an experiment along these lines which would be both realistic enough to be valid and harmless enough to be ethical.

If we assume, however, that these methodological problems do not invalidate the basic finding, how may it be explained? Why would unskilled workers accused but acquitted of assault have great difficulty getting jobs, while doctors accused of malpractice—whether acquitted or not—are left unharmed or more sought after than before?

First, the charge of criminal assault carries with it the legal allegation and the popular connotation of intent to harm. Malpractice, on the other hand, implies negligence or failure to exercise reasonable care. Even though actual physical harm may be greater in malpractice, the element of intent suggests that the man accused of assault would be more likely to repeat his attempt and to find the mark. However, it is dubious that this fine distinction could be drawn by the lay public.

Perhaps more important, all doctors and particularly specialists may be immune from the effects of a malpractice suit because their services are in short supply.[10] By contrast, the unskilled worker is one of many and therefore likely to be passed over in favor of someone with a "cleaner" record.

Moreover, high occupational status, such as is demonstrably enjoyed by doctors,[11] probably tends to insulate the doctor from imputations of incompetence. In general, professionals are assumed to possess uniformly high ability, to be oriented toward community service, and to enforce adequate standards within their own organization.[12] Doctors in particular receive deference just because they are doctors, not only from the population as a whole but even from fellow professionals.[13]

Finally, individual doctors appear to be protected from the effects of accusation by the sympathetic and powerful support they receive from fellow members of the occupation, a factor absent in the case of unskilled, unorganized laborers.[14] The medical society provides advice on handling malpractice actions, for instance, and referrals by other doctors sometimes increase as a consequence of the sympathy felt for the malpractice suit victim. Such assistance is further evidence that the professional operates as "a community within a community," [15] shielding its members from controls exercised by formal authorities in the larger society.

In order to isolate these factors, additional studies are needed. It would be interesting to know, for instance, whether high occupational status would protect a doctor acquitted of a charge of assault. Information on this question is sparse. Actual instances of assaults by doctors are probably very rare. When and if they do occur, it seems unlikely that they would lead to publicity and prosecution, since police and prosecutor discretion might usually be employed to quash charges before they are publicized. In the rare instances in which they come to public attention, such accusations appear to produce a marked effect because of the assumption that the pressing of charges, despite the status of the defendant, indicates probable guilt. Nevertheless, instances may be found in which even the accusation of first degree murder followed by acquittal appears to have left the doctor professionally unscathed.[16] Similarly, as a test of the group protection hypothesis, one might investigate the effect of an acquittal for assault on working men who are union members. The analogy would be particularly instructive where the union plays an important part in employment decisions, for instance in industries that make use of a union hiring hall.

In the absence of studies that isolate the effect of such factors, our findings cannot readily be generalized. It is tempting to suggest after an initial look at the results that social class differences provide the explanation. But subsequent analysis and research might well reveal significant intra-class variations, depending on the distribution of other operative factors. A lower class person with a scarce specialty and a protective occupational group who is acquitted of a lightly regarded offense might benefit from the accusation. Nevertheless, class in general seems to correlate with the relevant factors to such an extent that in reality the law regularly works to the disadvantage of the already more disadvantaged classes.

Conclusion

Legal accusation imposes a variety of consequences, depending on the nature of the accusation and the characteristics of the accused. Deprivations occur, even though not officially intended, in the case of unskilled workers who have been acquitted of assault charges. On the other hand, malpractice actions—even when resulting in a judgment against the doctor—are not usually followed by negative consequences and sometimes have a favorable effect on the professional position of the defendant. These differences in outcome suggest two conclusions: one, the need for more explicit clarification of legal goals; two, the importance of examining the attitudes and social structure of the community outside the courtroom if the legal process is to hit intended targets, while avoiding innocent bystanders. Greater precision in communicating goals and in appraising consequences of present practices should help to make the legal process an increasingly equitable and effective instrument of social control.

NOTES

1. Legal sanctions are defined as changes in life conditions imposed through court action.
2. The generality of these results remains to be determined. The effects of criminal involvement in the Catskill area are probably diminished, however, by the temporary nature of employment, the generally poor qualifications of the work force, and the excess of demand over supply of unskilled labor there. Accordingly, the employment differences among the four treatment groups found in this study are likely, if anything, to be smaller than would be expected in industries and areas where workers are more carefully selected.
3. Employers were not approached in pre-selected random order, due to a misunderstanding of instructions on the part of the law student who carried out the experiment during a three-and-one-half week period. Because of this flaw in the experimental procedure, the results should be treated with appropriate caution. Thus, *chi*-squared analysis may not properly be utilized. (For those used to this measure, $P < .05$ for Table 69–1.)
4. Sol Rubin, *Crime and Juvenile Delinquency* (New York: Oceana, 1958), pp. 151–156.
5. Harold Garfinkel, "Conditions of Successful Degradation Ceremonies," *American Journal of Sociology*, LXI (March, 1956), 420–424.
6. Severe negative effects of conviction on employment opportunities have been noted by Rubin, *Crime and Juvenile Delinquency, op. cit.* A further source of employment difficulty is inherent in licensing statutes and security regulations that sometimes preclude convicts from being employed in their pre-conviction occupation or even in the trades that they may have acquired during imprisonment. These effects may,

however, be counteracted by bonding arrangements, prison associations, and publicity programs aimed at increasing confidence in, and sympathy for, ex-convicts. See also B. F. McSally, "Finding Jobs for Released Offenders," *Federal Probation,* XXIV (June, 1960), 12–17; Harold D. Lasswell and Richard C. Donnelly, "The Continuing Debate over Responsibility: An Introduction to Isolating the Condemnation Sanction," *Yale Law Journal,* LXVIII (April, 1959), 869–899; Johs Andeneas, "General Prevention—Illusion or Reality?" *Journal of Criminal Law,* XLIII (July–August, 1952), 176–198.

7. 28 United States Code, Secs. 1495, 2513.

8. A spot check of one county revealed that the Company's records covered every malpractice suit tried in the courts of that county during this period.

9. No relationship was found between any of these characteristics and the legal or extra-legal consequences of the lawsuit.

10. See Eliot Freidson, "Client Control and Medical Practice," *American Journal of Sociology,* LXV (January, 1960), 374–382. Freidson's point is that general practitioners are more subject to client control than specialists are. Our findings emphasize the importance of professional as compared to client control, and professional protection against a particular form of client control, extending through both branches of the medical profession. However, what holds for malpractice situations may not be true of routine medical practice.

11. National Opinion Research Center, "Jobs and Occupations: A Popular Evaluation," *Opinion News,* IX (September, 1947), 3–13. More recent studies in several countries tend to confirm the high status of the physician. See Alex Inkeles, "Industrial Man: The Relation of Status to Experience, Perception, and Value," *American Journal of Sociology,* LXVI (July, 1960), 1–31.

12. Talcott Parsons, *The Social System* (Glencoe, Ill.: Free Press, 1951), pp. 454–473; and Everett C. Hughes, *Men and Their Work* (Glencoe, Ill.: Free Press, 1958).

13. Alvin Zander, Arthur R. Cohen, and Ezra Stotland, *Role Relations in the Mental Health Professions* (Ann Arbor: Institute for Social Research, 1957).

14. Unions sometimes act to protect the seniority rights of members who, discharged from their jobs upon arrest, seek re-employment following their acquittal.

15. See William J. Goode, "Community Within A Community: The Professions," *American Sociological Review,* XXII (April, 1957), 194–200.

16. For instance, the acquittal of Dr. John Bodkin Adams after a sensational murder trial, in which he was accused of deliberately killing several elderly women patients to inherit their estates, was followed by his quiet return to medical practice. *New York Times,* November 24, 1961, p. 28. Whether the British regard acquittals as more exonerative than Americans is uncertain.

SECTION FOURTEEN *Opportunities and Limits of the Legal Process*

70

On the Nature and Limits of Adjudication: Collective Bargaining

LON L. FULLER

I believe there is open to us a relatively simple way of defining the procedural restraints to which the judicial role is subject. We can do this by looking at adjudication, not through the eyes of the judge, but through the eyes of the affected litigant. Adjudication we may define as a social process of decision that assures to the affected party a particular form of participation, that of presenting proofs and arguments for a decision in his favor.

Viewed in this light, adjudication is only one form of social decision in which the affected party is afforded an institutionally guaranteed participation. Elections grant to the affected party participation through voting; contracts grant to him participation through negotiation, either in person or through representatives. No procedure of decision guarantees any particular outcome and least of all an outcome favorable to any particular participant. But the essence of the rule of law lies in the fact that men affected by the decisions that emerge from social processes should have some formally guaranteed opportunity to affect those decisions.

Within this frame of thought we may say, then, that adjudication is a process of decision in which the affected party—"the litigant"—is afforded an institutionally guaranteed participation, which consists of the opportunity to present proofs and arguments for a decision in his favor. Whatever protects and enhances the effectiveness of that participation, advances the integrity of adjudication itself. Whatever impairs that participation detracts from its integrity. When that participation becomes a matter of grace, rather than of right, the process of decision ceases to deserve the name of adjudication.

From the analysis just presented can be derived, I believe, all of the restraints usually associated with an adjudicative role. Thus, interest or bias on the part of the adjudicator constitutes an obvious impairment of the interested party's participation through presenting proofs and arguments. So does the holding of private conferences, for the party not included in such a conference cannot know toward what he should be directing the presentation of his case. Matters are not squared when both parties are separately consulted, for then both are dependent on the candor and intelligence of the adjudicator in learn-

From "Collective Bargaining and the Arbitrator," *Wisconsin Law Review* (January, 1963), pp. 19–24, 30–34. Reprinted by permission of the publisher. Abridged with renumbered notes.

ing what the other side is saying, not to mention the more usual objections, such as the lack of an opportunity to cross-examine.

The test here suggested by no means coincides with popular prejudice concerning the judicial role. In this country there is a strong inclination to identify judicial behavior with passiveness, the judge being viewed as an umpire over a game in which he takes no active part until called upon by one of the parties to do so. The test here proposed renders a quite different judgment. If the arbiter of a dispute judges prematurely without hearing what both sides have to say, he obviously impairs the effectiveness of the parties' participation in the decision by proofs and arguments. On the other hand, that participation may be equally impaired if the parties are given no inkling at any time as to what is happening in the arbiter's mind. One cannot direct an effective argument into a vacuum. Accordingly it is the part of the wise arbitrator at some time, usually toward the end of the hearing, to convey to the parties some notion of the difficulties he finds in supporting or in answering certain of the arguments that have been addressed to him. He may find it useful also to summarize the arguments on each side, asking the parties to make corrections or additions so that he may be sure he fully grasps what each is contending for. Such discussions, initiated by the arbitrator himself, take him out of a purely passive role. It is plain, however, that they enhance meaningful participation by the parties in the decision and thus enhance the integrity of adjudication itself.

Perhaps the crassest infringement of adjudicative integrity consists in what has been called the "rigged award." In its most extreme form this means that although the affected parties think their case is being submitted to arbitrational decision, in fact their representatives have already agreed on the outcome to be incorporated in the award. It might seem that this procedure involves not so much an abuse of arbitration as a fraud by representatives on their constituents. But it should not be forgotten that the object of the whole manipulation is to secure the moral force of adjudication for what is in fact not adjudicated at all. The apparent participation of the affected party— through proofs and arguments presented on his behalf—is an empty sham. This problem of the "rigged," or more politely, the "informed" award deserves some analysis. Such an analysis will reveal that, while in some cases to clothe an agreement with the trappings of an award will constitute a plain abuse of adjudicative power, in other instances the appraisal is less obvious.

Let me take two extreme cases, beginning with an instance where the practice is presented in its most innocent form. Six grievances are scheduled for hearing over a three-day period. These grievances are all closely related, involving, let us say, a series of work-load or machine-assignment problems. Late on the third day the sixth case has still not been heard. If it is to be heard at all, a new hearing will have to be scheduled and this will be difficult. Though the arbitrator has as yet rendered no formal award in any of the cases heard, the drift of his mind has become apparent during the hearing of the first five cases, and the disposition of the sixth is not hard to predict. The parties' representatives agree on a solution of it and ask the arbitrator to incorporate their settlement in an award. If the first five cases were reported to the membership as settled by arbitration, while the sixth was reported as settled by agreement, quite unjustified suspicions and doubts would be aroused. Hence the arbitrator is willing to put the agreed settlement "in series," as it were, with its five companions. It would take a purist indeed to discern any real wickedness in this action.[1]

At the other extreme is the case where an arbitrator is paid handsomely to hold extended hearings, where a parade of witnesses is heard, where lawyers plead with heart-stirring eloquence, when all the while the whole thing has been rigged and fixed from the beginning and the whole hearing is a farce from start to finish. I agree with Willard Wirtz that even if awards rendered in cases like this always produced a short-run advantage judged from the standpoint of public welfare, the long-run cost would be too high to pay.[2] Such an arbitrational practice is essentially parasitic. It takes advantage of the fact that most awards are honest, for if all awards were known to be fixed there would be no point in masquerading an agreement as the decision of an arbitrator. One recalls here the remark of Schopenhauer, that the prostitute owes her bargaining power to the restraint of virtuous women.

It should be observed that in cases like that just suggested, the "fixed" award may involve a by-passing of procedural guarantees surrounding the negotiation of the collective bargaining agreement itself. Those representing the union in an arbitration would seldom possess the power acting by themselves to negotiate a contract binding on the union. Thus, in the typical case where the arbitration involves the wages to be paid under a new contract, the arbitrator becomes an accomplice in circumventing limitations on the agency of the union's representatives.

At the extremes, passing judgment on the "agreed" award is relatively easy. In the middle area of gray, arriving at a valid appraisal requires a greater exercise of individual responsibility.[3] One thing seems to me clear, however. In deciding what he should do the arbitrator is not entitled to take the easy way out by saying, "After all, the purpose of arbitration is to promote good labor relations. If I can head off an unjustified and futile strike by issuing as an arbitrator's decision what is really an agreed settlement, then my conscience is clear." Before taking this escape the arbitrator should reflect that he is trustee for the integrity of the processes of decision entrusted to his care. He should ask himself whether the argument for bending his powers for good is not like that of the man who, in order to give to a worthy charity, embezzles funds entrusted to his care for an undeserving nephew. In practice the temptation to take short cuts to do good is a much greater threat to the integrity of arbitration than the temptation to use its forms for evil purposes.

Before leaving this question of the "informed" award—so that none of its nuances may be left unnoticed—it should be remarked that the problem can arise within the framework of an arbitration wholly conducted within the strictest judicial restraints. Effective advocacy sometimes suggests that the advocate give some intimation in his argument of the most acceptable form of an adverse decision in the event such a decision should be rendered. It needs hardly to be said that such intimations, though conveyed "in open court" and in the presence of all affected, are not always perceived by an inattentive audience. This tincturing of the argument with intimations of settlement, instead of employing more direct and reliable channels of communication, may seem to some the essence of hypocrisy. To others it will represent that deference for symbolism without which social living is impossible.

There remains the difficult problem of mediation by the arbitrator who, instead of issuing an award, undertakes to persuade the parties to reach a settlement, perhaps reinforcing his persuasiveness with "the gentle threat" of a decision. Again, there is waiting a too-easy answer: "Judges do it." Of course, judges sometimes mediate, or at least bring pressure on the parties for a voluntary settlement. Sometimes this is done usefully and sometimes in ways that involve an abuse of office. In any event the judiciary has evolved no uniform code with respect to this problem that the arbitrator can take over ready-made. Judicial practice varies over a wide range. If the arbitrator were to pattern his conduct after the worst practices of the bench, arbitration would be in a sad way.

Analysis of the problem as it confronts the arbitrator should begin with a recognition that mediation (or conciliation, the terms being largely interchangeable) has an important role to play in the settlement of labor disputes. There is much to justify a system whereby it is a prerequisite to arbitration that an attempt first be made by a skilled mediator to bring about a voluntary settlement. This requirement has at times been imposed in a variety of contexts. Under such systems the mediator is, I believe, invariably someone other than the arbitrator. This is as it should be.

Mediation and arbitration have distinct purposes and hence distinct moralities. The morality of mediation lies in optimum settlement, a settlement in which each party gives up what he values less, in return for what he values more.[4] The morality of arbitration lies in a decision according to the law of the contract. The procedures appropriate for mediation are those most likely to uncover that pattern of adjustment which will most nearly meet the interests of both parties. The procedures appropriate for arbitration are those which most securely guarantee each of the parties a meaningful chance to present arguments and proofs for a decision in his favor. Thus, private consultations with the parties, generally wholly improper on the part of an arbitrator, are an indispensable tool of mediation.

Not only are the appropriate procedures different in the two cases, but the facts sought by those procedures are different. There is no way to define "the essential facts" of a situation except by reference to some objective. Since the objective of reaching an optimum settlement is different from that of rendering an award according to the contract, the facts relevant in the two cases are different, or, when they seem the same, are viewed in different aspects. If a person who has mediated unsuccessfully attempts to assume the role of arbitrator, he must endeavor to view the facts of the case in a completely new light, as if he had previously known nothing about them. This is a difficult thing to do. It will be hard for him to listen to proofs and arguments with an open mind. If he fails in this attempt, the integrity of adjudication is impaired.

• • •

I come now to another kind of situation of much more fundamental importance than those I have so far discussed. An understanding of this situation is, I believe, essential not only for an understanding of labor arbitration, but of adjudication generally. The point I wish now to develop is this: There are certain kinds of problems that by their nature are unsuited to solution by the adjudicative process.

Let me return to the starting point. I have defined adjudication as a process of decision characterized by a particular form of participation accorded to the affected party, that of presenting proofs and arguments for a decision in his favor. The question then becomes, in what kinds of cases can this participation be meaningful? At this point I am no longer concerned with the availability of standards of decision. I am raising the more basic question of the kinds of problems that are amenable to solution by the adjudicative process. The question I have in mind is the counterpart of that which can be raised about elections. An election, too, is a method of decision in which the interested party is accorded a particular form of participation, in this case, that of voting. A good many questions can be decided by voting: who shall be president, whether a bond issue shall be authorized, and so forth. But there are other questions that do not lend themselves to such a decision: how troops shall be deployed to meet an enemy attack, what is the cheapest way to build a bridge, and so forth. There are, in other words, intrinsic limits to the kinds of questions that can be resolved by elections.[5] I want now to discuss whether the method of decision known as adjudication is subject to similar limits.

Let me begin with typical cases that fall neatly within the competence of the adjudicative process. One such case is that which calls for a yes-or-no decision between parties with opposed interests, no other interests being directly affected by the outcome. The claim is made that a particular employee is entitled to a week's vacation. The company argues that under a proper construction of the contract the employee is entitled to no vacation at all. The decision of such a case can be reached entirely within the limits of normal adjudicative propriety, each party advancing his proofs and arguments in the presence of the other. To be sure, an inexperienced company representative might wish to convey privately to the arbitrator his concern that a decision for the grievant might have an expensive carry-over to somewhat similar situations. He might explain that he does not want to make this statement in front of the union for fear it might be taken later as an admission on his part that the carry-over effect was justified; if decision goes against him, he wants an unimpeded opportunity to oppose the carry-over as if it were a new problem. Clearly this wish to have one's cake and eat it too cannot be gratified. All formal procedures of decision inevitably involve inconveniences and side costs. If every guarantee surrounding adjudication were relaxed the minute it rubbed either party, adjudication would lose its integrity as a distinct form of social decision.

A second kind of case that normally puts no strain on the forms of adjudication may be called the more-or-less case. In a lawsuit a party asks for $10,000 damages. The possible decisions run from zero to $10,000. The plaintiff of course argues for $10,000, the defendant for zero, the actual judgment may lie somewhere in between. The important thing is that all of the possible decisions may be represented within a single dimension, as points along a straight line.

In practice more-or-less questions are normally compounded with yes-or-no questions: does the defendant owe anything, and if so, how much? Thus, in a discharge case the arbitrator may be asked to decide, yes or no, whether the employee shall be reinstated. If he is reinstated, the arbitrator may then have to decide how much back pay, more or less, he is entitled to. Though this makes the issues more complex, there is nothing in the nature of the case as a whole that makes it unsuitable for decision within the adjudicative frame.

Now let me present a case in which the question is not simply yes or no, more or less, or a combination of the two. To emphasize that the problem is a general one, I shall begin with a case falling completely outside the field of labor relations.

In 1959 a wealthy lady by the name of Timken died in New York City. She left a collection of paintings valued at millions of dollars. The pictures were drawn from different periods, different nations, different schools of art. Her will devised the collection to the Metropolitan Museum and the National Gallery of Art "in equal shares." The will prescribed no apportionment and set up no procedure for accomplishing any apportionment.

Here obviously the problem of effecting a division "in equal shares" does not permit of a yes-or-no answer. Similarly the available solutions do not lie along a straight line of more-or-less, but are scattered in an irregular pattern across a checkerboard of possibilities. One can imagine an optimum solution, yielding the greatest utility to both donees, that might lie only a few moves away from the worst possible solution. If one were to seek the best solution by a series of approximations, the movement of a single picture across the line might call for a host of compensatory adjustments in the allotment of other pictures. For it should be remembered that the problem here is not merely that of giving to the two museums collections that might produce an equal dollar return if offered for sale—a conjectural standard in any event—but also that of giving to each those pictures that will most effectively supplement the extensive collection it already has.

The division under Mrs. Timken's will was in fact effected by an agreement of the two museums. The solution was reached through a somewhat complex procedure designed not merely to achieve "fairness" in monetary terms, but to produce a maximum satisfaction of the needs of both museums.[6]

What difficulty would have been encountered in attempting to effect an equal division of the paintings within the usual adjudicative frame? The difficulty lies in the fact that meaningful participation by the litigants through proofs and arguments would become virtually impossible. There is no single solution, or simple set of solutions, toward which the parties meeting in open court could address themselves. If an optimum solution had to be reached through adjudicative procedures, the court would have had to set forth an almost endless series of possible divisions and direct the parties to deal with each in turn.

Similar problems can plague adjudication in all fields. In international law the classic problem is that of apportioning the rights in an international river system, including the interrelated rights of diversion, pollution, power uses, navigation, and fishing. In constitutional law we have the problem presented by a demand that the courts reapportion election districts to make them more representative of the distribution of population. In administrative law those agencies most likely to fall short of judicial proprieties are almost invariably those entrusted with tasks of apportionment, such as that of allotting air routes or radio and TV channels. In controlled economies (including those of this country in times of war) the adjudicative function is likely to get badly confused with managerial direction because many of the problems that require solution do not yield themselves to solution within the adjudicative frame.

Adopting a term introduced by Michael Polanyi [7] I have called problems like that presented by Mrs. Timken's will "polycentric," that is, "many-centered." One may illustrate the essential idea by a spider web. Pull a strand here, and a complex pattern of adjustments runs through the whole web. Pull another strand from a different angle, and another complex pattern results. As I have said, the essential point does not lie in the presence or absence of rational grounds for action. Constructing a bridge, for example, is a rational procedure, but there is no rational ground on which one can determine, in abstraction from the structure of the bridge as a whole, that Girder A should intersect Girder B at a particular angle, say, 18 degrees. Needless to say, placing all the elements of the bridge in proper relationship with one another is not a problem solvable within the adjudicative frame.

NOTES

1. To forestall a possible inference of self-justification at this point, I should like to say that I have never as an arbitrator had anything to do with a situation of the sort described in the text. On the other hand, I certainly would not like to pretend that I have never been influenced by intimations conveyed during argument as to the lines of an acceptable settlement.
2. Wirtz, "Due Process of Arbitration," *The Arbitrator and the Parties* (National Academy of Arbitrators, 1958), esp. p. 27.
3. "The Code of Ethics for Arbitration," *Labor Arbitration,* XV (1951), 961, offers a sparse guidance.

Part II, § 5(c):

"It is discretionary with the arbitrator, upon the request of all parties [who are *all* parties?], to give the terms of their voluntary settlement the status of an award."

Part III, § 10:

"If the parties reach a settlement of their dispute but desire nevertheless to have an award made, they should give the arbitrator a full explanation of the reasons therefor in order that he may judge whether he desires to make or join such an award."

4. In exchange ". . . the rule must be that you give, so far as possible, what is less valuable to you but more valuable to the receiver; and you receive what is more valuable to you and less valuable to the giver. This is common sense, good business sense, good social sense, good technology, and is the enduring basis of amicable and constructive relations of any kind. This does not mean that you give as little as you can from the receiver's point of view. . . . What conceals this simple fact of experience so often is that subsequent evaluations may change, though this is then beside the point. I may pay a man $10 today with pleasure, and find tomorrow that I need $10 very badly, but cannot use the service I paid for. I am then perhaps disposed to think I made a bad exchange. I read the past into the present. This leads to the false view that what exchange should be is as little as possible of what the receiver wants, regardless of its value to me. This philosophy of giving as little as possible and getting as much as possible in the other man's values is the root of bad customers' relations, bad labor relations, bad credit relations, bad supply relations, bad technology. The possible margins of cooperative success are too limited to survive the destruction of incentives that this philosophy implies." Barnard, *The Functions of the Executive* (1950), pp. 254–255.

Barnard may simplify the matter somewhat in this passage. If in making a deal today I look forward to possible future deals with the same party tomorrow, then it may sometimes be wise to hold back something he wants badly, even if it would cost me little to give it. By doing so I improve my bargaining position tomorrow. But without doubt this consideration is in practice grossly overemphasized. Barnard is certainly right in pointing up the social destructiveness of the conception that you have won an important victory just because you have deprived the other party of something he wanted badly. One of the most important tasks of the mediator is to keep the discussions within the frame recommended by Barnard, so that this conception will have no chance to work its havoc.

5. Arrow, *Social Choice and Individual Values* (1951); Black, *The Theory of Committees and Elections* (1958); a comprehensive bibliography will be found in Riker, "Voting and the Summation of Preferences," *American Political Science Review,* LV (1961), 900.

6. *New York Times,* May 15, 1960, p. 77.

7. Polanyi, *The Logic of Liberty* (1951), pp. 170–184.

71

Poverty and Legal Competence

JEROME E. CARLIN, JAN HOWARD, AND
SHELDON MESSINGER

One view of the citizen's role in the legal system stresses his capacity to evoke favorable consideration from officials in the application of established rules.[1] We would suggest another image of the competence required to use the legal system, one that emphasizes the ability to further and protect one's interests through active assertion of legal rights. We call the relevant ability "legal competence." The legally competent person will want and expect government officials to take his interests into account in both their dealings with him and with others; but he will see their propensity to do so as closely connected with his own actions. The competent subject will take initiative. Moreover, like other practical men, he is concerned with creating, preserving, and expanding his capacity to initiate action. He may expect government officials (and others) to accord him "equal treatment" and "serious consideration," [2] but he will continuously lay a basis for this expectation through his own actions.

As we see him, the competent subject will see law as a resource for developing, furthering, and protecting his interests. This is partly a matter of knowledge. The competent subject will be aware of the relation between the realization of his interests and the machinery of law-making and administration. He will know how to use this machinery and when to use it. Moreover, he will see assertion of his interests through legal channels as desirable and appropriate. This is not to say that he will view law as omni-relevant, as a sort of all-purpose tool. He will be aware of the limits of law. But it is important to stress that he will not be hostile to extension of the rule of law. When he believes it proper, he will make an effort to bring his interests under the aegis of authoritative rules. This will call for "a creative act of influence" that will affect the content of official decisions.

It is implicit in what we have said that the competent subject will have a sense of himself as a possessor of rights, and in seeking to validate and implement these rights through law he will be concerned with holding authorities accountable to law. With respect to the latter, Almond and Verba contend that in seeking favorable rulings from legal and other government authorities the subject may appeal to "the set of administrative rules that are supposed to

From "Civil Justice and the Poor," *Law and Society Review* (November, 1966), pp. 69–71, 85–87. Abridged with renumbered notes. Reprinted by permission of the authors and publisher.

guide the action of the government official, or he may appeal to his considerateness." [3] We suggest that the legally competent subject does more than appeal to the considerateness of officials; he insists that official actions and decisions be consistent with authoritative rules.

In doing so he changes or reinforces his relationship to those who make and administer law. He changes it in a direction compatible with the rule of law, for his manner of winning "consideration" tends to reduce his dependence on the good will and whims of those who govern.[4] The competent subject demands that there be reasons for official decisions and actions, and that these reasons be consonant with both "reason" and "law." Power, however benevolent, is not for him its own justification.

In sum, it is evident that "legal competence" is a complex quality. Broadly speaking, it would appear to consist of one part awareness and one part assertiveness. The legally competent person has a sense of himself as a possessor of rights, and he sees the legal system as a resource for validation of these rights. He knows when and how to seek validation. Beyond this, the legally competent person takes action: he not only "knows his rights" and how to validate them, he turns to the legal system and uses it when his interests can be served by doing so. In the process, he tends to extend the rule of law.

•   •   •

We have suggested that the poor no less than the rich have legal problems, that they are even more likely than the rich to suffer injustices resulting from the operation of our economic and governmental systems. We have said that many of the abuses experienced by the poor arise from institutionalized practices, and that these collective problems are often unaffected by, if not exacerbated by, traditional legal controls. In fact, however, we know very little about the range or incidence of injustices experienced by individuals in different segments of the society. In the consumer area we need systematic studies of the incidence of missed payments on installment contracts, the frequency with which missed payments result in repossession or garnishment, and the extent to which garnishment leads to loss of job. Repossessions are said to be made in illegal ways, deficiency judgments granted without due notice to the debtor, and wage attachments applied to larger portions of the debtor's wages than legally justified. How common are these practices, and what are the conditions that give rise to and sustain them? The public sphere, too, contributes its share of important legal problems, probably an increasing share. What is the experience of those who must deal with welfare and unemployment insurance agencies, county hospitals, public housing authorities? What kinds of abuses are routinely met in these situations? How are they dealt with?

We are interested not only in a description of injustices and their incidence in different social classes. Research is also required to illuminate the character of the institutional settings in which injustices arise, the various pressures leading to the initiation and establishment of abusive practices, and the capacity of firms and agencies for institutionalizing procedures that might prevent or restrict such practices.

Law

The law is, above all, a means of creating and protecting rights. We must inquire more fully into the extent to which it performs this essential function for the poor. For example, to what extent do potential recipients of public assistance have recourse through law when they are denied assistance, or when benefits are reduced, or are less than the recipient is entitled to? To the extent that the law provides determinate criteria for eligibility decisions and regular procedures for challenging these decisions, the benefit takes on the character of a "right." To the extent that the criteria are vague—or to the extent that the law fails to require public assistance administrators to make their criteria known —the benefit remains "a privilege." We know something of the conditions under which "privileges" are transformed into "rights"—this has happened, for example, to benefits for the aged.[5] More inquiry is needed.

But this is not the only issue. We must also inquire into the character of the rights which may be accorded by law. An important fact about assistance is that many persons who are apparently qualified do not enter a claim. There are a number of reasons for this, some of which have been considered in our discussion of "legal competence." One of the reasons is that many people apparently consider a claim for public assistance to be an admission of "failure"; given current definitions it seems to connote that one is less than whole. Is there any alternative? It is worth noting that others receive public benefits (such as subsidies) without suffering the degradation allegedly experienced by those on "public assistance." We should inquire more closely into the consequences of transforming "assistance" into a "pension." Study of this process among the aged might provide a useful beginning. A simple change of terms —the invention of euphemisms for public assistance or relief investigation, for example—is not enough. What is needed is the conviction, which can be expressed in law, that those receiving benefits have given something in the past for which they are now being remunerated, or that they are giving something now.

Research is obviously required to document areas of inequality in the law (*de facto* as well as *de jure*), and to explore criteria for determining the nature and extent of inequality. Studies should also be directed at what is perhaps a more fundamental issue: what are the potential resources within existing areas of law for promoting the interests and aspirations of the poor and for insuring conformity of official action to the rule of law?

Administration of Justice

We have suggested that justice is administered in many settings. One of the principal problems, regardless of setting, is that agencies administering justice tend to be large-scale organizations faced with the task of processing an ever increasing volume of cases. To what extent is it possible to preserve minimal standards of fairness within a framework of mass-production justice? Can we provide decent justice at low cost?

The tendency to conceive of treatment and rehabilitation as the primary objectives of tribunals and agencies serving the poor may also weaken the adjudicative process. How extensive is this development; what are the conditions that sustain it; and to what extent are these newer goals in fact realizable? More important, to what extent is this development necessarily inconsistent with the preservation of certain standards of procedural fairness?

Study of agencies applying law to the poor reveals the difficulties of maintaining a commitment to serving the needs and interests of poor constituents. Welfare agencies, for example, have apparently been more zealous to see that those not entitled to benefits did not receive them than they have been to insure that those entitled did in fact receive them. The history of the development of internal controls within public assistance agencies remains to be written. When it is written it will probably show that controls developed first to see that assistance officials did not extend benefits to the ineligible and to prevent fraud on the part of applicants. Lately, it appears that controls are developing which at least permit the agency to rectify another sort of administrative error, the denial of benefits to those entitled to them. This implies, of course, that those who are entitled apply for benefits. We know that many do not. To date there appears to be little activity on the part of agencies to see that those entitled to benefits do apply.

Controlling administrative behavior is ordinarily taken to mean controlling "arbitrariness." This is crucially important. But the term itself requires more analysis than it has received to date. To do nothing is also a form of official arbitrariness. When this occurs on a mass scale—as it apparently has in public assistance—it is not obvious that traditional forms of litigation will serve to change the situation.

The problem we have discussed here applies beyond public assistance; in many ways it is the same problem confronted by Blumrosen in his study of the New Jersey Civil Rights Division: moving public agencies to positive action.[6] Is this a matter that is appropriately dealt with through adjudication? Or, are administrative or legislative reforms called for? This is clearly an area requiring careful and serious study.

NOTES

1. Such an image is implicit in G. Almond and S. Verba, *The Civic Culture* (1965). The authors characterize administrative or subject competence (as distinguished from political competence) as follows:

   The subject does not participate in making rules, nor does his participation involve the use of political influence. His participation comes at the point at which general policy has been made and is being applied. The competence of the subject is more a matter of being aware of his rights under the rules than of participating in the making of the rules. And though the subject may attempt to make the government official responsive, he appeals rather than demands. His appeal may be to the set of administrative rules that are supposed to guide the action of the government official, or he may appeal to his considerateness. If the government official responds, it is because he is following these rules or because he is being considerate —not because influence has been applied to him. . . . The (competent) subject . . . may want and expect beneficial outputs from government. But he does not expect them to be accorded to him because he demands them. The government official who acts to benefit him responds, not to the subject's demands, but to some other force. . . . This kind of competence is more circumscribed, more passive than that of the citizen. It may set in motion an action that will affect the way in which a rule is interpreted or enforced against an individual. It is not a creative act of influence that can affect the content of the decisions themselves, except in an indirect way.

2. Almond and Verba asked their respondents whether they expected government officials and the police to accord them "equal treatment" and "serious consideration." If they did expect it, respondents were classified as having a "sense of administrative competence," that is, as competent "subjects." *Id*. at 70, 72, 168.

3. *Id*. at 168.

4. In discussing administrative competence Almond and Verba suggest that even if subjects "exert pressure on bureaucrats to follow the administrative rules" (versus seeking "a particular decision in favor of a particular individual or group"), "it does not change the relationship of the individual to the administration—he still comes as a subject, albeit a competent one, whose appeal is to the rules of the bureaucracy." See *Id*. at 171–172. We would argue that the competent subject does change this relationship.

5. See F. Pinner, P. Jacobs, and P. Selznick, *Old Age and Political Behavior: A Case Study* (1959).

6. A similar recommendation was proposed many years ago by Ludwig Bendix "Richter, Rechtsanwälte und Arbeitsgerichte," *Die Justez,* II (1926), 188–189.

72

The New Property

CHARLES REICH

Toward Individual Stakes in the Commonwealth

Ahead there stretches—to the farthest horizon—the joyless landscape of the public interest state. The life it promises will be comfortable and comforting. It will be well planned, with suitable areas for work and play. But there will be no precincts sacred to the spirit of individual man.

There can be no retreat from the public interest state. It is the inevitable outgrowth of an interdependent world. An effort to return to an earlier economic order would merely transfer power to giant private governments which would rule not in the public interest, but in their own interest. If individualism

From *Yale Law Journal*, LXXIII (April, 1964), 778–787. Reprinted by permission of the author, The Yale Law Journal Company, and Fred B. Rothman & Company.

and pluralism are to be preserved, this must be done not by marching backward, but by building these values into today's society. If public and private are now blurred, it will be necessary to draw a new zone of privacy. If private property can no longer perform its protective functions, it will be necessary to establish institutions to carry on the work that private property once did but can no longer do.

In these efforts government largess must play a major role. As we move toward a welfare state, largess will be an ever more important form of wealth. And largess is a vital link in the relationship between the government and private sides of society. It is necessary, then, that largess begin to do the work of property.

The chief obstacle to the creation of private rights in largess has been the fact that it is originally public property, comes from the state, and may be withheld completely. But this need not be an obstacle. Traditional property also comes from the state, and in much the same way. Land, for example, traces back to grants from the sovereign. In the United States, some was the gift of the King of England, some that of the King of Spain. The sovereign extinguished Indian title by conquest, became the new owner, and then granted title to a private individual or group.[1] Some land was the gift of the sovereign under laws such as the Homestead and Pre-emption Acts.[2] Many other natural resources—water, minerals, and timber—passed into private ownership under similar grants. In America, land and resources all were originally government largess. In a less obvious sense, personal property also stems from government. Personal property is created by law; it owes its origin and continuance to laws supported by the people as a whole. These laws "give" the property to one who performs certain actions. Even the man who catches a wild animal "owns" the animal only as a gift from the sovereign, having fulfilled the terms of an offer to transfer ownership.[3]

Like largess, real and personal property were also originally dispensed on conditions, and were subject to forfeiture if the conditions failed. The conditions in the sovereign grants, such as colonization, were generally made explicit, and so was the forfeiture resulting from failure to fulfill them. In the case of the Pre-emption and Homestead Acts, there were also specific conditions.[4] Even now land is subject to forfeiture for neglect; if it is unused it may be deemed abandoned to the state or forfeited to an adverse possessor. In a very similar way, personal property may be forfeited by abandonment or loss.[5] Hence, all property might be described as government largess, given on condition and subject to loss.

If all property is government largess, why is it not regulated to the same degree as present-day largess? Regulation of property has been limited, not because society had no interest in property, but because it was in the interest of society that property be free. Once property is seen not as a natural right but as a construction designed to serve certain functions, then its origin ceases to be decisive in determining how much regulation should be imposed. The conditions that can be attached to receipt, ownership, and use depend not on where property came from, but on what job it should be expected to perform. Thus in the case of government largess, nothing turns on the fact that it originated in government. The real issue is how it functions and how it should function.

To create an institution, or to make an existing institution function in a new way, is an undertaking far too ambitious for the present article. But it is possible to begin a search for guiding principles. Such principles must grow out of what we know about how government largess has functioned up to the present time. And while principles must remain at the level of generality, it should be kept in mind that not every principle is equally applicable to all forms of largess. Our primary focus must be those forms of largess that chiefly control the rights and status of the individual.

A. CONSTITUTIONAL LIMITS

The most clearly defined problem posed by government largess is the way it can be used to apply pressure against the exercise of constitutional rights. A first principle should be that government must have no power to "buy up" rights guaranteed by the Constitution.[6] It should not be able to impose any condition on largess that would be invalid if imposed on something other than a "gratuity." [7] Thus, for example, government should not be able to deny largess because of invocation of the privilege against self-incrimination.[8]

This principle is in a sense a revival of the old but neglected rule against unconstitutional conditions, as encunciated by the Supreme Court:

> Broadly stated, the rule is that the right to continue the exercise of a privilege granted by the state cannot be made to depend upon the grantee's submission to a condition prescribed by the state that is hostile to the provisions of the federal constitution.[9]

> If the state may compel the surrender of one constitutional right as a condition of its favor, it may in like manner compel a surrender of all. It is inconceivable that guaranties embedded in the Constitution of the United States may thus be manipulated out of existence.[10]

The courts in recent times have gone part of the distance toward this principle. In 1958 the Supreme Court held that California could not use the gratuity theory to deny a tax exemption to persons engaged in certain political activities:

> To deny an exemption to claimants who engage in certain forms of speech is in effect to penalize them for such speech. Its deterrent effect is the same as if the state were to fine them for this speech. The appellees are plainly mistaken in their argument that, because a tax exemption is a "privilege" or a "bounty," its denial may not infringe speech.[11]

In 1963 the Court followed this reasoning in the important case of *Sherbert v. Verner*.[12] South Carolina provided unemployment compensation, but required recipients to accept suitable employment when it became available, or lose their benefits. An unemployed woman was offered a job requiring her to work Saturdays, but she refused it because she was a Seventh Day Adventist, to whom Saturday was the Sabbath, a day when work was forbidden. The state thereafter refused to pay her any unemployment benefits. The Supreme Court reversed this action:

> The ruling forces her to choose between following the precepts of her religion and forfeiting benefits, on the one hand, and abandoning one of the precepts of her religion in order to accept work, on the other hand. Governmental imposition of such a choice puts the same kind of burden upon the free exercise of religion as would a fine imposed against appellant for her Saturday worship.
>
> Nor may the South Carolina Court's construction of the statute be saved from constitutional infirmity on the ground that unemployment compensation benefits are not appellant's "right" but merely a "privilege." It is too late in the day to doubt that the liberties of religion and expression may be infringed by the denial of or placing of conditions upon a benefit or privilege. . . . [To] condition the availability of benefits upon this appellant's willingness to violate a cardinal principle of her religious faith effectively penalizes the free exercise of her constitutional liberties.[13]

In a somewhat different setting, the District of Columbia Court of Appeals reached an analogous result. The Civil Aeronautics Board attempted to issue a letter of registration to an irregular carrier in terms making the registration subject to suspension without a hearing. The agency claimed that, since it was granting the carrier an exemption from statutory requirements, a form of gratuity, it could provide that suspension might be without a hearing. The Court said:

> The government cannot make a business dependent upon a permit and make an otherwise unconstitutional requirement a condition to the permit.[14]

On the state level there have been some rather similar decisions.[15]

The problem becomes more complicated when a court attempts, as current doctrine seems to require, to "balance" the deterrence of a constitutional right against some opposing interest. In any balancing process, no weight should be given to the contention that what is at stake is a mere gratuity. It should be recognized that pressure against constitutional rights from denial of a "gratuity" may be as great or greater than pressure from criminal punishment. And the concept of the public interest should be given a meaning broad enough to include general injury to independence and constitutional rights.[16] It is not possible to consider detailed problems here. It is enough to say that government should gain no power, as against constitutional limitations, by reason of its role as a dispenser of wealth.

B. SUBSTANTIVE LIMITS

Beyond the limits deriving from the Constitution, what limits should be imposed on governmental power over largess? Such limits, whatever they may be, must be largely self-imposed and self-policed by legislatures; the Constitution sets only a bare minimum of limitations on legislative policy. The first type of limit should be on relevance. It has proven possible to argue that practically anything in the way of regulation is relevant to some legitimate legislative purpose. But this does not mean that it is desirable for legislatures to make such use of their powers. As Justice Douglas said in the *Barsky* case:

> So far as I know, nothing in a man's political beliefs disables him from setting broken bones or removing ruptured appendixes, safely and efficiently. A practicing surgeon is unlikely to uncover many state secrets in the course of his professional activities.[17]

Courts sometimes manage, by statutory construction, to place limits on relevance. One example is the judicial reaction to attempts to ban "disloyal tenants" from government aided housing projects. The Illinois Court said:

> The purpose of the Illinois Housing Authorities Act is to eradicate slums and provide housing for persons of low-income class. . . . It is evident that the exclusion of otherwise qualified persons solely because of membership in organizations designated as subversive by the Attorney General has no tendency whatever to further such purpose. . . . A construction of section 27 that would enable the housing authority to prescribe conditions of eligibility having no rational connection with the purpose of the act would raise serious constitutional questions.[18]

And the Wisconsin Court said:

> Counsel for the defendant Authority have failed to point out to this court how the occupation of any units of a federally aided housing project by tenants who may be members of a subversive organization threatens the successful operation of such housing projects.[19]

It is impossible to confine the concept of relevance. But legislatures should strive for a meaningful, judicious concept of relevance if regulation of largess is not to become a handle for regulating everything else.

Besides relevance, a second important limit on substantive power might be concerned with discretion. To the extent possible, delegated power to make rules ought to be confined within ascertainable limits, and regulating agencies should not be assigned the task of enforcing conflicting policies. Also, agencies should be enjoined to use their powers only for the purposes for which they were designed.[20] In a perhaps naïve attempt to accomplish this, Senator Lausche introduced a bill to prohibit United States government contracting officers from using their contracting authority for purposes of duress. This bill, in its own words, would prohibit officials from denying contracts, or the right to bid on contracts, with the intent of forcing the would-be contractor to perform or refrain from performing any act which such person had no legal obligation to perform or not perform.[21] Although this bill might not be a very effective piece of legislation, it does suggest a desirable objective.

A final limit on substantive power, one that should be of growing importance, might be a principle that policy making authority ought not to be delegated to essentially private organizations. The increasing practice of giving professional associations and occupational organizations authority in areas of government largess tends to make an individual subject to a guild of his fellows. A guild system, when attached to government largess, adds to the feudal characteristics of the system.

C. PROCEDURAL SAFEGUARDS

Because it is so hard to confine relevance and discretion, procedure offers a valuable means for restraining arbitrary action. This was recognized in the strong procedural emphasis of the Bill of Rights, and it is being recognized in the increasingly procedural emphasis of administrative law. The law of government largess has developed with little regard for procedure. Reversal of this trend is long overdue.

The grant, denial, revocation, and administration of all types of government largess should be subject to scrupulous observance of fair procedures. Action should be open to hearing and contest, and based upon a record subject to judicial review. The denial of any form of privilege or benefit on the basis of undisclosed reasons should no longer be tolerated.[22] Nor should the same person sit as legislator, prosecutor, judge and jury, combining all the functions of government in such a way as to make fairness virtually impossible. There is no justification for the survival of arbitrary methods where valuable rights are at stake.

Even higher standards of procedural fairness should apply when government action has all the effects of a penal sanction. In *Milwaukee Social Democratic Publishing Co. v. Burleson,*[23] where the postmaster general revoked the second-class mail privileges of a newspaper because he found its contents in violation of the Espionage Act, Justice Brandeis wrote a far-seeing dissent on the penal nature of such a denial of government benefits:

> It would in practice deprive many publishers of their property without due process of law. Would it not also violate the Fifth Amendment? It would in practice subject publishers to punishment without a hearing by any court. Would it not also violate Article III of the Constitution? It would in practice subject publishers to severe punishment without trial by jury. Would it not also violate the Sixth Amendment? And the punishment inflicted—denial of a civil right—is certainly unusual. Would it also violate the Eighth Amendment?
>
> • • •
>
> The actual and intended effect of the order was merely to impose a very heavy fine, possibly $150 a day, for supposed transgression in the past. But the trial and

punishment of crimes is a function which the Constitution, Article III, § 2, cl. 3, entrusts to the judiciary.

• • •

What is in effect a very heavy fine has been imposed by the Postmaster General. It has been imposed because he finds that the publisher has committed the crime of violating the Espionage Act. And that finding is based in part upon "representations and complaints from sundry good and loyal citizens" with whom the publisher was not confronted. It may be that the court would hold, in view of Article Six in our Bill of Rights, that Congress is without power to confer upon the Postmaster General, or even upon a court, except upon the verdict of a jury and upon confronting the accused with the witnesses against him, authority to inflict indirectly such a substantial punishment as this.[24]

Today many administrative agencies take action which is penal in all but name. The penal nature of these actions should be recognized by appropriate procedures.[25]

Even if no sanction is involved, the proceedings associated with government largess must not be used to undertake adjudications of facts that normally should be made by a court after a trial. Assuming it is relevant to the grant of a license or benefit to know whether an individual has been guilty of a crime or other violation of law, should violations be determined by the agency? The consequence is an adjudication of guilt without benefit of constitutional criminal proceedings with judge, jury, and the safeguards of the Bill of Rights. In our society it is impossible to "try" a violation of law for any purpose without "trying" the whole person of the alleged violator. The very adjudication is punishment, even if no consequences are attached. It may be added that an agency should not find "guilt" after a court has found innocence. The spirit, if not the letter, of the constitutional ban against double jeopardy should prevent an agency from subjecting anyone to a second trial for the same offense.

D. FROM LARGESS TO RIGHT

The proposals discussed above, however salutary, are by themselves far from adequate to assure the status of individual man with respect to largess. The problems go deeper. First, the growth of government power based on the dispensing of wealth must be kept within bounds. Second, there must be a zone of privacy for each individual beyond which neither government nor private power can push—a hiding place from the all-pervasive system of regulation and control. Finally, it must be recognized that we are becoming a society based upon relationship and status—status deriving primarily from source of livelihood. Status is so closely linked to personality that destruction of one may well destroy the other. Status must therefore be surrounded with the kind of safeguards once reserved for personality.

Eventually those forms of largess that are closely linked to status must be deemed to be held as of right. Like property, such largess could be governed by a system of regulation plus civil or criminal sanctions, rather than a system based upon denial, suspension, and revocation. As things now stand, violations lead to forfeitures—outright confiscation of wealth and status. But there is surely no need for these drastic results. Confiscation, if used at all, should be the ultimate, not the most common and convenient penalty. The presumption should be that the professional man will keep his license, and the welfare recipient his pension. These interests should be "vested." If revocation is necessary, not by reason of the fault of the individual holder, but by reason of overriding demands of public policy, perhaps payment of just compensation would be appropriate. The individual should not bear the entire loss for a remedy primarily intended to benefit the community.

The concept of right is most urgently needed with respect to benefits like unemployment compensation, public assistance, and old age insurance. These benefits are based upon a recognition that misfortune and deprivation are often caused by forces far beyond the control of the individual, such as technological change, variations in demand for goods, depressions, or wars. The aim of these benefits is to preserve the self-sufficiency of the individual, to rehabilitate him where necessary, and to allow him to be a valuable member of a family and a community; in theory they represent part of the individual's rightful share in the commonwealth.[26] Only by making such benefits into rights can the welfare state achieve its goal of providing a secure minimum basis for individual well-being and dignity in a society where each man cannot be wholly the master of his own destiny.[27]

Conclusion

The highly organized, scientifically planned society of the future, governed for the good of its inhabitants, promises the best life that men have ever known. In place of the misery and injustice of the past there can be prosperity, leisure, knowledge, and rich opportunity open to all. In the rush of accomplishment, however, not all values receive equal attention; some are temporarily forgotten while others are pushed ahead. We have made provision for nearly everything, but we have made no adequate provision for individual man.

This article is an attempt to offer perspective on the transformation of society as it bears on the economic basis of individualism. The effort has been to show relationships; to bring together drivers' licenses, unemployment insurance, membership in the bar, permits for using school auditoriums, and second class mail privileges, in order to see what we are becoming.

Government largess is only one small corner of a far vaster problem. There are many other new forms of wealth: franchises in private businesses, equities in corporations, the right to receive privately furnished utilities and services, status in private organizations. These too may need added safeguards in the future. Similarly, there are many sources of expanded governmental power aside from largess. By themselves, proposals concerning government largess would be far from accomplishing any fundamental reforms. But, somehow, we must begin.

At the very least, it is time to reconsider the theories under which new forms of wealth are regulated and by which governmental power over them is measured. It is time to recognize that "the public interest" is all too often a reassuring platitude that covers up sharp clashes of conflicting values, and hides fundamental choices. It is time to see that the "privilege" or "gratuity" concept, as applied to wealth dispensed by government, is not much different from the absolute right of ownership that private capital once invoked to justify arbitrary power over employees and the public.

Above all, the time has come for us to remember what the framers of the Constitution knew so well—that "a power over a man's subsistence amounts to a power over his will." We cannot safely entrust our livelihoods and our rights to the discretion of authorities, examiners, boards of control, character committees, regents, or license commissioners. We cannot permit any official or agency to pretend to sole knowledge of the public good. We cannot put the independence of any man—least of all our Barskys and our Anastaplos—wholly in the power of other men.

If the individual is to survive in a collective society, he must have protection against its ruthless pressures. There must be sanctuaries or enclaves where no majority can reach. To shelter the solitary human spirit does not merely make possible the fulfillment of individuals; it also gives society the power to change, to grow, and to regenerate, and hence to endure. These were the objects which property sought to achieve, and can no longer achieve. The challenge of the future will be to construct, for the society that is coming, institutions and laws to carry on this work. Just as the Homestead Act was a deliberate effort to foster individual values at an earlier time, so we must try to build an economic basis for liberty today—a Homestead Act for rootless twentieth-century man. We must create a new property.

NOTES

1. *Johnson v. McIntosh,* 21 U.S. (8 Wheat.) 543 (1823).
2. 5 Stat. 453, 455 (September 4, 1841), 12 Stat. 392 (May 20, 1862).
3. *Pierson v. Post,* 3 Cai. R. 175 (1805).
4. The Homestead Act had conditions of age, citizenship, intention to settle was cultivated, and loyalty to the United States. 12 Stat. 392 (1862).
5. *Mullett v. Bradley,* 24 Misc. 695, 53 N.Y. Supp. 781 (1898); *Bridges v. Hawkesworth,* 21 L.J. Rep. 75 (Q.B. 1851).
6. Note, "Unconstitutional Conditions," *Harvard Law Review,* LXXIII (1960), 1595, 1599.
7. Compare Calabresi, "Retroactivity: Paramount Powers and Contractual Changes," *Yale Law Journal,* LXXI (1962), 1191. In the context of legislation dealing with government obligations, Professor Calabresi argues that certain regulation can only be justified by a "paramount power of government" (for example, the commerce power) rather than power merely incidental to the obligation itself.
8. Judge Curtis Bok wrote:
   > We are unwilling to engraft upon our law the notion, nowhere so decided, that unemployment benefits may be denied because of raising the bar of the [Fifth] Amendment against rumor or report of disloyalty or because of refusing to answer such rumor or report. The possible abuses of such a doctrine are shocking to imagine.
   Ault Unemployment Compensation Case, 398 Pa. 250, 259, 157 A.2d 375, 380 (1960).

9. *United States v. Chicago,* M., St. P. & P.R.R., 282 U.S. 311, 328–329 (1931).
10. *Frost & Frost Co. v. Railroad Commission,* 271 U.S. 583, 594 (1926); Hale, "Unconstitutional Conditions and Constitutional Rights," *Columbia Law Review,* XXXV (1935), 321. The latter is an elaborate study of the older cases on the Federal conditioning power.
11. *Speiser v. Randall,* 357 U.S. 513, 518 (1958).
12. 374 U.S. 398 (1963).
13. *Id.* at 404–406.
14. *Standard Airlines v. CAB,* 177 F.2d 18, 20 (D.C. Cir. 1949).
15. In California a political test for use of school auditoriums for holding public meetings was upset:

   > Nor can it [the State] make the privilege of holding them dependent on conditions that would deprive any members of the public of their constitutional rights. A state is without power to impose an unconstitutional requirement as a condition for granting a privilege even though the privilege is the use of state property.

   Danskin v. San Diego Unified School District, 28 Cal. 2d 536, 545–546, 171 P.2d 885 (1946); *ACLU v. Board of Education,* 55 Cal. 2d 167, 10 Cal. Rptr. 647, 359 P.2d 45 (1961). See also *Syrek v. California Unemployment Insurance Appeals Board,* 2 Cal. Rptr. 40, 47 (Ct. App. 1960), *affirmed,* 54 Cal. 2d 519, 7 Cal. Rptr. 97 (1960).
16. The approach of the Court of Appeals for the Ninth Circuit in *Parker v. Lester,* 227 F.2d 708 (9th Cir. 1955) might serve as a model:

   > What we must balance in the scales here does not involve a choice between any security screening program and the protection of individual seamen. Rather we must weigh against the rights of the individual to the traditional opportunity for notice and hearing, the public need for a screening system whic... denies such right to notice and hearing. Granted that the Government may adopt appropriate means for excluding security risks from employment on merchant vessels, what is the factor of public interest and necessity that requires that it be done in the manner here adopted?

   Id. at 718.

   Later the Court added:

   > It is not a simple case of sacrificing the interests of a few to the welfare of the many. In weighing the considerations of which we are mindful here, we must recognize that if these regulations may be sustained, similar regulations may be made effective in respect to other groups as to whom Congress may next choose to express its legislative fears.

   Id. at 721.
17. *Barsky v. Board of Regents,* 347 U.S. 442, 472, 474 (1954) (Douglas, J., dissenting).
18. *Chicago Housing Authority v. Blackman,* 4 Ill. 2d 319, 326, 122 N.E.2d 522, 526 (1954). See also *Housing Authority v. Cordova,* 130 Cal. App. 2d 883, 279 P.2d 215 (Super. Ct. 1955).
19. *Lawson v. Housing Authority,* 270 Wis. 269, 287, 70 N.W.2d 605, 615 (1955).
20. Compare *Housing Authority v. Cordova,* 130 Cal. App. 2d 883, 889, 279 P.2d 215, 218 (1955):

   > We fail to find in the act, pursuant to which the plaintiff Housing Authority was created, anything to suggest that it is authorized to use the powers conferred upon it to punish subversives or discourage persons from entertaining subversive ideas by denying to such the right of occupying its facilities. . . .
21. *Congressional Record,* CIX (March 4, 1963), 3258–3259. The Senator, while denouncing coercion and government by men rather than laws, failed to discuss the question whether there is any "right" to a government contract.
22. The Administrative Conference of the United States has recommended "drastic changes" in the procedures by which persons or firms may be debarred from government contracting. The Conference said that such action should not be taken without prior notice, which includes a statement of reasons, and a trial-type hearing before an impartial trier of facts, all within a framework of procedures. Thus, protections would surround even that form of largess which is closest to being a matter within the managerial function of government. *Final Report of the Administrative Conference of the United States,* p. 15, and Recommendation "No. 29" (1962).

23. *United States ex rel. Milwaukee Social Democratic Publishing Co. v. Burleson,* 255 U.S. 407 (1921).
24. *Id.* at 434–435 (dissenting opinion).
25. Recently the Supreme Court, in a case involving revocation of citizenship for evading the draft, held that any action that is in fact punishment cannot be taken "without a prior criminal trial and all its incidents, including indictment, notice, confrontation, jury trial, assistance of counsel, and compulsory process for obtaining witnesses." *Kennedy v. Mendoza-Martinez.* 372 U.S. 144, 167 (1963).
26. The phrase is adapted from Hamilton and Till's definition of the word "property": "a general term for the miscellany of equities that persons hold in the common-wealth." Hamilton and Till, "Property," *Encyclopedia of the Social Sciences,* XII.
27. Experts in the field of social welfare have often argued that benefits should rest on a more secure basis, and that individuals in need should be deemed "entitled" to benefits. See tenBroek and Wilson, "Public Assistance and Social Insurance—A Normative Evaluation," *U.C.L.A. Law Review,* I (1954), 237; Kieth-Lucas, *Decisions about People in Need* (1957). The latter author speaks of a "right to assistance" that is a corollary of the "right to self-determination" (*id.* at 251) and urges public assistance workers to pledge to respect the rights and dignity of welfare clients (*id.* at 263). See also Wynn, *Fatherless Families* (1964), pp. 78–83, 162–163. The author proposes a "fatherless child allowance," to which every fatherless child would be entitled.

Starting from a quite different frame of reference—the problem of the rule of law in the welfare state—Professor Harry Jones has similarly argued that the welfare state must be regarded as a source of new rights, and that such rights as Social Security must be surrounded by substantial and procedural safeguards comparable to those enjoyed by traditional rights of property. Jones, "The Rule of Law and the Welfare State," *Columbia Law Review,* LVIII (1958), 143, 154–155. See also Note, "Charity Versus Social Insurance in Unemployment Compensation Laws," *Yale Law Journal,* LXXIII (1963), 357.

A group called the Ad Hoc Committee on the Triple Revolution recently urged that, in view of the conditions created by the "cybernation revolution" in the United States, every American should be guaranteed an adequate income as a matter of right whether or not he works. *New York Times,* March 23, 1964, p. 1.

73

University Governance by Rules: Socio-Legal Issues

TERRY F. LUNSFORD

The "free speech" controversy at Berkeley has given impetus to an already growing scholarly enterprise: the study of universities as "private govern-

From *The "Free Speech" Crises at Berkeley, 1964–1965: Some Issues for Social and Legal Research.* A Report from the Center for Research and Development in Higher Education, University of California, Berkeley, pp. 123–132. Reprinted by permission of the author. Abridged.

ments." Along with a general development of administrative law, there is today a developing body of legal and scholarly opinion that views the large, complex administrative structures of formally "autonomous" or "private" organizations (such as business corporations, labor unions, universities, etc.) as wielding "governmental" powers and carrying out governmental functions, which require that traditional problems of government be considered in assessing the rights and obligations within them. Among the principal problems that arise are the scope and bases of administrative officials' discretion, the applicability of "due process" traditions to administration, and the character and sources of administrative authority. Study of such problems requires an intermixture of legal and sociological perspectives. Issues in each of these problem areas were raised in vivid form by the Berkeley disputes. Some are discussed below, along with problems concerning the effectiveness of university "legal" action and the bases of demands for freedom on the campus.

The Scope and Bases of Administrative Discretion

As we have seen, the Free Speech Movement (FSM) objected to the enforcement of specific rules of on-campus conduct by the University in 1964. However, the organization and its successors also have taken strong stands against the broad character of the University's rules, especially as to their generality and the broad discretion that they lodge in administrative officials. The FSM argued that the size and impersonality of the modern university, the apparent desire of administrators to preserve order at the expense of important freedoms, and the manifest political pressures from the outside community have made university officials unable to use discretion fairly in student disciplinary matters. The FSM thus demanded that constitutional standards of specificity and clarity be applied to University rules, and urged that jurisdiction over disciplinary cases involving political expression or activity be lodged in a committee of faculty members. On November 20, the Regents approved President Kerr's recommendation:

> That rules and regulations be made more clear and specific and thus, incidentally and regrettably, more detailed and legalistic; and explicit penalties, where possible, be set forth for specific violations.

Subsequent events resulted in University-wide rules being kept broad and general, with authority or direction to the individual Chancellors to implement them with more specific regulations. A greater range and diversity of penalties was included in the President's rules of July 1, 1965.

Even at the campus level, however, it has been argued that specificity and detail in rules is inappropriate to a university. Such detail destroys much of the flexibility necessary for judgmental application of rules to diverse and unforeseen circumstances, it is said. Moreover, once created, rules are troublesome and time-consuming to change. Yet the students of later years may find them wholly unsuitable to the times.

SOCIAL BASES OF "PARENTAL" DISCRETION

These complaints find parallels in scholarly discussions of the social context of developing legal forms. For example, one focus of student complaint elsewhere for some years now has been the legal doctrine that university authorities stand *in loco parentis*—a piece of judicial imagery that has allowed courts to approve the broadest kinds of discretionary rulings by university and college officials in student disciplinary matters. As noted above, some modifications of this doctrine now appear in the cases, and some scholars forecast further changes. Moreover, social bases for such changes have been suggested; these call for much further study: How important is the Southern civil rights movement in producing judicially imposed restraints that will modify the "parental" discretion of university administrators? As full-time administrative officials, rather than teaching faculty members, increasingly impose student discipline, how is the tenability of the "parental" analogy affected? What is the effect on the analogy of modern universities' great size, complexity, and impersonality? How relevant is the increased number of university students aged 21 years and over, with adult experience and responsibility for their own affairs? How relevant is the heightened importance of a university education for economic and professional opportunity, or the military obligation expected of 18-year-olds? What is the significance of long-term changes in universities' social functions—for example, from general moral and cultural conditioning for a social and economic elite to more specific vocational and professional training for members of diverse social classes? Are judges or university officials more socially "competent" to establish the rights of students against universities' "institutional" interests in survival, economic prosperity, and general order? How have such social factors affected legal changes in the discretion allowed administrative officials of other organizations besides universities?

RESTRAINTS IN THE TASK-COMMITTED ORGANIZATION

The concerns of university administrators over "legalism" and inflexible, time-consuming procedural mechanisms also have a meaningful foundation in the socio-legal literature, however. Like most other "private governments," the university is an organization charged with performance of a special function for society. Its main functions—the advanced education of growing sectors of the population, and the discovery and dissemination of new knowledge—are complex and demanding tasks that defy easy routinization and require flexible judgments adapted to changing circumstances. Fuller has pointed to the difficulty with which judicial organs assess the judgments of "marginal utility" required in the management of complex enterprises.

In addition, Max Weber long ago pointed out that the growth of "legal-rational" regulation in human affairs carried with it disadvantages for the handling of particular cases. He saw that the growing "formality" of Western European law, with bureaucracy as the "pure" form of its administration, sacrificed "substantive rationality" in specific cases for the "legal certainty" that detailed and unambiguous rules make possible.

Thus basic, not illusory, dilemmas are posed by the disputes illustrated in the Berkeley controversy over administrative arbitrariness and legalism. It would appear that the modern university provides a rich social laboratory for the study of socio-legal issues in this area.

"DUE PROCESS" IN THE UNIVERSITY

The desire to restrain University administrators' discretion early led FSM leaders to call not only for more clear and specific rules but also for a series of procedural safeguards in disciplinary cases. These safeguards they grouped under the general rubric of "due process," as represented in the Anglo-American legal tradition.

Within that broad rubric, FSM leaders at various times demanded the following guarantees: (1) a pre-existent, "impartial" faculty tribunal, appointed independent of the administration, to have final authority over student discipline; (2) a deliberate and open hearing before provisional sanctions are imposed on students charged with violations; (3) prohibition of *ex parte* communications to or from the hearing committee; (4) adequate notice in writing of an alleged violation and scheduled hearing; (5) a clear statement of charges to the accused; (6) no selective or exemplary enforcement of rules (for example, against leaders of a protest movement); (7) trial before a jury of one's peers; (8) a clear statement of the tribunal's jurisdiction (for example, over matters concerning political expression or not); (9) charges based on pre-existent rules that are specific enough to allow the accused's prior knowledge of his guilt, and are reasonably related to University purposes; (10) an opportunity to challenge the bases of rules that one is charged with violating; (11) suspension of University discipline while legal proceedings are pending on related charges, so as to avoid "double jeopardy" or "self-incrimination"; (12) no "bullying" by University counsel to admit the validity of charges; (13) the right to confront one's accusers; (14) the right to present evidence on one's behalf and to call and cross-examine witnesses; (15) counsel of one's own choosing at the hearing; (16) committee findings of fact and rulings in writing; (17) penalties reasonably related to the gravity of the offense; and (18) no subjection to "trial" on the unsupported testimony of a single administrative official.

In an immediate and practical sense, these demands are the heart of the matter: they are attempts to apply strong Anglo-American legal traditions directly to the restraint of administrative actions. The Legal Advisory Committee report of December 14, 1964, at Berkeley indicated that for the want of "those institutional and procedural safeguards that are available to a defendant in a criminal court of law," the U.S. Supreme Court "has denied to administrative tribunals and other non-judicial bodies certain powers to regulate the content of expression that have been given to the courts." However, as we have seen, University attorneys have denounced the FSM "due process" demands as "pseudo-legalism"; other officials have simply declared them unworkable and undesirably "adversary" in character for a university setting. More importantly, legal scholars on the campus have pointed out that no single, universal set of procedural safeguards is required by the courts in the name of due process; instead, the procedures allowed vary widely with the nature of the case. In this connection, some faculty members have proposed simpler, "fair hearing" standards for University use in student discipline.

President Kerr's new University-wide *Policies,* effective July 1, 1965, provide that campus regulations must be "in accordance with basic standards of fairness." Consistent with this, rules are to be "simple" and "appropriate to the nature of the case and the severity of the potential discipline." University violations may be disciplined "whether or not such violations are also violations of law, and whether or not proceedings are or have been pending in the courts involving the same acts." Student or faculty committees may advise the Chancellor on student discipline, but the final authority is his, except that expulsion requires approval of the President. The Chancellor "in his discretion, may immediately impose warning or interim suspension upon a student when circumstances warrant such action."

Thus disagreements about the proper scope of "due process" in university disciplinary proceedings remain. Research by legal scholars already has been done on this subject. However, it may not be amiss to suggest some questions that deserve further study. For example:

What is the pattern of procedural restraints on administrative disciplinary action in U.S. universities? How closely does this pattern follow the requirements laid down in U.S. legal precedent (a) for courts and (b) for administrative tribunals other than those of universities? What elements of "due process" have been required of universities by courts in the past?

What are the specific purposes of each major "due process" requirement imposed in the U.S. legal tradition, and how applicable is each to the university setting? Are some procedural restraints more important than others, for students in the large university? Are some less burdensome on university officials? What specific interests and values would be sacrificed if universities' discipline were made to conform more closely to legal standards of due process?

Finally, are there changing social conditions that alter the relevance of "due process" restraints to university procedures? How relevant are the procedures typically used in determining the dismissal of a university faculty member?

"LEGALITY" IN THE UNIVERSITY

Beyond the immediate and practical issues of specific restraints in university settings, the FSM protests raised more general questions about the nature of authority. The course of the protests provided a shocking reminder that authority depends on consent—consent that may be withdrawn at any time, with dramatic consequences for all concerned.When this occurred on a large scale in the University of California, that community was faced with some of the difficult questions that have been faced by the society at large since mass "civil disobedience" gained currency as a means of social protests. The socio-legal questions involved reach close to the core of all "legal" systems, some scholars believe.

Authority is taken to mean many things. One persuasive view (that of Simon) sees authority as a relation between two persons that influences one of them to accept a decision of the other without "deliberation," or "critical review" of its validity. Thus the acceptance of another's authority involves a "suspension of judgment" in deference to that of the other person. T. D. Weldon has suggested this typically involves a presumption that the person exercising authority "could produce reasons, if challenged," and that these reasons would satisfy us that the decision asserted was appropriate. Thus we do *not* challenge the "authoritative" person's decision—except in the unusual case, when the tenuousness of the relation is revealed. In such a terminology, *power* (such as physical force) may be employed without the acquiescence of its subject, but *authority* refers to a relationship that depends primarily on characteristics which the subordinate imputes to the authority-wielder. Fear of the power he can invoke may be one of those characteristics; citizens may obey laws at times solely for fear of physical arrest and detention. But such incentives are poor substitutes for belief by the governed that those who govern them do so by "right"—by authority that is "legitimate." All reasonably stable societies, Max Weber argued, depend on such beliefs.

Building on such conceptions, Selznick and others have suggested the emergence in Western society of a tradition of "egality," under which all *exercise* of authority is seen as restrained by the need for reasoned justification. Selznick argues that any system of "governance by rules" that is to be stable and effective must do more than establish its basic "legitimacy," as "right" authority in general. It must also develop patterns of criticism and justification for specific official acts. These patterns must—upon proper challenge—allow public examination of the reasons for particular rules and applications, in light of the principles that give the system and its officials their legitimacy.

Recent events indicate that study of the origins, implications, and limits of "legality" in the complex modern university holds many opportunities for productive scholarship. As before, closer analysis is the first need. For example: (1) The university has a strong tradition of consensual governance, and an inherent concern for exploring the reasons, assumptions, and principles of validation behind any assertion. These facts suggest that universities should have well-developed systems of reasoned restraint on the arbitrary use of authority. However, modern universities are also "formal" organizations, chartered by the state for the "efficient" achievement of special purposes upon the regular allocation of public funds. This fact has tended to produce a hierarchic administrative structure, and demands for central responsiveness to the public's view of those functions. (2) There is growing emphasis on a "counter-principle" of authority that operates in the university, based on certified expertise. These facts have received attention primarily as illustrating one source of restraint on *bureaucratic* authority. However, more attention is due the fact that the expert's authority itself is very hard to restrain "reasonably" without destroying its value altogether. (3) In the past, an open paternalism has been assumed to be necessary in the relations of both faculty members and administrators with university students. This necessity is now being subjected to reasoned challenge in the administrative sphere, albeit with uncertain success. Even murkier questions concerning the authority of teacher over student remain largely unexplored in today's university. (4) Finally, the university is a complex of distinct status groups, each with its own peculiar—but ambiguous and overlapping—aspirations, values, spheres of authority, and views on the uses of "law." The effects of their interplay on the development of "legal" forms of university governance has yet to be adequately described.

Thus issues concerning "legality" in the modern university are not simple. A number of questions suggest themselves: Why has the U.S. university historically not developed more systematic, reasoned justification for its rules? Do U.S. universities differ in this regard from those of other cultures? From other "private governments"? What social conditions foster the growth of incipient "legal" systems within "non-governmental" organizations? What problems are inherent in any movement toward "legality" as an ideal of university governance? What kinds of reasons are given today by university authorities to justify official, discretionary restrictions on the conduct of university members? Are there trends in the kinds of reasons given? If so, what are their directions? What trends are observable in the bases of student challenges to university officials' actions?

Clearly, open challenges to university rules, such as have occurred at Berkeley and other U.S. universities in the recent past, offer a prime opportunity for study of issues such as these. In addition, parallels in other cultures and eras should not be overlooked, for the important perspective they can provide on our own place and time.

THE LEGITIMACY OF UNIVERSITY ADMINSITRATION

A closely related "socio-legal" approach begins with a different focal point: the "legitimacy" ascribed to authority-relations whose continuation is accepted. The Free Speech Movement involved more than student objections to particular University restrictions on speech and activity, and more than open refusal to obey the specific rules being contested. For complex reasons, FSM leaders explicitly denied the basic legitimacy of the University's unqualified administrative authority over students' conduct. By words and by symbolic acts of civil disobedience (such as the December 3 sit-in) the FSM challenged *both* specific "abuses" of authority *and* the basic impropriety of a university's having rules made and enforced solely by administrators and Regents.

For example, the FSM asserted that specific administrators had shown "arbitrariness" by refusing to continue discussions of the reasons for the disputed rules; this charge suggests only changes in behavior, or perhaps at most the unfitness of specific persons. The FSM also urged that a pattern of past restrictions revealed a conscious design among administrators and Regents to stifle student political expression; this charge suggests more widespread misfeasance, and possibly a conspiracy to violate a public trust. It was argued that persons in administrative positions generally are too subject to political pressure to deal fairly with questions of political expression, and that an independent committee of faculty members should have final authority in such matters. It was argued by the Graduate Coordinating Committee that only students can represent students' legitimate interests adequately, so that students must have voting membership in University planning councils. It was contended by the Free Student Union that students, "as students, . . . have certain rights that no agency can legitimately grant or deny." Both the FSM and the FSU demanded that "negotiation" or "collective bargaining" by students with University authorities replace the "advisory" consultation generally prevalent at present.

Responding to such attacks, University authorities referred to the Constitution of the State of California, under which "ultimate authority" was vested in the Regents by "the people" of the State. Appeal was made to the advantages of a lay governing board for separation of university life from direct political intervention by government and party officials. The necessity for University authorities to enforce "law and order" against rule violators was asserted as a condition of university "self-government." The reasonableness, tolerance, decency, and good will of University officials were asserted, and called upon as evidence that their discretion was appropriate in a society where "the rule of law" protects rights amid great ideological diversity.

The principles by which authority gains legitimacy among its subordinates have been discussed by a number of social and political thinkers. Max Weber's well-known "types" of authority (traditional, charismatic, and legal-rational) are based on the principles that make each type seem "right" to the people whose consent must be engendered. Weber was interested in principles applicable not only to explicitly "political" states but to all "corporate groups." He emphasized the emergence of legal-rational legitimacy in Western society. In the same vein, Selznick has suggested that some principles of legitimacy are more conducive than others to the development of what he calls "legality." At a very general level, for example, a principle that treats authority as a rational means to specified ends is more conducive to reasoned justification of specific rules than one that accepts history (tradition) as its own justification. More specifically, if legitimacy is attached to unfettered discretion in the hands of "duly constituted" administrative officials, there is little room for reasoned dialogue over specific rules. By contrast, if structures of rules are legitimized by reference to values shared among the members of an organization, this keeps open the possibility of reasoned criticism of the rule-structure and particular rules within it.

If such considerations are taken as important for universities and other "private governments," a number of significant questions arise which are relevant to the recent student protests. For example: What principles are put forward to "legitimize" the present structure of authority in U.S. universities? Are these principles well accepted by the different status groups within the university, such as faculty, students, and professional research staffs? What are the typical grounds of challenge to administrative, regental, or faculty authority? What are the implications of specific legitimating principles for the development of stable university rule-systems? How explicit, and how widely accepted, are the principles used to justify specific university rules, or the character of a university's rule-system? How do the reasons given for particular official rules and acts affect popular acceptance of an administrative regime's legitimacy? If a specific administrative structure "loses" legitimacy with many persons in a university, what consequences are to be expected? How is administrative legitimacy re-established, once it has been seriously questioned?

Such questions imply a thorough look at universities as "private governments." They suggest a view of the university as a complex political-legal system, whose officials and administrative arrangements depend for their effectiveness in part upon acceptance by subordinates as well as superiors. The events of 1964–1965 at Berkeley would seem to lend much credence to such an approach.

The Effectiveness of University "Legal" Action

The uses and limits of formal law enforcement as a means of social control are matters of concern today in many areas of society. One complex and puzzling set of questions surrounds the increased use of mass civil disobedience as a form of social protest, and the responses to it. These problems were prominent in the Berkeley controversy. They cannot be discussed in depth here, but a number of issues especially relevant to the university context may be briefly suggested.

ACADEMIC AIMS AND LAW ENFORCEMENT

As we indicated above, the University of California's *Policies* and official declarations in 1964 suggested that rules regulating on-campus political expression were designed in part to safeguard academic standards in extracurricular discussions on University premises. The University wished officially to discourage "propaganda," encourage regard for "the reasoned argument as against the simplistic slogan," and foster "higher standards of conduct and work" in the academic community than those that prevail outside. In addition, the University's posture of support for "law and order" on and off the campus was an issue by May, 1964, and it became more so with student civil disobedience on the campus in the fall. In the face of these official concerns, some faculty members have suggested that the University places undue reliance on the effectiveness and propriety of formal rule enforcement as the means to its ends.

In the view of some scholars, some affirmative goals, such as the maintenance of "responsibility" in public speech and expression, cannot be enforced effectively by formal rules. These faculty members believe that, if such goals are to be attained in a community, they must be supported by values shared widely among the community's members, and reinforced by informal respect accorded those who uphold the values in question. Attempts to create "higher" standards of expression by legislation and police action, it is said, usually result only in equating "higher" with "more restrictive."

In this view, the activity of rule enforcement generally places a university's officials in a punitive, restrictive posture; this inevitably does violence to the development of the intellectual community that universities seek, and competes with attempts to help students evolve their own independent and coherent codes of self-directed conduct. Thus, while some rules of student conduct may always be necessary, they should be minimized as far as possible, and should be left largely to the law-enforcement agencies which are better equipped to perform them. The university should avoid assuming elaborate law-enforcement functions, particularly in regard to events that are of primary concern to the community at large rather than to the distinctive goals of academic life. Restrictive rules should be avoided especially in the area of speech and expression, this view argues—first, because of expression's close relation to the university's goals of free inquiry and discussion; second, because of the many difficult and ambiguous judgments that have plagued the courts themselves in dealing with the basic constitutional liberties involved. If the university thus "gets out of the law-enforcement business" as much as possible, it is argued, the problem of student civil disobedience also is reduced: The occasions for violation or enforcement, the distance between administrators and students, and the confrontations of principle that rally students around protest leaders all are minimized.

By contrast, as we have seen, some University of California officials and faculty members continue to feel that the University has a function and duty, along with its other purposes, to uphold affirmatively the principle of respect for "law and order" in general. They believe that the minimal order necessary for normal University functions, and for the protection of involuntary audiences from a tyrannous few, requires the University to accept responsibility for some restraints on speech and expression. These restraints may even legitimately involve matters of content, some believe, and if established they must be rigorously enforced. Finally, many feel that the University's internal order is necessary to safeguard University "self-government" from outside intervention, which in turn is a pre-condition to the fulfillment of University goals. Thus it is felt that overt student disobedience of University rules, no matter what its intent or origins, cannot long be tolerated.

Whatever the merits of the case at hand, more study seems indicated on these underlying questions: Are there inherent limits to what can be accomplished by enforcing formal rules of human conduct? What is their special relevance to a community with the university's distinctive goals? Are some university goals impeded by administrative enforcement of any rules? Or do such problems arise primarily from special restraints on matters of speech and expression? What objective consequences might be expected from universities' minimizing rule enforcement generally on their campuses?

Further: Is student civil disobedience on the campus a cause of increased rule-enforcement activity, an effect of it, or both? What are the alternatives to formal rule enforcement, for maintaining reasonable order in a university community? Is there increasing dependence throughout American society on formal means of social control? If so, what are the social and economic forces that foster this trend, and how far do they affect the university? What means, if any, could be used to combat them, consistent with university goals?

74

Controlling Official Behavior in Welfare Administration

JOEL F. HANDLER

Lawyers have always been concerned with controlling the actions of government. What is new today is that attention has shifted to welfare administration. The shift, of course, reflects the larger national interest in civil rights and poverty. The legal profession's reaction to the national interest has been an increasing awareness and apparent (if somewhat halting) willingness to do something about providing legal services for the underprivileged, the Negro, and the dependent poor. Within these broader shifts in attitudes, it is natural that lawyers would begin to concern themselves with the problems raised by government activity in the welfare field. Public welfare has been around a long time; attention is now being directed at it as part of the broad national movement for civil justice.

To a very considerable extent, lawyers cast the problem in traditional terms: How can the socially approved interests of the individual be protected in the government welfare programs? The concern of lawyers in the welfare field is timely. Existing welfare programs, which were aimed primarily at assistance or income maintenance, are being extended. But more important, government welfare programs are taking on new goals and purposes. The dependent poor are not only to be helped financially, but the new programs are designed to strengthen family life and to move the dependent poor toward self-

From Jacobus tenBroek, ed., *The Law of the Poor* (San Francisco: Chandler, 1966), pp. 155–166. Reprinted by permission of the publisher.

support and independence, to improve their life chances by "breaking the cycle of poverty." The War on Poverty is the most popular example. The Social Security Act,[1] particularly in its recent amendments concerning aid to families with children, bristles with the new approach. The Aid to Dependent Children program (ADC) has been changed to "aid and services to needy families with children" (AFDC).[2] The purposes have been re-stated "to help such parents or relatives to attain or retain capability for maximum self-support and personal independence consistent with the maintenance of continuing parental care and protection. . . ."[3] The amendments call for increased services such as accelerated programs in education, vocational rehabilitation, counselling, mental health, and community organization work.[4] The War on Poverty and the changes in the Social Security Act offer new hope for the dependent poor to escape many of the problems that they have known. But the new programs also pose new threats to the interests and freedom of the welfare clients; they may further weaken or debilitate family life and result in further loss of personal dignity.[5]

It is to the danger or threats to the freedom and dignity of the individual that the recent literature of the lawyers has turned. A good way to discuss the issues is to examine the work of Professor Charles Reich. His three articles— "Midnight Welfare Searches and the Social Security Act,"[6] "The New Property,"[7] and "Individual Rights and Social Welfare: The Emerging Legal Issues"[8]—have received a great deal of attention. They purport to define some of the more important issues, and suggest how we should solve them. Much new legal research adopts Reich's analysis and approach.[9]

Reich catalogues certain "ills" of present-day welfare administration. Welfare officials have attempted to impose moral codes on welfare recipients. Privacy has been unnecessarily invaded under the guise of eligibility and need investigations. Welfare laws sometimes impose financial responsibility on relatives of welfare recipients that are much broader than duties imposed on relatives of non-welfare persons. The residence of welfare recipients is usually restricted; in some states, there are "removal" laws. Several states require work or vocational retraining as a condition of receiving aid. Public housing authorities may deny admission or terminate leases of people who have police records or whom the authorities think keep undesirable company or engage in immoral conduct. Often welfare recipients are required to take loyalty oaths not required of the general public. Under the means test, welfare officials have great powers over the family budget; independence is restricted by official supervision.[10]

The "ills" that Reich (as well as others) is concerned with fall into two broad categories. On the one hand, the day-to-day administration has resulted in many instances of plainly lawless administrative behavior; that is, administrative officials are acting contrary to the Constitution and statutory terms, and clients are being deprived of rights embodied in constitutional and statutory law. On the other hand, there is concern over unwarranted interferences in the interests of welfare clients that are not clearly defined legal rights. These would include various aspects of privacy, moral behavior, and the manipulation of welfare clients in such matters as employment, retraining, counselling, mental health, and other rehabilitative services. In this latter category there is a feeling that welfare clients are being made to adopt behavior not required of other people by the state, or that welfare clients are made to forego activities and enjoyments that other people are allowed to enjoy.

The ills come about in two ways. First, there is bad substantive legislation. Welfare statutes often contain provisions that impose unnecessary hardships on the recipients. These would include residence requirements, responsibility provisions, loyalty oaths (included in the Economic Opportunity Act),[11] and the notice to law enforcement provision in the ADC program. Second, there are broad delegations of authority to welfare agencies that allow them to define critical substantive matters. Generally, the federal welfare statutes allow the states to determine the criteria of need, levels of income and resources, and the minimum level of living for the recipients.[12] When eligibility criteria are set forth in the legislation (federal and state), the criteria often conflict, or are vague, and the agencies have choice over which criteria to choose in any given situation. Or, the statutes are silent as to critical substantive areas, giving the agencies an even freer hand. In the day-to-day administration, the power granted through delegations of authority is increased by the agency practice of deciding issues on a case-by-case basis rather than promulgating and publishing rules in advance, the discretionary powers of enforcement, the power to delay, investigate, and harass, and the fact that people dependent on welfare are over-anxious to please officials rather than run the risk of punishment.

The remedies or solutions that Reich proposes have a ring familiar to lawyers. In welfare the government should not be allowed to impose any conditions that would be unconstitutional if imposed on persons not on welfare; government can't "buy up" constitutional rights. The substantive provisions of welfare statutes must be stripped of all that is not relevant to the purposes of the programs, such as loyalty requirements for tenants in government housing. In addition, "to the extent possible, delegated power to make rules ought to be confined within ascertainable limits, and regulating agencies should not be assigned the task of enforcing conflicting policies. Also agencies should be enjoined to use their powers only for the purposes for which they were designed." [13] But because it is so difficult to define in statutes what is relevant and to confine administrative discretion, Reich puts heavy emphasis on "basic" procedural safeguards. "In the case of a decision removing a family from public housing, or a decision denying aid to families with dependent children, generally the matter is finally determined at some level within the appropriate agency, after investigation by the agency, and with comparatively informal procedures, if any, available to the persons affected." [14] He calls for "full adjudicatory procedures." [15] Reich is not very specific about what he means by this ("procedures can develop gradually and pragmatically") [16] but appears to favor quite strongly the following: advance notification and publication of regulations that will govern future agency decisions; notice of proposed action, including a "full statement of the basis for it"; a trial-type hearing with the right to be represented by counsel; a separation of functions of investigator and judge; a decision based on competent evidence in the record; reasons in support of the decision; and "some form of review" (perhaps "within the agency, and, ultimately, in the courts").[17] Finally, Reich develops his idea of "entitlement." His conclusion is that the poor are entitled to welfare as a matter of "right" and not of "privilege." "The idea of entitlement is simply that when individuals have insufficient resources to live under conditions of health and decency, society has obligations to provide support, and the individual is entitled to that support as of right." At the risk of oversimplification, the objective of this position is to promote individual security by rejecting the case law justifying government interference on the ground that what the individual is claiming is a "mere gratuity" rather than a "right."[18]

Reich's strategy is quite clear. What he wants to do, in essence, is elevate the position of the welfare recipient to a position similar to that of a person whose business interests are regulated by government. In business regulation, government agencies are dealing with a "right"—property. Constitutional limits, more or less, are applicable. Through the years statutory and judicially imposed procedural safeguards have developed. Reich introduces his argument for procedural safeguards in the welfare field by talking about and listing specifically the types of procedural safeguards developed in business regulation. (These were basically the "full adjudicatory" procedures discussed above.)

> These procedures, however cumbersome they may seem, have come to represent a fundamental standard of fairness in administrative process. They may be exaggerated and misused until they produce inordinate delay and expense, but they represent effective checks on the characteristic evils of proceedings in any large public or private organization: closed doors, Kafka-like uncertainty, difficulty in locating responsibility, and rigid adherence to a particular point of view. They are fundamental safeguards for those who must deal with government.[19]

What Reich is doing, then, is giving welfare recipients legally protectible rights (similar to "standing"), procedural safeguards with which to assert those rights, and, he adds, the ability to protect the rights through representation by counsel. Welfare clients would then be in a position similar to regulated industries, and in "business regulation . . . lawyers have made paper procedures a practical reality."[20]

In analyzing this very appealing approach, I will first examine the assumptions underlying Reich's view as to what the process of business regulation is like. We will see how much lawyers have in fact made a "practical reality" out of "paper procedures." More important, an examination of the administrative process in business regulation will shed light on some basic institutional and structural problems that apply to welfare administration. Second, I will discuss some of the particular problems of judicializing welfare administration. The main example will be the AFDC program. Third, I will suggest different avenues if we are to accomplish Reich's, as well as our, goal of civil justice.

The Analogy to Administrative Regulation of Business Interests

The procedural safeguards in the administration of business interests, which Reich has in mind, arise in many types of situations. Typically, they come into operation when a person or business is claiming that an agency is acting contrary to law. The person may claim, for example, that the agency is taxing him illegally, or is wrongly applying a health regulation to his restaurant. The person may also be complaining about the failure of an agency to give him permission to do something, such as denying an application for a zoning variance. In situations like these (and if the matter cannot be settled), the claimant, with counsel, presents his claim to the agency which then conducts a trial-type hearing. The agency (or a hearing officer) acts like a judge. Although agencies are generally not bound by formal rules of evidence, the decision usually must be based on evidence in the record and the type of evidence cannot stray too far afield from that typically presented in court. If the claimant is still unhappy with the agency decision, he can seek judicial review. Again there are variations, but we will assume that the review will be appellate court review rather than a trial *de novo*. The appellate court is asked to "review" the administration action, to see whether the administrative behavior was authorized by law. The claim can be that there was no authority for the agency to act at all in this situation (for example, no statutory jurisdiction), or that the agency misapplied the statute, or that there was insufficient evidence to support the decision, or that there was bias, and so forth.

If the court thinks that the claimant is correct, the remedy may be to nullify the administrative decision and thus to allow the claimant to use his property as he intended free from official interference. Such would be the case, for example, if the court decided that the particular health regulation did not apply to the claimant's business. On the other hand, if the court decides that there was insufficient evidence to support the agency decision, the court may send the case back to the agency for a "new trial." This may also happen even if the court thinks that the agency has misconstrued the statute. The court may still think that the basic substantive decision should be made by the agency rather than the court. But the court will insist that the administrative decision be legal.

In these examples we note that there is no question about the protectibility of the claimant's interest; he is seeking to prevent interference with land or money or other types of property in which he has "rights." In addition, there is generally no question about knowledge or resources on the part of the claimant. He knows what he wants to do with his property; the agency has told him what he can or cannot do with the property; he has legal counsel of his own choosing to advise him. Reich's solutions would place the welfare recipient in a similar position—he would have rights, he would have procedural safeguards, and he would be given counsel.

The fact of the matter is that even in the administration of business regulation, very little of the type of control of administrative behavior that Reich talks about exists. It is now commonplace to reiterate that the informal procedures are truly "the lifeblood of the administrative process." [21] Davis estimates that "perhaps 80 or 90 per cent of the impact of the administrative process involves discretionary action in absence of safeguards of hearing procedures." [22] These are cases that are disposed of without a trial-type hearing or a record upon which the decision is based. Sometimes the informal adjudication consists of "settlement cases"—the party is entitled to a formal hearing if he wants one, but the case is settled prior to the hearing. In others, sometimes called the "pure administrative process," no formal hearings are provided prior to the formal decision (for example, inspection or tests of physical properties).[23] I cannot here describe in any detail the characteristics and range of problems encompassed by the informal administrative process. I will point out instead some highlights and examples of some aspects that have particular relevance to the problems raised by welfare administration and the program of "rights" that Reich calls for.

A great deal of informal adjudication is present when agencies have the power to enforce statutes. These agencies are able to negotiate settlements and regulate behavior without using formal procedures and without judicial review. In non-administrative law contexts, the regulatory practices of the police and the administrators of juvenile justice are familiar examples. These officials "settle" cases and impose sanctions without any resort to courts or other formal procedures.[24] This is also true of many administrative agencies. One prominent example is the Federal Trade Commission. The statute provides for hearings, findings of fact, and orders to cease and desist.[25] The vast majority of the results obtained by the FTC are through stipulation and consent orders rather than cease and desist orders. Many deceptive practices are disposed of through administrative treatment upon assurance that the party will discontinue the practice. It is claimed that "if the Federal Trade Commission were compelled to discontinue its stipulation and consent order procedures, it would have to forego a major part of its activity." [26] It is also said that "the fact that stipulation and consent orders are based on consent does not mean that parties are necessarily protected against exercise of arbitrary power." [27] There is little difference between the "quasi-judicial" independent Commission and the wholly non-judicial Antitrust Division of the Justice Department in the matter of informal adjudication. In recent years, between 85 and 90 per cent of the antitrust decrees were obtained under consent procedures.[28] The FTC, with its judicialized structure and procedural rights and safeguards, operates to a large extent as strictly a prosecuting agency.

The regulation of banking is another prominent example.

The striking fact is that the banking agencies use methods of informal supervision, almost always without formal adjudication, even for the determination of controversies. . . . A single example will suggest the spirit of the regulatory system. The Board of Governors of the Federal Reserve System has authority, after hearing, to suspend any member bank for "undue use" of its credit for speculative purposes inconsistent with sound credit conditions. . . . What happens is that the Board enforces the statute through methods of bank examiners, who call to the bank's attention the items that require correction. A bank that is inclined to disagree does not typically stand on its supposed rights and defy the Board to start a formal proceeding; suspension is too drastic a remedy for the bank to risk. The bank deals informally with the Board's representatives until some mutually satisfactory solution is worked out. Adjudication gives way almost entirely to supervision. . . . The sanction is not the power of suspension but the power of instituting proceedings.[29]

A third example involves the Securities and Exchange Commission's power over registration and acceleration. Because the mere announcement of a stop-order proceeding is so harmful, the decisive administrative determination, as far as the registrant is concerned, is the letter of comment from the SEC staff suggesting changes in the registration statement. "The registrant may be inclined to disagree with the staff's policies and may even think that the staff is arbitrary or unreasonable. But even if the registrant could convince a reviewing court that this is so, the registrant is in practical effect at the mercy of the Commission." [30] The statute provides that the effective date of a registration statement is 20 days after filing.[31] Registrants, however, usually want the date accelerated, and the Commission has discretionary power to grant the request.[32]

Business reasons usually make acceleration . . . so compelling that the registrant is willing to yield to onerous conditions. The SEC uses its discretionary power . . . to bargain for what it thinks the public interest may require; indeed, it sometimes requires substantive action having nothing to do with full disclosure. . . . The manner in which the SEC uses the acceleration power has long been highly controversial, but no registrant has been able to challenge it in a reviewing court.[33]

The SEC example, as well as the others, raises another aspect of the informal administrative process—regulation by fear of prosecution or publicity. The main weapon in the arsenal of the SEC, in the above example, is the potentially disastrous effects of publicity and delay. There are numerous examples in the literature of regulation by threats of adverse publicity. The Food and Drug Administration decided to stop salad oil and margarine makers from making claims about cholesterol and heart disease. According to H. Thomas Austern:

The FDA did not reach that conclusion by taking evidence or by offering any facts or opinions for expert discussion and criticism at a public hearing. It did not issue any formal regulation. It held no hearings. It made no formal findings. Instead, it published what it called a "Statement of Policy." It simply announced that it would hereafter consider as false and misleading any label claim that the use of a non-animal fat had any relation to heart disease. In the accompanying press release, which was hardly a legal document, it went even further. It announced that any label reference to "cholesterol" would also be illegal, because it might falsely imply some relation to heart disease. . . .

Whether the FDA was right or wrong, the fact is that every margarine manufacturer has acquiesced.[34]

After discussing other FDA examples of this type of regulation (including the cranberries), Austern concludes:

That is why no experienced Food and Drug lawyer resorts to court save *in extremis*—why here the conventional talk about the "administrative process" and "'court review" is largely academic, why seizures usually go uncontested, why what I shall call "jawbone enforcement" is the real area of administrative activity, why reported decisions and formal regulations bear as little relation to what really goes on as the visible top of an iceberg to the whole, and why the question of enforcement of administrative views by Madison Avenue techniques of publicity demands such close scrutiny in this field.[35]

Reich, in drawing upon the analogy of the administration of business regulation to support his arguments for "judicializing" welfare administration, seems to give the impression that administrative decisions are generally carried out with all the procedural safeguards: advance publication of rules, notice, formal trial-type hearings, competent and relevant evidence, decisions based on the record. His description leaves out the most significant area: informal administration, where none of these procedural safeguards are used. He is quite wrong in asserting that lawyers have made a "practical reality" of the judicial-type procedures. The existing evidence points in the opposite direction. According to persons intimate with the administrative process, it seems rare indeed when judicial-type procedures are used to attempt to control administrative behavior.

It might be argued that the fact that judicial-type procedures are not used or are circumvented in business regulation does not detract from their value; it only means that reform is needed with business regulation as well as welfare administration. The fact is, however, that arguments over procedures in administration have been raging for years, and many able and serious students of the administrative process argue for *less,* not more, judicial-type procedure. It is claimed, for example, that many regulatory agencies simply could not administer their programs if all decisions on cases and policies had to go through formalized hearing procedures.[36] The same is true with regard to enforcement agencies. In many situations the parties may be better off if minor infractions can be settled informally.[37] Several critics take issue with the popular notion (usually put forward by lawyers) that adjudication can be considered separate from policy formulation. They argue that many administrative policies have to be formulated on a case-by-case approach, with observation of a gradual de-velopment, rather than the promulgation of rules in advance.[38] Marver Bern-stein suggests, as a hypothesis, that the "continuing judicialization of adminis-trative regulation . . . has encouraged the growth of non-adversary methods to dispose of regulatory business and may have stimulated wider recourse to *ex parte* contacts and communications." [39] That is to say, more stringent "due process" requirements may result in more non-formal regulations or less regu-lations altogether; more rigid and formal hearing requirements may result in increased pressures for informal settlements. Running through many of the ar-guments of informed critics like Massel, Bernstein, Gellhorn, Byse, as well as many others, is the view that lawyers have wrongly looked at administrative agencies through judicial-colored glasses and have evaluated the administrative process in terms of how well administrative procedures match up to court procedures. This approach concentrates on the independent regulatory agen-cies and ignores the vast amount of regulation carried on by executive depart-ments; it fails to recognize that the agencies were set up, in part, because the courts and legislatures could not handle the programs that the agencies are charged with; it misses the very important regulatory activity that goes on without judicial-type procedures and the value of the informal process; and it has resulted in sometimes harmful and sometimes futile attempts to engraft on agencies procedural requirements unsuited for the conduct of their business.[40]

But, it may be argued that even though "rights" embodied in judicial-type procedures are not used very often, it is still important that they exist; it is still within the power of private citizens and companies to check illegal and unwar-ranted official behavior if the need should arise. This argument may or may not be true. First, as some of the above examples show (and these are not atypical cases), in many instances people and businesses are not *able* to use the judicial-type procedures. The costs or the risks involved are too high—even in situations where they feel that government action is unwarranted.

Second, the argument is dangerous and, if implemented, can be productive of much harm. By ignoring the realities of administration, and particularly the informal process, it leads one into thinking that the important problems of controlling official behavior will be solved by enacting a program of rights. The informal process exists. It cannot be legislated away. In many situations, there is persuasive evidence that the informal process works fairly and fulfills legislative goals.[41] No doubt there are many instances where this is not true.[42] But the informal process is intimately connected with the formal proc-ess. Enacting a formal program of rights and judicializing the administrative procedure may make the informal process more fair. On the other hand, changing the formal process may destroy much of the value of the informal process; in other instances, it may lead to even more lawless administrative behavior.[43] Reich pays little or no attention to the problem of implementing his program or to whether the harm caused by an effective use of these rights (if that is ever possible) outweighs the good. It is premature to defend his po-sition on the ground that "it is good as far as it goes" because of his failure to calculate the costs of judicializing administrative procedures. The easy assumption that because agencies decide individual cases they are therefore like courts and should act like courts ignores the very different institutional and structural characteristics of administrative agencies.

NOTES

1. 49 Stat. 620 (1935), as amended, 42 U.S.C. §§ 301–1394 (1964), as amended, 42 U.S.C. §§ 302–1369d (Supp. I, 1965).
2. 76 Stat. 185 (1962), as amended, 42 U.S.C. §§ 601–609 (1964), as amended, 42 U.S.C. §§ 602, 603, 606 (Supp. I, 1965).
3. 70 Stat. 848 (1956), as amended, 42 U.S.C. § 601 (1964).
4. See 76 Stat. 173 (1962), 42 U.S.C. §§ 603(a)(3), (c)(1) (1964) (the states are offered a 75 per cent grant-in-aid to develop these new programs); Bureau of Family Service, United States Department of Health, Education, and Welfare, *Handbook of Public Assistance Administration*, Part IV §§ 4050–53.5 (Rev. November 30, 1962).
5. Some of the far-reaching implications of the new welfare programs are discussed in Handler and Rosenheim, "Privacy in Welfare: Public Assistance and Juvenile Justice," *Law and Contemporary Problems*, XXXI (1966).
6. *Yale Law Journal*, LXXII (1963), 1347.
7. *Ibid.*, LXXIII (1964), 733.
8. *Ibid.*, LXXIV (1965), 1245.
9. See, for example, the statement of purposes of the newly established Project on Social Welfare Law at the New York University School of Law, *Welfare Law Bulletin*, I (December, 1965), 1, and Columbia University School of Social Work: Center on Social Welfare Policy and Law, Memorandum on the "social welfare law testing" function of the Center. This memorandum has been reprinted in *Practical Lawyer*, April, 1966.
10. Reich, *supra*, note 8, at 1247–1251.
11. 79 Stat. 973, 42 U.S.C. § 2714(d) (Supp. I, 1965).
12. See Burns, *Social Security and Public Policy* (1956), pp. 228–231.
13. Reich, *supra*, note 7, at 782–783.
14. Reich, *supra*, note 8, at 1252.
15. *Id*. at 1253.
16. *Ibid*.
17. *Ibid*.
18. *Id*. at 1256.
19. *Id*. at 1253.
20. *Id*. at 1252.
21. Attorney-General's Commission on Administrative Procedure, *Report*, S. Doc. No. 8, 77th Cong., 1st Sess, 35 (1941).
22. Davis, *Administrative Law—Cases, Text, Problems* (1965), p. 70.
23. On the "pure administrative process," see Gellhorn and Byse, *Administrative Law* (4th ed. 1960), pp. 657–665.
24. See generally Note, *Harvard Law Review*, LXXIX (1966), 775.
25. 38 Stat. 719 (1914), as amended, 15 U.S.C. § 45 (1964).
26. Massel, "The Regulatory Process," *Law and Contemporary Problems*, XXVI (1961). 181, 187.
27. Davis, *op. cit. supra*, note 22, at 75.
28. Massel, *supra*, note 26, at 192.
29. Davis, *op. cit. supra*, note 22, at 76.
30. *Id*. at 73.
31. 48 Stat. 79 (1933), as amended, 15 U.S.C. § 77h (1964).
32. *Ibid*.
33. *Davis, op. cit. supra*, note 22, at 73–74.

34. Address by H. Thomas Austern, *Sanctions in Silhouette,* Second Annual Charles Wesley Dunn Food and Drug Law Lecture, delivered at the Harvard Law School, March 22, 1960, reprinted in Gellhorn and Byse, *op. cit. supra,* note 23, at 671–672.
35. *Id.* at 673.
36. Massel, *supra,* note 26, at 187.
37. *Ibid.*
38. Mark Massel, of the Brookings Institution, for example, states: "The criticisms of policy-making seem to be founded on the assumption that the agencies refuse to issue rules because of timidity, inability, and ineffectiveness. There seems to be no room allowed for the possibility that there exist reasonable grounds for the agency practice or institutional pressures against such a practice." *Id.* at 189. See generally Shapiro, "The Choice of Rule-making or Adjudication in the Development of Administrative Policy," *Harvard Law Review,* LXXVIII (1965), 921.
39. Bernstein, "The Regulatory Process: A Framework for Analysis," *Law and Contemporary Problems,* XXVI (1961), 329, 345.
40. Gellhorn and Byse, in commenting on informal adjudication, say:
    Procedural forms are not fetishes. They are means to ends. The ends are correct determinations of disputable questions, with safeguards against abusive exercises of governmental authority.
    In some circumstances it has been concluded, and rightly so, that a record of past happenings can be reconstructed with greatest fidelity by requiring narrations concerning them to be made with full solemnity—under oath, in a public forum, and subject to that process of refinement and qualification known as cross-examination. . . .
    In other circumstances . . . a different method seems warranted. An investigatory technique supplants the judicialized hearing. It is the technique which, after all, is employed almost exclusively—except by government—to develop the facts on which the gravest judgments turn. To suggest that it is no longer an apt tool merely because it is in official hands, would be an absurdity. The groupings of cases mentioned in these pages . . . suffice to refute . . . the contention that administration is necessarily defective to the extent that it tolerates basic departures from the procedure of courts. . . .
    The extension of unconventional processes presupposes a subordinate personnel equipped to use them fairly and an administrative hierarchy fired with a sense of responsibility for scrupulously just results. There is no reason to suppose that public administration through official agencies is incapable of developing professional traditions and standards comparable with those developed by public administration through the courts.
    It is here that the experience of life offers lessons: the formalized hearing is a method of getting at the truth and of assuring justice; but it is only one of many methods. No particular means is invariably synonymous with the fair result. No one device can properly assert a monopoly over the procedural virtues, and thus debar efforts to build new, perhaps more direct roads to justice.
    Gellhorn and Byse, *op. cit. supra,* note 23, at 644–665.
41. For an excellent and exhaustive analysis of the intimate relationship between the formal and informal process in the administration of the automobile dealers' statutes, see Macaulay, "Changing A Continuing Relationship Between A Large Corporation and Those Who Deal With It: Automobile Manufacturers, Their Dealers, and The Legal System" (Parts 1, 2), *Wisconsin Law Review* (1965), p. 483, 740. Professor Macaulay presents a persuasive case that the informal process in Wisconsin better serves the competing interests than the formal legal system.
42. See Levy, "Protecting the Mentally Retarded: An Empirical Survey and Evaluation of the Establishment of State Guardianship in Minnesota," *Minnesota Law Review,* XLIX (1965), 821.
43. See LaFave, *Arrest: The Decision to Take a Suspect into Custody* (1965); and LaFave and Remington, "Controlling the Police: The Judge's Role in Making and Reviewing Law Enforcement Decisions," *Michigan Law Review,* LXIII (1965), 987.

75

The Privatization of Public Welfare

PHILIPPE NONET

Perhaps the most striking feature of this pattern of legal development is its dependence upon a close relation of law and politics. This is apparent in the crucial role that interest groups and political controversy have played in the evolution of the California Industrial Accidents Commission (IAC). We have discussed earlier the significance of political resources in the growth of legal competence; we have also seen how the sponsorship of representative groups gives impetus to legal advocacy by gearing it to the needs and aspirations of a constituency. This link of advocacy to class interests made law politically effective and meaningful, and provided a source of dynamic legal development.

It is worth noting at this point how much the administrative philosophy of the early IAC contributed to the emergence of this pattern. Those features of the IAC that made for its weakness as an administrator of public policy also helped to transform the agency into a site of flourishing legalization. The emphasis on self-help and voluntarism tended to tie administration to political interests and to blur the distinction between public ends and the private aims of the parties. The agency had thus placed itself in a position where it would be inclined, and indeed compelled, to be responsive to the demands of affected persons and groups. Furthermore, the adversary structure of the compensation system underscored the necessity for the parties to have effective means of pressing their claims. As the agency retreated from its active role, labor was continuously reminded that workers could not count on much protection from the IAC and would eventually have to rely upon their own strength. Finally, the weaker the competence of the agency became, the less authority its administrative judgments were able to carry. The agency had lost its qualifications for prescribing what were the best interests of employer and employee. The parties themselves had become the judges of that question. It was, therefore, easier for them to press the IAC to renounce administrative discretion, and easier for the IAC to settle for the role of an adjudicator. Thus although the agency had expressly sought to avoid the intrusion of law and adversary contentions in its program, its own strategy of administration helped lay the foundations for a quite different institutional outcome.

From *Administrative Justice: Advocacy and Change in a Government Agency* (New York: Russell Sage Foundation, 1968), pp. 261–268. Reprinted by permission of the author and publisher.

The Privatization of Public Policy

This institutional link between judicialization and the growing political initiative of interested groups had important implications for the character of compensation policies. Briefly, one might say that the legalization of workmen's compensation went along with a privatization of its public welfare aims.

Initially workmen's compensation was seen as entirely divorced from the employment relation and the concerns of the private law of employer and employee. Its purpose was to remove industrial accident problems from the realm of free contract, and to make them a responsibility of society. The new legislation was interested in the injured man as a poor man rather than as an employee; it was a welfare program, a War on Poverty, and not a regulation of employment. Compensation was a matter of public concern: injured men's claims were demands to the state, not to the employer. In practice, of course, this idea received important qualifications. Compensation was based on a liability, and responsibility for payment was in effect vested in the employer. But liability was considered only a means of financing the program, one that did not detract from its public character; and the "direct payment" system was conceived of as a kind of delegation of state authority to the employers, who were thus entrusted with a public mandate, always liable to be revoked. Those views fitted nicely in the ideology of welfare capitalism, which envisioned that industry would, out of good will and a sense of civic responsibility, provide for the welfare of its employees beyond and apart from its strict legal contractual obligations to them. That welfare was not seen as an ingredient of the law of employment is indicated by the policy, continued well into the 1930's, of avoiding the incorporation of private benefit plans in collective agreements or individual contracts of services. Welfare was a matter of public or civic responsibility, not a duty between employer and employee.

However, this purported segregation of welfare and the contract of employment could not long be maintained. By assuming control over the administration of workmen's compensation, industry inevitably committed itself to the program. Operationally, if not in theory, liability and "direct payment" established a bridge between public welfare and the relation of employer and employee. Workmen's compensation became, for most practical purposes, a responsibility of the employer, independent of the aims and control of the state. Public welfare therefore tended to be "privatized." It implicitly became a duty of the employer *qua* employer. Labor's own emphasis on self-help and voluntarism would further contribute to remove welfare from the ambit of the state. When workers acquired independent means of promoting their interests through unions, welfare matters increasingly became a bargaining issue between them and employers, with the state confined to a role of support and arbitration. Just as private and formerly unilateral welfare plans have been made objects of bargaining between unions and industry, so have public welfare programs, including workmen's compensation, been supplemented, adapted, and refashioned through collective agreements. Thus, legally and institutionally, workmen's compensation has been absorbed into the private setting of the employment relation. This outcome was accomplished in two ways: (1) First, by assuming control over the program, industry implicitly accepted compensation as a responsibility of its own. (2) Later, through collective bargaining, the compensation legislation was woven into the contractual law of employment. Today, each policy issue is a controversy between industry and organized labor, and each particular claim is a challenge by the worker against his employer.

This does not mean that the welfare ideals of early workmen's compensation have been entirely lost. The incorporation of public policy into the law of employment has fostered important changes in legal ideas governing the relations of employer and employee. Welfare made the concrete human problems of the employee relevant again to the conduct of work relations. The worker would no longer be regarded as a mere object on the market and otherwise a stranger. The focus of attention was displaced from contract, the mere exchange of services for wages, to the broader set of social conditions created by the employment relation. This paved the way toward an enlargement of the legal concept of employment and a recognition of the employee as a person with a status and rights to be legally protected.

By itself, however, welfare was unable to accomplish this evolution: it treated the worker as a human being, but not as a person. The effort to help the "whole man" tended to divest him of his rights. It took a return to the law and its impersonal system of governance by rules to transform the values evolved through welfare into a secure set of rights. This return was facilitated by the privatization of public welfare. Welfare was redefined as a set of definable interests to be aggressively and self-servingly pursued by the parties. From a provider of care, the employer became a debtor. The needs the worker had as a man, dependent upon the understanding and generosity of his master, were transformed into specific claims he asserted as an employee. The resources of private law, including the law of employment, were made relevant as tools for vesting benefits as legally protected rights. From a stranger, and later a human being, the disabled employee became a person with rights that took account of his condition and needs, that protected his autonomy and dignity by a web of impersonal rules.

But the attenuation of public aims and governmental responsibility that went along with this evolution has entailed important costs. This is quite apparent in the declining significance of rehabilitation and public health as goals of workmen's compensation. More important, privatization has profoundly weakened the idea that government is responsible for bringing assistance to the more incompetent and helpless members of its constituency. It has promoted a view of the injured claimant as a full-fledged citizen, equal under law, and to be treated accordingly. While this evolution made law more responsive to his demands, more ready to recognize him as a carrier of rights, it also left many needs unfulfilled: to the many workers who have no connection with a union, and no way of getting to a lawyer, to the many whose union is tame or resourceless, or who fall in the hands of incompetent attorneys, to all those who have no opportunity to learn their rights and no support in asserting their claims, the attenuation of public responsibility has been a considerable loss.

This dependence of the legal process on self-help and self-serving advocacy can give impetus and direction to legal change. But for the very reason that it makes law more responsive to political demands, it also tends to distort the balance of interests in the legal order. The recognition of legal interests becomes dependent upon those interests as they are defined by affected groups, and upon what resources those groups are able to muster for political and legal action. Even where representative groups are powerful and articulate, the citizen tends to be a captive of their special commitments and perspectives. It is no unmitigated blessing for employers and injured workers that insurance and unions have provided for their representation. Among workers there are many for whom organized labor has had little concern, and whom it has sacrificed to the narrower interests of its active membership. The increased richness and vitality of the law are therefore purchased at the price of added obstacles to the realization of legal ideals. Justice develops greater potentials, but equality becomes more problematic.

Political Tensions in the Legal Order

This problem is all the more significant as political tensions tend to strain the capacity of legal institutions to define and affirm the values and policies of the legal order. The reduction of public responsibilities we have observed in the IAC is but one aspect of a larger phenomenon. When legal advocacy acquires greater political significance and the legal process becomes an arena of political controversy, the authority of legal institutions becomes more vulnerable. One characteristic response that is illustrated by the IAC is to evade the responsibility for making and affirming legal policies. Therefore, those very features of the legal process that enhance its potentials also make the realization of those potentials more difficult.

One traditional source of strength and security for legal institutions was relative insulation from political controversy. The making of policy and the creation of rights have always been central tasks of the judicial system; but the system was sparingly used and its work had little visibility, being viewed as focused on particular cases of narrowly confined import. As long as the claims dealt with remain isolated individual disputes, as long as decisions appear bound to the case at hand, as long as precedents are made almost without knowing it, it is comparatively easy for the courts to assert their authority in defining the values and standards of the legal order. These conditions change when the pursuit of legal interests is organized under the sponsorship of groups. The aggregation of legal demands underscores their political import, and authority is then exposed to more serious challenges. This tendency to politicize legal debate is by no means confined to the narrow setting of workmen's compensation. It corresponds to a characteristic trend of the modern social and legal order. The increasing demands on government to solve the problems of society, the growth of representative organizations, and the extension of citizenship all contribute to make law and legal institutions the target of more active and more deliberately concerted appeals.

It is about this process, and the kinds of strains and responses it arouses in the administration of justice, that we can learn from the experience of the IAC. When a court enjoys a well-guarded political immunity, it may be capable of withstanding a high exposure to political controversy. The blurring of law and politics serves then to create opportunities for extending the role of law in society, and legal institutions can assume leadership in defining and affirming the moral commitments of the political community.

But when judicial authority lacks political immunity, the response is more likely to resemble that of the IAC: a defensive retreat from politics and a flight from policy. It is through the appellate courts, not through the IAC, that the legal development of workmen's compensation has proceeded. In the IAC, the impoverishment of the legal process was particularly visible in the efforts of the agency to avert legal controversies. In a more subtle form, it was apparent in the growth of legalistic modes of adjudication. We speak of "legalism" when insistence on legal rules or modes of reasoning tends to frustrate the purposes of public policy. Law is then presented as abstract, rigid, and unable to respond to actual needs; those who invoke it are made to appear irrational or irresponsible. Legalism tends to weaken the authority of the law in the eyes of those whose needs and aspirations are frustrated; legal institutions come to seem ineffective and arbitrary and tend to lose their claim to reasoned obedience.

Basically, legalism is an issue about the competence of the law as an instrument of problem-solving. This is not to say that whenever the law frustrates certain aspirations or grows costly to certain interests it then becomes legalistic. The legal process, like any other mode of social ordering, affects and can expressly be used to alter the balance of interests. The law also tends to promote certain values, such as accountability and respect for the person, at the expense of other social aims. But the idea of legalism suggests more than merely the range of costs attendant on the normal functioning of legal institutions. What it points to is a pathology of the legal order, an impoverishment of its competence, rather than any cost flowing from the use or development of the law. Legalism develops when emphasis on specific rules and technicalities of the law prevents responding to problems and demands that the legal order would otherwise be competent and inclined to meet by a creative use of its own principles.

Symptoms of legalism in the IAC were its rigid and myopic interpretations of rules pertaining to the assessment of disability, even when the very rationale of those rules called for greater openness and flexibility. Even more significant was its appeal to the standards of judicial office as requiring that it renounce its authority over matters such as medical expertise and counseling of unrepresented claimants in which the integrity of its judicial processes was directly at stake. It has never occurred to the IAC that, as a judicial guardian of the principles of workmen's compensation, it might have to assume responsibility for promoting the legal competence of its constituents. This failure occurred in spite of a long tradition of administrative concern, and indeed at a time when the courts and government, in other domains of the law, were recognizing new responsibilities for making citizens equal and effective participants in the legal order.

Today, the agency seems to cling to those very concepts of law that, in its administrative role, it once abhorred; yet, as a court, its responsibilities call for a kind of affirmative authority that has much in common with what it formerly aspired to. The concessions the early IAC made to the values of self-help, and which reduced its power as an administrator, also laid the foundations for those patterns of legal advocacy which today would require that the agency return to a more assertive use of its authority.

One may conceive of this historical dilemma of the IAC as a quest for a new conception of the mission of state and law in society; one that would reconcile the concerns of the liberal state for the demands and interests of the person with the efforts of the welfare state to play a more active role in the pursuit of social aspirations. The IAC has not succeeded in resolving this problem: it remains, now as before, torn between an overly ambitious notion of government action and an overly restrictive view of the limits of law. In more positive terms, the problems of the commission point to a basic dilemma of government: How can authority respond to demands for participation without impairing its ability to preserve the integrity of policy? This dilemma cannot be resolved until agencies of government find means to overcome the contradictory requirements of authority and participation, and learn to keep their self-confidence while being responsive. What is needed is a more humble and realistic conception of authority that would acknowledge the dependence of power on criticism and free government from a too severe test of acceptance and respect; and a more positive view of the value of participation as enhancing the competence of authority to define and realize public aims. The ideals and experience of the legal process have much to contribute to this reconstruction of authority, and there are signs that this may come about. The attempt to construct a "welfare law," where the purposes of social action would be related to the development of citizenship and the rights of persons, is a characteristic concern of the contemporary legal order. The IAC may eventually find in those efforts an answer to its own institutional problems.

76

There Oughta Be a Law

RONALD DWORKIN

Martin Mayer's accusation that the "legal approach" neglects policy is misguided. He fails to notice the difference between a policy argument and an argument of right, and so fails to see that there are occasions that call for one but not the other. Some lawyers will mistake these occasions, of course, and fail to attend to policy when they should. Fifty years ago policy arguments that should have been made were not made. That is not a central problem today, however; and, moreover, the examples Mayer gives are not cases in which this mistake has occurred.

Mayer criticizes, for example, the lawyers who are trying to attack urban poverty by calling attention to the social rights of the poor. He feels that their arguments divert attention from the research and planning that are necessary if we are to improve housing and education. But this confuses two issues, each important: What goals must the community have? What political and economic means must it use to reach these goals? The lawyers who are concerned with rights are speaking to the first issue, and Mayer can hardly claim that there is nothing to argue about. Recent American history shows no agreement that the poor, as a group, have any right to better housing or education; what they have so far been given is often thought of as charity or as the by-product of national economic goals (like subsidies to farmers). The "legal approach" argues that the poor have rights that the majority must recognize even if it is not feeling generous, and even if its larger economic goals are not served thereby.

Lawyers who make this claim follow the strategy I have described. They point to some recognized practice of obligation, and then argue that consistency requires extending to the poor the rights this practice generates. This strategy determined the successful arguments in the Supreme Court that a state cannot refuse an appeal from a criminal conviction because the defendant cannot pay for a transcript, and that a state cannot limit the vote to those who can pay a poll tax. It also suggests a more general argument, which should be urged in the legislatures. The states now offer a wide variety of public services, ranging from police protection and public education to public health and zoning. Few citizens could afford these services independently, and a state that did

From a review of Martin Mayer, *The Lawyers* in *The New York Review of Books*, X No. 5 (1968), 19–21. Reprinted by permission of the author and *The New York Review of Books*. Copyright © 1968 by The New York Review.

not provide them for the majority would be thought derelict in its duties, and callous of the rights of its constituents. If so, then these state services constitute a practice of obligation, and form a sound basis for asserting the general duty of a state to provide its citizens the essential of a decent and effective life. It is inconsistent, and a breach of duty, to cut off the minority in the economic cellar, even if extending the practice to them would be vastly more expensive and troublesome, and therefore in contradiction to other policies of the majority. The force of this argument may be clear to some, but it is not generally accepted. Lawyers must try to document and support it, not abandon it.

The same confusion of policies and rights is involved in another of Mayer's examples. He is unhappy about some of the rules the Supreme Court has recently developed to protect persons accused of crimes. "A certain irreducible idiocy underlies the argument of some civil libertarians," he says, "that a cop who finds a man driving a stolen car does not have the right to ask the man how he came by the car." He fails to understand the contrary argument: that since the driver is free not to answer, because he is free not to incriminate himself, it is wrong of the state to take advantage of him if he is too poor or ignorant to understand his position. The force of that argument depends on the justification that can be made for the principle of freedom from self-incrimination. If this freedom rests simply on a judgment of policy that is the most effective safeguard against police brutality, then it would be silly to carry the safeguard so far as to stop the police from asking any questions at all before a lawyer arrives. But if the freedom rests, as Mayer's civil libertarians argue, on an individual's moral right not to condemn himself, then the state has a duty to take whatever steps are necessary to insure that a waiver of that right is voluntary and considered, even at the cost of policy efficiency. It may be that silencing the police goes a bit further than is necessary, but that is arguable, and the suggestion is far from irreducible idiocy.

Index